A Companion to the Study of *Epistle to the Son of the Wolf*

BY THE SAME AUTHOR

Islam at the Crossroads

A Companion to the Study of *Epistle to the Son of the Wolf*

Lameh Fananapazir

GR
GEORGE RONALD
OXFORD

George Ronald, Publisher
Oxford
www.grbooks.com

A catalogue record for this book
is available from the British Library

ISBN 978-0-85398-631-7

Cover design: Steiner Graphics

CONTENTS

FOREWORD

There has long been a need for helpful background information to accompany the reading and study of the English edition of Bahá'u'lláh's monumental *Epistle to the Son of the Wolf*. This singular work, addressed by the Messenger of God for this Day to one of His most virulent and active opponents, constitutes a divine and majestic summary – an overview of His historic prophetic Mission. Bahá'u'lláh Himself has culled, from the entire range of His own revelatory Writings, extensive passages which best characterize and define the purpose of His Faith and its meaning for humanity.

These inspiring quotations have been combined with numerous exhortations to Shaykh Muḥammad-Taqí, appealing to him to weigh afresh his views on the Bahá'í teachings and the transforming influence they have had on the saintly and heroic actions of His early followers. Apart from these passages from Bahá'u'lláh's own Writings, the work cites numerous quotations from previous divine scriptures in support of His claims. Direct textual evidence has been included from authentic Jewish, Christian, Islamic and Bábí sources in support of His assertions. Apart from these selections Bahá'u'lláh enriches His offering with many additional passages of His own Words, unique to this singular work. In the course of gathering and relating His Teachings, the narrative is laden with many rich elucidations and clarifications of a number of historic episodes related to His Cause.

Dr Lameh Fananapazir, author and compiler of the present volume, through his impressive familiarity with the Holy Books of past and present Revelations, leads us gently and convincingly to important sources and parallel citations. In the process he has provided a volume rich with thoughtful connections and useful cross-references – inspired table-settings, so to speak, for a sumptuous feast.

This version of the Epistle was rendered into English in 1940 by

Shoghi Effendi in his capacity as Guardian of the Bahá'i Faith (1921–1957). Upon dispatching his manuscript to the United States Bahá'í National Spiritual Assembly, he cabled:

> DEVOUTLY HOPE ITS STUDY MAY CONTRIBUTE FURTHER ENLIGHTENMENT, DEEPER UNDERSTANDING VERITIES ON WHICH EFFECTUAL PROSECUTION TEACHING, ADMINISTRATIVE UNDERTAKINGS ULTIMATELY DEPEND.[1]

Notice how the Guardian disabuses us of any notion that the contents of the volume may in some way be limited to the particular circumstances of the Shaykh to whom it is addressed. By linking its study to our dependence on 'further enlightenment' and 'deeper understanding' of the 'verities' of the Faith, Shoghi Effendi establishes the immediacy and universal import of the text for each and every believer.

In earlier messages, particularly *The Dispensation of Bahá'u'lláh* (1934), the Guardian had set forth those fundamental verities which lie at the basis of the Bahá'í Revelation. Then some years later he provided us with his masterful translation of this veritable omnibus work of Bahá'u'lláh as a means for an even further and deeper grasp of such essentials. Moreover, he re-emphasizes that the effectiveness of our teaching and administrative activities depend on such a knowledge and understanding.

In reviewing, four years later, the salient events of the first Bahá'í century in *God Passes By*, Shoghi Effendi included the *Epistle to the Son of the Wolf* in his survey of Bahá'u'lláh's major works:

> Finally, mention must be made of His Epistle to Shaykh Muḥammad Taqí, surnamed 'Ibn-i-Dhi'b (Son of the Wolf), the last outstanding Tablet revealed by the pen of Bahá'u'lláh, in which He calls upon that rapacious priest to repent of his acts, quotes some of the most characteristic and celebrated passages of His own writings, and adduces proofs establishing the validity of His Cause.
>
> With this book, revealed about one year prior to His ascension, the prodigious achievement as author of a hundred volumes, repositories of the priceless pearls of His Revelation, may be said to have practically terminated . . .[2]

This summary description in the words of the Guardian identifies three major aspects of the book:

1. Admonitions and warnings to Shaykh Muḥammad-Taqí, the Son of the Wolf
2. Passages quoted by Bahá'u'lláh from His own Writings
3. Proofs of the validity of Bahá'u'lláh's Cause

In effect, as Shoghi Effendi is said to have stated, the *Epistle to the Son of the Wolf* is in itself a library and, further, it was a book Bahá'u'lláh enjoyed composing.

Hooper C. Dunbar

ACKNOWLEDGEMENTS

I wish to express my profound gratitude to Mr Hooper C. Dunbar for his encouragement. I am particularly indebted to Dr Khazeh Fananapazir and Dr Ghaneh Fananapazir for their many generous contributions and insights. I would also like to express my heartfelt gratitude to my wife for her many valuable suggestions. I am profoundly grateful to Dr May Hofman for depth of experience, patience, and amazing editorial skills, without which this manuscript would not have been completed.

INTRODUCTION

Bahá'u'lláh revealed the *Epistle to the Son of the Wolf* (*Lawḥ-i-Ibn-i-Dhi'b*), His last major work, in the final years of His life.[1] The Epistle was written mostly in Persian but with many Arabic citations.

It is addressed to Shaykh Muḥammad Taqíy-i-Najafí, also known as Áqá Najafí (1846–1914), an influential and wealthy Shí'ih cleric of Isfahan, Persia, stigmatized by Bahá'u'lláh as the 'Son of the Wolf'. He was an inveterate and relentless enemy of the new religion, who had made it his life mission to extirpate Bahá'u'lláh's Faith and to persecute His followers.

However, the Epistle is of far wider interest than the concerns with the admittedly horrendous and widespread persecutions of the followers of Bahá'u'lláh by the Shaykh, as it elaborates and summarizes many aspects of His Revelation.

Bahá'u'lláh, the promise of all ages

In the Epistle Bahá'u'lláh states unequivocally that He is the long-awaited World Redeemer expected by the adherents of the religions of mankind, anticipated to rehabilitate the spiritual fortunes of their faiths and to usher in an age of righteousness and unity.

The Jews have now been expecting their Messiah or Saviour for more than three thousand years, an event that would coincide with the return of the dispersed of Judah to the Holy Land. The Christians have been promised a Second Coming of Christ revealed in the Glory of the Father, and have prayed for more than two thousand years that the Father may hasten the advent of His Kingdom, when 'Thy will be done on earth, as it is in heaven', and when they shall receive their portion of the divine 'daily bread'.[2] Similarly, the Muslims have anticipated for more than fourteen hundred years the advent of the 'Lord', 'the Great

Announcement'[3] and 'the Day of Judgement or Resurrection'.[4] They have prayed to be guided to the right Path[5] and not be disgraced when 'the Day of God'[6] finally dawns,[7] a Day when 'the earth will shine with light of its Lord'.[8] Additionally, the three religions have predicted a time of unity, when the divers flocks will be brought together by the Great Shepherd.

In 1844 CE, equivalent to 1260 AH, the dates repeatedly alluded to in the Bible[9] and in Muslim traditions, a young merchant of Shiraz, Persia, declared that the cycle of prophecy was complete, the Day of resurrection had at long last arrived, and that He was the Qá'im,[10] the Forerunner of 'He Whom God shall make manifest', Who would soon appear and reestablish faith.

The Message of Bahá'u'lláh could not have been clearer. As summarized succinctly by Shoghi Effendi, He declared Himself unequivocally to be the One promised in the Writings of the Báb, the Qur'án, the New Testament, the Hebrew Bible, the Bhagavad-Gita, and the scriptures of Buddha and Zoroaster:

> To Israel He was neither more nor less than the incarnation of the 'Everlasting Father,' the 'Lord of Hosts' come down 'with ten thousands of saints'; to Christendom Christ returned 'in the glory of the Father,' to Shí'ah Islám the return of the Imám Ḥusayn; to Sunní Islám the descent of the 'Spirit of God' (Jesus Christ); to the Zoroastrians the promised Sháh-Bahrám; to the Hindus the reincarnation of Krishna; to the Buddhists the fifth Buddha.[11]

Persia in the nineteenth century

Shí'ih Islam, the dominant religion in Iran, was in the powerful grip of clergy when Bahá'u'lláh announced His mission in 1863. Persia, the cradle of the Bábí Dispensation, had been the land from which in earlier times the Zoroastrian Magi travelled to find the newly born Christ, and Salmán Farsi set out on his spiritual quest to find Muhammad. In the mid-eighteenth century the civil and religious life of Persia was in an 'indescribable state of decadence, with its attendant corruption, confusion, intolerance, and oppression'.[12] As often depicted by 'Abdu'l-Bahá, the son and successor of Bahá'u'lláh, 'of all the peoples and nations of the civilized world, that race and nation' Persia 'had sunk to such ignominious depths, and manifested so great a perversity, as to find no parallel among its contemporaries.'[13] Despotic and uxorious Shahs controlled the provinces through their innumerable corrupt and autocratic progenies. Perhaps even more overbearing and repressive were the Shí'ih clergy who, hand-in-glove with the civil authorities, had absolute control of the servile and largely uneducated masses. Beyond the very basics, education and pursuit of scientific knowledge were almost non-existent. What passed for justice was largely based on interpretations of the Sharia law. Religious minorities such as the Jews, Christians and Zoroastrians were barely tolerated and treated as second class citizens.

Mír Muḥammad-Ḥusayn, the 'She-Serpent'; and Shaykh Muḥammad Báqir, the 'Wolf'

Mír Muḥammad-Ḥusayn's brother, the Sultánu'l-'Ulamá, 'the foremost ecclesiastical authority of that province',[14] had hosted the Báb in his house where the Báb had penned His *Tafsir Súrih val-Asr* (Commentary on the Chapter on Time and Age, that is, the Advent of the Qá'im).

In contrast, Mír Muḥammad-Ḥusayn, the head priest or Imám-Jum'ih[15] who led the prayers in the Friday mosque in Isfahan, was a cruel individual. When he later owed a great deal of money to two wealthy brothers who were followers of Bahá'u'lláh, Mírzá Muḥammad-Ḥasan Iṣfáhání and Mírzá Muḥammad-Ḥusayn Iṣfáhání, he denounced them as Bábís to evade paying the debt. Consequently, in 1879,

> their beautiful houses were at once given over to the mob and stripped, and even the trees and flowers in their gardens were torn away. Whatever they had was taken. Then Shaykh Muḥammad-Báqir . . . pronounced their death sentence. The Prince-Governor, Ẓillu's-Sulṭán, eldest son of the Sháh, ratified it. The brothers were chained. Their heads were severed. Their bodies were dragged to the great open square of the city, and there they were exposed to every indignity the mob could inflict. 'In such wise', 'Abdu'l-Bahá has written, 'was the blood of these two brothers shed that the Christian priest of Julfa[16] cried out, lamented and wept on that day.'[17]

The following is another account of the tragic events:

> [Mír Muḥammad-Ḥusayn] left the management of his financial affairs in the hands of the two brothers who were the most trustworthy persons he could find.
>
> Time passed, during which the Imám-Jum'ih became rich and prosperous through the many financial transactions negotiated for him. He was quite satisfied with the handling of his financial affairs until he was informed that he owed the two brothers a considerable sum of money. It was at this point that the ferocious and beastly nature of the Imám-Jum'ih came to the surface and he turned his evil thoughts to one course of action only – to take the lives of the two who had served him with absolute faithfulness and honesty . . .
>
> To carry out his evil intentions, he combined forces with . . . Shaykh Báqir, the leading mujtahid[18] of the city whom Bahá'u'lláh later denounced as *Dhi'b* (Wolf).[19] They both knew that taking the lives of the two brothers would not be difficult. All that the mujtahid had to do was to write their death warrant on the grounds that they were Bahá'ís . . . these two embodiments of wickedness approached Mas'úd Mírzá, the Ẓillu's-Sulṭán (Shadow of the King),[20] the Governor of Iṣfahán, and asked him to implement their sinister designs. They demanded the execution of the brothers and promised him a giant share of their estate after its confiscation.[21]

The underlying reason for seeking the deaths of the two brothers was therefore largely avarice – two clerics coveted their properties but pretended to be concerned for the welfare of Islam. Bahá'u'lláh condemns Shaykh Báqir, the Wolf, in a Tablet entitled Lawḥ-i-Burhán (Tablet of the Proof) revealed about twelve years before the *Epistle to the Son of the Wolf.* Addressing the She-Serpent in the same Tablet Bahá'u'lláh writes:

> Thou hast clung to tyranny and cast away justice; whereupon all created things have lamented, and still thou art among the wayward. Thou hast put to death the aged, and plundered the young. Thinkest thou that thou wilt consume that which thine iniquity hath amassed? Nay, by Myself! Thus informeth thee He Who is cognizant of all. By God! The things thou possessest shall profit thee not, nor what thou hast laid up through thy cruelty. Unto this beareth witness Thy Lord, the All-Knowing. Thou hast arisen to put out the light of this Cause; ere long will thine own fire be quenched, at His behest.[22]

Bahá'u'lláh predicts a miserable end to both of them, and, in particular, the She-Serpent, Mír Muḥammad-Ḥusayn:

> O heedless outcast! Ere long will the breaths of chastisement seize thee, as they seized others before thee. Wait, O thou who hast joined partners with God, the Lord of the visible and the invisible.[23]

The Lawḥ-i-Burhán arrived in Tehran thirty-eight days after the martyrdom of the two brothers (1879 CE). Two copies were made and sent to Mír Muḥammad-Ḥusayn and Shaykh Muḥammad Báqir.

> It took only a few days after the martyrdom of the 'twin shining lights' before a serious quarrel broke out between the Prince and the Imám-Jum'ih (the She-Serpent) over the sharing out of the plundered wealth. About twenty-five days after the martyrdom, the Imám gathered a great number of his followers who accompanied him to the government house to pressurize the Prince for a much larger share than previously envisaged for him. The crowd gathered and soon there was a commotion outside the government headquarters. Day by day the situation grew worse and soon the central government in Ṭihrán became involved. Soldiers were secretly despatched. They arrested the Imám, ransacked his home, plundered all his possessions and took him to Khurásán as an exile. Eventually he was permitted to return to his native town and retire to his home where he died in great misery. This was two years after the martyrdom of the King and Beloved of the Martyrs.
>
> > . . . expelled from Iṣfáhán, [he] wandered from village to village, contracted a disease that engendered so foul an odor that even his wife and daughter could not bear to approach him, and died in such ill-favor with the local authorities that no one dared to attend his funeral, his corpse being ignominiously interred by a few porters.[24]
>
> The disease mentioned above is said to have been a cancer of the throat which caused a huge abscess on his neck; the pain and the foul odour were intolerable. It is reported that when the martyrdom of the King and Beloved of the Martyrs was being discussed, some

were hesitant to put them to death. The Imám became very angry at this: placing his hands upon his neck he said, 'If there be any sin in this let it be upon my neck!'

> Shaykh Muḥammad Báqir witnessed the steady decline of his prestige, and died in a miserable state of acute remorse . . .[25]

The Prince, Ẓillu's-Sulṭán, whom Bahá'u'lláh has stigmatized as 'the infernal tree' also fell from grace. He who once ruled over two-thirds of Persia, who made the greatest effort and even secured the support of the British government in fulfilling his long-cherished ambition to become the heir to the throne, and who had assembled such pomp and majesty around himself as to rival those of the King – such a man went steadily into decline, his position and authority lowered, and his hopes and aspirations frustrated. In the end he was sent to Europe as an exile, and was only allowed to return home when suffering from melancholia. Later he died in ignominy.[26]

The recipient of the *Epistle to the Son the Wolf*: Shaykh Muḥammad Taqí

Shaykh Muḥammad-Ḥasan-i-Najafí received his early education under his father Shaykh Muḥammad Báqir in Isfahan. He is also known as Áqá Najafí because of his education in Najaf where he studied *Usúl al-fiqh* (jurisprudence)[27] and *Usúl al-Din* (roots of religion). On his return to Isfahan, he cooperated with his father on various religious activities including the persecution of the Bahá'ís.

After the death of his father, Shaykh Muḥammad Taqí was confirmed as a *mujtahid* (an authority in Islamic law) and judge. He rose in the rank of clerics becoming the leading mujtahid of Persia. He was extolled as '*Ayatalláh* (Sign of God), the deputy of the Twelfth Imám (*Náyib-i Imám Zamán*), and *Hujjat al-Islám* (Proof of Islám)'.[28] He is reported to have authored about a hundred books on obscure and metaphysical aspects of Islam, largely the products of his own imagination. These he reportedly published at his own expense.[29] Others have maintained that he plagiarized the works of others, and that 'these were not Áqá Najafí's own, but were written by others and published in his name'.[30] Nonetheless Bahá'u'lláh refers to him as 'the acknowledged exponent and repository' of arts and sciences.[31] The historian Nabíl has described him as a 'proud and fanatic leader'.[32] Others have maintained that Áqá Najafí 'never attained a reputation of high scholarly achievement, and was called into question by critics for his mediocre academic learning and lack of erudition'.[33] Yet some of his supporters made exaggerated claims about him – that he possessed divine inspiration, and that his knowledge was revealed to him by the Imáms and therefore transcended all fallible worldly knowledge.

The Shaykh allegedly loved his food and drink, and adding to his vast wealth, often illegitimately:

> Áqá Najafí was well connected with the leading merchants of the city; he had managed to establish his authority over legal and economic matters, by accumulating extraordinary riches and financial power which secured both his religious and political influence. On these grounds he had acquired a controversial reputation. Orthodox and post-revolutionary Iranian historians portrayed him as an achieved scholar, and advocate of popular interests, who was selfless and charitable; more critical scholars as . . . a bigoted opportunist, a ruthless murderer, and a voracious magnate.[34]

> To avoid paying government taxes, Āqā Najafī manipulated revenue officers; one he publicly treated as unbeliever (Nūrallāh Dānešvar 'Alawī, *Tārīḵ-e mašrūṭa-ye Īrān o jonbeš-e waṭanparastān-e Eṣfahān o Baḵtīārī*, Tehran, 1956, p. 189); in the end he had to pay taxes of at least 60,000 tomans a year (Dawlatābādī, *Tārīḵ* I, p. 339). According to M. Malekzāda, during a famine Ḥājjī Moḥammad Ja'far, the mayor of Isfahan, complained that people were dying of hunger while Āqā Najafī had stored thousands of *ḵarvārs* (one *ḵarvār* = 300 kilos) of wheat that he would not sell at any reasonable price; the mayor was then tortured to death in the street (*Tārīḵ-e enqelāb-e mašrūṭīyat-e Īrān* I, Tehran, 1327 Š./1948, p. 166).[35]

Like the father, he too would get excited by the kill, martyring large numbers of Bahá'ís without just cause or due process. Despite his pretences to holiness, he too was motivated by materialism and greed – despite his enormous wealth he coveted the modest land and properties of the Bahá'ís who lived in the small villages around Isfahan:

> Isfahán's rich and fertile hinterlands contributed essentially to the wealth of the city's nobility, who owned most of the villages and land, of which the Zill al-Sultán and Áqá Najafí owned the lion's share.[36]

He initiated a campaign of persecution of the Bahá'ís of Najafabad and Sidih (towns in the province of Isfahan) in 1889 and 1890, driving over a hundred people out of the villages,[37] and resulting in the revelation of *Epistle to the Son of Wolf*. The persecution of the Bahá'ís seemed to have been 'part of the unrelenting power politics among the rank of the 'ulemá (religious scholars), who sought to advance their personal authority and reputation' by campaigns against the religious minorities.[38]

Áqá Najafí was not averse to testing the will of Náṣiri'd-Dín Sháh and the governor, Ẓillu's-Sulṭán, who tried to moderate the cleric's blood-thirsty atrocities against the Bahá'ís and the Jews. When the Shah curtailed the power of Ẓillu's-Sulṭán, 'Áqá Najafí tested the opportunity for the reestablishment of his name through pogroms against the Bábís as well as the Jews':[39]

> In the early summer of 1889 . . . Áqá Najafí embarked on a campaign against the Jews . . . the Zill al-Sultán swiftly intervened and Áqá Najafí turned his efforts against the Bábís of Najafábád and Sidih of Márbín . . . His motion was again forestalled by the Zill al-Sultán . . . Four months later, when the prince had left Isfahán for his annual trip to Ṭihrán, Áqá Najafí resumed his lapsed crusade against the Bábís of Sidih and Najafábád. Disregarding the Sháh's orders to allow these men to return to their village unharmed Áqá Najafí endorsed the massacre of the Sidihís . . .[40]

> The methods of inciting a pogrom were unsophisticated, blunt, time-honored, and if not stopped by the government or foiled by the opposition of rival mujtahids always worked. The *tulláb* (students), or the *lútís* (thugs) . . . were swiftly mobilized and petty disputes . . . were frequently exploited to embroil a whole city quarter. At the same time there was a dramatic difference in the nature of harassment; while particularly lower class Bábís could literally be hounded and massacred in a pogrom, transgressions against the Jews surfaced usually in threats, petty discrimination, and oppressive economic sanctions . . .[41]

He also engineered a massacre of the Bahá'ís in 1902. The ferocity of the campaigns alarmed even the central government and Áqá Najafí was summoned to the capital on two occasions to reduce tensions.

> The murders of Bábís and Bahá'ís, commissioned by Shaykh Muhammad Báqir and his son Áqá Najafí were central to their political and juridical rationale . . . Even partisan biographers admitted the excessive brutality of their pogroms, but defended these as divine will and as a just resistance against evil.[42]

The unrest which he caused resulted in his eventual banishment from Isfahan.

The *Epistle to the Son of the Wolf*

Like many of Bahá'u'lláh's other Writings, the style of the Epistle may be described as pulsatile – many closely-related subjects are dealt with intensely and energetically, and the important issues are referred to again and again.

Bahá'u'lláh also seamlessly cites, directly and indirectly, many verses of the Bible and Qur'án in the *Epistle to the Son of the Wolf.* Thus in His last major work He follows the style of the *Kitáb-i-Íqán*, revealed the year prior to the declaration of His Mission in Baghdad, which by frequently referring to scriptural passages illustrates that 'all the Prophets are the Temples of the Cause of God, Who have appeared clothed in divers attire . . . all abiding in the same tabernacle, soaring in the same heaven, seated upon the same throne, uttering the same speech, and proclaiming the same Faith.'[43]

In this manner, the *Epistle to the Son of the Wolf* powerfully reinforces belief in the singleness of the aims and purposes of the various Messengers of God, and inculcates hope of the 'ultimate reconciliation of their teachings and followers'. Indeed, a 'cardinal truth which is of the essence of the Faith of Bahá'u'lláh' is that 'all the Prophets of God – including Jesus Christ and the Apostle of God, the two greatest Manifestations preceding the Revelation of the Báb' are divine in origin. The followers of Bahá'u'lláh 'unreservedly and unshakably' uphold 'the fundamental unity of these Messengers of God' and affirm 'the continuity of their Revelations', and admit 'the God-given authority and correlative character of their Books'.[44] As attested by Bahá'u'lláh, 'These principles and laws, these firmly-established and mighty systems, have proceeded from one Source, and are the rays of one Light. That they differ one from another is to be attributed to the varying requirements of the ages in which they were promulgated.'[45]

In Paris 'Abdu'l-Bahá stated, 'The Heavenly Books, the Bible, the Qur'án, and the other Holy Writings have been given by God as guides into the paths of Divine virtue, love, justice and peace,'[46] and wrote in the pulpit Bible in London's City Temple, 'This book is the Holy Book of God, of celestial Inspiration. It is the Bible of Salvation, the Noble Gospel. It is the mystery of the Kingdom and its light. It is the Divine Bounty, the sign of the guidance of God.'[47] Furthermore, 'Abdu'l-Bahá in the *Tablets of the Divine Plan*, the second of three charters for the World Order of Bahá'u'lláh, relates the creation of unity to elucidation of the mysteries of the Bible and of the Qur'án.[48]

The recipient of the Epistle, Shaykh Muḥammad Taqí, as a prominent Muslim clergyman and scholar would have been familiar with the references to the verses of the Qur'án, but perhaps had never considered these in the light of Bahá'u'lláh's explanations. Notably, Bahá'u'lláh exhorts the Shí'ih cleric: 'Hearken unto the melodies of the Gospel with the ear of fairness'.[49]

In light of the above, the following annotations attempt to provide succinct additional explanations of themes in the Bible and Qur'án. The English translations from these holy books are the King James version and the translation by Yusuf Ali respectively, unless otherwise indicated.

Major themes

Unique in religious experience, Bahá'u'lláh towards the end of His earthly life reviews the salient events associated with the history of His Faith, and re-reveals parts of His earlier Writings. The Epistle is remarkable in the manner with which Bahá'u'lláh deals with His venal, cruel and blood-thirsty adversary. He traces for him the path for his redemption and reveals for him a prayer of forgiveness and remorse for his seemingly unpardonable sins. He should not despair of God's mercy and grace, as there was still the opportunity to recognize the truth and to serve God's Faith.

Quoting His Tablet to Náṣiri'd-Dín Sháh, His royal adversary, Bahá'u'lláh describes Himself as unlettered (*ummi*) and explains the easily verifiable fact that He had no formal education. His Revelation was therefore not His own, but emanated from the Lord God.

Bahá'u'lláh expounds in the Epistle:

> Religion is, verily, the chief instrument for the establishment of order in the world, and of tranquillity amongst its peoples. The weakening of the pillars of religion hath strengthened the foolish, and emboldened them, and made them more arrogant. Verily I say: The greater the decline of religion, the more grievous the waywardness of the ungodly. This cannot but lead in the end to chaos and confusion.[50]

And He admonishes:

> Gird up the loins of your endeavor, O people of Bahá, that haply the tumult of religious dissension and strife that agitateth the peoples of the earth may be stilled, that every trace of it may be completely obliterated. For the love of God, and them that serve Him, arise to aid this most sublime and momentous Revelation. Religious fanaticism and hatred are a world-devouring fire, whose violence none can quench. The Hand of Divine power can, alone, deliver mankind from this desolating affliction.[51]

Lameh Fananapazir

A SUMMARY OF
EPISTLE TO THE SON OF THE WOLF

¶0 – ¶2

The opening sentence praises God, 'the One' and 'Incomparable'. Unconstrained, He has revealed His Cause and Most Exalted Word amidst all peoples. By revealing the Qur'án, the God of Mercy has transformed man into the spiritual being fit to receive the Bayán.

The Supreme Mediator Who manifests the divine names and attributes is then praised. 'Through Him the light of unity and the law of oneness hath been revealed amidst the nations.'

¶3 – ¶7

Bahá'u'lláh respectfully counsels Shaykh Muḥammad Taqíy-i-Najafí to heed His admonitions which are offered purely out of consideration for his spiritual well-being: 'Know thou that the ear of man hath been created that it may hearken unto the Divine Voice on this Day that hath been mentioned in all the Books, Scriptures and Tablets.' As a preliminary he must purify his soul with the waters of renunciation, fear God, and place his reliance on Him. Having set his face towards the Most Great House in Baghdad, he must offer the prayer that is revealed for him to assist him to supplicate forgiveness for his many misdeeds and cruelties.

He should not despair, for no one is beyond God's redemption, but put his trust in the One Who 'turnest darkness into light' and commit his affairs to His care.

¶ 8 – ¶ 9

Bahá'u'lláh informs the Shaykh that none of the calumnies, denials, or cavils of men can harm him – He has not spoken of His own impulse but has been given a voice by One Who 'hath given a voice unto all things, that they may praise and glorify Him'.

¶ 10 – ¶ 11

Bahá'u'lláh reveals a second prayer so that the Shaykh may inhale the breath of detachment and have pity upon himself and others. God is potent to exalt or abase whomsoever He wishes.

Now is the time for mankind to be adorned 'with a fresh attire' through the transformative power of His Revelation. He entreats God to aid the Shaykh to be just and fair-minded, to be acquainted with the things that were hidden from the eyes of men, to reflect upon that which has been revealed, to be fair and just in his speech, truthful and sincere, and that he may thus be delivered from the darkness of ignorance, and arise to illumine the world with the light of knowledge.

Bahá'u'lláh reiterates that He has frequented no school, nor 'attended the controversies of the learned' – He has not revealed Himself, but God has manifested Him.

¶ 12

Excerpts from the Lawḥ-i-Sulṭán, Bahá'u'lláh's Tablet to Náṣiri'd-Dín Sháh. Bahá'u'lláh describes His intimations of His Revelation and Mission. His knowledge is innate: 'The learning current amongst men I studied not; their schools I entered not'; God's 'all-compelling summons hath reached Me, and caused Me to speak His praise amidst all people'.

¶ 13

Now is the time for the Shaykh to cleanse himself with the waters of detachment, and to strive to quench 'through the power of wisdom and the force of thy utterance, the fire of enmity and hatred which smouldereth in the hearts of the peoples of the world'. The purpose of the successive Messengers who have been sent down, and their Revelations, has been 'promoting the knowledge of God, and of furthering unity and fellowship amongst men . . .'

¶ 14 – ¶ 15

Emphasis on justice and equity – attributes that will ensure 'the well-being of the world and the protection of the nations'.

¶ 16

Oneness of God and His Divine Plan: 'the purpose of the one true God . . . hath been to bring forth the Mystic Gems out of the mine of man – they Who are the Dawning-Places of His Cause . . .'

¶ 17– ¶ 18

Oneness of faith: 'That the divers communions of the earth, and the manifold systems of religious belief, should never be allowed to foster the feelings of animosity among men, is, in this Day, of the essence of the Faith of God . . .' – all religions 'have proceeded from one Source, and are rays of one Light'. Their teachings have been adapted to the needs of 'the ages in which they were promulgated'.

The task of Bahá'u'lláh's followers is to obliterate religious dissension and strife – only God's transforming power can deliver mankind from the 'desolating affliction' and 'world-devouring fire' of religious fanaticism and hatred.

¶ 19 – ¶ 21

Oneness of mankind: 'Ye are the fruits of one tree, and the leaves of one branch'; 'So powerful is the light of unity that it can illuminate the whole earth.'

Bahá'u'lláh therefore commands His followers to: 'Consort with all men, O people of Bahá, in a spirit of friendliness and fellowship;' and to share the truth of His Revelation 'in a language of utmost kindliness and goodwill'.

¶ 22 – ¶ 27

By 'divines', whom Bahá'u'lláh admonishes, 'is meant those men who outwardly attire themselves with the raiment of knowledge, but who inwardly are deprived therefrom'. He asks them why they 'wear the guise of the shepherd, when inwardly ye have become wolves, intent upon My flock?' He castigates them as heedless, occupied with worldly matters, outwardly virtuous but inwardly corrupt.

Conversely, He praises 'those divines who are truly adorned with the ornament of knowledge and of a goodly character'; they are 'as a head to the body of the world, and as eyes to the nations'.

¶ 28

Bahá'u'lláh is aware that the Shaykh has turned against Him, and has 'bidden the people to curse' Him. He expresses His willingness to sacrifice His life: 'I fear no tribulation in [God's] path.'

¶ 29

He reveals a third prayer for the Shaykh to ask God to grant him forgiveness and mercy, and admonishes him: 'Set thine heart towards Him Who is the Kaaba of God.'

¶ 30 – ¶ 31

God has fulfilled His promise and unsealed the Choice Wine of His Revelation. It is therefore futile for the divines to study 'arts and sciences' that begin and end with words. He reminds the Shaykh that God in the past transformed unlearned individuals and made them effective promoters of His Faith.

Man-made learning cannot be made a standard of truth.

¶ 32 – ¶ 36

Description of events and Bahá'u'lláh's sufferings following the attempt on the life of the Shah and false accusations against Him; His detention and imprisonment in the Síyáh-Chál; and the fierce ensuing persecution. Following His release He set Himself the task of regenerating the faith of the Bábís.

Bahá'u'lláh's intimations of His Revelation in the prison of Tehran, and God's promise: 'Verily, We shall render Thee victorious by Thyself and by Thy Pen . . .'

His subsequent exile to Baghdad. 'We exhorted all men, and particularly this people, through Our wise counsels and loving admonitions, and forbade them to engage in sedition, quarrels, disputes and conflict. As a result of this, and by the grace of God, waywardness and folly were changed into piety and understanding, and weapons converted into instruments of peace.'

¶ 37 – ¶ 53

The essentials of faith – some of the moral and ethical laws Bahá'u'lláh revealed in Baghdad designed primarily to transform the character of the Bábís but also addressed to the 'peoples of the earth'.

He enjoins honesty and piety. What harms Him is when His followers forget their high calling and make mischief. They must exemplify purity, patience, awareness of the presence of God, chastity, respect for the property and privacy of others, and must wage war in the path of God with the armies of wisdom and utterance, of a goodly character and praiseworthy deeds. Contention and conflict are forbidden. The peoples are forbidden to revile one another, for He has come 'to unite and weld together all that dwell on earth'. He forbids the shedding of blood, and abrogates the law to wage holy war (allowed by earlier Dispensations including that of the Báb).

His followers are to pursue art and sciences that profit humanity.

The civil and religious leaders must uphold religion, for it is 'the chief instrument for the establishment of order in the world, and of tranquillity amongst its peoples'.

He pleads: 'Strive that haply the tribulations suffered by this Wronged One and by you, in the path of God, may not prove to have been in vain.'

¶ 54

Bahá'u'lláh teaches that the individual should not consider the things that profit him but instead what profits mankind, and choose for his neighbour that which he wishes for himself. Humility exalts man, whilst pride abases him. He lauds the greatness of His Day, and warns that 'ears that are defiled with lying tales have never been, nor are they now, fit to hear' the Voice of God.

¶ 55 – ¶ 57

He invites the rulers to establish the Lesser Peace to ensure the tranquility of the nations: 'convene an all-inclusive general assembly' to establish unity and concord, and thus avoid the need to maintain excessively large armies. The exercise of justice is 'a powerful force' that conquers the 'hearts and souls of men', reveals truths, and is 'the standard-bearer of love and bounty'.

He refers to knowledge 'concealed in the treasuries of the knowledge of God' which 'when applied, will largely, though not wholly, eliminate fear' but advises that this knowledge should be 'taught from childhood'.

¶ 58 – ¶ 62

Assailed from all sides, Bahá'u'lláh reiterates that He has never desired earthly leadership. His sole aim has been the betterment of the world and to suppress the causes of contention and disunity of the nations, 'so that all men may be sanctified from every earthly attachment . . .' He warns against misrepresenting the truth and recounting miracles and prodigies as proof of His Cause.

He acknowledges that 'all are earnestly striving to put out this glorious and shining light', including the dissemination of false reports by Mírzá Yaḥyá's followers in Istanbul (Constantinople) designed to cause difficulties for the prisoners in 'Akká, for example, that Bahá'u'lláh has been receiving vast amounts of money from Persia when in fact the 'Akká exiles are 'denied the barest means of subsistence.'

He prays that God may protect His loved ones, and aid them to be patient and long-suffering. He promises that although the Ark of God has been battered by waves, the dawn will break and the storms will pass.

¶ 63 – ¶ 64

Bahá'u'lláh attests that 'the true Faith' laments at what has been inflicted on God's religion today, but in reality Judaism, Christianity and Islam rejoice at the reappearance of the One Who authored their Revelations. He exhorts humanity: 'Withhold not yourselves from that which hath been revealed through His grace. Seize ye the living waters of immortality . . .' As in earlier Dispensations, God has today 'enjoined on men what is right, and forbidden what is wrong'.

As opposed to the practices of Shí'ih Islam and the Covenant-breakers, Bahá'u'lláh and His followers shun dissimulation (*taqíyyah*, conveniently hiding the truth).

¶ 65 – ¶ 67

Quoting from His Tablet to Náṣiri'd-Dín Sháh, Bahá'u'lláh states that the summons of God had transformed Him and instructed Him to reveal the divine purpose. He counsels the king to be just – the people that surround him love him for their own sakes, whereas Bahá'u'lláh loves him for his sake. Had he the bounty of recognizing Bahá'u'lláh, he would regard his 'sovereignty as the most contemptible of [his] possessions, abandoning it to whosoever might desire it'. He would not be willing to bear the 'burden of dominion' save for the purpose of helping God's Faith.

¶ 68 – ¶ 76

Bahá'u'lláh refutes the allegation of the Wolf and the Son of the Wolf that the Bábís believe in 'his Divinity and Godhead', and their assertion that Bahá'ís should read the Súrih of Tawḥíd which declares the Oneness of God. He explains that God has 'everlastingly been sanctified above the mention and praise' of anyone but Himself. The connection of God to His Prophets is an identity of purpose and not of personalities. They are the manifestation of self-effacement – they say nothing from themselves but speak only as God bids them. They are thus one with Him. Bahá'u'lláh illustrates this point from the sayings of Imám 'Alí: it was the same self-effacement that allowed Moses to heed the Voice of God which addressed Him through the Burning Bush. The subject of the relation of the Prophets to God has created idle fancies.

Bahá'u'lláh prays God 'to grant unto men hearing ears, and sharp sight, and dilated breasts, and receptive hearts'.

¶ 76 – ¶ 77

In a Tablet sent from Adrianople, Bahá'u'lláh announced His mission to Napoleon III, and responded to some of his statements in relation to the Crimean War. The Emperor did not reply and abjectly failed this test of his sincerity, reportedly saying, 'if this man is God, I am two Gods'. When Bahá'u'lláh was in 'Akká He received a letter from Napoleon's Minister, and laments the fact that His Tablet had been misunderstood as a request for material assistance.

¶ 78 – ¶ 82

This section consists in part of realized eschatology. Bahá'u'lláh states that there is no need for the priests to ring the church bells to gather the faithful, for 'The Most Mighty Bell hath appeared in the form of Him Who is the Most Great Name . . .' The 'Ancient of Days' had come. His was the voice that addressed Moses on Mount Sinai and He was the One Who sent Christ to announce His Light. The peoples should set their faces towards Bahá'u'lláh and arise 'to serve God and help His Cause'. He is the' Face of God', 'His Testimony and Guide', the 'Desired One'.

But when He came as Christ promised, the priests failed to recognize Him. They have thus become the fallen stars foretold in the Gospels.

¶ 83

Bahá'u'lláh commands the Christian monks not to seclude themselves in their 'churches and cloisters', and to abandon celibacy. He explains that Christ, who did not marry, 'could find no place wherein to abide, nor where to lay His head'.

¶ 84 – ¶ 94

Bahá'u'lláh upbraids Napoleon III for his insincerity and his rejection of His summons. He urges him to arise and make amends, and warns him: 'Erelong the world and all that thou possessest will perish . . .' 'For what thou hast done, thy kingdom shall be thrown into confusion, and thine empire shall pass from thine hands . . . Commotions shall seize all the people in that land, unless thou arisest to help this Cause, and followest Him Who is the Spirit of God (Jesus Christ) in this, the Straight Path.'

Bahá'u'lláh informs Napoleon of His banishments and imprisonment in 'Akká by the 'King of Islám' (the Ottoman Sultan) for the crime of introducing a new religion. He asks the Emperor, if he prefers a more ancient Dispensation why does he ignore the teachings of the Bible? He warns him not to allow 'wolves to become the shepherds of the fold'. He admonishes him that the thing that deters him is 'worldliness in its essence'. 'Exultest thou over the treasures thou dost possess, knowing they shall perish? Rejoicest thou in that thou rulest a span of earth, when the whole world, in the estimation of the people of Bahá, is worth as much as the black in the eye of a dead ant?'

¶ 95 – ¶ 99

Bahá'u'lláh re-reveals sections of the Súriy-i-Haykal addressed to the Czar of Russia. He invites him to listen to the voice of God: 'Beware that nothing deter thee from setting thy face towards thy Lord, the Compassionate, the Most Merciful.' He informs the Czar that He has heard his prayer, and acknowledges the help of his Minister whilst imprisoned in the Black Pit of Tehran. He announces to him that His advent signifies that 'He Who is the Father is come', as anticipated 'mounted upon the clouds'. He reminds him that when Christ appeared at the First Coming, Herod the king gave judgement against Him.

¶ 100 – ¶ 106

Bahá'u'lláh quotes from His Tablet to Queen Victoria, saying that in quoting from these Tablets he wishes the Shaykh to share their contents with other divines.

He tells Victoria that the promises of the Gospel have been fulfilled. He praises her for forbidding the slave trade, but advises her: 'Man's actions are acceptable after his having recognized (the Manifestation).' He also praises her for promoting constitutional monarchy, noting however that the elected members must be trustworthy and regard themselves the representatives of all humanity. He encourages consultation at national and international levels for the betterment of mankind. Bahá'u'lláh further explains that God has ordained 'one common Faith' as the sovereign remedy for the healing of the world, but: 'This can in no wise be achieved except through the power of a skilled, an all-powerful, and inspired Physician.' He further announces to her that the 'World Reformer', the 'Ancient Beauty' has come that 'He may quicken the world and unite its peoples', but that at all times He has been at the mercy of 'wicked doers'.

¶ 107 – ¶ 109

Fomenting discord, a charge that has been used to inflict injustice on the Báb and Bahá'u'lláh and their followers, was also levelled against Moses by the Pharaohs from fear that He wished to change the religion of the people. Indeed, 'men have, at all times, considered every World Reformer a fomenter of discord'. The test was even greater for Pharaoh as he had reared Moses in his family, and prior to His Revelation on Mount Sinai Moses had in fact disturbed the peace by killing an Egyptian.

¶ 110 – ¶ 115

The real mischief was caused by the supporters of Mírzá Yaḥyá who, in collaboration with Persian dignitaries, had been constantly plotting in Istanbul to dishonour Bahá'u'lláh and to discredit His followers. Bahá'u'lláh prays that God will 'assist them that have been led astray to be just and fair-minded . . . to dispel the mists of idle fancy, and to tear away the veils of vain imaginings and hopes'. For His part, He has been occupied 'in the daytime and in the night-season . . . with that which would edify the souls of men, until the light of knowledge prevailed over the darkness of ignorance'.

¶ 116 – ¶ 129

For about forty years Bahá'u'lláh had assisted the Shah in maintaining the peace. He pays tribute to some of the many individuals who had testified to the truth of His Cause with their lives and bore their torments with patience, resignation and contentment. He mentions the sufferings of His followers in Mázindarán, Rasht and Isfahan, mentioning Ḥájí Náṣir, the King of Martyrs and the Beloved of Martyrs, Káẓim, As͟hraf, Mírzá Muṣṭafá, Badí‘, Najaf-‘Alí, Mullá ‘Alí-Ján, ‘Abá-Básir, Siyyid As͟hraf-i-Zanjání, the mother of As͟hraf, the father of Badí‘, and Siyyid Ismá‘íl.

He exhorts the S͟hayk͟h to arise and serve his Lord, reminding him that God accepted the faith and service of Balál, the Ethiopian slave who could not even pronounce correctly the Arabic phrase ‘I testify’.

He provides a brief account of His own severe trials: ‘O S͟hayk͟h! That which hath touched this Wronged One is beyond compare or equal.’

He describes the remarkable instance when following the martyrdom of Ḥájí Muḥammad-Riḍá in Ashgabat (‘Is͟hqábád), whose family and friends interceded on behalf of the murderers rather than seek revenge.

He entreats God to assist the Shah to ‘ponder upon these things, and to judge with equity and justice’. He states: ‘We, verily, have announced unto men this Most Great Revelation, and yet the people are in a state of strange stupor.’

¶ 130 – ¶ 138

Bahá’u’lláh quotes from the Lawḥ-i-Burhán revealed following the martyrdom of the King of Martyrs and the Beloved of Martyrs to the S͟hayk͟h’s father, the ‘Wolf’. Addressing the Wolf as ‘O thou who are reputed for thy learning!’, Bahá’u’lláh once again describes the enormity of his action: ‘Thou hast pronounced sentence against them for whom the books of the world all scriptures have wept, and in whose favour the scriptures of all religions have testified.’ He informs the persecutor of His Faith: ‘There is no hatred in Mine heart for thee nor for anyone.’

The fanaticism and hatred of the Wolf are compared to those who opposed Christ, Muhammad, and indeed all earlier prophets. Although he may have considered his persecution of Bahá’u’lláh’s followers as a great service to Islam, he had in fact dismayed Muhammad and His Holy Family whom he claimed to revere. His unreasonableness and injustice were at variance with the moral and ethical principles of the Qur’án, and he had behaved as the ‘Pharisees and the idolatrous [Meccan] priests’; rather, he had ‘surpassed them in their cruelty’, and in the damage he had done to the Cause of God.

¶ 139 – ¶ 141

In contrast to the martyrs of the Faith, the faint-hearted Mírzá Hádí Dawlat-Ábádí is upbraided, he who claimed to have believed in the Báb but when accused of being a Bábí ascended the pulpits and reviled Him.

He mentions some of the most harrowing and poignant episodes in Bábí–Bahá'í history that resulted in the martyrdom of many believers: Zanján, Nayríz, Ṭabarsí, and the upheaval in the aftermath of the attempted assassination of Náṣiri'd-Dín Sháh by two crazed Bábís.

¶ 142 – ¶ 145

It was now incumbent upon the Shah to 'deal with this people with loving-kindness and mercy': 'A just king enjoyeth nearer access unto God than anyone.' His teachings were that His followers respect and obey the civil authorities. The divines must support the king and not undermine his authority. They should 'cleave unto that which will insure the protection, the security, the welfare and prosperity of men'.

¶ 146

If the Shaykh were to ponder even briefly upon the fate of earlier Dispensations he would have endeavoured to become the means for exalting God's Word – all God's Messengers were ridiculed, rejected and persecuted, some were held to be possessed, others were called impostors. Bahá'u'lláh's Revelation was therefore no exception.

¶ 147 – ¶ 148

Mention of other virtues that must characterize the followers of Bahá'u'lláh: 'Be generous in prosperity . . .' He explains that His admonishment of the Shaykh is no harsher than His treatment of a wayward son.

¶ 149 – ¶ 150

Bahá'u'lláh has always faced dire peril, and spent most of the days of His life sitting under a sword of Damocles. However, He asks God, 'But for the tribulations which are sustained in Thy path, how could

Thy true lovers be recognized; and were it not for the trials which are borne for love of [God], how could the station of such as yearn for Thee be revealed?' He prays, 'Raise up, I implore Thee, O my God, as helpers to this Revelation such as shall be counted worthy of Thy Name and of Thy sovereignty, that they may remember Thee among Thy creatures, and hoist the ensigns of Thy victory in Thy land, and adorn them with Thy virtues and Thy commandments.'

He declares, 'I am the true Faith of God amongst you. Beware that ye deny Me not.'

¶ 151 – ¶ 157

Bahá'u'lláh re-reveals sections of the Lawḥ-i-Burhán, addressed to the Shaykh's father; the Voice of God has commanded him to 'recite' the remaining passages to the Shaykh. Also, the *Kitáb-i-Íqán* and the Tablet to Napoleon III should be read. Bahá'u'lláh advises that what profits man is setting his face towards the Most Sublime Word. He warns the Wolf, 'Rely not on thy glory, and thy power. Thou art even as the last trace of sunlight upon the mountain-top. Soon will it fade away.' He wonders why the Shah had chosen to turn a blind eye to the mischief he was inciting in Persia. He also rebukes the Muslim divines collectively, 'Because of you the people were abased, and the banner of Islám was hauled down, and its mighty throne subverted. Every time a man of discernment hath sought to hold fast unto that which would exalt Islám, ye raised a clamor, and thereby was he deterred from achieving his purpose, while the land remained fallen in clear ruin.'

¶ 158

The accomplice of the Wolf, the Imám-Jum'ih of Isfahan, is castigated as the 'She-Serpent' for his role in the martyrdom of the two Siyyid brothers for financial gain – he is warned of his impending punishment.

¶ 159 – ¶ 160

Bahá'u'lláh declares to the Shaykh, 'This Cause is too evident to be obscured, and too conspicuous to be concealed. It shineth as the sun in its meridian glory. None can deny it unless he be a hater and a doubter.'

In a prayer He supplicates God, 'Thou hast lighted the lamp of Thy Cause with the oil of wisdom; protect it from contrary winds. The lamp is Thine, and the glass is Thine, and all things in the heavens and on earth are in the grasp of Thy power. Bestow justice upon the rulers, and fairness upon the divines . . .'

¶ 161 – ¶ 166

Bahá'u'lláh alerts the Shaykh that God 'had seized the reins of authority' from the ecclesiastics, who will be 'afflicted with the retribution which their acts must entail'. He mentions the ongoing mischief designed to embarrass God's Faith resulting from an evil collaboration between by the followers of Mírzá Yaḥyá and the Persian Embassy in Istanbul. The false accusations had resulted in the suicide of one the followers of Bahá'u'lláh. However, God would divulge their machinations: 'The time is at hand when whatsoever lieth hid in the souls and hearts of men will be disclosed.' He would nullify the efforts of the mischief-makers through the influence of His Word.

¶ 167 – ¶ 171

Bahá'u'lláh returns to the important issue of divinity and Godhead. He explains that Imám Ṣádiq hath said: 'Servitude is a substance, the essence of which is Divinity.' Clearly, the Prophets are the essence of servitude and thus divine. He further frames the advent of the Qá'im as the coming of the Lord. The Qur'án anticipates that God Himself will come. In several of his statements, Imám 'Alí claims divinity.

Bahá'u'lláh also alludes to scriptural references that explicitly anticipate the 'Divine Presence', namely, 'the Presence of Him Who is the Dayspring of the signs, and the Dawning-Place of the clear tokens, and the Manifestation of the Excellent Names, and the Source of the attributes, of the true God . . .'.

¶ 172

Bahá'u'lláh instructs the Shaykh: 'Bid men to do that which is praiseworthy, and be not of such as tarry,' for 'the Sun of Truth shineth resplendently' from 'the prison-city of 'Akká'. 'Repudiation hath not veiled it, and all were powerless to withhold it from shining. Thou canst excuse thyself no longer. Either thou must recognize it, or . . . deny all the Prophets!'

¶ 173 – ¶ 178

This section describes how the Shí'ih sect had because of their idle fancies and vain imaginings denied their Qá'im and put Him to death. It was the followers of Shaykh Aḥmad-i-Aḥsá'í who had understood the signs. Bahá'u'lláh encourages the divines to sent a representative to 'Akká to investigate His truth, and also evaluate Mírzá Yaḥyá who had been banished to Cyprus. So far, they were attacking Bahá'u'lláh without ever having met him.

He describes the holding of the ceremony of *Rawḍih-khání* (traditional lamentation for the Imám Ḥusayn), which some prominent Bábís were commemorating in their houses, as an error, explaining that according to tradition, during the Revelation of the Qá'im (the Báb) the Imáms have been resurrected.

¶ 179 – ¶ 190

Bahá'u'lláh reiterates that the community of His followers has for many years now not been 'inclined to mischief'. Such is their transformation that their hearts 'are illumined with the light of the fear of God, and adorned with the adornment of His love. Their concern hath ever been and now is for the betterment of the world. Their purpose is to obliterate differences, and quench the flame of hatred and enmity, so that the whole earth may come to be viewed as one country.'

In contrast, the officials of the Persian Embassy in Istanbul were assiduously seeking to put out God's Light and to exterminate His Faith.

He describes the people of Bahá as 'men who if they came to cities of pure gold will consider them not; and if they meet the fairest and most comely of women will turn aside'. There is therefore no basis to the stories that are being spread to discredit Him. He adjures the Shah to investigate these matters fairly.

He rhetorically asks the cause of the waywardness of the Shí'ih sect 'which regardeth itself as the most learned, the most righteous, and the most pious of all the peoples of the world', for it to commit such cruelty. Figuratively, Bahá'u'lláh describes that the pulpits are protesting at what the clergy are preaching from them. He for His part has repeatedly admonished the divines and invited them to fulfil a higher calling. He warns the 'leaders of religion' not to measure the worth of His Revelation by the criteria known to them. He declares that the true Faith groans because it has been hamstrung by the efforts of those who wish to extinguish God's light. He invites the Shaykh to exert himself so that 'the wings of men may be sanctified from the mire of self and desire, and be made worthy to soar in the atmosphere of God's love'.

¶ 191 – ¶ 193

This section deals with realized eschatology of the Qur'án. To appreciate the fulfilment of the expectations, the Shaykh and his fellow Muslims must not be laden down by the mire of 'vague fancies', 'vain imaginings' and selfish desires.

¶ 194 – ¶ 198

Once again, Bahá'u'lláh admonishes that the fear of God is 'the fountain-head of all goodly deeds and virtues. It is the commander of the hosts of justice in the city of Bahá'. Any man who upholds its standard has been true to the Covenant of Bahá'u'lláh mentioned by the Báb in His Writings.

The people of God must be adorned with trustworthiness and piety. They must assist Him through goodly deeds and praiseworthy character.

¶ 199 – ¶ 202

Bahá'u'lláh restates that He 'hath, at all times, summoned the peoples of the world unto that which will exalt them, and draw them nigh unto God'.

He once again urges the Shaykh to encourage the divines to unite with the Shah to 'exalt the station of both the government and the nation'. In this context he mentions the necessity of a universal auxiliary language, and recommends that to aid the creation of unity humanity must 'choose one of the divers languages' or 'create a new language and a new script to be taught children in schools throughout the world'.

¶ 203 – ¶ 205

Bahá'u'lláh alludes to the fact that His Name 'Bahá' is specifically mentioned in an important Shí'ih prayer read at dawn during the fasting month of Ramadan: 'I beseech Thee by Thy most glorious light (Bahá) . . .'

He gives details of the prophecies of His Forerunner, the Báb, recorded in the *Bayán* with regard to 'He Whom God shall make manifest', and the year 'nine'. Bahá'u'lláh states that the Báb 'laid down His life for this Great Announcement . . .'

¶ 206 – ¶ 215

Bahá'u'lláh invites the Shaykh to listen to the 'melodies of the Gospel' which state clearly that the exact knowledge of that Day is with the Father only. He quotes realized eschatology with reference to many Biblical prophets. He alludes to the fact that 'the blast of the trumpet must needs spread confusion throughout the world'. He states that the truths that 'lie concealed' in the Words of Jesus have now been announced 'by the Most Sublime Pen'.

¶ 216 – ¶ 219

Reassurances about the city of Tehran, chosen 'to be the source of the joy of all mankind'. Quoting His earlier Writings (the Lawḥ-i-Fu'ád and the Tablet to Napoleon III), Bahá'u'lláh states that all the 'perspicuous signs' will be revealed, but at present 'men are, for the most part, deprived of the privilege of beholding and of comprehending them. We beseech God to bestow His aid, that all men may recognize the pearls that lie hid within the shells of the Most Great Ocean . . .'

¶ 220 – ¶ 257

Bahá'u'lláh quotes some of the references made to Him by His Forerunner, the Báb, warning the Bábís not to use His Revelation to dispute with and to reject 'Him Whom God shall make manifest'. Despite these admonitions, several of the Bábís denied Bahá'u'lláh and rose up against Him. In their opposition they behaved 'as the followers of John (the

Baptist)', and the disciples of Muhammad who opposed His successor, Imám 'Alí. To sow confusion and dismay, some of the faithful disciples of Bahá'u'lláh were falsely claimed to be the followers of Mírzá Yaḥyá.

Bahá'u'lláh remarks on the 'complaint of the Primal Point' (the Báb) against the 'Mirrors' of the Bábí Faith. He also comments that after all their expressions of love for the promised Qá'im, the S͟hí'íhs 'in the end all pronounced the sentence of His death, and caused Him to suffer martyrdom'.

In this section Bahá'u'lláh revisits the activities of His main adversaries. He addresses Ḥáji Mírzá Hádíy-i-Dawlat-Ábádí, a follower of Mírzá Yaḥyá: 'thou hast striven to lay hands on and destroy every copy of the Bayán'; Mírzá Yaḥyá, who had 'ascribed the authorship of the *Kitáb-i-Íqán* and of other Tablets unto others', ordered the death of the faithful believer Dayyán, and inflicted dishonour upon the Primal Point; Siyyid Muḥammad-i-Iṣfáhání, the Antichrist of the Bábí Faith who 'was but one of Our servants' but 'surreptitiously duped' Mírzá Yaḥyá and 'committed that which . . . hath caused the Pen of the Most High to weep and His Tablet to groan'; and Bahá'u'lláh's own half-sister S͟háh Sulṭán K͟hánum and her mother, Kult͟húm K͟hánum-i-Núrí who were followers of Mírzá Yaḥyá.

This section also deals with the misappropriation of the House of Bahá'u'lláh in Tehran, and objections that the Dispensations of the Báb and Bahá'u'lláh were separated by too short a time – the Bábís are urged not to follow in the footsteps of John the Baptist in this regard.

Bahá'u'lláh concludes by declaring that 'He that was hidden in the Treasury of Knowledge, and inscribed by the Pen of the Most High in His Books, and His Scriptures, and His Scrolls, and His Tablets, is come!'

¶ 258 – ¶ 269

The *Epistle* ends with a number of references that eulogize 'Akká where Bahá'u'lláh was incarcerated in 1868 and lived until His passing in 1892. These represent realized eschatology concerning Muslim traditions.

ANNOTATIONS

1. p. 1 ¶ 0.

This opening sentence of the Epistle praises God as part of an exordium (a formal address, sermon, oration, homily or discourse) known in Arabic as *khutbih*. Notably, the Universal House of Justice chose the exordium and the second paragraph as the opening passage of its Constitution, which was adopted and signed in 1972.[1]

The Arabic word *Bismilláh* in the exordium consists of five words in English, 'In the name of God'. Each of the 114 chapters (*Súrihs*) of the Qur'án except the ninth, *at-Taubah* (Repentance), begins with *Bis'mi-láhi l-raḥmáni l-raḥimi,* a phrase which consists of 19 letters and which means 'In the name of God, the Most Compassionate, and the Most Merciful'. There are, however, still 114 occurrences of the phrase in the Qur'án, as it is revealed twice in the 27th Súrih, *an-Naml* (the Ant).

The *al-Raḥmán* specifically refers to the Divine Messenger, as He is the Author of divine Revelation, such as the Qur'án, described as divine Mercy. In a sense the phrase refers to the Manifestation of God, for God in His essence is unapproachable, inaccessible and far beyond human comprehension. His Manifestations represent the 'Godhead in both the Kingdom of His Cause and the world of creation'.[2] They are the bearers of His titles amongst His servants.[3]

God becomes identified predominantly with one of His many names in every Dispensation. For instance, He is known as Yahweh or Jehovah in the Torah, the Father in the Gospels, and Allah (Arabic for God) in the Qur'án. Today He is associated with Glory or *Bahá*, an appellation anticipated in both Shí'ih and Sunni traditions.

The phrase 'In the name of' in Arabic consists of three letters: 'B S M'. An Islamic tradition describes that the first letter signifies the name

Bahá'u'lláh (the Glory or Beauty of God), the second letter S signifies *Saná'u'lláh* (Radiance or Praise of God), and the third letter M signifies *Majd'u'lláh* (Grandeur of God).[4]

See also Annotation 625.

2. p. 1 ¶ 0. the One, the Incomparable

God is referred to by about thirty names in the Hebrew Bible. He is also known by a similar number of descriptions in the New Testament. Traditionally, in addition to God, the Qur'án contains ninety-nine 'Beautiful Names of God' (*Asmá al-Husná*) which describe the divine attributes (Qur'án 7:180; 17:110; 20:8; 59:24). The designations are often paired.

Similarly, God is invoked by one of His many names and attributes in the Bahá'í Writings,[5] some of which are mentioned at the beginning of the Epistle: the One (*al-Fard*); the Incomparable (*al-Wáhid*); the All-Powerful (*al-Muqtadir*); the All-Knowing (*al-'Alim*); the All-Wise (*al-Hakim*); the Eternal (*al-Báqí*). the Everlasting (*al-Dá'im*), the Self-Subsisting (*al-Qá'im*); He Who is transcendent in His Sovereignty (*al-Muhaymin*); the Manifest (*az-Záhir*); and the Hidden (*al-Bátin*).

Usage of dissimilar names may give the false impression that the followers of the various belief systems worship different gods. In this connection, the *Shemá* prayer in the Torah (Deut. 6:4) proclaims: 'Hear, Israel, the Lord is our God, the Lord is One' (*echad*). Christ described the *Shemá* as 'the first of all the commandments' (Mark 12:29). The Apostle Paul wrote that 'there is but one God, the Father, of whom are all things' (I Cor. 8:6).

The Qur'án also describes God as *al-Wáhid* or the 'Incomparable One' or the 'Unique One' and the 'One and Only'; and as *al-Ahad* or the 'Indivisible', and *Ahadun* (related to the word *wáhid*), that is, single, unique and peerless – He has no partner.

However, the emphasis on God's singleness by no means implies that the divine nature, the infinite and 'Unknowable Essence', is defined by the finite number 'one'. Instead, these attributes convey the sense that God is the one and only source of inspiration of all religions. It also follows that those who convey His Message also have only one purpose – the spiritualization of humanity through an evolving but one common Faith.

In keeping with this belief, the Qur'án (29:46) moreover states that God is the same Lord as that worshipped by Jews and Christians – He is the Cherisher and Sustainer (Lord of the worlds, Qur'án 1:2) and the Educator of all Dispensations.

Bahá'u'lláh states that 'God . . . is in His Essence sanctified above all names and exalted beyond even the loftiest attributes'.[6] He admonishes: 'Tear ye asunder the veils of names', and announces that today 'He Who is the Monarch of all names is come'.[7]

3. p. 1 ¶ 0. the All-Powerful, the All-Knowing, the All-Wise

The Names of God in the Qur'án (24:45; 57:2) and in the Bahá'í Writings include *al-Qádir* or the 'All-Powerful'; and *al-Muqtadir* or 'the Creator of All Power' (18:45). The prefix 'al-' denotes the 'All' or the 'Omni' God: for example, the Omniscient, the Omnipotent, the All-Merciful, etc.

4. p. 1 ¶ 1. Praise be to God

God is praised as the Source of guidance to all humanity.

There are numerous passages in the Bible (e.g. I Chron. 16: 24–28; Dan. 2:20; Heb. 12:28) that call on the Jews and Christians to 'give unto the Lord glory' and praise or worship the Lord God for His many bounties.

The Qur'án also opens (1:2) with divine praise or *hamd*: 'Praise be to God, the *Rabb* or Lord of the Worlds'. Notably, it anticipates a Day when humanity will be summoned to praise Him (17:52). In Arabic, *al-ḥamdu lilláhi* has the additional implication that the praise belongs to God, in other words in every age and Dispensation He defines, through His Chosen One, the praise that best befits Him. Hence, in Bahá'u'lláh's Tablet of Visitation, God is praised with the best praise possible, that is, the praise that emanates from His twin Manifestations, the Báb and Bahá'u'lláh:

> The praise which hath dawned from Thy most august Self [*Alá*, the Báb, the August or Exalted Lord], and the glory [*Bahá*] which hath shone forth from Thy most effulgent Beauty, rest upon Thee, O Thou Who art the Manifestation of Grandeur, and the King of Eternity, and the Lord of all who are in heaven and on earth![8]

5. p. 1 ¶ 1. the Self-Subsisting that altereth not

The term 'self-subsisting' is often used by Bahá'u'lláh to characterize God. It denotes the dependence of humanity on the Creator for spiritual food and existence. Through the divine teachings and heavenly daily bread (c.f. the Lord's Prayer), the individual and human society evolve and mature. However, the Creator is independent of His creation and remains immutable. The Universal House of Justice has provided the following explanation about 'self-subsisting':

> It is likely that this term signifies in some way a basic concept of the Faith; namely, that creation is an emanation from God, without Whose continuing bounty and grace it would cease to exist. The term thus underscores the immense contrast between our reality, which is related to the contingent world, and His reality which is independent of any cause and which entirely transcends the world of being. Indeed, the point is that He is the Cause of being itself. There is a way to deduce such a meaning, however, solely from the common meaning of the words. According to its primary dictionary definition, 'to subsist' means to have existence, to persist or continue. The addition of 'self' makes it reflexive. Knowing just these two things, can we not then say that if God is self-subsisting it means that there is nothing other than Himself upon which He depends for His continuing existence? In other words, He exists in and of Himself without being dependent on any other cause: He has no creator and there is nothing prior to Him.[9]

The Bible teaches (Heb. 6:17) that God's purpose is unchangeable. The Qur'án states (6:115): 'none can change His words', that is, the essentials of faith remain unchanged throughout God's Dispensations.

6. p. 1 ¶ 1. Who is manifest through His signs

Verses (*áyát*), also translated 'Signs', refers to the scriptural lines or to the Revelation as whole. They constitute proofs or evidences of God's intervention in human affairs.

Signs and verses also describe individuals who have been recreated through the transformative power of God's Revelation and bear witness to its truth. 'Abdu'l-Bahá prays that Bahá'u'lláh will make His followers the manifestations of His glorious Signs,[10] and verses of His glorious Book.[11]

7. p. 1 ¶ 1. is hidden through His mysteries

The following is also revealed in the Epistle: 'I beseech Thee . . . by the mysteries of Thy Book, and by the things hid in Thy knowledge, and by the pearls that lie concealed within the shells of the ocean of Thy mercy' [¶ 7]. Bahá'u'lláh has declared that He is

> the Hidden Secret, the Impenetrable Mystery, Whose advent hath been foretold in the Book of God and hath been heralded by His Prophets and Messengers. Through Him the mysteries have been unravelled, the veils rent asunder and the signs and evidences disclosed . . . He hath now been made manifest. He bringeth to light whatsoever He willeth, and treadeth upon the high places of the earth, invested with transcendent majesty and power.[12]

Again:

> Call out to Zion, O Carmel, and announce the joyful tidings: He that was hidden from mortal eyes is come! His all-conquering sovereignty is manifest; His all-encompassing splendor is revealed.[13]

Bahá'u'lláh teaches that 'within every word [of His Revelation] a new spirit is hidden . . .'[14] And:

> He Who hath come from the heaven of divine revelation is the Hidden Secret, the Impenetrable Mystery, Whose advent hath been foretold in the Book of God and hath been heralded by His Prophets and Messengers. Through Him the mysteries have been unravelled, the veils rent asunder and the signs and evidences disclosed. Lo! He hath now been made manifest. He bringeth to light whatsoever He willeth.[15]

> I implore Thee, O my God, by Thy Most Great Name, to enrapture the nations through the potency of the Word which Thou didst

> ordain to be the king of all words, the Word whereby the goodly pearls of Thy hidden wisdom were uncovered, and the gem-like mysteries which were wrapped up within Thee were unravelled.[16]

'Abdu'l-Bahá explains that this is akin to the potential of the fruit hidden in the tree:

> The form of the seed was sacrificed for the tree, but its perfections were revealed and manifested by virtue of this sacrifice: For the tree, its branches, its leaves, and its blossoms were latent and hidden within the seed, but when the form of the seed was sacrificed, its perfections were fully manifested in the leaves, blossoms, and fruit.[17]

The Qur'án explains that there are two aspects to the Revelation of Muhammad:

> He it is Who has sent down to thee the Book [revelation]: in it are verses that are clear (of established meaning); they are the foundation of the Book: others are allegorical. But those in whose hearts is perversity follow the part thereof that is allegorical, seeking discord, and searching for its hidden meanings, but no one knows its hidden meanings [*ta'wil*] except God. (3:7)

It admonishes (7:53) Muslims to await the Day when God will reveal the interpretation (*ta'wil*).

Similarly, there are many hidden truths in the Bible (Deut. 29:29). Thus, the Prophet Daniel (Dan. 12:4, 8–10) is told that the meaning of his visions are hidden: 'the words are shut up and sealed till the time of the end' – even then, only those who are spiritually receptive will understand. In the Book of Jeremiah (33:3) God invites the individual to call unto Him and He will answer 'and shew thee great and mighty things, which thou knowest not'. Christ in the Gospel of Luke (10:23–24) emphasizes the importance of receptivity and perception: 'And he (Jesus) turned him unto his disciples, and said privately, Blessed are the eyes which see the things that ye see: For I tell you, that many prophets and kings have desired to see those things which ye see, and have not seen them; and to hear those things which ye hear, and have not heard them.' The Apostle Paul confirms (I Cor. 2:9): 'But as it is written, Eye hath not seen, nor ear heard, neither have entered into the heart of man, the things which God hath prepared for them that love him.' Christ promised:

> For there is nothing hid, which shall not be manifested; neither was any thing kept secret, but that it should come abroad [New International Version: 'For whatever is hidden is meant to be disclosed, and whatever is concealed is meant to be brought out into the open.']. (Mark 4:22; also Luke 8:17; 12:2–3)

The Book of Revelation (2:17) also states that God will provide hitherto 'hidden manna' (spiritual food), along with a 'white stone' (new Dispensation) and 'a new name . . . which no man knoweth saving he that receiveth it'.

As anticipated in the Gospel of John (16:12), Bahá'u'lláh has come to guide Christians to the truth that was hidden from them because they could not bear it at the First Coming. The Book of Revelation (5:3) warns that other than God, 'no man in heaven, nor in earth, neither under the earth, was able to open the book [explain the mysteries], neither to look thereon'. Therefore, the Apostle Paul (I Cor. 4:5) urged Christians not to pass any premature opinions because of the likelihood that they would be deceived in their judgement – they should instead wait 'until the Lord come, who both will bring to light the hidden things of darkness, and will make manifest the counsels of the hearts: and then shall every man have praise of God.'

8. p. 1 ¶ 1. the Most Exalted Word

Promoting the Most Exalted Word, also referred to in the Epistle as the Most Sublime Word, is the most befitting way to praise (exalt) God in this day. Teaching the Faith of Bahá'u'lláh is hence referred to as 'exalting . . . [His] Word'.[18] The Báb also urged Ṭáhírih to proclaim His Faith and to 'deliver the summons of the most exalted word' to her kindred.[19]

The creative Word of God was referred to as 'Logos' by the Greeks. It is distinguishable from human philosophies by its ability to effect a spiritual transformation of individuals and societies. Thus, the Gospel of John (1:1–13) explains that what we can understand as God is His Divine Word which has been the source of guidance for every human being and which overcomes darkness. Bahá'u'lláh states that this Divine

Word establishes truth and eliminates idle fancies and vain imaginings.[20] All God's Prophets proclaim this Word – Christ is identified with the Logos and in this connection the Qur'án refers to Him as the Word of God. Bahá'u'lláh refers to Himself as the revealed and manifest Letter, and in turn refers to the Báb as the most exalted Word.[21] Bahá'u'lláh explains that every man can respond to this Divine Word.[22] In many of His Writings He emphasizes the transformative or 'the pervasive power [or influence]' of the 'most exalted Word',[23] 'the Divine Elixir'[24] that can transmute base metal into gold and 'revive the souls of all men'.[25] He exhorts His followers to avail themselves of this spiritual power and use it to promote His Revelation:

> Every body calleth aloud for a soul. Heavenly souls must needs quicken, with the breath of the Word of God, the dead bodies with a fresh spirit. Within every word a new spirit is hidden. Happy is the man that attaineth thereunto, and hath arisen to teach the Cause of Him Who is the King of Eternity.[26]

> Fortify him, then, that he may cling to Thy most exalted Word, and to unloose his tongue to celebrate Thy praise, and cause him to be gathered unto such of Thy people as are nigh unto Thee . . .[27]

9. p. 1 ¶ 1. He doeth whatsoever He willeth

The recipient of the Epistle would have believed that Islam was a complete religion from God (Qur'án 5:3), and that no additions or future revelations were necessary, particularly as Muhammad was the 'Seal of the Prophets' (33:40). He would therefore have denounced the followers of Bahá'u'lláh as having gone astray (1:7), causing mischief or corruption (*fasád*) on earth and 'warring with God' (5:33), and worked assiduously to exterminate them. Similarly, the Jews rejected the new teachings of Christ because of a ruling (Deut. 4:2) that nothing should be added to, or subtracted from, the Torah. The Christians in turn rejected Islam because of their belief that Christ was the Way and, as warned in Revelation (22:18–19), nothing should be added to or subtracted from their book. This belief in the supremacy, exclusivity and finality of Judaism, Christianity and Islam is perhaps the biggest obstacle to acceptance of God's Faith today.

The restrictions not to add or subtract were imposed on the religious leaders who have ignored the warning and adulterated the pristine purity of God's Message beyond recognition. It was never the intention to suggest that God could not bring a fuller version of His Truth.

Bahá'u'lláh, quoting the Qur'án (2:106) reminds the Muslim clergyman that God is neither constrained by human understanding nor fettered by the provisions of earlier Dispensations – He is free to bring a new revelation: 'None of Our revelations do We abrogate or cause to be forgotten, but We substitute something better or similar: knowest thou not that God hath power over all things?' The Qur'án (5:64) also emphasizes that God is not restricted in what He ordains:

> The Jews say: 'God's hand is tied up.' Be their hands tied up and be they accursed for the (blasphemy) they utter. Nay, both His hands are widely outstretched: (of His bounty) as He pleaseth . . .

Bahá'u'lláh, quoting this verse in the *Kitáb-i-Íqán*, explains that Muslims have committed the same error today:

> When the Unseen, the Eternal, the divine Essence, caused the Day-star of Muḥammad to rise above the horizon of knowledge, among the cavils which the Jewish divines raised against Him was that after Moses no Prophet should be sent of God. Yea, mention hath been made in the scriptures of a Soul Who must needs be made manifest and Who will advance the Faith, and promote the interests of the people, of Moses, so that the Law of the Mosaic Dispensation may encompass the whole earth. Thus hath the King of eternal glory referred in His Book to the words uttered by those wanderers in the vale of remoteness and error: ' "The hand of God," say the Jews, "is chained up." Chained up be their own hands! And for that which they have said, they were accursed. Nay, outstretched are both His hands!' 'The hand of God is above their hands.'
>
> He saith: How false is that which the Jews have imagined! How can the hand of Him Who is the King in truth, Who caused the countenance of Moses to be made manifest, and conferred upon Him the robe of Prophethood – how can the hand of such a One be chained and fettered? How can He be conceived as powerless to raise up yet another Messenger after Moses?[28]

Bahá'u'lláh explains further:

> 'All things lie imprisoned within the hollow of His mighty Hand; all things are easy and possible unto Him.' He accomplisheth whatsoever He willeth, and doeth all that He desireth. Whoso sayeth 'why' or 'wherefore' hath spoken blasphemy![29]

This theme has likewise been included in the Most Holy Book:

> Whenever My laws appear like the sun in the heaven of Mine utterance, they must be faithfully obeyed by all, though My decree be such as to cause the heaven of every religion to be cleft asunder. He doeth what He pleaseth. He chooseth; and none may question His choice. Whatsoever He, the Well-Beloved, ordaineth, the same is, verily, beloved.[30]

'Abdu'l-Bahá comments on this verse in *Some Answered Questions*:

> the 'Dayspring of Revelation' . . . 'doeth whatsoever He willeth' . . . the supreme Manifestations certainly possess essential infallibility, therefore whatever emanates from Them is identical with the truth, and conformable to reality. They are not under the shadow of the former laws. Whatever They say is the word of God, and whatever They perform is an upright action. No believer has any right to criticize; his condition must be one of absolute submission . . .[31]

The Psalms (115:3; 135:6) also declare God's omnipotence, and warn that none may question His deeds (Rom. 9:20). The Gospel of John (5:21) states that Christ gives life to 'whom he will'. In considering why one brother (Jacob) was preferred over another (Esau), the Apostle Paul (Rom. 9:18) states that God showers His mercy and has compassion on whomsoever He wishes.

10. p. 1¶ 1. amidst all peoples

Earlier Dispensations have been limited to certain peoples and regions, but their scriptures foretell a Revelation that will address the needs of all peoples. Thus Zechariah (14:9) anticipated a Day when 'the Lord shall be king over all the earth; in that day shall there be one Lord, and His Name one'. Similarly, Joel (3:2) envisages the advent of a universal Faith when God 'will gather all nations'. The Prophet Isaiah (66:23) has similarly promised: 'And it shall come to pass, that from one new moon to another, and from one sabbath to another, shall all flesh come to worship before me, saith the Lord.' And again (40:5):

> And the glory of the Lord shall be revealed, and all flesh shall see it together: for the mouth of the Lord hath spoken it.

And (2: 2–5):

> And it shall come to pass in the last days, that the mountain of the Lord's house shall be established in the top of the mountains, and shall be exalted above the hills; and all nations shall flow unto it. And many people shall go and say, Come ye, and let us go up to the mountain of the Lord, to the house of the God of Jacob; and he will teach us of his ways, and we will walk in his paths: for out of Zion shall go forth the law, and the word of the Lord from Jerusalem. And he shall judge among the nations, and shall rebuke many people: and they shall beat their swords into plowshares, and their spears into pruninghooks: nation shall not lift up sword against nation, neither shall they learn war any more. O house of Jacob, come ye, and let us walk in the light of the Lord.

These prophecies apply more aptly to Bahá'u'lláh than to Christ, as Jesus stated that He had been sent primarily to the Jews (Matt. 10:5–6; 15:24). Bahá'u'lláh has in these 'end times' brought salvation to many nations that include the Jews as well as the *goyim* or non-Jews. They all have the opportunity to perceive the divine truth and to play their role in God's Faith.

11. p. 1 ¶ 1. He it is Who hath revealed His Cause for the guidance of His creatures

Humanity has an absolute need for divine spiritual direction and transformation. Bahá'u'lláh states here that God has again revealed His guidance for today.

The Hebrew Bible (Ps. 119:102, 104–105) teaches Jews and Christians to pray to God for guidance:

> for thou hast taught me . . . Through thy precepts I get understanding . . . Thy word is a lamp unto my feet, and a light unto my path.

And (Ps. 25:4–5):

> Shew me thy ways, O Lord; teach me thy paths. Lead me in thy truth, and teach me: for thou art the God of my salvation; on thee do I wait all the day.

The supplicant is reassured (Is. 58:11): 'The Lord will guide you continually . . .' One of the Names of God in the Qur'án is *al-Hádí* or 'the Guide', that is, He Who leads humanity out of spiritual darkness. The Qur'an (31:2–3) is also described as a mercy and guidance to humanity. It in turn predicts (2:2) a future Book, referred to as 'that Book' (*Th͟álika alkitáb*) destined to similarly guide humanity.

However, there comes a time when the guidance given to humanity is no longer heeded. The New Testament (II Tim. 4:3) warns of a time when people of faith will not listen to the divine guidance and teachings:

> For the time will come when they will not endure sound doctrine; but after their own lusts shall they heap to themselves teachers, having itching ears.

The hadith (traditions) speak of a time characterized by dearth of spiritual guidance when Muslims will imitate the errors of the Jews and Christians:

> *Amir al-mu'minin*, peace be upon him said: A time will come when nothing will remain of the Qur'án except its writing, and nothing of Islám except its name. The mosques in those days will be busy with regards to construction [*baná*] but desolate with regard to guidance [*hudá*]. Those staying in them and those visiting them will be the worst of all on earth. From them mischief will spring up and towards them all wrong will turn. If anyone isolates himself from it

> (mischief) they will fling him back to it. And if any one steps back from it they will push him towards it.[32]

> The Prophet said, 'Surely you will follow the ways, of those nations who were before you, span by span and cubit by cubit (i.e. inch by inch) so much so that even if they entered a hole of a lizard, you too would follow them,' We said, 'O God's Messenger! Do you mean the Jews and the Christians?' He replied, 'Whom else?'[33]

12. p. 1 ¶ 1. and sent down His verses

In the Gospel of John (6:35) Christ described Himself as 'the bread of life which came down from heaven'. He added (6:38): 'For I came down from heaven, not to do mine own will, but the will of him that sent me.' Clearly, He was referring to His teachings, as He was born to Mary in Bethlehem. The Book of Revelation (21:1–3) in turn promised that a new Revelation, the City of God, the New Jerusalem, would descend from a New Heaven at the time of the Second Coming.

The Revelation of the Qur'án is described as a divine inspiration (17:105; 26:192–5; 53:3–5) – knowledge and truth, sent down (*anzala*) by God Who is the 'All-Truth', and Who is the Lord of the worlds. It represents a 'Divine Visitation' and is the greatest testimony of the very existence of God, reaffirming His earlier interventions in human affairs to guide humanity along its true spiritual path.

Bahá'u'lláh informs the Shaykh that His Revelation had also descended from the heaven of Divine Will; that is, it was not a product of human learning. See also ¶ 7: 'How often hast Thou sent down the food of Thine utterance out of the heaven of Thy bounty . . .'

13. p. 1 ¶ 1. to demonstrate His Proof and His Testimony

The Qur'án (2:23; 10:38; 17:88) describes God's Revelation as a sufficient proof – human beings are incapable of producing it 'even should they combine to assist one another'. Bahá'u'lláh also spoke of His Revelation in a similar vein:

> If these verses be indeed contrived, then by what proof have ye believed in God? Produce it, if ye be men of understanding![34]

> O people, if ye deny these verses, by what proof have ye believed in God? Produce it, O assemblage of false ones.
>
> Nay, by the One in Whose hand is my soul, they are not, and never shall be able to do this, even should they combine to assist one another.[35]

The Epistle itself is a sufficient testimony, as Bahá'u'lláh states in ¶ 159:

> And when thou enterest into the place of resurrection, and God asketh thee by what proof thou hast believed in this Revelation, draw forth the Tablet and say: 'By this Book, the holy, the mighty, the incomparable.'

14. p. 1 ¶ 1. embellished the preface of the Book of Man with the ornament of utterance

The Book of Man (*Kitáb-i-Insán*) refers to the Perfect or Complete Man (*al-Insán al-Kámil*) who reveals the divine Purpose and has the power of Utterance or *Bayán* – that is, a divine Manifestation.

The Apostle Paul (I Cor. 15:22; Heb. 2:5–9) considered Christ 'the Perfect Man', the 'second Adam' who brought forth life. Irenaeus,[36] a second-century Father of the Church, and Tertullian,[37] a third-century Father of the Church, based their concepts of Christ as the Perfect Man on the incarnation of the Logos in Christ, for according to the Gospel of John (1:1–3) the Word or Logos pre-existed and was perfect.

The Perfect Man is also an honorific title of Prophet Muhammad, based on a tradition quoted by Ibn Arabi (1165–1240 CE), a prominent Muslim scholar, poet, mystic and philosopher. Muhammad is reputed to have said: 'I was a prophet when Adam was between water and clay.'[38]

Shaykh Aḥmad-i-Ahsá'í, the forerunner of the Báb, taught that apart from the Imáms a contemporary Perfect Man would arise to reflect the light of Divinity.

'Abdu'l-Bahá explains that the Perfect Man is also an allusion to the Manifestation of God, the embodiment of the Divine Word and the most complete and perfect Revealer of the Divine Attributes,[39] and also:

> Man is the sum of Creation, and the Perfect Man is the expression

of the complete thought of the Creator – the Word of God.[40]

The title of the principal Writing of the Báb is called *Bayán* (Utterance or Exposition). The Epistle also refers to Bahá'u'lláh as the 'Tongue of Utterance' (¶ 2). God's Faith is promoted by individuals uttering His divine teachings:

> This is the day in which to speak. It is incumbent upon the people of Bahá to strive, with the utmost patience and forbearance, to guide the peoples of the world to the Most Great Horizon. Every body calleth aloud for a soul. Heavenly souls must needs quicken, with the breath of the Word of God, the dead bodies with a fresh spirit . . .[41]

As explained by the Apostle Peter (I Peter 1:21) only God's Chosen Ones have been empowered with utterance and revelation.

15. p. 1 ¶ 1. The God of Mercy hath taught the Qur'án, hath created man, and taught him articulate speech

Chapter 55 of the Qur'án is known as the Súrih of *Raḥmán* or the Merciful. Verses 1–4 are cited by Bahá'u'lláh here (also in the opening of the *Seven Valleys*, and alluded to by 'Abdu'l-Bahá in the opening of *The Secret of Divine Civilization*):

> (God) Most Merciful! [*ar-Raḥmán*]
> It is He Who has taught the Qur'án [*alamal Qur'án*].
> He has created man [*khalagha insán*]:
> He has taught him utterance (speech) [*alamu al Bayán*].

The passage does not make sense if taken literally, for surely God would first create man and then teach him the Qur'án. The explanation is that through the creative power of the Revelation of Islam, the Spiritual Man was created who then would transmit the next Revelation – the *Bayán* (Utterance) of the Báb. Notably, the Gospel of Luke (1:50) states that in every generation those who fear God receive His mercy, that is, perceive His Revelation.

16. p. 2¶ 2. The light that is shed from the heaven of bounty

Revelation is often denoted as 'light'. The first creation of God in the Torah is light (Gen. 1:3): 'And God said, Let there be light: and there was light.' The Gospel of John (1:4–5, 9, 12–13) equates this light with divine guidance – a light that darkness cannot overcome. It moreover proclaims that the divine light has been the source of illumination of every man that has come into the world and transforms those that receive it.

The Súrih of Light or *Nur* in the Qur'án (24:35) contains the following statement that is quoted by 'Abdu'l-Bahá in *Tablets of the Divine Plan*:

> God is the Light of the heavens and the earth. The similitude of His light is as a niche wherein is a lamp. The lamp is in a glass. The glass is as it were a shining star. (This lamp is) kindled from a blessed tree, an olive neither of the East nor of the West, whose oil would almost glow forth (of itself) though no fire touched it. Light upon light. God guideth unto His light whom He will . . .[42]

The Qur'án (39:69) moreover anticipates a time when 'the earth shall shine with the light of her Lord'. In this context, Bahá'u'lláh proclaims:

> Say: 'The light hath shone forth from the horizon of Revelation, and the whole earth hath been illumined at the coming of Him Who is the Lord of the Day of the Covenant!'[43]

He explains that 'in every Dispensation the light of Divine Revelation hath been vouchsafed unto men in direct proportion to their spiritual capacity'.[44] Notably today, as attested by Bahá'u'lláh, the divine light is shining with unparalleled intensity:

> Centuries, nay, countless ages, must pass away ere the Day-Star of Truth shineth again in its mid-summer splendor, or appeareth once more in the radiance of its vernal glory . . .[45]

17. p. 1 ¶ 2. from the dawning-place of the will of God

An allusion to the divine realm from which emanates God's truth. In this Dispensation, Bahá'u'lláh is 'the Dawning-Place of His most excellent names' and 'the Dayspring of His most excellent attributes'.

In the Psalms (130:5–6) King David states that his soul waits for the dawn of the Lord's Day. The Proverbs (4:18) refers to 'the path of the just [righteous] 'as as the shining light [of dawn], that shineth more and more unto the perfect day'. Isaiah (60:1), anticipating the advent of Bahá'u'lláh, announced: 'Arise, shine; for your light has come, and the glory of the Lord has risen upon thee.' Malachi (4:2) spoke of the rise of 'the sun of righteousness . . . with healing in his wings'. The Apostle Peter (II Peter 1:19) speaks of the Second Coming as 'a light that shineth in a dark place, until the day dawn, and the day star arise in your hearts'. A short early Súrih in the Qur'án (113:1) refers to Divinity as 'the Lord of the Dawn or Daybreak'. The 89th Súrih of the Qur'án revealed in Mecca is also entitled *al-Fajr*, 'the Dawn' or 'the Daybreak'.

18. p. 2 ¶ 2. the Supreme Mediator

The Manifestations of God mediate between God and His creation (Man) and, as perfect mirrors, transmit the light of His Revelation. They connect Man to his Creator and cause his actions to be more in accordance with the Divine Will.

Christ (I Tim. 2:5) mediated for the sins of humanity and thus is referred to as a 'Mediator' in the New Testament. In the Qur'án (4:64) forgiveness of sin is also based on Muhammad's mediation.

Bahá'u'lláh is referred to here as the Supreme Mediator as He mediates today between God and followers of all Dispensations.

19. p. 2 ¶ 2. Most Exalted Pen

Also rendered by Shoghi Effendi as 'the Pen of the Most High' or 'the Supreme Pen' and identified with Bahá'u'lláh, the Author of God's Revelation.[46]

The Bible consists of 66 books which were based on oral tradition. They were written by about 40 different authors residing on three continents in three different languages over a period of about two thousand years. The Qur'án (96:1) is derived from the word *iqra* or 'read'. When inspired, Muhammad would reveal the verses orally, and His followers would then memorize the Revelation or write it down on palm leaves or skin or shoulder bones of animals.

In contrast, the Revelations of the Báb and Bahá'u'lláh were inscribed either by themselves or by their amanuenses. While Bahá'u'lláh was in the subterranean dungeon of Tehran God promised Him, 'Verily, We shall render Thee victorious by Thyself and by Thy Pen' (¶ 34; see also ¶ 65: 'Nay by Him (God) Who taught the Pen the eternal mysteries . . .')

20. p. 2 ¶ 2. Him Whom God hath made the dawning-place of His most excellent names and the dayspring of His most exalted attributes

God in His Essence is Unknowable. He loves His creation, and has made Himself known to man through His Messengers and Mediators who 'are the Manifestations of His most excellent names, the Revealers of His most exalted attributes, and the Repositories of His Revelation in the kingdom of creation . . . through them every soul hath found a path unto the Lord of the Throne on high'.[47] Today, Bahá'u'lláh is the Manifestation of the divine names and attributes.

The Qur'án (17:110) admonishes humanity: 'Call upon God, or call upon Rahman [the Merciful]: by whatever name ye call upon Him, (it is well): for to Him belong the Most Beautiful Names.' Hence, the followers of the various Dispensations should avoid remaining divided by adhering to one of His names.

The specific purpose of the Faith of Bahá'u'lláh is to eliminate religious differences and to unify mankind. His followers testify in a prayer that God and His Faith are 'sanctified above all attributes and holy above all names'.[48]

21. p. 2 ¶ 2. Through Him the light of unity hath shone forth . . . and the law of oneness hath been revealed amidst the nations

The Light of Bahá'u'lláh dispels the spiritual darkness of religious and sectarian divisions and hostilities. The fundamental verities of the Faith of Bahá'u'lláh may be defined as the unity of God, the unity of His Prophets and the unity of mankind:

> The great and fundamental teachings of Bahá'u'lláh are the oneness of God and unity of mankind.[49]

> The Bahá'í Faith upholds the unity of God, recognizes the unity of His Prophets, and inculcates the principle of the oneness and wholeness of the entire human race. It proclaims the necessity and the inevitability of the unification of mankind, asserts that it is gradually approaching, and claims that nothing short of the transmuting spirit of God, working through His chosen Mouthpiece in this day, can ultimately succeed in bringing it about.[50]

> Likewise the divine religions of the holy Manifestations of God are in reality one though in name and nomenclature they differ. Man must be a lover of the light no matter from what day-spring it may appear. He must be a lover of the rose no matter in what soil it may be growing. He must be a seeker of the truth no matter from what source it come.[51]

The oneness of God implies that the Educator of mankind is one and the same. The oneness of His Prophets indicates that the various Dispensations are the different expressions of one common Faith. In the words of Bahá'u'lláh, 'This is the changeless Faith of God, eternal in the past, eternal in the future.'[52] The third verity, 'the principle of the Oneness of Mankind, is the pivot round which all the teachings of Bahá'u'lláh revolve.'[53] Indeed the Bahá'í Faith maintains that 'the well-being of mankind, its peace and security are unattainable unless and until its unity is firmly established'.[54] Science has relatively recently demonstrated that mankind is indeed one: we all share an identical number of genes – the Human Genome Project has shown there is no such thing as race. The unity of mankind, anticipated in the scriptures, requires elimination of all forms of prejudice – humanity can no longer afford to be divided by false concepts of race, Jew *vs.* Gentile; circumcised *vs.* uncircumcised; believer (*momen*) *vs.* unbeliever (*káfir*); touchable *vs.* untouchable and pure (*táhir*) *vs.* unclean (*najis*), and so on.

See also Annotations 111 and 112.

22. p. 2 ¶ 2. the Supreme Horizon

A title of Bahá'u'lláh, as depicted by Shoghi Effendi in his variant translation, 'the All-Highest Horizon':

> He was formally designated Bahá'u'lláh, an appellation specifically recorded in the Persian Bayán, signifying at once the glory, the light and the splendor of God, and was styled the 'Lord of Lords,' the 'Most Great Name,' the 'Ancient Beauty,' the 'Pen of the Most High,' the 'Hidden Name,' the 'Preserved Treasure,' 'He Whom God will make manifest,' the 'Most Great Light,' the 'All-Highest Horizon,' the 'Most Great Ocean,' the 'Supreme Heaven,' the 'Pre-Existent Root,' the 'Self-Subsistent,' the 'Day-Star of the Universe,' the 'Great Announcement,' the 'Speaker on Sinai,' the 'Sifter of Men,' the 'Wronged One of the World,' the 'Desire of the Nations,' the 'Lord of the Covenant,' the 'Tree beyond which there is no passing'.[55]

23. p. 2 ¶ 2. the Tongue of Utterance

A further reference to Bahá'u'lláh; see also ¶ 4. Compare:

> O Tongue of this Temple! We, verily, have created thee through Our name, the All-Merciful, have taught thee whatsoever had remained concealed in the Bayán, and have bestowed upon thee the power of utterance, that thou mayest make mention of Mine exalted Self amidst My creatures . . . Through thee have We unloosed the Tongue of Utterance to expound all that hath been . . .[56]

24. p. 2 ¶ 2. Earth and heaven, glory and dominion, are God's, the Omnipotent, the Almighty, the Lord of grace abounding!

In other words, the spiritual and social content of Dispensations, including the Revelation of Bahá'u'lláh, belong to God, and man cannot impose any conditions or limitations on His grace and bounty. Compare:

> Lo, the All-Possessing is come. Earth and heaven, glory and dominion are God's, the Lord of all men, and the Possessor of the Throne on high and of earth below![57]

The title 'the Lord of grace abounding' in reference to divinity is often used by the Báb and Bahá'u'lláh, including in the Epistle: see ¶ 2, ¶ 61, ¶ 92 and ¶ 202. It also occurs in the Qur'án (57:29), and would therefore have resonated with the recipient of the Epistle:

> That the People of the Book [religious leaders] may know that they have no power whatever over the Grace of God, that Grace is (entirely) in His hand, to bestow it on whomsoever He wills. For God is the Lord of Grace abounding.

25. p. 2 ¶ 3. Give ear, O distinguished divine

Religious leaders or scholars are often referred to in the Bahá'í Writings as 'divines'. The title Shaykh (literally, 'elder' or 'venerable authority') applies to eminent Muslim religious leaders.

The particular divine addressed in the Epistle and in this sentence is Shaykh Muḥammad-Taqíy-i-Najafí, the 'Son of the Wolf' (14 April 1846–September 1914). He was a Muslim cleric of Isfahan, and was known as Áqá Najafí to his contemporaries. His father, Shaykh Muḥammad Báqir-i-Iṣfáhání, the 'Wolf', had instigated the martyrdom of the King of Martyrs and the Beloved of Martyrs. The 'Son of the Wolf' arranged for the killing of numerous Bahá'ís. Bahá'u'lláh admonishes him to pay attention to what He is saying, for it will draw him closer to God. Further information about him can be found in the Introduction to the present book.

26. p. 2 ¶ 3. this Wronged One

A reference to Bahá'u'lláh Who suffered endless wrongs and tribulations at the hands of so many enemies.[58] Compare: 'the eye of creation hath never gazed upon One wronged like Thee'.[59]

In the context of the unity of the Messengers of God, and one common faith, the wrongs suffered by His earlier Manifestations in the same Divine Path were also the sufferings of Bahá'u'lláh:

> Praise be to Thee, O Lord my God, for the wondrous revelations of Thine inscrutable decree and the manifold woes and trials Thou hast destined for myself. At one time Thou didst deliver me into

the hands of Nimrod [Abraham]; at another Thou hast allowed Pharaoh's rod to persecute me [Moses] . . . Again Thou didst cast me into the prison-cell of the ungodly for no reason except that I was moved to whisper into the ears of the well-favored denizens of Thy kingdom an intimation of the vision with which Thou hadst, through Thy knowledge, inspired me and revealed to me its meaning through the potency of Thy might. And again Thou didst decree that I be beheaded by the sword of the infidel [John the Baptist]. Again I was crucified for having unveiled to men's eyes the hidden gems of Thy glorious unity, for having revealed to them the wondrous signs of Thy sovereign and everlasting power [Christ]. How bitter the humiliations heaped upon me, in a subsequent age, on the plain of Karbilá! [Imám Ḥusayn] How lonely did I feel amidst Thy people; to what state of helplessness I was reduced in that land! Unsatisfied with such indignities, my persecutors decapitated me and carrying aloft my head from land to land paraded it before the gaze of the unbelieving multitude and deposited it on the seats of the perverse and faithless. In a later age I was suspended and my breast was made a target to the darts of the malicious cruelty of my foes. My limbs were riddled with bullets and my body was torn asunder [the Báb]. Finally, behold how in this day my treacherous enemies have leagued themselves against me, and are continually plotting to instill the venom of hate and malice into the souls of Thy servants. With all their might they are scheming to accomplish their purpose [Bahá'u'lláh] . . .[60]

27. p. 2 ¶ 3. the All-Possessing, the Exalted

God holds all humanity and the kingdoms of Revelation in His Hands. The 'Exalted' is an attribute of God, but in some of the Bahá'í Writings it is a specific reference to the Primal Point (the Báb).

28. p. 2 ¶ 3. Know thou that the ear of man hath been created that it may hearken unto the Divine Voice

Bahá'u'lláh paraphrases the admonishment in the Qur'án (17:36): 'pursue not that of which thou hast no knowledge; for every act of hearing, or of seeing or of [feeling in] the heart will be enquired into [on the Day of Reckoning]'. The Qur'án (16:78) further reassures the seeker that he has been endowed with the ability to explore reality. Each individual is required to seek the Straight Path by his own efforts (6:164; 17:15; 29:69; 35:18; 39:7; 53:38). Compare ¶ 6:

> Thou hast given me eyes to witness Thy signs, and to behold Thy verses, and to contemplate the revelations of Thine handiwork, but I have rejected Thy will, and have committed what hath caused the faithful among Thy creatures and the detached amidst Thy servants to groan. Thou hast given me ears that I may incline them unto Thy praise and Thy celebration, and unto that which Thou didst send down from the heaven of Thy bounty and the firmament of Thy will. And yet, alas, alas, I have forsaken Thy Cause . . .

The spiritual health of man is dependent on the extent to which he heeds the divine Call. The Psalms (85:5–14) express an intense yearning for God's salvation and mercy, and a willingness to heed the divine Word. The Proverbs (3:5–6) admonish: 'Trust in the Lord with all thine heart; and lean not unto thine own understanding. In all thy ways acknowledge him, and he shall direct thy paths.' Isaiah (44:18) bemoaned the deafness and lack of receptivity of the people of His time. Christ (Matt. 13:15–17) and Muhammad (Qur'án 2:7, 18; 7:179) echoed the same sentiment and frustration.

29. p. 2 ¶ 3. this Day that hath been mentioned in all the Books, Scriptures, and Tablets

Day (or Hour) refers to the Dispensation of Bahá'u'lláh.[61] Its advent has been promised in all scriptures:

> In this Day the inner ear exclaimeth and saith: Indeed well is it with me, today is my day, inasmuch as the Voice of God is calling aloud . . .
>
> The glory with which this Day is invested hath been explicitly mentioned and clearly set forth in most heavenly Books and Scriptures. However, the divines of the age have debarred men from this transcendent station, and have kept them back from this Pinnacle of Glory, this Supreme Goal.[62]

Shoghi Effendi summarizes some of the titles of Bahá'u'lláh in the Bible and the Qur'án but explains:

> To attempt an exhaustive survey of the prophetic references to Bahá'u'lláh's Revelation would indeed be an impossible task. To this the pen of Bahá'u'lláh Himself bears witness: 'All the Divine Books and Scriptures have predicted and announced unto men the advent of the Most Great Revelation. None can adequately recount the verses recorded in the Books of former ages which forecast this supreme Bounty, this most mighty Bestowal.'[63]

30. p. 2 ¶ 3. all the Books

Refers to the successive divine Revelations and the scriptures associated with earlier Dispensations, such as the Tanakh, the New Testament, the Qur'án, and the Bhagavad-Gita.

31. p. 2 ¶ 3. Purify thou, first, thy soul

This is a necessary condition in the Qur'án (26:89) for attaining to the Presence of God.

The Psalmist (51:10–14) prays for a clean heart, that is, one purified from the contamination and dross of earlier understandings, and for restoration of 'the joy of salvation'. He also admonishes (24:3–4) that individuals 'shall ascend into the mountain of the Lord . . . and stand in His holy place' only if they possess 'clean hands and a pure heart'. Christ also taught (Matt. 5:8) that only those blessed with a pure heart will see God, that is, recognize His Manifestation. The followers of Bahá'u'lláh likewise supplicate:

> Create in me a pure heart, O my God, and renew a tranquil conscience within me, O my Hope![64]

Bahá'u'lláh teaches:

> O Son of Spirit! My first counsel is this: Possess a pure, kindly and radiant heart, that thine may be a sovereignty ancient, imperishable and everlasting.[65]

'Abdu'l-Bahá observes:

> It is easy to read the Holy Scriptures, but it is only with a clean heart and a pure mind that one may understand their true meaning.[66]

32. p. 2 ¶ 3. waters of renunciation

Renunciation is an act of relinquishing, abandoning, repudiating, or sacrificing something, such as a right, title, person, or ambition. Bahá'u'lláh emphasizes renunciation several times in the Epistle, referring to the virtue in various contexts: 'horizon of renunciation'; 'arena of renunciation,'; 'the light of renunciation'; 'the sea of renunciation'; the 'ocean of renunciation' (¶ 89, ¶ 118, ¶ 119, ¶ 120). He exhorts the Shaykh to cleanse himself (*táhir*) with the waters of renunciation – that is, through the power of faith renounce his worldly desires and ambitions. In a sense, this commandment is amusing as the Shaykh was apparently known for his meticulous attention to ritual purity (*tahárat*) and to his physical cleanliness.

The exhortation reminds one of the prayer of David (Ps. 51:2), 'Wash me thoroughly from mine iniquity, and cleanse me from my sin' and Christ's observation (Luke 11:39): 'Now do ye Pharisees make clean the outside of the cup and the platter; but your inward part is full of ravening and wickedness.'

Later in the Epistle Bahá'u'lláh returns to this topic: 'ponder thereon with a heart rid of all attachment, and with ears that are pure and sanctified, be attentive to its meaning' (¶ 9). He further explains in His other Writings:

> With the hands of renunciation draw forth from its life-giving waters, and sprinkle therewith all created things, that they may be cleansed from all man-made limitations and may approach the mighty seat of God, this hallowed and resplendent Spot.[67]

> Purge thou thy heart that We may cause fountains of wisdom and utterance to gush out therefrom, thus enabling thee to raise thy voice among all mankind.[68]

The Báb underlined His role in purifying mankind of the misunderstandings that prevented recognition of Bahá'u'lláh:

> O peoples of the earth! Verily His Remembrance is come to you from God . . . that He may purge and purify you from uncleanliness in anticipation of the Day of the One true God . . .[69]

Martyrdom, a word whose original Greek meaning is 'witness' or 'testimony', is the ultimate expression of renunciation and of the individual's witness to the truth of his faith. Bahá'u'lláh contrasts this testimony by so many of His followers with the materialistic greed of those, such as the Shaykh, who were responsible for their sacrifice:

> Doth not the testimony of these holy souls, who have so gloriously risen to offer up their lives for their Beloved that the whole world marvelled at the manner of their sacrifice, suffice the people of this day? Is it not sufficient witness against the faithlessness of those who for a trifle betrayed their faith, who bartered away immortality for that which perisheth . . . and whose one aim in life is to usurp the property of others?[70]

'Abdu'l-Bahá in His *Will and Testament* exhorts the friends to emulate the self-sacrifice of the disciples of Christ:

> The disciples of Christ forgot themselves and all earthly things, forsook all their cares and belongings, purged themselves of self and passion and with absolute detachment scattered far and wide and engaged in calling the peoples of the world to the Divine Guidance, till at last they made the world another world, illumined the surface of the earth and even to their last hour proved self-sacrificing in the pathway of that Beloved One of God. Finally in various lands they suffered glorious martyrdom. Let them that are men of action follow in their footsteps![71]

Shoghi Effendi, quoting the Apostle Paul (Rom. 12:1), calls on the American Bahá'ís to achieve their destiny by becoming a living sacrifice.[72]

During the ritual of baptism the Christian renounces his past sins and uses water to symbolically wash himself of spiritual impurities. Using a farming analogy, Christ clarified this need for sacrificial efforts. He taught that a kernel of wheat only realizes its full potential when it sacrifices itself and becomes a plant, which in turn yields 'much fruit' (John 12:24–26). He elaborated (Luke 13:19) that the sacrifice of small mustard seed results in the growth of a mighty tree. He further added:

> If any man will come after me, let him deny himself, and take up his cross daily, and follow me. For whosoever will save his life shall lose it: but whosoever will lose his life for my sake, the same shall save it. For what is a man advantaged, if he gain the whole world, and lose himself, or be cast away? (Luke 9:23–25)

33. p. 2 ¶ 3. adorn thine head with the crown of the fear of God

The fear of God (*taqwá*) – being conscious of the Creator and cognizant of His Presence – stays the hand of the oppressor and aids the individual to empathize with his fellow human beings, to be more equitable, and to be charitable and compassionate towards those who are less fortunate. It should according to the Qur'án (4:9), for example, persuade one to be more careful about the management of the estate of orphans.

Bahá'u'lláh has affirmed that the 'essence of wisdom is the fear of God',[73] and citing the Qur'án (2:282), He states in the *Kitáb-i-Íqán*: 'Fear ye God; God will teach you'.[74] In several of His Writings He also stresses the importance of the fear of God. For example:

> Walk ye in the fear of God.[75]

> The fear of God hath ever been a sure defence and a safe stronghold for all the peoples of the world. It is the chief cause of the protection of mankind, and the supreme instrument for its preservation.[76]

> We have admonished Our loved ones to fear God, a fear which is the fountainhead of all goodly deeds and virtues. It is the commander of the hosts of justice in the city of Bahá. Happy the man that hath entered the shadow of its luminous standard, and laid fast hold thereon.[77]

> 'Religion,' He, in another Tablet, has stated, 'is a radiant light and an impregnable stronghold for the protection and welfare of the peoples of the world, for the fear of God impelleth man to hold fast to that which is good, and shun all evil. Should the lamp of religion be obscured, chaos and confusion will ensue, and the lights of fairness, of justice, of tranquillity and peace cease to shine.'[78]

In a letter Shoghi Effendi explains:

> perhaps the friends do not realize that the majority of human beings need the element of fear in order to discipline their conduct? Only a relatively very highly evolved soul would always be disciplined by love alone. Fear of punishment, fear of the anger of God if we do evil, are needed to keep people's feet on the right path. Of course we should love God – but we must fear Him in the sense of a child fearing the righteous anger and chastisement of a parent; not cringe before Him as before a tyrant, but know His mercy exceeds His justice![79]

Nurturing the fear of God is also an important virtue in Judaism, Christianity and Islam. The Hebrew Bible (Eccles. 5:7) exhorts: 'fear thou God', and (Ps. 2:11): 'serve the Lord with fear and rejoice with trembling'. Proverbs (8:13) defines fear of God as aversion to evil, pride and arrogance, and advises (1:7) that 'the fear of the Lord is the beginning of knowledge', and (9:10) 'the fear of the Lord is the beginning of wisdom'. In this context, the Torah (Ex. 9:29–31) explains that the main reason for the disaster brought on Egypt by Pharaoh was that he did not fear God. Malachi (4:2) promised that 'unto you that fear my [God's] name shall the Sun of righteousness arise with healing in his wings . . .' The Apostle Paul (II Cor. 7:1) said that Christians should work towards spiritual purification because of fear or reverence for God. He stated (Rom. 3:10–18) that the unrighteous were bereft of understanding and did not seek God, they did not know the way of peace, and had no 'fear of God'. The Apostle Peter (Act 10:35) further stated that 'in every nation he that feareth him [God] and worketh righteousness is accepted by him'. The Qur'án (9:119) also teaches, 'fear God and be with those who are true (in word and deed),' and (3:130; 3:200) 'fear God; that ye may prosper'.

See also ¶ 50; and Annotations 198 and 200.

34. p. 2 ¶ 3. ornament of reliance upon Him

Bahá'u'lláh states that God ranks contentment with God's Will, patience, thankfulness in the midst of tribulation, and complete reliance upon Him as 'among the highest and most laudable of all acts'.[80]

The Bible (Prov. 3:5–6) teaches that we should place our hope (reliance) on the divine teachings: 'Trust in the Lord with all thy heart, and lean not upon thine own understanding.' Jeremiah states (17:7–8): 'Blessed is the man that trusteth in the Lord, and whose hope the Lord is. For he shall be as a tree planted by the waters, and that spreadeth out her roots by the river, and shall not see when heat cometh, but her leaf shall be green; and shall not be careful in the year of drought, neither shall cease from yielding fruit.'

Similarly, the Qur'án teaches (3:159): 'put thy trust in God. For God loves those who put their trust (in Him).'

35. p. 2 ¶ 3. Arise

Lying prone symbolizes spiritual somnolence and death. In the Hidden Words Bahá'u'lláh writes:

> O ye that are lying as dead on the couch of heedlessness! Ages have passed and your precious lives are well-nigh ended, yet not a single breath of purity hath reached Our court of holiness from you. Though immersed in the ocean of misbelief, yet with your lips ye profess the one true faith of God. Him whom I abhor ye have loved, and of My foe ye have made a friend. Notwithstanding, ye walk on my earth complacent and self-satisfied, heedless that My earth is weary of you and everything within it shunneth you. Were ye but to open your eyes, ye would, in truth, prefer a myriad griefs unto this joy, and would count death itself better than this life.[81]

'Arise' invites the individual to discard heedlessness and to become spiritually alive. Notably, Christ (Matt. 17:7; Mark 5:41; Luke 5:24 and 7:14) on several occasions addressed the sick with the command 'arise'.

Bahá'u'lláh outlines for the Shaykh the preliminary conditions he must fulfil in this regard: (1) undergo baptism of renunciation; (2) fear God; (3) put his entire reliance on God; (4) arise from his posture of defiance and heedlessness; and (5) recite the prayer revealed specifically for him by Bahá'u'lláh.

36. p. 2 ¶ 3. Most Great House

A reference to the principal residence of Bahá'u'lláh during His exile in the then Ottoman or Turkish province of Baghdad (present-day Iraq). As Shoghi Effendi explains:

> Within a few years after Bahá'u'lláh's return from Sulaymáníyyih the situation had been completely reversed. The house of Sulaymán-i-Ghannám, on which the official designation of the Bayt-i-A'ẓam (the Most Great House) was later conferred, known, at that time, as the house of Mírzá Músá, the Bábí, an extremely modest residence, situated in the Karkh quarter, in the neighborhood of the western bank of the river, to which Bahá'u'lláh's family had moved prior to His return from Kurdistán, had now become the focal center of a great number of seekers, visitors and pilgrims, including Kurds, Persians, Arabs and Turks, and derived from the Muslim, the Jewish and Christian Faiths.[82]

And again with reference to this House's destiny:

> 'Grieve not, O House of God,' Bahá'u'lláh Himself has significantly written, 'if the veil of thy sanctity be rent asunder by the infidels. God hath, in the world of creation, adorned thee with the jewel of His remembrance. Such an ornament no man can, at any time, profane. Towards thee the eyes of thy Lord shall, under all conditions, remain directed.' 'In the fullness of time,' He, in another passage, referring to that same House, has prophesied, 'the Lord shall, by the power of truth, exalt it in the eyes of all men. He shall cause it to become the Standard of His Kingdom, the Shrine round which will circle the concourse of the faithful.'[83]

Shoghi Effendi provides an account of the unlawful seizure of this House by the Shí'ihs of Iraq during the early 1920s in *God Passes By*.[84]

37. p. 2 ¶ 3. the Spot round which . . . all that dwell on earth must circle

The Most Great House in Baghdad has been designated by Bahá'u'lláh as a centre for Bahá'í pilgrimage. Shoghi Effendi explains:

> It was during those same days [in Adrianople] that Bahá'u'lláh instructed this same Nabíl to recite on His behalf the two newly revealed Tablets of the Pilgrimage, and to perform, in His stead, the rites prescribed in them, when visiting the Báb's House in Shíráz and the Most Great House in Baghdád – an act that marks the inception of one of the holiest observances, which, in a later period, the *Kitáb-i-Aqdas* was to formally establish.[85]

Bahá'u'lláh entered Baghdad as an exile and there announced His mission. Previously, that city had been called 'Dar'al-Salám' meaning 'Abode of Peace' or 'Dwelling of Peace'. The Qur'án refers to Baghdad as follows:

> But God doth call to the Home of Peace [Dar'al-Salám]: He doth guide whom He pleaseth to a Way that is straight. (10:25)

And:

> For them will be a Home of Peace [Dar'al-Salám] in the presence of their Lord: He will be their Friend. Because they have practised (righteousness). (6:127)

38. p. 3 ¶ 4. holding fast unto the cord of Thy bounty

The word 'cord' is a translation of the Arabic word '*habl*' and occurs several times in the Epistle:

¶ 6	severed the cord of my hope
¶ 8	clung to the cord of the grace
¶ 53	hold fast to the cord of trustworthiness and piety
¶ 63	cord of patience and fortitude
¶ 85	unless thou holdest fast by this firm cord
¶ 116	the firm cord of patience and of the shining hem of fortitude

¶ 156 It behooveth whosoever hath set his face towards the Most Sublime Horizon to cleave tenaciously unto the cord of patience, and to put his reliance in God, the Help in Peril, the Unconstrained

¶ 164 haply men may take fast hold of the cord of justice and truthfulness

¶ 164 I cleave tenaciously to the cord of His bounty, and cling unto the hem of His generosity

The cord of hope and salvation is belief in God's Manifestation and the spiritual teachings that He brings. The cord of bounty refers to divine rewards and mercies.

The Qur'án (3:103) teaches that the Muslims must hold fast steadfastly to the rope of faith and revelation, expressions of divine bounty. It equates 'the rope' with the provisions of 'the Book', and warns that moral and ethical teachings must be adhered to resolutely if they are to avoid sectarianism:

> And hold fast, all together, by the Rope Which God (stretches out for you), and be not divided among yourselves; and remember with gratitude God's favour on you; for ye were enemies and He joined your hearts in love, so that by His Grace, ye became brethren . . .

A tradition also refers to God's Revelation as God's rope or cord: 'Behold, for I am leaving amongst you two weighty things, one of which is the Book of Alláh, the Exalted and Glorious, and that is the rope of Alláh. He who holds it fast would be on right guidance and he who abandons it would be in error.'[86]

39. p. 3 ¶ 4. the hem of Thy generosity

The word 'hem' frequently occurs elsewhere in Bahá'í Writings, referring to Bahá'u'lláh and His Revelation as in 'hem of the mercy' (¶ 8); 'hem of His robe' (¶ 105 and ¶ 109); 'hem of bounty' (¶ 189); 'hold fast unto My hem' (¶ 196); and,

> Suffer not the hem of My sacred vesture to be smirched and mired with the things of this world . . .[87]

Kissing or touching someone's garment is a mark of respect and reverence, and expresses servitude. It was a common practice amongst the Turks. It is also depicted in an account related in the New Testament:

> And, behold, a woman, which was diseased with an issue of blood twelve years, came behind him, and touched the hem of his garment: For she said within herself, If I may but touch his garment, I shall be whole. But Jesus turned him about, and when he saw her, he said, Daughter, be of good comfort; thy faith hath made thee whole. And the woman was made whole from that hour. (Matt. 9:20–22)

40. p. 3 ¶ 4. Thou didst not take unto Thyself a partner in Thy dominion, nor didst Thou choose a peer for Thyself upon earth

Association of anyone with God (such as the Trinity), worshipping gods other than God, or adulterating the Divine Word are serious sins (*shirk*) in the Qur'án and are proscribed by Bahá'u'lláh:

> Beware, beware, lest thou be led to join partners with the Lord, thy God. He is, and hath from everlasting been, one and alone, without peer or equal, eternal in the past, eternal in the future, detached from all things, ever-abiding, unchangeable, and self-subsisting. He hath assigned no associate unto Himself in His Kingdom, no counsellor to counsel Him, none to compare unto Him, none to rival His glory.[88]

> No peer or partner has been, or can ever be, joined with Him. No name can be compared with His Name. No pen can portray His nature, neither can any tongue depict His glory. He will, for ever, remain immeasurably exalted above any one except Himself.[89]

> We testify that He is One in His Essence, One in His Attributes. He hath none to equal Him in the whole universe, nor any partner in all creation. He hath sent forth His Messengers, and sent down His Books, that they may announce unto His creatures the Straight Path. (¶ 155)

The Shí'ih clergy in Persia made themselves into gods and their pronouncements were considered inspired. Here Bahá'u'lláh indirectly warns clergymen such as Shaykh Najafí to renounce this *shirk*. Elsewhere in the Epistle Bahá'u'lláh calls the Shaykh openly a *mushrik* (one who is guilty of *shirk*):

> O thou who hast joined partners with God, and turned aside from His sovereignty that hath encompassed the worlds! (¶ 133)

> O thou who hast joined partners with God . . . This is the day which God hath announced through the tongue of His Apostle. Reflect, that thou mayest apprehend what the All-Merciful hath sent down in the Qur'án and in this inscribed Tablet. (¶ 158)

> Woe betide thee, O thou who hast joined partners with God, and woe betide them that have taken thee as their leader, without a clear token or a perspicuous Book. (¶ 158)

> O thou who dost associate a partner with God and doubtest. (¶ 192)

41. p. 3 ¶ 4. Tongue of Thy grandeur

The magnificent and glorious voice of God speaking through Bahá'u'lláh.

42. p. 3 ¶ 4. Thou wast sanctified from the mention of Thy servants, and exalted above the description of Thy creatures

Compare:

> Too high art Thou for the praise of those who are nigh unto Thee to ascend unto the heaven of Thy nearness, or for the birds of the hearts of them who are devoted to Thee to attain to the door of Thy gate.[90]

Also:

> Far be it, then, from Thy glory that anyone should gaze on Thy wondrous beauty with any eye save Thine own eye, or hear the melodies proclaiming Thine almighty sovereignty with any ear except Thine own ear. Too high art Thou exalted for the eye of any creature

to behold Thy beauty, or for the understanding of any heart to scale the heights of Thine immeasurable knowledge.[91]

43. p. 3 ¶ 4. Thou beholdest, O Lord, the ignorant seeking the ocean of Thy knowledge, the sore athirst the living waters of Thine utterance

Compare the following lines from the Long Obligatory Prayer:

> Thou seest, O my Lord, this stranger hastening to his most exalted home beneath the canopy of Thy majesty and within the precincts of Thy mercy; and this transgressor seeking the ocean of Thy forgiveness; and this lowly one the court of Thy glory; and this poor creature the orient of Thy wealth . . .
>
> Thou seest, O my Lord, this wretched creature knocking at the door of Thy grace, and this evanescent soul seeking the river of everlasting life from the hands of Thy bounty.[92]

Living waters or flowing water such as in a river are more likely to sustain life than a stagnant pool. The Bible (Is. 14:23, NET translation) refers to conditions characterized by dearth of spirituality as 'pools of stagnant water'. It describes (Zeph. 1:12, New American Standard Bible) individuals affected by spiritual malaise as 'the men Who are stagnant in spirit', that is, self-satisfied and complacent. Baptism was therefore originally performed in running water such as the River Jordan. The Prophet Jeremiah (17:13) refers to the Lord God as 'the fountain of living waters'. Christ (John 7:37–39) declared, 'If any man thirst, let him come unto me, and drink. He that believeth on me, as the scripture hath said, out of his belly shall flow rivers of living water. (But this spake he of the Spirit . . .)' The Book of Revelation (21:6) promises, 'I will give unto him that is athirst of the fountain of the water of life freely.'

The reference to living waters, which appears several times in this Epistle, is a translation of Kaw<u>th</u>ar as in ¶ 6: 'the living waters of Thy pardon'; ¶ 63: 'Living waters of immortality'; ¶ 100: 'the living waters of God's counsels'; ¶ 135: 'the living waters of the love of the Most Merciful'; ¶ 177: 'the living waters of certitude'; and ¶ 245: 'the living waters of faith'. *Al-Kaw<u>th</u>ar* (the Abundant, the All-Good) is the shortest chapter (108th) of the Qur'án. Kaw<u>th</u>ar is derived from the word *ka*<u>*th*</u>*ír* (plentiful) and refers to the abundant heavenly bestowals.

Living waters is twice a translation of the word *Furát* – metaphorically, the name of a river in paradise. Furát is figuratively and literally the Arabic name for the river Euphrates, as in ¶ 158: 'living waters of the mercy of his Lord'; and in ¶ 234: 'the living waters of acknowledgment'.

The phrase 'living waters of Thine utterance' is synonymous with terms used in other Bahá'í Writings such as 'waters of life',[93] 'the water which is life indeed',[94] 'soft-flowing streams',[95] 'soft-flowing waters'[96] and 'life-giving waters'.[97] Bahá'u'lláh is identified as 'the water which is life indeed . . . Every drop of that water would suffice to quicken the dead.'[98] The sources for the 'living waters' include the 'mouth' of God's Will,[99] the 'Sublime Pen',[100] the 'cup' of God's Revelation,[101] the 'hands' of His bounteousness,[102] the 'fingers' of His mercy,[103] and His 'tongue'.[104] It is noted that there are a variety of 'living waters' such as 'living fountain of Thy grace',[105] 'of Thy love',[106] 'of Thy bounty',[107] 'of Thine utterance',[108] 'the living fountain of Thy presence',[109] 'of friendliness and charity',[110] 'the living waters of reunion',[111] 'the living waters of uprightness and understanding',[112] and 'divine knowledge'.[113]

Among these passages we discover the prerequisites of search, recognition and attainment of the 'living waters': 'Thou art He Who watereth the hearts of all that have recognized Thee from Thy plenteous stream and the fountain of Thy living waters';[114] 'Give them, then, to drink what will quicken their hearts in Thy days . . . Bless . . . them . . .who have hastened with their whole hearts toward Thy grace, until they finally quaffed the water that is life indeed.'[115] Other passages reveal the promises related to those who attain to these 'waters': 'Every one that hath partaken of them' is enabled 'to rid himself of all attachment to any one save Thee, and to soar into the atmosphere of detachment from all Thy creatures, and to fix his gaze upon Thy loving providence and Thy manifold gifts.'[116] Again, 'Wert thou to attain to but a dewdrop of the crystal waters of divine knowledge, thou wouldst readily realize that true life is not the life of the flesh but the life of the spirit.'[117]

The following extract from the opening passage of Bahá'u'lláh's Lawḥ-i-Manik<u>ch</u>í-Ṣáḥib also reveals the central importance of this theme to His Revelation:

> Praise be to the all-perceiving, the ever-abiding Lord Who, from a dewdrop out of the ocean of His grace, hath reared the firmament of

> existence, adorned it with the stars of knowledge, and admitted man into the lofty court of insight and understanding. This dewdrop, which is the Primal Word of God, is at times called the Water of Life, inasmuch as it quickeneth with the waters of knowledge them that have perished in the wilderness of ignorance.[118]

44. p. 3 ¶ 4. the tabernacle of Thy glory

The Tabernacle was a portable sanctuary or dwelling place of God that the Children of Israel carried with them during their wanderings in the desert. There were three parts to the place where Jews worshipped God: the Outer Courtyard, the Holy Place, and the Holy of Holies which contained the Ark or the Ten Commandments and which was separated from the Holy Place by a thick curtain that acted as a veil or barrier to all of the congregation but the High Priest.

Two Arabic words are translated as 'tabernacle(s)' by Shoghi Effendi: *Khibá* (a concealed tent) and *Surádiq* (a tent, canopy or pavilion; also the curtain before the door of a house or tent). For example, 'tabernacle (*Khibá*) of Thy glory' [¶ 4]; 'the dwellers of the Tabernacles (*Surádiq*) of Thy majesty' [¶ 7].

Today, the Tabernacle of Glory is personified by Bahá'u'lláh. Entering this Tabernacle and the Holy of Holies is synonymous with recognition of Him, as alluded to by Bahá'u'lláh, referring to the Báb:

> Sanctify your souls, O ye peoples of the world, that haply ye may attain that station which God hath destined for you and enter thus the tabernacle [*Surádiq*] which, according to the dispensations of Providence, hath been raised in the firmament of the Bayán.[119]

Again:

> The King of Glory proclaimeth from the tabernacle of majesty and grandeur His call, saying: O people of the Gospel! They who were not in the Kingdom have now entered it, whilst We behold you, in this day, tarrying at the gate. Rend the veils asunder by the power of your Lord . . .[120]

See also Annotations 63 and 665.

45. p. 3 ¶ 4. the dumb

This is consistent with Biblical pronouncements describing individuals who are spiritually dumb, deaf and blind (Ex. 4:11; Is. 56:10; Mark 7:37), and the promise that God will make 'the tongue of the dumb sing' (Is. 35:6). The Qur'án (2:171; 6:39) also refers to those who reject faith and disbelieve as spiritually dumb.

46. p. 3 ¶ 5. I testify, O my God, and my King, that Thou hast created me to remember Thee, to glorify Thee, and to aid Thy Cause

Bahá'u'lláh alerts the cleric to the wide gulf that existed between his deeds and the purpose of his existence, as also stated in the Short Obligatory Prayer: 'I bear witness, O my God, that Thou hast created me to know Thee and to worship Thee.'[121]

47. p. 3 ¶ 5. I have aided Thine enemies, who have broken Thy Covenant

The Shaykh would have been quite familiar with the term 'Covenant' (*Ahd* and *Míthdáq*) as it appears fifty-four times in the Qur'án. He would also have been aware (Qur'án 2:40) that in every Dispensation, God had established a covenant concerning a future Prophet and Revelation, and of God's warning (Qur'án 2:27) that 'those who break God's Covenant after it is ratified, and sunder what God has ordered to be joined. And do mischief on earth: these cause loss (only) to themselves'. He knew well (Qur'án 3:187) that the Jews and Christians had earlier violated their Covenant, as confirmed by Jeremiah (31:31–34). Now he was following in their footsteps and, in persecuting God's Faith, he had assisted and given comfort to His enemies.

48. p. 4 ¶ 5. my waywardness . . . My heedlessness

'Waywardness' and 'heedlessness' are translations of the Arabic word *ghaflati* derived from *ghaflat* which means negligence or inattention to one's spiritual duties. Waywardness and heedlessness may be defined as reckless disregard of the consequences of one's actions. When persons are heedless of the divine admonishments, they are still aware that there is a God and they are accountable to Him, but choose to ignore this knowledge.

The Qur'án (10:92) observes that 'many among mankind are heedless of Our Signs [Revelation]'. Addressing the religious leaders of His time Muhammad states (Qur'án 3:70): 'Ye People of the Book (with revealed scripture)! Why reject ye the Signs of God [latest divine Revelation], of which ye are (Yourselves) witnesses (bear witness to its truth)?' The Prophet Jeremiah (3:22) tried to 'cure' the people of their 'backsliding' and waywardness. Christ (Matt. 17:17) also decried the faithlessness and perversity of the people of His time. The Apostle Paul (Rom. 5:19) wrote that due to the heedlessness of one man many are made sinners, and 'by the obedience of one shall many be made righteous'.

49. p. 4 ¶ 6. by reason of mine iniquity

Iniquity here is the translation of the Arabic word *zulm* which is defined as injustice, evildoing, immorality, sinfulness, cruelty or unjust acts of exploitation, oppression and wrongdoing, whereby a person either deprives others of their rights or does not fulfil his obligations towards them. The 'Son of the Wolf' was responsible for inflicting a great deal of injustice, suffering and death upon the religious minorities. The Epistle refers to him as 'the mountain of iniquity' [¶ 6].

Iniquity is an important sin in Judaism – the Hebrew word *awon* means crookedness, perverseness, to err, or go astray. Thus the Psalms (25:11) supplicate: 'O Lord, Pardon mine iniquity, for it is great.'

Christ stated (Matt. 7:21–23) that entrance into the heavenly kingdom was contingent on doing the will of the Father (Bahá'u'lláh) in that Day. Acceptance would not depend on merely calling on His name, doing good works, and performing miracles. He prophesied (Matt. 24:12) that iniquity would abound at the Second Coming and 'the love of many shall wax cold'.

The Qur'án (6:82) condemns *zulm*, and considers *shirk* (31:13), which Bahá'u'lláh accuses the Shaykh of committing, as the worst variety of *zulm*.

50. p. 4 ¶ 6. the fruits of the tree of Thy justice have fallen

The Tree of Faith today is Bahá'u'lláh's Dispensation. The Shaykh's persistent attacks had left the marks of his 'sword on its boughs, and its branches, and its leaves' [¶ 135], and had managed to prevent it from bearing its fruits of love, compassion, unity, justice, and the other divine principles designed to bring about a spiritual civilization.

51. p. 4 ¶ 6. Such of Thy creatures as enjoy near access to Thee

'Abdu'l-Bahá provides the following explanation:

> It is through self-sacrifice that the individual achieves near access to God: However, when we ponder carefully it will be observed that these unceasing trials and afflictions, these successive ordeals, though they break one's back, crush one's strength, and exhaust one's endurance, are among the greatest gifts of God . . . sacrifice which certain souls are prompted to make in His path, enabling them to attire their heads with the glorious crown of martyrdom . . . Such hath ever been the qualification of them that enjoy near access unto God, such are the attributes of the pure in heart.[122]

The Qur'án (3:49) explains that Christ came to heal the blind and the leper, and to resuscitate the dead. 'Abdu'l-Bahá explains that Christ 'sacrificed Himself for the life of the world',[123] for its salvation, and 'so that mankind might be freed from the imperfections of the material nature and endowed with the virtues of the spiritual nature'.[124]

See also ¶ 87.

52. p. 5 ¶ 6. Thou seest the sinner

The word for sin is *hamartian* in Greek, a derivation of the word *hamartia* which translates as 'error', 'defect', or 'to miss the mark'. Sin is therefore a relative term – any individual may appear sinful when compared to a righteous person endowed with greater virtues. Such a person may, through prayer and sincere efforts, discard the robe of sinfulness and achieve his or her destiny. Sin is therefore a rectifiable error or aberration – it provides an opportunity for redemption and spiritual transformation. As stated in Proverbs (28:13): 'He that covereth his sins shall not prosper; but whoso confesseth and forsaketh them shall obtain mercy.' In the Apostle Paul's opinion (Rom. 3:23), 'all have sinned and come short of the glory of God,' but perhaps there is nothing more sinful than for individuals to cavil against God and His Messenger and refute His latest Revelation. Christ (John 9:39–41) admonished the Jewish religious leaders that their sin was that much greater because they believed that they perceived the truth when in reality they were spiritually blind.

The Qur'án (74:45–46) defines sinners as those who 'talk vanities with vain talkers' and 'deny the Day of Judgment'. The dawn of every Revelation represents the resurrection of earlier Dispensations. Therefore every prophet faces enemies among the sinners and deniers (25:31).

53. p. 5 ¶ 6. I am he that hath failed in duty towards Thee

This is an allusion to the Shaykh's negligence and heedlessness (see Annotation 48). The Qur'án (39:56) states, 'Say: "Ah! woe is me! – In that I neglected (my duty) towards God, and was but among those who mocked!"'

54. pp. 5–6 ¶ 6. I have . . . clung to the dictates of my passions, and have cast away the statutes of Thy Book, and seized the book of mine own desire

In other words, the Shaykh has not only violated the eternal moral and ethical principles of faith, but has also been negligent in investigating the truth of Bahá'u'lláh's Revelation. Instead he has followed his own worldly desires and passions.

55. p. 6 ¶ 6. As mine iniquities waxed greater and greater, Thy forbearance towards me augmented, and as the fire of my rebelliousness grew fiercer, the more did Thy forgiveness and Thy grace seek to smother up its flame

Bahá'u'lláh had addressed the iniquities of the Shaykh's father in the Lawḥ-i-Burhán. It is in the last year of His earthly life that He addresses in the Epistle the iniquities of the son – an Epistle that, in spite of the enormity of his sins, holds out the promise of redemption.

56. p. 6 ¶ 6. O Thou Who art the desire of the world and the Best-Beloved of the nations

'Desire of the world' is a title of Bahá'u'lláh in the Hebrew Bible (Hagg. 2:6–7): 'For thus saith the Lord of hosts . . . I will shake the heavens, and the earth, and the sea, and the dry land; And I will shake all nations, and the desire of all nations shall come: and I will fill this house with glory saith the Lord of hosts.' The Torah (Num. 14:20–21) promised that 'all the earth shall be filled with the Glory of the Lord'. Similarly Isaiah (40:5) announced: 'And the glory of the Lord shall be revealed. And all flesh shall see it together' [all humanity will see the divine Revelation].

Christ (Luke 3:6) also stated that the Father would bring a universal Revelation and address all nations at the Second Coming, 'And all flesh shall see the salvation of God'. He further predicted 'And I say unto you, That many shall come from the east and west, and shall sit down with Abraham, and Isaac, and Jacob, in the kingdom of heaven' (Matt. 6:11).

In the Qur'án (56:50) all sections of humanity will be gathered in the Day of Resurrection.

57. p. 6 ¶ 6. Thy long-suffering hath puffed me up, and Thy patience hath emboldened me

God is gracious. He is rich in kindness, forbearance and patience, but these same qualities can misguidedly cause sinners such as the Shaykh to confidently manipulate situations for their own material benefit. Ecclesiastes (8:11–12) states.

> Because sentence against an evil work is not executed speedily, therefore the heart of the sons of men is fully set in them to do evil. Though a sinner do evil an hundred times, and his days be prolonged, yet surely I know that it shall be well with them that fear God, which fear before him.

Joel (2:13) describes God as gracious and compassionate, slow to anger, abounding in loving-kindness and relenting of evil. II Peter (3:9) also states:

> The Lord is not slack concerning his promise, as some men count slackness; but is longsuffering to us-ward, not willing that any should perish, but that all should come to repentance.

One of the names of God in the Qur'án is the Patient One (*al-Sabur*). It exhorts Muhammad to be patient (68:48): 'So wait with patience for the Command of your Lord . . .' Although man possesses free will, the Qur'án (2:9–10) teaches that if he has a spiritual disease for which he does not seek healing then the malady is likely to worsen: 'Fain would they deceive God and those who believe, but they only deceive themselves, and realize (it) not. In their hearts is a disease; and God has increased their disease: and grievous is the penalty they (incur), because they are false (to themselves).'

58. p. 6 ¶ 6. Thou seest me in the midst of a sea of despair and of hopelessness . . . Thou didst cause me to hear Thy words 'Despair not'

By quoting the phrase 'Despair not' (*lá taqnaṯoo*) which occurs in the Qur'án (39:53), Bahá'u'lláh indicates to the Shaykh that it is not too late to repent of his sins:

> Say, 'O My servants who have transgressed against their souls, despair not of the Mercy of God: for God forgives all sins. Indeed, He is Oft-forgiving, Most Merciful.'

The Bible reassures the despairing soul (Deut. 31:8): 'And the Lord, he it is that doth go before thee; he will be with thee, he will not fail thee, neither forsake thee: fear not, neither be dismayed.'

59. p. 6 ¶ 6. hath darkened my face before the throne of Thy justice

The Psalms (34:5) state that the faces of those who turn to God and His Manifestation are not darkened by regret, sin, anger and gloominess, but are radiant.

The Qur'án (3:106; 39:60; 80:38–42) states that on the Day of Resurrection the faces of some people will be radiant because they have accepted God's Faith, but other faces will be 'black' (indicating gloominess and depression) because of their rejection of the Faith.

60. p. 6 ¶ 6. Thou beholdest, O my God, him who is as one dead

Death is a metaphor for lack of spiritual life. God states in Ezekiel (37:14): 'I will put My Spirit within you and you shall live.' According to the Qur'án (30:19), by accepting God's Revelation some spiritually dead individuals are resurrected, but others by denying His message die a spiritual death:

> It is He [God] Who brings out the living from the dead, and brings out the dead from the living . . .

See also Annotation 82.

61. p. 7 ¶ 6. the sincere

'Sincere' or 'sincerity' is a translation of *tamim* in the Hebrew Bible meaning 'complete' and 'entire'. The Hebrew Bible demands sincerity (Joshua 24:14): 'Now, therefore, fear the Lord and serve Him in sincerity and truth . . .' In the New Testament (I Peter 2:2) 'sincere', a translation of *adolos*, implies 'without guile', 'uncorrupted', and 'unadulterated'. Sincerity is also a necessary virtue in the Qur'án (2:225; 37:40–41, 73–74). This is contrasted in scripture to the prevarication and dissimulation of the hypocrites and the insincere.

See other examples: ¶ 84 and ¶ 135.

62. p. 8 ¶ 7. every pulpit be set apart for Thy mention

See ¶ 185 and ¶ 238 regarding the lamentation and 'moaning' of the pulpits (*minbar*). In other words, Bahá'u'lláh's Revelation should be preached from the places of worship of former Dispensations, but instead the religious podium of Islam was being used to attack Him. This was particularly true in the case of the pulpit of the Royal Mosque or Masjid Shah in Isfahan used by the 'Wolf', the 'She-Serpent', and the 'Son of the Wolf' to denounce the Faith.

Muhammad used to lean against a date palm in the first mosque, the Mosque of the Prophet (*Masjid-e-Nabawi*), when delivering His sermon (*khutbah*) to the believers. Later when a *minbar* and a pillar was constructed, according to tradition the tree lamented at the change and at its separation from the 'Remembrance of God' (*Zikr* of God or 'Mention of God: the Manifestation of God). Hence, the pillar is known as *Ustuwaanah Hannanah* (the weeping pillar).

The Báb used the *minbars* of the mosques to proclaim His Faith. However, Bahá'u'lláh abolished the use of pulpits by the clergy in His Most Holy Book.[125]

63. p. 8 ¶ 7. dwellers of the Tabernacle of Thy majesty and the denizens of the Cities of Thy wisdom

The Messengers of God are manifested from God's Tabernacle of majesty and of ancient glory. They and their favoured ones are the denizens of the cities of His wisdom. Bahá'u'lláh writes:

> Leave this people unto themselves, and repair unto the Tabernacle of majesty and glory, wherein Thou shalt encounter a people whose faces shine as brightly as the sun in its noontide splendour, and who praise and extol their Lord in this Name that hath arisen, in the plenitude of might and power, to assume the throne of independent sovereignty.[126]

See also Annotations 44 and 665.

64. p. 8 ¶ 7. How often hast Thou sent down the food of Thine utterance out of the heaven of Thy bounty, and I denied it

The prayer revealed by Bahá'u'lláh for the Shaykh requires him to understand and admit that by his actions against God's Revelation, the clergyman had denied all earlier Dispensations and deprived himself and others of divine sustenance. Bahá'u'lláh thus describes divine Revelation:

> That which is preeminent above all other gifts . . . is the gift of Divine Revelation . . . the Bread which cometh down from Heaven. It is God's supreme testimony, the clearest evidence of His truth, the sign of His consummate bounty, the token of His all-encompassing mercy, the proof of His most loving providence, the symbol of His most perfect grace. He hath, indeed, partaken of this highest gift of God who hath recognized His Manifestation in this Day.[127]

Again:

> This is the food that conferreth everlasting life upon the pure in heart and the illumined in spirit. This is the bread of which it is said [Matt. 6:11]: 'Lord, send down upon us Thy bread from heaven.' This bread shall never be withheld from them that deserve it, nor can it ever be exhausted. It groweth everlastingly from the tree of grace; it descendeth at all seasons from the heavens of justice and mercy. Even as He saith: 'Seest thou not to what God likeneth a good word? To a good tree; its root firmly fixed, and its branches reaching unto heaven: yielding its fruit in all seasons [Qur'án 14:24].'[128]

And:

> Blessed the insatiate soul who casteth away his selfish desires for love of Me and taketh his place at the banquet table which I have sent down from the heaven of divine bounty for My chosen ones.[129]

It is in this context that Jesus (John 6:58) declared: 'this is that bread which came down from heaven: not as your fathers did eat manna, and are dead: he that eateth of this bread shall live for ever.' Clearly, He was not referring to physical bread but to spiritual sustenance, because He had said earlier (John 6:27): 'Labour not for the meat which perisheth, but for that meat which endureth unto everlasting life, which the Son of man shall give unto you . . .'

Similarly, according to the Qur'án (5:112), the disciples asked Jesus, 'Can thy Lord send down to us a table set (with viands) from heaven?'

65. p. 8 ¶ 7. O Thou that turnest darkness into light

King David attested (Ps. 18:28; II Sam. 22:29): 'For thou art my lamp, O Lord: and the Lord will lighten my darkness.' The Apostle Paul (Acts 26:18) states that Christ's purpose was also 'to open their eyes, and to turn them from darkness to light, and from the power of Satan unto God . . .'

The Qur'án (2:257) similarly states:

> God is the Protector of those who have faith: from the depths of darkness He will lead them forth into light. Of those who reject faith the patrons are the evil ones: from light they will lead them forth into the depths of darkness . . .

Again (14:1):

> A Book which We have revealed unto thee, in order that thou mightest lead mankind out of the depths of darkness into light . . .

The Qur'án also mentions (39:5) that, in the past, the bright day of the Dispensations turned into darkness but the darkness eventually gave way to the bright dawn of a fresh Revelation: 'He makes the night overlap the day, and the day overlap the night.' A prayer revealed by Bahá'u'lláh reads:

> Praise be to Thee, O Lord my God! I beseech Thee by this Revelation whereby darkness hath been turned into light . . .[130]

66. p. 8 ¶ 7. and revealest Thy mysteries on the Sinai of Thy Revelation

In the Torah (Ex. 3:1; 24:13) Sinai is referred to as the Mountain of God. It predicts (Deut. 33:1–2) four successive Dispensations beginning with that of Moses:

> And this is the blessing, wherewith Moses the man of God blessed the children of Israel before his death. And he said, The Lord came from Sinai [mountain associated with Moses where God spoke to Him through the Burning Bush], And rose from Seir [mountain in Galilee associated with Jesus] unto them; He shined forth from mount Paran [in Arabia], and he came with myriads holy [Orthodox Jewish Bible: ten thousands of kodesh or saints; a reference to Bahá'u'lláh], At his right hand went a fiery law for them.[131]

The Arabic word used for Sinai is *Túr* (the mountain; Mount Sinai; *Jebel Musa* or Mountain of Moses). The 52nd Súrih opens with the oath of the Divine One swearing by the Mount of Revelation (Sinai) where the Torah was revealed to Moses. The Prophet is urged to bide His time, to continue to deliver His message, and to wait with confidence for God's judgements. God swears by, among other things, Mount Sinai, that the Day of Judgement is inevitable. The Súrih addresses many of the objections of the disbelievers of Mecca, and contrasts the bliss that awaits the believers to the torments of hell destined for unbelievers.

Bahá'u'lláh likens His Revelation to that of Moses on Mount Sinai, a further illustration of the oneness of Faith:

> Purge ye your ears and set your hearts towards Him that ye may hearken to the most wondrous Call which hath been raised from Sinai, the habitation of your Lord, the Most Glorious. It will, in truth, draw you nigh unto the Spot wherein ye will perceive the splendour of the light of His countenance which shineth above this luminous Horizon.[132]

67. p. 8 ¶ 7. Make me, then, O my God, content with that which the finger of Thy decree hath traced, and the pen of Thy ordinance hath written

Here Bahá'u'lláh counsels the Shaykh to become reconciled to His Revelation which is the decree of God, to acknowledge his many sins and heedlessness, and put his trust in God's bounteousness.

68. p. 9 ¶ 8. O Shaykh! Know thou that neither the calumnies which men may utter, nor their denials, nor any cavils they may raise, can harm him that hath clung to the cord of the grace, and seized the hem of the mercy, of the Lord of creation

God's Faith has always faced seemingly impossible difficulties and opposition. However, the Divine Light eventually triumphs and overcomes the darkness. If the believer holds on to God's grace and mercy he will not be hurt by the evil that men do or say. The Shaykh could also have taken this statement as assurance that God would protect him if he were to accept Bahá'u'lláh and His Revelation.

See also Annotation 225.

69. p. 9 ¶ 8. By God! He, the Glory of God (Bahá), hath spoken not from mere impulse

Bahá'u'lláh states that His Revelation did not emanate from Himself but was divinely ordained – He was impelled by the Holy Spirit to speak:

> O my God, when lo, the gentle winds of Thy grace and Thy loving-kindness passed over me, and wakened me through the power of Thy sovereignty and Thy gifts, and bade me arise before Thy servants, and speak forth Thy praise, and glorify Thy word.[133]

> Thou knowest full well that I have not spoken a word but by Thy leave, that my lips have never been opened except at Thy bidding and in accordance with Thy pleasure, that every breath I have breathed hath been animated with Thy praise and Thy remembrance, that I have summoned all men to naught else except that whereunto Thy chosen ones have through all eternity been summoned . . .[134]

> Had it been in my power, I would have, under no circumstances, consented to distinguish myself amongst men, for the Name I bear utterly disdaineth to associate itself with this generation whose tongues are sullied and whose hearts are false. And whenever I chose to hold my peace and be still, lo, the voice of the Holy Ghost, standing on my right hand, aroused me, and the Supreme Spirit appeared before my face, and Gabriel overshadowed me, and the Spirit of

Glory stirred within my bosom, bidding me arise and break my silence.[135]

See also Annotations 70, 87 and 88; and ¶ 11: 'By My life! Not of Mine own volition have I revealed Myself, but God, of His own choosing, hath manifested Me.'

This represents the fulfilment of Christ's promise (John 16:12–13): 'I have yet many things to say unto you, but ye cannot bear them now. Howbeit when he, the Spirit of truth, is come, he will guide you into all truth: for he shall not speak of himself; but whatsoever he shall hear, that shall he speak: and he will shew you things to come.' The Qur'án also declares (53:3) that Muhammad had not said anything from His own 'desire' (whim or volition).

70. p. 9 ¶ 8. He that has given Him a voice

As noted earlier, the divine Messengers only speak what God has revealed to them. Thus, Christ stated (John 14:24): 'the word which ye hear is not mine, but the Father's which sent me.' The Qur'án (41:20) explains that it is God Who gives speech to all things. The divine Messengers voice His commands and declare His will and purpose.

See also Annotations 69, 87 and 88.

71. p. 9 ¶ 9. They whose sight is keen, whose ears are retentive, whose hearts are enlightened, and whose breasts are dilated, recognize both truth and falsehood, and distinguish the one from the other

Perception is an essential quality for recognizing truth. Compare the following verse of the Qur'án (46:26) about the people of Ád: 'We had endowed them with (faculties of) hearing, seeing, heart and intellect but of no profit to them were their (faculties of) hearing, sight, and heart and intellect, when they went on rejecting the Signs (revelation) of God; and they were (completely) encircled by that which they used to mock at!'

Christ told the Jewish leaders (John 5:46) that had they truly believed in Moses they would also have reconized His truth. The New Testament (I John 4:6) further teaches: 'We are of God: he that knoweth God heareth us; he that is not of God heareth not us . . .'

72. p. 9 ¶ 9. the breath of detachment

This is detachment from all else but God. Bahá'u'lláh calls upon His followers to ascend to a station where no created thing will hold them back from the love of God. Detachment, however, does not mean to deprive oneself of the material benefits of this world, but rather consists of trusting in God and fixing one's eyes upon Him. True detachment is attachment to God:

> The essence of detachment is for man to turn his face towards the courts of the Lord, to enter His Presence, behold His Countenance, and stand as witness before Him.[136]

> they that tread the path of faith, they that thirst for the wine of certitude, must cleanse themselves of all that is earthly – their ears from idle talk, their minds from vain imaginings, their hearts from worldly affections, their eyes from that which perisheth.[137]

The Prophet Isaiah admonished that evaluation of divine precepts should be unfettered by preconceived notions (43:18): 'Remember ye not the former things, neither consider the things of old.' Christ encouraged seekers to be objective at the Second Coming (Matt. 7:16, 2). The Qur'án teaches (49:6) that Muslims should investigate the truth of a message even if its author has been dismissed as evil.

73. pp. 9–10 ¶ 10. Whosoever Thou exaltest is raised above the angels and attaineth the station: 'Verily, We uplifted him to a place on high!'

The phrase 'Verily, We uplifted him to a place on high [lofty station]' is from the Qur'án (19:57), and refers to the Prophet Idris who was raised to the station of Prophethood and provided with a Revelation.

The concept that some individuals are of a rank higher than the angels is also part of the New Testament. For example, the Apostle Paul (Heb. 1:13–14) states that the position of believers is said to be higher than the angels.

See also Bahá'u'lláh, *Prayers and Meditations*, CLX, p. 252.

74. p. 10 ¶ 10. and whosoever Thou dost abase is made lower than dust, nay, less than nothing

Those who have an exalted position in an earlier Dispensation but reject God's promised Revelation are abased. For example, figuratively, as recounted in the Qur'án (2:30–34) God taught Adam knowledge, and then instructed the angels to worship him. All of them did except for Iblis, who was cast out of heaven and became the fallen angel (Diabolis or Satan). In a related verse the Qur'án (6:39) states, 'whom God willeth, He leaveth to wander: whom He willeth, He placeth on the Way that is Straight.'

Christ (Matt. 23:12) also warned. 'And whosoever shall exalt himself shall be abased; and he that shall humble himself shall be exalted.'

75. p. 10 ¶ 10. 'a seat of truth'

God is the 'All-Truth' (*Al Haqq* in the Qur'án). The Manifestations of God reveal a measure of truth as bidden by God – Their Revelations are the 'seat of truth'.

The Psalms (89:14) praise the Lord of hosts: 'Justice and judgment are the habitations of thy throne: mercy and truth shall go before thy face.' Isaiah prophesied (16:5): 'And in mercy shall the throne be established: and he shall sit upon it in truth.' The Gospel of John (16:13) anticipates the advent of the Spirit of Truth Who will guide humanity to all truth (see also below, Annotation 80). The phrase 'seat of truth' originates in the Qur'án (54:54–55), and refers to a heavenly state reserved for the pious who will be in the presence of the 'seat of truth' and the 'Omnipotent King', 'amid gardens and rivers'.

The Báb also specifically referred to the 'Remembrance of God' (Bahá'u'lláh) as the 'Seat of Holiness' and 'Mercy-seat'.[138] Addressing Bahá'u'lláh, the Báb wrote:

> O Lord, my Best Beloved! Make me steadfast in Thy Cause and grant that I may be reckoned among those who have not violated Thy Covenant nor followed the gods of their own idle fancy. Enable me, then, to obtain a seat of truth in Thy presence, bestow upon me a token of Thy mercy and let me join with such of Thy servants as shall have no fear nor shall they be put to grief.[139]

Bahá'u'lláh refers to Himself and His Revelation as the 'Seat of Glory'[140] and the 'Seat of Grace'.[141] He affirms that His presence is the seat of truth:

> Write down for me, moreover, the good of this world and of the world which is to come, and ordain for me a seat of truth in Thy presence . . .[142]

> Stablish me also on the seat of truth in Thy presence, and join me with the sincere among Thy servants.[143]

> Grant that I may be seated in Thy presence on the seat of truth, within the Tabernacle of Glory.[144]

Bahá'u'lláh equates the seat of truth also with heaven and nearness to God: 'Call thou to mind the behaviour of Ashraf's mother, whose son laid down his life in the Land of Zá (Zanján). He, most certainly, is in the seat of truth, in the presence of One Who is the Most Powerful, the Almighty.'[145]

'Abdu'l-Bahá writes: 'After the ascension of Muḥammad, and His passing to "the seat of truth, in the presence of the potent King," the tribes around Medina apostatized from their Faith.'[146]And also: 'By "heaven" is not meant this infinite phenomenal space, but "heaven" signifies the world of the divine kingdom which is the supreme station and seat of the Sun of Truth.'[147] And, 'Although his [Mullá 'Alí, a martyr] body lies under the earth, his pure spirit lives on, "in the seat of truth, in the presence of the potent King."'[148]

Notably, Ṭáhirih used the same words at the conference of Badasht, implying that Bahá'u'lláh was the 'seat of truth'. In the Qur'án the gardens or paradise refer to the anticipated twin Manifestations and the rivers of Revelation that flow through Them, and heaven, the abode the righteous – nearness to Them:

> Without the least premeditation, and in language which bore a striking resemblance to that of the Qur'án she delivered her appeal with matchless eloquence and profound fervour. She concluded her address with this verse of the Qur'án: 'Verily, amid gardens and rivers shall the pious dwell in the seat of truth, in the presence of the

> potent King.' As she uttered these words, she cast a furtive glance towards both Bahá'u'lláh and Quddús . . .[149]

76. p. 10 ¶ 10. long to behold the countenance of the Omnipotent King

From the Qur'án (54:55); see Annotation 75. For 'countenance' see Annotations 260, 287, 510; and the Lawḥ-i-Liqá (Tablet of the Meeting with God).[150] The Arabic word *liqá* translates 'countenance', and 'face' as in the 'Face of God', or 'meeting with God'. There are many Qur'anic verses (6:31; 6:154; 10:45; 13:2; 18:110; 29:5; 30:8; 32:10; 33:44) that describe meeting with God (the Omnipotent King), that is, His Manifestation, Bahá'u'lláh.

The Lord thus blesses the Israelites in the Hebrew Bible (Num. 6:25–26): 'the Lord make His face shine on you, And be gracious to you; The Lord lift up His countenance on you, And give you peace.' Again: 'seek His [the Lord's] face continually.' These may be taken as anticipations of His Prophet(s). The Apostle Paul (I Cor. 13:12) wrote, 'For now we see through a glass, darkly; but then face to face: now I know in part; but then shall I know [fully] . . .' Referring to the Second Coming, the author of the Book of Revelation (22:4–5) writes: 'And they shall see his face; and his name shall be in their foreheads. And there shall be no night there; and they need no candle, neither light of the sun; for the Lord God giveth them light . . .'

77. p. 10 ¶ 10. pure justice . . . the very essence of grace

Justice (*adl*) is a measured response to a transgression. In contrast, grace is an undeserved favour and bestowal of blessings – the Arabic word *fazl* translates as grace or bounty. Here Bahá'u'lláh explains that His Revelation represents simultaneously both divine justice and grace. We fear His justice and supplicate His mercy:

> I pray Thee by Him Who is the sovereign Lord of Names to write down for me with the Pen of Thy bounty that which will enable me to draw nigh unto Thee and will purge me from my trespasses which have intervened between me and Thy forgiveness and Thy pardon.[151]

A perfect example of grace is provided in ¶ 6 (Annotation 55) – the worse the sins committed by the Shaykh, the greater the divine mercy towards him.

The Qur'án (5:54) explains: 'That is the Grace of God, which He will bestow on whom He pleaseth.' Again (35:45): 'If God were to punish men according to what they deserve, He would not leave on the back of the (earth) a single living creature: but He gives them respite for a stated term . . .'

The Psalms (96:13) announce the tidings: 'for he [the Lord] cometh, for he cometh to judge the earth: he shall judge the world with righteousness, and the people with his truth.'

78. p. 10 ¶ 10. One gleam from the splendors of Thy Name

A gleam is a faint or brief light, especially one reflected from something; in Arabic, a *tajallí* (gleam or illumination) from the *tajallíyát* (splendours, effulgences or lights radiating). *Tajallí* refers here to the light that is reflected in the mirror of man's heart. This light penetrates the veils that obscure the truth of the divine Manifestation.

See also Bahá'u'lláh, *Prayers and Meditations*, CLX.

79. p. 10 ¶ 10. Thy Name, the All-Merciful

God's mercy is synonymous with divine Revelation. Christ (Matt. 5:45) stated that God 'maketh his sun to rise on the evil and on the good, and sendeth rain on the just and on the unjust'.

The All-Merciful (*ar-Rahmán*) is one of the Beautiful Names of God in the Qur'án. Specifically, the Revelation of Muhammad is described (21:107) 'as a Mercy for all creatures'. The Qur'án (7:56) adds that this 'Mercy of God is (always) near to those who do good'.

Bahá'u'lláh also often refers to God, the Source of Revelation, as the Lord or God of Mercy. Today, to an extent never previously experienced, God's boundless mercy is in the reach of all humanity and His Revelation addresses all mankind. As the Mouthpiece of God, Bahá'u'lláh identifies Himself with the All-Merciful:

> Set your faces towards Him (Bahá'u'lláh), on this Day which God hath exalted above all other days, and whereon the All-Merciful

> hath shed the splendor of His effulgent glory upon all who are in heaven and all who are on earth. (¶ 80)

> The breezes of the Most Merciful have passed over all created things; happy the man that hath discovered their fragrance, and set himself towards them with a sound heart. Attire thy temple with the ornament of My Name, and thy tongue with remembrance of Me, and thine heart with love for Me, the Almighty, the Most High. (¶ 81)

> Blessed is that man that hath recognized the fragrance of the All-Merciful and been numbered with the steadfast. (¶ 154)

Further examples:

> The breeze of the All-Merciful hath wafted, and the souls have been quickened in the tombs of their bodies.[152]

> The seas of Divine wisdom and divine utterance have risen under the breath of the breeze of the All-Merciful.[153]

> The fragrances of the All-merciful have wafted over all creation. Happy the man that hath forsaken his desires, and taken hold of guidance.[154]

> Blessed art thou, O My servant, inasmuch as thou hast recognized the Truth, and withdrawn from him who repudiated the All-Merciful . . . Walk thou steadfastly in the love of God, and keep straight on in His Faith, and aid Him through the power of thine utterance. Thus biddeth thee the All-Merciful Who is suffering imprisonment at the hands of His oppressors.[155]

Bahá'u'lláh thus addresses the father of the Epistle's recipient, Shaykh Muḥammad Báqir, denounced as the 'Wolf':

> This is the day whereon every man endued with perception hath discovered the fragrance of the breeze of the All-Merciful in the world of creation, and every man of insight hath hastened unto the living waters of the mercy of His Lord, the King of Kings.[156]

80. p. 10 ¶ 10. a single breath from the breezes of the Day of Thy Revelation

In Persian, *yek nassim (*or single breeze) from the *nassáim* (breezes).

According to the Hebrew Bible (Gen. 2:7; Job 33:4; Ezek. 37:5) the breath of the Almighty (divine inspiration) endows life and (Job 32:8) understanding.

The Gospel of John (16:13–15) speaks of the advent of the Spirit of Truth. The phrase used for the Spirit of Truth in the original Greek is *Pneuma tēs alētheias*. 'Pneumo' translates as 'air' or 'breath' and has no gender. However, the 'One who is coming' is specified as a male and is referred to multiple times as a 'He'. Moreover, this individual will be able to 'hear' and to 'speak' – again, to make a clear distinction from the Holy Ghost that appeared to the disciples at Pentecost which inspired them but did not reveal any additional truth.

A closely related synonym for revelation used throughout the Qur'án (3:49*;* 15:29; 21:91; 42:7, 51 and 53:3–5) is also inspiration (Arabic, *Wahy* – a divine outpouring that provides the breath of spiritual life without which individuals 'expire' or die).

'Breezes' refers to divine inspiration and the Holy Spirit: 'O King! I was but a man like others, asleep upon My couch, when lo, the breezes of the All-Glorious were wafted over Me . . .' (¶ 12).

81. p. 10 ¶ 10. adorn mankind with a fresh attire

The type of clothing often identifies an individual's profession and beliefs. The terms attire, garment, or clothing are frequently used in scripture, including the Bahá'í Writings, to refer to God's Revelation, His laws or principles, and outer aspects or characteristics of a Dispensation. The 'fresh attire' signifies the unsullied and new outpouring of God's will for mankind today.

'Abdu'l-Bahá explains that the Holy Spirit 'is the mediator between God and His creation . . . Whensoever it appears, the world is revived, a new cycle is ushered in, and the body of humanity is clothed in a fresh attire.' The Apostle Paul in Galatians (3:27) states, 'for all of you who were baptized into Christ have clothed yourselves with Christ'.

The person to be baptized symbolically removed his old clothes before he went into the water, and put on new or clean raiment when he came out of it; to signify that he had put off his old nature, with all his former effete principles and corrupt practices, and become a new man. Hence, the Apostle Paul's expression (Ephes. 4:22, 24) of putting off the old man, and putting on the new man.

Judaism, Christianity and Islam expect a fresh Revelation, a new heaven, a new earth, a new Jerusalem, a new name, etc. The Acts of the Apostles (3:20) promises that 'the times of refreshing' and 'times of restitution (restoration) of all things' will come. God promises in the Book of Revelation (21:5) 'to make all things new'. To accept the new, Jesus said (Matt. 9:16), one has to discard the old garment: 'No man putteth a piece of new cloth unto an old garment, for that which is put in to fill it up taketh from the garment, and the rent is made worse.' We also read in the Book of Revelation (22:14, English Standard Version): 'Blessed are those who wash their robes, so that they may have the right to the tree of life, and may enter the city by the gates.'

The Qur'án (2:42) warns the religious leaders not to veil the new truth with falsehoods. Hence, Bahá'u'lláh's summons:

> God grant that through His gracious and invisible assistance, thou mayest divest thy body and soul of the old garment, and array thyself with the new and imperishable attire.[157]

> How high the reward of him that hath not deprived himself of so great a bounty, nor failed to recognize the beauty of his Best-Beloved in this, His new attire.[158]

> Attire, O my Lord, both my inner and outer being with the raiment of Thy favors and Thy loving-kindness . . .[159]

'Abdu'l-Bahá wrote in this regard:

> Whensoever it [the Holy Spirit] appears, it invests the world of humanity with a new life and endows human realities with a new spirit. It clothes all existence with a glorious attire, disperses the darkness of ignorance, and causes the light of human perfections to shine resplendent.[160]

> As regards the teachers, they must completely divest themselves

from the old garments and be invested with a new garment . . . They must be baptized with the water of life, the fire of the love of God and the breaths of the Holy Spirit.[161]

82. p. 10 ¶ 10. quicken them who are as dead

'Quicken' here means to revive, refresh, and to increase the life of the spiritually dead. Notably, the Psalms (119:37, 40, 88) indicate that this quickening in God's Path had previously occurred but pray for it to be repeated. (The Hebrew word for the phrase 'quicken me' and 'revive me' is *ḥay·yé·ní*, which is very similar to *thayyeni* in Arabic which means 'give me life').

Christ (John 5:25) declares that both in His day and on the day of His return those who hear and respond to the divine message will be spiritually resuscitated and live.

One of the Names of God in the Qur'án is *al-Muhyi*, or 'the Bestower (or Giver) of Life'. The Qur'án (2:28) claims that the Arabs were dead during the pre-Islamic period of ignorance or *Jahiliyyah*, and that they will die again but will once again be resuscitated spiritually.

Bahá'u'lláh admonishes:

Arise, and lift up your voices, that haply they that are fast asleep may be awakened . . . Whoso hath been reborn in this Day, shall never die; whoso remaineth dead, shall never live.[162]

83. p. 10 ¶ 10. divers tongues of the world

The world is home to an immense diversity of cultures, languages, ethnic groups and religious traditions. Whatever his background, man's greatest bounty and achievement is that his heart and tongue is illuminated with the knowledge of his Lord, and his energies serve the cause of unity and amity of mankind:

The diffusion of the instructions of God and the descent of His law, were all in order to establish agreement and union and to strengthen love and harmony among nations of different customs and thoughts, of diverse beliefs, doctrines, rites and habits; of various classes, tribes and races . . .[163]

84. p. 10 ¶ 10. If such tongues, however, be deprived of that fragrance, they assuredly would be unworthy of any mention, in word or yet in thought

If souls have not been brought to life by the divine teachings, their existence will be mundane. These statements treat all nationalities similarly – any section of humanity that responds to God's commands is praised and any that does not deprives itself of the divine grace.

85. p. 11 ¶ 11. the splendors of the daystar of truthfulness and sincerity may shine forth

Bahá'u'lláh beseeches God to aid the Shaykh to become just and fair-minded, to remove the veils from his eyes, and to be delivered from the darkness of ignorance. He exhorts him to reflect on what has been revealed to him.

The original word is the 'Sun' which is translated as 'Daystar'. It appears eighteen times in the Epistle, referring to God and His Teachings, and to divine attributes that illuminate individuals: Daystar of Truth (¶ 19 and ¶ 231); daystar of truthfulness and sincerity (¶ 11); Daystar of Thy Revelation (¶ 74); Daystar of Divine Revelation (¶ 108); Daystar of the world [that] shone forth from the horizon of 'Iráq (¶ 39); Daystar of God's Testimony (¶ 115); daystar of justice (¶ 20, ¶ 124 and ¶ 175); Daystar of God's loving-kindness and bounty (¶ 129); Daystar of knowledge (¶ 131 and ¶ 154); Daystar of Certitude (¶ 148); Daystar of Justice (¶ 20, ¶ 125 and ¶ 175); and Daystar of grace (¶ 216).

Daystar means 'light-bringer'. Although it refers primarily to Bahá'u'lláh and His Revelation, all Manifestations of God, such as Christ and Muhammad, may also be described as Daystars. For example, in the *Kitáb-i-Íqán* Bahá'u'lláh refers to Christ as 'the Daystar of Jesus',[164] 'the Daystar of the beauty of Jesus',[165] and 'the Daystar of the heaven of divine Revelation'.[166]

The historian Nabíl movingly describes Mullá Ḥusayn's final sacrifice in the path of the Báb, fixing the time of his sortie from Fort Ṭabarsí with the appearance of the morning star, which for him represented symbolically the Báb:

> soon after midnight, as soon as the morning-star had risen, the star that heralded to him the dawning light of eternal reunion with his Beloved, he started to his feet and, mounting his charger, gave the signal that the gate of the fort be opened. As he rode out at the head of three hundred and thirteen of his companions to meet the enemy, the cry of 'Yá Ṣáḥibu'z-Zamán (O Thou, the Lord of the age)!'. . .[167]

'Abdu'l-Bahá urged the followers of Bahá'u'lláh to become as resplendent as the morning-star and illuminate a dark world:

> each one of you may shine forth from the horizon of Reality like unto the morning star, divine illumination may overcome the darkness of nature, and the world of humanity may become enlightened.[168]

Some translations of the Bible use 'Daystar' and others use 'morning star'. The Daystar or morning star refers to the bright star which precedes and accompanies the rising of the sun (the appearance of Venus in the sky signalled the emergence of the day from the night, so in the spiritual sense the appearance of a new Manifestation of God signalled the emergence of light from out of the darkness).

Isaiah (9:2) anticipated the appearance of this light piercing the darkness of spiritual night: 'The people that walked in darkness have seen a great light: they that dwell in the land of the shadow of death, upon them hath the light shined.' Notably, John the Baptist is called a 'bright morning star' in Eastern Orthodox Church hymnology. In the Book of Revelation (22:16), the terms refer to the Manifestation of Christ Who imparted spiritual light and comfort: 'I [Jesus] am the root and the offspring of David, and the bright and morning star.' The Apostle Peter (II Peter 1:19) spoke of when 'the day star [shall] arise in your hearts'.

A source of confusion for some Christians is the description of Satan in Isaiah (14:12) as the morning star (Latin: Lucifer or bearer of light): 'How you have fallen from heaven, morning star [Lucifer or Satan, son of the morning, in the King James version], son of the dawn! You have been cast down to the earth, you who once laid low the nations!' They question how both Lucifer and Christ could have the same appellation. The explanation may be that certain individuals who could have been the source of illumination at the dawn of a new Revelation later become the cause of the spiritual demise of others. This is particularly likely to affect religious leaders who, drunk with their own self-worth, rise to put out God's Light:

> O ye that are foolish, yet have a name to be wise! Wherefore do ye wear the guise of shepherds, when inwardly ye have become wolves, intent upon My flock? Ye are even as the star, which riseth ere the dawn, and which, though it seem radiant and luminous, leadeth the wayfarers of My city astray into the paths of perdition.[169]

Bahá'u'lláh likens what the learned could have been, that is, guides that reflected the divine light and illuminated the path of their followers, and what they had become, that is 'earth' devoid of reflective power:

> O ye seeming fair yet inwardly foul! Ye are like clear but bitter water, which to outward seeming is crystal pure but of which, when tested by the divine Assayer, not a drop is accepted. Yea, the sunbeam falls alike upon the dust and the mirror, yet differ they in reflection even as doth the star from the earth: nay, immeasurable is the difference![170]

Súrih 53 of the Qur'án is entitled 'the Star'. Súrih 86 is entitled *al-Tariq* or 'that which comes by night (in the sky)' – a piercing star (pierces the darkness). Súrih 89 is called *al-Fajr* (the Dawn) and Súrih 113 *al-Falaq* (the Daybreak). The Qur'án also speaks of the setting, falling and retreat of stars (53:1; 56:75; 81:15).

86. p. 11 ¶ 11. perchance the splendors of the daystar of truthfulness and sincerity may shine forth, and may deliver thee from the darkness of ignorance, and illumine the world with the light of knowledge

Bahá'u'lláh declares:

> I am the Sun of Wisdom and the Ocean of Knowledge. I cheer the faint and revive the dead. I am the guiding Light that illumineth the way. I am the royal Falcon on the arm of the Almighty. I unfold the drooping wings of every broken bird and start it on its flight.[171]

Again,

> At a time when darkness had encompassed the world, the ocean of divine favour surged and His Light was made manifest. . . This, verily, is that Light which hath been foretold in the heavenly scriptures. Should the Almighty so please, the hearts of all men will be purged and purified through His goodly utterance, and the light of unity will shed its radiance upon every soul and revive the whole earth.[172]

He exhorts the Shaykh to reflect on His Revelation, the Source of divine light in this day, to be just and fair-minded, that perhaps he may escape the darkness of his heedlessness.

Light often symbolically represents truth, knowledge and divine teachings in the scriptures. Conversely, darkness represents the evil of ignorance, prejudice and hatred. It describes the condition of the Shaykh.

The New Testament states (I John 2:10–11): 'He that loveth his brother abideth in the light, and there is none occasion of stumbling in him. But he that hateth his brother is in darkness, and walketh in darkness, and knoweth not whither he goeth, because that darkness hath blinded his eyes.' The Qur'án states (2:257) that God will bring the believers out of darkness into light. In contrast, the unbelievers will pass out of light into darkness. It also promises a time (39:69) when the earth of human understanding will be illuminated with the Light of the knowledge of its Lord.[173]

87. p. 11 ¶ 11. This Wronged One hath frequented no school, neither hath He attended the controversies of the learned

Bahá'u'lláh refers to Himself in the Epistle as 'this unlettered One' (*ummi*, unschooled, bereft of training in scriptures) (¶ 188). Compare:

> The learning current amongst men I studied not; their schools [Arabic *madáris*: centres of Islamic instruction] I entered not. Ask of the city wherein I dwelt, that thou mayest be well assured that I am not of them who speak falsely. (¶ 12)

> We have not entered any school, nor read any of your dissertations. Incline your ears to the words of this unlettered One, wherewith He

> summoneth you unto God, the Ever-Abiding. Better is this for you than all the treasures of the earth, could ye but comprehend it.[174]

Born in 1817, Bahá'u'lláh did not have access to the type of education that we are familiar with today; modern education and the printing press were introduced in Iran only in the closing decades of the 19th century. Islamic education was for those aspiring to become part of the ecclesiastical system and, as a member of the nobility, this was not the path that Bahá'u'lláh could take or would take:

> In those days, the scions of noble houses were taught such matters as befitted their station in life, such as riding, handling a gun, wielding a sword, calligraphy, acquaintance with the work of great classical poets of the land, a good reading knowledge of the Holy Book, the Qur'án and hardly ever anything more. They were given such instructions by tutors, specially engaged by the parents, who were also required to teach them good manners.[175]

> Although Bahá'u'lláh did not attend any of the schools for the divines or learned classes, yet men of letters have testified that His Writings both in Arabic and Persian, viewed solely from the literary point of view, are unsurpassed in their beauty, richness and eloquence. Although unfamiliar with the Arabic language, its vast vocabulary and the complexities of its grammar, which normally took the divines a lifetime to master, Bahá'u'lláh has so enriched Arabic literature with His Writings that He has created, as Muḥammad did in His day, a style which has inspired Bahá'í scholars and writers ever since. The same is true of His Persian Writings.[176]

> But as Mírzá Ḥusayn-'Alí, the son of the Vazír-i-Núrí, grew up, the fame of His keen intelligence, His alert mind, His upright character, His benign, compassionate, benevolent nature, spread.
>
> By the time Mírzá Ḥusayn-'Alí was fourteen, His rare understanding, His complete mastery of argument, and His unparalleled powers of exposition were remarked in all circles.[177]

> It was a fact well known that He had never attended a theological college, nor ever sat at the feet of a famed theologian, teacher,

philosopher or guide. It was also well known that He was a master of argument, a fount of knowledge, a model of eloquence.[178]

Concerning His knowledge and lack of formal education, Bahá'u'lláh states in the Lawḥ-i-Hikmat:

> We have decreed, O people, that the highest and last end of all learning be the recognition of Him Who is the Object of all knowledge; and yet, behold how ye have allowed your learning to shut you out, as by a veil, from Him Who is the Dayspring of this Light, through Whom every hidden thing hath been revealed.
>
> Thou knowest full well that We perused not the books which men possess and We acquired not the learning current amongst them, and yet whenever We desire to quote the sayings of the learned and of the wise, presently there will appear before the face of thy Lord in the form of a tablet all that which hath appeared in the world and is revealed in the Holy Books and Scriptures.[179]

According to the Gospel of Luke (2:42–43, 46–47, 49), Jesus also did not have formal rabbinical training but his profound knowledge of the scriptures at a young age amazed His elders. Similarly, the Qur'án (7:157) refers to the Prophet Muhammad as *al-nabi al-ummi*, translated as 'the unlettered prophet'.

88. p. 11 ¶ 11. Not of Mine own volition have I revealed Myself, but God, of His own choosing, hath manifested Me

Indeed, it is an essential feature of Prophethood that God's Messenger does the bidding of God and only speaks as bidden by God. Thus God tells Moses that the Prophet Who will follow Him will similarly abide only by God's command:

> I will raise them up a Prophet from among their brethren [Arabs], like unto thee, and will put my words in his mouth; and he shall speak unto them all that I shall command him. And it shall come to pass, that whosoever will not hearken unto my words which he shall speak in my name, I will require it of him. (Deut. 18:18–19)

It is in this same context that Christ stated:

> I can of mine own self do nothing: as I hear, I judge and my judgment is just; because I seek not mine own will, but the will of the Father which hath sent me. (John 5:30)

Again:

> Verily, verily, I say unto you, The Son can do nothing of himself, but what he seeth the Father do: for what things soever he doeth, these also doeth the Son likewise. (John 5:19)

And:

> For I came down from heaven, not to do mine own will, but the will of him that sent me. (John 6:38)

> And the Jews marvelled, saying, How knoweth this man letters, having never learned? Jesus answered them, and said, My doctrine is not mine, but his that sent me. (John 7:15–16)

> When ye have lifted up [crucified] the Son of man, then shall ye know that I am he, and that I do nothing of myself; but as my Father hath taught me, I speak these things. (John 8:28)

> Jesus cried and said, He that believeth on me, believeth not on me, but on him that sent me. (John 12:44)

> . . . the word which ye hear is not mine, but the Father's which sent me. (John 14:24)

He added that the Spirit of Truth Who would succeed Him would also speak only as bidden by the Father:

> I have yet many things to say unto you, but ye cannot bear them now. Howbeit when he, the Spirit of Truth, is come, he will guide you into all truth: for he shall not speak of himself; but whatsoever he shall hear, that shall he speak. (John 16:12–13)

Bahá'u'lláh's statement should therefore have resonated with the <u>Shaykh</u>, particularly as Muhammad states in the Qur'án:

> Your Companion is neither astray nor being misled, nor does he say (aught) of (his own) desire. It is no less than inspiration sent down to him: He was taught by one Mighty in Power. (53:2–5)

Again:

> Say: I am but a man like yourselves, (but) the inspiration has come to me, that your God is One God: whoever expects to meet his Lord, let him work righteousness, and, in the worship of his Lord, admit no one as partner. (18:110)

See also Annotations 69, 70, 87, 92 and 93.

89.   p. 11 ¶ 11.   the Tablet, addressed to His Majesty the <u>Sháh</u>

This is a reference to the Lawḥ-i-Sulṭán, the Tablet to Náṣiri'd-Dín <u>Sh</u>áh of Persia. It is Bahá'u'lláh's lengthiest epistle to any single sovereign.[180] Revealed in Adrianople and later dispatched from 'Akká, it was delivered to the Shah in 1869 by Bahá'u'lláh's seventeen-year-old messenger, the 'illustrious' Badí'.

See also Annotations 244 and 377.

90.   p. 11 ¶ 11.   His Majesty the <u>Sháh</u>

Náṣiri'd-Dín <u>Sh</u>áh was the monarch of Persia from 1848 to 1896. He was a member of the Qájár dynasty, a Turkoman tribe which usurped the Persian throne and ruled from 1794 to 1925. Shoghi Effendi describes him as 'the despotic ruler of Persia and the mightiest potentate of <u>Sh</u>í'ih Islám', 'a selfish, capricious, imperious monarch'[181] and stigmatized by Bahá'u'lláh as one who had 'perpetrated what hath caused the denizens of the cities of justice and equity to lament'.[182] He was not only cruel to the general population, but was ultimately responsible for the martyrdom of the Báb, the imprisonment and deaths of many thousands of Bábís/Bahá'ís, and the confinement and torture of Bahá'u'lláh in the Síyáh-<u>Ch</u>ál and His banishment in severe winter to Baghdad.

Shoghi Effendi writes of him:

> The vain and despotic Náṣiri'd-Dín Shấh, denounced by Bahá'u'lláh as the 'Prince of Oppressors'; of whom He had written that he would soon be made 'an object-lesson for the world'; whose reign was stained by the execution of the Báb and the imprisonment of Bahá'u'lláh; who had persistently instigated his subsequent banishments to Constantinople, Adrianople and 'Akká; who, in collusion with a vicious sacerdotal order, had vowed to strangle the Faith in its cradle, was dramatically assassinated, in the Shrine of Sháh Abdu'l-'Aẓím on the very eve of his jubilee, which, as ushering in a new era, was to have been celebrated with the most elaborate magnificence, and was to go down in history as the greatest day in the annals of the Persian nation. The fortunes of his house thereafter steadily declined, and finally through the scandalous misconduct of the dissipated and irresponsible Aḥmad Sháh, led to the eclipse and disappearance of the Qájár dynasty.[183]

91. p. 11 ¶ 12. O King! I was but a man like others . . . the breezes of the All-Glorious were wafted over Me

This is para. 192 of the Súriy-i-Haykal. Compare with the following passages:

> How can I thank Thee for having singled me out and chosen me above all Thy servants to reveal Thee, at a time when all had turned away from Thy beauty! . . . I lay asleep on the bed of self when lo, Thou didst waken me with the divine accents of Thy voice, and didst unveil to me Thy beauty, and didst enable me to listen to Thine utterances, and to recognize Thy Self, and to speak forth Thy praise, and to extol Thy virtues, and to be steadfast in Thy love.[184]

> I lay asleep on my couch, O my God, when lo, the gentle winds of Thy grace and Thy loving-kindness passed over me, and wakened me through the power of Thy sovereignty and Thy gifts, and bade me arise before Thy servants, and speak forth Thy praise, and glorify Thy word. Thereupon most of Thy people reviled me.[185]

'Abdu'l-Bahá, interpreting the meaning of this passage to the Shah, has stated:

> This is the station of divine revelation. It is not a sensible, but an intelligible reality. It is sanctified from and transcendent above past, present, and future. It is a comparison and an analogy – a metaphor and not a literal truth. It is not the condition that is commonly understood by the human mind when it is said that someone was asleep and then awoke, but signifies a passage from one state to another. For example, sleeping is the state of repose, and wakefulness is the state of motion. Sleeping is the state of silence, and wakefulness is the state of utterance. Sleeping is the state of concealment, and wakefulness is that of manifestation . . .
>
> Briefly, the Manifestations of God have ever been and ever will be luminous Realities, and no change or alteration ever takes place in Their Essence. At most, before Their revelation They are still and silent, like one who is asleep, and after Their Revelation They are eloquent and effulgent, like one who is awake.[186]

92. p. 11 ¶ 12. taught Me the knowledge of all that hath been

A further reference to Bahá'u'lláh's innate divine knowledge – His Revelation was not the product of His environment and human learning.

93. p. 11 ¶ 12. This thing is not from Me

The Messengers of God have all denied that their teachings are theirs – instead they have attributed their Revelation to God alone.

See also Annotations 69, 70, 87, 88 and 92.

94. p. 11 ¶ 12. He bade Me lift up My voice between earth and heaven

Bahá'u'lláh experienced intimations of His Revelation whilst incarcerated in the subterranean dungeon of the Siyáh-Chál of Tehran.

> It was on that occasion that the 'Most Great Spirit,' as designated by Bahá'u'lláh Himself, revealed itself to Him, in the form of

> a 'Maiden,' and bade Him 'lift up' His 'voice between earth and heaven' – that same Spirit which, in the Zoroastrian, the Mosaic, the Christian, and Muḥammadan Dispensations, had been respectively symbolized by the 'Sacred Fire,' the 'Burning Bush,' the 'Dove,' and the 'Angel Gabriel.'[187]

See also Annotations 69, 70, 87, 88, 92, 93 and 162.

95. p. 11 ¶ 12. Ask of the city wherein I dwelt

A reference to the city of Tehran where Bahá'u'lláh's background and upbringing were well-known.

96. p. 12 ¶ 12. His all-compelling summons hath reached Me, and caused Me to speak His praise amidst all people . . . The hand of the will of thy Lord, the Compassionate, the Merciful, transformed Me

As noted earlier, Bahá'u'lláh states that He was 'but a man like others' and 'as one dead' prior to being entrusted with a divinely ordained mission. He was compelled by God to proclaim God's Revelation to all humanity:

> 'By My Life!' He asserts in another Tablet, 'Not of Mine own volition have I revealed Myself, but God, of His own choosing, hath manifested Me.' And again: 'Whenever I chose to hold My peace and be still, lo, the Voice of the Holy Spirit, standing on My right hand, aroused Me, and the Most Great Spirit appeared before My face, and Gabriel overshadowed Me, and the Spirit of Glory stirred within My bosom, bidding Me arise and break My silence.'[188]

See also Annotations 69, 70, 87 and 88.

97. p. 12 ¶ 13. Now is the moment in which to cleanse thyself with the waters of detachment . . . and to ponder . . . those things which, time and again, have been sent down

The Book of Certitude (the *Kitáb-i-Íqán*) begins with the assertion and challenge that no one 'shall attain the shores of the ocean of true understanding' and certitude of faith, 'except he be detached' (sanctified or cleansed) from 'worldly affections' and human theological learning, and unless and until he ceases to regard the words and deeds of mortal men as a standard for the true understanding and recognition of God and His Prophets. It then follows with the admonishment that the individual must consider 'the past' (what transpired in earlier Dispensations). Study of the expectations, the denials and persecutions at the dawn of every Dispensation confirms the belief they are all part of the same eternal faith of God, and that the Revelation of Bahá'u'lláh is the latest expression of the Divine Will.

Thus the Qur'án (3:3) states that the divine Revelation has been revealed in steps, and that Muhammad's Dispensation confirms earlier Dispensations. Muslims must therefore investigate the veracity of any message (49:6): 'O ye who believe! If a wicked person comes to you with any news, ascertain the truth, lest ye harm people unwittingly, And afterwards become full of repentance for what ye have done.'

Christ (John 5:45–46) stated that if the Jewish leaders had truly understood the preceding Dispensation of Moses and understood the teachings of Moses, they would also have recognized Him as the Messiah, as like recognizes like. He commanded (Matt. 7:7) His disciples 'to ask, seek, and knock' – only then will they attain to the truth.

The Torah (Deut. 13:14) requires that the children of Israel 'inquire, and make search, and ask diligently; and behold, if it be truth, and the thing certain . . .' Jeremiah (6:16) taught that the seeker must investigate the past paths and determine 'where is the good way and walk therein'.

Faith should accord with science and reason, as they are both divine gifts. Faith that is not based on reason and verifiable premises is unreliable and unconvincing and, therefore, ultimately of limited value. Thus God says in the Book of Isaiah (1:18): 'Come now, and let us reason together . . .' Similarly, the Qur'án (12:108) states that God's Way is to invite humanity 'on evidence clear as the seeing with one's eyes . . .'

It states further (10:36) that most people 'follow nothing but fancy (conjecture; false imagination)'. It admonishes (2:42): 'And cover not truth with falsehood, nor conceal the truth when ye know (what it is)'; and (33:70): 'Fear God, and (always) say a word directed to the right (favours the truth).'

98. p. 12 ¶ 13. cleanse thyself with the waters of detachment that have flowed out from the Supreme Pen

The Arabic word used is *Ma'ín*, which means 'flowing and living water'. The 'Supreme Pen' is also rendered by Shoghi Effendi as 'the Pen of the Most High' and 'the Most Exalted Pen', and is identified with Bahá'u'lláh and His Revelation.[189]

99. p. 12 ¶ 13. the fire of enmity and hatred

This refers specifically to the frenzy of hatred that was whipped up against the Bábís in the aftermath of the attempted assassination of the Shah. There are other rare mentions of 'enmity and hatred' in the Writings but the mention in the Epistle relates directly and exclusively to the conflagration and persecution that engulfed the Bábís and Bahá'u'lláh following the attempted assassination of the Shah.

See also Annotation 109.

100. p. 12 ¶ 13. The Divine Messengers have been sent down, and their Books were revealed, for the purpose of promoting the knowledge of God, and of furthering unity and fellowship amongst men

Compare the following statement by Bahá'u'lláh:

> The aim of this Wronged One in sustaining woes and tribulations, in revealing the Holy Verses and in demonstrating proofs hath been naught but to quench the flame of hate and enmity, that the horizon of the hearts of men may be illumined with the light of concord and attain real peace and tranquillity.[190]

'Abdu'l-Bahá taught that God's Messengers came to foster unity:

> The divine Prophets came to establish the unity of the Kingdom in human hearts. All of them proclaimed the glad tidings of the divine bestowals to the world of mankind. All brought the same message of divine love to the world. Jesus Christ gave His life upon the cross for the unity of mankind . . . Through His death and teachings we have entered into His Kingdom. His essential teaching was the unity of mankind and the attainment of supreme human virtues through love. He came to establish the Kingdom of peace and everlasting life.[191]

101. pp. 12–13 ¶ 14–15. Attire mine head with the crown of justice . . . Justice and equity are twin Guardians that watch over men

There are two Arabic terms often translated by Shoghi Effendi as 'justice'. The first, *'adl*, as in the title House of Justice, is the counterbalance to mercy. The second is *insáf*, here rendered as 'equity' in the sense of fair-mindedness, impartiality and the like. This is the term rendered as 'justice' in the Hidden Word: 'The best beloved of all things in My sight is justice.'[192]

The advent of divine justice has been the promise of the scriptures of the past. Justice and equity are ensured by the principle inculcated by Bahá'u'lláh, namely, the oneness of humanity. Bahá'u'lláh warns:

> The well-being of mankind, its peace and security, are unattainable unless and until its unity is firmly established. This unity can never be achieved so long as the counsels which the Pen of the Most High hath revealed are suffered to pass unheeded.[193]

102. p. 13 ¶ 15. perspicuous

Perspicuous means clear and lucid, that is, there is no need for translation, interpretation or explanation. The Arabic word used is *muhkam* which is related to the word *muhkammat* used in the Qur'án:

> He it is Who has sent down to thee the Book: In it are verses basic [perspicuous] or fundamental (of established meaning); they are the foundation of the Book: others are allegorical. But those in

whose hearts is perversity follow the part thereof that is allegorical, seeking discord, and searching for its hidden meanings, but no one knows its hidden meanings except God. (3:7)

103. p. 13 ¶ 16. one of His Tablets

This refers to the Tablet to Ḥáji Siyyid Javád Karbilá'í. The following account is provided by the historian Nabíl concerning this venerable early believer:

> While Vaḥíd was still in Shíráz, Ḥájí Siyyid Javád-i-Karbilá'í arrived and was introduced by Ḥájí Mírzá Siyyid 'Alí into the presence of the Báb. In a Tablet which He addressed to Vaḥíd and Ḥájí Siyyid Javád, the Báb extolled the firmness of their faith and stressed the unalterable character of their devotion. The latter had met and known the Báb before the declaration of His Mission, and had been a fervent admirer of those extraordinary traits of character which had distinguished Him ever since His childhood. At a later time, he met Bahá'u'lláh in Baghdád and became the recipient of His special favour. When, a few years afterwards, Bahá'u'lláh was exiled to Adrianople, he, already much advanced in years, returned to Persia, tarried awhile in the province of 'Iráq, and thence proceeded to Khurásán. His kindly disposition, extreme forbearance, and unaffected simplicity earned him the appellation of the Siyyid-i-Núr [radiant Siyyid].
>
> Ḥájí Síyyid Javád, one day, while crossing a street in Ṭihrán, suddenly saw the Sháh as he was passing on horseback. Undisturbed by the presence of his sovereign, he calmly approached and greeted him. His venerable figure and dignity of bearing pleased the Sháh immensely. He acknowledged his salute and invited him to come and see him. Such was the reception accorded him that the courtiers of the Sháh were moved with envy. 'Does not your Imperial Majesty realise,' they protested, 'that this Ḥájí Siyyid Javád is none other than the man who, even prior to the declaration of the Siyyid-i-Báb, had proclaimed himself a Bábí, and had pledged his undying loyalty to his person?' The Sháh, perceiving the malice which actuated their accusation, was sorely displeased, and rebuked them for their temerity and low-mindedness. 'How strange!' he is reported to have exclaimed;

'whoever is distinguished by the uprightness of his conduct and the courtesy of his manners, my people forthwith denounce him as a Bábí and regard him as an object worthy of my condemnation!'

Ḥájí Siyyid Javád spent the last days of his life in Kirmán and remained until his last hour a staunch supporter of the Faith. He never wavered in his convictions nor relaxed in his unsparing endeavours for the diffusion of the Cause.[194]

104. p. 13 ¶ 16. The purpose of the one true God

He is the one true God as He is the one source of all Truth revealed in all Dispensations. The purpose of our creation is to know Him, worship Him and recognize His Manifestation:

> I bear witness, O my God, that Thou hast created me to know Thee and to worship Thee. I testify, at this moment, to my powerlessness and to Thy might, to my poverty and to Thy wealth. There is none other God but Thee, the Help in Peril, the Self-Subsisting.[195]

The purpose and the essence of His Faith in this Day are to ensure that 'the diverse communions of the earth, and the manifold systems of religious belief, should never be allowed to foster the feelings of animosity among men' (¶ 17).

105. p. 13 ¶ 16. Mystic Gems

The Writings also speak of 'pearls of My mysteries',[196] and 'gems of Thy knowledge'.[197] In one sense they refer to the inner realities concealed in God's Revelation. The *Kitáb-i-Íqán* also refers to the Manifestations of God as 'hidden Gems':

> they Who are the Luminaries of truth and the Mirrors reflecting the light of divine Unity, in whatever age and cycle they are sent down from their invisible habitations of ancient glory unto this world, to educate the souls of men and endue with grace all created things, are invariably endowed with an all-compelling power, and invested with invincible sovereignty. For these hidden Gems, these concealed and invisible Treasures, in themselves manifest and vindicate the reality

of these holy words: 'Verily God doeth whatsoever He willeth, and ordaineth whatsoever He pleaseth.'[198]

106. p. 13 ¶ 16. the mine of man

God 'hast endowed each and all with talents and faculties'.[199] The Purpose of God is to once again reveal these spiritual treasures or 'mystic gems (*jawáher maání*) from the mine of man'. A slightly different translation is 'to lay bare those gems that lie hidden within the mine of their true and inmost selves . . .'[200]

All men have the potential to be educated spiritually and to reflect the divine attributes revealed by God's Mediator:

> Regard man as a mine rich in gems of inestimable value. Education can, alone, cause it to reveal its treasures, and enable mankind to benefit therefrom.[201]

The Arabic word *Murabbi* means educator and is derived from *Rabb* or Lord. In this sense Bahá'u'lláh writes 'He [God], verily, is the True Educator, and the Spiritual Teacher.' [¶ 206.]

107. p. 13 ¶ 16. No vision taketh in Him, but He taketh in all vision

This is a quotation from Qur'án 6:103 (Rodwell translation). In other words, the reality of God is incomprehensible but He is the All-Knowing, the All-Seeing and the All-Wise. The Infinite cannot be understood by the finite mind of man. The following passage was revealed by the Báb and is reiterated in the *Kitáb-i-Íqán*:

> Far be it from me to extol Thy virtues save by what Thou hast extolled Thyself in Thy weighty Book where Thou sayest, 'No vision taketh in Him but He taketh in all vision. He is the Subtile, the All-Perceiving.' Glory be unto Thee, O my God, indeed no mind or vision, however keen or discriminating, can ever grasp the nature of the most insignificant of Thy signs . . . I bear witness that Thou Thyself alone art the sole expression of Thine attributes, that the praise of no one besides Thee can ever attain to Thy holy court

nor can Thine attributes ever be fathomed by anyone other than Thyself.[202]

Far be it from His glory that human tongue should adequately recount His praise, or that human heart comprehend His fathomless mystery. He is and hath ever been veiled in the ancient eternity of His Essence, and will remain in His Reality everlastingly hidden from the sight of men. 'No vision taketh in Him, but He taketh in all vision; He is the Subtile, the All-Perceiving [Qur'án 6:103].'[203]

108. p. 13 ¶ 17. These principles and laws . . . are rays of one Light

White light is light but may be refracted into the distinct colours of the rainbow, each with a defined wavelength. When recombined they once again appear as one light and one colour. Similarly, the various Dispensations are different expressions of the same faith.

Only the practical and social aspects change with each Dispensation. The spiritual aspect – the moral and ethical considerations – never change. As stated by 'Abdu'l-Bahá: 'All the Manifestations of God and His Prophets have taught the same truths and given the same spiritual law. They all teach the one code of morality. There is no division in the truth. The Sun has sent forth many rays to illumine human intelligence, the light is always the same.'[204]

109. p. 14 ¶ 18. Religious fanaticism and hatred are a world-devouring fire, whose violence none can quench. The Hand of Divine power can, alone, deliver mankind from this desolating affliction

This statement represents a triple prediction, the truth of which has become increasingly evident: (a) there are numerous religious and sectarian wars and acts of terrorism being conducted world-wide in the name of Judaism, Christianity, Islam, Buddhism and Hinduism; (b) the fanaticism, hatred and bloodshed is immune to military intervention or social engineering; and (c) the spiritual disease requires the spiritual solutions brought by Bahá'u'lláh.

110. p. 14 ¶ 18. Consider the war that hath involved the two Nations

This refers to a futile conflict between Russia and the Ottoman Empire between the 16th and 20th centuries.

Revealed previously in the Ishráqát, Bahá'u'lláh explains in the original Persian version that this refers to a series of hostilities between Russia and the Áliyé government,[205] that is, the Áliyé Osmaniye or the Sublime Ottoman Empire. The protracted wars resulted in a great deal of death and destruction with no positive outcome for either side.

The Ottoman Empire had maintained military parity with Russia until the second half of the eighteenth century. In 1853 Russia destroyed the entire Ottoman fleet. Britain and France then carried out armed intervention on the side of the Ottomans to prevent a massive Russian expansion. Even though Ottomans and Russians were on opposing sides, the roots of the ensuing Crimean War lay in the rivalry between the British and the Russians. The war ended unfavourably for the Russians, with the signing of the Treaty of Paris in 1856.[206] The weakened and demoralized Ottoman Empire progressively lost many of its territories. During this period, Abdul-Aziz, the ruler of the Ottoman Empire, wasted valuable resources on building and furnishing great palaces.

111. p. 14 ¶ 19. Ye are the fruits of one tree, and the leaves of one branch

This is one of nine verses from the Writings of Bahá'u'lláh selected by Shoghi Effendi to be inscribed in the interior of the Bahá'í Temple in Wilmette, Illinois. The implication of such a statement is the oneness of mankind, which Shoghi Effendi refers to as 'the cornerstone of the message of Bahá'u'lláh',[207] and 'the pivot round which all the teachings of Bahá'u'lláh revolve'.[208]

Christ (Matt. 7:16–19) emphasized that if the gifts of revelation were good, the tree was divine. Muhammad stated (Qur'án 14:24) that the Dispensations have derived their life-giving water from the same water table, spread their branches towards heaven, and in due time yielded divine fruits. Bahá'u'lláh uses a similar analogy to emphasize the unity of mankind and the oneness of faith:

> The most glorious fruit of the tree of knowledge is this exalted word: Of one tree are all ye the fruit, and of one bough the leaves. Let not man glory in this that he loveth his country, let him rather glory in this that he loveth his kind.[209]

See also Annotation 182.

112. p. 14 ¶ 19. So powerful is the light of unity

This is one of the nine selected verses chosen for inscription in the interior of the Bahá'í House of Worship in Wilmette, albeit with a slightly different rendering.

Unity of mankind and oneness of Faith are powerful beacons of light and optimism in a spiritually dark world:

> The principle of the Oneness of Mankind . . . is no mere outburst of ignorant emotionalism or an expression of vague and pious hope. Its appeal is not to be merely identified with a reawakening of the spirit of brotherhood and good-will among men, nor does it aim solely at the fostering of harmonious cooperation among individual peoples and nations. Its implications are deeper, its claims greater than any which the Prophets of old were allowed to advance. Its message is applicable not only to the individual, but concerns itself primarily with the nature of those essential relationships that must bind all the states and nations as members of one human family. It does not constitute merely the enunciation of an ideal, but stands inseparably associated with an institution adequate to embody its truth, demonstrate its validity, and perpetuate its influence. It implies an organic change in the structure of present-day society, a change such as the world has not yet experienced . . .[210]

> The principle of the Oneness of Mankind, as proclaimed by Bahá'u'lláh, carries with it no more and no less than a solemn assertion that attainment to this final stage in this stupendous evolution is not only necessary but inevitable, that its realization is fast approaching, and that nothing short of a power that is born of God can succeed in establishing it.[211]

113. p. 14 ¶ 20. the thick clouds of oppression, which obscure the day-star of justice

Zephaniah (1:14–15) describes a day of clouds and thick darkness. The Qur'án (2:210) anticipates a day when God will descend in clouds: 'What can such expect but that God should come down to them overshadowed with clouds, and the angels also, and their doom be sealed?'

Clouds prevent the light of the sun from shining through. In this connection they refer to the spiritual hurdles, referred to as in the Bible, that prevent the light of divine sun from shining through – the false teachings, dogmas, trappings and hallowed traditions and superstitions of former Dispensations that conceal the divine light. Bahá'u'lláh explains:

> By the term 'clouds' is meant those things that are contrary to the ways and desires of men . . . These 'clouds' signify, in one sense, the annulment of laws, the abrogation of former Dispensations, the repeal of rituals and customs current amongst men, the exalting of the illiterate faithful above the learned opposers of the Faith. In another sense, they mean the appearance of that immortal Beauty in the image of mortal man, with such human limitations as eating and drinking, poverty and riches, glory and abasement, sleeping and waking, and such other things as cast doubt in the minds of men, and cause them to turn away. All such veils are symbolically referred to as 'clouds'.
>
> These are the 'clouds' that cause the heavens of the knowledge and understanding of all that dwell on earth to be cloven asunder.[212]

> . . . the changes brought about in every Dispensation constitute the dark clouds that intervene between the eye of man's understanding and the Divine Luminary which shineth forth from the day spring of the Divine Essence. Consider how men for generations have been blindly imitating their fathers, and have been trained according to such ways and manners as have been laid down by the dictates of their Faith. Were these men, therefore, to discover suddenly that a Man, Who hath been living in their midst, Who, with respect to every human limitation hath been their equal, had risen to abolish every established principle imposed by their Faith – principles by which for

> centuries they have been disciplined, and every opposer and denier of which they have come to regard as infidel, profligate and wicked, – they would of a certainty be veiled and hindered from acknowledging His truth. Such things are as 'clouds' that veil the eyes . . .
>
> It behoveth us, therefore, to make the utmost endeavor, that, by God's invisible assistance, these dark veils, these clouds of Heaven-sent trials, may not hinder us from beholding the beauty of His shining Countenance, and that we may recognize Him only by His own Self.[213]

He further explains that one of the greatest oppressions is the inability of souls to investigate the truth at the dawn of every Dispensation because of the actions and control of the clergy:

> As to the words – 'Immediately after the oppression of those days' – they refer to the time when men shall become oppressed and afflicted, the time when the lingering traces of the Sun of Truth and the fruit of the Tree of knowledge and wisdom will have vanished from the midst of men, when the reins of mankind will have fallen into the grasp of the foolish and ignorant, when the portals of divine unity and understanding – the essential and highest purpose in creation – will have been closed, when certain knowledge will have given way to idle fancy, and corruption will have usurped the station of righteousness. Such a condition as this is witnessed in this day . . . On their tongue the mention of God hath become an empty name; in their midst His holy Word a dead letter. Such is the sway of their desires, that the lamp of conscience and reason hath been quenched in their hearts, and this although the fingers of divine power have unlocked the portals of the knowledge of God, and the light of divine knowledge and heavenly grace hath illumined and inspired the essence of all created things . . .
>
> What 'oppression' is more grievous than that a soul seeking the truth, and wishing to attain unto the knowledge of God, should know not where to go for it and from whom to seek it?[214]

Bahá'u'lláh explains that if humanity does not see the spiritual sun because it is hidden by clouds it is not a proof of its absence:

> Consider again the sun when it is completely hidden behind the clouds. Though the earth is still illumined with its light, yet the measure of light which it receiveth is considerably reduced. Not until the clouds have dispersed, can the sun shine again in the plenitude of its glory. Neither the presence of the cloud nor its absence can, in any way, affect the inherent splendour of the sun.[215]

He announced to the 'Bishop of Rome' that He had indeed come in the clouds, 'O Pope! Rend the veils asunder. He Who is the Lord of Lords is come overshadowed with clouds . . .'[216]

See also Annotations 279, 498, 499 and 609.

114. p. 15 ¶ 20. exponents of idle fancies and vain imaginings

This refers to the religious leaders who obscure the Divine Light by blinding their followers with their rank and spurious scriptural knowledge, and by promoting outworn dogmas, rituals and traditions.

Christ (Matt. 15:14) castigated them as blind guides: 'Let them alone: they be blind leaders of the blind. And if the blind lead the blind, both shall fall into the ditch.' The Apostle Paul (Col. 2:8) warned against rejecting Christ and God's Revelation due to being taken in by vain and fallacious philosophical imaginings and the traditional stance of religious leaders: 'Beware lest any man spoil you through philosophy and vain deceit, after the tradition of men, after the rudiments of the world.'

The Qur'án (3:65, 69–71) addresses them as 'the people of the Book' because they considered themselves authoritative scribes and interpreters of the scripture. The Jewish and Christian religious leaders, relying on their limited scriptural understanding, were the first to oppose and dispute with Muhammad in Medina.

Bahá'u'lláh thus admonishes the religious leaders:

> O concourse of divines! When My verses were sent down, and My clear tokens were revealed, We found you behind the veils. This, verily, is a strange thing. Ye glory in My Name, yet ye recognized Me not at the time your Lord, the All-Merciful, appeared amongst you with proof and testimony. We have rent the veils asunder. Beware lest ye shut out the people by yet another veil. Pluck asunder the

> chains of vain imaginings, in the name of the Lord of all men, and be not of the deceitful.[217]

115. p. 15 ¶ 20. At one time We spoke in the language of the lawgiver; at another in that of a truth-seeker and the mystic

Bahá'u'lláh in the Súratu'l-Haykal (the Súrih of the Temple) states that the verses of His Revelation have been sent down in nine different styles, and that each style by itself constitutes sufficient proof of the divine source of His verses. In the following passage Shoghi Effendi appraises the vastness and diversity of approach that Bahá'u'lláh employs in the Epistle (and elsewhere in His Writings) to explain His Revelation:

> With this book, revealed about one year prior to His ascension, the prodigious achievement as author of a hundred volumes, repositories of the priceless pearls of His Revelation, may be said to have practically terminated – volumes replete with unnumbered exhortations, revolutionizing principles, world-shaping laws and ordinances, dire warnings and portentous prophecies, with soul-uplifting prayers and meditations, illuminating commentaries and interpretations, impassioned discourses and homilies, all interspersed with either addresses or references to kings, to emperors and to ministers, of both the East and the West, to ecclesiastics of divers denominations, and to leaders in the intellectual, political, literary, mystical, commercial and humanitarian spheres of human activity . . .[218]

116. p. 15 ¶ 21. Consort with all men

To 'consort' means to associate or keep company with, but it also implies moving in the same direction, as with consort ships that protected the merchant ships in World War II. In this way, fostering shared values and goals effectively removes barriers between individuals and social groupings. This is essential if the followers of Bahá'u'lláh wish to teach His Faith, promote religious unity, and establish the oneness of humanity:

> . . . to consort with the followers of all religions in a spirit of friendliness and fellowship, to proclaim that which the Speaker on Sinai hath set forth and to observe fairness in all matters.[219]

It is a law of the *Kitáb-i-Aqdas*:

> Consort with all religions with amity and concord, that they may inhale from you the sweet fragrance of God.[220]

'Abdu'l-Bahá similarly wrote:

> Wherefore, O my loving friends! Consort with all the peoples, kindreds and religions of the world with the utmost truthfulness, uprightness, faithfulness, kindliness, good-will and friendliness, that all the world of being may be filled with the holy ecstasy of the grace of Bahá, that ignorance, enmity, hate and rancor may vanish from the world and the darkness of estrangement amidst the peoples and kindreds of the world may give way to the Light of Unity.[221]
>
> Bahá'u'lláh has announced that the foundation of all the religions of God is one, that oneness is truth and truth is oneness which does not admit of plurality. This teaching is new and specialized to this Manifestation.[222]

Shoghi Effendi cites this passage when presenting the characteristics of those followers of Bahá'u'lláh who are engaged in the teaching field:

> Every labourer in those fields, whether as travelling teacher or settler, should, I feel, make it his chief and constant concern to mix, in a friendly manner, with all sections of the population, irrespective of class, creed, nationality, or colour, to familiarize himself with their ideas, tastes, and habits . . .[223]

By contrast, the Torah and the Talmud strongly discourage intimate contact with non-Jews – the priority at that time was to protect the Jews from the prevalent pagan practices that were abhorrent to the God of Israel. Likewise, the Epistle of the Apostles Paul and Timothy sent in 56 CE to the struggling Christian community of Corinth (II Cor. 6:14–17) recommends that Christians avoid unbelievers:

> Be ye not unequally yoked together with unbelievers: for what

> fellowship hath righteousness with unrighteousness? And what communion hath light with darkness?
>
> And what concord hath Christ with Belial? or what part hath he that believeth with an infidel?
>
> And what agreement hath the temple of God with idols? . . .
>
> Wherefore come out from among them, and be ye separate, saith the Lord, and touch not the unclean thing [New Living Translation: don't touch their filthy things], and I will receive you.

The Qur'án has numerous verses that sanction war against the unbelievers. Moreover, given the idolatrous dogma and practices that had crept into Judaism and Christianity, it admonishes Muslims (5:51):

> O ye who believe! Take not the Jews and the Christians for your friends and protectors: They are but friends and protectors to each other . . .

117. p. 15 ¶ 21. If ye be aware of a certain truth. . .

Compare with the following passage from the eighth Is͟hráq, accounted by Bahá'u'lláh as belonging to the *Kitáb-i-Aqdas:*

> Set forth that which ye possess. If it be favourably received, your end is attained; if not, to protest is vain. Leave that soul to himself and turn unto the Lord, the Protector, the Self-Subsisting. Be not the cause of grief, much less of discord and strife.[224]

Christians are instructed (II Tim. 2:23–25): 'But foolish and unlearned questions avoid, knowing that they do gender strifes. And the servant of the Lord must not strive; but be gentle unto all men, apt to teach, patient, in meekness instructing those that oppose themselves; if God peradventure will give them repentance to the acknowledging of the truth . . . '

Muslims must also avoid contentious situations (Qur'án 3:105), enervating disputations and divisions, and engaging in false arguments (Qur'án 18:56) as was practised by the unbelievers in the past. They must instead provide better reasonings (Qur'án 16:125; 29:46), exercise patience and perseverance (Qur'án 8:46; 16:126), and rely on God and

His Messenger, as the divisions sap faith and the power vested in the Revelation. Indeed, the Qur'án (2:263) warns: 'Kind speech and forgiveness are better than charity . . .'

118. p. 15 ¶ 21. If anyone should refuse it

Compare Shoghi Effendi: 'The Revelation, of which Bahá'u'lláh is the source and centre . . . is [not] arrogant in the affirmation of its claims.'[225] Bahá'u'lláh, likewise, states:

> Beware lest ye contend with any one, nay, strive to make him aware of the truth with kindly manner and most convincing exhortation. If your hearer respond, he will have responded to his own behoof, and if not, turn ye away from him, and set your faces towards God's sacred Court, the seat of resplendent holiness.
>
> Dispute not with any one concerning the things of this world and its affairs, for God hath abandoned them to such as have set their affection upon them.[226]

The Qur'án (2:256) teaches that no one should in any way be coerced to change his beliefs or religion. 'Let there be no compulsion in religion: Truth stands out clear from error . . .' Further, an individual's faith is a matter between him and his creator – there should be no pressure to convert anyone to Islam – God guides whomsoever He wishes to Himself (42:8, 13).

119. p. 15 ¶ 22. Hidden Words

A previously revealed work of Bahá'u'lláh, regarding which Shoghi Effendi writes:

> Next to this unique repository of inestimable treasures [the *Íqán*] must rank that marvelous collection of gemlike utterances, the 'Hidden Words' with which Bahá'u'lláh was inspired, as He paced, wrapped in His meditations, the banks of the Tigris. Revealed in the year 1274 A.H. partly in Persian, partly in Arabic . . . The significance of this dynamic spiritual leaven cast into the life of the world for the reorientation of the minds of men, the edification of their souls and the

rectification of their conduct can best be judged by the description of its character given in the opening passage by its Author: 'This is that which hath descended from the Realm of Glory, uttered by the tongue of power and might, and revealed unto the Prophets of old. We have taken the inner essence thereof and clothed it in the garment of brevity, as a token of grace unto the righteous, that they may stand faithful unto the Covenant of God, may fulfil in their lives His trust, and in the realm of spirit obtain the gem of Divine virtue.'[227]

120. p. 15 ¶ 22. Abhá Pen

Literally, 'the Pen of the All-Glorious'; i.e. revealed by Bahá'u'lláh. See also Annotation 19, and also ¶ 17, ¶ 50, ¶ 74 and *Gleanings from the Writings of Bahá'u'lláh*, CXXXII, pp. 287–8.

121. p. 15 ¶ 22. Book of Fáṭimih

The 'Hidden Book of Fáṭimih' was the original title of the *Hidden Words*. It was revealed by Bahá'u'lláh as He paced, wrapped in His meditations, the banks of the Tigris, 1274 AH (about 1857):

> [It] was identified by its Author with the Book of that same name, believed by Shí'ah Islám to be in the possession of the promised Qá'im, and to consist of words of consolation addressed by the angel Gabriel, at God's command, to Fáṭimih, and dictated to the Imám 'Alí, for the sole purpose of comforting her in her hour of bitter anguish after the death of her illustrious Father.[228]

122. p. 15 ¶ 22. Fáṭimih

Fáṭimih Zahrá was the youngest daughter of Muhammad. She was also the wife and consort of 'Alí, who was the Prophet's cousin, had been the first to believe in Him, and became His indicated successor. It is alleged that following a violent act by Umar, a companion of the Prophet, she aborted her child and died soon after the passing of Muhammad. Of her several children, Ḥasan and Ḥusayn were greatly distinguished and became the second and third Shí'ih Imáms after their father. The Báb Himself is a direct descendant of Muhammad through Fáṭimih from both His parents. According to Shoghi Effendi, she 'outshone every member of her sex' in the Islamic Dispensation.[229]

123. p. 16 ¶ 23. O ye that are foolish, yet have a name to be wise! . . . Ye are even as the star, which riseth ere the dawn, and which, though it seem radiant and luminous, leadeth the wayfarers of My city astray into the paths of perdition

A quotation from *Hidden Words* (Persian no. 24), in reference to religious leaders who do not give proper consideration to weighty matters, are unwise in their deliberations and decisions, and consequently mislead their followers in the early days of a Dispensation.

The idea is that a star should be dependable for guidance because of the regularity of its movements within the planetary system. In the Bible those religious leaders who do not shine like stars in respect of the light (knowledge and guidance) that they convey but instead become teachers of error are represented as wandering stars, going astray themselves and leading others astray (Jude 1:4–13).

124. p. 16 ¶ 23. Wherefore do ye wear the guise of the shepherd, when inwardly ye have become wolves, intent upon My flock?

There are four other mentions of 'wolves' in the Epistle:

> O ye followers of this Wronged One! Ye are the shepherds of mankind; liberate ye your flocks from the wolves of evil passions and desires. (¶ 53)

> Know of a truth that your subjects are God's trust amongst you. Watch ye, therefore, over them as ye watch over your own selves. Beware that ye allow not wolves to become the shepherds of the fold, or pride and conceit to deter you from turning unto the poor and the desolate. (¶ 89)

> Hath the <u>Sh</u>áh been informed, and chosen to close his eyes to thine acts? Or hath he been seized with fear at the howling of a pack of wolves who have cast the path of God behind their backs and

> followed in thy way without any clear proof or Book? We have heard that the provinces of Persia have been adorned with the adornment of justice. When We observed closely, however, We found them to be the dawning-places of tyranny and the daysprings of injustice. We behold justice in the clutches of tyranny. (¶ 156)

> O Land of Ṭá (Ṭihrán)! Let nothing grieve thee, for God hath chosen thee to be the source of the joy of all mankind. He shall, if it be His Will, bless thy throne with one who will rule with justice, who will gather together the flock of God which the wolves have scattered. (¶ 216)

A hadith predicts:

> Abú Hurairah narrated that the Messenger of Alláh said: 'In the end of times there shall come men who will swindle the world with religion, deceiving the people in soft skins of sheep, their tongues are sweeter than sugar and their hearts are the hearts of wolves . . .[230]

Amos (8:3) predicted a time when the temple will resonate with the cries of wolves:

> And the songs of the temple shall be howlings in that day, saith the Lord God: there shall be many dead bodies in every place . . .

Zechariah (11:3) states:

> There is a voice of the howling of the shepherds; for their glory is spoiled . . .

Christ (Matt. 7:15) warned His followers:

> Beware of false prophets, which shall come to them in sheep's clothing (similar in outward appearances to His other followers), but inwardly they are ravening [predatory and rapacious] wolves.

The Apostle Paul wrote (Acts 20:29):

> For I know this, that after my departing shall grievous wolves enter in among you, not sparing the flock.

See also Annotations 312 and 398.

125. p. 16 ¶ 24. O ye seeming fair . . . immeasurable is the difference

Bahá'u'lláh provides another extract from *Hidden Words* (Persian no. 25). In the *Kitáb-i-Íqán* He observes:

> Such a condition as this is witnessed in this day when the reins of every community have fallen into the grasp of foolish leaders, who lead after their own whims and desire.[231]

'Ye are like clear but bitter water' is reminiscent of the following passages from the Qur'án (25:48–49, 53):

> We send down pure water from the sky [heaven], – that with it We may give life to a dead land, and slake the thirst of things We have created . . .
>
> It is He Who has let free the two bodies of flowing water: one palatable and sweet, and the other salt and bitter; yet has He made a barrier between them, a partition that is forbidden to be passed.

See also Qur'án 35:12: 'Nor are the two bodies of flowing water alike, – the one palatable, sweet, and pleasant to drink, and the other, salt and bitter.'

Christ also underlined this dichotomy (Matt. 6:24): 'No man can serve two masters: for either he will hate the one, and love the other; or else he will hold to the one, and despise the other. Ye cannot serve God and mammon.' Similarly, Matt. 7:18: 'A good tree cannot bring forth evil fruit, neither can a corrupt tree bring forth good fruit.' He added (Matt. 23:27–28): 'Woe unto you, scribes and Pharisees, hypocrites! for ye are like unto whited sepulchres, which indeed appear beautiful outward, but are within full of dead men's bones, and of all uncleanness. Even so ye also outwardly appear righteous unto men, but within ye are full of hypocrisy and iniquity.'

The Apostle James (3:11–12) asked rhetorically: 'Doth a fountain send forth at the same place sweet water and bitter? Can the fig tree, my brethren, bear olive berries? either a vine, figs? so can no fountain both yield salt water and fresh.'

126. p. 16 ¶ 25. O essence of desire . . . hosts of holiness

This is the third extract Bahá'u'lláh quotes from *Hidden Words* (Persian no. 28).

The voracious appetite of the Shaykh to amass wealth by any means at his disposal may be contrasted with Bahá'u'lláh's statements on detachment, such as in ¶ 63:

> The betterment of the world hath been the sole aim of this Wronged One. Unto this beareth witness every man of judgment, of discernment, of insight and understanding. Whilst afflicted with trials, He held fast unto the cord of patience and fortitude, and was satisfied with the things which have befallen Him at the hands of His enemies, and was crying out: 'I have renounced My desire for Thy desire, O my God, and My will for the revelation of Thy Will.'

127. p. 16 ¶ 26. O bond slave of the world! Many a dawn hath the breeze of My loving-kindness wafted over thee and found thee upon the bed of heedlessness fast asleep. Bewailing then thy plight it returned whence it came

This is the fourth extract Bahá'u'lláh quotes from *Hidden Words* (Persian no. 30). It implies that the individual is a slave to the mundane rather than doing God's will.

The Apostle Paul described himself as a bond slave (the Greek *doulos* means purchased slave), who is bought by the blood and sacrifice of Christ (Rom 1:1), indicating his total surrender to the divine will. By contrast, a 'bond slave of the world' is an individual who is attached to the mundane.

Muhammad refers to Himself as 'Abd' (Qur'án 17:1); hence His title 'Abd'u'lláh, the servant or the slave of God. A hadith attributed to Imám Ja'far aṣ-Ṣádiq explains that the Arabic word for servant or slave, *'Abd,* is composed of three letters: '*ayn*', '*ba*', and '*dal*'. The '*ayn*' indicates *'ilm*, knowledge and certainty that a servant has of God. The '*ba*' indicates *bu'd*, the separation and distance he has from other than God. And the letter '*dal*' denotes *dunuw*, his closeness to God.[232]

128. p. 16 ¶ 27. Those divines . . . who are truly adorned with the ornament of knowledge and of a goodly character

This passage is cited by Shoghi Effendi in *The Promised Day Is Come*, along with others on the same theme:

> Nor should it be thought for a moment that the followers of Bahá'u'lláh either seek to degrade or even belittle the rank of the world's religious leaders, whether Christian, Muslim, or of any other denomination, should their conduct conform to their professions, and be worthy of the position they occupy . . . 'The divine whose conduct is upright, and the sage who is just, are as the spirit unto the body of the world. Well is it with that divine whose head is attired with the crown of justice, and whose temple is adorned with the ornament of equity.' And yet again: 'The divine who hath seized and quaffed the most holy Wine, in the name of the sovereign Ordainer, is as an eye unto the world. Well is it with them who obey him, and call him to remembrance.' 'Great is the blessedness of that divine,' He, in another connection, has written, 'that hath not allowed knowledge to become a veil between him and the One Who is the Object of all knowledge, and who, when the Self-Subsisting appeared, hath turned with a beaming face towards Him. He, in truth, is numbered with the learned. The inmates of Paradise seek the blessing of his breath, and his lamp sheddeth its radiance over all who are in heaven and on earth. He, verily, is numbered with the inheritors of the Prophets. He that beholdeth him hath, verily, beheld the True One, and he that turneth towards him hath, verily, turned towards God, the Almighty, the All-Wise.' 'Respect ye the divines amongst you,' is His exhortation, 'They whose acts conform to the knowledge they possess, who observe the statutes of God, and decree the things God hath decreed in the Book. Know ye that they are the lamps of guidance betwixt earth and heaven. They that have no consideration for the position and merit of the divines amongst them have, verily, altered the bounty of God vouchsafed unto them.'[233]

129. p. 17 ¶ 28. God requite him who said: 'Willingly will I obey the judge who hath so strangely decreed that my blood be spilt at Ḥill and at Ḥaram!'

A quotation from the collection of poetry (*Diwán*) of Ibn al-Fáriḍ, also known as Sharaf al-Dín Abú Ḥafṣ and 'Umar ibn al-Fáriḍ (c. 1181–1235 CE), a famous Egyptian poet. His expressions of Sufi mysticism are regarded as the finest in the Arabic language. He spent several years in Mecca and in his poems (*qaṣídah* or odes) he describes his yearning to return to Mecca and, at a deeper level, professes a lover's longing for reunion with his beloved, and a desire to be assimilated into the spirit of Muhammad. In this poem quoted by Bahá'u'lláh he expresses his eagerness to sacrifice himself if it is God's decree that his blood be shed in the sacred vicinity or outside it. Bahá'u'lláh quotes his poetry in *Seven Valleys*, *Jawáhiru'l-Asrár* (*Gems of Divine Mysteries*) and the *Kitáb-i-Íqán*.

Shoghi Effendi provides the following account relating to this poet:

> Amazed by the profundity of His [Bahá'u'lláh's] insight and the compass of His understanding, they [the learned instructors and students of the seminary in Sulaymaníyyih] were impelled to seek from Him what they considered to be a conclusive and final evidence of the unique power and knowledge which He now appeared in their eyes to possess. 'No one among the mystics, the wise, and the learned,' they claimed, while requesting this further favour from Him, 'has hitherto proved himself capable of writing a poem in a rhyme and meter identical with that of the longer of the two odes,[234] entitled Qaṣídiy-i-Tá'íyyih composed by Ibn-i-Fáriḍ. We beg you to write for us a poem in that same meter and rhyme.' This request was complied with, and no less than two thousand verses, in exactly the manner they had specified, were dictated by Him, out of which He selected one hundred and twenty-seven, which He permitted them to keep, deeming the subject matter of the rest premature and unsuitable to the needs of the times. It is these same one hundred and twenty-seven verses that constitute the Qaṣídiy-i-Varqá'íyyih, so familiar to, and widely circulated amongst, His Arabic speaking followers.[235]

130. p. 17 ¶ 28. at Ḥill and at Ḥaram

There are two hills, Safa and Marwa, now located in the Great Mosque (also known as *al-Masjid al-Ḥarám* – the Arabic word *ḥaram* means sacred or forbidden) in Saudi Arabia. The Mosque also encloses the Kaaba, a cube-shaped structure that is the cynosure of Islam. According to tradition, Hagar rushed seven times to see if she could find water, or anyone who could provide water, for her infant son Isaac (Ismail). Muslims travel back and forth between the two hills seven times, during the ritual pilgrimages of Hajj. The area is sacred and a sanctuary from punishment and blood revenge. The term *ḥaram* is commonly used to refer to certain other holy sites, such as the Temple Mount (*Ḥaram ash Sharif*) in Jerusalem.

131. p. 17 ¶ 28. Deadly poison in His path is pure honey

Bahá'u'lláh expresses His complete submission to the Divine Will. Elsewhere, He eulogizes suffering in the Path of God:

> Perish that lover who discerneth between the pleasant and the poisonous in his love for his beloved![236]

'Abdu'l-Bahá also writes:

> Therefore think not that this fierce opposition and cruelty hath brought humiliation and abasement upon you. Nay, I swear by God, besides Whom there is none other God, they redound to imperishable glory and unfading bounty. Indeed this persecution is a cooling draught and these trials a source of delight. This poison is but sugar and this venom the essence of sweetness. This stab in the breast is a soothing balm to heart and soul, and this bitter medicine a healing remedy. One's sense of taste must be unimpaired to perceive its sweetness and to savour its relish.[237]

132. p. 17 ¶ 28. I fear no tribulation in His path, nor any affliction in My love for Him

This is part of Bahá'u'lláh's experience in the Siyáh-Chál when He had the first intimation of His Mission. The content of His Revelation was independent of His adverse experiences:

> Under all conditions, whether in adversity or at ease, whether honoured or afflicted, this Wronged One hath directed all men to show forth love, affection, compassion and harmony.[238]

133. p. 17 ¶ 28. Verily God hath made adversity as a morning dew upon His green pasture, and a wick for His lamp which lighteth earth and heaven

Bahíyyih Khánum, the Greatest Holy Leaf, quotes this passage in one of her letters:

> . . . earthly cares and have prevented blessed souls, so overflowing with love, to shine in this dark and dismal world. Nevertheless, dear sister, rest assured and never be sorrowful. It is in one of the foremost Tablets of Bahá'u'lláh that He says: 'Verily God hath made adversity as a morning dew upon His green pasture, and a wick for His lamp which lighteth earth and heaven.' Meaning thereby that physical illnesses and misfortunes certainly make a person nearer and nearer to his Lord. Why then should we sorrow over earthly hindrances when we have done what we possibly could, and when we are sure that this, our little service, will certainly be acceptable in His Sight?[239]

In the words of Shoghi Effendi, the Faith of the Báb and Bahá'u'lláh has been 'cradled in adversity'.[240] However, elsewhere, Bahá'u'lláh explains that adversity has always served to promote His Faith:

> Say: Adversity is the oil which feedeth the flame of this Lamp and by which its light is increased, did ye but know. Indeed, the repudiation of the froward serveth but to proclaim this Faith and to spread the Cause of God and His Revelation throughout the world.[241]

134. p. 17 ¶ 29. Set thine heart towards Him Who is the Kaaba of God

The Kaaba – the Islamic Point of adoration (Qiblih) to which Muslims turn in prayer at the centre of the great Mosque in Mecca. The structure is reputed to have originally been built by Abraham. Prior to Islam it housed 360 idols. Here, the Kaaba of God is used symbolically to signify the Person of the Manifestation of God, who in this Dispensation is Bahá'u'lláh Himself.

See also Annotations 438 and 509.

135. p. 18 ¶ 29. say: 'Thou seest me, O my Lord, with my face turned towards the heaven of Thy bounty

A reference to Bahá'u'lláh and His Revelation. Cited in *Bahá'í Prayers*, p. 76.

136. p. 18 ¶ 29. God is our Lord, the Lord of all who are in heaven and all who are on earth

The statement paraphrases Qur'án (7:56, Rodwell translation): 'Your Lord is God, who in six days created the Heavens and the Earth, and then mounted the throne . . .' Also (45:36, Rodwell translation): 'Praise then be to God, Lord of the Heavens and Lord of the Earth; the Lord of the worlds!'

It is similar to the following verses of the Torah (Deut. 10:14): 'Behold, the heaven and the heaven of heavens is the Lord's thy God, the earth also, with all that therein is,' and the Psalms (89:11): 'The heavens are thine, the earth also is thine: as for the world and the fullness thereof, thou hast founded them.'

See also: The Báb, *Selections from the Writings of the Báb*, p. 7; Bahá'u'lláh, *Prayers and Meditations*, p. 171; Medium Obligatory Prayer in *The Kitab-i-Aqdas*, p. 99; *Kitáb-i-Íqán*, pp. 48 and 67.

137. p. 18 ¶ 30. O Shaykh! Verily I say, the seal of the Choice Wine hath, in the name of Him Who is the Self-Subsisting, been broken

The Choice Wine refers to the beginning of a new Revelation. Reference to the use of 'wine' in an allegorical sense – such as being the cause of spiritual ecstasy and intoxication – is found not only in the Revelation of Bahá'u'lláh, but also in the Bible and the Qur'án.

In the Acts of the Apostles, Peter speaking for the disciples explains that they are not drunk with literal wine but with the spirit of their new-found faith in Christ. Hence 'wine' is sometimes used in the Bible as a metaphor for Revelation. Evaporation and the process of fermentation of literal wine were controlled by sealing it with beeswax in airtight jars. Daniel is promised that God will open the sealed wine of divine Words at the end of times (Dan. 12:4, 8–9). Using the same metaphor, Christ explained (Matt. 9:17) that if a new wine is poured into old goatskins the skins would absorb the water and burst – a new wine required new goatskins, in other words, a new Revelation requires the outward form of a new Dispensation. In this context, Amos (9:13) promises a new wine or Revelation, 'Behold, the days come, saith the Lord that . . . the mountains shall drop sweet wine . . .'

In the Qur'án (83:22–26) the righteous are promised that their thirst will be satisfied by a drink of the 'choice sealed wine, the seal thereof will be Musk'.

Compare the following verse from the *Kitáb-i-Aqdas*: 'Think not that We have revealed unto you a mere code of laws. Nay, rather, We have unsealed the choice Wine with the fingers of might and power.'[242]

> Bahá'u'lláh identifies the 'choice Wine' with His Revelation whose 'musk-laden fragrance' has been wafted 'upon all created things'. He states that he has 'unsealed' this 'Wine', thereby disclosing spiritual truths that where hitherto unknown, and enabling those who quaff thereof to 'discern splendors of the light of divine unity' and to 'grasp the essential purpose underlying the Scriptures of God'.[243]

Bahá'u'lláh also refers to God's 'choice Wine of justice'[244] and 'the choice Wine of utterance'.[245] In one of His meditations, Bahá'u'lláh entreats God to supply the believers with the 'the choice Wine of Thy mercy, that it may cause them to be forgetful of anyone except Thee, and to arise to serve Thy Cause, and to be steadfast in their love for Thee'.[246]

Also,

> How great the multitude of the poor who have quaffed the choice wine of divine revelation and how many the rich who have turned away, repudiated the truth and voiced their disbelief in God, the Lord of this blessed and wondrous Day![247]

Referring to the *Kitáb-i-Íqán*, Shoghi Effendi wrote,

> Revealed on the eve of the declaration of His Mission, it proffered to mankind the 'Choice Sealed Wine,' whose seal is of 'musk,' and broke the 'seals' of the 'Book' referred to by Daniel, and disclosed the meaning of the 'words' destined to remain 'closed up' till the 'time of the end'.[248]

138. p. 18 ¶ 30. Self-Subsisting

Jehovah in the Torah (Ex. 3:14) explains that His Name I AM THAT I AM indicates the unchanging and eternal God, Who exists by virtue of His own nature; that is, He is Self-Existing or Self-Subsisting. God in Mal. 3:6 states 'For I am the Lord, I change not . . .' Also (Rev. 1:8): 'I am Alpha and Omega, the beginning and the ending, saith the Lord, which is, and which was, and which is to come, the Almighty.' The Manifestations of God reflect this attribute, as illustrated by Christ's statements (John 8:58): 'Before Abraham was, I am.' The Apostle Paul explains (Heb. 13:8): 'Jesus Christ the same yesterday, and today and for ever.'

The Arabic word is *qayyum*, which means self-subsisting and eternal – *al-Qayyum* is one of the names of God in the Qur'án (2:255) as in 'God! There is no god but He, the Living, the Self-subsisting, Eternal . . .'

A letter on behalf of the Universal House of Justice explains:

> It is likely that this term signifies in some way a basic concept of the Faith; namely, that creation is an emanation from God, without Whose continuing bounty and grace it would cease to exist. The

term thus underscores the immense contrast between our reality, which is related to the contingent world, and His reality which is independent of any cause and which entirely transcends the world of being. Indeed, the point is that He is the Cause of being itself. There is a way to deduce such a meaning, however, solely from the common meaning of the words. According to its primary dictionary definition, 'to subsist' means to have existence, to persist or continue. The addition of 'self' makes it reflexive. Knowing just these two things, can we not then say that if God is self-subsisting it means that there is nothing other than Himself upon which He depends for His continuing existence? In other words, He exists in and of Himself without being dependent on any other cause: He has no creator and there is nothing prior to Him.[249]

139. p. 19 ¶ 30. Dust-made Adam was raised up

In the account of the Torah (Gen. 2:7) God formed Adam out of 'the dust of the ground' and 'breathed into his nostrils the breath of life'. Adam is etymologically related to *Adamah*, a Hebrew word which means earth, red ground or red clay. As a collective name Adam refers to humanity. The Qur'án (3:59; 22:5; 30:20; 35:11) relates the same story and explains that all humanity has been created from the same dust.

In *Hidden Words* Bahá'u'lláh frequently addresses man as begotten of 'dust': 'O Offspring of Dust!'; 'O Children of Dust!'; 'O Son of Dust!'; 'O Moving Form of Dust!'; and 'O Weed that Springeth out of Dust!' He elsewhere remarks: 'the universe is darkened with the dust of sin'.[250] His prescription elucidates the meaning of 'dust': 'Strive that your deeds may be cleansed from the dust of self and hypocrisy.'[251]

Through Bahá'u'lláh, humanity's earthly preoccupations have been transmuted to heavenly aspirations:

> O Son of Spirit! The bird seeketh its nest; the nightingale the charm of the rose; whilst those birds, the hearts of men, content with transient dust, have strayed far from their eternal nest, and with eyes turned towards the slough of heedlessness are bereft of the glory of the divine presence. Alas! How strange and pitiful; for a mere cupful, they have turned away from the billowing seas of the Most High, and remained far from the most effulgent horizon.[252]

> O My friends that dwell upon the dust! Haste forth unto your celestial habitation.[253]

Referring to the creative power of the Divine Word 'Abdu'l-Bahá explains:

> There is a power which purifies the mirror from dust and transforms its reflection into intense brilliancy and radiance so that spiritual susceptibilities may chasten the hearts and heavenly bestowals sanctify them. What is the dust which obscures the mirror? It is attachment to the world, avarice, envy, love of luxury and comfort, haughtiness and self-desire; this is the dust which prevents reflection of the rays of the Sun of Reality in the mirror. The natural emotions are blameworthy and are like rust which deprives the heart of the bounties of God. But sincerity, justice, humility, severance, and love for the believers of God will purify the mirror and make it radiant with reflected rays from the Sun of Truth.[254]

He exhorts those who arise to proclaim the Message of Bahá'u'lláh: 'Just as His Holiness Christ says: "Shake off the very dust from your feet [Matt. 10:14; Luke 9:5]."'[255]

In another sense, the 'obscuring dust' refers to acquired knowledge and theology which can also dim the mirror of the seeker's heart and the light of his faith.[256] In yet another sense, 'same dust' refers to our common molecular-genetic composition, an illustration that humanity is one:

> O Children of Men! Know ye not why We created you all from the same dust? That no one should exalt himself over the other. Ponder at all times in your hearts how ye were created. Since We have created you all from one same substance it is incumbent on you to be even as one soul, to walk with the same feet, eat with the same mouth and dwell in the same land, that from your inmost being, by your deeds and actions, the signs of oneness and the essence of detachment may be made manifest.[257]

140. p. 19 ¶ 30. through the Word of God

Bahá'u'lláh explains to the Shaykh that humanity's necessary spiritual transformation through the creative power of the Divine Word has been the primary purpose of all religions, including His Revelation.

> . . . is not the object of every Revelation to effect a transformation in the whole character of mankind, a transformation that shall manifest itself, both outwardly and inwardly, that shall affect both its inner life and external conditions? For if the character of mankind be not changed, the futility of God's universal Manifestations would be apparent.[258]

> 'Every body calleth aloud for a soul. Heavenly souls must needs quicken, with the breath of the Word of God, the dead bodies with a fresh spirit. Within every word a new spirit is hidden. Happy is the man that . . . hath arisen to teach the Cause of Him Who is the King of Eternity.' 'Say: O servants! The triumph of this Cause hath depended, and will continue to depend, upon the appearance of holy souls, upon the showing forth of goodly deeds, and the revelation of words of consummate wisdom.'[259]

> Every word that proceedeth out of the mouth of God is endowed with such potency as can instill new life into every human frame . . .[260]

The Gospel of John (1:1–2, 3–5, 11–13) asserts that what we appreciate as 'God' is through the Divine Word or 'Logos'. This at the First Coming was incarnated in Christ and those who believed in His Word became transformed into new spiritual beings and were born of God. Confirming the Bible, the Qur'án (3:45; 4:171) refers to Jesus as God's 'Word' (*Kalimah*) and 'A word from Him', that is, 'The Word of God' (*Kalimatulláh).* Also (2:287) as 'One inspired by the Holy Spirit', and (58:22) as 'A Spirit from God' (*Ruhulláh*). Today Bahá'u'lláh incarnates the Divine Word.

141. p. 19 ¶ 30. a mere fisherman

This refers to Simon, later named Peter by Christ. Together with his brother Andrew, Simon was the first disciple to believe in Jesus. As a simple unschooled fisherman, his unquestioning and immediate response to Christ's Message (Matt. 4:18–20) is quite endearing and instructive: 'And he [Jesus] saith unto them, Follow me, and I will make you fishers of men. And they straightway left their nets, and followed him.'

> 'Peter,' 'Abdu'l-Bahá has testified, 'according to the history of the Church, was also incapable of keeping count of the days of the week. Whenever he decided to go fishing, he would tie up his weekly food into seven parcels, and every day he would eat one of them, and when he had reached the seventh, he would know that the Sabbath had arrived, and thereupon would observe it.' If the Son of Man was capable of infusing into apparently so crude and helpless an instrument such potency as to cause, in the words of Bahá'u'lláh, 'the mysteries of wisdom and of utterance to flow out of his mouth,' and to exalt him above the rest of His disciples, and render him fit to become His successor and the founder of His Church, how much more can the Father, Who is Bahá'u'lláh, empower the most puny and insignificant among His followers to achieve, for the execution of His purpose, such wonders as would dwarf the mightiest achievements of even the first apostle of Jesus Christ![261]

Concerning the successorship of Peter, Shoghi Effendi writes:

> the primacy of Peter, the Prince of the Apostles, is upheld and defended. The Founder of the Christian Faith is designated by Bahá'u'lláh as the 'Spirit of God', is proclaimed as the One Who 'appeared out of the breath of the Holy Ghost', and is even extolled as the 'Essence of the Spirit'. His mother is described as 'that veiled and immortal, that most beauteous, countenance', and the station of her Son eulogized as a 'station which hath been exalted above the imaginings of all that dwell on earth', whilst Peter is recognized as one whom God has caused 'the mysteries of wisdom and of utterance to flow out of his mouth'.[262]

According to Christian tradition, Peter was crucified in Rome during the rule of Emperor Nero Augustus Caesar, at a time when Christians were being persecuted. It is traditionally held that he was crucified upside down at his own request, since he saw himself unworthy to be crucified in the same way as Jesus.

142. p. 19 ¶ 30. Abú <u>Dh</u>ar

Abú <u>Dh</u>ar <u>Gh</u>ifárí was an illiterate Bedouin tribesman, known for his strict piety, who was an outstanding and much esteemed disciple of Muhammad. After the passing of Muhammad, he became a firm upholder of the primacy of 'Alí ibn Abí Tálib, in defence of whose mission he eventually gave his life (652 CE). The following are accounts that describe his life:

> A man of the Bani Ghifár named Abú Dhar – his tribe lived to the north-west of Mecca, not far from the Red Sea – had already heard of the Prophet and of the opposition to him. Like most of his tribesmen, Abú Dhar was a highwayman; but unlike them he was a firm believer in the Oneness of God, and he refused to pay any respect to idols. His brother Unays went to Mecca for some reason, and on his return he told Abú Dhar that there was a man of Quraysh who claimed to be a Prophet, and who said 'there is no god but God,' and his people had disowned him in consequence. Abú Dhar immediately set off for Mecca, in the certainty that here was a true Prophet, and on his arrival those of the Quraysh who manned the approach told him all he wished to know before he had time to ask. Without difficulty he found his way to the Prophet's house. The Prophet was lying asleep on a bench in the courtyard, with his face covered by a fold of his cloak. Abú Dhar woke him and wished him good morning. 'On thee be Peace!' said the Prophet. 'Declaim unto me thine utterances,' said the Bedouin. 'I am no poet,' said the Prophet, 'but what I utter is the Koran, and it is not I who speak but God who speaketh.' 'Recite for me,' said Abú Dhar, and he recited to him a súrah, whereupon Abú Dhar said: 'I testify that there is no god but God, and that Muhammad is the messenger of God.' 'Who are thy people?' said the Prophet, and at the man's answer he looked him up and down in amazement and said: 'Verily God guideth whom He

> will.' It was well known that the Bani Ghifár were mostly robbers. Having instructed him in Islam the Prophet told him to return to his people and await his orders. So he returned to the Bani Ghifár, many of whom entered Islam through him. Meantime he continued his calling as highwayman, with special attention to the caravans of Quraysh. But when he had despoiled a caravan he would offer to give back what he had taken on condition that they would testify to the Oneness of God and the prophethood of Muhammad.[263]

> Jundub 'ibn Junadah, known as Abú Dhar Al-Ghifarí, was a shepherd of the Ghafarí tribe which lived in the Waddan valley, near Mecca. He was known for his courage, his calmness and his far sightedness and also for the repugnance he felt against the idols which his people worshipped. Hearing of the new Prophet, he journeyed to Mecca and was taught the new Faith by 'Alí and attained the presence of Muḥammad Upon returning to the Waddan, he converted a large number of his tribe. After the battle of Khandaq, he was accepted as a personal servant of the Prophet, Who was greatly pleased with him. After the passing of Muḥammad, because of his sharp criticism of the worldliness of the Muslim community, 'Uthmán, the third Sunní *Khalíf*, sent him to Rubdhah, a small village near Madinah, where he lived a life of renunciation. It was there that he died in 32 AH (about 653 CE). According to tradition, the Prophet had said, 'The earth does not carry nor the heavens cover a man more true and faithful than 'Abú Dhar . . .'[264]

Bahá'u'lláh calls Abú Dhar 'a prince of the nations', and in a Tablet to Karím states that the moment Abú Dhar turned to the Self-Subsistent, the seas of wisdom and utterance flowed forth from his heart and lips.

143. p. 19 ¶ 31. This Day, O Shaykh, hath never been, nor is it now, the Day whereon man-made arts and sciences can be regarded as a true standard for men . . . He Who was wholly unversed in any of them

This is a reference to Mullá Muḥammad Ja'far-i-Iṣfáhání, the first Bábí from Isfahan, 'the sifter of wheat' (*gandum-pák-kun*), one of the martyrs at Shaykh Ṭabarsí and the only believer honoured by having been mentioned in both the *Bayán* and the *Kitáb-i-Aqdas*. The following is recounted by Nabíl:

> The first to embrace the Cause of the Báb in that city was a man, a sifter of wheat, who, as soon as the Call reached his ears, unreservedly accepted the Message. With marvellous devotion he served Mullá Ḥusayn, and through his close association with him became a zealous advocate of the new Revelation. A few years later, when the soul-stirring details of the siege of the Fort of Shaykh Ṭabarsí were being recounted to him, he felt an irresistible impulse to throw in his lot with those heroic companions of the Báb who had risen for the defence of their Faith. Carrying his sieve in his hand, he immediately arose and set out to reach the scene of that memorable encounter. 'Why leave so hurriedly?' his friends asked him, as they saw him running in a state of intense excitement through the bazaars of Iṣfáhán. 'I have risen,' he replied, 'to join the glorious company of the defenders of the fort of Shaykh Ṭabarsí! With this sieve which I carry with me, I intend to sift the people in every city through which I pass. Whomsoever I find ready to espouse the Cause I have embraced, I will ask to join me and hasten forthwith to the field of martyrdom.' Such was the devotion of this youth, that the Báb, in the Persian Bayán, refers to him in such terms: 'Iṣfáhán, that outstanding city, is distinguished by the religious fervour of its Shí'ah inhabitants, by the learning of its divines, and by the keen expectation, shared by high and low alike, of the imminent coming of the Ṣáḥibu'z-Zamán. In every quarter of that city, religious institutions have been established. And yet, when the Messenger of God had been made manifest, they who claimed to be the repositories of learning and the expounders of the mysteries of the Faith of God rejected His Message. Of all the inhabitants of that seat of learning, only one person, a sifter of wheat, was found to recognise the Truth, and was invested with the robe of Divine virtue!'[265]

144. p. 19 ¶ 31. the acknowledged exponent and repository of these arts and sciences

A reference to the 'far-famed' Shaykh Muḥammad-Ḥasan-i-Najafí, the leading mujtahid of Persia and a great enemy of the Cause of the

Báb and of Bahá'u'lláh; characterized by Nabíl as a 'proud and fanatic leader'.[266] Bahá'u'lláh writes of him:

> Call ye to mind the shaykh whose name was Muḥammad-Ḥasan, who ranked among the most learned divines of his day. When the True One was made manifest, this shaykh, along with others of his calling, rejected Him, while a sifter of wheat and barley accepted Him and turned unto the Lord. Though he was occupied both night and day in setting down what he conceived to be the laws and ordinances of God, yet when he Who is the Unconstrained appeared, not one letter thereof availed him, or he would not have turned away from a Countenance that hath illumined the faces of the well-favoured of the Lord. Had ye believed in God when He revealed Himself, the people would not have turned aside from Him, nor would the things ye witness today have befallen Us. Fear God, and be not of the heedless.[267]

145. p. 19 ¶ 31. By 'arts and sciences' is meant those which begin with words and end with words

It should be noted that Bahá'u'lláh extols 'arts and sciences that add to man's exaltation' in ¶ 47:

> Arts, crafts and sciences uplift the world of being, and are conducive to its exaltation. Knowledge is as wings to man's life, and a ladder for his ascent. Its acquisition is incumbent upon everyone. The knowledge of such sciences, however, should be acquired as can profit the peoples of the earth, and not those which begin with words and end with words.

A letter written on behalf of Shoghi Effendi to a student further clarifies this point:

> Philosophy, as you will study it and later teach it, is certainly not one of the sciences that begins and ends in words. Fruitless excursions into metaphysical hair-splitting is meant, not a sound branch of learning like philosophy.[268]

146. p. 19 ¶ 32 vindicating

An attempt had been made on the life of the Shah of Persia in 1852 (see Annotation 150), following which Bahá'u'lláh was falsely charged with complicity in this action and was sent to prison. This is the event that He is here vindicating himself of. It transpired that the would-be assassin of the Shah confessed to the crime and completely exonerated the Bábí leaders and Bahá'u'lláh of any involvement. By itself, the ill-conceived manner by which the attempt was made proved the falsity of the accusation that Bahá'u'lláh was involved:

> Now when Bahá'u'lláh was interrogated on this matter He answered in reply, 'The event itself indicates the truth of the affair and testifies that this is the action of a thoughtless, unreasoning, and ignorant man. For no reasonable person would charge his pistol with shot when embarking on so grave an enterprise. At least he would so arrange and plan it that the deed should be orderly and systematic. From the very nature of the event it is clear and evident as the sun that it is not the act of such as Myself.'
>
> So it was established and proven that the assassin had on his own responsibility engaged in this grievous action and monstrous deed with the idea and design of taking blood revenge for his Master, and that it concerned no one else. And when the truth of the matter became evident the innocence of Bahá'u'lláh from this suspicion was established in such wise that no doubt remained for anyone; the decision of the court declared His purity and freedom from this charge . . .[269]

147. p. 20 ¶ 32. At the time when His Majesty the Sháh . . . was planning a journey to Iṣfahán, this Wronged One . . . visited the holy and luminous resting- places of the Imáms

The historian Nabíl writes:

> The seventh Naw-Rúz after the Declaration of the Báb fell on the sixteenth day of the month of Jamádiyu'l-Avval in the year 1267 A.H. [1851 CE], a month and a half after the termination of the struggle of Zanján. That same year, towards the end of spring, in the early days

> of the month of Sha'bán, Bahá'u'lláh left the capital for Karbilá . . .
>
> The month of Shavval, in the year 1267 A.H., witnessed the arrival of Bahá'u'lláh at Karbilá. On His way to that holy city, He tarried a few days in Baghdád, that place which He was soon to visit again and where His Cause was destined to mature and unfold itself to the world . . .
>
> It was during that visit to Karbilá that Bahá'u'lláh encountered, as He was walking through the streets, Shaykh Ḥasan-i-Zunúzí, to whom He confided the secret He was destined to reveal at a later time in Baghdád. He found him eagerly searching after the promised Ḥusayn, to whom the Báb had so lovingly referred and whom He had promised he would meet in Karbilá. We have already, in a preceding chapter, narrated the circumstances leading to his meeting with Bahá'u'lláh. From that day, Shaykh Ḥasan became magnetised by the charm of his newly found Master, and would, but for the restraint he was urged to exercise, have proclaimed to the people of Karbilá the return of the promised Ḥusayn whose appearance they were awaiting.[270]

Najaf and Karbila are the sites of Imám 'Alí's Mosque, and *Maqam al-Imám al-Ḥusayn ibn 'Ali*, the Mosque and burial site of Imám Ḥusayn. Within his shrine and at the foot of Imám Ḥusayn's grave may be found a mass grave of all the seventy-two individuals who were martyred with him in Karbila. The site also contains the remains of Siyyid Kázim-i-Rashtí. Thus, Bahá'u'lláh visited the shrine of His namesake, Imám Ḥusayn, Whose return He would come to represent.

148. p. 20 ¶ 32. Imáms

The Imáms were the twelve descendants and Shí'ih successors of Muhammad – all were likely killed, by Muslim enemies of the Imamate:

1. 'Alí ibn Abí Ṭálib. Assassinated on 26 January 661 CE by Ibn Muljam, a Khawarij or member of a breakaway sect that was against 'Alí's agreement to accept arbitration with Mu'áwiya following the Battle of Siffin. The Imám 'Alí Mosque in Najaf, (80 km from Karbilá) Iraq contains his tomb (the exact location of his remains is however uncertain).

2. Ḥasan, son of 'Alí, died at the age of 47 years on 9 March 670 CE as a result of being poisoned by his wife on instructions from Mu'áwiya. He is buried in Medina next to his mother, Fáṭimih, in Al-Baqi.

3. Ḥusayn, son of 'Alí, beheaded in the Battle of Karbila by the forces of Yazid, the son of Mu'áwiya, on 10 October 689 CE, and buried with his son, 'Alí al-Asg͟har ibn Ḥusayn, in the Imám 'Alí Mosque.

4. 'Alí ibn Ḥusayn, also known as Zaynu'l-Abidin (the adornment of the worshippers) and Imám Sajjád (the Prostrating Imám). He was poisoned by Umayyad ruler Al-Walid, and died 713–714 CE. He is buried in Medina, alongside his uncle Ḥasan and grandmother in Al-Baqi.

5. Muḥammad al-Báqir, also known as 'Abú-Ja'far and al-Báqir (abbreviation of Báqir al 'Ilm, literally, the one who opens knowledge). By some accounts he was poisoned by the Umayyad Ibrahim ibn Walid ibn Abdallah (733 CE). He is buried in Al-Baqi in Medina.

6. Ja'far-i-Ṣádiq, known as Aṣ-Ṣádiq, son of the fifth Imám, al-Baqir. He is believed to have been poisoned on orders of the Umayyad Mansur (765 CE) and is buried in Al-Baqi in Medina.

7. Músá al-Káẓim, son of the sixth Imám, buried in Kazimayn.

8. 'Alí ar-Riḍá, full name 'Alí ibn Músá. He was poisoned by Caliph Ma'mún (c. 799 CE), and is buried in Mashhad (literally. the place of martyrdom).

9. Muḥammad ibn 'Alí ibn Músá, also known as Ibn al-Riḍá and al-Jawád (the Generous) and al-Taqí (the Pius). He was poisoned by his wife at the urging of Caliph al-Mu'tasim. He died at the age of 25 years (835 CE) and is buried in Kazimayn.

10. 'Alí ibn Muḥammad ibn 'Alí, also known as 'Alí Naqi and al-Hádí, son of the ninth Imám. He is reported to have been poisoned

by the Abbasid Caliphs, al-Mutawakkil or al-Mu'tamid, and is buried in Samarra, Iraq.

11. Ḥasan al-'Askarí, son of the tenth Imám poisoned at the age of 28 on the orders of the Abbasid Caliph al-Mu'tamid (874 CE). He is buried with his father in Samarra, Iraq.

12. Muḥammad al-Mahdi, also known as Imám Zamán, Muḥammad al-Qá'im, son of the eleventh Imám. Behind the shrine of the eleventh Imám is the Mosque of the Occultation, beneath which is the underground chamber in which the twelfth Imám is said to have disappeared (260 AH). The S͟hí'ihs expect him to return and bring justice and peace to the world accompanied by Jesus (Ísá).

149.   p. 20 ¶ 32.   Upon Our return, we proceeded to Lavásán

A rural district of Tehran where in 1852 CE Bahá'u'lláh stayed at the summer residence of Ja'far-Qulí K͟hán, the brother of the Grand Vizir:

> Bahá'u'lláh, when that attempt had been made on the life of the sovereign, was in Lavásán, the guest of the Grand Vizir, and was staying in the village of Afchih when the momentous news reached Him.[271]

150.   p. 20 ¶ 32.   the attempt upon the life of His Majesty

On 15 August 1852 CE two Bábí youths made an attempt upon the life of Náṣiri'd-Dín S͟háh. Shoghi Effendi recounts the circumstances. The historian Nabíl provides the following details:

> That criminal act was committed towards the end of the month of Shavvál, in the year 1268 AH (Shavvál 28; August 15, 1852 A.D.) by two obscure and irresponsible young men, one named Ṣádiq-i-Tabrízí, and the other Fatḥu'lláh-i-Qumí, both of whom earned their livelihood in Ṭihrán. At a time when the imperial army, headed by the S͟háh himself, had encamped in S͟himírán, these two ignorant youths, in a frenzy of despair, arose to avenge the blood of their slaughtered brethren.[272]

151. p. 20 ¶ 32. fires of hatred burned high

The following summary by Shoghi Effendi explains:

> No sooner had this act been perpetrated than its shadow fell across the entire body of the Bábí community. A storm of public horror, disgust and resentment, heightened by the implacable hostility of the mother of the youthful sovereign, swept the nation, casting aside all possibility of even the most elementary inquiry into the origins and the instigators of the attempt. A sign, a whisper, was sufficient to implicate the innocent and loose upon him the most abominable afflictions. An army of foes – ecclesiastics, state officials and people, united in relentless hate, and watching for an opportunity to discredit and annihilate a dreaded adversary – had, at long last, been afforded the pretext for which it was longing. Now it could achieve its malevolent purpose. Though the Faith had, from its inception, disclaimed any intention of usurping the rights and prerogatives of the state; though its exponents and disciples had sedulously avoided any act that might arouse the slightest suspicion of a desire to wage a holy war, or to evince an aggressive attitude, yet its enemies, deliberately ignoring the numerous evidences of the marked restraint exercised by the followers of a persecuted religion, proved themselves capable of inflicting atrocities as barbarous as those which will ever remain associated with the bloody episodes of Mázindarán, Nayríz and Zanján. To what depths of infamy and cruelty would not this same enemy be willing to descend now that an act so treasonable, so audacious had been committed? What accusations would it not be prompted to level at, and what treatment would it not mete out to, those who, however unjustifiably, could be associated with so heinous a crime against one who, in his person, combined the chief magistracy of the realm and the trusteeship of the Hidden Imám? [273]

152. p. 20 ¶ 32. We were in no wise connected with that evil deed, and Our innocence was indisputably established by the tribunals

See Shoghi Effendi, *God Passes By*, pp. 61–71.

153. p. 20 ¶ 32. Níyávarán

Bahá'u'lláh was at His country house in the village of Níyávarán, a village in Shimírán to the north of Tehran and at the foot of the Damavand mountains, where people went to escape the heat of the summer. The Shah also had a residence in Níyávarán.

154. p. 20 ¶ 32. with bared head and bare feet

Bahá'u'lláh was forced by a troop of executioners and officials on horseback to walk hurriedly before them, and at their pace, from Niyávarán to Tehran, a distance of about fifteen miles:

> Delivered into the hands of His enemies, this much-feared, bitterly arraigned and illustrious Exponent of a perpetually hounded Faith was now made to taste of the cup which He Who had been its recognized Leader had drained to the dregs. From Níyávarán He was conducted 'on foot and in chains, with bared head and bare feet,' exposed to the fierce rays of the midsummer sun, to the Síyáh-Chál of Ṭihrán. On the way He several times was stripped of His outer garments, was overwhelmed with ridicule, and pelted with stones. As to the subterranean dungeon into which He was thrown, and which originally had served as a reservoir of water for one of the public baths of the capital, let His own words, recorded in His 'Epistle to the Son of the Wolf,' bear testimony to the ordeal which He endured in that pestilential hole.[274]

155. p. 20 ¶ 32 the dungeon of Ṭihrán

The Síyáh-Chál, literally the 'Black Pit', was a loathsome subterranean prison in Tehran, where Bahá'u'lláh was confined from mid-August to December 1852. Shoghi Effendi recounts:

> Wrapped in its stygian gloom, breathing its fetid air, numbed by its humid and icy atmosphere, His feet in stocks, His neck weighed down by a mighty chain, surrounded by criminals and miscreants of the worst order, oppressed by the consciousness of the terrible blot that had stained the fair name of His beloved Faith, painfully aware

> of the dire distress that had overtaken its champions, and of the grave dangers that faced the remnant of its followers . . .[275]

Bahíyyih Khánum, 'Abdu'l-Bahá's sister, has provided following description of Bahá'u'lláh's conditions in the Síyáh-Chál:

> My noble father was hurled into this black hole, loaded with heavy chains; five other Bábís were chained to him night and day, and here he remained for four months. Picture to yourself the horror of these conditions. Any movement caused the chains to cut deeper and deeper not only into the flesh of one, but of all who were chained together; whilst sleep or rest of any kind was not possible. No food was provided, and it was with the utmost difficulty that my mother was able to arrange to get any food or drink taken into that ghastly prison.
>
> Meanwhile, the spirit which upheld the Bábís never quailed for a moment, even under these conditions. To be tortured to a death, which would be the Martyr's Crown of Life, was their aim and great desire. They chanted prayers night and day.
>
> Every morning one or more of these brave and devoted friends would be taken out to be tortured and killed in various ways of horror. When religious fanaticism was aroused against a person or persons, who were accused of being infidels, as was now the case with the Babis, it was customary not simply to condemn them to death and have them executed by the State executioner, but to hand the victims over to various classes of the populace. The butchers had their methods of torture; the bakers theirs; the shoemakers and blacksmiths yet others of their own. They were all given opportunities of carrying out their pitiless inventions on the Babis.[276]

156. p. 20 ¶ 32. Ṭihrán

Tehran, the capital of Iran:

> a city which, by reason of so rare a privilege conferred upon it, had been glorified by the Báb as the 'Holy Land', and surnamed by Bahá'u'lláh as 'the Mother of the world', the 'Dayspring of Light', the 'Dawning-Place of the signs of the Lord', the 'Source of the joy of all mankind'.[277]

157. p. 20 ¶ 32. A brutal man, accompanying Us on horseback, snatched off Our hat

The Arabic word used for 'a brutal man' is '*zálim*', that is, one who acts unjustly (with *zulm*). The Qur'án (4:168) states that God does not forgive those who commit *zulm*. A hadith by Abú Dhar (see Annotation 142) reports: 'The Messenger of Alláh said, "My servants, I have made oppression unlawful for Me and unlawful for you, so do not commit oppression against one another. My servants, all of you are liable to err except one whom I guide on the right path, so seek right guidance from Me so that I should direct you to the right path . . ."'[278]

Professor E. G. Browne describes Bahá'u'lláh as wearing 'a felt head-dress of the kind called "táj" by dervishes (but of unusual height and make), round the base of which was wound a small white turban' when he met Him at Bahjí in 1890.[279]

The Greatest Holy Leaf relates that His turban had been removed during the forced march to the dungeon:

> Suddenly and hurriedly a servant came rushing in great distress to my mother. 'The master, the master, he is arrested – I have seen him! He has walked many miles! Oh, they have beaten him! They say he has suffered the torture of the bastinado! His feet are bleeding! He has no shoes on! His turban has gone! His clothes are torn! There are chains upon his neck!' [280]

Without His headgear, which in those days was the very symbol of a man's rank and dignity, Bahá'u'lláh's head was unprotected from the fierce rays of the sun.

158. p. 20 ¶ 32. troop of executioners

The Shah and provincial governors had executioners called *Mir Ghazab*, or literally, Masters of Wrath.

> . . . wearing black hats and bright red coats, the Masters of Wrath led royal processions and displayed to the public the brute power of their sovereign.[281]

> Nineteenth-century Iran – like most traditional societies – punished transgressions not with prolonged imprisonment but with various forms of physical torment and violent death . . . They [*Mir Ghazabs*] gouged out eyes. They amputated fingers, feet, and ears. They hanged, decapitated, strangled, impaled, disemboweled, crucified, hurled from cliffs, buried alive, and drew-and-quartered. Most common of all, they flogged the soles of the feet in a process known as *falak*.[282]
>
> Lady Sheil, the British envoy's wife, writes that once the guilty had received their just 'deserts' the Master of Wrath distributed sweets among the participants as a token of gratitude . . .[283]

159. p. 20 ¶ 32. four months

Bahá'u'lláh was imprisoned between August and December 1852.

160. p. 21 ¶ 32. a hundred and fifty souls

Amongst these were 81 Bábís, 38 of whom were leading members of the Bábí community.

161. p. 21 ¶ 33. the task of regenerating this people

Bahá'u'lláh increasingly dedicated Himself to this task during the period of His exile in Baghdad:

> The dissociation of the Bábí Faith from every form of political activity and from all secret associations and factions; the emphasis placed on the principle of non-violence; the necessity of strict obedience to established authority; the ban imposed on all forms of sedition, on back-biting, retaliation, and dispute; the stress laid on godliness, kindliness, humility and piety, on honesty and truthfulness, chastity and fidelity, on justice, toleration, sociability, amity and concord, on the acquisition of arts and sciences, on self-sacrifice and detachment, on patience, steadfastness and resignation to the will of God – all these constitute the salient features of a code of ethical conduct to which the books, treatises and epistles, revealed during

those years, by the indefatigable pen of Bahá'u'lláh, unmistakably bear witness.[284]

162. p. 21 ¶ 34. One night, in a dream

It was in October 1852 that Bahá'u'lláh received the intimation of His Revelation. He also describes this experience in the Súriy-i-Haykal:

> While engulfed in tribulations I heard a most wondrous, a most sweet voice, calling above My head. Turning My face, I beheld a Maiden – the embodiment of the remembrance of the name of My Lord – suspended in the air before Me. So rejoiced was she in her very soul that her countenance shone with the ornament of the good pleasure of God, and her cheeks glowed with the brightness of the All-Merciful. Betwixt earth and heaven she was raising a call which captivated the hearts and minds of men. She was imparting to both My inward and outer being tidings which rejoiced My soul, and the souls of God's honoured servants.
>
> Pointing with her finger unto My head, she addressed all who are in heaven and all who are on earth, saying: By God! This is the Best-Beloved of the worlds, and yet ye comprehend not. This is the Beauty of God amongst you, and the power of His sovereignty within you, could ye but understand. This is the Mystery of God and His Treasure, the Cause of God and His glory unto all who are in the kingdoms of Revelation and of creation, if ye be of them that perceive. This is He Whose Presence is the ardent desire of the denizens of the Realm of eternity, and of them that dwell within the Tabernacle of glory, and yet from His Beauty do ye turn aside.[285]

See also Annotation 94.

163. p. 21 ¶ 34. by Thyself and by Thy Pen

Bahá'u'lláh is assured of victory by virtue of the power invested in Him and His Revelation. Shoghi Effendi quotes this passage in *God Passes By*, and relates:

> 'One night in a dream,' He Himself, calling to mind, in the evening

> of His life, the first stirrings of God's Revelation within His soul, has written, 'these exalted words were heard on every side: "Verily, We shall render Thee victorious by Thyself and by Thy pen . . ."'[286]

Both the Báb and Bahá'u'lláh quote Muhammad (Qúr'an 29:51) that the greatest testimony and proof of His Faith is the Qur'án. The Muslim clergy must likewise evaluate their Revelations by their Writings:

> 'The mightiest, the most convincing evidence of the truth of the Mission of the Prophet of God,' the Báb replied, 'is admittedly His own Word. He Himself testifies to this truth: "Is it not enough for them that We have sent down to Thee the Book?" The power to produce such evidence has been given to Me by God.'[287]

164. p. 21 ¶ 34. treasures of the earth

A reference to individuals, the heavenly and earthly hosts, and the saints that God will raise up to assist His Cause:

> The Blessed Beauty hath promised this servant that souls would be raised up who would be the very embodiments of guidance, and banners of the Concourse on high, torches of God's oneness, and stars of His pure truth, shining in the heavens where God reigneth alone. They would give sight to the blind, and would make the deaf to hear; they would raise the dead to life.[288]

> O people of the Bayán! If ye aid Him not, God will assuredly assist Him with the powers of earth and heaven, and sustain Him with the hosts of the unseen through His command 'Be', and it is! The day is approaching when God will have, by an act of His Will, raised up a race of men the nature of which is inscrutable to all save God, the All-Powerful, the Self-Subsisting. He shall purify them from the defilement of idle fancies and corrupt desires, shall lift them up to the heights of holiness, and shall cause them to manifest the signs of His sovereignty and might upon earth. Thus hath it been ordained by God, the All-Glorious, the All-Loving.[289]

165. pp. 21–2 ¶ 35. And when this Wronged One went forth out of His prison, We journeyed, in pursance of the order of His Majesty the <u>Sh</u>áh – may God, exalted be He, protect him – to 'Iráq

Shoghi Effendi writes:

> The relative peace and tranquillity accorded Bahá'u'lláh after His tragic and cruel imprisonment was destined, by the dictates of an unerring Wisdom, to be of an extremely short duration. He had hardly rejoined His family and kindred when a decree from Náṣiri'd-Dín <u>Sh</u>áh was communicated to Him, bidding Him leave the territory of Persia, fixing a time-limit of one month for His departure and allowing Him the right to choose the land of His exile.[290]

Bahá'u'lláh arrived in Baghdad with His family and companions on 8 April 1853 CE.

166. p. 22 ¶ 35. 'Iráq

Modern-day Iraq covers approximately the same area as ancient Mesopotamia. During the time of Bahá'u'lláh, Iraq was part of the Turkish Ottoman Empire and consisted of the three Turkish provinces of Basra, Baghdad and Mosul. It was ruled by successive governors appointed by the Sultan in Istanbul. The area to the south, from Baghdad to the Persian Gulf, was dominated by <u>Sh</u>í'ih Muslims. The resting places of three of the twelve Imáms are found in Iraq: Kazimayn contains the Shrine of the seventh and ninth Imáms; the Shrine of Imám 'Alí is located in Najaf; and the Shrine of Imám Ḥusayn is found in Karbila.

167. p. 22 ¶ 35. escorted by officers in the service of the esteemed and honored governments of Persia and Russia

Shoghi Effendi writes:

> The Russian Minister, as soon as he was informed of the Imperial decision, expressed the desire to take Bahá'u'lláh under the protection of his government, and offered to extend every facility for His removal to Russia. This invitation, so spontaneously extended, Bahá'u'lláh

declined, preferring, in pursuance of an unerring instinct, to establish His abode in Turkish territory, in the city of Baghdád. 'Whilst I lay chained and fettered in the prison,' He Himself, years after, testified in His epistle addressed to the Czar of Russia, Nicolaevitch Alexander II, 'one of thy minsters extended Me his aid. Whereupon God hath ordained for thee a station which the knowledge of none can comprehend except His knowledge. Beware lest thou barter away this sublime station.' 'In the days,' is yet another illuminating testimony revealed by His pen, 'when this Wronged One was sore-afflicted in prison, the minister of the highly esteemed government (of Russia) – may God, glorified and exalted by He, assist him! – exerted his utmost endeavour to compass My deliverance. Several times permission for My release was granted. Some of the 'ulamás of the city, however, would prevent it. Finally, My freedom was gained through the solicitude and the endeavour of His Excellency the Minister . . . His Imperial Majesty, the Most Great Emperor – may God, exalted and glorified be He, assist him! – extended to Me for the sake of God his protection – a protection which has excited the envy and enmity of the foolish ones of the earth.'[291]

168. p. 22 ¶ 35. After Our arrival, We revealed, as a copious rain . . . Our verses

The verses that streamed during those years from His pen, described as 'a copious rain' by Himself, whether in the form of epistles, exhortations, commentaries, apologies, dissertations, prophecies, prayers, odes or specific Tablets, contributed, to a marked degree, to the reformation and progressive unfoldment of the Bábí community, to the broadening of its outlook, to the expansion of its activities and to the enlightenment of the minds of its members. So prolific was this period, that during the first two years after His return from His retirement, according to the testimony of Nabíl, who was at that time living in Baghdád, the unrecorded verses that streamed from His lips averaged, in a single day and night, the equivalent of the Qur'án! As to those verses which He either dictated or wrote Himself, their number was no less remarkable than either the wealth of material they contained, or the diversity of subjects to which they referred. A vast, and indeed the greater, proportion of these writings were, alas,

> lost irretrievably to posterity. No less an authority than Mírzá Áqá Ján, Bahá'u'lláh's amanuensis, affirms, as reported by Nabíl, that by the express order of Bahá'u'lláh, hundreds of thousands of verses, mostly written by His own hand, were obliterated and cast into the river. 'Finding me reluctant to execute His orders,' Mírzá Áqá Ján has related to Nabíl, 'Bahá'u'lláh would reassure me saying: "None is to be found at this time worthy to hear these melodies." . . . Not once, or twice, but innumerable times, was I commanded to repeat this act.' A certain Muḥammad Karím, a native of Shíráz, who had been a witness to the rapidity and the manner in which the Báb had penned the verses with which He was inspired, has left the following testimony to posterity, after attaining, during those days, the presence of Bahá'u'lláh, and beholding with his own eyes what he himself had considered to be the only proof of the mission of the Promised One: 'I bear witness that the verses revealed by Bahá'u'lláh were superior, in the rapidity with which they were penned, in the ease with which they flowed, in their lucidity, their profundity and sweetness to those which I, myself saw pour from the pen of the Báb when in His presence. Had Bahá'u'lláh no other claim to greatness, this were sufficient, in the eyes of the world and its people, that He produced such verses as have streamed this day from His pen.'[292]

169. p. 22 ¶ 35. particularly this people

'This people' is a reference to the Bábís. See ¶ 33, ¶ 37, ¶ 120, ¶ 121, ¶ 126, ¶ 142, ¶ 177, ¶ 178, ¶ 179, ¶ 199, ¶ 239.

170. p. 22 ¶ 36. the galling weight of the chains

Bahá'u'lláh refers later in ¶ 125 to these two chains, one of which is known as *Qará-Guhar*, and the other as *Salásil.*

> Bahá'u'lláh's feet were placed in stocks, and around His neck were fastened the Qará-Guhar chains of such galling weight that their mark remained imprinted upon His body all the days of His life. 'A heavy chain,' 'Abdu'l-Bahá Himself has testified, 'was placed about His neck by which He was chained to five other Bábís; these fetters were locked together by strong, very heavy, bolts and screws. His

> clothes were torn to pieces, also His headdress. In this terrible condition He was kept for four months.'[293]

Qará-Guhar or 'Black Jewel': *Qará* is Turkish for 'black'; *guhar* is Persian for a 'pearl' or other jewel. The *Qará-Guhar* was worn around the neck and was thus a necklace of torture. *Salásil* is the Arabic word for 'chains'. *Qará-Guhar*, heavier than *Salásil*, weighed about seventeen *man* (51 kilos, or 113 pounds).

171. p. 22 ¶ 36. I felt as if something flowed from the crown of My head over My breast, even as a mighty torrent

Shoghi Effendi writes:

> He describes, briefly and graphically, the impact of the onrushing force of the Divine Summons upon His entire being – an experience vividly recalling the vision of God that caused Moses to fall in a swoon, and the voice of Gabriel which plunged Muḥammad into such consternation that, hurrying to the shelter of His home, He bade His wife, Khadíjih, envelop Him in His mantle.[294]

See also Annotations 94 and 162–164.

172. p. 23 ¶ 38. O ye friends of God . . . This Wronged One enjoineth on you honesty and piety

The original of this passage can be found in the book *La'Aaliyul Hikmat.*[295]

173. p. 23 ¶ 39. We enjoin the servants of God and His handmaidens to be pure and to fear God

The origin of this Tablet is uncertain. Purity and fear of God are enjoined on both genders. Women are called to engage in activities that will exalt the Divine Word:

> We beseech the True One to adorn His handmaidens with the ornament of chastity, of trustworthiness, of righteousness and of purity . . . We make mention of the handmaidens of God at this time and

> announce unto them the glad-tidings of the tokens of the mercy and compassion of God and His consideration for them . . . We supplicate Him for all His assistance to perform such deeds as are the cause of the exaltation of His Word.[296]

In this context, purity means being righteous, chaste and holy, being sanctified from self and passion, being unsullied by prejudice and uncontaminated by idols of vain imaginings. In a sense, a corrupt desire is one that is not grounded in spiritual concerns and seeking the truth but is instead focused on selfish and mundane desires.

174. p. 23 ¶ 39. that they may shake off the slumber of their corrupt desires

The pursuit of desires that are not consistent with divine teachings induces spiritual somnolence. Bahá'u'lláh states in the Lawḥ-i-Ra'ís:

> Our purpose is that thou mayest lift up thy head from the couch of heedlessness, shake off the slumber of negligence, and cease to oppose unjustly the servants of God.[297]

> Say: The breeze of God hath wafted over you from the retreats of Paradise, but ye have neglected it and chosen to persist in your waywardness. Guidance hath been given unto you from God, but ye have failed to follow it and preferred to reject its truth. The Lamp of God hath been lit within the niche of His Cause, but ye have neglected to seek the radiance of its glory and to draw nigh unto its light. And still ye slumber upon the couch of heedlessness![298]

He rhetorically asks:

> How long will ye persist in your waywardness? How long will ye refuse to reflect? How long ere ye shake off your slumber and are roused from your heedlessness? How long will ye remain unaware of the truth?[299]

The following beatitudes are revealed in the Lawḥ-i-Aqdas (The Most Holy Tablet), sometimes referred to as the Tablet to the Christians:

> Say: Blessed the slumberer who is awakened by My Breeze. Blessed the lifeless one who is quickened through My reviving breaths . . .[300]

The Book of Job (14:11–12) laments that people 'shall not awake, nor be raised out of their sleep'. The Apostle Paul (Rom. 11:8) bemoans the tragic stupor that had become prevalent at the First Coming: 'God hath given them the spirit of slumber, eyes that they should not see, and ears that they should not hear, unto this day.' Christians have been repeatedly warned to remain awake and to be vigilant (II Peter 3:10; also, I Thess. 5:2), for 'the day of the Lord will come as a thief in the night'. The Apostle Paul wrote (Ephes. 5:14–16), 'Awake thou that sleepest, and arise from the dead, and Christ shall give thee light.'

The Qur'án promises (39:68) that with a second blast of the divine trumpet humanity will arise and pay attention. It reassures (11:49) that the end or final outcome of those who are righteous and follow the limits of faith is good. *Jihád* or holy war for the defence of religion is one of the pillars of faith in Shí'ih Islam. However, the real *jihád* is considered to be the war against one's own corrupt desires and inclinations.

It is profoundly regrettable that despite all the admonitions, prophecies and experiences of earlier Dispensations, most followers of the religions prefer to sleep through the Revelation of Bahá'u'lláh. This tragic state of affairs is summarized by John E. Esslemont (1874–1925):

> The state of the world today surely affords ample evidence that, with rare exceptions, people of all religions need to be reawakened to the real meaning of their religion; and that reawakening is an important part of the work of Bahá'u'lláh.[301]

See also Annotation 605.

175. p. 23 ¶ 39. the Day-Star of the world shone forth

In addition to the 'Day-Star of the world' Bahá'u'lláh is referred to as 'the Day-Star of ancient mysteries',[302] and 'the Day-Star of the Universe . . .'[303] This passage is a reference to His efforts to rehabilitate and reform the Bábís during His sojourn in Iraq (1853–1863).

176. p. 23 ¶ 39. the horizon of 'Iráq

The transformation of the Bábí community in Iraq during the above-mentioned ten-year sojourn culminated in Bahá'u'lláh's Declaration which took place in Baghdad on 21 April 1863.

177. p. 23 ¶ 39. My imprisonment doeth me no harm . . . That which harmeth Me is the conduct of those who, though they bear my name, yet commit that which maketh My heart and My pen to lament

This passage is also quoted by Bahá'u'lláh in the Kalímát-i-Firdawsíyyih:

> My counsels and admonitions have compassed the world. Yet, instead of imparting joy and gladness they have caused grief, because some of those who claim to love Me have waxed haughty and have inflicted upon Me such tribulations as neither the followers of former religions nor the divines of Persia did ever inflict.
>
> We have said: 'My imprisonment doeth Me no harm, nor do the things that have befallen Me at the hands of My enemies. That which harmeth Me is the conduct of my loved ones who, though they bear My name, yet commit that which maketh My heart and My pen to lament.' Such utterances as these have again and again been revealed, yet the heedless have failed to profit thereby, since they are captive to their own evil passions and corrupt desires. Beseech thou the One true God that He may enable everyone to repent and return unto Him. So long as one's nature yieldeth unto evil passions, crime and transgression will prevail.[304]

178. p. 23 ¶ 39. enter a house without leave of its owner

The Torah protects the privacy of the individual (Deut. 24:10–11).

The Qur'án (24:27) forbids entering a house uninvited. According to the *Tafsir Ibn Kathir*, a classic Sunni commentary on the Qur'án, Islamic etiquette dictates that Muslims seek permission three times before entering a house.

Bahá'u'lláh has emphasized respect for the privacy of others: 'no man should enter the house of his friend save at his friend's pleasure, nor lay hands upon his treasures nor prefer his own will to his friend's, and in no wise seek an advantage over him'.[305] This concern is linked to other considerations for the welfare of others that define a follower of Bahá'u'lláh: 'Take heed that ye enter no house in the absence of its owner, except with his permission. Comport yourselves with propriety under all conditions, and be not numbered with the wayward.'[306]

179. p. 24 ¶ 40. war ye valiantly, as it behooveth you to war, for the sake of proclaiming His resistless and immovable Cause. We have decreed that war shall be waged in the path of God with the armies of wisdom and utterance, and of a goodly character and praiseworthy deeds

The origin of this Tablet is uncertain. The Arabic phrases used for war are *jihád* (holy war) and the related word *jahd* (strive). Bahá'u'lláh here advocates warring against inordinate desires – an internal spiritual struggle, considered the greater *jihád* in Islam. The purpose is to become more effective in teaching His Faith. In this connection, He explains the prerequisites of possessing penetrating power of utterance in the Lawḥ-i-Siyyid Mihdíy-i-Dahají:

> Utterance must needs possess penetrating power. For if bereft of this quality it would fail to exert influence. And this penetrating influence dependeth on the spirit being pure and the heart stainless. Likewise it needeth moderation, without which the hearer would be unable to bear it, rather he would manifest opposition from the very outset. And moderation will be obtained by blending utterance with the tokens of divine wisdom which are recorded in the sacred Books and Tablets.[307]

> A goodly character is a means whereby men are guided to the Straight Path and are led to the Great Announcement. Well is it with him who is adorned with the saintly attributes and character of the Concourse on High.[308]

Shoghi Effendi often describes teaching as spiritual warfare, or a crusade:

> The time during which so herculean a task is to be performed is alarmingly brief. The period during which so gigantic an operation must be set in motion, prosecuted and consummated, coincides

with the critical, and perhaps the darkest and most tragic, stage in human affairs. The opportunities presenting themselves to them are now close at hand. The invisible battalions of the Concourse on High are mustered, in serried ranks, ready to rush their reinforcements to the aid of the vanguard of Bahá'u'lláh's crusaders in the hour of their greatest need, and in anticipation of that Most Great, that Wondrous Jubilee in the joyfulness of which both heaven and earth will partake.[309]

180. p. 24 ¶ 40. There is no glory for him that committeth disorder on the earth after it hath been made so good

In the light of Bahá'u'lláh's Revelation, committing disorder consists today of promoting views that are based on superstition and prejudice, and create division and disunity.

181. p. 24 ¶ 40. Fear God, O people, and be not of them that act unjustly

Bahá'u'lláh indicates that if man was aware of God's presence and feared Him, he would, as stated in the Qur'án (5:8), observe justice and fair-dealing: 'O ye who believe! Stand out firmly for God, as witnesses to fair dealing, and let not the hatred of others to you make you swerve to wrong and depart from justice. Be just: that is next to piety: and fear God . . .'

The Hebrew Bible asks (Micah 8:8): 'O man, what is good; and what doth the Lord require of thee, but to do justly, and to love mercy, and to walk humbly with thy God?'

182. p. 24 ¶ 41. Revile ye not one another. We, verily, have come to unite and weld together all that dwell on earth

This passage is recorded in *Á<u>th</u>ár-i-Qalam-i-A'lá* (Traces of the Supreme Pen), a compilation of the Writings of Bahá'u'lláh in Arabic and Persian.[310]

Bahá'u'lláh forbids backbiting and disparaging one another. Notably, the New Testament (I Peter 2:23) states in reference to Christ: 'when he was reviled, reviled not again; when he suffered, he threatened not;

but committed himself to him that judgeth righteously.' The Qur'án (6:108) instructs that Muslims should not revile non-Muslims. The Muslim clergymen in Iran have for than 150 years been engaged in insulting and slandering the Faiths of the Báb and Bahá'u'lláh. Shoghi Effendi writes:

> Of the principles enshrined in these Tablets the most vital of them all is the principle of the oneness and wholeness of the human race, which may well be regarded as the hall-mark of Bahá'u'lláh's Revelation and the pivot of His teachings. Of such cardinal importance is this principle of unity that it is expressly referred to in the Book of His Covenant, and He unreservedly proclaims it as the central purpose of His Faith. 'We, verily,' He declares, 'have come to unite and weld together all that dwell on earth.'[311]

Compare ¶ 88, where Bahá'u'lláh expresses His willingness to die for the cause of unity: 'O would I had been severed in Thy path, so that the world might be quickened, and all its peoples be united!' Notably, 'Abdu'l-Bahá stated:

> Jesus Christ gave His life upon the cross for the unity of mankind. Those who believed in Him likewise sacrificed life, honor, possessions, family, everything, that this human world might be released from the hell of discord, enmity and strife. His foundation was the oneness of humanity.[312]

Division, disintegration, and fragmentation are the hallmarks of physical or spiritual death. Bahá'u'lláh has come to resuscitate and unite mankind:

> Consider these days in which He Who is the Ancient Beauty hath come in the Most Great Name, that He may quicken the world and unite its peoples. (¶ 106)

> Night and day hath this Wronged One been occupied in that which would unite the hearts, and edify the souls of men. (¶ 141)

Indeed, all Revelations have promoted the same aim:

> The divine Prophets came to establish the unity of the Kingdom in human hearts. All of them proclaimed the glad tidings of the divine bestowals to the world of mankind. All brought the same message of divine love to the world.[313]

See also Annotations 111 and 414.

183. p. 24 ¶ 41. the Book of God

A reference to the *Kitáb-i-Aqdas* (the Most Holy Book), the repository of Bahá'u'lláh's laws and ordinances.

184. p. 24 ¶ 41. ye have been forbidden to engage in contention and conflict

This admonition of Bahá'u'lláh appears in the *Kitáb-i-Aqdas*: 'Ye have been forbidden in the Book of God to engage in contention and conflict, to strike another, or to commit similar acts whereby hearts and souls may be saddened.'[314] Again: 'Take heed not to stir up mischief in the land after it hath been set in order. Whoso acteth in this way is not of Us, and We are quit of him.'[315]

A similar statement appears in the Qur'án (7:56): 'Do no mischief on the earth, after it hath been set in order, but call on Him with fear and longing (in your hearts): for the Mercy of God is (always) near to those who do good.' Again (7:85): 'do no mischief on the earth after it has been set in order: that will be best for you, if ye have Faith.'

See also Annotation 180.

185. p. 24 ¶ 41. His Most Great Name

Shoghi Effendi writes: 'He was formally designated Bahá'u'lláh . . . signifying at once the glory, the light and the splendor of God.'[316] Bahá'u'lláh Himself refers to 'Thy name which Thou hast chosen above all other names and set up over all that are in heaven and on earth'.[317] And:

> This is the day whereon nothing amongst all things, nor any name amongst all names, can profit you save through this Name which

God hath made the Manifestation of His Cause and the Dayspring of His Most Excellent Titles unto all who are in the kingdom of creation. (¶ 154)

186. p. 25 ¶ 42. Beware lest ye shed the blood of any one

This passage is also found in *Á<u>th</u>ár-i-Qalam-i-A'lá* (Traces of the Supreme Pen).[318]

The Torah (Ex. 20:13) teaches: 'Thou shalt not kill.' Although it does not specifically use the term 'holy war', it does celebrate God (Ps. 24:8) as 'the Lord mighty in battle' and (Jer. 20:11) 'a warrior' who vanquished Pharaoh and the Egyptian army. There are too many instances of religious warfare and killings in the Hebrew Bible to mention here, but the destruction of the Amalekites, Joshua's conquest of Ai, and the battles of King David are some prominent examples.

The three most important imperatives of the Gospel message (Luke 10:27) are to 'love God', love 'thy neighbour as thyself', and (Matt. 5:44) 'love your enemies, bless them that curse you, do good to them that hate you, and pray for them which despitefully use you, and persecute you'. Despite this emphasis, fighting for God, perhaps borrowed from the Old Testament, entered early into the teachings and practices of the Church. The recommendation of the Church that Christians engage in 'justifiable war' and holy war was based in part on two instances when Christ (Matt. 10:34 and Luke 22:35–38) appears to condone violence.

In practice, instead of a sword, Christ used the sharp weapon of his tongue to fend off the verbal abuse and physical attacks of the Pharisees and Sadducees. The reason, He explained (John 18:33, 36) to the Roman governor, Pontius Pilate, that His followers did not fight was because it was not His mission to establish an earthly kingdom but to proclaim the good news of its advent.

Nevertheless, when the Roman Empire became Christian about three hundred years later, the Church leaders found themselves almost overnight in charge of an empire that they had to defend against the barbarian forces that frequently attacked Rome. They therefore reinterpreted the Gospel message in ways that allowed them to justify the use of force.

The Qur'án (5:32) confirms the sacredness of life taught in the Torah: 'We ordained for the Children of Israel that if any one slew a person – unless it be for murder or for spreading mischief in the land – it would be as if he slew the whole people: and if any one saved a life, it would be as if he saved the life of the whole people. Then although there came to them Our Apostles with Clear Signs, yet, even after that, many of them continued to commit excesses in the land.' Again (6:151): 'take not life, which God hath made sacred, except by way of justice and law: thus doth He command you, that ye may learn wisdom.'

Islam faced the same hostile desert environment as Judaism. As noted, the Qur'án teaches the importance of forgiveness, mercy, compassion, high-mindedness, justice, equity, and avoiding killing any innocent individual. No individual should be forced to change his or her religion. However, the Qur'án (2:212–14) does prescribe equitable retaliation (2:178–179), and condones holy war or *jihád*, and the use of the sword to safeguard the community, promote the interests of faith, and ensure the dominance of Islam.

It must also be said that the three main battles fought during Muhammad's time (Badr, Uhud and the Battle of Khandaq or the 'Battle of the Moat') were essentially defensive.

Instead of waging war, Bahá'ís use the power of reason, logic and example to demonstrate the validity of their Faith and to promote its vision. Thus, for the first time in religious history, war in defence of religion or to advance its interests has been eliminated from God's Faith. Bahá'u'lláh declares:

> O people of the earth! The first Glad-Tidings which the Mother Book hath, in this Most Great Revelation, imparted unto all the peoples of the world is that the law of holy war hath been blotted out from the Book. Glorified be the All-Merciful, the Lord of grace abounding, through Whom the door of heavenly bounty hath been flung open in the face of all that are in heaven and on earth.[319]

187. p. 25 ¶ 42. sword of your tongue

Compare:

> O people of Bahá! Subdue the citadels of men's hearts with the swords of wisdom and of utterance. They that dispute, as prompted by their desires, are indeed wrapped in a palpable veil. (¶ 92)

Again,

> Aid ye your Lord with the sword of wisdom and of utterance. This indeed well becometh the station of man. To depart from it would be unworthy of God, the Sovereign Lord of all, the Glorified.[320]

188. p. 25 ¶ 42. We have abolished the law to wage holy war

Holy war is one of the laws of the Qur'án. The <u>Sh</u>í'ihs include it as one of their 'pillars of faith'. The subject of 'justifiable war' and 'holy war' is of particular interest nowadays due to escalating terrorism in the name of religion.

See also Annotation 186.

189. p. 25 ¶ 43. O people! Spread not disorder in the land

Every prophet is denounced as a mischief maker (*fasád*) even though the new faith ushers in peace and order. The accusation has been commonly levelled against the followers of the Báb and Bahá'u'lláh, justifying their torture and martyrdom. Bahá'u'lláh states that it is the religious leaders that have waged *fasád*. Addressing these, He had earlier revealed a similar injunction in the *Kitáb-i-Aqdas* stating that all the Manifestations of God had issued the same admonition:

> O concourse of divines! . . . Should ye turn unto God and embrace His Cause, spread not disorder within it, and measure not the Book of God with your selfish desires. This, verily, is the counsel of God aforetime and hereafter, and to this God's witnesses and chosen ones, yea, each and every one of Us, do solemnly attest.[321]

The Prophets Isaiah (59:4) and Ezekiel (7:26) remarked that man has a propensity for creating disorder. Psalm 28:3 speaks of 'the wicked' and 'the workers of iniquity, which speak of peace to their neighbours but mischief is in their hearts'.

Disorder or *fasád* is also a major theme in the Qur'án (2:11) and is strictly forbidden. It is in contrast to 'setting things right' (*islah* in Arabic): 'When it is said to them: "Make not mischief on the earth," They say: "Why, we only want to make peace!"' The prescribed

punishment for *fasád* in the Qur'án (5:33) is death or exile.
See also Annotations 180 and 184.

190. p. 25 ¶ 44. The Sun of Divine Utterance can never set

That is, although certain provisions of earlier Dispensations may become abrogated, there is no finality to divine Revelation. 'The Sun of Divine Utterance' and 'the Sun of Utterance' (¶ 108) refer to Bahá'u'lláh but the terms also refer to divine Revelation in general. Bahá'u'lláh in the *Kitáb-i-Íqán* states that the Prophets of God have one reality, utter the same speech and proclaim the same Faith:

> all the Prophets are the Temples of the Cause of God, Who have appeared clothed in divers attire. If thou wilt observe with discriminating eyes, thou wilt behold them all abiding in the same tabernacle, soaring in the same heaven, seated upon the same throne, uttering the same speech, and proclaiming the same Faith.[322]

Shoghi Effendi elaborates on this, referring to Revelation and divine mercies as incessant:

> From the 'beginning that hath no beginning,' these Exponents of the Unity of God and Channels of His incessant utterance have shed the light of the invisible Beauty upon mankind, and will continue, to the 'end that hath no end,' to vouchsafe fresh revelations of His might and additional experiences of His inconceivable glory.[323]

Another point worth considering, and one specific to the Revelation of Bahá'u'lláh because of the power of its Covenant, is the fact that this is a Day that will not be followed by the darkness of sectarianism:

> This is but an evidence of the bounty which God hath vouchsafed unto Thee, a bounty which shall last until the Day that hath no end in this contingent world. It shall endure so long as God, the Supreme King, the Help in Peril, the Mighty, the Wise, shall endure. For the Day of God is none other but His own Self, Who hath appeared with the power of truth. This is the Day that shall

> not be followed by night, nor shall it be bounded by any praise, would that ye might understand![324]

That the Sun of Truth shall not set is also the promise of the Bible (Is. 60:20):

> Thy sun shall no more go down; neither shall thy moon withdraw itself: for the Lord shall be thine everlasting light, and the days of thy mourning shall be ended.

Also, Rev. 21:23, 25:

> And the city had no need of the sun, neither of the moon, to shine in it: for the Glory of God [in Arabic, Bahá'u'lláh] did lighten it . . .
>
> And the gates of it shall not be shut at all by day for there shall be no night there.

And Rev. 22:5:

> And there shall be no night there; and they need no candle, neither light of the sun; for the Lord God giveth them light: and they shall reign for ever and ever.

191. p. 25 ¶ 44. Lote-Tree beyond which there is no passing

This is a symbolic reference to the Manifestation of God, beyond which there is no understanding. The Lote tree is mentioned in the Qur'án (53:14): 'near the Lote-tree beyond which none may pass'. According to Islamic belief, it marks the boundary beyond which no creation can pass. During *Isra* and *Mi'raj* (the two parts of the Night Journey), the Prophet Muhammad, being the only one allowed, travelled with the archangel Gabriel to the *Sadratu'l-Muntaha* where it is said God assigned the five daily prayers to be recited by Muslims.

See also Annotations 333, 239 and 250.

192. p. 25 ¶ 45. Ye are the letters of the words, and the words of the Book

The original source of this statement is uncertain but it is a theme of the Writings of Bahá'u'lláh:

> O friends! Be not careless of the virtues with which ye have been endowed, neither be neglectful of your high destiny. Suffer not your labors to be wasted through the vain imaginations which certain hearts have devised. Ye are the stars of the heaven of understanding, the breeze that stirreth at the break of day, the soft-flowing waters upon which must depend the very life of all men, the letters inscribed upon His sacred scroll.[325]

Consider the following explanation of 'Abdu'l-Bahá:

> It is evident that the Letter is a member of the Word, and this membership in the Word signifieth that the Letter is dependent for its value on the Word, that is, it deriveth its grace from the Word; it has a spiritual kinship with the Word, and is accounted an integral part of the Word. The Apostles were even as Letters, and Christ was the essence of the Word Itself; and the meaning of the Word, which is grace everlasting, cast a splendour on those Letters. Again, since the Letter is a member of the Word, it therefore, in its inner meaning, is consonant with the Word.[326]

The description of the early disciples as letters in the Bible 'written not with ink but with the Spirit of the living God. Not in tables of stone. But in fleshy tables of the heart' appears in II Cor. 3:3.

193. p. 26 ¶ 46. the fourth I<u>sh</u>ráq

Bahá'u'lláh revealed the Lawḥ-i-I<u>sh</u>ráqát (Tablet of Splendours) in Bahjí (c. 1885) in answer to questions posed by Jalíl-i-<u>Kh</u>u'í, a coppersmith and a believer from Azerbaijan. Bahá'u'lláh explains that His Faith is to be assisted by good deeds. The phrase 'Every cause needeth a helper' appears only in the Epistle:

> In this Revelation the hosts that can render it victorious are the hosts of praiseworthy deeds and upright character. The leader and commander of these hosts hath ever been the fear of God, a fear that encompasseth all things and reigneth over all things.[327]

194. p. 26 ¶ 46. The leader and commander of these hosts hath ever been the fear of God

See Annotations 33, 198 and 200.

195. p. 26 ¶ 47. In the third Tajallí (effulgence) of the Book of Tajallíyát (Book of Effulgences)

Revealed in honour of Ustád 'Alí-Akbar who was a staunch believer from Yazd. He designed the Mashriqu'l-Adhkár of Ishqábád (Ashgabat) and his design was approved by 'Abdu'l-Bahá. Ustád 'Alí-Akbar offered up his life as a martyr in Yazd in 1903.

The Tablet describes four Tajallís:

1. The knowledge of God, which is attainable only through His Manifestation.
2. Steadfastness in the Cause of God through faith in His wisdom.
3. The value of those arts and sciences which profit mankind, 'not those which begin with words and end with words'.
4. The recognition of Divinity in its Manifestation.

196. p. 26 ¶ 47. Arts, crafts and sciences uplift the world of being, and are conducive to its exaltation . . .The knowledge of such sciences, however, should be acquired as can profit the peoples of the earth, and not those which begin with words and end with words

The passage 'Arts, crafts and sciences uplift the world of being, and are conducive to its exaltation' appears only in the Epistle. The passage in Tajallíyát (Effulgences) reads:

> The third Tajallí is concerning arts, crafts and sciences. Knowledge is as wings to man's life, and a ladder for his ascent. Its acquisition is incumbent upon everyone. The knowledge of such sciences,

> however, should be acquired as can profit the peoples of the earth, and not those which begin with words and end with words.[328]

Also: 'Great indeed is the claim of scientists and craftsmen on the peoples of the world.' (¶ 47)

197. p. 27 ¶ 47. the Mother Book

The Bahá'í Writings explain that the 'Mother Book' refers to both the Author of Revelation in every age and His Book.

> The term 'Mother Book' is generally used to designate the central Book of a religious Dispensation. In the Qur'án and Islamic Ḥadíth, the term is used to describe the Qur'án itself. In the Bábí Dispensation, the Bayán is the Mother Book, and the Kitáb-i-Aqdas is the Mother Book of the Dispensation of Bahá'u'lláh. Further, the Guardian in a letter written on his behalf has stated that this concept can also be used as a 'collective term indicating the body of the Teachings revealed by Bahá'u'lláh'. This term is also used in a broader sense to signify the Divine Repository of Revelation.[329]

The Báb states that His Revelation was the promised Mother Book:

> Hearken unto the Voice of Thy Lord calling from Mount Sinai, 'Verily there is no God but Him, and I am the Exalted One Who hath been veiled in the Mother Book according to the dispensations of Providence.'[330]

Bahá'u'lláh also refers to the Revelation of the Báb in the Tablet of Aḥmad as the 'Mother Book':

> Say: O people be obedient to the ordinances of God, which have been enjoined in the Bayán by the Glorious, the Wise One. Verily He is the King of the Messengers and His Book is the Mother Book did ye but know.[331]

But He also announces that God has once again revealed the 'Mother Book', 'Say, this, verily, is the heaven in which the Mother Book is treasured, could ye but comprehend it' (¶ 188). Again, 'He is the sovereign Truth, the Knower of things unseen. The Mother Book is revealed and the Lord of Bounty is established upon the most blessed seat of Glory. The Dawn hath broken, yet the people understand not.'[332]

The phrase 'Mother Book' (*Ummul Kitáb*) occurs three times in the Qur'án where it refers to an essential and unchangeable Faith of God: As the omnipotent God, *al-Qádir* (Qur'án 24:45; 57:1), He can ordain that certain of its provisions be abrogated with the advent of a new Dispensation (13:39): 'God doth blot out or confirm what He pleaseth: with Him is the Mother of the Book' [that is, He is the Source of all Revelations]. The Qur'án (2:2) may also be taken as an allusion to a future Book, 'That is the book! there is no doubt therein; a guide to the pious.'

The New Testament (Rev. 20:12) promises that there will be an additional 'Book':

> And I saw the [spiritually] dead, small and great, stand before God; and the books were opened: and another book was opened, which is the book of life: and the dead were judged out of those things which were written in the books, according to their works.

198. p. 27 ¶ 49. The fear of God hath ever been the prime factor in the education of His creatures

Taqwá, translated here as 'fear of God', is an Arabic phrase for being conscious and cognizant of God, and promotes self-restraint and virtuous living.

The Proverbs (2:2–5) admonish:

> So that thou incline thine ear unto wisdom, and apply thine heart to understanding;
>
> Yea, if thou criest after knowledge, and liftest up thy voice for understanding;
>
> If thou seekest her as silver, and searchest for her as for hid treasures;
>
> Then shalt thou understand the fear of the Lord, and find the knowledge of God.

Again (Prov. 9:10): 'The fear of the Lord is the beginning of wisdom, and knowledge of the Holy is understanding.'

The Qur'án (35:28) also teaches that the fear of God, or *taqwá*, is a potent source of spiritual guidance, 'Those truly fear God among His servants who have knowledge.' And (2:282): 'So fear God; for it is God that teaches you. And God is well acquainted with all things.' Again, 3:200: 'fear God; that ye may prosper,' and (39:10): 'Say: O ye My servants who believe! Fear your Lord. Good is (the reward) for those who do good in this world.'

See also ¶ 3 and ¶ 50, and Annotations 33 and 200.

199. p. 27 ¶ 50. the first leaf of Paradise

The Kalimát-i-Firdawsíyyih (Words of Paradise) was revealed by Bahá'u'lláh two years before His passing in honour of his trusted disciple Ḥájí Mírzá Ḥaydar-'Alí, who was an outstanding Bahá'í teacher and author. He spent nine years in prison and exile in Khartoum, travelled extensively in Iran, and passed away in 1920 in the Holy Land. Western pilgrims knew him as the 'Angel of Mount Carmel'.

The Tablet has eleven sections known as 'leaves', and largely consists of counsels, a number of which are directed to the rulers of society. Among other teachings, Bahá'u'lláh reveals the following:

- people will be exalted through honesty, virtue, wisdom and saintly character
- the fear of God is a safe stronghold for all the peoples of the world
- living in seclusion or practising asceticism is not acceptable
- all should work towards the betterment of humanity as a whole rather than pursue individual self-interest
- charity and the use of sciences and arts to promote the well-being of humankind are praiseworthy
- moderation is desirable in all matters – anything taken to an excess is a source of evil
- the moral education of children is of supreme importance
- choosing for your neighbour that what you wish for yourself
- enjoins the kings and rulers of the world to uphold the cause of religion
- enjoins all nations to cleave tenaciously to unity, which will lead to the well-being of humankind
- the use of an international auxiliary language to increase the unity of the world

- the basis of world order is established on the twin principles of reward and punishment
- religion is the chief instrument for promoting unity and fellowship among people
- the members of the Universal House of Justice are authorized 'to take counsel together regarding those things which have not been outwardly revealed in the Book', referring to its legislative authority and infallibility in those matters. He commands them 'to ensure the protection and safeguarding of men, women and children'.

200. pp. 27–8 ¶ 50. Verily I say: The fear of God hath ever been a sure defence and a safe stronghold for all the peoples of the world

Bahá'u'lláh warns the rulers to uphold religion as true faith instils the fear of God in all. He re-reveals in part the Kalimát-i-Firdawsíyyih (Words of Paradise), stressing the importance of being aware of the Divine Presence and admonitions. Had the Shaykh and his fellow clergymen truly feared God they would not have committed so many atrocities in the name of religion.

He adds: 'there existeth in man a faculty which deterreth him from, and guardeth him against, whatever is unworthy and unseemly, and which is known as his sense of shame. This, however, is confined to but a few; all have not possessed, and do not possess, it.'

Shame is an unpleasant emotional feeling caused by the consciousness of wrong and unworthy behaviour. The Arabic word *ḥayá* used here is one variant of 'shame' and is considered an appropriate emotion – it indicates feeling embarrassed, ashamed or shy.

A defining characteristic of sociopathic individuals is their profound lack of conscience – they lack empathy. These individuals may be entirely incapable of shame or guilt. Faith can provide the strong moral compass needed to cultivate *ḥayá* and steer people away from breaking humanitarian rules and treating others indecently.

In the Epistle Bahá'u'lláh adds at the end of the paragraph: 'It is incumbent upon the kings and the spiritual leaders of the world to lay fast hold on religion, inasmuch as through it the fear of God is instilled in all else but Him.' It should be noted that this sentence is not part of the Kalimát-i-Firdawsíyyih as printed in *Tablets of Bahá'u'lláh*.

See also Annotations 33 and 198.

201. p. 28 ¶ 51. Religion is, verily, the chief instrument for the establishment of order in the world

In the Tablet of Is_h_ráqát Bahá'u'lláh writes:

> In truth, religion is a radiant light and an impregnable stronghold for the protection and welfare of the peoples of the world, for the fear of God impelleth man to hold fast to that which is good, and shun all evil. Should the lamp of religion be obscured, chaos and confusion will ensue, and the lights of fairness and justice, of tranquillity and peace cease to shine.[333]

Again, He writes:

> As the body of man needeth a garment to clothe it, so the body of mankind must needs be adorned with the mantle of justice and wisdom. Its robe is the Revelation vouchsafed unto it by God. Whenever this robe hath fulfilled its purpose, the Almighty will assuredly renew it. For every age requireth a fresh measure of the light of God. Every Divine Revelation hath been sent down in a manner that befitted the circumstances of the age in which it hath appeared.[334]

Shoghi Effendi observes:

> No wonder, therefore, that when, as a result of human perversity, the light of religion is quenched in men's hearts, and the divinely appointed Robe, designed to adorn the human temple, is deliberately discarded, a deplorable decline in the fortunes of humanity immediately sets in, bringing in its wake all the evils which a wayward soul is capable of revealing.[335]

202. p. 28 ¶ 52 light of equity and the sun of justice

Equity (treatment of human rights equally; desiring to give to each man his due, according to reason; fairness in determination of conflicting claims; impartiality) and justice are translation of '*insáf*' and '*adl*', respectively. The two attributes are mostly mentioned together (see ¶ 14, ¶ 15, ¶ 32, ¶ 37, ¶ 116, ¶ 124, ¶ 127, ¶ 167, ¶ 190, ¶ 191 and ¶ 205).

Bahá'u'lláh admonishes: 'The light of men is justice. Quench it not with the contrary winds of oppression and tyranny. The purpose of justice is the appearance of unity among men.'[336] He recommends that the king and clergy judge with equity and justice, but observes that 'equity is rarely to be found, and justice hath ceased to exist' (¶ 191) and that pride and vanity have 'laid waste the home of justice and of equity' (¶ 124). In contrast, the Manifestations of God 'are the exponents of justice and equity' (¶ 190).

Shoghi Effendi explains the importance of justice in Bahá'u'lláh's Dispensation:

> Justice He extols as 'the light of men' and their 'guardian', as 'the revealer of the secrets of the world of being, and the standard-bearer of love and bounty'; declares its radiance to be incomparable; affirms that upon it must depend 'the organization of the world and the tranquillity of mankind.' He characterizes its 'two pillars' – 'reward and punishment' – as 'the sources of life' to the human race; warns the peoples of the world to bestir themselves in anticipation of its advent; and prophesies that, after an interval of great turmoil and grievous injustice, its day-star will shine in its full splendor and glory.[337]

He wrote further that Bahá'u'lláh has come to establish 'the Most Great Justice . . .

> . . . upon which the structure of the Most Great Peace can alone, and must eventually, rest, while the Most Great Peace will, in turn, usher in that Most Great, that World Civilization which shall remain forever associated with Him Who beareth the Most Great Name.[338]

The Manifestations of God re-establish justice – through them truth is distinguished from error and the wisdom of every command is tested.[339] The Epistle also refers to the Qur'án as a Book that judged between truth and falsehood with a justice which turned into light the darkness of the earth (¶ 132).

203. p. 29 ¶ 53. the Book of Utterance

The term 'Bayán', literally 'utterance' or 'exposition', appears in the Qur'án (55:4). It often refers to the Writings of the Báb collectively but is also the title of two of His outstanding works containing the laws and ordinances of the Bábí Dispensation: the Persian *Bayán* and the shorter Arabic *Bayán*.

The Persian *Bayán* is a lengthy but incomplete work of nine sections, each consisting of nineteen chapters, except for the last, which has only ten chapters (see also Annotation 723). It was the last major work of the Báb and contains many exhortations and homilies, and the laws and ordinances of His Dispensation. It is characterized by over three hundred references to 'He Whom God shall make manifest' (*Man Yuzhiruhu'lláh*).[340]

While the Persian and Arabic *Bayán* are parallel and complementary in content, the one is not a translation of the other – both books are unique and original.

Here, the 'Book of Utterance' refers to the Revelation of Bahá'u'lláh – His light has eclipsed the earlier 'suns of utterance'.[341]

204. p. 29 ¶ 53. Strive that haply the tribulations suffered by this Wronged One and by you, in the path of God, may not prove to have been in vain

Bahá'u'lláh here speaks beyond the Shaykh and addresses the Bahá'ís, admonishing them not to act in any manner that would negate all the suffering that has gone into rearing this precious Faith. He adds later in the same paragraph: 'The sword of a virtuous character and upright conduct is sharper than blades of steel [*jihád*].'

Christ stated that the good fruits of the Tree of Revelation establish its validity. Therefore, Shoghi Effendi explains in some detail in *The Advent of Divine Justice* the importance of the world witnessing the transformation of individuals through the Faith of Bahá'u'lláh, a powerful and valid proof of its divine source. He wrote earlier on:

> Humanity, through suffering and turmoil, is swiftly moving on towards its destiny; if we be loiterers, if we fail to play our part surely others will be called upon to take up our task as ministers to

> the crying needs of this afflicted world.
>
> Not by the force of numbers, not by the mere exposition of a set of new and noble principles, not by an organised campaign of teaching – no matter how worldwide and elaborate in its character – not even by the staunchness of our faith or the exaltation of our enthusiasm, can we ultimately hope to vindicate in the eyes of a critical and sceptical age the supreme claim of the Abhá Revelation. One thing and only one thing will unfailingly and alone secure the undoubted triumph of this sacred Cause, namely, the extent to which our own inner life and private character mirror forth in their manifold aspects the splendour of those eternal principles proclaimed by Bahá'u'lláh.[342]

205. p. 29 ¶ 53. Cling ye to the hem of virtue

Virtues are morally good qualities, meant to benefit the individual as well as mankind.

> All men have been created to carry forward an ever-advancing civilization. The Almighty beareth Me witness: To act like the beasts of the field is unworthy of man. Those virtues that befit his dignity are forbearance, mercy, compassion and loving-kindness towards all the peoples and kindreds of the earth.[343]

206. p. 29 ¶ 53. O ye followers of this Wronged One! Ye are the shepherds of mankind; liberate ye your flocks from the wolves of evil passions and desires, and adorn them with the ornament of the fear of God

Here 'wolves' are not individuals but corrupt inclinations that destroy faith. For more information, see Annotations 124, 312 and 398.

207. p. 29 ¶ 53. The voice of the true Faith calleth aloud, at this moment . . .

The phrase 'true Faith' (Arabic: *fiṭrah* or *fiṭrat*) appears several times in the Epistle (¶ 63, ¶ 136, ¶ 149 (x2), ¶ 188 (x3), ¶ 191 (x2) and refers to original faith. It is akin to the phrase 'pristine purity' used by Shoghi Effendi:

> Far from aiming at the overthrow of the spiritual foundation of the world's religious systems, its avowed, its unalterable purpose is to widen their basis, to restate their fundamentals, to reconcile their aims, to reinvigorate their life, to demonstrate their oneness, to restore the pristine purity of their teachings . . .[344]

Fiṭrat also refers to the primordial purity in every soul before the human essential reality becomes sullied by definitions and attachments. At its primordial level faith is unschooled, sanctified from man-made vain imaginings and theological accretions, and is One. Here Bahá'u'lláh declares that today He is 'the Voice of the true Faith'. He further states explicitly 'I am the true Faith of God amongst you' (¶ 150). A hadith states:

> Abu Huraira narrated that the Prophet said, 'Every child is born with a true faith (i.e. to worship none but Allah Alone) but his parents convert him to Judaism or to Christianity or to Magainism, as an animal delivers a perfect baby animal. Do you find it mutilated?'[345]

208. p. 29 ¶ 53. the Day is come, and My Lord hath made Me to shine forth with a light whose splendor hath eclipsed the suns of utterance

The Writings of Bahá'u'lláh emphasize that the various Dispensations are expressions of one Faith:

> 'They differ . . . only in the intensity of their revelation and the comparative potency of their light.' And this, not by reason of any inherent incapacity of any one of them to reveal in a fuller measure the glory of the Message with which He has been entrusted, but rather because of the immaturity and unpreparedness of the age He lived in to apprehend and absorb the full potentialities latent in that Faith.[346]

Today, the Sun of Truth is shining at its zenith.[347] Hence, Isaiah (30:26) and Joel (3:15) predict that the sun of the expected Revelation will be transcendently more bright and glorious than ever it was before.

209. p. 29 ¶ 54. If thine eyes be turned towards mercy, forsake the things that profit thee, and cleave unto that which will profit mankind

In other words, if you have put your trust in God and His Revelation, eschew self-interest and turn your eyes from the world and all who seek it, and instead, cling faithfully to what would benefit humanity. This passage comes from the 'third leaf' of the Kalimát-i-Firdawsíyyih.[348]

210. p. 30 ¶ 54. Humility exalteth man . . . whilst pride abaseth him

Humility, especially towards God's Manifestation and Revelation, is an essential virtue if one desires to be guided to true faith. Man's cup must be empty before it can be filled. The scriptures testify that those who confess their spiritual poverty will be rewarded.

The Hebrew Bible teaches (Prov. 22:4–5): 'humility and the fear of the Lord are riches, and honour, and life. Thorns and snares are in the way of the froward: he that doth keep his soul shall be far from them.' Also (Prov. 11:2): 'When pride cometh, then cometh shame; But with the lowly is wisdom'; (Ps. 25:9): 'The meek will he guide in judgment: and the meek will he teach his way'; and (Ps. 34:18): 'the Lord is nigh unto them that are of a broken heart, and saveth such as are of a contrite spirit.'

In the New Testament, the key to spiritual success is humility. In His first Beatitude Jesus (Matt. 5:3) proclaimed that a Christian will gain the anticipated Kingdom of God if he confesses his spiritual poverty. Also (James 4:10): 'Humble yourselves in the sight of the Lord, and he shall lift you up'; and (I Peter 5:6): 'Humble yourselves therefore under the mighty hand of God, that he may exalt you in due time . . .'

The Qur'án (25:63) also instructs Muslims to exhibit a spirit of humility: 'And the servants of (God) the All-Merciful are those who move on the earth in humility, and when the ignorant address them, they say: "Peace!"'; and (31:18): 'And swell not thy cheek (for pride) at men, nor walk in insolence through the earth; for God loveth not any arrogant boaster.'

211. p. 30 ¶ 54. Great is the Day

'Day' in this context refers to the Dispensation of Bahá'u'lláh. 'Great is the Day' is a translation of the Arabic *yawmin Azím,* which is a phrase from the Qur'án (6:15 and 83:5) usually rendered 'A Mighty Day'. 'A Great day' (*yawmin kabir*) is a similar phrase in the Qur'án (11:13) describing the Day of Bahá'u'lláh. Other descriptions testifying to its greatness in the Qur'án (Rodwell translation) mentioned by Shoghi Effendi in *God Passes By*, p. 96 include:

'Last (latter) Day' (2:8, 2:228 and 2:232; 65:2)

'Day(s) of God' (14:5 and 45:13)

'Day . . . which none can hinder God from bringing on' (30:43)

'Day of Resurrection or Judgement' (39:67)

'Day of Reckoning' (1:4; 38:15)

'Day of Mutual Deceit' (64:9)

'Day of Severance' (78:17)

'Day of Sighing' (19:40)

'Day of Meeting' (40:15)

'Day when the Decree shall be accomplished' (19:40)

'Day whereon the second Trumpet will be sounded' (79:7)

'Day when mankind shall stand before the Lord of the worlds' (83:6) and 'all shall come to Him in humble guise' (27:89)

Day 'wherein account shall be taken', 'the approaching Day, when men's hearts shall rise up, choking them, into their throats' (40:17–18)

> Day when 'all that are in the heavens and all that are in the earth shall be terror-stricken, save him whom God pleaseth to deliver; and all shall come to him in humble guise'
>
> 'And thou shalt see the mountains, which thou thinkest so firm, pass away with the passing of a cloud! 'Tis the work of God, who ordereth all things! of all that ye do is He well aware' (27:89–90)
>
> Day whereon 'every suckling woman shall forsake her sucking babe, and every woman that hath a burden in her womb shall cast her burden' (22:2)
>
> Day 'when the earth shall shine with the light of her Lord, and the Book shall be set, and the Prophets shall be brought up, and the witnesses; and judgement shall be given between them with equity; and none shall be wronged' (39:69)

Zephaniah (1:14) proclaimed: 'The great day of the Lord is near, it is near and hasteth greatly.' Malachi prophesied (4:5): 'Behold, I will send you Elijah the prophet before the coming of the great and dreadful day of the Lord . . .' Joel characterizes that day (2:31) as: 'the great and the terrible day of the Lord . . .' The Acts of the Apostles state (2:20): the 'great day of the Lord comes in glory'.

As quoted by Shoghi Effendi, Bahá'u'lláh's Writings are replete with numerous references to the greatness of this Day:

> 'The Day of the Promise is come . . . Happy is the eye that seeth, and the face that turneth towards, the Countenance of God, the Lord of all being.' 'Great indeed is this Day! The allusions made to it in all the sacred Scriptures as the Day of God attest its greatness. The soul of every Prophet of God, of every Divine Messenger, hath thirsted for this wondrous Day. All the divers kindreds of the earth have, likewise, yearned to attain it.' 'This Day a door is open wider than both heaven and earth. The eye of the mercy of Him Who is the Desire of the worlds is turned towards all men . . .' 'This is the Day whereon the unseen world crieth out, "Great is thy blessedness, O earth, for thou hast been made the footstool of thy God, and been chosen as the seat of His mighty throne."' 'The

world of being shineth, in this Day, with the resplendency of this Divine Revelation. All created things extol its saving grace, and sing its praises. The universe is wrapt in an ecstasy of joy and gladness. The Scriptures of past Dispensations celebrate the great Jubilee that must needs greet this most great Day of God. Well is it with him that hath lived to see this Day, and hath recognized its station.' . . . 'This is the Day whereon human ears have been privileged to hear what He Who conversed with God [Moses] heard upon Sinai, what He Who is the Friend of God [Muḥammad] heard when lifted up towards Him, what He Who is the Spirit of God [Jesus] heard as He ascended unto Him, the Help in Peril, the Self-Subsisting.' 'This Day is God's Day, and this Cause His Cause. Happy is he who hath renounced this world, and clung to Him Who is the Dayspring of God's Revelation.' 'This is the King of Days, the Day that hath seen the coming of the Best Beloved, He Who through all eternity hath been acclaimed the Desire of the World.' 'This is the Chief of all days and the King thereof. Great is the blessedness of him who hath attained, through the sweet savor of these days, unto everlasting life, and who, with the most great steadfastness, hath arisen to aid the Cause of Him Who is the King of Names. Such a man is as the eye to the body of mankind.' 'Peerless is this Day, for it is as the eye to past ages and centuries, and as a light unto the darkness of the times.'[349]

212. p. 30 ¶ 54. mighty the Call!

The Arabic word used by Bahá'u'lláh for 'Call' is *nedá*, which is related to one of the titles of the Promised One (Qur'án 50:41): *al-Munádi* or 'the Caller'. Muslims are expecting *al-Munádi* who will raise his call from a place quite near (*min makánin qaríbin*), a declaration of faith that is described as a trumpet blast of truth. Notably, after the declaration of His Mission in Shiraz, the Báb travelled to Mecca where He proclaimed to the Muslim world that He was the Promised One of Islam. Bahá'u'lláh received the intimations of His Revelation in Tehran but declared His Mission in Baghdad. Thus both Manifestations of God proclaimed their Missions in close proximity to where Muhammad revealed this verse.

A well-known Shí'ih hadith also predicts that the Promised Qá'im will make His Announcement while leaning on Hajar Aswad, the Black Stone in Mecca:

> Imam Muhammad Baqir said: 'By Allah, as if I can see Imam Qaim leaning his back against Hajar Aswad and adjuring people in the name of Allah and saying: "O people, Whoever argues with me about Allah, I am the worthiest for Allah. Whoever argues with me about Adam, I am the worthiest of Adam. Whoever argues with me about Nuh [Noah], I am the worthiest of Nuh. Whoever argues with me about Ibrahim [Abraham], I am the worthiest of Ibrahim. Whoever argues with me about Musa [Moses], I am the worthiest of Musa. Whoever argues with me about Isa [Jesus], I am the worthiest of Isa. Whoever argues with me about Muhammad, I am the worthiest of Muhammad. Whoever argues with me about the Book of the Almighty Allah, I am the worthiest of the Book of Allah."'[350]

This Caller or Summoner is also referred to in the Qur'án (54:6–8) as *al-Dá'í*, who will invite (call) humanity to a 'difficult affair of great import': 'therefore, turn away from them. The Day that the Caller will call (them) to a terrible affair. They will come forth, their eyes humbled – from (their) graves, like locusts scattered abroad Hastening, with eyes transfixed, towards the Caller! – hard is this Day!, the unbelievers will say.' Again: (20:108): 'On that Day will they follow the Caller): no crookedness (can they show) him: all sounds shall humble themselves in the Presence of (God) Most Gracious: nothing shalt thou hear but the tramp of their feet.'

213. p. 30 ¶ 54. In one of Our Tablets We have revealed these exalted words: 'Were the world of the spirit to be wholly converted into the sense of hearing, it could then claim to be worthy to hearken unto the Voice that calleth from the Supreme Horizon

The passage quotes an unnamed Tablet also quoted in the Kalímát-i-Firdawsíyyih (Words of Paradise), third leaf.[351] It underlines the importance of intensely focusing on hearing the Word of God and being receptive to the divine message. Were all the spiritual endeavours of all humanity to be engaged fully in perceiving the Voice of God, they would then be deemed worthy of receiving the Revelation that was promised in all their scriptures. Unfortunately the majority of the followers of earlier Dispensations are deaf today to God's Revelation.

214. p. 30 ¶ 54. these ears that are defiled with lying tales have never been, nor are they now, fit to hear it

By 'lying tales' is meant superstitions and theological fallacies as distinct from the pristine purity of the teachings of the divine Messengers. The Apostle Paul warned (II Tim. 4:3–4):

> For the time will come when they will not endure sound doctrine; but after their own lusts shall they heap to themselves teachers, having itching ears;
>
> And they shall turn away their ears from the truth, and shall be turned unto fables [many translations, e.g. 'myths'].

As attested by Bahá'u'lláh, this prediction is a reality today:

> The accumulations of vain fancy have obstructed men's ears and stopped them from hearing the Voice of God, and the veils of human learning and false imaginings have prevented their eyes from beholding the splendour of the light of His countenance . . . With the arm of might and power We have rescued a number of souls from the slough of impending extinction and enabled them to attain the Dayspring of glory . . . Nevertheless some people . . . abandon God . . . He before Whose revelation of a single verse, all the Scriptures of the past and of more recent times pale into lowliness and insignificance – and set their hearts on lying tales and follow empty words.[352]

215. p. 30 ¶ 55. the Lesser Peace

In His Tablet to Queen Victoria Bahá'u'lláh invites the monarchs 'to hold fast to "the Lesser Peace", since they had refused "the Most Great Peace"'[353] . . . 'that haply ye may in some degree better your own condition and that of your dependents'.[354] In the Bis<u>h</u>árát Bahá'u'lláh writes:

> The sixth Glad-Tidings is the establishment of the Lesser Peace,

> details of which have formerly been revealed from Our Most Exalted Pen.[355]

And he explains:

> It is incumbent upon the ministers of the House of Justice to promote the Lesser Peace so that the people of the earth may be relieved from the burden of exorbitant expenditures. This matter is imperative and absolutely essential, inasmuch as hostilities and conflict lie at the root of affliction and calamity.[356]

> The time must come when the imperative necessity for the holding of a vast, an all-embracing assemblage of men will be universally realized. The rulers and kings of the earth must needs attend it, and, participating in its deliberations, must consider such ways and means as will lay the foundations of the world's Great Peace amongst men. Such a peace demandeth that the Great Powers should resolve, for the sake of the tranquillity of the peoples of the earth, to be fully reconciled among themselves. Should any king take up arms against another, all should unitedly arise and prevent him. If this be done, the nations of the world will no longer require any armaments, except for the purpose of preserving the security of their realms and of maintaining internal order within their territories. This will ensure the peace and composure of every people, government and nation.[357]

The following clarification has been provided by the Universal House of Justice:

> You should also take note of the distinction between the unity of nations and the Lesser Peace. Shoghi Effendi, in response to questions from believers, clarified that 'unity in the political realm', to which 'Abdu'l-Bahá referred in his enunciation of the seven candles of unity, 'is a unity which politically independent and sovereign states achieve among themselves' . . . the Lesser Peace will initially be a political unity arrived at by decision of the various governments of the world. The unity of nations can be taken as that unity which arises from a recognition among the peoples of the various nations, that they are members of one common human family.[358]

216. p. 31 ¶ 55. must arise to deter him

See Shoghi Effendi's reference to the principle of collective security.[359]

217. p. 31 ¶ 56. In this land, every time men are conscripted for the army, a great terror seizeth the people

A reference to a system of conscription in the Ottoman Empire introduced as part of the *Tanzimát Fermání* (Imperial Edict of Reorganization) proclaimed in 1839 by Sulṭán 'Abdu'l-Majid I, who sought, amongst other reforms, to increase the military defence of his empire. The Muslim population was required to serve in the army, and draft for non-Muslims was introduced in 1856. Conscription could be avoided by paying an exemption tax. The system was complex, not equitable and prone to abuse and bribery. The rich evaded the military burdens. Once a year, a young man would be forcibly recruited from every family, often resulting in hardship and anguish.[360]

218. p. 32 ¶ 56. We have learned that the government of Persia . . . have, likewise decided to reinforce their army

Bahá'u'lláh recommends that the Shah of Persia drastically reduce his standing armies and armaments as they consume a great deal of the country's resources. The large armies maintained by the various competing countries do not ultimately lead to the peace and security of mankind – there is a desperate need for an alternative and spiritual solution to the maintenance of security.

219. p. 32 ¶ 56. Justice is a powerful force. It is, above all else, the conqueror of the citadels of the hearts and souls of men

In the spiritual clash between the forces of darkness and the army of light, the exercise of justice is vitally important if rulers wish to conquer 'the citadels of the hearts and souls of men'.

> Justice hath a mighty force at its command. It is none other than reward and punishment for the deeds of men. By the power of this force the tabernacle of order is established throughout the world,

causing the wicked to restrain their natures for fear of punishment.[361]

See also Annotation 202.

220. p. 32 ¶ 57. In the treasuries of the knowledge of God there lieth concealed a knowledge

Shoghi Effendi in a letter written on his behalf states:

> Unfortunately it would seem that the knowledge 'which could largely eliminate fear' has not been disclosed or identified by Bahá'u'lláh so we do not know what it is.[362]

It is notable, however, that because of their certitude of faith, many of the martyrs utterly lacked fear while they were being tortured prior to their martyrdom.

221. p. 32 ¶ 57. A word hath . . . been written down . . . in the Crimson Book which is capable of fully disclosing that force which is hid in men, nay of redoubling its potency

The Book of the Covenant states:

> A mighty force, a consummate power lieth concealed in the world of being. Fix your gaze upon it and upon its unifying influence, and not upon the differences which appear from it.[363]

> O ye that dwell on earth! The religion of God is for love and unity; make it not the cause of enmity or dissension.[364]

Bahá'u'lláh ensured this unity through the appointment of 'Abdu'l-Bahá as His successor. This in turn provided the certitude that the unity of mankind will be realized, thus eliminating undue fear and anxiety. It prompted individuals not to waver but to rely on God and confidently proclaim the Faith of Bahá'u'lláh:

> The source of courage and power is the promotion of the Word of God, and steadfastness in His Love.[365]

'Abdu'l-Bahá explains the importance and power of the Covenant of Bahá'u'lláh thus:

> Today the dynamic power of the world of existence is the power of the Covenant which like unto an artery pulsateth in the body of the contingent world and protecteth Bahá'í unity.
>
> The Bahá'ís are commanded to establish the oneness of mankind . . .
>
> The purpose of the Blessed Beauty in entering into this Covenant and Testament was to gather all existent beings around one point so that the thoughtless souls, who in every cycle and generation have been the cause of dissension, may not undermine the Cause.[366]

222. p. 32 ¶ 57. Crimson Book

Bahá'u'lláh's Will and Testament, designated by Him as His 'Most Great Tablet' and 'the Book of My Covenant' (*Kitáb-i-'Ahdí*), was written in His own hand, probably not long before He revealed the *Epistle to the Son of the Wolf*, and was entrusted shortly before His passing to His eldest son, 'Abdu'l-Bahá. In it Bahá'u'lláh clearly designates 'Abdu'l-Bahá as His successor and as the Centre of His Covenant, providing for the continuation of divine authority over the affairs of the Faith in the future:

> unsealed, on the ninth day after His ascension in the presence of nine witnesses chosen from amongst His companions and members of His Family; read subsequently, on the afternoon of that same day, before a large company assembled in His Most Holy tomb, including His sons, some of the Báb's kinsmen, pilgrims and resident believers, this unique and epoch-making Document, designated by Bahá'u'lláh as His 'Most Great Tablet', and alluded to by Him as the 'Crimson Book' in His 'Epistle to the Son of the Wolf', can find no parallel in the Scriptures of any previous Dispensation, not excluding that of the Báb Himself.[367]

223. p. 33 ¶ 58. This Wronged One hath never had, nor hath He now any desire for leadership

Bahá'u'lláh states that God wishes only to possess the hearts of men:

> O Son of Dust! All that is in heaven and earth I have ordained for thee, except the human heart, which I have made the habitation of My beauty and glory; yet thou didst give My home and dwelling to another than Me; and whenever the manifestation of My holiness sought His own abode, a stranger found He there, and, homeless, hastened unto the sanctuary of the Beloved.[368]

In contrast, the clergy are tenaciously holding on to their leadership with its attendant earthly rewards:

> In leadership they have recognized the ultimate object of their endeavor, and account pride and haughtiness as the highest attainments of their hearts' desire. They have placed their sordid machinations above the Divine decree, have renounced resignation unto the will of God, busied themselves with selfish calculation, and walked in the way of the hypocrite. With all their power and strength they strive to secure themselves in their petty pursuits, fearful lest the least discredit undermine their authority or blemish the display of their magnificence.[369]

Bahá'u'lláh castigates those 'who are so enslaved by their lust for leadership that they would not hesitate to destroy themselves in their desire to emblazon their fame and perpetuate their names'.[370]

The Psalmist (62:6) declares: 'He [God] only is my rock and my salvation: he is my defence; I shall not be moved.' Christ declared (John 5:41) 'I receive not honour from men,' and castigated the religious leaders of His time (John 5:44) for coveting earthly honour: 'How can ye believe, which receive honour one of another, and seek not the honour that cometh from God only?' Imitating Christ, the Apostle Paul acknowledged (I Thess. 2:6): 'Nor of men sought we glory, neither of you, nor yet of others . . .'

224. p. 33 ¶ 58. We entreat Our loved ones not . . . to allow references to what they have regarded as miracles and prodigies to debase Our rank and station, or to mar the purity and sanctity of Our name

Although miracles are mostly unreliable in establishing the validity of the claims of a prophet, while in Baghdad Bahá'u'lláh did at one time agree to perform a miracle:

> Frustrated in their designs, but unrelenting in their hostility, the assembled divines delegated the learned and devout Ḥájí Mullá Ḥasan-i-'Ammú, recognized for his integrity and wisdom, to submit various questions to Bahá'u'lláh for elucidation. When these were submitted, and answers completely satisfactory to the messenger were given, Ḥájí Mullá Ḥasan, affirming the recognition by the 'ulamás of the vastness of the knowledge of Bahá'u'lláh, asked, as an evidence of the truth of His mission, for a miracle that would satisfy completely all concerned. 'Although you have no right to ask this,' Bahá'u'lláh replied, 'for God should test His creatures, and they should not test God, still I allow and accept this request . . . The 'ulamás must assemble, and, with one accord, choose one miracle, and write that, after the performance of this miracle they will no longer entertain doubts about Me, and that all will acknowledge and confess the truth of My Cause. Let them seal this paper, and bring it to Me. This must be the accepted criterion: if the miracle is performed, no doubt will remain for them; and if not, We shall be convicted of imposture.' This clear, challenging and courageous reply, unexampled in the annals of any religion, and addressed to the most illustrious Shí'ah divines, assembled in their time-honored stronghold, was so satisfactory to their envoy that he instantly arose, kissed the knee of Bahá'u'lláh, and departed to deliver His message. Three days later he sent word that that august assemblage had failed to arrive at a decision, and had chosen to drop the matter, a decision to which he himself later gave wide publicity, in the course of his visit to Persia, and even communicated it in person to the then Minister of Foreign Affairs, Mírzá Sa'íd Khán.[371]

Followers of all religions ascribe miraculous deeds to their founders.

Clearly, it is reasonable to assume that the Prophets, in their capacity as the agents of the Ruler and Fashioner of the universe, can suspend the laws of nature and perform the miraculous. However, as proof of faith miracles have their limitations. They are often observed only by a limited number of eyewitnesses during a snapshot in humanity's history. Many come to label them several centuries later as mere fables. Even the onlookers can dismiss them as a trick on the senses. Many miracles are attributed to Moses, but perhaps there could not have been a miracle more dramatic than His parting of the sea (Ex. 14:21). However, these narratives are only convincing and of value to those who already believe. Others deny that the events are historical or ever transpired. Notably, we read a few chapters later (Ex. 32:1) that the Jews who presumably witnessed this event and the other miracles reverted to idolatry and the worship of the golden calf when 'Moses delayed to come down out of the mount'.

It is therefore futile to try to establish the validity and superiority of a Dispensation by accounts of impressive physical miracles. The Jew may point out the miracle of Balaam's perceptive and talking donkey (Num. 22:21–39) which in contrast to the prophet saw an angel blocking the road and protested, refusing to proceed. (In this case it is not quite clear whether the miracle was attributable to the prophet or to his gifted donkey!) Moses's changing His staff into a serpent before Pharaoh, partitioning the sea, providing manna from heaven, and making water gush from a rock in the desert can all be related as examples of miracles. One also notes (I Sam. 28:6–17) that a female medium brought the High Priest Samuel back to life.

A Christian may also consider the many miracles attributed to Christ or His disciples as literally true. He may not consider that most, if not all, of these may have been allegories for more profound spiritual truths. For example, when the disciples of John the Baptist asked Jesus (Matt. 11:26): 'Art thou he that should come, or do we look for another?' His answer (Matt. 11:4–5) may be taken as a catalogue of physical miracles or as referring to the manifold transformative effects of His teachings: 'Go and shew John again those things which ye do hear and see: The blind receive their sight, and the lame walk, the lepers are cleansed, and the deaf hear, the dead are raised up, and the poor have the gospel preached to them.' If the disciples of John the Baptist expected to witness physical miracles then they would have been 'offended' (English Standard Version) by what Christ said and did, and this would have caused them to stumble (Matt. 11:6).

If bringing the physically dead, such as Lazarus, back to life was critical to belief, Christ would not have been so dismissive when He stated earlier (Matt. 8:22): 'Let the dead bury their dead,' or explained on another occasion (John 3:6): 'That which is born of the flesh is flesh; and that which is born of the Spirit is spirit.'

Notably, Jesus stated (Matt. 7:22–23) that in spite of many claiming in His name to drive out demons and perform many miracles, He will tell them plainly, '. . . I never knew you, depart from me, ye that work iniquity.' In his commentary on the Bible, the Methodist leader Joseph Benson provides the following explanation for the above sobering prediction of Christ concerning some of His followers:

> Then will I profess unto them, I never knew you – Though I called you to be my servants, and you professed yourselves such, I never knew you to be such, nor approved of you. So that even the working of the greatest miracles, and the uttering the most undoubted prophecies, is not a sufficient proof that a man possesses saving faith, nor will any thing of that kind avail to prove that we are now accepted of God, or are in the way to meet with acceptance of him at the day of final accounts, without the faith productive of true and universal holiness.[372]

One must also consider the fact that Christ refused to perform a miracle at the request of the Pharisees and Sadducees (Matt. 16:4).

Muslim traditions claim that Muhammad performed several supernatural events that are not credible. The Qur'án (17:88) states that the supreme miracle of Muhammad was the Book (Revelation) itself, which should have been sufficient for the Meccan people (Quraysh). Nevertheless, they constantly requested Muhammad to show them miracles. He refused, explaining (Qur'án 6:37 and 17:59) that such signs did not result in increased faith.

225. p. 33 ¶ 59. all are earnestly striving to put out this glorious and shining light

This statement appears twice in the Qur'án, which explains that in spite of the objections, verbal and written attacks, opposition to and persecution of the believers, God will accomplish His Purpose (61:8): 'Their intention is to extinguish God's Light (by blowing) with their mouths: But God will complete (the revelation of) His Light, even though the Unbelievers may detest (it).' And (9:32): 'Fain would they extinguish God's Light with their mouths, but God will not allow but that His Light should be perfected, even though the unbelievers may detest (it)'. The fire of faith and God's love cannot be extinguished by blowing on it. Instead, the opposition will cause it to rage even more fiercely. Notably, Christ exclaimed (Luke 12:49, English Standard Version): 'I came to cast fire on the earth, and would that it were already kindled!'

Bahá'u'lláh repeats the assertion of the Qur'án several times in the Epistle (¶ 157 (x2), ¶ 169, ¶ 179, ¶ 188, ¶ 249), and thereby reminds the Shaykh and his ilk that they will be powerless to stem the tide of God's irresistible Faith, just as the Meccan idolaters and the Medina hypocrites failed to do in the Dispensation of Muhammad:

> Say: The springs that sustain the life of these birds are not of this world. Their source is far above the reach and ken of human apprehension. Who is there that can put out the light which the snow-white Hand of God hath lit? Where is he to be found that hath the power to quench the fire which hath been kindled through the might of thy Lord, the All-Powerful, the All-Compelling, the Almighty? It is the Hand of Divine might that hath extinguished the flames of dissension. Powerful is He to do that which He pleaseth. He saith: Be; and it is. Say: The fierce gales and whirlwinds of the world and its peoples can never shake the foundation upon which the rock-like stability of My chosen ones is based.[373]

226. p. 33 ¶ 59. One of Our friends hath reported that among the residents of the Great City (Constantinople)

Whilst Bahá'u'lláh was incarcerated in 'Akká, there was a group of Persians in Constantinople (Istanbul) who worked tirelessly to stir up trouble for Bahá'u'lláh, undermine His Faith and bring it to disrepute by spreading rumours. These included Shaykh Muḥammad Yazdí and Áqá Muḥammad Tabrízí (editor of the *Akhta*r (Star) magazine, founded in 1875 at the suggestion of the Persian ambassador and closed in 1896 by the Ottoman government) collaborating with Siyyid Muḥammad-i-Iṣfáhání (at whose instigation Mírzá Yaḥyá had betrayed the trust of the Báb and was designated the Antichrist of the Bahá'í Revelation); and Muḥammad-'Alí Iṣfáhání (not to be confused with Muḥammad-'Alíy-i-Iṣfáhání mentioned in *Memorials of the Faithful*). Bahá'u'lláh dispatched Jináb Názir to Istanbul to investigate the matter. He reported to Bahá'u'lláh that the group was accusing the Bahá'ís of stealing and of sending each year 50,000 tumans to 'Akká (1 tuman was equivalent to 60 to 100 gm of silver).[374]

227. p. 33 ¶ 59. 'Akká

'Akká is referred to in the Bahá'í Writings as 'the prison city';[375] 'the Most Great Prison';[376] 'this Resplendent Spot';[377] 'The fortress-town';[378] 'penal colony';[379] 'prison-fortress';[380] 'the Strong City';[381] 'the Holy Land';[382] 'the Blessed Spot';[383] 'the Resort of spirits';[384] 'the land of desire';[385] 'the citadel';[386] 'the silver-white city';[387] and 'the resplendent city'.[388] Shoghi Effendi writes that it was

> girt about by a double system of ramparts; was inhabited by a people whom Bahá'u'lláh stigmatized as 'the generation of vipers'; was devoid of any source of water within its gates; was flea-infested, damp and honey-combed with gloomy, filthy and tortuous lanes. 'According to what they say,' the Supreme Pen has recorded . . . 'it is the most desolate of the cities of the world, the most unsightly of them in appearance, the most detestable in climate, and the foulest in water. It is as though it were the metropolis of the owl.' So putrid was its air that, according to a proverb, a bird when flying over it would drop dead.[389]

It is clear from the description by 'Abdu'l-Bahá of the dire circumstances of Bahá'u'lláh in 'Akká that it would not have been feasible for Him to receive the reported substantial assistance from Iran:

> the Most Great Name was held prisoner and confined nine years in the fortress-town of 'Akká; and at all times, both in the barracks and afterward, from without the house, the police and farrá<u>sh</u>es had Him under constant guard. The Blessed Beauty lived in a very small house, and He never set foot outside that narrow lodging, because His oppressors kept continual watch at the door.[390]

See also Annotations 648, 649 and 814.

228. p. 35 ¶ 60. Within the walls of this prison a highly esteemed man was for some time obliged to break stones that he might earn a living

To illustrate the sheer falsity and enormity of the accusation that He and His fellow prisoners were receiving vast amounts of money from Iran, Bahá'u'lláh describes the reduced circumstances of one of His followers, Ustád Ismá'íl Mi'már (*Mi'már* means builder in Persian). He had been a prosperous architect in Iran, but in 'Akká he was reduced to cutting stones and selling trinkets to survive. His life is summarized by 'Abdu'l-Bahá in *Memorials of the Faithful*.[391]

229. p. 35 ¶ 60. to nourish themselves with that Divine sustenance which is hunger!

Bahá'u'lláh here explains that, instead of living lavishly in the Great Prison on an alleged large stipend from Persia, He and His companions suffered severe deprivation and hunger.

All of the Prophets have suffered similarly. During the boycott by the Meccans, the Prophet Muhammad and the tribe that befriended Him had to endure hunger and tribulation for about three years. During the digging of the trenches (Battle of the Trench or *<u>Kh</u>andaq*), even the Prophet was involved in the hard work of labour, sustained by a few dates. He would dig the trench as well as carry the sand and rocks on his shoulders. The Muslims struggled on, even though there was a shortage of food and other supplies. In one incident, a companion complained to the Prophet about the extreme hunger he was suffering. He showed Muhammad that he had tied a rock to his stomach to subdue the pain of hunger. The Prophet also lifted his shirt and revealed to him that he had two rocks tied to his stomach – He shared the suffering of His companions.

Christ (Matt. 21:18; Luke 4:2) also led a life of poverty, and suffered pangs of physical hunger. At the same time He offered (Matt 5:6) His followers spiritual food and drink, 'Blessed are they which do hunger and thirst after righteousness: for they shall be filled.' Again (John 6:35), 'I am the bread of life: he that cometh to me shall never hunger; and he that believeth on me shall never thirst.'

230. p. 36 ¶ 62. it behooveth every fair-minded person to succor Him

> To assist Me is to teach My Cause . . .This is the changeless commandment of God, eternal in the past, eternal in the future.[392]

> O ye beloved of God! Repose not yourselves on your couches . . . hasten to His assistance. Unloose your tongues, and proclaim unceasingly His Cause. This shall be better for you than all the treasures of the past and of the future, if ye be of them that comprehend this truth.[393]

To effectively teach His Cause requires that one's life reflect the moral and ethical principles proclaimed by Him.[394]

231. p. 36 ¶ 62. Most men have until now failed to discover the purpose of this Wronged One, nor have they known the reason for which He hath been willing to endure countless afflictions

Steeped in imitation and selfish concerns most people cannot fathom why God's Messengers choose to suffer for the betterment of humanity. Their endurance, resignation, patience and forbearance are evidence of their Mission but are attributed to ulterior motives. Hence, Bahá'u'lláh clarifies:

> The betterment of the world hath been the sole aim of this Wronged One . . . Whilst afflicted with trials, He held fast unto the cord of patience and fortitude, and was satisfied with the things which have befallen Him at the hands of His enemies, and was crying out: 'I

> have renounced My desire for Thy desire, O my God, and My will for the revelation of Thy Will. By Thy glory! I desire neither Myself nor My life except for the purpose of serving Thy Cause, and I love not My being save that I may sacrifice it in Thy path . . .' (¶ 63)

232. p. 36 ¶ 62. Waves have encompassed the Ark of God

In Judaism the Ark of God was a sacred chest that housed and protected the core of faith, God's Testimony, that is, the Ten Commandments (Ex. 40:20) written on two stone tablets.

Early Christians referred to the tribulations that they endured as waves encompassing the Ark, as in the following early hymn: 'Lo! all the billows trouble me; and Thou hast given more favour to the ark: for waves alone encompassed it, mounds and weapons and waves encircle me. It was unto Thee a storehouse of treasures, but I have been a storehouse of debts: it in Thy love subdued the waves . . .'[395]

In the Qur'án (23: 27) Noah admonished His son to symbolically enter the Ark of God for his safety, but he refused and was drowned by waves (of misfortune).

Bahá'u'lláh states here that the Ark of God and His Revelation, representing the salvation of humanity today, is once again buffeted by the waves of disbelief and opposition.

233. p. 36 ¶ 62. He Who causeth the dawn to appear is, verily, with Thee in this darkness

Bahá'u'lláh informs the Shaykh that the Omnipotent Lord and the Source of His Revelation is with Him. He is therefore assured of the eventual triumph of His Cause. No worldly power can thwart the purpose of the Most Exalted Pen:

> Know ye that I am afraid of none except God. In none but Him have I placed My trust; to none will I cleave but Him, and wish for naught except the thing He hath wished for Me . . . I have offered up My soul and My body as a sacrifice for God, the Lord of all worlds. Whoso hath known God shall know none but Him, and he that feareth God shall be afraid of no one except Him, though the powers of the whole earth rise up and be arrayed against him. I

speak naught except at His bidding, and follow naught, through the power of God and His might, except His truth.[396]

His followers take heart that He is with them at all times:

> Arise to further My Cause, and to exalt My Word amongst men. We are with you at all times, and shall strengthen you through the power of truth. We are truly almighty. Whoso hath recognized Me will arise and serve Me with such determination that the powers of earth and heaven shall be unable to defeat his purpose.[397]

> The glory of God rest upon you, O people of Bahá. Rejoice with exceeding gladness through My remembrance, for He is indeed with you at all times.[398]

The Qur'án (16:128) states that 'God is with those who restrain themselves, and those who do good.'

Christ (Matt. 28:20) had similarly reassured His followers: 'Lo, I am with you alway, even unto the end of the world.'

234. pp. 36–7 ¶ 63. The betterment of the world hath been the sole aim of this Wronged One . . . I have renounced My desire for Thy desire, O my God

This statement is akin to Edward G. Browne's account of what Bahá'u'lláh shared with him around the same time in 'Akká:

> We desire but the good of the world and the happiness of the nations; yet they deem Us a stirrer up of strife and sedition worthy of bondage and banishment . . . That all nations should become one in faith and all men as brothers; that the bonds of affection and unity between the sons of men should be strengthened; that diversity of religion should cease, and differences of race be annulled – what harm is there in this? . . . Yet so it shall be; these fruitless strifes, these ruinous wars shall pass away, and the 'Most Great Peace' shall come . . . Yet do We see your kings and rulers lavishing their treasures more freely on means for the destruction of the human race than on that which would conduce to the happiness of mankind . . . These strifes

> and this bloodshed and discord must cease, and all men be as one kindred and one family . . . Let not a man glory in this, that he loves his country; let him rather glory in this, that he loves his kind . . .[399]

Bahá'u'lláh states in the Book of the Covenant:

> We further admonish you to serve all nations and to strive for the betterment of the world.[400]

235. p. 37 ¶ 63. Openly they were with Me, yet secretly they assisted My foes, who have arisen to dishonor Me

Throughout His life Bahá'u'lláh had to face the duplicity and pretensions of some of the Bábís and the hypocrisy of certain so-called believers. Regarding the iniquity of such behaviour, Bahá'u'lláh admonishes:

> Tell . . . the loved ones of God that equity is the most fundamental among human virtues. The evaluation of all things must needs depend upon it. Ponder a while on the woes and afflictions which this Prisoner hath sustained. I have, all the days of My life, been at the mercy of Mine enemies, and have suffered each day, in the path of the love of God, a fresh tribulation. I have patiently endured until the fame of the Cause of God was spread abroad on the earth. If any one should now arise and, prompted by the vain imaginations his heart hath devised, endeavor, openly or in secret, to sow the seeds of dissension amongst men – can such a man be said to have acted with equity? No, by Him Whose might extendeth over all things! By My life! Mine heart groaneth and mine eyes weep sore for the Cause of God and for them that understand not what they say and imagine what they cannot comprehend.[401]

Earlier Dispensations also had their hypocrites. In response to the sanctimonious questions of the Pharisees and teachers of the law, Christ (Mark 7:6 quoting Is. 29:13) said: 'Well hath Esaias prophesied of you hypocrites, as it is written, This people honoureth me with their lips, but their heart is far from me.' And again, (Matt. 23:24–28):

> Ye blind guides, which strain at a gnat, and swallow a camel.

> Woe unto you, scribes and Pharisees, hypocrites! for ye make clean the outside of the cup and of the platter, but within they are full of extortion and excess.
>
> Thou blind Pharisee, cleanse first that which is within the cup and platter, that the outside of them may be clean also.
>
> Woe unto you, scribes and Pharisees, hypocrites! for ye are like unto whited sepulchres, which indeed appear beautiful outward, but are within full of dead men›s bones, and of all uncleanness. Even so ye also outwardly appear righteous unto men, but within ye are full of hypocrisy and iniquity.

In a chapter of the Qur'án (63:1–4) entitled 'Hypocrites' (*al-Muáfiqun*), Muhammad also warned His followers:

> When the Hypocrites come to thee, they say, 'We bear witness that thou art indeed the Messenger of God' . . . God beareth witness that the Hypocrites are indeed liars.
>
> They have made their oaths a screen (for their misdeeds): thus they obstruct (men) from the Path of God: truly evil are their deeds.
>
> That is because they believed, then they rejected Faith: so a seal was set on their hearts: therefore they understand not.
>
> When thou lookest at them, their exteriors please thee; and when they speak, thou listenest to their words. They are as (worthless as hollow) pieces of timber propped up (unable to stand on their own).

236. p. 38 ¶ 63. The voice and the lamentation of the true Faith have been raised

Bahá'u'lláh is the well-spring of truth in this day, and the true Faith laments that humanity has not heeded the Call of the Manifestation of God but instead has risen to inflict sufferings on Him and His followers:

> How grievously Bahá'u'lláh suffered to regenerate the world! Wrongly accused, imprisoned, beaten, chained, banished from country to country, betrayed, poisoned, stripped of material possessions, and 'at every moment tormented with a fresh torment': such was the cruel reception that greeted the Everlasting Father, Him Who is the Possessor of all Names and Attributes. For two score years, until the

end of His earthly days, He remained a prisoner and exile – persecuted unceasingly by the rulers of Persia and the Ottoman Empire, opposed relentlessly by a vicious and scheming clergy, neglected abjectly by other sovereigns to whom He addressed potent letters imparting to them that which, in His truth-bearing words, 'is the cause of the well-being, the unity, the harmony, and the reconstruction of the world, and of the tranquility of the nations'.[402]

237. p. 38 ¶ 63. This is the Day whereon Sinai hath smiled at Him Who conversed upon it

Sinai is the mountain where according to the Torah (Ex. 3:1–17) God spoke to Moses from the Burning Bush. The occasion is referred to frequently in the Qur'án (2:63; 4:154, 164; 19:52; 20:80; 23:20; 28:46; 52:1 and 95:2). Sinai is called *Ṭúr* in Arabic, the Mount (of Revelation). In one sense, the ultimate purpose of the Dispensation of Moses was to free the Children of Israel from slavery and guide them to the Promised Land and to the advents of the Messiah and the Lord of Hosts. Here Bahá'u'lláh indicates that Mount Sinai rejoices that that promise has been fulfilled. In this context 'the beginning is the end and the end is the beginning', consistent with the understanding that the Voice that spoke through Bahá'u'lláh also addressed Moses through the Burning Bush. Hence Bahá'u'lláh is also known as the Speaker on Mount Sinai. Divine reality is one and His Faith is one. Compare ¶ 29: 'I ask of Thee, by the splendours of the Sun of Thy revelation on Sinai . . .'

The identity of the Báb and Bahá'u'lláh is exemplified by the following statement of the Báb:

> Indeed We conversed with Moses by the leave of God from the midst of the Burning Bush in the Sinai and revealed an infinitesimal glimmer of Thy Light upon the Mystic Mount and its dwellers, whereupon the Mount shook to its foundations and was crushed into dust . . .[403]

238. p. 38 ¶ 63. Carmel [hath smiled] at its Revealer

Carmel is a mountain in Israel. It is closely associated with Bahá'u'lláh and is where the Shrines of the Báb and 'Abdu'l-Bahá, and the world administrative centre of the Bahá'í Faith are located.

The mountain had metaphorically anticipated for more than two and a half thousand years that it will witness the Glory of God. Therefore it greeted the fulfilment of the prophecies with great joy (Is. 35:1–2):

> The wilderness and the solitary place shall be glad for them; and the desert shall rejoice, and blossom as the rose.
>
> It shall blossom abundantly, and rejoice even with joy and singing: the glory of Lebanon shall be given unto it, the excellency of Carmel and Sharon, they shall see the glory of the Lord, and the excellency of our God.

239. p. 38 ¶ 63. and the Sadrah [hath smiled] at Him Who taught it

Sadrah means literally 'Tree' and the *Sadratu'l- Muntahá* is the Divine Lote-Tree beyond which there is no passing. The phraseology is derived from the Qur'án (53:5–15). The passage reveals that Muhammad's Revelation was not His but a divine inspiration – He had been taught by the Omnipotent Lord (*shadid'ul Ghuwá*) in the exalted horizon. He saw the Omnipotent Lord twice by the Lote-Tree [*sadrati almuntahá*] in paradise.

In pre-Islamic Arabia, the *sadrati almuntahá* was a tree planted at the end of a road to serve as guide in the desert. In Islam, it has been traditionally understood as a tree that marks the end of the seventh heaven beyond which is the Throne of God and through which no one can pass. In the Bahá'í Writings it refers to the Manifestation of God, Who is the ultimate Source of Truth in each Dispensation.

Man can only know God to the extent he can perceive the divine attributes reflected in the mirror of the His Manifestations. Hence, recognition of the Manifestation and His Revelation constitute the profoundest level of man's ability to know God – it is the limit of humanity's access to God.

In the above passage, Bahá'u'lláh indicates that the *Sadrah* (Muhammad) is also smiling as He observes the One Who taught Him, the *Shadid'ul Ghuwá,* seated on God's Throne.

240. p. 38 ¶ 63. Withhold not yourselves from that which hath been revealed through His grace

The followers of every Dispensation have been expecting a new Revelation. Now is the time to discard imitation and investigate the truth that has been revealed to them through His infinite mercy, with the understanding that their success is contingent on making a sincere effort. Christ (Matt. 7:7–8) exhorted the people of His time, 'Ask, and it shall be given you; seek, and ye shall find; knock, and it shall be opened unto you: For every one that asketh receiveth; and he that seeketh findeth; and to him that knocketh it shall be opened.' The Apostle Paul (I Thess. 5:21) instructed Christians to 'Prove all things; hold fast that which is good.'

God also states in the Qur'án (29:69):

> And those who strive in Our (Cause), – We will certainly guide them to Our Paths: for verily God is with those who do right.

241. p. 38 ¶ 63. Seize ye the living waters of immortality

That is, partake of the Revelation that confers spiritual immortality. The Hebrew Bible predicts a time when this spiritual life-conferring water will flow in the lifeless arid desert (Is. 35:6–7): 'for in the wilderness shall waters break out, and streams in the desert. And the parched land shall become a pool, and the thirsty ground springs of water . . .' Again (Is. 43:19), 'Behold, I will do a new thing . . . I will even make a way in the wilderness, and rivers in the desert.' The Beatitudes (Matt. 5:6) teach that to be successful, the Christian must possess a sincere spiritual thirst and hunger. God (Rev. 21:5–6) will make all things new, and He will 'give unto him that is athirst of the fountain of the water of life freely'. The Qur'án teaches that true guidance flows from God (2:272), but man must strive for the truth (9:19 and 29:69).

'Abdu'l-Bahá is reported to have advised:

> The first thing to do is to acquire a thirst for Spirituality, then Live the Life! Live the Life! Live the Life! The way to acquire this thirst is to meditate upon the future life. Study the Holy Words, read your Bible, read the Holy Books, especially study the Holy Utterances of Bahá'u'lláh; Prayer and Meditation. . .

> Then will you know this Great Thirst, and then only can you begin to Live the Life![404]

He exhorts:

> O thou who are athirst for the water of Life! This manifest Book is the fountainhead of the Water of Life eternal. Drink so much as thou art able from the fountain of the living water . . .[405]

242. p. 38 ¶ 64. We have . . . enjoined on men what is right, and forbidden what is wrong

In every Dispensation, Revelation has a dual purpose: to prescribe what is right and is consistent with God's good pleasure; and to forbid what is wrong, including earlier teachings that no longer serve the best interests of humanity.

Thus, Bahá'u'lláh has enjoined the essential and eternal virtues enjoined in earlier Dispensations, but has expanded them and endowed them with new life:

> The virtues and attributes pertaining unto God are all evident and manifest, and have been mentioned and described in all the heavenly Books. Among them are trustworthiness, truthfulness, purity of heart while communing with God, forbearance, resignation to whatever the Almighty hath decreed, contentment with the things His Will hath provided, patience, nay, thankfulness in the midst of tribulation, and complete reliance, in all circumstances, upon Him. These rank, according to the estimate of God, among the highest and most laudable of all acts. All other acts are, and will ever remain, secondary and subordinate unto them . . .[406]

He has today also forbidden previously accepted principles of conduct, such things as racial and religious prejudice, holy war, and gender inequality.

Enjoining what is right and forbidding what is wrong is an important instruction in the Qur'án (3:104): 'Let there arise out of you a band of people inviting to all that is good, enjoining what is right, and forbidding what is wrong: They are the ones to attain felicity.' Again,

(9:71; also 3:110; 9:112; 31:17): 'The believers . . . enjoin what is just, and forbid what is evil.'

243. p. 38 ¶ 64. This Wronged One is not capable of dissimulation

Bahá'u'lláh states that He has not concealed or covered up the truth (Arabic word used here, *satr*). Dissimulation (also known as *taqíyyah* in Arabic) refers to concealing one's true feelings or intentions, hiding or denying one's true faith, or breaking one's oath in order to avoid persecution. Bahá'u'lláh and His followers do not resort to this practice:

> This Wronged One hath never acted hypocritically towards any one, in the Cause of God, and hath loudly proclaimed the Word of God before the face of His creatures. Let him who wisheth turn thereunto, and let him who wisheth turn aside. (¶ 165)

> God knows that at no time did We attempt to conceal Ourself or hide the Cause which We have been bidden to proclaim. Though not wearing the garb of the people of learning, We have again and again faced and reasoned with men of great scholarship in both Núr and Mázindarán, and have succeeded in persuading them of the truth of this Revelation. We never flinched in Our determination; We never hesitated to accept the challenge from whatever direction it came. To whomsoever We spoke in those days, We found him receptive to our Call and ready to identify himself with its precepts.[407]

A very early instance of dissimulation, recorded in the Torah, occurs when, to avoid trouble, Abraham misrepresents his wife Sarah as his sister to Pharaoh (Gen. 12:12–20). He does it a second time to King Abimelech (Gen. 26:1–16). Similarly, Isaac tells the Philistines that his wife, Rebecca, is really his sister (Gen. 26:1–33). The Jews of Spain practised dissimulation in the 1400s when thousands of them were either massacred or forced to convert to Catholicism during the Inquisition that was established to root out and punish the Crypto-Jews or Marrano Jews among the new Christian converts.

Christ frequently asked those who were healed by Him to conceal His identity and actions (Matt. 8:4; 9:30; 12:16; 16:20; 17:9). However, it would be difficult to interpret being cautious as dissimulation.

Taqíyyah is an approved practice in Usuli Shi'ih Islam. It has been justified by interpretation of certain verses of the Qur'án such as 2:225:

> God will not call you to account for thoughtlessness in your oaths, but for the intention in your hearts; and He is Oft-forgiving Most Forbearing.
> (See also: 3:28; 3:54, 8:30; 9:3; 10:21; 16:106; 40:28; 66:2.)

It was sanctioned by reference to the seclusionist policies of the later Imáms and, in particular, during the alleged *ghayba* (occultation) of the Twelfth Imám, who went into hiding out of fear of his enemies. However, the practice was expected to be annulled by the Promised One. A hadith attributed to the eighth Shí'ih Imám, 'Alí bin Musá, states:

> 'The one who is not pious has no religion and the one who does not practice Taqiyyah has no *Imán* (deep faith).' So he was asked, 'O grandson of the Messenger, until when (is one required to practice taqiyyah)?' He replied, 'Until a certain day (i.e. the day Imám Mahdi appears). Whoever does not practise taqiyyah before the appearance of Imám Mahdi, is not one of us.'[408]

Another word used in the Qur'án for a hypocrite is *munáfiqh*, and *al-Munafiqún* or the Hypocrites is the title of the 63rd Súrih of the Qur'án. It describes a group in Medina who hid their true intentions – they attested to the Prophethood of Muhammad and swore fealty to Him, but hid their true intentions of causing dissension and confusion in the Muslim community, and secretly continued to ally themselves with His enemies.

Taqíyyah was also practised by the Shaykhis. Although the Báb did not formally abrogate it during His short and turbulent ministry, many of His followers openly announced that He was the Qá'im, at great risk to their lives. The Báb had no hesitation in stating openly at His arraignment in Tabriz that He was the Qá'im:

> At last the stillness which brooded over them was broken by the Niẓámu'l-'Ulamá'. 'Who do you claim to be,' he asked the Báb, 'and

> what is the message which you have brought?' 'I am,' thrice exclaimed the Báb, 'I am, I am, the promised One! I am the One whose name you have for a thousand years invoked, at whose mention you have risen, whose advent you have longed to witness, and the hour of whose Revelation you have prayed God to hasten. Verily I say, it is incumbent upon the peoples of both the East and the West to obey My word and to pledge allegiance to My person.'[409]

The followers of Mírzá Yaḥyá (Azalis) frequently resorted to dissimulation to sow seeds of dissension and confusion. A historian writes:

> Bahá'u'lláh clearly announced that the recognition of the manifestation of God and 'steadfastness' [in] His Cause is more important than observing any of the other teachings. Gradual abandonment of taqíyyah amongst the Bahá'ís was one of the distinguishing feature[s] of the new religion from the Bábí era. After this time the practice of taqíyyah became unofficially superseded. In contrast the Azali Bábís glorified taqíyyah in their literature. Taqíyyah was considered a virtue and classified into various levels of concealment. Prominent Azali leaders openly recanted their faith and even abused Báb and Azal in the process. The extent of taqíyyah in their words and actions caused Mírzá Abu'l-Faḍl to question Edward Browne's method of portraying of Azali Bábís. Taqíyyah became one of the distinguishing features of the Azali-Bahá'í split.[410]

244. p. 39 ¶ 65. the Tablet to His Majesty the Sháh

This is a reference to Bahá'u'lláh's Tablet to Náṣiri'd-Dín Sháh, known as Lawḥ-i-Sulṭán,[411] in which Bahá'u'lláh explains His Station as the One Who has 'the knowledge of all that hath been'. He asks the Shah to be just in his treatment of his citizens, especially the Bahá'ís, and to beware of those who claim to love him for their own benefit. He explains that if the Shah saw clearly he would not value his earthly sovereignty but rather abandon it for nearness to God.

In the Tablet, Bahá'u'lláh explains that distinction for man lies in his deeds of righteousness, not in the pomp and grandeur of this world. He also offers to meet with the divines and argue His Cause if given the opportunity. He points out the insincerity of the clergy and extols the courage of the Bábí martyrs. Most of the martyrs were distinguished and virtuous, and their choice of martyrdom could only have been because of the love for God burning in their breasts. Bahá'u'lláh relates some of His tribulations and the suffering of the Bahá'ís but assures the Shah that He has counselled His followers to abandon strife and the use of the sword in defending their Faith. He prophesies the ultimate triumph of His Faith.

The Tablet was revealed shortly before leaving Adrianople (late 1867 to mid-1868). Written in 'Abdu'l-Bahá's handwriting, it was delivered by Mírzá Buzurg surnamed Badí' who travelled on foot for four months from 'Akká to Tehran in early to mid-1869. On delivering the Tablet personally to Náṣiri'd-Dín Sháh, Badí' was tortured and martyred.

See also Annotation 377.

245. p. 39 ¶ 65. O King! I was but a man like others

Bahá'u'lláh sheds further light on the divine origin of His mission. Writing earlier to Muḥammad Sháh, the Báb had written: 'That which devolveth upon Me is but to mention the Book of thy Lord and to deliver this clear Message. If thou wishest to enter the gates of Paradise, lo, they are open before thy face . . .'[412] In His turn, Bahá'u'lláh had but to deliver the divine message, and consequently suffered unimaginable torments.

246. p. 39 ¶ 65. The learning current amongst men I studied not; their schools I entered not. Ask of the city wherein I dwelt . . .

Continuing the quotation from the Lawḥ-i-Sulṭán, addressed to Náṣiri'd-Dín Sháh, Bahá'u'lláh stresses further that His Revelation is not the product of human learning but is divine in origin. He points out the easily verifiable fact that He did not receive the type of education that was available at that time to those who aspired to become a member of the ecclesiastical system. Nor may it be said that the theological training, such as Shaykh Najafí had received and the source of his pride and arrogance, could possibly have yielded the truths of Bahá'u'lláh's vast Revelation and new teachings.

The Báb wrote in the same vein:

> God beareth Me witness, I was not a man of learning, for I was trained as a merchant. In the year sixty [1260 AH /1844 CE] God graciously infused my soul with the conclusive evidences and weighty knowledge which characterize Him Who is the Testimony of God . . . until finally in that year I proclaimed God's hidden Cause and unveiled its well-guarded Pillar, in such wise that none could refute it.[413]

See also Annotations 70 and 87.

247. p. 40 ¶ 66. Look upon this Wronged One, O King, with the eyes of justice . . . Judge thou between Us and them that have wronged Us without proof

Bahá'u'lláh does not plead for Náṣiri'd-Dín Sháh's mercy or bounty but appeals to his atrophied sense of justice and fairness. The Tablet, as translated in *The Summons of the Lord of Hosts*, reads:

> Look upon this Youth, O King, with the eyes of justice; judge thou, then, with truth concerning what hath befallen Him. Of a verity, God hath made thee His shadow amongst men, and the sign of His power unto all that dwell on earth. Judge thou between Us and them that have wronged Us without proof and without an enlightening Book . . . this Youth . . . hath had no desire except to draw thee nigh unto the seat of grace, and to turn thee toward the right-hand of justice.[414]

248. p. 40 ¶ 66. They that surround thee love thee for their own sakes, whereas this Youth loveth thee for thine own sake

In other words, the advice that your fawning ministers, court officials, and clergymen give you is biased by their own political interest and financial gain, but Bahá'u'lláh's admonishments are given solely out of consideration for the Shah's welfare.

249. p. 40 ¶ 67. O King! Wert thou to incline thine ears unto the shrill voice of the Pen of Glory

The Revelation was written using pens made from bamboo. Literally, this made a high-pitched sound as it traced certain letters on paper, and it appeared as if the Pen voiced the 'shrill' and penetrating Divine Word. See also ¶ 147.

250. p. 40 ¶ 66. the cooing of the Dove of Eternity, which on the branches of the Lote-Tree beyond which there is no passing, uttereth praises to God

The Dove of Eternity refers to the Manifestations of God, and their loving messages and entreaties are likened to 'cooing'. The branches of the Lote-Tree, or *Sadratu'l-Muntahá*, refer to the tree of Revelation that transforms humanity through the creative power of the Divine Word.

Christ (Matt. 7:17–18) stated that a good tree (divine Manifestation; Revelation) is known by its fruits. The Qur'án (14:24–26) states that a good tree brings forth fruit in every period and Dispensation. Bahá'u'lláh uses the analogy of the tree to emphasize the principles of the oneness of the divine purpose and the oneness of mankind:

> The utterance of God is a lamp, whose light is these words: Ye are the fruits of one tree, and the leaves of one branch.[415]

And,

> These Lights have proceeded from but one Source, and these fruits are the fruits of one Tree. Thou canst discern neither difference nor distinction among them.[416]

The tree of humanity (man) must reflect the divine attributes:

> Man is like unto a tree. If he be adorned with fruit, he hath been and will ever be worthy of praise and commendation . . . The fruits of the human tree are exquisite, highly desired and dearly cherished. Among them are upright character, virtuous deeds and a goodly utterance. The springtime . . . for human trees appeareth in the Days of God . . .[417]

This passage in the Epistle is similar to the beginning of the Tablet of Aḥmad where *varqá* (dove) is translated as 'nightingale':

> Lo, the Nightingale of Paradise singeth upon the twigs of the Tree of Eternity [*Sadratu'l-Baghá*], with holy and sweet melodies . . . '

Again:

> The All-Merciful is come invested with power and sovereignty. Through His power the foundations of religions have quaked and the Nightingale of Utterance hath warbled its melody upon the highest branch of true understanding.[418]

251. p. 41 ¶ 68. Either thou or someone else hath said: 'Let the Súrih of Tawḥíd be translated . . .'

The Súrih of Tawḥíd (divine unity), also known as *al-Ikhlás* (sincerity or purity of Faith); *al-Ma'rifah* (Recognition or True Knowledge); and *al-Mudhakirrah* (the Reminder), is the 112th Súrih of the Qur'án and consists of only four verses. It is believed to have been revealed in the early part of the Mecca period (chronologically, it is Súrih 22 of the Qur'án). It is reported in the hadith that Muhammad regarded the content of this chapter as being equivalent to one-third of the Qur'án.

The four verses of the Súrih of Tawḥíd were allegedly revealed in response to a question asked by members of the idolatrous Quraysh tribe in Mecca, which had many tribal gods, as to the lineage of God. According to other accounts it was revealed in response to a similar question by the Jews and Christians. It proclaims (112:1–4) the unity of God – that He is One in His Essence, attributes and actions:

> Say: He is God, The One and Only;
> God, the Eternal, Absolute;
> He begetteth not, nor is He begotten;
> And there is none like unto Him.

The Súrih thus asserts that God is sanctified above numbers and does not admit plurality, and affirms that all created things are dependent upon Him for their spiritual growth.

252. p. 41 ¶ 68. so that all may know and be fully persuaded that the one true God begetteth not, nor is He begotten. Moreover, the Bábís believe in his (Bahá'u'lláh's) Divinity and Godhood

In his memoirs, Ḥájí Mírzá Ḥaydar-'Alí writes:

> The story is told that the brutal Shaykh Muḥammad-Báqir who was responsible for the martyrdom of so many Bahá'ís and whom Bahá'u'lláh named 'The Wolf' because of his evil plots, once shouted from his pulpit, 'Translate the chapter of the Qur'án in which the Prophet Muḥammad proclaims that God is one, has always existed, and can never be born. Give this to the Bahá'ís who have taken Bahá'u'lláh as their God.[419]

The son, Shaykh Muḥammad Najafí, is reported to have similarly repeated mischievously at a gathering in Tehran that the Súrih of Tawḥíd should be translated into Farsi so that people may become aware that God begetteth not nor was begotten and thus be able to reject the claims of divinity advanced by the Bábís.[420] In this manner, the Shaykh and his father tried to misconstrue Bahá'u'lláh's Words as indicating that He was claiming to be God.

The 'Wolf' and the 'Son of the Wolf' failed to explain that Bahá'u'lláh, as with Christ and Muhammad, had not spoken of His own will but entirely as directed by God. Hence, it was the Voice speaking through Him that was divine. Indeed, again as with Christ and Muhammad, Bahá'u'lláh de-emphasized His own role: for example, He states 'The evanescent is as nothing before Him Who is the Ever-Abiding' (¶ 65). He warns:

> Beware, beware, lest thou be led to join partners with the Lord, thy God. He is, and hath from everlasting been, one and alone, without peer or equal, eternal in the past, eternal in the future, detached from all things, ever-abiding, unchangeable, and self-subsisting. He hath assigned no associate unto Himself in His Kingdom, no counsellor to counsel Him, none to compare unto Him, none to rival His glory. . . Bear thou witness in thine inmost heart unto this testimony which God hath Himself and for Himself pronounced, that there is none other God but Him, that all else besides Him have

> been created by His behest, have been fashioned by His leave, are subject to His law, are as a thing forgotten when compared to the glorious evidences of His oneness, and are as nothing when brought face to face with the mighty revelations of His unity.[421]

Expounding on this theme, Bahá'u'lláh states that God, 'the invisible and Unknowable Essence of essences' must not be confused with His creation:

> He, in truth, hath, throughout eternity, been one in His Essence, one in His attributes, one in His works. Any and every comparison is applicable only to His creatures, and all conceptions of association are conceptions that belong solely to those that serve Him. Immeasurably exalted is His Essence above the descriptions of His creatures. He, alone, occupieth the Seat of transcendent majesty, of supreme and inaccessible glory. The birds of men's hearts, however high they soar, can never hope to attain the heights of His unknowable Essence. It is He Who hath called into being the whole of creation, Who hath caused every created thing to spring forth at His behest. Shall, then, the thing that was born by virtue of the word which His Pen hath revealed, and which the finger of His Will hath directed, be regarded as partner with Him, or an embodiment of His Self? Far be it from His glory that human pen or tongue should hint at His mystery, or that human heart conceive His Essence. All else besides Him stand poor and desolate at His door, all are powerless before the greatness of His might, all are but slaves in His Kingdom.[422]

And Shoghi Effendi comments:

> The divinity attributed to so great a Being and the complete incarnation of the names and attributes of God in so exalted a Person should, under no circumstances, be misconceived or misinterpreted. The human temple that has been made the vehicle of so overpowering a Revelation must, if we be faithful to the tenets of our Faith, ever remain entirely distinguished from that 'innermost Spirit of Spirits' and 'eternal Essence of Essences' – that invisible yet rational God Who, however much we extol the divinity of His Manifestations on earth, can in no wise incarnate His infinite, His unknowable, His

> incorruptible and all-embracing Reality in the concrete and limited frame of a mortal being. Indeed, the God Who could so incarnate His own reality would, in the light of the teachings of Bahá'u'lláh, cease immediately to be God.[423]

Nevertheless, for the purposes of human understanding and obeying the divine exhortations, there is no difference between God and the Will of His Manifestation and the Will of the Unknowable Essence. What the Muslim cleric did not appreciate was that the Báb and Bahá'u'lláh have revealed once again the attributes of the Divinity today, including His Unity and Oneness:

> The essence of belief in Divine unity consisteth in regarding Him Who is the Manifestation of God and Him Who is the invisible, the inaccessible, the unknowable Essence as one and the same. By this is meant that whatever pertaineth to the former, all His acts and doings, whatever He ordaineth or forbiddeth, should be considered, in all their aspects, and under all circumstances, and without any reservation, as identical with the Will of God Himself.[424]

There are statements in earlier scriptures that confirm this thesis. For example, in the Torah (Ex. 4:16; 7:1) the Lord states that Moses 'shalt be to him [Aaron] instead of God'. Again, the Lord decrees (Ex. 7:1): 'I have made thee a god to Pharaoh: and Aaron thy brother shall be thy prophet.' Similarly, Christ declared (John 10:30): 'I and my Father are one.'

Verses of the Qur'án which demonstrate that Muhammad represented God on this earth may be similarly misconstrued. For instance, the Qur'án (4:80) states: 'He who obeys the Messenger, obeys God'; (48:10): 'Verily those who plight their fealty to thee do no less than plight their fealty to God'; and (8:17): 'It is not ye who slew them; it was God: When thou threwest [in the face of the enemy] (a handful of dust), it was not Thy act, but God's . . .' These illustrate identity of purpose rather than identity of God with His creatures.

In reality it was the Shaykh and his father who, by denying God's twin Manifestations, were guilty of *shirk*, that is, calling on other gods of their vain imaginings (Qur'án 10:106; 16:20). It is in this context that Bahá'u'lláh castigates the 'Son of the Wolf' and the 'She-Serpent' as *mushrik*, individuals who in their pursuit of leadership corrupted the meaning of the text (Qur'án 2:75; 3:77–79), and committed *s͟hirk*. Without merit, they also allowed themselves to be idolized and worshipped by their followers.

253. p. 41 ¶ 69. O S͟hayk͟h! This station is the station in which one dieth to himself and liveth in God. Divinity, whenever I mention it, indicateth My complete and absolute self-effacement. This is the station in which I have no control over mine own weal or woe nor over my life nor over my resurrection

In answer to the S͟hayk͟h's assertions that the Bábís (Bahá'ís were grouped in the same category) claimed that Bahá'u'lláh is God, He explains that the station is instead one of *faná* (annihilation). In this state He has no will of His own but is subject entirely to the Divine Will – the Voice that speaks through Him that is the Voice of God. This is an identity of purpose and not an identity with the Divine Essence. Regarding His relationship to God, He testifies:

> Know thou of a certainty that the Unseen can in no wise incarnate His Essence and reveal it unto men. He is, and hath ever been, immensely exalted beyond all that can either be recounted or perceived. From His retreat of glory His voice is ever proclaiming: 'Verily, I am God; there is none other God besides Me, the All-Knowing, the All-Wise. I have manifested Myself unto men, and have sent down Him Who is the Day Spring of the signs of My Revelation. Through Him I have caused all creation to testify that there is none other God except Him, the Incomparable, the All-Informed, the All-Wise.' He Who is everlastingly hidden from the eyes of men can never be known except through His Manifestation, and His Manifestation can adduce no greater proof of the truth of His Mission than the proof of His own Person.[425]

> When I contemplate, O my God, the relationship that bindeth me to Thee, I am moved to proclaim to all created things 'verily I am God'; and when I consider my own self, lo, I find it coarser than clay![426]

Again:

> Were any of the all-embracing Manifestations of God to declare: 'I am God!' He verily speaketh the truth, and no doubt attacheth thereto.For it hath been repeatedly demonstrated that through their Revelation, their attributes and names, the Revelation of God, His name and His attributes, are made manifest in the world . . .[427]

In the Gospel of John (14:7–10), Christ states:

> If ye had known me, ye should have known my Father also: and from henceforth ye know him, and have seen him.
>
> Philip saith unto him, Lord, shew us the Father, and it sufficeth us.
>
> Jesus saith unto him, Have I been so long time with you, and yet hast thou not known me, Philip? he that hath seen me hath seen the Father; and how sayest thou then, Shew us the Father?
>
> Believest thou not that I am in the Father, and the Father in me? the words that I speak unto you I speak not of myself: but the Father that dwelleth in me, he doeth the works.

Again (John 12:44): 'And Jesus cried out and said, "He that believeth on me, believeth not on me, but on him that sent me."'

For similar explanations from the Qur'án see Annotation 252.

254. p. 41 ¶ 70. O Shaykh! How do the divines of this age account for the effulgent glory which the Sadrah of Utterance hath shed upon the Son of 'Imrán (Moses) on the Sinai of Divine knowledge?

Here, Bahá'u'lláh refers to the Burning Bush (*Sadrah*) on Mount Sinai (Ex. 3:2; Horeb in this verse is another name for Sinai) through which God conferred upon Moses the mantle of Prophethood. His meekness, self-effacement, and trusting heart, cleansed and attuned to God, enabled Him to recognize and respond to the Word of God. With the mantle of Prophethood so suddenly thrust on Him, He became the Voice of God amidst a rebellious people – hence, the Torah (Ex. 7:1) describes Moses as 'God' to Pharaoh.

'Imrán is the Arabic equivalent of the Hebrew name *'Amrám* (Friend of the Most High). He was the father of Moses, Aaron and Miriam (Ex.

6:20; 15:20; I Chron. 23:13), and is praised in the New Testament (Heb. 11:23). *Al-Imrán* (The Family of Imrán) is the title of the third Súrih of the Qur'án. The 'Son of 'Imrán' refers to Moses and the phrase is used by Bahá'u'lláh in this context in His Writings.[428] For example, Bahá'u'lláh states: 'Present thyself before Me that thou mayest hear the mysteries which were heard by the Son of 'Imrán upon the Sinai of Wisdom.'[429]

See also ¶ 136.

255. p. 41 ¶ 70. He (Moses) hearkened unto the Word which the Burning Bush had uttered, and accepted it

Namely, Moses responded without hesitation to the Voice of God that addressed Him from the Burning Bush and obeyed the divine command, illustrating the importance of man's willingness to learn what God wishes to communicate to him and to show subservience rather than being busy creating other priorities.

256. p. 41 ¶ 70. the Siyyid of Findirisk hath well said: 'This theme no mortal mind can fathom

A noted Persian poet, thinker and author, also known as Mír-Abu'l Qásim Findiriski (16th century CE). Bahá'u'lláh quotes one verse from his poetry that states that the relationship of the Manifestation of God to the Unknowable Essence is beyond any human comprehension, including that of the profound thinkers Abú-Nasr and Abú-'Alí Síná (Avicenna).

257. p. 41 ¶ 70. Abú-Naṣr

Abú Naṣr al-Fárábí (c. 872–950 CE) was known in the West as Alpharabius. He was a renowned philosopher of the ninth century, considered second only to Aristotle.

258. p. 41 ¶ 70. Abú-'Alí Síná (Avicenna)

The expertise of Abú-'Ali Síná (980–1037 CE) spanned many different subject areas such as medicine, philosophy, logic, science, astronomy, poetry, and Islamic theology.

259. p. 42 ¶ 70. Seal of the Prophets

This is one of the many titles of Muhammad in the Qur'án (33:40): 'Muhammad is not the father of any of your men, but (he is) the Messenger of God (*rasúl-ulláh)*, and the Seal of the Prophets (*khátam al-nabiyyín*) and God has full knowledge of all things.' Bahá'u'lláh also refers to Muhammad by the titles 'Seal of the Prophets'[430] and the 'Seal of Thy Prophets and of Thy Messengers'.[431]

The designation is often misinterpreted by Muslims to mean that the Qur'án is the final Word of God and that there will be no Messengers or Apostles after Muhammad. More accurately, it signifies that the period of prophecy concerning the Promised One ended with Muhammad. There would be no further prophets until the appearance of the expected Qá'im. The next phase would represent the cycle of fulfilment and ushering in of the Day of God. That divine Revelation is continuous and not final is supported by the following verses of the Qur'án:

> And if all the trees on earth were pens and the ocean (were ink), with seven oceans behind it to add to its (supply), yet would not the words of God be exhausted (in the writing): for God is Exalted in Power, full of Wisdom. (31:27)

> None of Our revelations do We abrogate or cause to be forgotten, but We substitute something better or similar: Knowest thou not that God has power over all things? (2:106)

> Every nation hath its set time. And when their time is come, they shall not retard it an hour; and they shall not advance it.
>
> O children of Adam! there shall come to you Apostles from among yourselves, rehearsing my signs to you; and whoso shall fear God and do good works, no fear shall be upon them, neither shall they be put to grief. (7:33–34, Rodwell)

This is further clarified in one of the Visitation Addresses (*Ziyárah*) of Imám 'Ali known as the Ziyárah for 'Íd al-Ghadir:

> Peace be to Muhammad, the Apostle Allah, the Seal of the Prophets, the Chief of the Envoys, the elect of the Lord of all the worlds, who

was entrusted by Allah with His revelations, and His prime commandments, and who is the seal (*Khátim*) of the previous prophecies and inaugurator (*Fátih*) of what is yet to come . . .[432]

260. p. 42 ¶ 70. Ye, verily, shall behold your Lord as ye behold the full moon on its fourteenth night

This is with reference to a hadith common to Sunnis and Shí'ihs, that humanity will see the Lord God as clearly as the full moon on the fourteenth night of the lunar month. It is for example recorded in *Sahih al-Bukhari*, a compendium of Sunni traditions:

> . . . some people said, 'O Alláh's Messenger! Shall we see our Lord on the Day of Resurrection?' the Prophet was asked if the righteous will see Allah on the Day of resurrection. He replied, 'Yes, do you have any difficulty in seeing the sun at midday when it is bright and there is no cloud in the sky?' They replied, 'No.' He said, 'Do you have any difficulty in seeing the moon on a full moon night when it is bright and there is no cloud in the sky?' They replied, 'No.' The Prophet said, '(Similarly) you will have no difficulty in seeing Alláh on the Day of Resurrection.'[433]

Also:

> Narrated Jarír bin 'Abdulláh: We were in the company of the Prophet on a fourteenth night (of the lunar month), and he looked at the (full) moon and said, You will your Lord as you see this moon, and you will have no trouble looking at Him.[434]

It is also recorded in *Tafsir-i-Safi*, a commentary on the Qur'án by Mohsen Fayz Káshani, a 17th-century Shí'ih scholar.

In the Torah (Ex. 33:18–23) Moses asks to see God's Glory but is told that He cannot see the Countenance of God. This episode is also recounted in the Qur'án (7:143): 'He (Moses) said: "O my Lord! Show (Thyself) to me (*rabbi arinee*), that I may look upon Thee." God said, "by no means canst thou see Me (*qála lan taránee*)."'

Christ stated that the 'pure in heart . . . will see God' (Matt: 5:8). The Book of Revelation (22:4–5) predicts a time when 'they shall see his [God] face; and his name shall be in their foreheads'. The Qur'án (75:22–23) states that 'some faces, that Day, will beam (in brightness and beauty; looking towards their Lord [that is recognize their Lord]. And some faces, that Day will be sad and dismal.' The latter (83:15): 'verily from (the Light of) their Lord, that Day, will be veiled.'

To see the Lord God today, the Day of Resurrection, is to recognize Bahá'u'lláh and to heed the divine Message. Sadly, as attested by Bahá'u'lláh, most of the followers of the diverse religions have turned away from the Face of God:

> And whensoever the portals of grace did open, and the clouds of divine bounty did rain upon mankind, and the light of the Unseen did shine above the horizon of celestial might, they all denied Him, and turned away from His face – the face of God Himself.[435]

> Happy is the eye that seeth, and the face that turneth towards, the Countenance of God, the Lord of all being.[436]

261. p. 42 ¶ 70. The Commander of the Faithful (Imám 'Alí)

The cousin and son-in-law of the Prophet Muhammad (married to Fáṭimih, also father to Imám Ḥasan and Imám Ḥusayn), he was the first male to believe in Muhammad. According to the Shí'ihs, he was the rightful successor of the Prophet Muhammad, and the first Imám; according to the Sunnis, he was the fourth Caliph succeeding Muhammad after Abu Bakr, Umar and Uthman. He is known by several titles, including the Commander of the Faithful, the Lion of God, and the Lord of Saintship. Saint and warrior, brilliant writer and administrator, he was killed at Kufah by Ibn-i-Muljam in 661 CE. The author Ameer Alí states: 'Ali was its (chivalry's) beau-idéal – an impersonation of gallantry, of bravery, of generosity; pure, gentle, and learned, "without fear and without reproach", he set the world the noblest example of chivalrous grandeur of character.'[437]

262. p. 42 ¶ 70. Khuṭbiy-i-Ṭutúnjíyyih

Khuṭbiy-i-Ṭutúnjíyyih or the Sermon of the Twin Gulfs is an address given by Imám 'Alí in the village of Ṭutúnjíyyih and is accepted by the Shí'ihs. Shaykh Aḥmad-i-Ahsá'í often referred to it in his writings, and Siyyid Kázim-i-Rashtí wrote an extensive two-volume treatise on it. There is also a commentary by Shaykh Háfiz Rajab al-Bursi, a Shí'ih theologian and 14th-century mystic (d. 1392/1394), in his main work *Masháriq al-Anwár al-Yaqin fi Asrár Amir al-Muminin.*

Bahá'u'lláh refers to this famous prediction (quoted by Bahá'u'lláh here in a slightly different wording): 'anticipate ye then the Revelation of the Speaker of Mount Sinai. This will appear with manifest signs visible unto all, clearly perspicuous to them.'[438] He describes this passage as the *Quṭb*, or 'Pivot', around which 'all the glad tidings of the past revolve'.[439]

See also Annotation 670.

263. p. 42 ¶ 70. Ḥusayn, the son of 'Alí

Imám Ḥusayn (born 625 CE) was the son of Imám 'Alí and Fáṭimih, and the grandson of Muhammad. He is the third Imám of the Shí'ihs and is referred to as part of the *Ahl-al-Bayt* (member of Muhammad's Household), a term derived from the Qur'án (30:33). The Shí'ihs believe that this designation applies to Fáṭimih, the daughter of Muhammad, and to the twelve Imáms.

It was understood by some Muslims in Kufah that leadership of the Muslim community correctly belonged to the descendants of Muhammad. They opposed the caliphate, and invited Imám Ḥusayn and his relatives to take refuge with them and proclaim Imám Ḥusayn as their leader. While journeying to Kufah, Imám Ḥusayn and his company were intercepted by the governor's army at Karbila, and a battle ensued, during which the army cut off all access to water for Imám Ḥusayn's family, making them suffer from thirst in the intense heat of the desert. Betrayed by his supporters in Kufah, Imám Ḥusayn was alone apart from a small band of followers and the opposing army was 5,000 strong. He was rapidly surrounded, killed and beheaded. His head was raised on a lance, and eventually taken to Damascus. Most of his family and companions, including his six-month-old son, 'Alí al-Asghar, were also massacred, and the women and children taken as prisoners. Yazid, the son of Mu'awiya and the second caliph of the Umayyad caliphate, celebrated the occasion with great pomp and show by displaying the head of Ḥusayn in his crowded and decorated court.

The annual commemoration of the pitiful events and his martyrdom is termed *Ashura* (a time dreaded by the Bábís and Bahá'ís as the emotions whipped up by ceremonies often result in greater persecution against them).

Bahá'u'lláh revealed a Tablet of Visitation in 'Akká for Imám Ḥusayn. The Imám was, as attested by Bahá'u'lláh in the *Kitáb-i-Íqán*,[440] endowed with special grace and power among the Imáms. To His Shí'ih followers, Bahá'u'lláh is the return of Imám Ḥusayn,[441] and He writes:

> Consider the eagerness with which certain peoples and nations have anticipated the return of Imám-Ḥusayn, whose coming, after the appearance of the Qá'im, hath been prophesied, in days past, by the chosen ones of God, exalted be His glory. These holy ones have, moreover, announced that when He Who is the Day Spring of the manifold grace of God manifesteth Himself, all the Prophets and Messengers, including the Qá'im [the Báb, a direct descendant of Imám Ḥusayn] will gather together beneath the shadow of the sacred Standard which the Promised One will raise. That hour is now come. The world is illumined with the effulgent glory of His countenance.[442]

Notably, the Báb alluded to the fact that the name of He Whom God shall make manifest will be Ḥusayn.[443] Shoghi Effendi also observes:

> In the name He (Bahá'u'lláh) bore He combined those of the Imám Ḥusayn, the most illustrious of the successors of the Apostle of God – the brightest 'star' shining in the 'crown' mentioned in the Revelation of St. John – and of the Imám 'Alí, the Commander of the Faithful.[444]

264. p. 42 ¶ 71. Most Great Prison

Later in the Epistle (¶ 208) Bahá'u'lláh explains:

> The Strong City is 'Akká, which hath been named the Most Great Prison, and which possesseth a fortress and mighty ramparts.

See Annotations 227, 648, 649 and 814.

265. p. 43 ¶ 73. Men have failed to perceive Our purpose in the references We have made to Divinity and Godhood

See ¶ 69 and Annotation 253.

266. p. 43 ¶ 73. Manifold are Our relationships with God. At one time, We are He Himself, and He is We Ourself. At another He is that He is, and We are that We are

Bahá'u'lláh states that this passage belongs originally to the Prophet Muhammad. As a hadith it is recorded in the *Kalimát al-Maknúnah* (Hidden Words) of Muhsen Feyz Kashani, a prolific Shí'ih Iranian writer (died 1680 CE) where it is attributed to the sixth Imám of the Shí'ihs, Imám Ja'far Aṣ-Ṣádiq (702–765 CE), but also revered by many Sunnis for his erudition and piety. It describes the stations of servitude and divinity present simultaneously in God's Chosen Ones.

267. p. 43 ¶ 74. O God, my God! I bear witness to Thy unity and Thy oneness

Compare:

> I bear witness to Thy unity and Thy oneness, and that Thou art God, and that there is none other God beside Thee. Thou hast, verily, revealed Thy Cause, fulfilled Thy Covenant, and opened wide the door of Thy grace to all that dwell in heaven and on earth. Blessing and peace, salutation and glory, rest upon Thy loved ones, whom the changes and chances of the world have not deterred from turning unto Thee, and who have given their all, in the hope of obtaining that which is with Thee. Thou art, in truth, the Ever-Forgiving, the All-Bountiful.[445]

268. p. 44 ¶ 75. Idle fancies have debarred men from the Horizon of Certitude, and vain imaginings withheld them from the Choice Sealed Wine

The following may be counted amongst idle fancies: unwarranted reliance on worldly desires and aspirations, dependence on corrupt hereditary beliefs and traditions, superstition and prejudice, blind allegiance to man-made dogmas, excessive dependence on the opinions of religious leaders rather than on the Word of God, spurious explanations of events and literal interpretations of the scriptures which defy science. Bahá'u'lláh thus describes 'the people of tyranny':

> They have gone astray and have caused the people to go astray, yet perceive it not. They worship vain imaginings but know it not. They have taken idle fancies for their lords and have neglected God, yet understand not. They have abandoned the most great Ocean and are hastening towards the pool, but comprehend not. They follow their own idle fancies while turning aside from God, the Help in Peril, the Self-Subsisting.[446]

The Qur'án (9:31) similarly rebukes the followers of earlier Dispensations: 'They take their priests and their anchorites to be their lords in derogation of God.'

Bahá'u'lláh indirectly equates idle fancies with the religious leaders, as they have prevented their followers from receiving the wine of His Revelation and attaining certitude of faith:

> O concourse of divines! Fling away idle fancies and imaginings, and turn, then, towards the Horizon of Certitude. I swear by God! All that ye possess will profit you not, neither all the treasures of the earth, nor the leadership ye have usurped. Fear God, and be not of the lost ones . . . Say: O concourse of divines! Lay aside all your veils and coverings. Give ear unto that whereunto calleth you the Most Sublime Pen, in this wondrous Day . . . The world is laden with dust, by reason of your vain imaginings, and the hearts of such as enjoy near access to God are troubled because of your cruelty. Fear God, and be of them that judge equitably.[447]

See also Annotations 114, 403 and 540.

269. p. 45 ¶ 76. Napoleon III

This paragraph introduces an extensive quotation (¶ 78–93) from Bahá'u'lláh's second Tablet to Napoleon III quoted in the Súriy-i-Haykal (compare Bahá'u'lláh, *The Summons of the Lord of Hosts*, pp. 67–83). These paragraphs quote a number of Biblical passages illustrating Jewish and Christian eschatology realized by the Revelation of Bahá'u'lláh.

Napoleon III (1808–1873) was the nephew of Napoleon Bonaparte. Elected President of France in 1848, he overthrew the Constitution in 1851, and became Emperor of France as Napoleon III (1852–1870). His rule was infamous for harsh repressive measures against his opponents and the imposition of severe censorship. Many thousands were imprisoned or sent to penal colonies.

He reasserted French influence in Europe and around the world. He allied with Great Britain in the Crimean War and successfully stopped Russian expansion toward the Mediterranean. His regime assisted Italian unification and, in the process, annexed Savoy and Nice to France; at the same time, his forces defended the Papal states against annexation by Italy. Napoleon doubled the area of the French overseas empire in Asia, the Pacific and Africa.

He went to war against Prussia in 1870 and was defeated at the Battle of Sedan. He surrendered, was deposed and went to live in exile in England. His empire collapsed and the Third French Republic was proclaimed.

270. p. 45 ¶ 76. made a certain statement, as a result of which We sent him Our Tablet while in Adrianople

Bahá'u'lláh sent two Tablets to Napoleon III, the first from Adrianople and the second while living in the barracks of 'Akká. The first Tablet has been left out of the Súriy-i-Haykal, but extracts are available in *The Promised Day Is Come*. Shoghi Effendi has provided the following summary:

> To Napoleon III Bahá'u'lláh addressed a specific Tablet, which was forwarded through one of the French ministers to the Emperor, in which He dwelt on the sufferings endured by Himself and His followers; avowed their innocence; reminded him of his two pronouncements on behalf of the oppressed and the helpless; and, desiring to test the sincerity of his motives, called upon him to 'inquire into the condition of such as have been wronged,' and 'extend his care to the weak,' and look upon Him and His fellow-exiles 'with the eye of loving-kindness'.[448]

Shoghi Effendi further explains:

> In His first Tablet Bahá'u'lláh, wishing to test the sincerity of the Emperor's motives, and deliberately assuming a meek and unprovocative tone, had, after expatiating on the sufferings He had endured, addressed him the following words: 'Two statements graciously uttered by the king of the age have reached the ears of these wronged ones. These pronouncements are, in truth, the king of all pronouncements, the like of which have never been heard from any sovereign. The first was the answer given the Russian government when it inquired why the war [Crimean] was waged against it. Thou didst reply: "The cry of the oppressed who, without guilt or blame, were drowned in the Black Sea wakened me at dawn. Wherefore, I took up arms against thee." These oppressed ones, however, have suffered a greater wrong, and are in greater distress. Whereas the trials inflicted upon those people lasted but one day, the troubles borne by these servants have continued for twenty and five years, every moment of which has held for us a grievous affliction. The other weighty statement, which was indeed a wondrous statement, manifested to the world, was this: "Ours is the responsibility to avenge the oppressed and succor the helpless."'[449]

In the year 1869 in His second Tablet to Napoleon III, Bahá'u'lláh rebukes the Emperor for his lust of war and for the contempt with which he had treated the former Tablet from Bahá'u'lláh. It is this Tablet that is quoted in the Epistle (¶ 84 and 85). Compare:

> We testify that that which wakened thee was not their cry (Turks drowned in the Black Sea), but the promptings of thine own passions, for We tested thee, and found thee wanting. . . Hadst thou been sincere in thy words, thou wouldst not have cast behind thy back the Book of God (previous Tablet), when it was sent unto thee by Him Who is the Almighty, the All-Wise.[450]

> For what thou has done, thy kingdom shall be thrown into confusion, and thine empire shall pass from thine hands, as a punishment for that which thou has wrought. Then wilt thou know how thou has plainly erred. Commotions shall seize all the people in that land,

> unless thou arisest to held this Cause, and followest Him Who is the Spirit of God (Jesus Christ) in this, the Straight Path. Hath thy pomp made thee proud? By My Life! It shall not endure; nay, it shall soon pass away, unless thou holdest fast by this firm Cord. We see abasement hastening after thee, whilst thou art of the heedless.[451]

271. p. 45 ¶ 76. his Minister

Bahá'u'lláh's first Tablet to Napoleon III was revealed in Adrianople and forwarded to the Emperor through César Ketfagou, the son of a French Consul in Syria who was known to the exiles in 'Akká.[452]

272. p. 45 ¶ 76. to our Minister in Constantinople

Refers to Napoleon III's minister and ambassador in Constantinople.

273. p. 45 ¶ 77. Súratu'l-Haykal

Súratu'l-Haykal (Súriy-i-Haykal), or the Tablet of the Temple, is the name of both a single Tablet as well as a Tablet that is combined with the Tablets to five secular and religious rulers. Bahá'u'lláh is both the addresser and the addressee of this Tablet. The Temple or Body has a number of meanings, including a reference to the Manifestation of God, man, and the prophecy of the Hebrew Bible (Zech. 6:12–13), 'The Lord of Hosts . . . whose name is the Branch. . . He shall build the temple of the Lord.' The circumstances of its revelation are described by the Universal House of Justice:

> The years following Bahá'u'lláh's arrival in Adrianople witnessed His Revelation's attainment, in the words of Shoghi Effendi, of 'its meridian glory' through the proclamation of its Founder's message to the kings and rulers of the world. During this relatively brief but turbulent period of the Faith's history, and in the early years of His subsequent exile in 1868 to the fortress town of 'Akká, He summoned the monarchs of East and West collectively, and some among them individually, to recognize the Day of God and to acknowledge the One promised in the scriptures of the religions professed by the recipients of His summons. 'Never since the beginning of the world',

> Bahá'u'lláh declares, 'hath the Message been so openly proclaimed.'
>
> . . . It was originally revealed during His banishment to Adrianople and later recast after His arrival in 'Akká [around 1869]. In this version He incorporated His messages addressed to individual potentates – Pope Pius IX, Napoleon III, Czar Alexander II, Queen Victoria, and Náṣiri'd-Dín Sháh.
>
> It was this composite work which, shortly after its completion, Bahá'u'lláh instructed be written in the form of a pentacle, symbolizing the human temple. To it He added, as a conclusion, what Shoghi Effendi has described as 'words which reveal the importance He attached to those Messages, and indicate their direct association with the prophecies of the Old Testament':
>
> Thus have We built the Temple with the hands of power and might could ye but know it. This is the Temple promised unto you in the Book. Draw ye nigh unto it.[453]

An authorized translation was published in 2002 in *The Summons of the Lord of Hosts*, which includes many passages that had been translated by Shoghi Effendi.

See also Annotation 162.

274. p. 46 ¶ 78. O King of Paris!

Napoleon III was best known for his grand reconstruction of Paris. He commissioned a vast public works programme which included the demolition of overcrowded and unhealthy medieval neighborhoods, the building of wide avenues. new parks and squares, the annexation of the suburbs surrounding Paris, and the construction of new sewers, fountains and aqueducts. The street plan and distinctive appearance of the center of Paris today is largely the result of these renovations.

275. p. 46 ¶ 78. Tell the priest to ring the bells no longer

The primary purpose of ringing church bells has been to summon the Christian faithful to gather for a church service. However: 'During the early persecutions, the [Christian] faithful, who had to worship in the catacombs, or in other retired places, were not called together by any loud signal whatever, for this would have been to betray them to the Pagan.'[454]

Paulinus of Nola is traditionally credited with the introduction of bells in association with Christian worship in a church in 400 CE. Allegedly, Pope Sabianus in 604 CE officially sanctioned the usage of bells.

With the advent of the Father, Bahá'u'lláh, Who is establishing the promised Kingdom of God on earth, there is no longer a need to toll church bells (see next item).

276. p. 46 ¶ 78. By God, the True One! The Most Mighty Bell hath appeared in the form of Him Who is the Most Great Name, and the fingers of the will of Thy Lord, the Most Exalted, the Most High, toll it out in the heaven of Immortality, in His name, the All-Glorious

Napoleon III portrayed himself as a protector of Christianity and the Church. In reality he 'attempted to use the [Catholic] clergy in France as a means to disseminate propaganda', and manipulated the Catholic Church to legitimize domestic and foreign policies.'[455] Reciprocating, 'the French clergy fervently rallied behind Louis Napoleon Bonaparte's presidential election in 1848 and approved of his coup on December 2, 1851':

> . . . a cordial relationship between the imperial government and the Catholic Church existed for pragmatic purposes. The Legitimists amongst the clergy viewed the empire as a more church-friendly governmental system than the republic, while those wealthy Catholics realized that by supporting Napoleon III, the emperor would reward the clergy and facilitate a period of prosperity for Catholicism in France that positively impacted Catholics of every social rank . . .[456]

Napoleon occupied the Papal states in order to restore Pope Pius IX to his holy capital. His Spanish wife, Eugenie, 'drove Napoleon III to misadventure by pushing for the war against Protestant Prussia in 1870, which resulted in final disaster for the Napoleonic Empire that saw the Second French Empire expire and the Second German Reich emerge'.[457]

Bahá'u'lláh's Tablet to Napoleon III thus addresses the most powerful potentate in Europe with religious pretensions, and an avid supporter of Pope Pius IX and the Christian denomination that centuries earlier had introduced the church bell.

The first and main part of the Lord's Prayer is a supplication that the Heavenly Father expedites the coming of His Kingdom when the divine purpose will be established on earth as it is in heaven. This promise was fulfilled by Bahá'u'lláh Who has brought once again the 'daily bread'. As indicated by Bahá'u'lláh to Napoleon III, there is no further need to ring the bell – the Great Bell, His Revelation, was the fulfilment of the Gospel and represented the Good News.

277. p. 46 ¶ 78. when all the tribes of the earth have mourned

This is a reference to Matt. 24:30 (also Rev. 1:7): 'And then shall appear the sign of the Son of man in heaven: and then shall all the tribes of the earth mourn, and they shall see the Son of man coming in the clouds of heaven with power and great glory.'

Mourning denotes the loss or death of a person or object of devotion. Thus the various peoples are expected to grieve at the passing of the earlier Dispensation and their hallowed traditions, rituals and dogmas. All the tribes (people) shall also mourn because they will be beset by great calamities when He comes to judge. All the wicked shall mourn at the prospect of their doom – their time-honoured understandings, rituals and worship will be abrogated.

278. p. 46 ¶ 78. the dust of irreligion hath enwrapped all men

Dust, earth and ashes are descriptive of death and mourning, as in Ecclesiastes 3:20: 'all are of the dust, and all turn to dust again,' and Isaiah (52:2): 'Shake thyself from the dust; arise, and sit down [sit in a place of honour], O Jerusalem.' Isaiah (32:1–3) also speaks of a day when a king will reign in righteousness and a person will be a shelter from the [dust-laden] wind – 'And the eyes of them that see shall not be dim, and the ears of them that hear shall hearken.' *The Expositor's Bible* provides the following explanation of this passage:

> History is swept by drifts: superstition, error, poisonous custom, dust-laden controversy. What has saved humanity has been the uprising of some great man to resist those drifts, to set his will, strong through faith, against the prevailing tendency, and to be a shelter of the weaker, but no less desirous, souls of his brethren.[458]

The Qur'án (80:38–42) predicts that in 'that Day' or the Day of Resurrection, the faces of some will be illuminated but others will be covered with dust or ashes of mourning'. Stated otherwise, the Qur'án (91:3–4) swears 'by the Day when it reveals its radiance' and 'by the night as it conceals it,' interpreted by Imám Ṣádiq as follows:

> ('the day') is an Imam from the children of Fatema who are the progeny of the Messenger of Allah – who will replace the darkness of oppression and inequity with light. Allah mentions him by saying, 'By the day when it reveals his radiance, referring to the Qa'em.'[459]

Bahá'u'lláh comments thus on the demise of faith:

> The vitality of men's belief in God is dying out in every land; nothing short of His wholesome medicine can ever restore it. The corrosion of ungodliness is eating into the vitals of human society; what else but the Elixir of His potent Revelation can cleanse and revive it?[460]

Therefore, in this paragraph, Bahá'u'lláh informs Napoleon III that He has come that 'He may quicken all created things . . . and unify the world'. 'Abdu'l-Bahá remarked in 1912 on the growing forces of irreligion:

> . . . alas, day by day the power of the Kingdom in human hearts is weakened, and material forces gain the ascendancy. The divine signs are becoming less and less, and human evidences grow stronger. They have reached such a degree that materialists are advancing and aggressive while divine forces are waning and vanishing. Irreligion has conquered religion.[461]

And Shoghi Effendi observes:

> That the forces of irreligion, of a purely materialistic philosophy, of unconcealed paganism have been unloosed, are now spreading, and, by consolidating themselves, are beginning to invade some of the most powerful Christian institutions of the western world, no unbiased observer can fail to admit . . . 'The world is in travail,' He has further written, 'and its agitation waxeth day by day. Its face is

> turned towards waywardness and unbelief. Such shall be its plight that to disclose it now would not be meet and seemly.'[462]

279. p. 46 ¶ 78. He Who is the Unconditioned is come, in the clouds of light

As depicted in the Psalms (147:5–6, 8), clouds provide rain and the water that satisfies thirsty souls: 'His understanding is infinite . . . Who covereth the heaven with clouds, Who prepareth rain for the earth.' Isaiah (45:8) in this vein stated: 'Drop down, ye heavens, from above, and let the skies pour down righteousness: let the earth open, and let them bring forth salvation, and let righteousness spring up together; I the Lord have created it.' Christ predicted (Matt. 24:30): 'they shall see the Son of man coming in the clouds of heaven with power and great glory.'

Divine light associated with God's new Revelation is one sense the phrase 'clouds of light' may be understood. In this context Bahá'u'lláh states:

> And whensoever the portals of grace did open, and the clouds of divine bounty did rain upon mankind, and the light of the Unseen did shine above the horizon of celestial might, they all denied Him, and turned away from His face – the face of God Himself. Refer ye, to verify this truth, to that which hath been recorded in every sacred Book.[463]

In another sense, bright light can also blind those who are used to darkness. Hence, the coming of a new Revelation can cloud understanding. Thus 'clouds of light' is also akin to 'veils of glory' (Annotation 365).

The 'Unconditioned' is a reference to Bahá'u'lláh Whose Revelation is not restricted by human understanding and what had been taught and understood in earlier Dispensations (Annotation 9).

See also Annotations 113, 498, 499, and 609.

280. p. 46 ¶ 78. gather all men around this Table which hath been sent down from heaven

The 'Table' refers to the banquet of God's Revelation. One of its functions today is to gather and unify humanity around divine principles, such as the oneness of God, the oneness of faith, and the oneness of man.

The Torah (Ex. 16:1–36) describes that 'manna', literally 'bread of heaven', rained down on the starving children of Israel as they wandered through the desert. Many of the Jews listening to Jesus believed that the manna was literally bread/food from the sky, but the use of the Hebrew word '*haš·šá·ma·yim*' – the heaven that also rains divine teachings – indicates that by 'manna' was meant the Children of Israel receiving their share of spiritual nourishment in the preceding Dispensation.

Christ, in the Gospel of John (6:58), also referred to His teachings as bread from heaven, 'This is that bread which came down from heaven: not as your fathers did eat manna, and are dead: he that eateth of this bread shall live for ever.' It is clear that Christ did not come down from the sky, nor did any loaves of bread descend on the disciples. His allusions to bread, and sometimes to Himself, coming down from heaven refer to His teachings that were necessary for the spiritual nourishment of His followers. Christ's promise of spiritual food is alluded to in the 5th Súrih of the Qur'án (5:112–115) entitled '*al-Má'idah*,' 'The Table' or 'the Table Spread'.

281. p. 46 ¶ 78. the breezes of forgiveness have been wafted from the direction of your Lord, the God of Mercy; whoso turneth thereunto, shall be cleansed of his sins, and of all pain and sickness

The followers of all religions who obey the precepts of their Faith have performed their spiritual duty. Those who do not follow the divine dictates are said to have sinned. In this context, through the mercy of God, recognition of Bahá'u'lláh, Whose Faith 'is at once, essence, the promise, the reconciler, and the unifier of all religions',[464] removes the shackles of tradition, dogma and imitation, revivifies and purifies the followers of earlier Dispensations of their sins of omission and commission, and relieves them of the spiritual pain of remoteness from their Lord. This is a promise in the New Testament:

> Behold, the tabernacle of God is with men, and he will dwell with them, and they shall be his people, and God himself shall be with them, and be their God. And God shall wipe away all tears from their eyes; and there shall be no more death, neither sorrow, nor crying, neither shall there be any more pain: for the former things are passed away. (Rev. 21:34)

282. p. 47 ¶ 80. Give ear, O King, unto the Voice

Bahá'u'lláh, the Voice of God, addressing Napoleon III.

283. p. 47 ¶ 80. the hallowed and snow-white Spot

In an allegorical sense this can be understood as a reference to the domain of the Manifestation of God, and the place of His Revelation. Bahá'u'lláh has also referred to the Holy Land as the 'snow-white spot' in which the Prophets of God have appeared and proclaimed their missions. More specifically it is a reference to 'Akká itself (see Annotation 648) where Bahá'u'lláh was residing when He revealed this Tablet to Napoleon III. Compare this related verse from another Tablet:

> This Holy Land hath been mentioned and extolled in all the sacred Scriptures. In it have appeared the Prophets of God and His chosen Ones. This is the wilderness in which all the Messengers of God have wandered, from which their cry, 'Here am I, here am I, O my God' was raised. This is the promised Land in which He Who is the Revelation of God was destined to be made manifest. This is the Vale of God's unsearchable decree, the snow-white Spot, the Land of unfading splendour.[465]

284. p. 47 ¶ 80. the Everlasting City

This seems to correspond with the use of 'city' as a location in the next world, as in 'city of eternity'.[466] However, the most characteristic symbolic use of 'city' is found in the *Kitáb-i-Íqán* where Bahá'u'lláh states that Prophet Ṣáliḥ, 'that eternal Beauty was summoning the people to no other than the city of God'.[467] He further declares:

> That city is none other than the Word of God revealed in every age and dispensation. In the days of Moses it was the Pentateuch; in the days of Jesus the Gospel; in the days of Muḥammad the Messenger of God the Qur'án; in this day the Bayán; and in the dispensation of Him Whom God will make manifest His own Book . . . In these cities spiritual sustenance is bountifully provided, and incorruptible delights have been ordained. The food they bestow is the bread of heaven, and the Spirit they impart is God's imperishable blessing.[468]

Also:

> All that existeth in this city shall indeed endure and will never perish. Shouldst thou, by the leave of God, enter this sublime and exalted garden, thou wouldst find its sun in its noontide glory, never to set, never to be eclipsed . . . Were I to recount, from this day unto the end that hath no end, its wondrous attributes, the love that My heart cherisheth for this hallowed and everlasting city would never be exhausted.[469]

285. p. 47 ¶ 80. We, in truth, have sent Him Whom We aided with the Holy Spirit (Jesus Christ) that He may announce unto you this Light that hath shone forth from the horizon of the will of your Lord

Bahá'u'lláh states that Jesus was sent to proclaim the good news of the Second Coming, that is His advent.

All the gospels describe the descent of the Holy Spirit on Christ at His baptism by John the Baptist (Matt. 3:16; Mark 1:10; Luke 3:21 and John 1:32). The Qur'án states that God strengthened Jesus with the Holy Spirit (2:87; 2:253 and 5:110).

Jesus gave the good news (Mark 13:26–27) that humanity will see the Son of Man coming in clouds with great power and glory. Notably, 'glory' (*doxēs* in Greek) also means brightness of light as in Acts 22:11. Christ emphasized that only those of His followers who did the Will of the Father at the Second Coming would enter heaven (Matt. 7:21; 12:50).

286. p. 47 ¶ 80. Whose signs have been revealed in the West

Two thousand years ago three Magi, Persian Zoroastrian priests known as *majus*, travelled from Persia westward to Bethlehem because they had seen the sign of Christ (Matt. 2:1–2), represented by a star, in the East. The Prophet Ezekiel was transported in a vision to the land of Israel and to a high mountain (40:2). From this vantage point he saw (43:2): 'the glory of the God of Israel came from the way of the east: and his voice was like a noise of many waters, and the earth shined with his glory.' In the Gospel of Matthew, Jesus (24:27) explains that He will come again from the East (of the Holy Land) but that God's Light will then shine to the West. The Light of the Báb and Bahá'u'lláh arose in Persia, which is to the East of where Jesus was. It has, however, illuminated the West with lightning speed, and indeed has now spread to virtually all parts of the world.

In this connection Bahá'u'lláh wrote: 'Say: In the East the light of His Revelation hath broken; in the West the signs of His dominion have appeared.'[470] 'Abdu'l-Bahá wrote:

> It is stated in certain prophecies that when the standard of God appears in the East, its signs will become evident in the West. This is truly good news . . . I hope that this promise may be fulfilled in you . . . saying, 'Verily, the standard of God did appear in the East, and its tokens have become resplendent in the West.' This realization will be a source of great joy to all the friends in the Orient who anticipate the good news and await the glad tidings from the land of the Occident. They look forward to hearing that the friends in the West have become firm and steadfast, that they have distinguished themselves by establishing the oneness of the world of humanity . . .[471]

Again,

> . . . it was the Love of God that gave to the East Bahá'u'lláh, and is now sending the light of His teaching far into the West, and from Pole to Pole.[472]

287. p. 48 ¶ 81. 'He, verily, is the Face of God amongst you, and His Testimony and His Guide unto you. He hath come to you with signs which none can produce.' The voice of the Burning Bush

is raised in the midmost heart of the world, and the Holy Spirit calleth aloud among the nations: 'Lo, the Desired One is come with manifest dominion!'

See Annotations 260 and 510.

288. p. 48 ¶ 82. The stars of the heaven of knowledge have fallen

One of the signs of the Second Coming is the falling of stars from heaven. Bahá'u'lláh explains the meaning of this allegory:

> O people of God! Righteous men of learning who dedicate themselves to the guidance of others and are freed and well-guarded from the promptings of a base and covetous nature are, in the sight of Him Who is the Desire of the world, stars of the heaven of true knowledge.[473]

> O concourse of bishops! Ye are the stars of the heaven of My knowledge. My mercy desireth not that ye should fall.[474]

Stars denote leaders of the community. For example, in one of his dreams, Joseph (Gen. 37:9) sees his brothers (later the heads of tribes of Israel) as eleven stars. The Magi saw the star of Christ (Matt. 2:1–2). Also, in Biblical times the caravans relied on the stars to lead them safely through the treacherous deserts. Using this allegory, Daniel (12:2–3) states: 'And many of them that sleep in the dust of the earth shall awake, some to everlasting life, and some to shame and everlasting contempt. And they that are wise shall shine as the brightness of the firmament; and they that turn the many to righteousness as the stars for ever and ever.'

The Bible additionally warns of a time when the 'stars' of the religious communities will fail to guide their flock; their light will be obscured; they will fall from grace; and their light will not be visible in the bright day of God's new Revelation. Thus, Joel predicts that 'the stars shall withdraw their shining', that is, lose their luminosity (2:10; 3:15). The Prophet Isaiah predicted (34:4): 'the heavens shall be rolled together as a scroll: and all their host [stars] shall fall down, as the leaf falleth off from the vine, and as a falling fig from the fig tree.' This concept is consistent with the description of a fallen angel (Is.14:12): 'How art thou fallen from heaven, O Lucifer [day-star], son of the morning! how art thou cut down to the ground . . .!'

Christ (Matt. 24:29) spoke of the falling of the stars as one of the signs of the Second Coming: 'the stars shall fall from heaven, and the powers of the heavens shall be shaken.' We also read in Revelation (6:13–14): 'And the stars of heaven fell unto the earth, even as a fig tree casteth her untimely figs, when she is shaken of a mighty wind.'

The event cannot refer literally to the falling on earth of the innumerable stars, all of which are many times larger than our planet, as no one would be left on earth to receive the new Revelation!

> In another sense, by these terms [stars] is intended the divines of the former Dispensation, who live in the days of the subsequent Revelations, and who hold the reins of religion in their grasp. If these divines be illumined by the light of the latter Revelation they will be acceptable unto God, and will shine with a light everlasting. Otherwise, they will be declared as darkened, even though to outward seeming they be leaders of men, inasmuch as belief and unbelief, guidance and error, felicity and misery, light and darkness, are all dependent upon the sanction of Him Who is the Day-star of Truth.[475]

Bahá'u'lláh lovingly exhorts:

> O friends! Be not careless of the virtues with which ye have been endowed, neither be neglectful of your high destiny. Suffer not your labors to be wasted through the vain imaginations which certain hearts have devised. Ye are the stars of the heaven of understanding, the breeze that stirred at the break of day, the soft-flowing waters upon which must depend the very life of all men, the letters inscribed upon His sacred scroll.[476]

He addresses the learned of His Dispensation in the same language:

> Happy are ye, O ye the learned ones in Bahá [Glory]. By the Lord! Ye are the billows of the Most Mighty Ocean, the stars of the firmament of Glory, the standards of triumph waving betwixt earth and

> heaven. Ye are the manifestations of steadfastness amidst men and the daysprings of Divine Utterance to all that dwell on earth.[477]

289. p. 48 ¶ 82. who make mention of God in My Name. And yet, when I came unto them in My glory, they turned aside. They, indeed, are of the fallen

Compare: 'Some have known God and remember Him; others remember Him, yet know Him not' (¶ 79). As discussed in the previous annotation, 'They . . . are of the fallen' means the religious leaders, 'the stars of the heaven of knowledge', who have fallen from grace.

Bahá'u'lláh, as the promised Christ in the Glory of the Father, also admonishes the heedless Christians:

> O Concourse of Christians! We have, on a previous occasion, revealed Ourself [Muhammad and/or the Báb] as unto you, and ye recognized Me not. This is yet another occasion vouchsafed unto you. This is the Day of God; turn ye unto Him . . . Ye make mention of Me, and know Me not. Ye call upon Me, and are heedless of My Revelation . . .[478]

290. 48 ¶ 82. This is, truly, that which the Spirit of God (Jesus Christ) hath announced, when He came with truth unto you

Bahá'u'lláh categorically explains that He is the good news that Christ promised and instructed His disciples to announce to the world.

Christ referred to the Comforter and the Spirit of Truth who would come in the future (John 14:17; 15:26; 16:7, 13): 'Howbeit when he, the Spirit of truth, is come, he will guide you into all truth.' Since God is the Truth, in a sense, the 'Spirit of truth' may be seen as equivalent to the 'Spirit of God'. The Apostle Peter reminded the Jews of the prophecy of the Prophet Joel (Acts 2:17): 'And it shall come to pass in the last days, saith God, I will pour out of my Spirit upon all flesh.'

291. p. 49 ¶ 83. O concourse of monks! Seclude not yourselves in your churches and cloisters . . . Seclude yourselves in the stronghold of My love. This, truly, is the seclusion that befitteth you

Monasticism was a prominent feature of Catholicism in France. Hence, in His Tablet to Napoleon III, Bahá'u'lláh includes an address to the monks.

Monasticism is an ascetic and cloistered life dedicated to worship. The Jewish sects of the Essenes and the Therapeutae practised asceticism. This belief is in contrast to several Biblical verses which encourage individuals to enjoy the bounties that God has provided, for example, Eccles. 5:18–19:

> Behold that which I have seen: it is good and comely for one to eat and to drink, and to enjoy the good of all his labour that he taketh under the sun all the days of his life, which God giveth him: for it is his portion.
>
> Every man also to whom God hath given riches and wealth, and hath given him power to eat thereof, and to take his portion, and to rejoice in his labour; this is the gift of God.

For early Christians, monasticism derived its inspiration from the example of John the Baptist who lived an ascetic life and (Luke 1:80): 'was in the deserts till the day of his shewing unto Israel', and also from Jesus's call to his disciples (Mark 10:21) to emulate His life of sacrifice and service and to follow Him.

The Qur'án (9:31) laments: 'They take their priests and their anchorites [monks, religious leaders and scholars] to be their lords in derogation of God . . .'

Bahá'u'lláh states:

> Living in seclusion or practising asceticism is not acceptable in the presence of God. It behoveth them that are endued with insight and understanding to observe that which will cause joy and radiance. Such practices as are sprung from the loins of idle fancy or are begotten of the womb of superstition ill beseem men of knowledge. In former times . . . some people have been taking up their abodes in the caves of the mountains while others have repaired to

> graveyards at night. Say, give ear unto the counsels of this Wronged One. Abandon the things current amongst you and adopt that which the faithful Counsellor biddeth you. Deprive not yourselves of the bounties which have been created for your sake.[479]

One may also question the value of lifelong piety if it does not lead to the recognition of Christ and Bahá'u'lláh:

> How numerous the Pharisees who had secluded themselves in synagogues in His name, lamenting over their separation from Him, and yet when the portals of reunion were flung open and the divine Luminary shone resplendent from the Dayspring of Beauty, they disbelieved in God, the Exalted, the Mighty . . .
>
> . . . how numerous . . . are the monks who have secluded themselves in their churches, calling upon the Spirit, but when He appeared through the power of Truth, [see John 16:12–13] they failed to draw nigh unto Him and are numbered with those that have gone far astray.[480]

It is more valuable for them to abandon fruitless self-mortification and follow the divine dictates for today:

> Say: O concourse of priests and monks! Eat ye of that which God hath made lawful unto you and do not shun meat . . . He Who is your Lord, the All-Merciful, cherisheth in His heart the desire of beholding the entire human race as one soul and one body. Haste ye to win your share of God's good grace and mercy in this Day that eclipseth all other created Days. How great the felicity that awaiteth the man that forsaketh all he hath in a desire to obtain the things of God! Such a man, We testify, is among God's blessed ones.[481]

> O concourse of monks! If ye choose to follow Me, I will make you heirs of My Kingdom; and if ye transgress against Me, I will, in My long-suffering, endure it patiently, and I, verily, am the Ever-Forgiving, the All-Merciful.[482]

292. p. 49 ¶ 83. Enter ye into wedlock, that after you another may arise in your stead

The purpose of man is to know God and to worship Him. This ability is enriched in marriage which also provides the opportunity of bringing others into the world who will in their turn recognize Bahá'u'lláh and testify to the truth of His Revelation.

293. p. 49 ¶ 83. We, verily, have forbidden you lechery, and not that which is conducive to fidelity

The New Testament forbids lewd and lustful behaviour. A chaste and holy life is also prescribed in the Bahá'í Writings. Bahá'u'lláh indicates here that marriage allows the couple to demonstrate the spiritual virtue of fidelity through their physical life together. We are reminded of this admonishment by the recent reports of widespread sexual abuse and paedophilia, which could certainly be defined as lechery, amongst unmarried Catholic clergymen.

294. p. 49 ¶ 83. He that married not (Jesus Christ) could find no place wherein to abide, nor where to lay His head, by reason of what the hands of the treacherous had wrought

Jesus embraced a life of poverty. He lived in meagre circumstances and not in royal palaces. The fact is that during His relatively brief and turbulent ministry He did not have a fixed abode with which to establish domestic life (Luke 9:57–58):

> . . . as they went in the way, a certain man said unto him, Lord, I will follow thee whithersoever thou goest.
>
> And Jesus said unto him, Foxes have holes, and birds of the air have nests; but the Son of man hath not where to lay his head.

Christ's nomadic existence, fraught with danger and uncertainty, was also imposed on him by the authorities that were intent on taking His life.

295. p. 50 ¶ 84. O King! We heard the words thou didst utter

Here Bahá'u'lláh includes sections of His first Tablet addressed to Napoleon III, revealed in Adrianople between 1866 and 1867.

See also Annotations 270 and 321.

296. p. 50 ¶ 84. Czar of Russia

This refers to Czar Alexander II (1818–1881), who was Emperor of Russia from 1855 to 1881. He succeeded to the throne at the height of the Crimean War. He introduced certain domestic reforms, the most important being the emancipation of serfs (1861). However, he firmly upheld autocratic principles, and was sincerely convinced both of his duty to maintain the God-given autocratic power he had inherited and his duty to resist constitutional reform. His regime after 1862 reacted with increasingly repressive measures to revolutionary movements. An attempted assassination in 1866 led to a further increase in repressive measures and a resurgence of revolutionary terrorism. The Czar was mortally wounded by bombs on 1 March 1881.

See also Annotation 319.

297. p. 50 ¶ 84. the war

Several countries were involved in the build-up to the Crimean War (1853–1856): the Ottoman Empire ruled by Sulṭán 'Abdu'l-Majid I (1823–1861); France under Napoleon III; Russia under Czar Nicholas I; Britain under Queen Victoria; and Austria under Emperor Franz Joseph I. Russia had ambitions to expand westward and Turkey stood in the way.

In 1850, Napoleon III, who boasted that he was the protector of the downtrodden, had decided to champion the cause of the Catholics as a pretext to control the Christian holy places, over which there was a dispute with the Russian Orthodox Church. He pretended to be a good Catholic and his demands on behalf of the Catholic Church allowed him to divert attention from problems in France.

Russia's right to protect Orthodox Christians was the immediate issue that caused the Crimean War. When Russia destroyed the Turkish Fleet in the Black Sea in November 1853, France and Britain sent warships into the Black Sea and joined the war against Russia in 1854. The war concluded with the signing of the Treaty of Paris in 1856.

298. p. 50 ¶ 84. thou wouldst have not cast behind thy back the Book of God, when it was sent unto thee by Him

As previously mentioned (Annotation 270) Bahá'u'lláh sent two Tablets to Napoleon III. The first was from Adrianople, between 1866 and 1867, which Napoleon received 'with discourtesy and disrespect. He is reported to have flung down the Tablet saying "If this man is God, I am two gods!"'[483] Bahá'u'lláh wrote His second Tablet to Napoleon III from 'Akká in 1869, rebuking him for his insincerity, lust for war and the contempt with which he had treated His first Tablet.

299. p. 51 ¶ 85. For what thou hast done, thy kingdom shall be thrown into confusion, and thine empire shall pass from thine hands, as a punishment for that which thou hast wrought

Bahá'u'lláh in His second Tablet to Napoleon III sternly warns the French Emperor of the divine retribution that awaited him. This arraignment of Napoleon III was published and spread. A year later, in July 1870, Napoleon entered the Franco-Prussian (German) War without allies and with inferior military forces. The French army was rapidly defeated and Napoleon III was captured at the Battle of Sedan. He was deposed two days later and the Third Republic was proclaimed in Paris. Napoleon went into exile in England, where he died in 1873. His only son was killed in 1879, fighting in the British Army during the Zulu War.

300. p. 51 ¶ 85. unless thou arisest to help this Cause

Here Bahá'u'lláh warns Napoleon III that his salvation depended on arising to support God's Faith.

301. 51 ¶ 85. and followest Him Who is the Spirit of God

Ruḥulláh is an Arabic name which means 'the Spirit of God', a reference to Jesus Christ. As the return of Christ, Bahá'u'lláh is also the Spirit of God. Napoleon III is being admonished to follow in the footsteps of

Christ, and when he hears His Voice 'calling from the seat of glory to cast away all that thou possessest, and cry out: "Here am I, O Lord of all that is in heaven and all that is on earth!"' (¶ 85).

When God called Abraham (just prior to being ordered to sacrifice his son), his immediate response was (Gen 22:1): 'Behold, here I am', demonstrating his devotion to God and his readiness to comply with the divine decree. Again, when Moses was addressed by God 'from with the [burning] bush, "Moses! Moses!"', his response to the divine summons was 'here I am' (Ex. 3:4). Here, the Emperor is being asked to show the same spirit of sacrifice and to respond to God's summons.

302. p. 51 ¶ 85. the Straight Path

The 'Straight Path' is mentioned several times in the Epistle: ¶ 124, 130, 154, 160, 169, 203 and 236. It is also referred to in Bahá'u'lláh's *Seven Valleys* and in the *Tablets of the Divine Plan* by 'Abdu'l-Bahá.

In Proverbs (4:11) God states: 'I have taught thee in the way of wisdom; I have led thee in right paths [New International Version: 'straight paths'].' Isaiah (40:2–5; 42:16) promised future divine paths and guidance – God will make 'crooked things straight'. Moses prayed (Ex. 33:13): 'shew me now thy way, that I may know thee . . .' The Psalmist also prayed (25:4–5): 'Shew me thy ways, O Lord; teach me thy paths. Lead me in thy truth, and teach me: for thou art the God of my salvation; on thee do I wait all the day.' In the sermon on the Mount (Matt. 7:14) Jesus warned that 'strait is the gate, and narrow is the way, which leadeth unto life, and few there be that find it'.

The invocation 'guide us to the straight path' (*ihdiná alṣṣiráṭa almustaqeema*) appears in the first Súrih of the Qur'án, *al-Fátiḥah* (1:6). This was revealed initially in Mecca, and subsequently re-revealed in Medina. It is part of a prayer that Muslims are required to repeat five times daily. They are thereby reminded not only to pursue God's good pleasure in their lifetime, but also to anticipate the Path of God and His Guidance. They are to pursue (1:7) 'the way on whom Thou hast bestowed Thy Grace. Those whose portion is not wrath, and who go not astray.' The Qur'án (41:30) promises that individuals who heed the admonition to follow the Straight Path (*fástaqímú*), i.e. 'be straightforward', shall be rewarded. However, divine guidance and access to God's paths is contingent in the Qur'án (29:69) on Muslims making a sincere effort to investigate the truth free of preconceived notions and imitation. Ultimately, (2:212–213): 'God bestows His abundance without measure on whom He will . . . God guides whom He will to a path that is straight.' There is therefore no need to compel anyone to accept Islam (2:256).

In Bahá'u'lláh's Writings, the Straight Path is also synonymous with the Divine Word: 'He hath clearly set forth His Straight Path in words and utterances of highest eloquence.'[484]

> The episode of Sinai hath been re-enacted in this Revelation and He Who conversed upon the Mount is calling aloud: Verily, the Desired One is come, seated upon the throne of certitude, could ye but perceive it. He hath admonished all men to observe that which is conducive to the exaltation of the Cause of God and will guide mankind unto His Straight Path.[485]

> We have revealed Ourself unto men, have unveiled the Cause, guided all mankind towards God's Straight Path, promulgated the laws and have enjoined upon everyone that which shall truly profit them both in this world and in the next.[486]

> We have truly revealed the signs, demonstrated the irrefutable testimonies and have summoned all men unto the Straight Path. Among the people there are those who have turned away and repudiated the truth, others have pronounced judgement against Us without any proof or evidence. The first to turn away from Us have been the world's spiritual leaders in this age – they that call upon Us in the daytime and in the night season . . .[487]

The Báb declared that He was the Straight Path, a path that leads to the recognition of Bahá'u'lláh:

> . . . this Path from 'Alí [the Báb] is none but the Straight Path in the estimation of your Lord.[488]

> Verily God hath revealed unto Me that the Path of the Remembrance which is set forth by Me is, in very truth, the Straight Path of God . . .[489]

Today Bahá'u'lláh is the Straight Path:

> He hath clearly set forth His straight Path in words and utterances of highest eloquence.[490]

> I am the guiding Light that illumineth the way.[491]

> This is a Book which hath become the Lamp of the Eternal unto the world, and His straight, undeviating Path amidst the peoples of the earth. Say: This is the Dayspring of Divine knowledge . . .[492]

> My Forerunner (the Báb), Who laid down His life for this Great Announcement, this Straight Path (¶ 204).

The declaration of the oneness of God is the Straight Path:

> I beg of Thee, O my God, by Thy power, and Thy might, and Thy sovereignty, which have embraced all who are in Thy heaven and on Thy earth, to make known unto Thy servants this luminous Way and this straight Path, that they may acknowledge Thy unity and Thy oneness . . .[493]

The declaration of the oneness of Faith (oneness of the ways of God) is also the Straight Path:

> Thus doth the Lord make plain the ways of truth and guidance, ways that lead to one way, which is this Straight Path. Render thanks unto God for this most gracious favour; offer praise unto Him for this bounty that hath encompassed the heavens and the earth; extol Him for this mercy that hath pervaded all creation.[494]

Hence, every Divine Prophet is the Way of God, and His Revelation guides humanity along the same Straight Path of truth, 'They Who are the Dawning-Places of Revelation and the Manifestations of the Cause of thy Lord, the Most Merciful, Who have sacrificed Their souls and all that They possessed in His Straight Path.'[495] Again: 'The Prophets and Messengers of God have been sent down for the sole purpose of guiding mankind to the straight Path of Truth.'[496]

303. p. 51 ¶ 86. O King! We were in 'Iráq, when the hour of parting arrived

In the words of Shoghi Effendi:

> It was on the fifth of Naw-Rúz (1863), while Bahá'u'lláh was celebrating that festival in the Mazra'iy-i-Vashsháash, in the outskirts of Baghdád, and had just revealed the 'Tablet of the Holy Mariner,' whose gloomy prognostications had aroused the grave apprehensions of His Companions, that an emissary of Námiq Páshá arrived and delivered into His hands a communication requesting an interview between Him and the governor.
>
> . . . Twenty-seven days after that mournful Tablet had been so unexpectedly revealed by Bahá'u'lláh, and the fateful communication, presaging His departure to Constantinople had been delivered into His hands, on a Wednesday afternoon (April 22, 1863), thirty-one days after Naw-Rúz, on the third of Dhi'l-Qa'dih, 1279 AH, He set forth on the first stage of His four months' journey to the capital of the Ottoman Empire.[497]

304. p. 51 ¶ 86. the King of Islám (Sulṭán of Turkey)

Sulṭán 'Abdu'l-'Azíz was the 32nd Sultan of the Ottoman Empire and the 111th Caliph of the Sunni Muslim community who, together with Náṣiri'd-Dín Sháh, was the author of the calamities heaped upon Bahá'u'lláh. He succeeded his brother 'Abdu'l-Majid I and ruled from 1861 to 1876. He attempted to introduce reforms with the help of two powerful chief ministers, Fu'ád Pashá and 'Ali Pashá.[498]

He was headstrong, wilful and autocratic. By 1871 his ally, France, was defeated by Germany and he turned to Russia for friendship. However, Russia's encouragement of insurrection in Bosnia and Herzegovina and Bulgaria caused ill-feeling against the Sultan's new ally. Public discontent was also heightened by a severe crop failure, and the lavish expenditures and mounting public debt of 'Abdu'l-'Azíz. He was deposed by his ministers in 1876.

305. p. 52 ¶ 87. they took Us forth from Our prison

Shoghi Effendi writes:

> On the morning of the 2nd of Jamádíyu'l-Avval 1285 AH (August 21, 1868) they all embarked in an Austrian-Lloyd steamer for Alexandria, touching at Madellí, and stopping for two days at Smyrna, where Jináb-i-Munír, surnamed Ismu'lláhu'l-Muníb, became gravely ill, and had, to his great distress, to be left behind in a hospital where he soon after died. In Alexandria they transshipped into a steamer of the same company, bound for Haifa, where they disembarked, in the course of the afternoon of the 12th of Jamádíyu'l-Avval 1285 AH (August 31, 1868). It was at the moment when Bahá'u'lláh had stepped into the boat which was to carry Him to the landing-stage in Haifa that 'Abdu'l-Ghaffár, one of the four companions condemned to share the exile of Mírzá Yaḥyá, and whose 'detachment, love and trust in God' Bahá'u'lláh had greatly praised, cast himself, in his despair, into the sea, shouting 'Yá Bahá'u'l-Abhá,' and was subsequently rescued and resuscitated with the greatest difficulty, only to be forced by adamant officials to continue his voyage, with Mírzá Yaḥyá's party, to the destination originally appointed for him.[499]

306. p. 52 ¶ 87. and made Us . . . enter the Most Great Prison

Shoghi Effendi writes:

> [Bahá'u'lláh's] arrival at the penal colony of 'Akká, far from proving the end of His afflictions, was but the beginning of a major crisis, characterized by bitter suffering, severe restrictions, and intense turmoil, which, in its gravity, surpassed even the agonies of the Síyáh-Chál of Ṭihrán, and to which no other event, in the history of the entire century can compare, except the internal convulsion that rocked the Faith in Adrianople. 'Know thou,' Bahá'u'lláh, wishing to emphasize the criticalness of the first nine years of His banishment to that prison-city, has written, 'that upon Our arrival at this Spot, We chose to designate it as the "Most Great Prison." Though

> previously subjected in another land (Ṭihrán) to chains and fetters, We yet refused to call it by that name. Say: Ponder thereon, O ye endued with understanding!'[500]

See also Annotation 227.

307. p. 52 ¶ 87. And if anyone ask them: 'For what crime were they imprisoned?' they would answer and say: 'They, verily, sought to supplant the Faith with a new religion!'

'They' refers to Bahá'u'lláh and His companions. Bahá'u'lláh alludes to the fact that Napoleon III will be held responsible for his failure to enquire about their incarceration – it will not be enough for him to say in the next world that he failed to investigate the new Faith because it had come in the guise of a new religion.

The passage echoes the question that the Qur'án (81:8) states will be asked of the Arabs as to why they killed their innocent female daughters by burying them alive.

308. p. 52 ¶ 87. If that which is ancient be what ye prefer, wherefore, then, have ye discarded that which hath been set down in the Torah and the Evangel?

Bahá'u'lláh points out an incongruence to Napoleon III: his desire not to accept the new Revelation and to adhere to the old Dispensation of Christianity necessarily means that he rejects the prophecies of the Bible that give the glad-tidings of His Dispensation.

309. p. 52 ¶ 87. Torah

The Torah (Instruction, Teaching or Law) consists of the first five books (the Pentateuch) of a total of 24 books of the Tanakh (also referred to as the Hebrew Bible, or the Old Testament by Christians). The Torah contains the law given to Moses, and is a comprehensive set of guidelines that originated about 3,400 years ago. Its purpose was to ensure the welfare of the Jewish people and to have their behaviour reflect their favoured status as Yahweh's (also written as Jehovah: both are Hebrew names for God) chosen people. These themes are confirmed and amplified in the other two parts of the Tanakh, namely, Nevi'im (Prophets) and Ketuvim (Writings).

310. p. 52 ¶ 87. Evangel

'Evangel' is a term used in the Qur'án for 'Gospel'. It is derived from the Greek *euangelion* which means the good news. Christians of all denominations have now recalled the glad-tidings of the Second Coming every Sunday, and on other occasions, for the past two thousand years. Christ's last instruction to His disciples (Mark 16:15) was that they should disperse far and wide and proclaim this glad-tidings or gospel to all humanity. Later the good news was couched in the language of Church dogma as, for instance, referring to the 'salvation' claimed to have been brought solely by Jesus.

Notably, in the Qur'án (11:2) Muhammad is also described as *Mubasher* or 'the Bearer of Good Tidings' of God's salvation and future Revelations.

311. pp. 52–53 ¶ 88. all that befell Me from the hosts of the wayward was powerless to deter Me from My purpose. Should they hide Me away in the depths of the earth, yet would they find Me riding aloft on the clouds, and calling out unto God, the Lord of strength and of might

The Prophet Daniel describes that in a vision he saw: (7:13): 'one like the Son of man came with the clouds of heaven, and came to the Ancient of days, and they brought him near before him.' The New Testament promises (Matt. 26:64): 'Hereafter shall ye see the Son of man sitting on the right hand of power, and coming in the clouds of heaven'; (Matt. 24:30; Mark 13:26): 'they shall see the Son of man coming in the clouds of heaven with power and great glory'; and (Rev. 1:7) 'Behold, he cometh with clouds; and every eye shall see him.'

See also Annotations 113, 279, 498 and 499.

312. p. 53 ¶ 89. Beware that ye allow not wolves to become the shepherds of the fold

The Bible differentiates between false shepherds and the true Shepherd. Notably, a title of God in the Bible is the 'Shepherd' (Ps. 23:1). The Messiah is also the loving and caring shepherd of the flock (Is. 40:11): 'He shall feed his flock like a shepherd: he shall gather the lambs with his arm, and carry them in his bosom, and shall gently lead those that are with young.'

The New Testament (I Peter 5:4) anticipates the advent of the Chief Shepherd when humanity 'will receive the crown of glory that will never fade away'. Christ explains that the Shepherd will unite the different religions at the Second Coming (John 10:16): 'And other sheep I have, which are not of this fold: them also I must bring, and they shall hear my voice; and there shall be one fold, and one shepherd.'

In contrast, the Prophet Jeremiah (50:6) speaks of shepherds who have caused the sheep to go astray. The Prophet Ezekiel (34:1–10) spoke of predatory shepherds – instead of feeding the sheep they feed on the flock. God promises to deliver His 'sheep from their mouth, that they may not be food for them'. Christ (Matt. 7:15) castigated false prophets as 'wolves' in the Bible. Today, many false teachers, disguised in the familiar outward trappings of the Church, live off the flock that they claim to shepherd. Their sermons and teachings do not address the real concerns of humanity. Rather than eliminating sectarianism and promoting unity of faith, they stoke division and foster belief in the exclusivity and finality of their own particular denominational belief system.

313. pp. 53–54 ¶ 90. arise, then, to teach My Cause. Better is this for thee than that which thou possessest. God will, thereby, exalt thy name among all the kings

Bahá'u'lláh shares with the Shaykh His Words of admonishment addressed to Napoleon III explaining that his salvation lay in promoting the divine Cause. By implication, this would also be the remedy for the Shaykh's spiritual affliction. The process of teaching transforms the individual as 'ere he proclaimeth His Message', he must 'adorn himself with the ornament of an upright and praiseworthy character, so that his words may attract the hearts of such as are receptive to his call. Without it, he can never hope to influence his hearers.'[501]

See also ¶ 84.

314. p. 54 ¶ 91. Verily, the thing that deterreth you, in this day, from God is worldliness in its essence. Eschew it, and approach the Most Sublime Vision, this shining and resplendent Seat

Bahá'u'lláh admonishes Napoleon III that, despite his pretence of piety and concern for the Catholic Church, his motivation and the cause of his heedlessness is his attachment to the material world.

315. p. 56 ¶ 93. the most desolate of cities ('Akká)

See Annotation 227.

316. p. 56 ¶ 93. the whole world . . . is worth as much as the black in the eye of a dead ant

All His life Bahá'u'lláh cared very little for the vanities of the world:

> Had the world been of any worth in His sight, He surely would never have allowed His enemies to possess it, even to the extent of a grain of mustard seed.[502]

The Bible (I John 2:15–17) makes a similar statement: 'Love not the world, neither the things that are in the world. If any man love the world, the love of the Father is not in him. For all that is in the world, the lust of the flesh, and the lust of the eyes, and the pride of life, is not of the Father, but is of the world. And the world passeth away, and the lust thereof: but he that doeth the will of God abideth for ever.' In much the same way, the Qur'án teaches (6:32): 'What is the life of this world but play and amusement? But best is the home in the hereafter, for those who are righteous. Will ye not then understand?'

317. p. 56 ¶ 94. We bade a Christian dispatch this Tablet, and he informed Us that he transmitted both the original and its translation

The second Tablet of Bahá'u'lláh to Napoleon III, revealed in 1869, was spirited out of the prison barracks in the lining of a hat worn by a Bahá'í pilgrim. It was dispatched by a Christian Arab, Louis Ketfagou (Catafago), French consular agent in 'Akká and Haifa at that time, who first translated it into French. His son became a Bahá'í after seeing the fulfilment of Bahá'u'lláh's prophecies regarding Napoleon come true.[503]

See also Annotation 271.

318. p. 56 ¶ 96. Czar of Russia

Czar Alexander II was the recipient of a Tablet from Bahá'u'lláh, part of which is incorporated here.

See also Annotation 296.

319. p. 56 ¶ 96. Beware that nothing deter thee from setting thy face towards thy Lord, the Compassionate, the Most Merciful

Many impediments prevented the autocratic Czar from recognizing the Revelation of the Prisoner of 'Akká, including the trappings of earthly power, exalted rank and immense fortune; the outdated teachings, rites and rituals of the Russian Orthodox Church; and an arrogant aristocracy that ignored the plight of the peasants. Nevertheless, as a devout Christian, Czar Alexander II should have been aware of the Biblical warnings that Christians would face hindrances at the Second Coming which would deter many from recognizing their Lord:

> Not every one that saith unto me, Lord, Lord, shall enter into the kingdom of heaven; but he that doeth the will of my Father which is in heaven.
>
> Many will say to me in that day, Lord, Lord, have we not prophesied in thy name? and in thy name have cast out devils? and in thy name done many wonderful works?
>
> And then will I profess unto them, I never knew you: depart from me, ye that work iniquity. (Matt. 7:21–23)

Many would be preoccupied with false beliefs and dishonest endeavours:

> Now the Spirit speaketh expressly, that in the latter times some shall depart from the faith, giving heed to seducing spirits, and doctrines of devils;
>
> Speaking lies in hypocrisy; having their conscience seared with a hot iron. (I Tim. 4:1–2)

> For the time will come when they will not endure sound doctrine; but after their own lusts shall they heap to themselves teachers, having itching ears;
>
> And they shall turn away their ears from the truth, and shall be turned unto fables. (II Tim. 4:3–4)

God's Faith would be treated disdainfully and ridiculed:

> . . . there shall come in the last days scoffers, walking after their own lusts,
>
> And saying, Where is the promise of his coming? . . .
>
> But the day of the Lord will come as a thief in the night . . . (II Peter 3:3, 4, 10)

Only those free from spiritual contamination would perceive the truth:

> Blessed are the pure in heart: for they shall see God. (Matt. 5:8)

Only those who truly waiting for the Lord would deserve His blessing:

> Blessed are those servants, whom the lord when he cometh shall find watching . . .
>
> Be ye therefore ready also: for the Son of man cometh at an hour when ye think not. (Luke 12:37, 40)

The Psalmist prays: 'Hold up my goings in thy paths, that my footsteps slip not (Ps. 17:5). The Apostle Paul warned (Rom. 12:21): 'Be not overcome of evil, but overcome evil with good.' Only those who are not deterred by the stumbling blocks will be rewarded by recognizing the Promised Day:

> To him that overcometh will I give to eat of the tree of life, which is in the midst of the paradise of God. (Rev. 2:7)

> To him that overcometh will I give to eat of the hidden manna, and will give him a white stone, and in the stone a new name written, which no man knoweth saving he that receiveth it. (Rev. 2:17)

> Him that overcometh will I make a pillar in the temple of my God . . . I will write upon him the name of my God, and the name of the city of my God, which is new Jerusalem, which cometh down out of heaven from my God: and I will write upon him my new name. (Rev. 3:12)

Christ had also warned that His followers should judge a tree by its fruits rather than by its foliage, bark or flowers (Matt. 7:16–20).

320. p. 57 ¶ 96. turn thou unto Paradise, the Spot wherein abideth He Who, among the Concourse on high, beareth the most excellent titles

In other words, Bahá'u'lláh, incarcerated in 'Akká.

321. p. 57 ¶ 96. We, verily, have heard the thing for which thou didst supplicate thy Lord, whilst secretly communing with Him

The following account regarding the Czar's supplication was related by Áqá Muḥammad-Raḥím, a native of Isfahan, who was an accomplished teacher of the Faith as well as a writer. He visited 'Akká twice during the lifetime of Bahá'u'lláh and attained His presence. Before going on his first pilgrimage he had a meeting at the invitation of a Russian Consul in Esterábád, who had read the Tablet and asked him the meaning of the above verse. Adib Taherzadeh's translation of his account is as follows:

> I did not know what to answer, so I said, 'God knows that.' 'That is obvious,' he said, 'but how do you interpret this passage?' I meditated for a little while on the subject and came to the conclusion that kings don't ask anything from God except victory in their conquests and defeat for their enemies . . . To reverse the situation after

Russia's defeat in the Crimean War, the Czar had prayed to God to make him victorious in his fight against the Ottomans and to enable him to conquer their cities. I conveyed all these thoughts to the Consul and suggested that he ought to write a letter to the Czar and inform him that his prayers would be answered and that he should carry out his plans and intentions.

After a few days he paid my travelling expenses and I returned home. But in my heart I was apprehensive lest my interpretation of the Tablet might have been incorrect. I was worried about this subject. Fear and hope dwelt together in my heart until I travelled to 'Akká and arrived at the Caravanserai. It did not take very long before Mírzá Áqá Ján [Bahá'u'lláh's amanuensis] came to see me. Among other things he asked me: 'What things did you say to the Russian Consul?' I remained silent and became apprehensive . . .

The following morning, the Most Great Branch ['Abdu'l-Bahá] came. I felt obliged to tell Him the whole story exactly as it had happened and I confessed to the mistake I had made in my statement. 'Abdu'l-Bahá said to me, 'Be happy and relieved, for the statement you have made was the truth, because on a certain day the Blessed Beauty intimated that at that very moment someone was reading the Tablet of the Czar. Then Bahá'u'lláh mentioned you. He said, "The Russian Consul asked one of Our servants: 'What was the prayer of the King?' The answer he received was a correct one." Then He revealed your name, saying, "That person was Áqá Muḥammad-Raḥím-i-Iṣfáhání."' I thanked God for this and was very happy to hear it.[504]

Taherzadeh comments:

These thoughts of Áqá Muḥammad-Raḥím, conveyed to the Russian Consul, refer to the war of 1877–1878 between Russia and Turkey. The Czar went to war apparently to avenge the defeat of his father in the Crimean War. At first his armies made considerable progress and were moving toward Constantinople. Then their progress was halted by the Turks and many Russian soldiers were killed in the battles which followed. The Czar saw the prospect of defeat again, and Áqá Muḥammad-Raḥím thought this must have been the time that the Czar had turned to God in prayer beseeching His help. Bahá'u'lláh states in His Tablet that the Czar's prayers were answered.[505]

322. p. 57 ¶ 96. Whilst I lay, chained and fettered, in the prison of Ṭihrán, one of thy ministers, extended Me his aid

Shoghi Effendi gives the following account:

> The Russian Minister, as soon as he was informed of the Imperial decision, expressed the desire to take Bahá'u'lláh under the protection of his government, and offered to extend every facility for His removal to Russia. This invitation, so spontaneously extended, Bahá'u'lláh declined, preferring, in pursuance of an unerring instinct, to establish His abode in Turkish territory, in the city of Ba<u>gh</u>dád. 'Whilst I lay chained and fettered in the prison,' He Himself, years after, testified in His epistle addressed to the Czar of Russia, Nicolaevitch Alexander II, 'one of thy ministers extended Me his aid. Whereupon God hath ordained for thee a station which the knowledge of none can comprehend except His knowledge. Beware lest thou barter away this sublime station.' 'In the days,' is yet another illuminating testimony revealed by His pen, 'when this Wronged One was sore-afflicted in prison, the minister of the highly esteemed government (of Russia) – may God, glorified and exalted by He, assist him! – exerted his utmost endeavor to compass My deliverance. Several times permission for My release was granted. Some of the 'ulamás of the city, however, would prevent it. Finally, My freedom was gained through the solicitude and the endeavor of His Excellency the Minister . . . His Imperial Majesty, the Most Great Emperor – may God, exalted and glorified be He, assist him! – extended to Me for the sake of God his protection – a protection which has excited the envy and enmity of the foolish ones of the earth.'[506]
>
> The persistent and decisive intervention of the Russian Minister, Prince Dolgorouki, who left no stone unturned to establish the innocence of Bahá'u'lláh; the public confession of Mullá <u>Sh</u>ay<u>kh</u> 'Alíy-i-Tur<u>sh</u>ízí, surnamed 'Aẓím, who, in the Síyáh-<u>Ch</u>ál, in the presence of the Ḥájibu'd-Dawlih and the Russian Minister's interpreter and of the government's representative, emphatically exonerated Him, and acknowledged his own complicity; the indisputable testimony established by competent tribunals; the unrelaxing efforts exerted by His own brothers, sisters and kindred, – all these combined to

effect His ultimate deliverance from the hands of His rapacious enemies.[507]

323. p. 57 ¶ 97. He Who is the Father is come

To His Jewish followers Bahá'u'lláh is the incarnation of the 'Everlasting Father' (Is. 9:6) and the 'Lord' or *Hashem* come down with 'ten thousands of saints' (Deut 33:2).

Christ referred to Himself as the 'Son' (Mark 13:32). But in the Lord's Prayer (Matt. 6:9–10) He anticipated the advent of the kingdom of the Father when God's 'will be done on earth, as it is in heaven'. The Book of Revelation (Rev. 21:3) declares that the tabernacle of God will be with men and 'God himself shall be with them and be their God'.

324. p. 57 ¶ 97. mounted upon the clouds

Compare Matt. 24:30: 'And then shall appear the sign of the Son of man in heaven: and then shall all the tribes of the earth mourn, and they shall see the Son of man coming in the clouds of heaven with power and great glory.'

See also Annotations 113, 279, 498, 499 and 609.

325. p. 58 ¶ 98. the Spirit of God (Jesus Christ) appeared, and Herod gave judgment against Him

Herod I, the Great, was the King of Judaea when Jesus was born. He is not to be confused with his son, Herod Antipas, who was responsible for beheading John the Baptist. According to the Gospel narrative Herod I expected the advent of the Messiah but feared His coming. When the three Zoroastrian priests, the Magi, informed him that according to their prophecies Christ had been born he asked to be informed of His exact whereabouts. However, the Magi, fearing that he would cause harm to the newly-born King, returned directly to Persia (Matt. 2:16):

> Then Herod, when he saw that he was mocked of the wise men, was exceeding wroth, and sent forth, and slew all the children that were in Bethlehem, and in all the coasts thereof, from two years old and

> under, according to the time which he had diligently inquired of the wise men.

326. p. 58 ¶ 98. God, however, aided Him with the hosts of the unseen, and protected Him with truth, and sent Him down unto another land

Jesus escaped the slaughter of the newborn infants in Bethlehem when Joseph and Mary took Him to Egypt (Matt 2:13–14):

> And when they [the Magi] were departed, behold, the angel of the Lord appeareth to Joseph in a dream, saying, Arise, and take the young child and his mother, and flee into Egypt, and be thou there until I bring thee word: for Herod will seek the young child to destroy him.
>
> When he arose, he took the young child and his mother by night, and departed into Egypt: And was there until the death of Herod: that it might be fulfilled which was spoken of the Lord by the prophet, saying, Out of Egypt have I called my son.

327. p. 58 ¶ 98. according to His promise

'His promise' appears to refer to the verse from the Hebrew Bible (Hosea 11:1): 'When Israel was a child, then I loved him, and called my son in out of Egypt.' The verse might be said to refer to God's calling His people out of Egypt, under Moses. It denotes deliverance from danger, and indeed Bahá'u'lláh continues the Epistle by saying: 'Thy Lord truly preserveth whom He willeth, be he in the midst of the seas or in the maw of the serpent, or beneath the sword of the oppressor.' Elsewhere, Bahá'u'lláh described the danger He Himself was in: 'This Wronged One findeth himself in the maw of the serpent, yet He faileth not to make mention of the loved ones of God.'[508]

The Gospel of Matthew (2:17–18) interprets and adapts a passage in the Book of Jeremiah (31:15) and applies it to the massacre of the children in Bethlehem by Herod: 'Then was fulfilled that which was spoken by Jeremy the prophet, saying, In Rama was there a voice heard, lamentation, and weeping, and great mourning, Rachel weeping for her children, and would not be comforted, because they are not.' However, some

Jewish scholars maintain that these statements were not about the Messiah but related to other events such as the exodus of the Jews from Egypt.

328. p. 58 ¶ 99. the things that have befallen My Beauty, at the hands of them that are the manifestations of My glory

A reference to Sulṭán 'Abdu'l-'Azíz and Náṣiri'd-Dín Sháh: their authority was a reflection of divine glory and sovereignty:

> . . . these words refer unto the kings and rulers – those through the brightness of whose justice the horizons of the world are resplendent and luminous. We fain would hope that His Majesty the Sháh will shine forth with a light of justice whose radiance will envelop all the kindreds of the earth. (¶ 141)

> The sovereigns of the earth have been and are the manifestations of the power, the grandeur and the majesty of God. (¶ 142)

An additional explanation is that the cruelties that Bahá'u'lláh suffered caused His glory to be revealed:

> I sorrow not for the burden of My imprisonment. Neither do I grieve over My abasement, or the tribulation I suffer at the hands of Mine enemies. By My life! They are My glory, a glory wherewith God hath adorned His own Self. Would that ye know it!
>
> The shame I was made to bear hath uncovered the glory with which the whole of creation had been invested, and through the cruelties I have endured, the Daystar of Justice hath manifested itself, and shed its splendour upon men.[509]

329. p. 59 ¶ 100. Tablet of Her Majesty, the Queen

Bahá'u'lláh wrote a Tablet in Arabic to Queen Victoria, replete with counsels and exhortations, proclaiming the advent of the promised Lord in His great glory, and summoning her to His Cause. In the Tablet Bahá'u'lláh also instructs the elected representatives of the people throughout the world: 'Take ye counsel together, and let your concern be only for that which profiteth mankind, and bettereth the condition thereof . . .'

330. p. 59 ¶ 100. Queen Victoria

Queen Victoria (1819–1901) was one of the greatest constitutional monarchs, reigning for 64 years (1837–1901). She believed her power was held in trust for the people, and she used it to win many reforms in a time of change. She gained the approval and loyalty of her people during a fruitful reign. Of her 'Abdu'l-Bahá said:

> Victoria, Queen of England, was really superior to all kings of Europe in ability, justness and equable administration. During her long and brilliant reign the British Empire was immensely extended and enriched, due to her political sagacity, skill and foresight.[510]

Notably, the dowager Queen Marie of Romania, who accepted the Bahá'í Faith through the teaching efforts of Martha Root, was a granddaughter of Queen Victoria.

331. p. 59 ¶ 100. In those regions distinguished divines are numerous

Britain had a large number of prominent religious leaders, and the Queen, as head of the Anglican Church, could have persuaded them to consider the teachings of Bahá'u'lláh detailed in the Tablet. And given the influence of Britain in the Middle East, the Queen could have suggested that the religious leaders in that part of the world assemble and consult on the communication.

Bahá'u'lláh in the Epistle informs Shaykh Najafí of some of His teachings in His Tablet to Queen Victoria that perchance the cleric may regret his actions and embrace the truth. As a positive step, he could have gathered the many other religious scholars and Siyyids residing in Isfahan and announce to them Bahá'u'lláh's teachings. In this way, they might have ceased their feuding and nefarious activities, and become the cause of unity and amity.

332. p. 59 ¶ 100. among whom are those Siyyids who are renowned for their eminence and distinction

Bahá'u'lláh here encourages the Shaykh to confer with his fellow clergy concerning the weighty matters that He had put before the Queen. Siyyids are descendants of the Prophet Muhammad. They were numerous in Persia, and in reality they were considered a burden, as observed by Lord Curzon:

> an intolerable nuisance to the country, deducing from their alleged descent and from the prerogative of the green turban, the right to an independence and insolence of bearing from which their countrymen, no less than foreigners, are made to suffer.[511]

333. p. 60 ¶ 101. Divine Lote-Tree

Sadratu'l-Muntahá: a title of the Manifestation of God, for example, Christ[512] and Bahá'u'lláh:

> By the righteousness of God! The Mother Book is made manifest, summoning mankind unto God, the Lord of the worlds, while the seas proclaim: The Most Great Ocean hath appeared, from whose waves one can hear the thundering cry: 'Verily, no God is there but Me, the Peerless, the All-Knowing.' And the trees raising their clamour exclaim: O people of the world! The voice of the Divine Lote-Tree is clearly sounding and the shrill cry of the Pen of Glory is ringing loud: Give ye ear and be not of the heedless.[513]

See also Annotations 191, 239 and 250.

334. p. 60 ¶ 101. Mosque of Aqṣá

Bahá'u'lláh indicates in His Tablet to Queen Victoria that not only have the prophecies of the Gospel been fulfilled by His advent, but that He is also the Promised One of Islam.

The Al-Aqṣá Mosque in Jerusalem is also known as 'The Most Remote' Mosque, the 'Holy House' (*Bayt al-Maqdis*), and 'The Rock' (*Ṣakhrah*). The Mosque was built on the Temple Mount and, apart from the Kaaba in Mecca and the Prophet's Mosque in Medina, is considered to be the most sacred site in Sunni and Shí'ih Islamic tradition. This is due largely to a journey reportedly made by Muhammad during one night from Mecca to the Mosque ('The Night Journey' or *Isra*), where He prayed and then ascended through seven heavens to attain the Presence of God (*Mi'ráj*). This spiritual experience is described in Súrih 17 of the Qur'án and embellished in the hadith (traditions).

335. p. 60 ¶ 101. Baṭḥá

Baṭḥá or Bakka is an ancient name for Mecca, particularly the region of Kaaba and the sacred site surrounding it.

336. p. 60 ¶ 102. We have been informed that thou hast forbidden the trading in slaves, both men and women

A reference to the abolition of slavery during Queen Victoria's time.

The Torah condones slavery but recommends that slaves should be treated kindly. The New Testament states that Christian slaves should obey their Christian or non-Christian masters. For example (Ephes. 6:5–9):

> Servants [slaves], be obedient to them that are your masters according to the flesh, with fear and trembling, in singleness of your heart, as unto Christ;
>
> Not with eyeservice, as menpleasers; but as the servants of Christ, doing the will of God from the heart;
>
> With good will doing service, as to the Lord, and not to men . . .'

Although the Bible accepted slavery and Queen Victoria was the head of the Anglican Church, during her reign legislation was enacted and enforced for the abolition of slavery and for parliamentary reform. The British Parliament had passed an Act abolishing the slave trade in 1807, and a further act in 1833 for the emancipation of all slaves in the British Empire, a process that was completed by 1838.

The oneness of humanity is a pivotal principle in the Bahá'í Faith and Bahá'u'lláh therefore approved of Queen Victoria's enactments in this regard. This principle is still relevant today, as there is still active global human trafficking, and there are currently about 30 million slaves in the world 'living as forced labourers, forced prostitutes, child soldiers, child brides in forced marriages and, in all ways that matter, as pieces of property, chattel in the servitude of absolute ownership'.[514]

337. p. 61 ¶ 102. Man's actions are acceptable after his having recognized (the Manifestation)

This relates to the passage at the beginning of the *Kitáb-i-Aqdas*:

> The first duty prescribed by God for His servants is the recognition of Him Who is the Dayspring of His Revelation and the Fountain of His laws, Who representeth the Godhead in both the Kingdom of His Cause and the world of creation. Whoso achieveth this duty hath attained unto all good; and whoso is deprived thereof hath gone astray, though he be the author of every righteous deed. It behooveth everyone who reacheth this most sublime station, this summit of transcendent glory, to observe every ordinance of Him Who is the Desire of the world. These twin duties are inseparable. Neither is acceptable without the other.

Christ similarly stated (Matt. 6:33): 'But seek ye first the kingdom of God, and his righteousness; and all these things shall be added unto you.'

338. p. 61 ¶ 103. We have also heard that thou hast entrusted the reins of counsel into the hands of the representatives of the people. Thou, indeed, hast done well

The Reform Acts of 1832, 1867 and 1884 successively extended the vote to a greater proportion of the adult population in Britain. The Ballot Act of 1872 introduced the principle of secret ballot in parliamentary and municipal elections.

Many of the European monarchs during Queen Victoria's reign tended to be autocratic and were not always as wise in the exercise of their powers and privilege. Few have survived. By comparison, the Victorian era was possibly the greatest period of stability and progress that Britain had ever known. The social, political and economic progress that was allowed to flourish under Victoria's constitutional monarchy was an important factor contributing to this phenomenon.

339. p. 62 ¶ 104. O ye members of Assemblies in that land and in other countries! Take ye counsel together

Bahá'u'lláh advocated that the various countries of the world should consult with one another on ways of improving the welfare of all humanity.

340. p. 62 ¶ 105. That which God hath ordained as the sovereign remedy and mightiest instrument for the healing of the world is the union of all its peoples in one universal Cause, one common Faith

Bahá'u'lláh wrote: 'the well-being of mankind, its peace and security are unattainable unless and until its unity is firmly established.'[515] It is probably equally true that the unity of mankind is unachievable unless and until oneness of Faith is firmly established. Hence, many of the Bahá'í Writings are centred on this vital issue:

> all the Prophets are the Temples of the Cause of God, Who have appeared clothed in divers attire. If thou wilt observe with discriminating eyes, thou wilt behold them all abiding in the same tabernacle, soaring in the same heaven, seated upon the same throne, uttering the same speech, and proclaiming the same Faith.[516]

> The Revelation, of which Bahá'u'lláh is the source and center . . . disclaims any intention of dwarfing any of the Prophets of the past, or of whittling down the eternal verity of their teachings. It can, in no wise, conflict with the spirit that animates their claims, nor does it seek to undermine the basis of any man's allegiance to their cause. Its declared, its primary purpose is to enable every adherent of these Faiths to obtain a fuller understanding of the religion with which he stands identified, and to acquire a clearer apprehension of its purpose . . . [The Bahá'í] teachings revolve around the fundamental principle that religious truth is not absolute but relative, that Divine Revelation is progressive, not final. Unequivocally and without the least reservation it proclaims all established religions to

> be divine in origin, identical in their aims, complementary in their functions, continuous in their purpose, indispensable in their value to mankind.[517]

341. pp. 62–63 ¶ 105. This can in no wise be achieved except through the power of a skilled, an all-powerful, and inspired Physician

Christ promoted the unity of mankind through the power of the divine Word:

> By the power of His Word He was able to unite people of the Roman, Greek, Chaldean, Egyptian and Assyrian nations. Whereas they had been cruel, bloodthirsty and hostile, killing, pillaging and taking each other captive, He cemented them together in a perfect bond of unity and love. He caused them to agree and become reconciled. Such mighty effects were the results of the manifestation of one single Soul. This proves conclusively that Christ was assisted by God.[518]

Today, Bahá'u'lláh, as anticipated in the Bible and the Qur'án, is establishing the oneness of religions and the oneness of humanity, through the creative power of His Word. Bahá'u'lláh writes in the *Kitáb-i-Íqán*:

> consider the welding power of His Word. Observe, how those in whose midst the Satan of self had for years sown the seeds of malice and hate became so fused and blended through their allegiance to this wondrous and transcendent Revelation that it seemed as if they had sprung from the same loins. Such is the binding force of the Word of God, which uniteth the hearts of them that have renounced all else but Him, who have believed in His signs, and quaffed from the Hand of glory the Kawthar of God's holy grace. Furthermore, how numerous are those peoples of divers beliefs, of conflicting creeds, and opposing temperaments, who, through the reviving fragrance of the Divine springtime, breathing from the Riḍván of God, have been arrayed with the new robe of divine Unity, and have drunk from the cup of His singleness![519]

Bahá'u'lláh explains that humanity's sickness 'waxeth more severe' as it has fallen 'under the treatment of ignorant physicians.' He writes further: 'We behold it, in this day, at the mercy of rulers, so drunk with pride that they cannot discern clearly their own best advantage, much less recognize a Revelation so bewildering and challenging as this' (¶ 104).

342. p. 63 ¶ 106. until in the end they imprisoned Him in the most desolate of cities, and broke the grasp of the faithful upon the hem of His robe

A reference to Bahá'u'lláh's banishment to 'Akká, where He was separated from most of His followers.

343. p. 63 ¶ 106. The World Reformer is come

The Prophet Isaiah (49:19) promised that God would do 'a new thing'. Consequently (43:18–20), the former things would need to be forgotten. The New Testament (Acts 3:19–21) promises a reformation, and that the 'times of refreshing' will come 'from the presence of the Lord', when God will restore everything, as he promised long ago through his holy Prophets.

The Qur'án devotes many verses to a future event of great significance when God's religion and human society will be reformed. To allow Islam to evolve, its social laws need to be replaced or modified. The Qur'án (2:106–107; 14:48) therefore explains that parts of the Revelation God may abrogate (*nasakh*), cause to be forgotten (*nunsihá*), substitute (*badala*) for other verses, or erase (*mahv*).

344. pp. 63–64 ¶ 106. At all times He was at the mercy of the wicked doers. At one time they cast Him into prison, at another they banished Him, and at yet another hurried Him from land to land

This refers to Bahá'u'lláh's unjust sufferings and enforced banishments under great difficulties.

345. p. 64 ¶ 107. This charge of fomenting discord is the same as that imputed aforetime by the Pharaohs of Egypt to Him Who

conversed with God (Moses). Read thou what the All-Merciful hath revealed in the Qur'án

The Qur'án (26:18) explains that when Moses went to Pharaoh and invited him to heed the Divine Will, Pharaoh protested 'Did we not cherish thee as a child among us, and didst thou not stay in our midst many years of thy life?' He (40:26) expressed his fear that Moses would change the religion of the Egyptians. To prevent this mischief and disorder (*fasád* in Arabic), it was better to put to Him to death.

The Apostle Paul (Acts 24:5) was also accused of being 'a mover of sedition [insurrection] among all the Jews throughout the world, and a ringleader of the sect [heresy; cult] of the Nazarenes'. The Qur'án (2:11–12) accuses religious leaders of being the cause of mischief and creating discord, while claiming in the process that they are creating peace. By opposing God's Revelation, they prevent interfaith unity and amity and thereby, directly or indirectly, cause mischief and disorder, which they then attribute to God's Messenger and His Faith. Like Pharaoh, their apprehension is that the new religion will imperil their livelihood and undermine their prestige.

In the Lawḥ-i-Ra'ís, one of three Tablets addressed to 'Alí Pá<u>sh</u>á, Bahá'u'lláh, referring to Himself as Life-giver and World Reformer, asks: 'in thine estimation guilty of sedition and strife, what crime could have been committed by a group of women, children, and suckling mothers that they should be thus afflicted with the scourge of thine anger and wrath? No faith or religion hath ever held children responsible.'[520]

346. p. 64 ¶ 107. Moreover We had sent Moses of old with Our signs and with clear authority to Pharaoh

This a reference to the following verses of the Qur'án (40:22–25):

> . . . there came to them their apostles with Clear (Signs), but they rejected them: so God called them to account . . .
>
> Of old We sent Moses, with Our Signs and an Authority manifest, to Pharaoh, Hámán, and Qárún; but they called (him) 'a sorcerer telling lies!'. . .
>
> Now, when he came to them in truth, from Us, they said, 'Slay the

> sons of those who believe with him, and keep alive their females' but the plots of unbelievers (end) in nothing but errors (and delusions)!

347. p. 64 ¶ 107. Hámán

Hámán was the grand vizier and high priest of the Pharaoh at the time of Moses. He was known to pander to the vanity of those in power. He is mentioned six times in the Qur'án, and is depicted as being involved in the confrontation between Moses and Pharaoh (40:36–37):

> Pharaoh said: 'O Haman! Build me a lofty palace, that I may attain the ways and means – The ways and means of (reaching) the heavens, and that I may mount up to the god of Moses: But as far as I am concerned, I think (Moses) is a liar!'

348. p. 64 ¶ 107. Qárún

In the Torah (Ex. 6:21; Num. 16:1–50), Korah (thought to be the same as Qárún mentioned in the Qur'án) is described as being the son of Izhar, son of Kohath, son of Levi. He was thus a member of the same tribe as Moses and Aaron. Korah with 250 Jewish leaders, 'princes of congregation', challenged the authority of Moses and Aaron, accusing them of exalting themselves above the congregation of the Lord: 'They assembled themselves together against Moses and against Aaron and said to them, "You have gone too far! For all in the congregation are holy, every one of them, and the Lord is among them. Why then do you exalt yourselves above the assembly of the Lord?"' (Num. 16:3). Korah and his co-conspirators were destroyed by God for their rebellion. Some of the Israelites did not like what had happened to Korah and objected to Moses. They too were destroyed by plague, as punishment for objecting to Korah's destruction.

According to the Qur'án (28:76–82), due to his proverbial wealth, Qárún became very arrogant and oppressive. He credited his good fortune to his knowledge rather than divine generosity:

> Qárún was . . . of the people of Moses; but he acted insolently towards them: Such were the treasures We had bestowed on him, that their very keys would have been a burden to a body of strong

> men. Behold, his people said to him: 'Exult not, for God loveth not those who exult (in riches).
>
> 'But seek, with the (wealth) which God has bestowed on thee, the Home of the Hereafter, nor forget thy portion in this world: but do thou good, as God has been good to thee, and seek not (occasions for) mischief in the land: For God loves not those who do mischief.'
>
> He said: 'This has been given to me because of a certain knowledge which I have.' Did he not know that God had destroyed, before him, (whole) generations, – which were superior to him in strength and greater in the amount (of riches) they had collected? But the wicked are not called (immediately) to account for their sins.
>
> So he went forth among his people in the (pride of his worldly) glitter. Said those whose aim is the Life of this World: 'Oh! that we had the like of what Qárún has got! For he is truly a lord of mighty good fortune!'
>
> But those who had been granted (true) knowledge said: 'Alas for you! The reward of God (in the Hereafter) is best for those who believe and work righteousness: but this none shall attain, save those who steadfastly persevere (in good).'
>
> Then We caused the earth to swallow up him and his house; and he had not (the least little) party to help him against God, nor could he defend himself.'

The similarities between Shaykh Najafí and Qárún are remarkable. The Shaykh too had accumulated vast wealth, had prided himself in his knowledge, and persecuted God's people. His ambitions fulfilled the following prophecy recorded in a Shí'ih hadith:

> A time will come when . . . the dinár (unit of currency) will constitute their 'deen' or religion (*wa danaaneeruhum deenhum*) . . . there will be left nothing left of the Faith except for its name, and nothing left of Islám except its rituals, and nothing left of the Qur'án except for provision of instructions, their Mosques will be beautifully constructed but will be devoid of guidance, their learned (ulemá, jurists) will be the worst inhabitants on earth . . .[521]

349. p. 65 ¶ 109. Did We not rear thee among us when a child? And hast thou not passed years of thy life among us?

This is a quotation from Qur'án 26:18–19 (Rodwell). The Pharaoh had looked after Moses from infancy. He expected that Moses would be bound by ties of gratitude and would not go against His traditional training in the ways of the Egyptians:

> He (Pharaoh) said, 'Did we not rear thee (Moses) among us when a child? And hast thou not passed years of thy life among us? And yet what a deed is that which thou hast done! Thou art one of the ungrateful.'

Pharaoh accused Moses of sorcery, fomenting mischief, and attempting to change the polytheistic religion of the Egyptians.

See also Annotation 345.

350. p. 66 ¶ 109. And He entered a city . . . and slew him

Before God sent Him as a Messenger to Pharaoh, in a momentary fit of righteous anger Moses killed an Egyptian who was ill-treating a Jewish slave. The Torah (Ex. 2:11–15) recounts the story as follows:

> . . . when Moses was grown up, that he went out unto his brethren, and looked on their burdens; and he saw an Egyptian smiting a Hebrew, one of his brethren.
>
> And he looked this way and that way, and when he saw that there was no man, he smote the Egyptian, and hid him in the sand.
>
> And he went out the second day, and, behold, two men of the Hebrews were striving together; and he said to him that did the wrong: 'Wherefore smitest thou thy fellow?'
>
> And he said: 'Who made thee a ruler and a judge over us? thinkest thou to kill me, as thou didst kill the Egyptian?' And Moses feared, and said: 'Surely the thing is known.'
>
> Now when Pharaoh heard this thing, he sought to slay Moses. But Moses fled from the face of Pharaoh.

The Qur'án (28:15–18), quoted by Bahá'u'lláh, gives the following account of the event and Moses' regret at having taken a life:

> And he entered a city at the time when its inhabitants would not observe him, and found therein two men fighting: the one, of his own people [an Israelite]; the other, of his enemies [Egyptian]. And he who was of his own people asked his help against him who was of his enemies. And Moses smote him with his fist and slew him. Said he, 'This is a work of Satan; for he is an enemy, a manifest misleader.'
>
> He said, 'O my Lord, I have sinned to mine own hurt: forgive me.' So God forgave him; for He is the Forgiving, the Merciful.
>
> He said, 'Lord, because thou hast showed me this grace, I will never again be the helper of the wicked.'
>
> And in the city at noon he was full of fear, casting furtive glances round him: and lo! The man whom he had helped the day before, cried out to him again for help. Said Moses to him, 'Thou art plainly a most depraved person.'

351. p. 66 ¶ 109. Moses Himself, moreover, acknowledged His injustice and waywardness

Moses regretted His action. Despite it, He later became one of the greatest Prophets of Israel, as stated in the Torah (Deut. 34:10): 'And there arose not a prophet since in Israel like unto Moses, whom the Lord knew face to face.' Standing accused before Pharaoh, He readily confessed His error (Qur'án 26:20). He said: 'I did it when I was in error. So I fled from you (all) when I feared you; but my Lord has (since) invested me with judgment (and wisdom) and appointed me as one of the apostles.'

The account of Moses should have impelled the Shaykh to admit his many injustices, become receptive to the Divine Call and undergo a spiritual transformation. Bahá'u'lláh admonishes him in this paragraph of the Epistle: 'Thine ears and thine eyes must needs now be cleansed and sanctified, that thou mayest be able to judge with fairness and justice. Moses Himself, moreover, acknowledged His injustice and waywardness, and testified that fear had seized Him, and that He had transgressed, and fled away. He asked God – exalted be His glory – to forgive Him, and He was forgiven.'

352. p. 67 ¶ 110. men as have invariably withdrawn themselves behind veils and curtains, and busied themselves about their own protection

This is a reference to Mírzá Yaḥyá Azal (1831–1912), a half-brother of Bahá'u'lláh. He died at the age of 88 years in Famagusta, Cyprus. He was assigned nominally the leadership of the Bábí community by the Báb until the time when 'He Whom God shall make Manifest' would come and abrogate the Dispensation of the Báb. However, his tenure of the leadership of the Bábís was controversial and, because of his own concern for his personal safety, was characterized by dissimulation (*taqíyyah*), frequent absenteeism and hiding. He took on the name *Záhir* (which means evident!) and wandered in disguise as an Arab.

See also Annotation 362.

353. p. 68 ¶ 110. As soon as someone leaveth the Great City (Constantinople) to visit this land, they at once telegraph and proclaim that he hath stolen money and fled to 'Akká

Constantinople (Istanbul) was the capital of the Ottoman Empire. The primary instigators of mischief in the city were the followers of Mírzá Azal.

> In this way Constantinople became a nest of conspiracy and intrigue against the Faith of Bahá'u'lláh.
>
> The situation grew worse as the years went by, and the campaign of hostility and vilification reached such proportions as to become a cause of distress to Bahá'u'lláh during the last ten years of His life.[522]

354. p. 68 ¶ 110. A highly accomplished, learned and distinguished man

This is a reference to Ḥájí Mírzá Siyyid Ḥasan known as Afnán-i-Kabír (the Great Afnán), a brother of the wife of the Báb. He was also a paternal cousin of the mother of the Báb. He was the victim of intrigues and slander by mischief-makers, primarily Muḥammad-Ali Iṣfáhání who constantly plotted against Bahá'u'lláh and His followers (see ¶ 163).

He was very much attracted to the person of the Báb, and became a believer in Yazd through the teaching efforts of Ḥájí Muḥammad-Ibráhím, entitled *Muballigh* (Bahá'í teacher) by Bahá'u'lláh. Afnán-i-Kabír was a pillar of strength to his sister Khadíjih Bagum, the wife of the Báb, during her days of loneliness and bereavement. He had a great love for Bahá'u'lláh and in the latter part of his life he was permitted to go the Holy Land and spend the rest of his days there, where he lived very close to the Mansion of Bahjí, and passed away about a year after the ascension of Bahá'u'lláh. 'Abdu'l-Bahá has paid tribute to him in *Memorials of the Faithful*.[523]

355. p. 68 ¶ 111. Mírzá Ḥusayn Khán, Mushíru'd-Dawlih

Mírzá Ḥusayn Khán, also known as Mushíru'd-Dawlih Sepahsálar (1828–1881) married the aunt of Náṣiri'd-Dín Sháh. Following a diplomatic career in Tiflis, Georgia, he became the ambassador to the Sublime Porte (Istanbul). While there, he became concerned about the growing influence of Bahá'u'lláh in Baghdad given His close proximity to Persia. Through his efforts and influence Bahá'u'lláh was banished from Baghdad to Istanbul (Constantinople) in 1863.[524]

He was recalled to Tehran in 1871 and was made Prime Minister or *Ṣadr-i-A'ẓam* (1871–1873).[525] The Sepahsalar Mosque in Tehran is named after him. He died of a heart attack at the age of 53 years.

356. p. 68 ¶ 111. Sublime Porte

This refers to the Ottoman imperial government. It is a French translation of the Turkish name *Bábíáli* ('High Gate' or 'Gate of the Eminent'), the official name of the gate giving access to the block of buildings in Istanbul that house the principal state departments[526] and residences of powerful grand viziers.

357. p. 68 ¶ 111. Prince Shuja'u'd-Dawlih

A Persian Prince attached to the Embassy at Istanbul during the reign of Sulṭán 'Abdu'l-'Azíz, Prince Shuja'u'd-Dawlih did not play a significant role in history. He was a grandson of Fath-'Ali Sháh and the son of the notorious and autocratic Qájár prince, Zill'uṣ-Ṣultán who ruled Isfahan from 1874 to 1907 and who had tried to take power after the death of his father.

Now that Bahá'u'lláh was in Istanbul, the Persian Ambassador was making a desperate bid to misrepresent Him to the authorities and thereby secure their support for banishing Him further. The day after Bahá'u'lláh's arrival, the Ambassador sent Prince Shujá'u'd-Dawlih and Ḥájí Mírzá Ḥasan-i-Ṣafá, the two most prominent men in his circle, to call on Bahá'u'lláh on his behalf. He expected that Bahá'u'lláh would return the call and see him in person, but he soon learned that this was not going to happen. In those days it was customary for prominent guests of the government, soon after their arrival in the capital, to call upon the Shaykhu'l-Islám, (the highest religious dignitary of the Muslim community), the Prime Minister and other high-ranking officials. It was on the occasion of these visits that people solicited all kinds of favours, made deals and secured the support of the authorities for themselves. Bahá'u'lláh refused to do this and did not even return the visits of some of the Sultan's ministers who had already called on him to pay their respects.

Kamál Páshá and a few others went so far as to remind Him of this custom. Bahá'u'lláh responded by saying that He was aware of the practice but had no demands to make of anyone nor did He require favours from them; therefore there was no reason for Him to call. Bahá'u'lláh refers to this in the Súriy-i-Mulúk (Súrih of the Kings) in these words:

> Call Thou to remembrance Thine arrival in the City, how the Ministers of the Sulṭán thought Thee to be unacquainted with their laws and regulations, and believed Thee to be one of the ignorant. Say: Yea, by My Lord! I am ignorant of all things except what God hath, through His bountiful favour, been pleased to teach Me. To this We assuredly testify, and unhesitatingly confess it.[527]

And Taherzadeh comments:

> His standards were exalted above human statesmanship which is based upon compromise, and often upon deceit and selfish exploits. The authorities became conscious of His spiritual powers born of God and were deeply impressed by His uprightness and dignity. Some of these men had urged Bahá'u'lláh to send a plea to the

> Sublime Porte for a thorough and just investigation of His case so that any misgivings in the minds of the Sultán and his ministers might be dispelled.[528]

Bahá'u'lláh is reported to have made this response:

> If the enlightened-minded leaders [of your nation] be wise and diligent, they will certainly make enquiry, and acquaint themselves with the true state of the case; if not, then [their] attainment of the truth is impracticable and impossible. Under these circumstances what need is there for importuning statesmen and supplicating ministers of the Court? We are free from every anxiety, and ready and prepared for the things predestined to us. 'Say, all is from God' is a sound and sufficient argument, and 'If God toucheth thee with a hurt there is no dispeller thereof save Him' is a healing medicine.[529]

In one of His Tablets revealed soon after His arrival in Istanbul, Bahá'u'lláh expresses disappointment in the people He had met, saying that their welcome for Him was an act of formality and that He found them cold as ice and lifeless as dead trees.[530] In the Súriy-i-Mulúk, in a passage addressing the inhabitants of Istanbul, Bahá'u'lláh states that He found their leaders as 'children gathered about and disporting themselves with clay'. And He further comments:

> We perceived no one sufficiently mature to acquire from Us the truths which God hath taught Us, nor ripe for Our wondrous words of wisdom. Our inner eye wept sore over them, and over their transgressions and their total disregard of the thing for which they were created. This is what We observed in that City, and which We have chosen to note down in Our Book, that it may serve as a warning unto them and unto the rest of mankind.[531]

358. p. 68 ¶ 111. Mírzá Ṣafá

A man of learning and a dervish. An intimate friend and a close confidant of the ambassador, and an accomplice of Ḥájí Mírzá Ḥusayn Khán, he exhibited hostility towards Bahá'u'lláh during His three-year stay in

Istanbul. He lived in Istanbul and died in Tehran. He met Bahá'u'lláh several times in Istanbul.

359. p. 68 ¶ 111. Kamál Páshá

A former *Sadr-i-A'zam* (Prime Minister) who was at that time one of the ministers of the Sultan. He knew several languages well and prided himself on this accomplishment. Some time between August and December 1863, he visited Bahá'u'lláh in Istanbul and was directed by Him to lay the matter of promoting an international language before his Government.

360. p. 69 ¶ 111. this Wronged One sojourned for a period of four months in that city

The twin Manifestations of God suffered intensely during Their earthly life in the service of humanity. Bahá'u'lláh refers to Himself as 'this Wronged One' about a hundred times in the Epistle. In a prayer Bahá'u'lláh and the Báb are thus addressed:

> O Thou Who art His Beauty! I bear witness that the eye of creation hath never gazed upon one wronged like Thee. Thou wast immersed all the days of Thy life beneath an ocean of tribulations. At one time Thou wast in chains and fetters; at another Thou wast threatened by the sword of Thine enemies. Yet, despite all this, Thou didst enjoin upon all men to observe what had been prescribed unto Thee by Him Who is the All-Knowing, the All-Wise.
>
> May my spirit be a sacrifice to the wrongs Thou didst suffer, and my soul be a ransom for the adversities Thou didst sustain.[532]

Bahá'u'lláh's ordeals included multiple banishments and numerous indignities inflicted on Him by the Ottoman Caliph of Islam:

> The initial phase of that Proclamation may be said to have opened in Constantinople with the communication (the text of which we, alas, do not possess) addressed by Bahá'u'lláh to Sulṭán 'Abdu'l-'Azíz himself, the self-styled vicar of the Prophet of Islám and the absolute ruler of a mighty empire. So potent, so august a personage was

the first among the sovereigns of the world to receive the Divine Summons, and the first among Oriental monarchs to sustain the impact of God's retributive justice. The occasion for this communication was provided by the infamous edict the Sulṭán had promulgated, less than four months after the arrival of the exiles in his capital, banishing them, suddenly and without any justification whatsoever, in the depth of winter, and in the most humiliating circumstances, to Adrianople, situated on the extremities of his empire.[533]

361. p. 69 ¶ 112. That which was done by his late Excellency (Mu<u>sh</u>íru'd-Dawlih)

Bahá'u'lláh explains that what was done by Mírzá Ḥusayn <u>Kh</u>án was not out of concern for His welfare but prompted by his desire to further the interests of the Persian government – adding that 'it was he who was responsible' for His further banishment from Adrianople (Edirnih) to 'Akká. Bahá'u'lláh writes: 'As he was faithful, however, in the discharge of his duty, he deserveth Our commendation.'

362. p. 70 ¶ 113. what hath befallen Me at the hands of one (Mírzá Yaḥyá) over whom We watched for successive years

Mírzá Yaḥyá was the treacherous half-brother of Bahá'u'lláh and 'arch-breaker of the Covenant of the Báb'.[534] He was about fourteen years younger than Bahá'u'lláh, and when their father died he was only eight years old. He therefore grew up under the care and protection of Bahá'u'lláh, who paid special attention to his education and upbringing.

See also Annotation 352.

363. p. 70 ¶ 113. Siyyid Muḥammad

Siyyid Muḥammad-i-Iṣfáhání is considered 'the Antichrist of the Bahá'í Revelation' ('*Dajjal*', a one-eyed evil figure in Islamic eschatology) who instigated the villainies of Mírzá Yaḥyá. He did not appear to have had a sincere faith in either the Báb or Bahá'u'lláh. He misled and persuaded Mírzá Yaḥyá to turn against Bahá'u'lláh in Baghdad. He followed Bahá'u'lláh to Istanbul with another of His inveterate enemies,

Aqá Ján Kaj-Kulláh, and later to Adrianople. In Istanbul he joined a clique of enemies of the Faith, including those who worked tirelessly to stir up trouble with the Ottoman authorities against Bahá'u'lláh and His faithful followers.[535] He was eventually dispatched by the Ottoman authorities to 'Akká with three of his friends, presumably to spy on the Bahá'ís in 'Akká. Of him Shoghi Effendi writes:

> The black-hearted scoundrel who befooled and manipulated this vain and flaccid man (Mírzá Yaḥyá) with consummate skill and unyielding persistence was a certain Siyyid Muḥammad, a native of Iṣfahán, notorious for his inordinate ambition, his blind obstinacy and uncontrollable jealousy. To him Bahá'u'lláh had later referred in the Kitab-i-Aqdas as the one who had 'led astray' Mírzá Yaḥyá, and stigmatized him, in one of His Tablets, as the 'source of envy and the quintessence of mischief', while 'Abdu'l-Bahá had described the relationship existing between these two as that of 'the sucking child' to the 'much-prized breast' of its mother. Forced to abandon his studies in the madrisiyi-i-Sadr of Iṣfahán, this Siyyid had migrated, in shame and remorse, to Karbilá, and there joined the ranks of the Báb's followers, and shown, after His martyrdom, signs of vacillation which exposed the shallowness of his faith and the fundamental weakness of his convictions. Bahá'u'lláh's first visit to Karbilá and the marks of undisguised reverence, love and admiration shown Him by some of the most distinguished among the former disciples and companions of Siyyid Káẓim, had aroused in this calculating and unscrupulous schemer an envy, and bred in his soul an animosity, which the forbearance and patience shown him by Bahá'u'lláh had served only to inflame. His deluded helpers, willing tools of his diabolical designs, were the not inconsiderable number of Bábís who, baffled, disillusioned and leaderless, were already predisposed to be beguiled by him into pursuing a path diametrically opposed to the tenets and counsels of a departed Leader.[536]

In His Tablet of Tribulations (Lawḥ-i-Baláyá) written between 1863 and 1892, Bahá'u'lláh alludes to calumnies directed against Him by two unnamed individuals who are suspected as having been the Persian Prime Minister and Siyyid Muḥammad-i-Iṣfáhání. The latter, even though he did not openly rebel against Bahá'u'lláh and was not expelled from the Faith until Adrianople, had begun plotting while Bahá'u'lláh was in Baghdad. He had become envious of Bahá'u'lláh's early influence over the Bábí community, and used Mírzá Yaḥyá as a pawn in his opposition to Bahá'u'lláh. Taherzadeh writes:

> Shortly after Mírzá Yaḥyá had settled in Baghdad, he decided to engage in a profession so as to hide his identity. At first he changed his headgear, adopting a large turban and assuming the name of Ḥájí 'Alíy-i-Las-Furúsh. He then took a shop in a dilapidated part of the city in a bazaar and started working. In the meantime, a man of great evil described by Bahá'u'lláh as 'the embodiment of wickedness and impiety', 'the prime mover of mischief' and 'one accursed of God', entered the scene to influence Mírzá Yaḥyá. He was the notorious Siyyid Muḥammad-i-Iṣfáhání, known as the 'Antichrist of the Baha'i Revelation'. In the early days of the Faith this man was a student at a theological school in Iṣfahán, but was expelled for reprehensible conduct. He embraced the Faith during the early part of the Ministry of the Báb and later went to Karbilá where he joined the ranks of the believers. In the *Kitáb-i-Íqán* (written in 1862) Bahá'u'lláh alludes to him as that 'one-eyed man (he had lost his right eye), who . . . is arising with the utmost malevolence against us.'[537]

364. p. 70 ¶ 113. And there befell Me at the hands of both of them

A reference to the evil collaborations of Mírzá Yaḥyá and Siyyid Muḥammad-i-Iṣfáhání. Shoghi Effendi writes of Mírzá Yaḥyá:

> A constant witness of the ever deepening attachment of the exiles to Bahá'u'lláh and of their amazing veneration for Him; fully aware of the heights to which his Brother's popularity had risen in Baghdád, in the course of His journey to Constantinople, and later through His association with the notables and governors of Adrianople; incensed by the manifold evidences of the courage, the dignity, and independence which that Brother had demonstrated in His dealings with the authorities in the capital; provoked by the numerous Tablets which the Author of a newly-established Dispensation had

> been ceaselessly revealing; allowing himself to be duped by the enticing prospects of unfettered leadership held out to him by Siyyid Muḥammad, the Antichrist of the Bahá'í Revelation . . . refusing to be admonished by prominent members of the community who advised him, in writing, to exercise wisdom and restraint; forgetful of the kindness and counsels of Bahá'u'lláh, who, thirteen years his senior, had watched over his early youth and manhood; emboldened by the sin-covering eye of his Brother, Who, on so many occasions, had drawn a veil over his many crimes and follies, this arch-breaker of the Covenant of the Báb, spurred on by his mounting jealousy and impelled by his passionate love of leadership, was driven to perpetrate such acts as defied either concealment or toleration.
>
> Irremediably corrupted through his constant association with Siyyid Muḥammad, that living embodiment of wickedness, cupidity and deceit, he had already in the absence of Bahá'u'lláh from Ba<u>gh</u>dád, and even after His return from Sulaymáníyyih, stained the annals of the Faith with acts of indelible infamy. His corruption, in scores of instances, of the text of the Báb's writings; the blasphemous addition he made to the formula of the a<u>dh</u>án by the introduction of a passage in which he identified himself with the Godhead; his insertion of references in those writings to a succession in which he nominated himself and his descendants as heirs of the Báb; the vacillation and apathy he had betrayed when informed of the tragic death which his Master had suffered; his condemnation to death of all the Mirrors of the Bábí Dispensation, though he himself was one of those Mirrors; his dastardly act in causing the murder of Dayyán, whom he feared and envied; his foul deed in bringing about, during the absence of Bahá'u'lláh from Ba<u>gh</u>dád, the assassination of Mírzá 'Alí-Akbar, the Báb's cousin; and, most heinous of all, his unspeakably repugnant violation, during that same period, of the honor of the Báb Himself . . .[538]

Shoghi Effendi has thus summarized Mírzá Yaḥyá's attempts to kill Bahá'u'lláh:

> Desperate designs to poison Bahá'u'lláh and His companions, and thereby reanimate his own defunct leadership, began, approximately a year after their arrival in Adrianople, to agitate his mind. Well

aware of the erudition of his half-brother, Áqáy-i-Kalím, in matters pertaining to medicine, he, under various pretexts, sought enlightenment from him regarding the effects of certain herbs and poisons, and then began, contrary to his wont, to invite Bahá'u'lláh to his home, where, one day, having smeared His tea-cup with a substance he had concocted, he succeeded in poisoning Him sufficiently to produce a serious illness which lasted no less than a month, and which was accompanied by severe pains and high fever, the aftermath of which left Bahá'u'lláh with a shaking hand till the end of His life . . .

On another occasion this same Mírzá Yaḥyá had, according to the testimony of one of his wives, who had temporarily deserted him and revealed the details of the above-mentioned act, poisoned the well which provided water for the family and companions of Bahá'u'lláh, in consequence of which the exiles manifested strange symptoms of illness.[539]

365. pp. 70–71 ¶ 114. Assist them to dispel the mists of idle fancy, and to tear away the veils of vain imaginings and hopes.

'Idle fancy' is a translation of *sobaháté-jalál* or 'veils of glory'. The term was first used by Imám 'Alí, the son-in-law of Muhammad, the legitimate successor of the Prophet according to Shí'ih belief, and the fourth Caliph of the Sunnis. Bahá'u'lláh uses the term *sobaháté-jalál* in the *Kitáb-i-Íqán* to refer to the temporal pomp and glory surrounding religious leaders and the glitter and tinsel associated with their rank and office that blind their supine and adoring followers to the truth, rendering them unable to independently investigate reality and accept the divine message:

> And, now, strive thou to comprehend the meaning of this saying of 'Alí, the Commander of the Faithful: 'Piercing the veils of glory, unaided.' Among these 'veils of glory' are the divines and doctors living in the days of the Manifestation of God, who, because of their want of discernment and their love and eagerness for leadership, have failed to submit to the Cause of God, nay, have even refused to incline their ears unto the divine Melody. 'They have thrust their fingers into their ears.' And the people also, utterly ignoring God

> and taking them for their masters, have placed themselves unreservedly under the authority of these pompous and hypocritical leaders, for they have no sight, no hearing, no heart, of their own to distinguish truth from falsehood.[540]

Sobaháté-jalál also pertains to the nominal titles conferred on Mírzá Yaḥyá by the Báb or assumed by him, and which blinded him and others from recognizing 'He Whom God shall make manifest' repeatedly promised in the *Bayán*.

In addition, it refers to apparently exclusivist scriptural statements such as 'the Seal of the Prophets' (Qur'án 33:40) and 'I am the way, the truth, and the life: no man cometh unto the Father, but by me' (John 14:6) that are misinterpreted as proof of the superiority, exclusivity, and finality of a particular Dispensation.

'The veils of vain imaginings and hopes' also refers to the futile aspirations of the two evil collaborators to take over the reins of authority from Bahá'u'lláh. It could also be seen to apply to the Wolf's false assumption that he would benefit from his evil gains: 'Thinkest thou that thou wilt consume that which thine iniquity hath amassed?'[541] and to the Son of the Wolf's belief that he could put out the light of Bahá'u'lláh's Cause (¶ 158).

366. p. 71 ¶ 115. until the light of knowledge prevailed over the darkness of ignorance

The Bahá'í Revelation had to contend with many forces of darkness, including the ignorance, blindness and animosity of the Muslims and the opposition of some of the followers of the Báb. With superhuman resolve Bahá'u'lláh overcame the difficulties by dedicating Himself 'in the daytime and in the night-season' to 'that which would edify the souls of men' and which would create a new race of men.

In the absence of light darkness prevails and evil flourishes. However, when the light of truth comes, the darkness of ignorance recedes.

The Hebrew Bible promises the advent of a 'great light' that will rescue humanity from a spiritual death: 'The people that walked in darkness have seen a great light: they that dwell in the land of the shadow of death, upon them hath the light shined' (Is. 9:2). The Gospel of John (1:4) refers to the Divine Word and Revelation as Life and Light.

It explains (John 1:5, 9) that the Divine Light has lit the path of every man that has come into the world – a light that 'shineth in darkness' but is not overcome by it.

The Qur'án also refers to the Revelation of Muhammad as light:

> O mankind! Verily there hath come to you a convincing proof from your Lord: for We have sent unto you a light (that is) manifest. (4:174)

Again:

> O People of the Book!. . . There hath come to you from God a (new) light and a perspicuous Book, –
>
> Wherewith God guideth all who seek His good pleasure To ways of peace and safety, And leadeth them out of darkness, by His Will, unto the light, – guideth them to a Path that is Straight. (5:15–16)

It promises (39:69) that at the time of the Promised Day of God 'the earth will shine with the light of its Lord'. However, the Qur'án (35:19–22) also contrasts 'the (spiritually) blind and the seeing [perceptive]', 'Darkness and the Light', 'the shade and the heat of the sun', and the 'living and those that are dead'. Individuals are judged by their response to the light (5:44–46).

Today, Bahá'u'lláh represents the divine light shining with utmost brilliance:

> He is a Light which is not followed by darkness and a Truth not overtaken by error. Were He to pronounce water to be wine or heaven to be earth or light to be fire, He speaketh the truth and no doubt would there be about it; and unto no one is given the right to question His authority or to say why or wherefore.[542]

367. p. 72 ¶ 116. in Mázindarán and at Rasht a great many have been most hideously tormented

Mazindaran is a province in northern Persia on the Caspian Sea, and is the native province of Bahá'u'lláh.[543] Rasht and Lahijan are towns in the province of Gílan in northern Persia near the Caspian seaport of Pahlaví.

A wave of persecution occurred in 1300 AH (1882 CE) when many Bahá'ís at various locations around Tehran, Lahijan and Rasht were arrested, imprisoned and tortured by the orders of Kámrán Mírzá Náyeb-al-Salṭana, third surviving and favourite son of Náṣiri'd-Dín Sháh:

> In his role as governor of Tehran and head of the military and police, Kámrán Mírzá was faced with the difficult task of overseeing the suppression of the Bábí and Bahá'í threat. Charged with this by Náṣiri'd-Dín Sháh, but also eager to prove himself against a movement which might threaten his own prerogatives, Kámrán Mírzá periodically initiated arrest and persecution. He employed spies (often clerics) and offered bounties on the heads of important figures in the movement, as well as authorizing outright police measures, deception, blackmail, and torture.[544]

368. p. 72 ¶ 116. Ḥájí Naṣír

Ḥájí Muḥammad-Naṣír Qazvíni was a merchant and a survivor of Shaykh Ṭabarsí. He was one of sixteen Bahá'ís, including his son, who were imprisoned in Rasht. There was a great effort to coerce the Bahá'ís to recant. Ḥájí Naṣír died in prison and his body was desecrated by the population. He was a devoted believer in whose honour Bahá'u'lláh revealed the Tablet of Naṣír. Part of this important Tablet has been translated by Shoghi Effendi into English.[545]

369. p. 72 ¶ 117. In the land of Ṣád (Iṣfahán) the fire of tyranny burned with such a hot flame that every fair-minded person groaned aloud

The letter 'S' in Persian is represented by three letters in Persian alphabet: 'sin', 'se', and 'ṣád'. 'The land of Ṣád' is a reference to Isfahan in the Writings of the Báb and Bahá'u'lláh.

This is an allusion to the martyrdoms of the King of Martyrs and the Beloved of Martyrs by order of the 'Wolf', as well as many other Bahá'ís, including Mullá Káẓim and Mírzá Ashraf, who were martyred by order of the 'Son of the Wolf' and other clerics in Isfahan.

See Annotations 371 and 468.

370. p. 72 ¶ 117. The cities of knowledge and of understanding

That is, all those with faith, understanding, and perception – in another passage they are referred to as 'the inmates of the cities of knowledge and wisdom' (¶ 184). However, the 'Birds of the cities of knowledge' (¶ 204) refers to the Manifestations of God.

371. p. 72 ¶ 117. The twin shining lights

Mírzá Muḥammad-Ḥusayn (*Máḥbúbu'sh-Shuhadá'*, Beloved of Martyrs) and Mírzá Muḥammad-Ḥasan (*Sulṭánu'sh-Shuhadá'* King of Martyrs) were two brothers who were held in high honour. They were Siyyids (that is, direct descendants of Muhammad) and wealthy merchants of Isfahan.[546] They were martyred at the instance of the Imám-Jum'ih (head priest) of that city.

See Annotation 468.

372. p. 72 ¶ 118. Káẓim and they who were with him

Mullá Muḥammad Káẓim was from Talkhunchih, a village in the neighbourhood of Isfahan. He was a learned and well respected divine of that province. He became a believer in 1288 AH (1871–72 CE) and began to teach the Faith to his people. Taherzadeh writes:

> The news spread and he was forced to leave his native village. For a time he lived in Iṣfahán where he succeeded in bringing a number of people under the shadow of the Cause. This news reached the powerful mujtahid of the city, the inveterate enemy of the Cause Shaykh Muḥammad-Báqir (the Wolf), who immediately wrote his death sentence. By this time, however, Mullá Káẓim had relinquished his clerical attire and was working as a labourer in a public bath in the city. He succeeded in slipping out of Iṣfahán back to his own village. Then followed a period of comings and goings to Iṣfahán, Shíráz and Ṭihrán. At last he was arrested in his native village and sent to Iṣfahán where he was put in prison. Prince Masú'd Mírzá the Ẓillu's-Sulṭán summoned Mullá Káẓim to his presence, and when he refused to recant his Faith the Prince implemented the death sentence and ordered his execution. This was in 1877.

> The execution took place in a large public square, the famous Maydán-i-Sháh, where great crowds had assembled to watch. Having refused to recant his Faith and be freed, Mullá Káẓim was beheaded by the executioner. Shaykh Muḥammad-Báqir ordered his corpse to be hung upside-down from a pole situated on the executioner's platform. The rope from which he was suspended broke and his body fell down from a great height. His smashed body was again suspended and the Shaykh announced that anyone who threw a stone at the corpse would assuredly secure a place for himself in paradise. A frenzied crowd carried out the attack. For two days men and women could be seen walking long distances carrying stones. Even pregnant women who could hardly walk took part in this shameful crime. When the body was deserted at night some men even gouged out the eyes and cut off the fingers, the nose, the lips and the ears.
>
> On the morning of the third day Shaykh Muḥammad-Báqir arrived on the scene. Not satisfied with the savage indignities which had been heaped upon the victim, he ordered the corpse to be lowered to the ground for a horseman to gallop over it. And when every part of the corpse was broken, it was delivered to the flames and the charred bones were thrown into a disused well.[547]

It is related that due to his purity, Mullá Káẓim was convinced that the Shaykh's error and animosity was due to his lack of understanding of the Faith. To help the Wolf get a better understanding of the power of of the new Revelation he had gathered some of the Holy Writings, and took them to the Shaykh. Sadly, the Shaykh's actions were motivated by pride.[548]

The Shaykh was aware that the Writings of the Báb and Bahá'u'lláh were often transcribed in those days in red. His reaction was to dismiss the writings in red. It is recounted that at one time one of the Bahá'ís presented the Shaykh with a prayer by Zaynu'l-Ábidin (*Imám al-Sajjad*) the revered fourth Imám, transcribed in red, and an Arabic prayer by Bahá'u'lláh written in black. Demonstrating his lack of faith and sincerity, Shaykh Báqir spoke of the majesty and the depth of meaning of the part written in black but dismissed the red portion of the documents in very derogatory terms.[549]

373. p. 72 ¶ 118. after them, his honor A<u>sh</u>raf

Not to be confused with the Siyyid A<u>sh</u>raf who was martyred in Zanján (Annotation 381; ¶ 118). Shoghi Effendi recounts:

> Mírzá A<u>sh</u>raf was slain in Iṣfáhán, his corpse trampled under foot by <u>Sh</u>ay<u>kh</u> Muḥammad Taqíy-i-Najafí, the 'son of the wolf,' and his pupils, savagely mutilated, and delivered to the mob to be burnt, after which his charred bones were buried beneath the ruins of a wall that was pulled down to cover them.[550]

374. p. 73 ¶ 118. Sardár 'Azíz <u>Kh</u>án

He was present with the Shah's troops during their attack on Bábís at Zanjan. During his tenure as governor of Tabriz several believers, including Mírzá Muṣṭafá Naráqí, were executed in that city. *Nabíl's Narrative* implicates him in the martyrdom of Ṭáhirih, as told by the wife of the Kalantár in whose house Ṭáhirih was imprisoned:

> Three hours later my son returned, his face drenched with tears, hurling imprecations at the Sardár and his abject lieutenants. I tried to calm his agitation, and, seating him beside me, asked him to relate as fully as he could the circumstances of her death. 'Mother,' he sobbingly replied, 'I can scarcely attempt to describe what my eyes have beheld. We straightway proceeded to the Ílkhání garden, outside the gate of the city. There I found, to my horror, the Sardár and his lieutenants absorbed in acts of debauchery and shame, flushed with wine and roaring with laughter. Arriving at the gate, Ṭáhirih dismounted and, calling me to her, asked me to act as her intermediary with the Sardár, whom she said she was disinclined to address in the midst of his revelry. 'They apparently wish to strangle me,' she said. 'I set aside, long ago, a silken kerchief which I hoped would be used for this purpose. I deliver it into your hands and wish you to induce that dissolute drunkard to use it as a means whereby he can take my life.'
>
> When I went to the Sardár, I found him in a state of wretched intoxication. 'Interrupt not the gaiety of our festival!' I heard him shout as I approached him. 'Let that miserable wretch be strangled and her body be thrown into a pit!'[551]

375. p. 73 ¶ 118. Mírzá Muṣṭafá

A detailed account of Mírzá Muṣṭafá Naráqí is provided by 'Abdu'l-Bahá.[552] He is described as a pure and goodly soul, a leading citizen of Naraq and one of the earliest believers to believe in the Báb. He met Bahá'u'lláh in Iraq. He was sent back to Persia where he served the Faith to his utmost ability. He tried to see Bahá'u'lláh in Adrianople but failed to do so. He was asked to return to Persia. He actively taught the Faith in Azerbaijan in collaboration with Shaykh Aḥmad-i-Khurásáni. They were arrested, tortured and martyred in Tabriz. Mírzá Muṣṭafá begged to be killed before Shaykh Aḥmad so that he would not witness his dear friend being killed. It was customary at the time of execution for the victim to turn his face towards the Qiblih of Islam. But Mírzá Muṣṭafá turned towards Adrianople. He was reminded to face the Qiblih but refused to do so. He said 'This is the true Qiblih,' and shouted '*Yá-Bahá'u'l-Abhá*'.

376. p. 73 ¶ 118. his fellow-martyrs

One such martyr was Shaykh Aḥmad-i-Khurásání (see Annotation 375). He was from the same province of Persia as Mírzá Muṣṭafá, and is described as renowned and a scholar. The two were partners in teaching the Faith in Azerbaijan and were martyred together in Tabriz. Their greatness has been recorded for all time in the Writings of Bahá'u'lláh. They received many a Tablet from Him, and after their death He set down, with His exalted pen, the anguish they endured.[553]

377. p. 73 ¶ 118. Badí'

Shoghi Effendi writes:

> Áqá Buzurg of Khurásán, the illustrious 'Badí'' (Wonderful); converted to the Faith by Nabíl, surnamed the 'Pride of Martyrs'; the seventeen-year old bearer of the Tablet addressed to Náṣiri'd-Dín Sháh; in whom, as affirmed by Bahá'u'lláh, 'the spirit of might and power was breathed,' was arrested, branded for three successive days, his head beaten to a pulp with the butt of a rifle, after which his body was thrown into a pit and earth and stones heaped upon it.

> After visiting Bahá'u'lláh in the barracks, during the second year of His confinement, he had arisen with amazing alacrity to carry that Tablet, alone and on foot, to Ṭihrán and deliver it into the hands of the sovereign. A four months' journey had taken him to that city, and, after passing three days in fasting and vigilance, he had met the Sháh proceeding on a hunting expedition to Shimírán. He had calmly and respectfully approached His Majesty, calling out, 'O King! I have come to thee from Sheba with a weighty message'; whereupon at the Sovereign's order, the Tablet was taken from him and delivered to the mujtahids of Ṭihrán who were commanded to reply to that Epistle – a command which they evaded, recommending instead that the messenger should be put to death. That Tablet was subsequently forwarded by the Sháh to the Persian Ambassador in Constantinople, in the hope that its perusal by the Sulṭán's ministers might serve to further inflame their animosity. For a space of three years Bahá'u'lláh continued to extol in His writings the heroism of that youth, characterizing the references made by Him to the sublime sacrifice as the 'salt of My Tablets'.[554]

See also Annotation 244.

378. p. 73 ¶ 119. Najaf-'Alí . . . We have kept both Bahá and the khún-bahá (bloodmoney)!

Áqá Najaf-'Alíy-i-Zanjání was an early follower of the Báb and a survivor of the Zanjan upheaval. He often conveyed Tablets from Bahá'u'lláh to His followers. Taherzadeh writes:

> A devoted believer who came to Adrianople in the early years of Bahá'u'lláh's sojourn . . . He was an admirer of Mullá Muḥammad-'Alíy-i-Ḥujjat, and had been one of his companions during the struggle of Zanján. After the horrid massacre there in 1851, forty-four of the survivors, including Áqá Najaf-'Alí, were despatched to Ṭihrán. All of them were put to death except for Áqá Najaf-'Alí whose life was saved by the kindness of a certain officer in the army. Later, he went to Baghdád and was permitted by Bahá'u'lláh to remain in 'Iráq. He was one of the devoted companions of Bahá'u'lláh who recognized His station during the days of Baghdád . . . In the year

> 1283 AH (1866–1867), Najaf-'Alí was in Adrianople. Bahá'u'lláh sent him to Persia and gave him some Tablets to carry. Upon his arrival in Ṭihrán, he was arrested and taken to prison on the charge of being a follower of Bahá'u'lláh. They tortured him in order that he might disclose the identity of those for whom he was carrying the Tablets. But Áqá Najaf-'Alí did not reveal any name. When the time for his execution arrived his body was already covered with deadly wounds as a result of these tortures.[555]

Shoghi Effendi has written this brief yet moving portrayal of the martyrdom of Áqá Najaf-'Alí:

> Among the sufferers may be singled out the intrepid Najaf-'Alíy-i-Zanjání, a survivor of the struggle of Zanján . . . who, bequeathing the gold in his possession to his executioner, was heard to shout aloud 'Yá Rabbíya'l-Abhá' [All-Glorious Lord] before he was beheaded.[556]

Islam (Qur'án 2:178) prescribes retaliation for murder. In some circumstances the victim's family is compensated financially by the culprit (blood-money or *khún-bahá*). This was clearly not so with the martyrs of this Faith. Instead of receiving compensation, many were grateful to their executioner for allowing them to sacrifice themselves in the path of their Beloved. Several of them, such as Áqá Najaf-'Alí, are recorded to have bestowed their money and prized possessions on the killer, before hastening to the realm above. Áqá Najaf-'Alí thus states that he retained both his faith and integrity and the inestimable honour associated with acting as a devoted witness for the Cause that he loved so much.

379. p. 73 ¶ 119. Mullá 'Alí-Ján

In the words of Shoghi Effendi:

> Mullá 'Alí Ján was conducted on foot from Mázindarán to Ṭihrán, the hardships of that journey being so severe that his neck was wounded and his body swollen from the waist to the feet. On the day of his martyrdom he asked for water, performed his ablutions, recited his prayers, bestowed a considerable gift of money on his executioner, and was still in the act of prayer when his throat was

slit by a dagger, after which his corpse was spat upon, covered with mud, left exposed for three days, and finally hewn to pieces.[557]

380. p. 73 ¶ 119. 'Abá-Baṣír

Muḥammad-'Alíy-i-Salmání, one of the early believers, writes in his memoirs:

> The original name of Abá-Baṣír was Áqá Naqd-'Alí. His father, a certain Ḥájí Muḥammad-Ḥusayn, was martyred in the struggle of Zanján. Áqá Naqd-'Alí was born blind but possessed such insight and understanding that Bahá'u'lláh gave him the title of Baṣír (the Seeing). He was one of the most steadfast followers of Bahá'u'lláh in Zanján. When it became clear to some members of his family that he had embraced the Cause of Bahá'u'lláh and was actively teaching it, they drove him out of his home. It was after this incident that Abá-Baṣír went to live with Siyyid Ashraf. The spiritual ties which united these two souls were further strengthened when Abá-Baṣír married the sister of Ḥájí Ímán, Ashraf's brother-in-law, and settled in that household permanently. Abá-Baṣír, in spite of his blindness, was a man of great capacity. He had memorized many verses of the Qur'án and the traditions, and had such a deep understanding of their meanings that many students of theology used to seek enlightenment from him.[558]

381. p. 73 ¶ 119. Siyyid Ashraf-i-Zanjání

Shoghi Effendi writes:

> Abá-Baṣír and Siyyid Ashraf, whose fathers had been slain in the struggle of Zanján, were decapitated on the same day in that city, the former going so far as to instruct, while kneeling in prayer, his executioner as to how best to deal his blow, while the latter, after having been so brutally beaten that blood flowed from under his nails, was beheaded, as he held in his arms the body of his martyred companion. It was the mother of this same Ashraf who, when sent to the prison in the hope that she would persuade her only son to recant, had warned him that she would disown him were he to denounce his

> faith, had bidden him follow the example of Abá-Baṣír, and had even watched him expire with eyes undimmed with tears.[559]

See also Annotations 380 and 382.

382. pp. 73–74 ¶ 119. the mother of A<u>sh</u>raf

A reference to the mother of Siyyid A<u>sh</u>raf-i-Zanjání. The following is an account by the historian Nabíil:

> Among the women who distinguished themselves by the tenacity of their faith was one named Umm-i-A<u>sh</u>raf [Mother of A<u>sh</u>raf], who was newly married when the storm of Zanján broke out. She was within the fort when she gave birth to her son A<u>sh</u>raf. Both mother and child survived the massacre that marked the closing stages of that tragedy. Years afterwards, when her son had grown into a youth of great promise, he was involved in the persecutions that afflicted his brethren. Unable to persuade him to recant, his enemies endeavoured to alarm his mother and convince her of the necessity of saving him, ere it was too late, from his fate. 'I will disown you as my son,' cried the mother, when brought face to face with him, 'if you incline your heart to such evil whisperings and allow them to turn you away from the Truth.' Faithful to his mother's admonitions, A<u>sh</u>raf met his death with intrepid calm. Though herself a witness to the cruelties inflicted on her son, she made no lamentation, neither did she shed a tear. This marvellous mother showed a courage and fortitude that amazed the perpetrators of that shameless deed. 'I have now in mind,' she exclaimed, as she cast a parting glance at the corpse of her son, 'the vow I made on the day of your birth, while besieged in the fort of 'Alí-Mardán <u>Kh</u>án. I rejoice that you, the only son whom God gave me, have enabled me to redeem that pledge.'[560]

383. p. 74 ¶ 120. This people have passed beyond the narrow straits of names, and pitched their tents upon the shores of the sea of renunciation

'This people' refers to the martyrs mentioned in the Epistle as well as many others who sacrificed their lives and their possessions in the path of Bahá'u'lláh – they were truly 'worthy recipients of the effulgent splendours of Him Who is the King of all names and attributes'.[561] They could not help but leave aside their own interests and desires and seek only the good pleasure of their Lord, testifying with their blood and sacrifice to the truth of His Cause. Their detachment is in sharp contrast to the selfish and mundane pursuits of their denouncers who constantly sought to add to their wealth and improve their rank and standing.

In earlier Dispensations such as Islam, God has been known by many attributes and names and the followers have often held to one or more of these and allowed them to blind their vision. The Revelation of Bahá'u'lláh, however, is 'sanctified above all attributes and holy above all names'.[562]

> In the Lawḥ-i-Naṣír, speaking with the voice of God, Bahá'u'lláh states that a name from among His names which He had created with one Word and into which He had breathed a new life, rose up against Him and opposed His authority. Because of attachment to this name, He testifies that some people of the Bayán rejected His Cause and deprived themselves of His glory. Here Bahá'u'lláh is alluding to the name 'Azal' [Eternity], the title of Mírzá Yaḥyá. Indeed, this name, which is one of the attributes of God, became a barrier for many who blindly followed him because of their attachment to an exalted title. Mírzá Yaḥyá himself was also misled by this name. He extolled its virtues and remained attached to it till the end of his life.[563]

384. p. 75 ¶ 122. the father of Badí'

Ḥájí 'Abdu'l-Majíd-i-Ní<u>sh</u>ápúrí, or Ábá Badí', was a survivor of the struggle of Fort Ṭabarsí. Shoghi Effendi writes:

> In the city of Ma<u>sh</u>had, notorious for its unbridled fanaticism, Ḥájí 'Abdu'l-Majíd, who was the eighty-five year old father of the aforementioned Badí' and a survivor of the struggle of Ṭabarsí, and who, after the martyrdom of his son, had visited Bahá'u'lláh and returned afire with zeal to <u>Kh</u>urásán, was ripped open from waist to throat, and his head exposed on a marble slab to the gaze of a multitude

of insulting onlookers, who, after dragging his body ignominiously through the bazaars, left it at the morgue to be claimed by his relatives.[564]

385. p. 75 ¶ 122. Siyyid Ismá'íl

Reference to Siyyid Ismá'íl-i-Zavari'í, who had been instrumental in teaching the Faith to Nabíl-i-Zarandí, chronicler of Bábí history and author of *The Dawn-Breakers*. Shoghi Effendi writes:

> . . . one of His ardent lovers, a native of Zavárih, Siyyid Ismá'íl by name, surnamed Dhabíḥ (the Sacrifice), formerly a noted divine, taciturn, meditative and wholly severed from every earthly tie, whose self-appointed task, on which he prided himself, was to sweep the approaches of the house in which Bahá'u'lláh was dwelling. Unwinding his green turban, the ensign of his holy lineage, from his head, he would, at the hour of dawn, gather up, with infinite patience, the rubble which the footsteps of his Beloved had trodden, would blow the dust from the crannies of the wall adjacent to the door of that house, would collect the sweepings in the folds of his own cloak, and, scorning to cast his burden for the feet of others to tread upon, would carry it as far as the banks of the river and throw it into its waters. Unable, at length, to contain the ocean of love that surged within his soul, he, after having denied himself for forty days both sleep and sustenance, and rendering for the last time the service so dear to his heart, betook himself, one day, to the banks of the river, on the road to Káẓimayn, performed his ablutions, lay down on his back, with his face turned towards Baghdád, severed his throat with a razor, laid the razor upon his breast, and expired (1275 AH).
>
> Nor was he the only one who had meditated such an act and was determined to carry it out. Others were ready to follow suit, had not Bahá'u'lláh promptly intervened, and ordered the refugees living in Baghdád to return immediately to their native land. Nor could the authorities, when it was definitely established that Dhabíḥ had died by his own hand, remain indifferent to a Cause whose Leader could inspire so rare a devotion in, and hold such absolute sway over, the hearts of His lovers. Apprized of the apprehensions that episode had evoked in certain quarters in Baghdád, Bahá'u'lláh is reported

to have remarked: 'Siyyid Ismá'íl was possessed of such power and might that were he to be confronted by all the peoples of the earth, he would, without doubt, be able to establish his ascendancy over them.' 'No blood,' He is reported to have said with reference to this same Dhabíḥ, whom He extolled as 'King and Beloved of Martyrs,' 'has, till now, been poured upon the earth as pure as the blood he shed.'[565]

386. p. 76 ¶ 124. In former times he that was chosen to be slain was but one person

This is a reference to the fact that there are limits imposed on retaliation in the Torah (Ex. 21:12, 23–24) and the Qur'án (2:178): 'The free for the free, the slave for the slave, the woman for the woman.'

Bahá'u'lláh here notes that in the Dispensation of Abraham only one sacrifice was demanded by God, namely that Abraham sacrifice his son. (The Qur'án does not specify which son. The Hebrew Bible states that it was Isaac but Muslims believe that it was their ancestor Ishmael as decreed by God.) Once Abraham and his son had demonstrated their willingness to obey the Divine decree, God rescinded His demand (Qur'án 37:102–105). In contrast to this one demanded sacrifice, Bahá'u'lláh states that His Revelation has required many sacrifices but few have returned from the field of martyrdom alive (see for example ¶ 252).

387. p. 76 ¶ 124. Balál, the Ethiopian . . . sín . . . shín

Balál or Bílál was an Ethiopian slave who was one of the early converts to Islam in Mecca. The Quraysh despised him, calling *ibn Sauda* (son of the black woman) because his mother had been an Abyssinian princess who was enslaved at the Battle of the Elephant. During the year when Muhammad was born, the Christian Ethiopian governor of Yemen, *Abraha al-Ashram*, who envied the reverence shown to the Kaaba by the Arabs, led an army fortified by elephants against Mecca. This was providentially defeated as described in the Súrih entitled 'Elephant' or 'Fil'). Due to his purity, the Meccans had entrusted him with the keys of the Kaaba. Balál's owner, Umayya bin Khalaf, and others tortured him in the savage glare of the torrid sun of Mecca to recant his new-found faith and to force him to worship the Meccan idols in place of the one God. He had therefore first-hand knowledge that the idols of Kaaba and those who worshipped them were 'deaf, dumb and blind' and incapable of guiding or becoming guided to the 'straight Path' (Qur'án 2:18). Balál's limbs were stretched out and tied to stakes. Whilst lying flat on desert sand and feeling the full intensity of the heat of the Arabian sun, he was whipped and then a large stone was placed on his chest. The boulder heated by the sun burned into his body while at the same time crushing him. However, he did not recant his faith and it is recounted that whilst in this parlous state Balál continued to mutter, '*Ahad, Ahad*' (He is One, One). He was eventually saved by Abu Bakr, an uncle of Muhammad, who purchased him from his master.

He served the Prophet in the battles of Badr, Uhud and Khandaq and had an exalted rank amongst the companions of Muhammad. He achieved additional fame by being chosen to become the first *muezzin* (the one who calls Muslims to prayer – the *adh'án*). Due to his sincerity, his mispronunciation of the Arabic letter *shín* (of *ash-hado*, I testify) as *sín* (*as-hado*) was more pleasing to Muhammad than the correct articulation of His Arab followers. After the passing of Muhammad, Balál no longer performed his duty as muezzin. He was also the first to be put in charge of the treasury (*Bayt-ul-Mál*) in Medina. He died of typhoid in Damascus at the age of sixty.

Bahá'u'lláh's reference to Balál draws parallels between the circumstances that confronted Islam at its inception, and those that His followers faced in the new Dispensation. The early Muslim believers had to endure persecution and martyrdom patiently, resolutely and faithfully, as did His followers many times over. In both circumstances, martyrdom and living sacrifice were a testimony to God's Faith. The cruel and unjust Meccans who arose to eliminate the Faith were defending their commercial interests and social standing; they were advocates of the continuation of a period known as *jáhaliyyah* (age of ignorance). The perpetrators of evil in Bahá'u'lláh's time similarly defended an abrogated Dispensation and their own self-interest. The wealth and power of the Shaykh and his ilk were similar to that of the Meccan idolaters, such as Abu-Sufyán, the self-appointed protectors of the Kaaba and true religion, and contrasted with the simple and sincere faith of the Ethiopian slave. The clear implication is that the Faith of Bahá'u'lláh will also triumph despite the best efforts of the Shaykh and his fellow clerics.

388. p. 77 ¶ 125. while confined in the prison of the Land of Mím

The Land of Mím is a reference to Mazindaran, a vast northern province. On His way to assist the defenders of Fort Ṭabarsí Bahá'u'lláh was arrested in the town of Amul in 1848, and was bastinadoed and imprisoned there.[566]

389. p. 77 ¶ 125. the dungeon of His Majesty the Sháh

A reference to the Síyáh-Chál (Black Pit), the underground dungeon south-east of the Golestán Palace of the Shah and near Sabzih-Maydan in Tehran. Here Bahá'u'lláh was imprisoned for four months from mid-August to mid-December 1852 with 30 or more Bábís. He was chained in pitch darkness three flights of stairs underground, with some 150 fellow prisoners who were thieves, assassins and highwaymen. Here He received the intimations of His divine mission. The dungeon has been described by Shoghi Effendi as the second holiest Bahá'í site in Iran.

390. p. 77 ¶ 125. Qará-Guhar, and . . . Salásil

The notorious chains of Qará-Guhar and Salásil, one of which was placed around Bahá'u'lláh's neck at all times, cut through His flesh and left their marks on His blessed body till the end of His life. They were so heavy that a special wooden fork was provided to support their weight. His neck became bruised and swollen from the pressure of a heavy steel collar, and His back was bent with the weight of the chains.

See also Annotation 170.

391. p. 77 ¶ 125. My grief exceedeth all the woes to which Jacob gave vent, and all the afflictions of Job are but a part of My sorrows!

This is a quotation from the poetry of Ibn al-Fáriḍ (see also ¶ 28).

Jacob was a son of Isaac and grandson of Abraham and is regarded as one the three Patriarchs of the Jews. His life was characterized by pain and sadness. In part, his sufferings were due to the wild and aggressive behaviour of his sons, ten of whom were jealous of the favours that the father had showered on their younger brother Joseph. They threw him into a well, from which he was rescued by some travellers who sold him into slavery in Egypt (Gen. 37:18–28). The brothers then told their father Jacob that Joseph had been killed by wild animals. As a result, Jacob suffered for many years and it was only when he was old and had become blind (Gen. 48:10) that he was reunited with his beloved Joseph.

The Hebrew Bible (Job 1:1–3) describes Job as a blameless, devout and upright man who was quite wealthy and who lived with his family and extensive flocks in the land of Uz (south-western Jordan and southern Israel). He remains faithful to God despite a series of tribulations, including the loss of his wealth, bearing the grief he suffered following the death of seven sons and three daughters, and the appearance of open sores on his body. He becomes loathsome to his wife and brothers and even little children felt contempt for him. He is considered a prophet in the Qur'án who endures many sufferings but never loses his faith, instead, he prays that the merciful Lord may alleviate his afflictions (21:83).

Bahá'u'lláh's ministry was a life of intense suffering and deprivation. It is noteworthy that He too was betrayed by His brother. Among the many tragic events He had to endure was the loss of His son, Mihdi, in the prison of 'Akká and sharing in the pain and suffering of His ardent followers. Shoghi Effendi, describing Bahá'u'lláh's pain and anguish in Baghdad, writes:

> In some of His prayers He poignantly confesses that 'tribulation upon tribulation' had gathered about Him, that 'adversaries with one consent' had fallen upon Him, that 'wretchedness' had grievously touched Him, and that 'woes at their blackest' had befallen Him. God Himself He calls upon as a Witness to His 'sighs and lamentations,' His 'powerlessness, poverty and destitution,' to the 'injuries' He sustained, and the 'abasement' He suffered. 'So grievous hath been My weeping,' He, in one of these prayers, avows, 'that I have been prevented from making mention of Thee and singing Thy praises.' 'So loud hath been the voice of My lamentation,' He, in another passage, avers, 'that every mother mourning for her child would be amazed, and would still her weeping and her grief.' 'The wrongs which I suffer,' He, in His Lawḥ-i-Maryam, laments, 'have blotted out the wrongs suffered by My First Name (the Báb) from the Tablet of creation.'[567]

And the orientalist E. G. Browne writes:

> In a tradition recorded by Jabír, which the Shí'ahs regard as authentic, we read: – In him shall be the perfection of Moses, the preciousness of Jesus, and the patience of Job; his saints shall be abased in his time, and their heads shall be exchanged as presents, even as the heads of the Turk and the Deylamite (Iranian people who inhabited the mountainous regions of northern Irán on the southern shore of the Caspian Sea. They were employed as soldiers from the time of the Sásánian Empire, and long resisted the Muslim conquest of Persia) are exchanged as presents; they shall be slain and burned, and shall be afraid, fearful and dismayed; the earth shall be dyed with their blood, and lamentation shall prevail amongst their women; these are my saints indeed.[568]

392. p. 77 ¶ 126. the martyrdom of Ḥájí Muḥammad-Riḍá . . . no less than thirty-two wounds were inflicted upon his blessed body

The episode is described by Shoghi Effendi:

> in the city of 'Ishqábád the newly established Shí'ah community, envious of the rising prestige of the followers of Bahá'u'lláh who were living in their midst, instigated two ruffians to assault the seventy-year old Ḥají Muḥammad-Riḍáy-i-Iṣfáhání, whom, in broad day and in the midst of the bazaar, they stabbed in no less than thirty-two places, exposing his liver, lacerating his stomach and tearing open his breast. A military court dispatched by the Czar to 'Ishqábád established, after prolonged investigation, the guilt of the Shí'ahs, sentencing two to death and banishing six others – a sentence which neither Náṣiri'd-Dín Sháh, nor the 'ulamás of Ṭihrán, of Mashhad and of Tabríz, who were appealed to, could mitigate, but which the representatives of the aggrieved community, through their magnanimous intercession which greatly surprised the Russian authorities, succeeded in having commuted to a lighter punishment.[569]

393. p. 77 ¶ 126. the City of Love

Refers to 'Ishqábád (Ashgabat) which was originally a part of Persia – the word means literally 'the city of love' in Persian. The city was ceded to the Russian Empire in 1881 and is now the capital of Turkmenistan. In 1908, the first Bahá'í House of Worship was built in Ashgabat. It was badly damaged in a series of earthquakes in 1948 and for structural and safety reasons was demolished in 1963.

394. p. 78 ¶ 127. pleaded with the governor on behalf of their murderers

A reference to the intercession of the Bahá'ís on behalf of the murderers of Ḥájí Muḥammad-Riḍá, as a result of which their death sentences were commuted to life imprisonment. This victory was a source of pride as it demonstrated the spiritual progress and transformation of the followers of Bahá'u'lláh since the dark days of Baghdad.

See Annotation 392.

395. p. 78 ¶ 128. He was cast into prison, in the Land of Ṭá (Ṭihrán)

A reference to the Síyáh-Chál, the dungeon south-east of the palace of Náṣiri'd-Dín Sháh and near the square known as Sabzih-Maydan in Tehran. In 1868 the dungeon was filled in and an opera house was built over the site. The site was Bahá'í property from 1954 until the Islamic Revolution of 1979. It has been described by Shoghi Effendi as the second holiest Bahá'í site in Iran.[570]

396. p. 78 ¶ 128. At one time I found Myself on the heights of mountains; at another in the depths of the prison of Tá (Ṭihrán), in chains and fetters

Here Bahá'u'lláh identifies Himself with His Forerunner – it is an illustration of the oneness of the Manifestations of God. 'The heights of mountains' refers to the Báb's incarceration in Mah-Kú and to the Báb. 'The prison of Ṭá' refers to the Síyáh-Chál in Tehran.

397. p. 79 ¶ 129. a Voice was raised from the direction of Ḥijáz

The 'Voice' refers to Muhammad, Who came from the holy land of Hijaz, a region in south-western Arabia that incorporates Mecca and Medina. Bahá'u'lláh here associates the Quranic verses regarding 'Akká, also situated in a holy land, with His Revelation.

398. p. 79 ¶ 130. Lawḥ-i-Burhán

The Lawḥ-i-Burhán (Tablet of the Proof) was revealed in the Holy Land by Bahá'u'lláh after the martyrdoms of the King and Beloved of Martyrs and others.[571] It severely condemns the acts perpetrated by 'Shaykh Muḥammad-Báqir, surnamed '*Dhi'b*' (Wolf), and Mír Muḥammad-Ḥusayn, the Imám-Jum'ih of Isfahan, surnamed '*Raqshá*' (She-Serpent)'.[572] Here and in subsequent paragraphs of the Epistle Bahá'u'lláh quotes extensively from that Tablet.

Wolves are repeatedly mentioned in the scriptures as an enemy of sheep: a metaphor for evil men with a lust for power and dishonest gain preying on the innocent.

According to the Avesta, the sacred text of the Zoroastrians, wolves are a creation from the 'darkness' of the evil spirit Ahriman. They are ranked among the most cruel of animals,[573] and belong to the *daevas* (noxious creatures that promote chaos and disorder, and are personifications of every imaginable evil).

The Bible contains a number of references to wolves, usually as metaphors for predatory behaviour, greed and destructiveness. In the Gospels, Christ (Matt. 7:15; 10:16) spoke of wolves in sheep's clothing, to illustrate the dangers His followers could face.

In nature, wolves do sometimes kill more than they can eat at one time – biologists call this 'surplus killing'. This has been documented in many carnivorous animals, including bears, coyotes and snow leopards.[574] Accounts of Shaykh Muḥammad-Báqir and his son indicate that, excited by the kill, they too killed Bábís and Bahá'ís indiscriminately.

Serpents are in some cultures a symbol of evil power and refer to a wily, treacherous, or malicious person.[575] It is a Biblical name (Gen. 3:1–5, Rev. 20) for Satan. The Book of Revelation (12:3–9) alludes to the Umayyad rulers who opposed the Law of God, Muhammad and the Imáms as a serpent or dragon which was waiting to also get possession of the Promised One.[576]

John the Baptist called the Pharisees and Sadducees a brood of vipers, a reference to their cunning and malignancy (Matt. 3:7): 'But when he saw many of the Pharisees and Sadducees come to his baptism, he said unto them, O generation of vipers, who hath warned you to flee from the wrath to come?' Christ similarly described the religious leaders of His time as serpents and vipers for their deviousness, deadliness, and pretensions of piety:

> O generation of vipers, how can ye, being evil, speak good things? for out of the abundance of the heart the mouth speaketh. (Matt. 12:34)

> Woe unto you, scribes and Pharisees, hypocrites! . . . Ye serpents, ye generation of vipers, how can ye escape the damnation of hell?' (Matt. 23:29–30, 33)

Relevant to the behaviour of the Imám-Jum'ih is a hadith which describes the accumulation of wealth that is not coupled with giving alms as a poisonous serpent in the Day of Resurrection:

> Narrated Abu Huraira: Allah's Apostle said, 'Whoever is made wealthy by Allah and does not pay the Zakat of his wealth, then on the Day of Resurrection his wealth will be made like a bald-headed poisonous male snake with two black spots over the eyes. The snake will encircle his neck and bite his cheeks and say, "I am your wealth, I am your treasure."'[577]

399. pp. 79–80 ¶ 131. The winds of hatred have encompassed the Ark of Baṭḥá (Mecca), by reason of that which the hands of the oppressors have wrought

This is the first sentence of Lawḥ-i-Burhán (Tablet of the Proof), Bahá'u'lláh's Tablet addressed to Shaykh Muḥammad Báqir, the 'Wolf', the father of Shaykh Muḥammad Taqíy-i-Najafí.

The 'Ark' refers to the boat of Noah in which creation found salvation. The Dispensation of Muhammad represented a further Ark of

Salvation. In keeping with the concept of oneness of Faith, the Ark of Salvation that originated in Mecca is today identified by the Dispensation of Bahá'u'lláh. Hence, the actions of the 'Wolf' were assaults on the entire Faith of God and His eternal Divine Covenant.

400. p. 80 ¶ 131. O thou who art reputed for thy learning!

This refers to Shaykh Muḥammad-Báqir. In the Lawḥ-i-Burhán addressed to him, Bahá'u'lláh states:

> O foolish one! Know thou that he is truly learned who hath acknowledged My Revelation, and drunk from the Ocean of My knowledge, and soared in the atmosphere of My love, and cast away all else besides Me, and taken firm hold on that which hath been sent down from the Kingdom of My wondrous utterance.[578]

The pride of the clergymen of Shí'ih Islam in their acquired religious learning is particularly perplexing considering that one of their well-known hadith describes the vastness of the knowledge that will be brought by their Promised One:

> Imám Ja'far ibn Muḥammad as-Sádiq . . . said: 'Knowledge is contained in twenty-seven letters (parts) and everything which all of the (previous) messengers brought was merely two of these letters and until the day (when al-Mahdi makes his advent), the people will not be given knowledge except of these two letters. So then when our Qa'im makes his advent, he will bring with him the other twenty-five letters (of knowledge) and he will spread these among the people and add these to the previous two letters (parts) such that he will have imparted the twenty-seven letters (of knowledge) to them.[579]

401. p. 80 ¶ 131. Thou hast pronounced sentence against them for whom the books of the world have wept

A reference to the death sentences Shaykh Muḥammad-Báqir pronounced against the 'King of Martyrs' and the 'Beloved of the Martyrs'.

The 'books of the world' refer to the scriptures of all earlier Dispensations. The Bible and the Qur'án contain a number of recurrent admonitions concerning the persecution of divine Revelations. For example, the Bible:

> Wherefore, behold, I send unto you prophets, and wise men, and scribes: and some of them ye shall kill and crucify; and some of them shall ye scourge in your synagogues, and persecute them from city to city:
>
> That upon you may come all the righteous blood shed upon the earth, from the blood of righteous Abel unto the blood of Zacharias son of Barachias [a Hebrew prophet], whom ye slew between the temple and the altar . . .
>
> O Jerusalem, Jerusalem, thou that killest the prophets, and stonest them which are sent unto thee, how often would I have gathered thy children together, even as a hen gathereth her chickens under her wings, and ye would not! (Matt. 23:34–35, 37; quoted by Shoghi Effendi in *The World Order of Bahá'u'lláh*, p. 176)

The Qur'án:

> So oft then as an apostle cometh to you with that which your souls desire not, swell ye with pride, and treat some as impostors, and slay others? (2:87, Rodwell translation; quoted by Bahá'u'lláh in the *Kitáb-i-Íqán*, p. 13)

> . . . each nation schemed against their apostle to lay violent hold on him, and disputed with vain words to refute the truth. (40:5, Rodwell translation; quoted by 'Abdu'l-Bahá, *A Traveler's Narrative*, p. 73)

402. p. 80 ¶ 131. There is no hatred in Mine heart for thee nor for anyone

Bahá'u'lláh tells the ruthless Shaykh that despite his cruelty and all the attempts of the clergy to malign and extirpate His Faith, He bears him and his fellow clerics no malice. Instead, His interest is clearly to open their eyes and ears and to show them their path to redemption (see Annotation 58).

We are reminded of Christ's prayer from the cross (Luke 23:34): 'Father, forgive them; for they know not what they do.' The first Christian martyr, Stephen, also while being stoned 'cried with a loud voice, Lord, lay not this sin to their charge' (Acts 7:60). When Christ's disciples wondered whether God would rain down fire on the people who had mistreated them, Christ explained sternly that He had come to save and not to destroy lives (Luke 9:54–56).

The names of God in the Qur'án include *al-Afuw* ('Eraser of sins' or 'the Pardoner'), and *al-Ghafur*, ('the all-Forgiving' or 'the Oft-Forgiving').

Bahá'u'lláh declares that humanity's sins are a means by which God demonstrates His attributes. He moreover stated in this connection: 'Had it not been for Thy name, the Concealer, and for Thy name, the Ever-Forgiving, and for the sweet savours of Thy name, the Most Merciful, all Thy chosen ones had been reckoned amongst the perverse and the wicked.'[580]

403. p. 80 ¶ 131. O thou who art even as nothing!

'Nothing' is a translation of the word *mauhúm*, which means 'figment of the imagination', and refers to the evanescent life of the Shaykh, and the fact that all his theological learning amounted to nothing but represented 'idle fancies and vain imaginings'.

404. p. 80 ¶ 131. Thou hast torn in pieces a remnant of the Prophet Himself

In other words, by killing the two brothers who were the descendants of the Prophet Muhammad, believers in *Qá'im al-Mahdi* ('the Guided Who will arise') and the best fruits of His Faith, the Shaykh had torn away (melted) part of the Soul of Muhammad (colloquially, a piece of his liver or raiment), and had deluded himself that he had done a great service to Islam (see Annotation 405).

Súrih 11:86 of the Qur'án sends salutations to the 'Remnant of God'. According to a Shí'ih tradition a title of the Promised One is 'Remnant of God':

> A man once asked Imám Ja'far ibn Muḥammad as-Sádiq (peace be upon both of them) how he should send his salutations upon Imám

> al-Qá'im (may Alláh hasten his advent) and the Imám replied: 'Say: Greetings be upon you, O' Remnants of God [*As-Salámu 'Alaykum Ya Baqiyatulláh*]!'[581]

In Judaism several Prophets such as Micah, Jeremiah and Zephaniah use the word 'remnant' to refer to the Jews who had survived exile and who were destined to return to the Holy Land.

405. pp. 80–81 ¶ 131. and imagined that thou hadst helped the Faith of God

The Shaykh most likely considered the followers of the Báb and Bahá'u'lláh as those 'who had gone astray' (Qur'án 1:7), who spread 'mischief' or 'corruption (*fasád*) in the land' and who waged 'a war against God' (Qur'án 5:33). Their eradication was therefore compulsory and in keeping with the many verses of the Qur'án that condone war (*jihád*) with non-believers (*káfirun*). He would have believed in this way that his obsession and nefarious activities were aiding God and Islam, and were in accordance with the Qur'án:

> Thou art our Protector; help us against those who stand against Faith [*káfirs*, unbelievers]. (2:286)

> God will certainly aid those who aid His (cause) . . . (22:40)

406. p. 81 ¶ 131. the soul of the Chaste One (Fáṭimih) melted, by reason of thy cruelty

A reference to Fáṭimih, the daughter of the Prophet Muhammad, wife of Imám 'Alí, and the mother of Imám Ḥasan and Imám Ḥusayn – hence a most revered individual in Shí'ih Islam (see Epistle, ¶ 22 and Annotation 122).

The Prophet Muhammad had three sons: al-Qásim, 'Abdu'lláh and Ṭáhir (also known as Ṭayib), and four daughters: Zaynab, Ruqayyá, Umm-Kulthum and Fáṭimih.

Muhammad was 35 years old when Fáṭimih was born. When she was five years old Muhammad assumed the mantle of prophethood. She accepted His Call and is considered the youngest Muslim in Islam.

Fáṭimih was also known by the titles 'Zahrá', 'Batul' (the Immaculate), 'Umm al-Ḥasan wal-Ḥusayn' (the mother of Ḥasan and Ḥusayn) and 'Ummu Abeeha' ('the mother of her father', because of her care of the Prophet). Her father died when she was 28 years old, and she died six months later.

It was Fáṭimih who continued the lineage of the Prophet. She had five children: Ḥasan, Ḥusayn, Muhsin, Ummu Kulthum, and Zaynab; Muhsin passed away as a child. Her male descendants are known as Siyyids. Thus the two brothers who gave their lives for Bahá'u'lláh – the King of Martyrs and Beloved of Martyrs – were the direct descendants of Fáṭimih.

Compare: 'The Chaste One (Fáṭimih) hath cried out by reason of thine iniquity, and yet thou dost imagine thyself to be of the family of the Apostle of God!' (¶ 157).

407. p. 81 ¶ 132. the Pharisees and the idolatrous priests

This reference is to the religious leaders of the Jews, the Meccan Quraysh tribe and the non-Muslim Arabs of Medina who opposed Muhammad.

'Pharisees' refers to members of a Jewish sect that flourished during the first century BCE and first century CE. Because of their treatment of Christ, the word 'Pharisee' came to mean a sanctimonious, self-righteous or hypocritical person. Although a minority in the Sanhedrin and amongst the priests, they seemed to control the decision-making of the Sanhedrin because they had the support of the people. They accepted the written Torah but gave equal weight to oral tradition and attempted to defend this position by saying it went all the way back to Moses. Evolving over the centuries, these traditions such as the Talmud added substantially to God's Word, which is forbidden in the Torah (Deut. 4:2), with the Pharisees insisting that these traditions must be obeyed along with the Torah. Even more tragically, the Pharisees and the Sadducees used the tradition to object to Christ's Revelation, earning numerous rebukes from Jesus.

The Jewish leaders raised similar objections to Muhammad in Medina. As Reuven Firestone comments:

> The Jews of Medina had no choice but to oppose Muhammad as a false prophet who, from their perspective, was distorting the truth

> of God's revelation that had already been fully disclosed and codified in the Torah. But from the perspective of Muhammad and his followers, the Medinan Jews were unequivocally trying to oppose God by resisting and delegitimizing his prophecy and the authentic redemptive message that he brought. Parallel scenarios are easily found with the emergence of Christianity and its revelation in relation to Judaism, the emergence of Islam and its revelation in relation to Christianity, and the emergence of post-Qur'anic religion and its revelation such as Bahaism in relation to Islam.[582]

The phrase 'idolatrous priests' is used in the Hebrew Bible to describe the priests of Baal who were destroyed by King Josiah (II Kings 23:5) who reigned c. 640 BCE; worshippers of calves (Hos. 10:5, c. 786–746 BCE); and the priests of Baal during the time of Zephaniah (1:4, 640–609 BCE). Here it refers to the pagan Meccan leaders, such as Amr ibn Hisham, often known as Abu Jahl Abu Tálib, and Abu Sufyán ibn al-Harith who tended to the 360 gods of the Kaaba during the pre-Islamic period, and who vehemently resisted Muhammad.

408. p. 81 ¶ 132. Muḥammad, the Apostle of God . . . came unto them with a Book that judged between truth and falsehood with a justice which turned into light the darkness of the earth

'A Book' is a translation of *Al-Furqán* which refers to the Qur'án and is the title of the 25th Súrih. It means the 'Criterion' or 'the Discriminator' between right and wrong. In each successive Dispensation, God redefines truth and re-establishes justice, and thereby differentiates good from evil, truth from falsehood and superstition, justice and equity from unjustness and wrongfulness, and spiritual light from the darkness of ignorance.

Notably, God in the Book of Isaiah (45:6–7) says:

> That they may know from the rising of the sun, and from the west, that there is none beside me. I am the Lord, and there is none else. I form the light, and create darkness: I make peace, and create evil: I the Lord do all these things.

See also Annotation 202.

409. p. 81 ¶ 132. thou hast produced, in this day, the same proofs which the foolish divines advanced in that age

The religious leaders at the time of Muhammad, described in the Qur'án as 'the chiefs of unbelievers', insisted that He was an imposter and 'no more than a man like yourselves' and 'only a man possessed' (23:24–25); 'only one of those bewitched' and 'a mortal like us' with pretentious and fabricated claims (26:153–154). They challenged Him to back up his claims by performing miracles on demand (17:90–93):

> They say: 'We shall not believe in thee, until thou cause a spring to gush forth for us from the earth,
>
> 'Or (until) thou have a garden of date trees and vines, and cause rivers to gush forth 1in their midst, carrying abundant water;
>
> 'Or thou cause the sky to fall in pieces, as thou sayest (will happen), against us; or thou bring God and the angels before (us) face to face:
>
> 'Or thou have a house adorned with gold, or thou mount a ladder right into the skies. No, we shall not even believe in thy mounting until thou send down to us a book that we could read.' Say: 'Glory to my Lord! Am I aught but a man, – an apostle?

That the 'return' of an earlier Manifestation of God is accompanied by a return of His detractors is a theme of the *Kitáb-i-Íqán*:

> Leaders of religion, in every age, have hindered their people from attaining the shores of eternal salvation, inasmuch as they held the reins of authority in their mighty grasp. Some for the lust of leadership, others through want of knowledge and understanding, have been the cause of the deprivation of the people. By their sanction and authority, every Prophet of God hath drunk from the chalice of sacrifice . . .[583]

> And whensoever the portals of grace did open, and the clouds of divine bounty did rain upon mankind, and the light of the Unseen did shine above the horizon of celestial might, they all denied Him, and turned away from His face – the face of God Himself. Refer ye, to verify this truth, to that which hath been recorded in every sacred Book . . .

> . . . Not one single Manifestation of Holiness hath appeared but He was afflicted by the denials, the repudiation, and the vehement opposition of the people around Him. Thus it hath been revealed: 'O the misery of men! No Messenger cometh unto them but they laugh Him to scorn' (Qur'án 36:30, Rodwell). Again He saith: 'Each nation hath plotted darkly against their Messenger to lay violent hold on Him, and disputed with vain words to invalidate [refute] the truth' (Qur'án 40:5, Rodwell).[584]

Therefore, Bahá'u'lláh equates the Shaykh and his fellow clergymen with the Pharisees who opposed Christ and the religious leaders who opposed Muhammad.

410. p. 81 ¶ 132. this great Prison

A reference to the Most Great Prison in 'Akká.[585]

411. p. 81 ¶ 132. Thou hast, truly, walked in their ways, nay, hast surpassed them in their cruelty, and hast deemed thyself to be helping the Faith and defending the Law of God

Here, the lack of faith, negligence, heedlessness, blindness, objections and opposition of the Shí'ih Muslim clergy is compared by Bahá'u'lláh to the Jewish religious leaders in Medina and the pagan Meccan priests in the time of Muhammad, who opposed Him.

Compare ¶ 131, Annotation 405.

412. p. 81 ¶ 132. Thine iniquity hath made Gabriel to groan

It was while in the Cave of Hira, outside the holy city of Mecca, that Muhammad first heard the voice of Gabriel (Qur'án 96:1, Rodwell) which bade Him 'Recite thou, in the name of thy Lord who created . . .'[586] In other words, the Archangel, the personification of the Divine Spirit who announced God's Revelation to Muhammad, also laments the cruelty of the Shaykh and his opposition to God's Faith.

413. p. 82 ¶ 132. the knowledge of all things as recorded in the preserved Tablet

The term 'preserved Tablet' (*Fee lawḫin maḫfooṯhin*) occurs in the Qur'án (85:22). It refers to the 'Mother Book', the Source of all Revelations, from which all Revelations emanate. Therefore, it may be taken to refer to the Revelation of Bahá'u'lláh, the Source of all truth.

414. p. 82 ¶ 133. How is it, then, that thou hast bidden men to curse Me? Didst thou, in this, follow the promptings of thine own desires, or didst thou obey thy Lord? Produce thou a sign, if thou art one of the truthful

The Qur'án forbids cursing and wishing ill on anyone, and condemns individual hostility. It decries the fact that man, out of his ill-considered decisions, prays for evil rather than good (17:11). Bahá'u'lláh challenges the 'Wolf' and the 'Son of the Wolf' to provide evidence that they are acting according to God's will and not merely from their own perversity.

415. p. 82 ¶ 133. Say not to every one who meeteth you with a greeting, 'Thou art not a believer'

This is a quotation from the following verse of the Qur'án (4:94, Rodwell):

> O believers! when ye go forth to the fight for the cause of God, be discerning, and say not to every one who meeteth you with a greeting, 'Thou art not a believer' in your greed after the chance good things of this present life! With God are abundant spoils. Such hath been your wont in times past; but God hath been gracious to you. Be discerning, then, for God well knoweth what ye do.

This verse was reportedly revealed after several incidents when individuals were killed for their possessions, under the pretence of waging *jihád*, even after they confessed their belief in God and His Prophet. Muslims were to accept a profession of belief from anyone who uttered it, and not reject it out of hand, seeking the ephemeral benefits of this earthly world.

The injunction of the Qur'án applies aptly to the 'Wolf' and the 'Son of Wolf' and all the Muslim clerics who, without having seen Bahá'u'lláh, had prejudged His Faith and accused His followers of being unbelievers – this in spite of the fact that Bahá'ís believe in God and the Prophet Muhammad and are the first to defend the truest interests of Islam.

416. pp. 82–83 ¶ 133. If thou deniest Me, by what proof canst thou vindicate the truth of that which thou dost possess? Produce it, then, O thou who hast joined partners with God, and turned aside from His sovereignty that hath encompassed the worlds!

Bahá'u'lláh calls the Shaykh a *mushrik* (a term originally reserved for the pagans of Mecca who considered their gods as equal associates of Allah, and thus 'joined partners with God') because he also without any proof had acted at his own behest and not according to the precepts of the Qur'án. Bahá'u'lláh challenges the Shaykh that to deny Him is to deny all past Revelations:

> O people, if ye deny these verses, by what proof have ye believed in God? Produce it, O assemblage of false ones.[587]

The following account is given by the historian Nabíl about Bahá'u'lláh's receipt of the Message of the Báb transmitted to Him by Mullá Ḥusayn:

> As I approached the house of Bahá'u'lláh, I recognised His brother Mírzá Músá, who was standing at the gate, and to whom I communicated the object of my visit. He went into the house and soon reappeared bearing a message of welcome. I was ushered into His presence, and presented the scroll to Mírzá Músá, who laid it before Bahá'u'lláh. He bade us both be seated. Unfolding the scroll, He glanced at its contents and began to read aloud to us certain of its passages. I sat enraptured as I listened to the sound of His voice and the sweetness of its melody. He had read a page of the scroll when, turning to His brother, He said: 'Músá, what have you to say? Verily I say, whoso believes in the Qur'án and recognises its Divine origin, and yet hesitates, though it be for a moment, to admit that these

soul-stirring words are endowed with the same regenerating power, has most assuredly erred in his judgment and has strayed far from the path of justice.'[588]

See also ¶ 132, ¶ 159, ¶ 165.

417. p. 83 ¶ 134. thy sins which have caused the leaves of the Divine Lote-Tree to be burnt up

A healthy tree is characterized by verdant leaves. Bahá'u'lláh informs the 'Son of the Wolf' that he has inflicted incalculable harm on the Tree of His Revelation and burnt the leaves of God's Manifestation, the Divine Lote-Tree, by his sinful actions – he had impeded the progress of God's Faith.

As the reality of God's prophets is one, the Lote-Tree may be considered to refer to the Tree of Muhammad as the two Siyyids that the 'Wolf' killed were its leaves (descendants), but at the same time the 'Wolf' had attacked the Tree of Bahá'u'lláh's Revelation. Later in the same paragraph Bahá'u'lláh states that this Tree 'hath been raised up in truth by God', and that 'notwithstanding the things that befell it by reason of thy (the Wolf's) cruelty and of the transgressions of such as are like thee, calleth aloud and summoneth all men' to the divine Revelation.

The Báb refers to His Revelation as 'only a leaf among the leaves of His (Bahá'u'lláh's) paradise' (see ¶ 221).

In His Tablet to Náṣiri'd-Dín Sháh Bahá'u'lláh refers to Himself as 'a leaf' which the winds of the will of thy Lord, the Almighty, the All-Praised, have stirred' (¶ 12 and ¶ 65).

Notably, in the Dispensations of the Báb and Bahá'u'lláh 'leaf' often refers to a pious woman, many of whom also suffered in the various upheavals. Bahá'u'lláh explains why He has bestowed this title on one of those pious women: 'We have designated thee "a leaf" that thou mayest, like unto leaves, be stirred by the gentle wind of the Will of God – exalted be His glory – even as the leaves of the trees are stirred by onrushing winds.'[589]

The Bible also mentions 'leaf' in the context of someone who lives life according to the will of God:

> Blessed is the man that walketh not in the counsel of the ungodly, nor standeth in the way of sinners, nor sitteth in the seat of the scornful.
>
> But his delight is in the law of the Lord; and in his law doth he meditate day and night.
>
> And he shall be like a tree planted by the rivers of water, that bringeth forth his fruit in his season; his leaf also shall not wither; and whatsoever he doeth shall prosper. (Ps. 1:1–3)

> He that trusteth in his riches shall fall: but the righteous shall flourish as a branch. (Prov. 11:28; English Standard Version: like a green leaf)

418. p. 83 ¶ 134. and the Rock to cry out

Christ called the Apostle Peter the 'rock' (*Petros* in Greek and *Cephas* in Aramaic) on which the foundational Christian faith and belief would be based (Matt. 16:15–19):

> He [Jesus] saith unto them [disciples], But whom say ye that I am? And Simon Peter answered and said, Thou art the Christ, the Son of the living God.
>
> And Jesus answered and said unto him, Blessed art thou, Simon Barjona: for flesh and blood hath not revealed it unto thee, but my Father which is in heaven.
>
> And I say also unto thee, That thou art Peter, and upon this rock I will build my church; and the gates of hell shall not prevail against it.
>
> And I will give unto thee the keys of the kingdom of heaven: and whatsoever thou shalt bind on earth shall be bound in heaven: and whatsoever thou shalt loose on earth shall be loosed in heaven.

The term 'Rock' is often used in the Writings of Bahá'u'lláh in this context:

> He it is Who hath caused the Rock to shout, and the Burning Bush to lift up its voice, upon the Mount rising above the Holy Land, and proclaim: 'The Kingdom is God's, the sovereign Lord of all, the All-Powerful, the Loving!'[590]

> This is the day whereon the Rock (Peter) crieth out and shouteth, and celebrateth the praise of its Lord, the All-Possessing, the Most High, saying: 'Lo! The Father is come, and that which ye were promised in the Kingdom is fulfilled!'[591]

'Abdu'l-Bahá has written that the faith of Peter remained strong until Christ was delivered into the hands of His enemies. His faith was restored when, as predicted by Jesus (Matt. 26:75), the rooster crowed after Peter had denied Christ:

> Peter, who was the Rock (of the Christian Dispensation), was firm and solid; but, in the moment of Christ's deliverance, that Rock quaked a little, until the crowing of the cock was raised.[592]

It is often forgotten that the foundational belief in Christianity is the good news (*injil*) of the coming of the Father and His Kingdom. Christ commissioned Peter and His other disciples to proclaim the glad-tidings to all nations and then the end would come. Hence, Bahá'u'lláh states that the foundations of Christianity lament as to what had befallen the good news and the Revelation of the Father at the hand of the Muslim clerics.

Shoghi Effendi writes, 'It was he (Pope Pius IX), who, claiming to be the successor of St. Peter, was reminded by Bahá'u'lláh that "this is the day whereon the Rock crieth out and shouteth . . . saying: 'Lo, the Father is come, and that which ye were promised in the Kingdom is fulfilled.'"'[593]

419. p. 83 ¶ 134. the Veil of Divinity was rent asunder

The 'Wolf' was required to 'Rend . . . asunder the veils of idle fancies and vain imaginings' (¶ 130) but instead, he rent asunder the Veil of Divinity of God's Revelation. The phrase is also an allusion to an event described in the Bible when the loud cry of the dying Christ coincided symbolically with the tearing of the veil of the temple:

> Jesus, when he had cried again with a loud voice, yielded up the ghost.
>
> And, behold, the veil of the temple was rent in twain from the top to the bottom; and the earth did quake, and the rocks rent . . . (Matt. 27:50–51)

The Temple of Jerusalem was divided into three parts: the Outer Court, open to all; the Holy Place, to which the ministering priests had daily access to burn incense and trim the lamps; and the Holy of Holies, which contained the Ark of the Covenant and was thought to be the equivalent of the Presence of God, and where only the High Priest was permitted to go once a year, on the great Day of Atonement to intercede on behalf of the congregation – for the other 364 days the shrine lay silent, untrodden and dark. Between it and the less sacred Holy Place hung a heavy veil. This separated sinful humanity from the symbol of the earthly dwelling-place of God.

The condemnation of Jesus by the Sanhedrin and the High Priest Caiaphas resulted in Christ's crucifixion. Through His sacrifice, and as symbolized by the torn Temple veil, the barrier between God and His creation was torn: There was no need for the intercession of man-made priests – Christ was the High Priest (Heb. 5:10; 6:20; 8:1). Similarly, the 'Wolf' had caused the Veil of Divinity to be torn in this day — man now has once again direct access to divine forgiveness and favours. The actions of the 'Wolf' underline the damage done by religious leaders who interpose themselves between man and true understanding of the Word of God.

420. p. 83 ¶ 134. the Ark has foundered

The 'Ark' refers symbolically to God's Dispensation on which depends the salvation of humanity. 'Foundered' means that the potential of the Dispensation to effect improvement in the spiritual life of humanity has been hampered.

In the Bible, the Ark refers to the ship of Noah and the Ark of the Covenant that contained the Ten Commandments. The Book of Revelation (11:19) promises that 'the Ark of his Testament' or Covenant will once again appear in the Temple of the Lord.

The Ark of Baṭḥá refers specifically to the Dispensation of Muhammad. 'The "Crimson Ark" refers to the Cause of Bahá'u'lláh. His followers are designated as "companions of the Crimson Ark", lauded by the Báb in the Qayyúmu'l-Asmá.'[594]

See also Annotations 567, 578 and 618.

421. p. 83 ¶ 134. the She-Camel was hamstrung

The account of the She-Camel of Ṣáliḥ is given in the Qur'án (7:73–79; 11:61–69; 26:141–158; 54:23–31, and 91:11–15). The female camel was a symbol of the miraculous gift that God gave to Thámúd, a tribe that lived in Al-Hijr in Arabia, at their request as a sign and proof that Ṣáliḥ had indeed been sent as His Messenger. They had previously rejected Messengers sent to them. The 'She-Camel' denotes the divine Revelation. It produced sufficient milk to supply the whole community, and thus symbolically represented the Prophet Ṣáliḥ's Revelation. The people of Thámúd broke the divine commandments, hamstrung and killed the She-Camel, that is, paralysed God's Faith, and were punished for it; all the disbelievers were killed in an earthquake.

See also Annotation 472.

422. p. 84 ¶ 134. Sadratu'l-Muntahá and the Supreme Horizon

This refers to the Manifestation of God and the Supreme Horizon, the horizon from which the spiritual Sun dawns.

See Annotation 239.

423. p. 85 ¶ 135. Wish ye, then, for death, if ye are sincere

Muhammad challenged the religious leaders of the Jewish and Christian communities of His time (Qur'án 2:94) to wish for death if they truly believed that salvation was theirs exclusively, and that they alone would be admitted to heaven. Instead they appeared to be determined to avail themselves of the fleeting pleasures of this life. The same challenge now applies also to those Muslims who believe that theirs is the only path to salvation.

In contrast, the followers of Bahá'u'lláh have not shown any reluctance in this respect. In the same paragraph of the Epistle, Bahá'u'lláh writes concerning His followers: 'So carried away have they been by the living waters of the love of the Most Merciful, that neither the arms of the world nor the swords of the nations have deterred them from setting their faces towards the ocean of the bounty of their Lord.'

424. p. 86 ¶ 136. the Son of 'Imrán

'Imrán is a reference to the father of Moses. See Annotation 254.

425. p. 86 ¶ 137. the Bayán

The *Bayán* (Utterance or Exposition) refers to the Book of the Báb which is 'the repository of the laws ordained by the Báb', and 'Peerless among the doctrinal works of the Founder of the Bábí Dispensation. It is interspersed with 'unnumbered passages . . . in which He fixes the date of the promised Revelation . . .'[595]

426. p. 86 ¶ 138. martyrs of this Revelation

See Annotations 368–386 for the previous references to martyrs.

427. p. 86 ¶ 139. Mírzá Hádí Dawlat-Ábádí

Mírzá Hádí-i-Dawlat-Ábádí (also written Mírzá Hádíy-i-Dawlat-Ábádí) was a Muslim clergyman in Isfahan. He was involved in politics and supported the constitutional party. He became a follower of the Báb but never actively taught His Faith. He later became an Azalí, and Mírzá Yaḥyá appointed him as his representative in Persia and his successor. Very corrupt and ambitious, Hádí succeeded in misleading some of the Bábís to follow Mírzá Yaḥyá. The latter bestowed on him the title *wadud* or 'beloved' which is numerically equal to Hádí. In response to the falsehood that this man had instilled into the minds of His followers, Bahá'u'lláh writes in the same paragraph of the Epistle:

> Certain faint-hearted ones, however, such as Hádí and others, have tampered with the Cause of God and have, in their concern for this fleeting life, said and done that which caused the eye of justice to weep and the Pen of Glory to groan, notwithstanding their ignorance of the essentials of this Cause.

Bahá'u'lláh warned the Bábís in the Ṭarazát:

> O people of the Bayán! It is men like unto Hádí Dawlat-Ábádí who,

> with turban and staff [the insignia of a mullá]. have been the source of opposition and hindrance and have so grievously burdened the people with superstitions that even at the present time they still expect the appearance of a fictitious person from a fictitious place.[596]

After allegations of his Bábí affiliations surfaced, he was taken into custody. In order to please Shaykh Najafí, the Mujtahid of Isfahan, and protect his financial interests, he agreed to attend a number of his ceremonies and publicly denounce and slander the Faith. His denunciation came during a heavy round of persecutions in nearby Najafabad in which many Bábís were arrested and killed. In private, he considered himself the successor of Mírzá Yaḥyá, but outwardly he pretended to be a devoted Muslim and a Shí'ih. He frequently held the Muslim ceremony of *Rawḍih-khání* in his house (¶ 177).

428. p. 86 ¶ 139. Ṣád-i-Iṣfáhání

Mírzá Murtiḍá, known as Ṣadru'l-'Ulamá, was a clergyman of low intelligence who became a Bábí and fell under the spell of Siyyid Muḥammad-i-Iṣfáhání, and thus became an inveterate opponent of Bahá'u'lláh.

429. p. 87 ¶ 139. He ascended the pulpits and spoke words which ill-befitted him

Shoghi Effendi comments:

> Mírzá Hádí Dawlat-Ábádí. . . on the occasion of the martyrdom of Mírzá Ashraf, was seized with such fear that during four consecutive days he proclaimed from the pulpit-top, and in a most vituperative language, his complete repudiation of the Bábí Faith, as well as of Mírzá Yaḥyá, his benefactor, who had reposed in him such implicit confidence.[597]

Following this betrayal, Shaykh Najafí who had attended the mosque declared him to be a true Muslim and a pure Shí'ih. Dawlat-Ábádí later announced his allegiance to Mírzá Yaḥyá and began to persecute the local Bahá'ís.

See Annotation 427.

430. p. 87 ¶ 139. the clay clods of the world

A 'clay clod' is a lump of earth or clay and here is likened to Mírzá Hádí Dawlat-Ábádí. It infers that individuals like him who are bound together by their love for material things, rank and privilege, fall apart and dissolve when in contact with the slightest moisture of persecution.

The imagery is present in the Book of Daniel (2:31–35). In a dream Daniel sees an imposing King Nebuchadnezzar but with feet of iron and clay – the clay feet made the figure vulnerable, presaging the breakup of his empire. They eventually broke into pieces and 'became like the chaff of the summer threshing-floors; and the wind carried them away, so that no place was found for them'. Similarly, Mírzá Hádí Dawlat-Ábádí had feet of clay and in the end disintegrated and became forgotten by history.

431. p. 87 ¶ 140. Thou hast gone unto My brother and hast seen him

A reference to Mírzá Yaḥyá, who was the half-brother of Bahá'u'lláh. His mother died during childbirth, and he was still young when his father died. He was committed to the care of his father's second wife, the mother of Bahá'u'lláh. He was cared for and protected by Bahá'u'lláh for many years. However, he broke the Covenant of the Báb concerning 'He Whom God shall manifest', and betrayed Bahá'u'lláh to the extent of poisoning Him and ordering the deaths of some of His followers.

Mírzá Hádí Dawlat-Ábádí paid a visit to Mírzá Yaḥyá in Cyprus but failed to be convinced of his worth. In this paragraph Bahá'u'lláh summons him to now turn to the Light:

> Set now thy face towards the court of this Wronged One, that haply the breezes of Revelation and the breaths of inspiration may assist thee and enable thee to attain thy goal. Whoever gazeth this day on My signs will distinguish truth from falsehood as the sun from shadow, and will be made cognizant of the goal.

432. p. 88 ¶ 140. they that have turned aside and denied Me have failed to recognize Who despatched that which was delivered unto the Herald – the Primal Point

Addressing Muḥammad S͟háh from the prison-fortress of Máh-Kú, the Báb stated:

> I am the Primal Point from which have been generated all created things . . .I am the Countenance of God Whose splendor can never be obscured, the light of God whose radiance can never fade . . . All the keys of heaven God hath chosen to place on My right hand, and all the keys of hell on My left . . . I am one of the sustaining pillars of the Primal Word of God. Whosoever hath recognized Me, hath known all that is true and right, and hath attained all that is good and seemly . . . The substance wherewith God hath created Me is not the clay out of which others have been formed. He hath conferred upon Me that which the worldly-wise can never comprehend, nor the faithful discover.[598]

Shoghi Effendi enumerates descriptions of the Báb's true identity:

> The Báb, acclaimed by Bahá'u'lláh as the 'Essence of Essences,' the 'Sea of Seas,' the 'Point round Whom the realities of the Prophets and Messengers revolve,' 'from Whom God hath caused to proceed the knowledge of all that was and shall be,' Whose 'rank excelleth that of all the Prophets,' and Whose 'Revelation transcendeth the comprehension and understanding of all their chosen ones,' had delivered His Message and discharged His mission. He Who was, in the words of 'Abdu'l-Bahá, the 'Morn of Truth' and 'Harbinger of the Most Great Light,' Whose advent at once signalized the termination of the 'Prophetic Cycle' and the inception of the 'Cycle of Fulfillment' . . . He, as affirmed by Himself . . . the 'Mystic Fane,' the 'Great Announcement,' the 'Flame of that supernal Light that glowed upon Sinai,' the 'Remembrance of God' concerning Whom 'a separate Covenant hath been established with each and every Prophet' had, through His advent, at once fulfilled the promise of all ages and ushered in the consummation of all Revelations. He the 'Qá'im' (He Who ariseth) promised to the S͟hí'ahs, the 'Mihdí'

> (One Who is guided) awaited by the Sunnís, the 'Return of John the Baptist' expected by the Christians, the 'U<u>sh</u>ídar-Máh' referred to in the Zoroastrian scriptures, the 'Return of Elijah' anticipated by the Jews . . .[599]

> He, unlike the Founder of the Christian religion, is not only to be regarded as the independent Author of a divinely revealed Dispensation, but must also be recognized as the Herald of a new Era and the Inaugurator of a great universal prophetic cycle.[600]

However, Bahá'u'lláh here states that He Himself was the same reality as the Author of the Revelation of the Báb.

433. 88 ¶ 140. The Sealed Wine is disclosed in this day before the faces of men

See Annotations 137, 268 and 458.

434. p. 88 ¶ 141. Zanján

A village in the west of Persia that witnessed one of the most tragic episodes of Bahá'í history in which 'no less than eighteen hundred' disciples 'drained the cup of martyrdom', including the illustrious Ḥujjat, 'Alíy-i-Zánjání, and the audacious Zaynab, 'a village maiden' who for a period of five months 'disguised herself in male attire, cut off her locks, girt a sword about her waist, and, raising the cry of "Yá Ṣáḥibu'z-Zamán!" [O Thou the Lord of the Age] rushed headlong in pursuit of the assailants.' The 'mournful episode' of Zanjan took place at the Fort of 'Alí-Mardán <u>Kh</u>án. The fort at one time 'sheltered not less than three thousand Bábís, including men, women and children'. The struggle was brought to a close by 'the foul treachery of the besiegers, who . . . had drawn up and written out an appeal for peace and, enclosing with it a sealed copy of the Qur'án as a testimony of their pledge, had sent it to Ḥujjat,' and who, faithless to their word, inflicted on the defenceless Bábís 'a massacre and pillage, unexampled in scope and ferocity'. Shoghi Effendi describes this episode as 'unprecedented in both its duration and in the number of those who were swept away by its fury', and 'characterized by Lord Curzon as a "terrific siege and slaughter"'.[601]

435. p. 88 ¶ 141. Nayríz

Nayriz is a village in the south of Persia in the province of Fars, not far from Shiraz, which became the scene of a great upheaval. The hero of the new conflagration was Siyyid Yaḥyáy-i-Darábí, better known as Vaḥíd. The arch villains included the base and fanatical governor of Nayríz, Zaynu'l-Ábidín Khán, and Prince Fírúz Mírzá, the governor of Shiraz.

> Once again a handful of men, innocent, law-abiding, peace-loving, yet high-spirited and indomitable, consisting partly, in this case, of untrained lads and men of advanced age, were surprised, challenged, encompassed and assaulted by the superior force of a cruel and crafty enemy, an innumerable host of able-bodied men who, though well-trained, adequately equipped and continually reinforced, were impotent to coerce into submission, or subdue, the spirit of their adversaries.[602]

The closing stage was marked by a devastating massacre of the defenceless Bábí community. The victims of the barbaric atrocities included women and children.

436. p. 88 ¶ 141. Ṭabarsí

A reference to the Fort of Shaykh Ṭabarsí situated in the forest of Mazindaran in the north of Persia. It became the scene of the heroic siege of the Bábís which lasted for 'no less than eleven months', and claimed the lives of 'no less than half of the Letters of the Living, not excluding Quddús and Mullá Ḥusayn, respectively the last and the first of these Letters'. This contest witnessed some of the greatest and most heroic battles of Bahá'í history, and proved the intrepid and indomitable spirit of its defenders, in contrast to the cowardly and shameful conduct of their adversaries. It was Prince Mihdí-Qulí Mírzá, who in the end, swearing on the holy Qur'án 'to set free all the defenders of the Fort', violated his 'irrevocable oath' a particularly despicable example of dissimulation. As a result of the Prince's violation of his covenant, 'the betrayed companions of Quddús were assembled in the camp of the enemy, were stripped of their possessions, and sold as slaves, the rest being either killed by the spears and swords of the officers, or torn asunder, or bound to trees and riddled with bullets, or blown from the mouths of cannon and consigned to the flames, or else being disemboweled and having their heads impaled on spears and lances'. Shoghi Effendi describes this 'stirring episode, so glorious for the Faith, so blackening to the reputation of its enemies', as one which must be regarded as 'a rare phenomenon in the history of modern times'.[603]

437. p. 88 ¶ 140. the episode of the Land of Ṭá

A reference to the failed attempt on the life of the Náṣiri'd-Dín Sháh, stigmatized by Bahá'u'lláh as the 'Tyrant of Persia' (*ẓálim-i-'ajam*). Shoghi Effendi writes:

> Obsessed by the bitter tragedy of the martyrdom of his beloved Master, driven by a frenzy of despair to avenge that odious deed, and believing the author and instigator of that crime to be none other than the Sháh himself, a certain Ṣádiq-i-Tabrízí, an assistant in a confectioner's shop in Ṭihrán, proceeded on an August day (August 15, 1852), together with his accomplice, an equally obscure youth named Fatḥu'lláh-i-Qumí, to Níyávarán where the imperial army had encamped and the sovereign was in residence, and there, waiting by the roadside, in the guise of an innocent bystander, fired a round of shot from his pistol at the Sháh, shortly after the latter had emerged on horseback from the palace grounds for his morning promenade. The weapon the assailant employed demonstrated beyond the shadow of a doubt the folly of that half-demented youth, and clearly indicated that no man of sound judgment could have possibly instigated so senseless an act . . .[604]

The maelstrom that ensued engulfed Bahá'u'lláh. He was immediately arrested and imprisoned in the Síyáh-Chál of Tehran. The government, the clergy, and the mob vented their anger against many innocent Bábís, many of whom were martyred.

See Annotation 150.

438. p. 89 ¶ 142. Divine Kaaba

The Kaaba is a cube-like, stone building at Mecca, containing in its eastern cornerstone the Black Stone, a Muslim relic which, according to Islamic tradition, dates back to the time of Adam. It is the Qiblih (the Point of Adoration toward which Muslims turn in prayer) and the holiest spot in the Muslim world. According to Islamic tradition it was built by Adam and reconstructed after the Flood by Abraham and Ishmael. The Qur'án (3:96) states: 'the first House (of worship) appointed for men was that at Bakka [Mecca]: full of blessing and of guidance for all beings.'

See Annotations 134 and 509.

439. p. 89 ¶ 142. He Who is the Spirit (Jesus) . . . was asked . . . Is it lawful to give tribute to Caesar or not?

The Pharisees asked Jesus if they should pay taxes (tribute) to the Roman Emperor (Matt. 22:15–17). In this way they laid a trap for Him: if Jesus replied in the negative they would be able to report Him to the Roman authorities, and if He answered in the affirmative He would not be considered the Messiah or the Saviour of the Jews. But 'Jesus perceived their wickedness, and said, Shew me the tribute money. And they brought unto him a penny. And he saith unto them, Whose is this image and superscription? They say unto him, Caesar's. Then saith he unto them, Render therefore unto Caesar the things which are Caesar's; and unto God the things that are God's' (Matt. 22:18–21).

440. p. 90 ¶ 142. Obey God and obey the Apostle, and those among you invested with authority

This is a reference to Qur'án 4:59. The verse is preceded by a command to rulers to observe justice. The two verses are of great interest as they indicate that obedience to the Manifestation of God is tantamount to obedience to God, and that obedience of those placed in authority is tantamount to obedience to the Prophet.

Some believe that 'those in authority' refers to commanders in battle. Sunnis and Shí'ihs have also different interpretations of 'those in authority'. The Sunnis believe that it refers to the Sunni Caliphs and rulers of Islam. The Shí'ihs interpret it as referring to the Imáms, as they succeeded Muhammad. By extension, others identify 'those in authority' with the Muslim religious leaders and scholars (*'ulemá*) because of their knowledge of the Qur'án and the Sunnah, through which God and the Prophet are obeyed.

Bahá'u'lláh explains that 'those in authority' refers primarily to the Imáms (not the *'ulemá*), but also to the kings and rulers. Hence His followers are to obey rulers, even though these be imperfect.

441. p. 91 ¶ 144. Epistle to the Romans

The Epistle to the Romans was written by the Apostle Paul to Christians residing in the city of Rome. Rome was the centre of the Empire and was ethnically diverse. In the first century CE it had a population of around one million people in an area less than ten square miles. Of this relatively large population, it is estimated that there were between 40,000 and 50,000 Jews in the city.

442. p. 91 ¶ 144. Saint Paul

The Apostle Paul, the author of several New Testament epistles, was born as an Israelite in Tarsus of Cilicia (Acts 22:3). His name was originally Saul. He studied under Gamaliel in Jerusalem and became a Pharisee. He facilitated the stoning of Stephen (Acts 7:58; 8:1). Before his conversion to Christianity he had acquired a zealot's hatred of all Jesus stood for, and he began to harass the Church (Acts 8:1–3; 22:4–5; Phil. 3:6), 'entering house after house and dragging out men and women, he handed them over for imprisonment'.

He underwent a spiritual conversion on the road to Damascus and his name became changed from Saul to Paul. Instead of persecuting the Christians he went on several journeys to bring the Gospel to the Gentiles (Apostle: 'one sent on a mission'). He was imprisoned in Rome on two occasions and was martyred under the Emperor Nero. Had he so chosen, the Shaykh could have followed in the footsteps of the Apostle Paul and relinquished his role as a chief persecutor of Bahá'u'lláh's Faith, and instead become one of His ardent supporters.

443. p. 91 ¶ 144. Let every soul be subject unto the higher powers

Bahá'u'lláh quotes the Apostle Paul who taught (Rom. 13.1–3):

> Let every soul be subject unto the higher powers [English Standard Version: governing authorities]. For there is no power but of God: the powers that be are ordained of God.
>
> Whosoever therefore resisteth the power, resisteth the ordinance of God: and they that resist shall receive to themselves damnation.
>
> For rulers are not a terror to good works, but to the evil. Wilt thou then not be afraid of the power? Do that which is good, and thou shalt have praise of the same.

The Muslim clergy are apt to accuse the Bahá'ís of creating mischief or *fasád* (see Annotation 460). In point of fact the Shaykh spent a lifetime opposing the governor of Isfahan and the King. Although the governor and King also exercised arbitrary and absolute power, and in their own right were cruel and unjust, yet it was not their wish that Áqá Najafí should disturb the peace by persecuting and killing the Bahá'ís. Áqá Najafí 'exercised his own judgements despite a government injunction to the contrary'.[605] Following his bloody campaigns against the innocent and defenceless community which he called the 'detested Bábís', Áqá Najafí was summoned twice to the capital to moderate his nefarious actions. He resisted paying taxes and became a leading clerical supporter of the Constitutional Revolution. He declared the enemies of the Persian constitution (the monarchy) to be 'in the rank of the murderers of Siyyid Shuhadá', that is, Imám Ḥusayn.[606] Furthermore, he and his brother, Hajj Áqá Nurulláh Nur, attacked the government's European concessions and declared tobacco to be unclean.[607] Finally, he and his brother mobilized the Bakhtiari clan and the merchants (*bázárís*) of Isfahan against the forces of the governor and the King. The rebellion was initially successful but met disaster when the Bakhtiari and the clerical rebels then marched towards Tehran to overthrow the King.[608]

444. p. 91 ¶ 144. For he is the minister of God

This is a further quotation from the Apostle Paul (Rom. 13:4) that elevates the rank of a ruler to one who is appointed by God to do his will, and to execute his purpose:

> For he is the minister of God [English Standard Version: he is the servant of God] to thee for good. But if thou do that which is evil, be afraid; for he beareth not the sword in vain: for he is the minister of God, a revenger to execute wrath upon him that doeth evil.

445. p. 91 ¶ 145. the traditions of old

The oral tradition of the Muslims is called *ḥadíth* (plural, *aḥádíth*). The word has come into the English language as 'hadith'. Bahá'u'lláh states that there are several traditions that support the thesis that civil rulers must be respected and obeyed. For example, a section of *Biḥár al-Anwár* (Seas of Lights), a comprehensive collection of traditions compiled by the Shí'ih scholar Mullá Muḥammad Báqir, known as al-Majlisi (d. 1110 AH/1698 CE), and quoting Imám Ṣádiq, deals with this subject.

446. p. 92 ¶ 146. to ponder, though it be but for an hour

A hadith recounted by Imám Jalál ud Din Suyuti in *Sahih Al-Jaami As-Sagheer* states: 'One hour of meditation (*taffakur*) is sometimes better that one year of praying.'[609] Bahá'u'lláh quotes this tradition also in the *Kitáb-i-Íqán*: 'the meditation referred to in the words "One hour's reflection is preferable to seventy years of pious worship" must needs be observed . . .'[610]

447. p. 92 ¶ 146. Hath . . . any Light or Revelation shone forth from the dayspring of the will of God which the kindreds of the earth have accepted, and Whose Cause they have acknowledged?

Bahá'u'lláh observes: 'the wretched behaviour of the people . . . who, despite the love and yearning for truth which they profess, curse the followers of Truth when once He hath been made manifest.'[611] He declares that all divine Dispensations have been rejected and persecuted – His is therefore no exception:

> Why is it that the advent of every true Manifestation of God hath been accompanied by such strife and tumult, by such tyranny and upheaval? This notwithstanding the fact that all the Prophets of God, whenever made manifest unto the peoples of the world, have invariably foretold the coming of yet another Prophet after them, and have established such signs as would herald the advent of the future Dispensation . . .
>
> . . . Whatever in days gone by hath been the cause of the denial and opposition of those people hath now led to the perversity of the people of this age.[612]

The Hebrew Bible describes resistance to successive divine Revelations more than two and a half thousand years ago:

> And the Lord God of their fathers sent to them by his messengers, rising up betimes, and sending [New International Version: again and again]; because he had compassion on his people, and on his dwelling place:
>
> But they mocked the messengers of God, and despised his words, and misused his prophets, until the wrath of the Lord arose against his people, till there was no remedy. (II Chron. 36:15–16)

Castigating the Jewish religious leaders, Christ stated (Matt. 23:31): 'you are the children of them which killed the prophets.' He blamed them for frustrating God's repeated attempts to reconcile humanity to Himself (Matt. 23:37):

> O Jerusalem, Jerusalem, who kills the prophets and stones those sent to her, how often I have longed to gather your children together, as a hen gathers her chicks under her wings, but you were unwilling!

Comforting His disciples, Christ stated that all God's Messengers had suffered a similar fate in the past (Matt. 5:11–12):

> Blessed are ye, when men shall revile you, and persecute you, and

> shall say all manner of evil against you falsely, for my sake.
> Rejoice, and be exceeding glad: for great is your reward in heaven: for so persecuted they the prophets which were before you.

He indicated that there was unlikely to be any change in the way prophets would be treated in the future (Luke 11:49):

> Therefore also said the wisdom of God, I will send them prophets and apostles, and some of them they shall slay and persecute.

During his arraignment before the Jewish Sanhedrin, Stephen, the first Christian martyr who was stoned to death, brought his speech to a stinging conclusion with the challenge (Acts 7:51–52):

> Ye stiffnecked and uncircumcised in heart and ears, ye do always resist the Holy Ghost: as your fathers did, so do ye.
> Which of the prophets have not your fathers persecuted? and they [your ancestors] have slain them which shewed before of the coming of the Just One; of whom ye have been now the betrayers and murderers . . .

God in the Qur'án states (22:51–52):

> But those who strive against Our Signs, to frustrate them [thwart Our revelations],– they will be Companions of the Fire.
> Never did We send an apostle or a prophet before thee, but, when he framed a desire, Satan threw some (vanity) into his desire [suggested opposition to what he had revealed]: but God will cancel anything (vain) that Satan throws in, and God will confirm (and establish) His Signs [revelations] . . .

Again (Qur'án 2:87):

> We gave Moses the Book and followed him up with a succession of Apostles; We gave Jesus the son of Mary clear (Signs) and strengthened him with the holy spirit. Is it that whenever there comes to you an Apostle with what ye yourselves desire not, ye are puffed up with pride? – Some ye called impostors, And others ye slay!

Nevertheless, the Qur'án instructs Muhammad to deal with His adversities with patience and fortitude (6:34):

> Rejected were the Apostles before thee: with patience and constancy they bore their rejection and their wrongs, until Our aid did reach them . . .

448. p. 92 ¶ 146. Some were held to be possessed, others were called impostors

The divine message has often been dismissed by religious leaders and scholars on the basis that the authors of the Revelations were pretenders, insane or possessed by demons (insanity was often attributed to demonic possession). Thus the Bible records that Christ's forerunner, John the Baptist, was accused of having 'a devil' (Matt. 11:18); Jesus's siblings did not believe in Him (John 7:5); and His own family and friends considered Him at one time as being 'beside himself' (Mark 3:21; English Standard Version: out of his mind). The Pharisees dismissed His miracles by explaining that 'He casteth out devils through the prince of the devils' (Matt. 9:34). They moreover said (John 10:20): 'He hath a devil, and is mad; why hear ye him?' The Pharisees also objected to Christ's disciples on the grounds that they were not in the rank of the religious leaders or Pharisees – the people who had accepted Him were deceived and simply did not know the law and were therefore 'accursed' (John 7:47–49). The Apostle Peter and his fellow disciples, intoxicated not with wine but with the Faith of Jesus, were accused of being drunk (Acts 2:15). At the Apostle Paul's final hearing before Festus, the Roman governor shouted at him (Acts 26:24): 'Paul, thou art beside thyself; much learning doth make thee mad. But he said, I am not mad, most noble Festus; but speak forth the words of truth and soberness.'

As attested to by Bahá'u'lláh, Muhammad similarly suffered at the hands of the clergy of His time:

> Remember the days in which the Sun of Baṭḥá [Muhammad] shone forth above the horizon of the Will of thy Lord, the Exalted, the Most High, and recall how the divines of that age turned away from Him, and the learned contended with Him, that haply thou mayest

> apprehend that which, in this day, remaineth concealed behind the veils of glory. So grievous became His plight on every side that He instructed His companions to disperse . . .[613]

Muhammad was accused of being possessed and mad (Qur'án 23:70; 25:8; 26:153; 34:46; 37:36; 44:14 and 52:29) and the Qur'án was dismissed as being 'forged' (34:43), and nothing other than 'mere poetry' (69:41–42). Furthermore, the Qur'án explains that Noah was also rejected as God's Messenger and accused of being possessed (54:9).

449. p. 93 ¶ 147. as Thou hast admonished one of Thy Branches (sons)

'Branches' (*Ag͟hṣán*: plural of the word *G͟husn*) refers to the sons and descendants of Bahá'u'lláh (for example, *G͟husn Aẓam*, the Most Great Branch, refers to 'Abdu'l-Bahá). Here it refers to Mírzá Badí'u'lláh, the youngest son of Bahá'u'lláh and the chief accomplice of his brother, Muḥammad-'Ali, the Arch-breaker of the Covenant of Bahá'u'lláh. Bahá'u'lláh explains that He admonished Badí'u'lláh in a Tablet (Lawḥ-i-'Andalib). This Tablet, revealed following His confinement in the Most Great Prison in the house of 'Údí K͟hammár in 'Akká also admonishes Badí'u'lláh's brother, Ḍíyá'u'lláh).[614] The two sons are addressed in the Tablet as 'Ya Badí' (O Badí'u'lláh) and 'Ya Ḍíyá (O Ḍíyá'u'lláh) and are exhorted by Bahá'u'lláh to demonstrate amongst others, the virtues of patience, resignation, contentment, certitude of faith, and steadfastness in the Covenant. All His followers are recommended to exhibit the same virtues.

Badí'u'lláh continued to be involved in many machinations and opposed both 'Abdu'l-Bahá and Shoghi Effendi. He is denounced in the Will and Testament of 'Abdu'l-Bahá as an 'alert and active worker of mischief'. At one stage, he briefly betrayed the cause of Muḥammad-'Alí, published a signed denunciation of his evil acts, but rejoined him again, only to be alienated from him in consequence of the scandalous behaviour of his own daughter.[615]

Bahá'u'lláh in a similar vein admonishes the S͟hayk͟h, in the hope that he may come to a realization of true faith. The S͟hayk͟h is exhorted to embrace a life that is the antithesis of the one he was leading – Bahá'u'lláh provides a list of virtues that he must make his priority.

450. p. 93 ¶ 148. a dew to the soil of the human heart

'Dew' is translated from *raqzáz*, which refers to a gentle and persistent rain that causes the earth to become verdant. In the Torah 'dew' refers to divine Revelation, as in Gen. 27:28: 'Therefore God give thee of the dew of heaven' and Deut. 32:2: 'My doctrine shall drop as the rain, my speech shall distil as the dew, as the small rain upon the tender herb, and as the showers upon the grass . . .'

451. p. 94 ¶ 148. the Lord of the Judgement Day

There are numerous references to the Day of Judgement in the Bible and the Qur'án. It is held to be the day when the good and the bad deeds that individuals have done are taken into account and they are sent to heaven or hell accordingly. In the Bahá'í Writings, it is a Day when the understanding of all that has taken place and been revealed in the past is measured against whether or not it accords with what God has ordained in the Revelations of the Báb and Bahá'u'lláh.[616]

452. p. 94 ¶ 149. sitting under a sword hanging on a thread

Damocles was a courtier who was made to sit by Dionysius II of Syracuse (4th century BCE) under a sword hanging by a single hair to show him the perilous nature of earthly happiness. Hence, the sword of Damocles represents situations that threaten imminent harm or disaster – Bahá'u'lláh faced constant danger almost every day of His life. The statement features also in a prayer by Bahá'u'lláh[617] and in the Súriy-i-Haykal.[618]

453. p. 95 ¶ 149. Glory to Thee, O my God!

This prayer is published in *Prayers and Meditations*, XCII, pp. 155–6 and in many other Bahá'í prayer books. It is part of a Tablet re-revealed for the poet Ná'ím who had endured imprisonment, torture and expulsion from his native city of Isfahan. In a dark night in Tehran he read this newly revealed prayer and desired in his heart that it had been revealed for him. Bahá'u'lláh responds from 'Akká to his unexpressed wish and includes the prayer in His Tablet to him. The Tablet graces the beginning of Ná'ím's compilation of poems demonstrating the proof of the Faith and its teachings.

454. p. 96 ¶ 153. the right hand of the Luminous Spot

The right hand denotes dominant power. For example, the Psalms (110:1) states: 'The Lord said unto my Lord, Sit thou at my right hand, until I make thine enemies my footstool.' Christ also explained (Matt. 20:23): 'to sit on my right hand, and on my left, is not mine to give, but it shall be given to them for whom it is prepared of my Father.' Hence, 'the right hand of the Luminous Spot' describes a spiritual domain that shines and radiates light, and in which resides God's ultimate authority. Bahá'u'lláh refers to 'Akká in the Súriy-i-Mulúk as 'this luminous and perspicuous Spot'.[619] Again:

> Hearken unto the Call of Thy Lord, raised from the Divine Lote-Tree in the holy and luminous Spot, that the sweet accents of Thy Lord, the All-Merciful, may fill Thy soul with joy and fervour, and that the breezes that waft from My name, the Ever-Forgiving, may dispel Thy cares and sorrows.[620]

> We have attired thee with the vesture of My good-pleasure in My heavenly Kingdom, and from the Divine Lote-Tree which is raised on the borders of the vale of security and peace, situate in the luminous Spot beyond the glorious City, We call aloud unto thee . . .[621]

Bahíyyih Khánum, the Greatest Holy Leaf, refers to the Shrines of the Báb and Bahá'u'lláh as 'luminous' and situated in the 'hallowed land, this luminous Spot'.[622] Shoghi Effendi makes a similar reference to 'Akká: 'the Qiblih of the people of Bahá – 'Akká, the resplendent city, and the sanctified, the luminous, the Most Holy Shrine'.[623]

455. p. 97 ¶ 153. Lawḥ-i-Burhán

See ¶ 130, 131; Annotations 398–401.

456. p. 97 ¶ 153. The Kingdom is God's

Bahá'u'lláh's Revelation occurred at a time when there were several powerful earthly rulers. Nevertheless, He pointed out in the Tablet of Aḥmad revealed in Adrianople that 'He [God] is the King, the All-Knowing, the Wise'.[624] Here He emphasizes that the spiritual and earthly Kingdom belongs ultimately to God alone.

The Bible anticipates the advent of the Revelation of God when the Kingdom belonging to the Father will be established on earth (Rev. 21:3, 5); in that Day the Occupant of the Throne will be God.

The word used by Bahá'u'lláh – *al-mulku* – means that 'sovereignty', 'dominion' or 'kingdom' belongs to God and not to His pretentious creatures. It is from verses of the Qur'án that must have been familiar to the Shaykh:

> O God, Lord of the kingdom! Thou givest the kingdom to whomsoever Thou pleasest, and strippest the kingdom from whomsoever Thou pleases . . . (3:26, Palmer translation)

> On that day the Kingdom shall be God's: He shall judge between them: and they who shall have believed and done the things that are right, shall be in gardens of delight. (22:55, Rodwell)

> It is He who is God your Lord: the kingdom is His. (39:6, Rodwell)

> His Throne doth extend over the heavens and the earth . . . (2:255)

457. p. 97 ¶ 153. the Lord of the worlds!

This is also to be found in the Qur'án (1:2; 2:131). The 'worlds' may be taken to mean the material and spiritual world; the seen and unseen world; and the manifold ethical and moral injunctions as well as the social prescriptions. God has ultimate authority as to what He reveals. The Qur'án also states: 'His Throne doth extend over the heavens and the earth' (2:255); and that God is the Lord 'of all things' (6:164). Also:

> Praise be to God, to Whom belong all things in the heavens and on earth . . . (34:1)

> . . . to God belong the treasures of the Heavens and the Earth . . . (63:7)

> Knower of what is hidden and what is open [the Invisible and the Visible], exalted in Might, Full of Wisdom. (64:18)

458. p. 97 ¶ 154. Peruse thou the Kitáb-i-Íqán (Book of Certitude)

The Book of Certitude is thus described by Shoghi Effendi:

> Foremost among the priceless treasures cast forth from the billowing ocean of Bahá'u'lláh's Revelation ranks the Kitáb-i-Íqán (Book of Certitude), revealed within the space of two days and two nights, in the closing years of that period (1278 A.H.–1862 A.D.). It was written in fulfilment of the prophecy of the Báb, Who had specifically stated that the Promised One would complete the text of the unfinished Persian Bayán, and in reply to the questions addressed to Bahá'u'lláh by the as yet unconverted maternal uncle of the Báb, Ḥájí Mírzá Siyyid Muḥammad, while on a visit, with his brother, Ḥájí Mírzá Ḥasan-'Alí, to Karbilá. A model of Persian prose, of a style at once original, chaste and vigorous, and remarkably lucid, both cogent in argument and matchless in its irresistible eloquence, this Book, setting forth in outline the Grand Redemptive Scheme of God, occupies a position unequalled by any work in the entire range of Bahá'í literature, except the Kitáb-i-Aqdas, Bahá'u'lláh's Most Holy Book. Revealed on the eve of the declaration of His Mission, it proffered to mankind the 'Choice Sealed Wine,' whose seal is of 'musk,' and broke the 'seals' of the 'Book' referred to by Daniel, and disclosed the meaning of the 'words' destined to remain 'closed up' till the "time of the end.'[625]

459. p. 97 ¶ 154. King of Paris

A reference to Napoleon III. See also Annotations 269–72, 274–76, 282.

460. p. 97 ¶ 154. We have not sought to spread disorder in the land after it had been well-ordered

Bahá'u'lláh denies that He or His followers have caused *fasád* as alleged by the civil and ecclesiastical authorities. On the other hand, the ferocity of the campaigns against Bahá'ís, instigated by Shaykh Áqá Najafí, alarmed even the central government and he was summoned to the capital on two occasions to reduce tensions. The unrest which he caused resulted in his eventual banishment from Isfahan. Even partisan biographers admitted the excessive brutality of the pogroms commissioned by Shaykh Muḥammad Báqir and his son Áqá Najafí.[626] The turmoil created by the Shaykh and his accomplices went against the following admonishment of the Qur'án that Bahá'u'lláh alludes to (7:56): 'Do no mischief on the earth, after it hath been set in order, but call on Him with fear and longing (in your hearts): For the Mercy of God is (always) near to those who do good.' The Qur'án (2:8–12) warns Muslims that *fasád* is also caused (sometimes unwittingly) by people who think that what they are doing is in the name of peace:

> Of the people there are some who say: 'We believe in God and the Last Day;' But they do not (really) believe.
>
> Fain would they deceive God and those who believe, but they only deceive themselves, and realize (it) not!
>
> In their hearts is a disease; and God has increased their disease: and grievous is the penalty they (incur), Because they are false (to themselves).
>
> When it is said to them: 'Make not mischief on the earth,' they say: 'Why, we only want to make peace!
>
> Of a surety, they are the ones who make mischief, but they realize (it) not.

Warnings against *fasád* (mischief or corruption) are found throughout the Qur'án. It denotes also morally egregious acts, serious sins, particularly violence against others and inciting others to do the same, and is in contrast to *iṣláh*, 'setting things aright or 'making amends', believing and having faith, and performing righteous deeds.[627]

If through sincere investigation the 'Wolf' had realized that the Faith of Bahá'u'lláh was indeed from God and the promise of the Qur'án, he would have concluded that, by disobeying the divine Will, he was responsible for creating mischief on earth.

Bahá'u'lláh here denies that either He or His followers deserve the accusation of causing mischief or *fasád*, which under the Shariah law of Islam carries the death sentence. The Revelation of Bahá'u'lláh has united many contending members of humanity. Whatever mischief occurred had been initiated through the agitation of the population by Muslim clerics such as the 'Wolf' and his son attempting to eradicate every trace of the Faith of Bahá'u'lláh from the face of the earth.

461. p. 98 ¶ 155. O thou who art gone astray! . . . There is none other God but Him . . . He is One in His Essence, One in His Attributes. He hath none to equal Him in the whole universe, nor any partner in all creation

In their daily supplication to be guided to the straight path, Muslims pray that they do not become counted as those who have been misled (Qur'án 1:6–7):

> Show us the straight way,
> The way of those on whom Thou hast bestowed Thy Grace, those whose (portion) is not wrath, and who go not astray.

The word *Gháfil* used here denotes one who is heedless or 'gone astray'. In the Qur'án (30:7) the word is used to describe the worldly-wise who are unaware of spiritual matters.

In their explanations of the scriptures and in their actions on behalf of divinity, the 'Son of the Wolf' and the 'She-Serpent' had falsely adopted the role of partners of God, that is, *mus̲h̲rik*.

See also Annotations 40, 252 and 416.

462. p. 98 ¶ 156. We have heard that the provinces of Persia have been adorned with the adornment of justice. When We observed closely, however, We found them to be the dawning-places

of tyranny and the daysprings of injustice. We behold justice in the clutches of tyranny

The Qajar kings (1785–1925) acted with absolute power. However, not only were they surrounded by doting ministers who flattered their egos and generally told them what they wanted to hear, but at the same time the powerful clergy subverted the efforts of the king at every turn. Therefore, in this atmosphere of 'mutual deceit' (title of Súrih 64 of the Qur'án), there was a disparity between what was truly happening in Persia and the good that the king was being told that his administration was accomplishing.

The Qajar kings had numerous wives and concubines; Fath-'Alí Sháh (d. 1834 CE) had about 1,000 women in his harem. The many thousands of princes controlled key positions in the country, ensuring loyalty to the king. The ruthless power of the princes in league with a venal, arrogant and corrupt clergy holding sway over a fanatical and uneducated people was not conducive to any form of justice. Náṣiri'd-Dín Sháh prided himself on modernizing Iran, but in effect resisted reform. Bahá'u'lláh disabuses him of his illusion that justice permeated the country.

463. p. 99 ¶ 157. O heedless one! Rely not on thy glory, and thy power. Thou art even as the last trace of sunlight upon the mountain-top. Soon will it fade away

Shoghi Effendi relates the fate of the 'heedless one', namely the 'Wolf', in *God Passes By*:

> Shaykh Muḥammad-Báqir, surnamed the 'Wolf,' who, in the strongly condemnatory Lawḥ-i-Burhán addressed to him by Bahá'u'lláh, had been compared to 'the last trace of sunlight upon the mountain-top,' witnessed the steady decline of his prestige, and died in a miserable state of acute remorse.[628]

464. p. 100 ¶ 157. O concourse of divines! Because of you the people were abased

With few exceptions, people follow their religious leaders blindly instead of exercising their God-given right to investigate the truth for themselves. Hence, because of the Shaykh and his fellow clergy, many Muslims were misled and committed heinous acts against the people of Persia and God's Faith. This tragedy occurred in spite of clear warnings in the Qur'án (33:67–68):

> And they would say: 'Our Lord! We obeyed our chiefs and our great ones, and they misled us from the (right) path.
>
> Our Lord! Give them double penalty and curse them with a very great curse!'

465. p. 100 ¶ 157. the banner of Islám was hauled down

The banners of Muhammad were a white flag and a black flag. The black flag was also the flag of the Abbasid Caliphate.

Pulling down the flag signifies defeat. Reversal of a banner is a sign of distress and Bahá'u'lláh indicates that the actions of the 'Wolf' and the 'She-Serpent', instead of exalting the Faith of the Prophet Muhammad, wrought irremediable damage to Islam and caused it to be brought into disrepute.

A hadith reports that Muhammad said that the advent of the Mahdi would be signalled by a 'Black Standard' proceeding from Khurasan and that it would be the flag of the army that would fight the Antichrist (*Dajjál*). On 21 July 1848, under orders from the Báb, Mullá Ḥusayn raised the Black Standard in Mashhad (in Iran's province of Khurasan) and began a march westwards. The mission was to proclaim the Faith of the Báb and possibly also to rescue Quddús, who was under house arrest in Sari. After being rebuffed at the town of Barfurush, the group started to build defensive fortifications at the Shrine of Shaykh Ṭabarsí. It is reported that the Black Standard flew above the Bábí fortress until the end of the Battle of Fort Ṭabarsí. The historian Nabíl provides the following account:

> It was in the masjid of Míyámay, to which Mullá Ḥusayn had repaired in order to offer the Friday congregational prayer, that he delivered his soul-stirring appeal in which he laid stress upon the fulfilment of the tradition relating to the hoisting of the Black Standard in Khurásán, and in which he declared himself to be its bearer.[629]

466. p. 100 ¶ 157. Islám

This refers to the Dispensation of Prophet Muhammad, but the word 'Islam' has connotations of peace, purity and the surrender of one's will to God. The Qur'án (3:19) states that 'the true religion with God is Islam'. This is often taken as indication of the superiority and exclusivity of Islam. However, the Qur'án states that a number of individuals who lived long before Muhammad were also Muslims, indicating that the word 'Islam' includes a more inclusive and generic definition. Thus, Abraham and His followers (2,500 years before the religion of Islam) (3:67; 22:78); Joseph (2,500 years) (12:101); followers of Moses (>2,000 years) (10:84); Pharaoh's magicians (>2,000 years) (7:126); and the disciples of Christ (>600 years) (3:52) are all described as having been Muslims, presumably because they too promoted peace and exemplified submission to the divine Will. Importantly, the Qur'án considers the earlier Dispensations as integral parts of the same religion (*deen*) as Islam (42:13; also 2:285; 3:84; 4:152; 5:48):

> The same religion has He established for you as that which He enjoined on Noah – the which We have sent by inspiration to thee – and that which We enjoined on Abraham, Moses, and Jesus: Namely, that ye should remain steadfast in religion, and make no divisions therein . . .

467. p. 100 ¶ 158. the She-Serpent

This refers to Mír Muḥammad-Ḥusayn. His brother, the Sulṭánu'l-'Ulamá, was a high-ranking ecclesiastical dignitary in Persia who had hosted the Báb in his house in Isfahan. It was during this stay that the Báb penned a commentary on a Súrih of the Qur'án that pertains to the Advent of the Qá'im:

> It was at the request of this same prelate that the Báb, one night, after supper, revealed His well-known commentary on the súrih of Va'l-'Aṣr. Writing with astonishing rapidity, He, in a few hours, had devoted to the exposition of the significance of only the first letter of that súrih – a letter which Shaykh Aḥmad-i-Ahsá'í had stressed, and which Bahá'u'lláh refers to in the Kitáb-i-Aqdas – verses that equalled in number a third of the Qur'án, a feat that called forth such an outburst of reverent astonishment from those who witnessed it that they arose and kissed the hem of His robe.[630]

In contrast, Mír Muḥammad-Ḥusayn, the head priest or Imám-Jum'ih[631] who led the prayers in the Friday mosque in Isfahan, was a singularly cruel individual. The accomplice of Shaykh Muḥammad-Báqir, he was surnamed by Bahá'u'lláh 'She-Serpent' and described by Him as infinitely more wicked than the oppressor of Karbila, Yazid bin Mu'awiya, who martyred Imám Ḥusayn. Bahá'u'lláh refers to him here as the one who stung 'the children of the Apostle of God' and 'the one who hast joined partners with God [*mushrik*],' and addresses him thus: 'O thou who hast withdrawn thyself from God', 'O heedless one', 'heedless outcast', 'O perverse hater', 'O foolish one!', and 'O ignorant one'.

See also Annotations 398, 468, 474.

468. p. 100 ¶ 158. O She-Serpent! For what crime didst thou sting the children of the Apostle of God (King of Martyrs and Beloved of Martyrs), and pillage their possessions?

Two brothers, the King of Martyrs and Beloved of Martyrs, had for years helped the 'She-Serpent' to manage his affairs, and made payments on his behalf which became quite a substantial sum. When they asked for the money which the Imám owed them, he stalled, and began to find ways of evading the payment. He met with Shaykh Muḥammad-Báqir (the 'Wolf'), and they hatched a plot to destroy the two of them. They approached Sulṭan-Maṣ'ud Mírzá, the governor of Isfahan, and he quickly agreed to have them thrown in jail, on the grounds that they were Bábís.

The two brothers were tortured but were promised release upon recanting their faith and cursing its leaders, which they never did. The collaborators wrote a letter to the Shah in Tehran, informing him that they had 'in their concern for the security of the sovereign' detained and imprisoned two Bahá'ís, and requested his permission to have them put to death. The Shah refused the request, and instead asked them to be sent as prisoners to Tehran.

> The Ulama [the 'Wolf' and the 'She-Serpent'] then decided that the brothers [the King and Beloved of Martyrs] would likely be set free due to their innocence. They then decided to ensure their death before departing for Tehran. They used their power as religious leaders to encourage over 50 other divines, each with his own crowd of rioters, to approach the house of the governor and demand the death of the brothers, chanting 'Oh for our Religion!' (Oh for the danger facing Islam!)
>
> The governor argued with the Ulama that the two brothers were not guilty of any treasonable act and had done nothing hostile to the State. He refused to give orders for their execution. One of the Ulama then offered to kill them with his own hands. A large sum of money was offered to the governor, which he accepted. Before the orders could be carried out, a crowd broke into the prison holding them and dragged them into the street, where they were torn apart.[632]

Shoghi Effendi gives the following account of

> . . . the tragedy of the two famous brothers Mírzá Muḥammad-Ḥasan and Mírzá Muḥammad-Ḥusayn, the 'twin shining lights,' respectively surnamed 'Sulṭánu'sh-Shuhudá' (King of Martyrs) and 'Maḥbúbu'sh-Shuhadá' (Beloved of Martyrs), who were celebrated for their generosity, trustworthiness, kindliness and piety. Their martyrdom was instigated by the wicked and dishonest Mír Muḥammad-Ḥusayn, the Imám-Jum'ih, stigmatized by Bahá'u'lláh as the 'she-serpent,' who, in view of a large debt he had incurred in his transactions with them, schemed to nullify his obligations by denouncing them as Bábís, and thereby encompassing their death. Their richly-furnished houses were plundered, even to the trees and flowers in their gardens, all their remaining possessions were confiscated; Shaykh Muḥammad-Báqir, denounced by Bahá'u'lláh as

the 'wolf,' pronounced their death-sentence; the Ẓillu's-Sulṭán ratified the decision, after which they were put in chains, decapitated, dragged to the Maydán-i-Sháh, and there exposed to the indignities heaped upon them by a degraded and rapacious populace. 'In such wise,' 'Abdu'l-Bahá has written, 'was the blood of these two brothers shed that the Christian priest of Julfá cried out, lamented and wept on that day.' For several years Bahá'u'lláh in His Tablets continued to make mention of them, to voice His grief over their passing and to extol their virtues.[633]

469. p. 100 ¶ 158. be, and it was

'Be' in Arabic is ***kun*** written as 'KN'. Bahá'u'lláh refers to this divine attribute symbolically as the connecting of K and N, and the equivalent in English is 'the letters B and E . . . joined and knit together' as included in the Long Obligatory Prayer.

It is an expression of the omnipotence of God – if He ordains something it will come to pass. Hence, certain occurrences that are the product of His divine Will are not conducive to human explanation (2:117; 6:73; 40:68). For example, the Qur'án states that it was through the exercise of this divine omnipotent Will that Jesus was born of the Virgin Mary (3:47; 3:59). Hence, Bahá'u'lláh asks the She-Serpent by what right 'gainsayest thou the signs of thy Lord . . .?'

470. p. 100 ¶ 158. 'Ád

'Ád was allegedly the grandson of Aram, who was the grandson of Noah. His tribe lived in Arabia and built large edifices and pillars in *al-Aḥqáf* (The Sand Dunes). They grew haughty because of their prosperity and were destroyed for rejecting their Prophet, Húd (Qur'án 7:65, 26:123–126; 41:15–16).

471. p. 100 ¶ 158 Húd

The first of five Prophets of God mentioned in the Qur'án as having been sent to the peoples of Arabia. The others are Ṣáliḥ, Abraham, Shu'ayb and Muhammad. Húd is possibly Eber or Heber of the Bible sent to Israelites and the Ishmaelites (Gen. 10:24; I Chron. 1:18–19).

472. p. 100 ¶ 158. Thámúd

Thámúd was a descendant of Shem, who was the son of Noah. It is also the name of an Arabian tribe which lived in Hejáz, Arabia (4th century BCE to the time of Muhammad). They moved to al-Ḥijr where they lived in habitations cut in the rocks (15:80). Their story in the Qur'án illustrates the transitoriness of worldly dominion and consequences of disregarding a divine Revelation. The tribe of Thámúd were a cruel people and merely wanted to continue worshipping the gods of their forefathers (Qur'án: 7:73). This people hamstrung the she-camel (54:31) that was miraculously produced as a sign of His mission by the Prophet, Ṣáliḥ, and were consequently destroyed by thunderbolts from heaven and earthquakes.

473. p. 100 ¶ 158. Ṣáliḥ

Ṣáliḥ was a prophet sent to the pre-Islamic Arab tribe of Thámúd. Some commentators identify Him with the Salah of Genesis (11:13). The translator Sale states that this Prophet lived after Húd but before Abraham, and identifies him with Phaleg. The Muslim historian Ibn Khatir describes him as Ṣáliḥ Ibn Ubeid from the progeny of Noah. Ṣáliḥ was known for his wisdom, purity and goodness and had been greatly respected by his people before he had a Revelation from God. Ṣáliḥ's people then said to him (Qur'án 11:62):

> O Ṣálih! You have been among us as a figure of good hope and we wished for you to be our chief, till this, new thing which you have brought that we leave our gods and worship your God (God) alone! Do you now forbid us the worship of what our fathers have worshipped? But we are really in grave doubt as to that which you invite us to monotheism.

474. p. 101 ¶ 158. Erelong will the breaths of chastisement seize thee

Also ¶ 157: 'ere long will thine own fire be quenched'.

> The . . . 'She-Serpent' was . . . expelled from Iṣfáhán, wandered

from village to village, contracted a disease that engendered so foul an odor that even his wife and daughter could not bear to approach him, and died in such ill-favor with the local authorities that no one dared to attend his funeral, his corpse being ignominiously interred by a few porters.[634]

475. p. 101 ¶ 158. The tale of the Sacrifice (Ishmael) hath been retold

Ishmael ('*Ismá'íl*' in Arabic) was the firstborn son of Abraham and the ancestor of the Arabs (the Jews are descended from Abraham's second son Isaac). Ishmael (the name means 'hearken unto the Lord') is also known as 'the Sacrifice' (*Dhabiḥ Alláh* in Arabic): the Qur'án tells of Abraham's dream in which He was instructed to sacrifice his son (37:99–111). Although the Qur'án does not mention the son's name, Shí'ih Muslims believe that Abraham was instructed to sacrifice Ishmael but notably, Jews and Christians believe that the Patriarch was required to sacrifice Isaac.

Bahá'u'lláh refers here to the martyrdom of the two brothers, Mírzá Muḥammad-Ḥasan and Mírzá Muḥammad-Ḥusayn, as a retelling of the sacrifice of Ishmael.

476. p. 101 ¶ 158. he who was to be offered up . . . returned not

God's Revelation entails sacrifice. While Ishmael survived his sacrifice and thus returned, the Báb was martyred and Bahá'u'lláh's life epitomized daily sacrifice. Hardly any of their followers returned from the field of martyrdom unscathed.

The nightingale (*andalib*) and the dove (*varqá*, see ¶ 6) refer to the Spirit speaking through Bahá'u'lláh (the same dove representing the Holy Spirit that the Gospels describe descending on Jesus). 'Melodies' refers to the Revelation as in 'Sweet melodies of the Doves of Utterance' (¶ 158); 'These melodies, uttered by the Birds of the cities of Knowledge' (¶ 203); and 'Hearken unto the melodies of the Gospel with the ear of fairness' (¶ 205).

One can surmise that endowing the Shaykh with the ability to hear and to perceive the truth is not only a blessing but also an unbearable punishment and torment, for it means that he will appreciate the enormity of his actions and sins.

477. p. 101 ¶ 158. Woe betide thee, O thou who hast joined partners with God

Shirk is an inclination to see distinctions, dichotomies and multiplicities where there is essential singleness and unity. It is associated with idolatry and a literal interpretation of trinity. By several criteria, the Shaykh was a *mushrik*, that is, guilty of the unpardonable sin of *shirk*. For example, because of his hatred the clergyman misconstrued the teachings of the new Revelations as indicating that the Báb and Bahá'u'lláh were claiming to be gods; a more reasonable understanding would have been that Their Will and Purpose was identical and one with God, the Source of all inspiration. Again, the Qur'án states that the Dispensations of Noah, Abraham, Moses, Jesus, and Muhammad were indivisible components of one common Faith. Hence, believers must not make artificial distinctions and divisions in this single religion. It follows that the other anticipated and succeeding Dispensations, such as those of the Báb and Bahá'u'lláh, would also be integral parts of the same *deen* or religion. The Qur'án (42:13) warns that *mushriks* have difficulty accepting this teaching of the oneness of faith and God's manifestations.

478. p. 104 ¶ 159. O thou who assumest the voice of knowledge! This Cause is too evident to be obscured, and too conspicuous to be concealed. It shineth as the sun in its meridian glory

The Son of the Wolf is reported to have authored about a hundred books on obscure and metaphysical aspects of Islam, largely the products of his own imagination. These he reportedly published at his own expense. Others have maintained that he plagiarized the work of others and that 'these were not Áqá Najafí's own, but were products of plagiarism, and were written by others and published in his name'.[635]

The brilliance of the spiritual sun varies in each Dispensation; today it is shining at maximum intensity ('meridian glory'), as Shoghi Effendi describes:

> 'Know of a certainty,' explains Bahá'u'lláh, 'that in every Dispensation the light of Divine Revelation has been vouchsafed to men in

direct proportion to their spiritual capacity. Consider the sun. How feeble its rays the moment it appears above the horizon. How gradually its warmth and potency increase as it approaches its zenith, enabling meanwhile all created things to adapt themselves to the growing intensity of its light . . . In like manner, if the Sun of Truth were suddenly to reveal, at the earliest stages of its manifestation, the full measure of the potencies which the providence of the Almighty has bestowed upon it, the earth of human understanding would waste away and be consumed; for men's hearts would neither sustain the intensity of its revelation, nor be able to mirror forth the radiance of its light . . .'[636]

479. p. 104 ¶ 159. None can deny it unless he be a hater and a doubter

In faith, doubt is the opposite of certitude, and wavering is the opposite of steadfastness and fidelity in the face of persecution. Bahá'u'lláh declares: 'Know thou of a truth that whatsoever hath been prescribed in the Book is indeed the truth, no doubt is there about it.'[637] And:

> . . . the people are in doubt and in contention with Him. They have denied the testimony of God and His proof, after He came from the heaven of power with the kingdom of His signs. They have cast away what had been prescribed, and perpetrated what had been forbidden them in the Book. They have abandoned their God, and clung unto their desires. They truly have strayed and are in error. They read the verses and deny them. They behold the clear tokens and turn aside. They truly are lost in strange doubt.[638]

Again:

> . . . be thou so steadfast in My love that thy heart shall not waver, even if the swords of the enemies rain blows upon thee and all the heavens and the earth arise against thee . . . be not of those who doubt.[639]

The Qur'án observes that those who oppose God's Revelation hate the truth (23:70). It also admonishes that Truth comes from God and, therefore, there can be no doubt or vacillation (2:147; 10:94). It states further (49:15):

> Only those are believers who have believed in God and His Messenger, and have never since doubted, but have striven with their belongings and their persons in the Cause of God: Such are the sincere ones.

And (2:209):

> If ye backslide after clear (Signs) have come to you. Then know that God is Exalted in Power, Wise.

The Epistle of James advises that wavering in faith is not appropriate (1:5–6):

> If any of you lack wisdom, let him ask of God, that giveth to all men liberally, and upbraideth not; and it shall be given him.
>
> But let him ask in faith, nothing wavering. For he that wavereth is like a wave of the sea driven with the wind and tossed.

The Apostle Paul wrote (Heb. 11:1): 'Now faith is the substance [certitude] of things hoped for, the evidence of things not seen.'

480. p. 104 ¶ 160. the Desired One

Haggai (2:7) announced the advent of the Desired One: 'And I will shake all nations, and the desire of all nations shall come: and I will fill this house with glory (Bahá), saith the Lord of hosts.' This prophecy has been fulfilled by Bahá'u'lláh Whose advent has been anticipated by all divine religions.

481. pp. 104–105 ¶ 160. O God, my God! Thou hast lighted the lamp of Thy Cause with the oil of wisdom; protect it from contrary winds. The lamp is Thine, and the glass is Thine, and all things in the heavens and on earth are in the grasp of Thy power . . . Thou art

the All-Powerful, Who, through the motion of Thy Pen, hast aided Thine irresistible Cause, and guided aright Thy loved ones

'Thou hast lighted the lamp of Thy Cause with the oil of wisdom' is a reference to the following verse of the Qur'án (24:35):

> God is the Light of the heavens and the earth. The Parable of His Light is as if there were a Niche and within it a Lamp: the Lamp enclosed in Glass: the glass as it were a brilliant star: Lit from a blessed Tree, an Olive, neither of the east nor of the west, whose oil is well-nigh luminous, though fire scarce touched it: Light upon Light! God doth guide whom He will to His Light . . .

It infers that God's Message pertains to both the East and the West and unifies all humanity. The enclosing 'glass' (the recipients of the God's Message, and the social teachings) has no intrinsic light but becomes a 'brilliant star' when the light of the Divine Manifestation and His Revelation shines through it.

'Guided aright Thy loved ones' is a reference to the last two verses of the first chapter of the Qur'án (1:6–7), which forms part of the prayer that Muslims read five times daily: 'Guide Thou us on the straight path, The path of those to whom Thou hast been gracious; – with whom thou art not angry, and who go not astray.'

Compare this with the following statement in Bahá'u'lláh's Tablet to Náṣiri'd-Dín Sháh: 'Say: He hath kindled the lamp of utterance, and feedeth it with the oil of wisdom and understanding . . .[640]

482. p. 105 ¶ 160. Sealed Wine

See Annotations 137, 268 and 458.

483. p. 106 ¶ 161. the secret progress of the Extended Cord

The Extended Cord very likely refers to the telegraph which was used to transmit and spread lies about Bahá'u'lláh and His followers in 'Akká and Istanbul – 'it incited and aided' adversaries in their nefarious activities coordinated in the 'Great City' (Istanbul) – 'rousing a considerable number of people in that city to oppose this Wronged

One' (¶ 161). The telegraph system began in Adrianople (Edirne) and went on line in 1865. Britain had a strong interest in the development of the telegraph. It had laid a 340-mile cable in the Black Sea and wished to connect up with the telegraph that it had set up in India. The expansion of the telegraph in the Ottoman Empire was a sensitive subject. It was resisted by local pashas and Muslim fundamentalists, as corrupt ideas could travel the lines, and a small army was needed to protect these lines.

484. p. 106 ¶ 161. A distinguished siyyid

Ḥájí Mírzá Siyyid Ḥasan, Afnán-i-Kabír (the Great Afnán), a brother of the wife of the Báb.

See Annotation 354.

485. p. 107 ¶ 162. Luqmán spoke unto his son

The identity of Luqmán, also known as Luqmán al-Hakím, is not known and most of the accounts written about this sage are perhaps apocryphal stories used to highlight certain words of wisdom. Some of the stories are mentioned in the 31st chapter of the Qur'án which is named after him. In the Qur'án, Luqmán often conveys his wisdom to his son. The poet Rumi refers to him as a Negro slave.

In Bahá'u'lláh's *Seven Valleys*, Luqmán presents the following analogy to his son to explain the inevitability of the afterlife:' O Son, if thou art able not to sleep, then thou art able not to die. And if thou art able not to waken after sleep, then thou shalt be able not to rise after death.'[641]

486. p. 107 ¶ 162. O my son! . . . informed of all

Bahá'u'lláh uses an anecdote from the Qur'án to admonish the Shaykh that God will eventually bring all his secret dealings and plots to light (31:16): 'O my son!"'(said Luqmán), 'if there be (but) the weight of a mustard-seed and it were (hidden) in a rock, 'or (anywhere) in the heavens or on earth, God will bring it forth . . .' He adds: 'The time is at hand when whatsoever lieth hid in the souls and hearts of men will be disclosed.' Bahá'u'lláh makes the same point as in the *Hidden Words*: 'O Children of Fancy! Know, verily . . . the satanic secrets and deeds done in the gloom of night shall be laid bare and manifest before the peoples of the world.'[642]

The Qur'án (9:94) also explains that God, Who knows what is hidden and what is evident, observes the actions of evil men, and in the end will show them the truth of all that they have done.

Notably, Christ also states (Luke 8:17): 'For nothing is secret, that shall not be made manifest, neither any thing hid, that shall not be known abroad'; and (Luke 12:2–3): 'For there is nothing covered, that shall not be revealed, neither hid, that shall not be known. Therefore whatsoever ye have spoken in the ear in closets shall be proclaimed upon the housetops.'

487.   p. 108 ¶ 163.   A<u>kh</u>tar

This is a reference to the weekly newspaper *A<u>kh</u>tar* (Star) which had existed since 1875 and which reflected liberal views that were anathema to Náṣiri'd-Dín <u>Sh</u>áh.[643] The Persian Ambassador in Istanbul, Mírzá Ḥusayn <u>Kh</u>án, Mu<u>sh</u>íru'd-Dawlih, had gathered a number of the enemies of the Faith around him and with Muḥammad Iṣfáhání constantly plotted against Bahá'u'lláh and His followers. The newspaper was published in Istanbul and was influenced by the followers of Mírzá Yaḥyá, including Siyyid Muḥammad-i-Iṣfáhání and two sons-in-law of Mírzá Yaḥyá, <u>Sh</u>ay<u>kh</u> Aḥmad Núrí and Mírzá Áqá <u>Kh</u>án. The latter became a sub-editor of the newspaper.

See also Annotations 226, 353.

488.   p. 108 ¶ 163.   nor the first goblet that hath been dashed to the ground

An Arab saying that describes that an event has occurred many times before (not the first disappointment).

489.   p. 108 ¶ 164.   Ḥájí <u>Sh</u>ay<u>kh</u> Muḥammad 'Alí

Ḥájí <u>Sh</u>ay<u>kh</u> Muḥammad 'Alí, known as Nabíl ibn Nabíl, was a brother of <u>Sh</u>ay<u>kh</u> Káẓim of Qazvin, to whom Bahá'u'lláh gave the surname Samandar (salamander). Both brothers were merchants of high repute. Their father, <u>Sh</u>ay<u>kh</u> Muḥammad, known as Nabíl, espoused the Faith of the Báb in the early days, and passed away in Baghdad one year before the Declaration of Bahá'u'lláh.

490. p. 108 ¶ 164. the Persian Embassy

Refers to the Persian Embassy in Istanbul, the capital of the Ottoman Empire. The Ambassador was Mírzá Ḥusayn Khán, Mushíru'd-Dawlih (see ¶ 111).

491. p. 110 ¶ 164. servant hath chosen to commit this most grievous sin

Ḥájí Shaykh Muḥammad-'Alí explains in his suicide note that he was driven to commit suicide by taking poison, as he could no longer abide the calumnies and intrigues of the followers of Mírzá Yaḥyá in Istanbul.

492. p. 110 ¶ 165. Ponder, now, O Shaykh, the influence of the word of God

Humanity's transformation through the creative power of the Divine Word has been the primary purpose of all religions including the Bahá'í Faith. 'The calling into being of a new race of men' is referred to in the Bahá'í Writings as 'the supreme and distinguishing function' of God's Faith'.[644] Hence,

> the Prophets of God, not excepting Bahá'u'lláh Himself, [have] chosen to appear, and deliver their Message in countries and amidst peoples and races, at a time when they were either fast declining, or had already touched the lowest depths of moral and spiritual degradation . . . For no more convincing proof could be adduced demonstrating the regenerative spirit animating the Revelations proclaimed by the Báb and Bahá'u'lláh than their power to transform what can be truly regarded as one of the most backward, the most cowardly, and perverse of peoples into a race of heroes, fit to effect in turn a similar revolution in the life of mankind.[645]

The Faith of Bahá'u'lláh has demonstrated its ability to assimilate the diversified elements of humanity, and to cleanse them of all forms of prejudice – evidences of a transformation, born of the Holy Spirit, 'which a disillusioned and sadly shaken society can ill afford to ignore'.[646] 'Abdu'l-Bahá has written:

> Praise be to God, today the splendour of the Word of God has illumined every horizon, and from all sects, races, tribes, nations, and communities souls have come together in the light of one Word, assembled, united and agreed in perfect harmony.[647]

See also Annotation 140.

493. p. 111 ¶ 167. Such references as have been made to Divinity and Godhead

See Bahá'u'lláh, Tajalliyát, in *Tablets of Bahá'u'lláh Revealed After the Kitáb-i-Aqdas*, p. 52; and Annotations 251, 252 and 256.

494. p. 111 ¶ 167. Imám Ṣádiq

Ja'far-i-Ṣádiq or simply al-Ṣádiq (the Truthful) was the sixth Imám of Shí'ih Islam. He was born in Medina and lived between 83 AH and 148 AH (702–765 CE). He inherited the mantle of Imám in his mid-30s from his father Muḥammad al-Báqir, the fifth Imám. On his mother's side he was related to Muḥammad ibn Abu Bakr (son of Abu Bakr). He formulated the 'Ja'fari jurisprudence' adhered to by the Shí'ihs. He is also revered in the Sunni sect as a transmitter of hadith and a prominent jurist and mystic.

A brother of the eleventh Imám, Ḥasan al-Askari, also had the name Ja'far and claimed the Imamate. He was declared Ja'far Kazáb, the Liar, and the sixth Imám was named Ja'far al-Ṣádiq, the Truthful, to distinguish between the two of them.

Al-Ṣádiq was harassed and arrested several times by the Umayyad and Abbasid Caliphs. He was poisoned at the behest of Manṣúr, the second Abbasid Caliph, at the age of 64 or 65. His eldest son Isma'il ibn Ja'far had died before Imám Ṣádiq and therefore did not succeed him. However, the sect of Isma'ilis consider his son, Muḥammad ibn Ismá'il, as the seventh Imám. The Twelver sect of Shí'ih Islam follows Músá al-Káẓim as the next Imám.

495. p. 111 ¶ 167. Servitude is a substance, the essence of which is Divinity

Bahá'u'lláh quotes this saying attributed to Imám Ja'far ibn Muḥammad aṣ-Ṣadiq[648] to refute further the Shaykh's contention that the Twin Manifestations had falsely claimed to be God.

The prophets of God are the essence of servitude to humanity, a servitude that has no equal or rival. Moses is called the servant of the Lord (Josh. 22:5), and the Torah describes Him as being 'very meek (Num. 12:3), beyond all the men that were upon the face of the earth. Christ taught (Matt. 23:11): 'The greatest among you will be your servant.' He stated further (Mark 10:44–45): 'And whosoever of you will be the chiefest, shall be servant of all. For even the Son of man came not to be ministered unto, but to minister, and to give his life a ransom for many.' To emphasize the importance of servitude He washed the feet of His disciples (John 13:4). Muhammad also stated that He was the servant/slave of God (Qur'án 19:30). In the Epistle Bahá'u'lláh frequently refers to Himself as 'servant'. Therefore, this attribute alone demonstrates the fact that they all manifest divinity.

496. p. 112 ¶ 167. The Imám Ṣádiq hath said: 'When our Qá'im will arise, the earth will shine with the light of her Lord

In a further defence of the divinity of the Manifestation of God, Bahá'u'lláh quotes the Qur'án (39:69) which states that the expected Qá'im ('He Who ariseth') will manifest the Divine Light: 'And the earth will shine with the Glory of its Lord.' The sixth Imám, Ja'far-i-Ṣádiq, explains this prophecy of the Qur'án about the Day of Resurrection:

> Mufaddal bin Umar has narrated that I heard Imám Ja'far Sadiq say: When our Qá'im rises, the earth will shine with the light of its Lord. Men will not need a light of the sun and darkness will vanish . . .[649]

497. p. 112 ¶ 167. Abí-'Abdi'lláh

Another reference to Ja'far-i-Ṣádiq.

498. p. 112 ¶ 167. Thereupon will He Who is the All-Compelling – exalted and glorified be He – descend from the clouds with the angels

This tradition is recorded in *Bihár al-Anwár*, a comprehensive collection of traditions (hadith, *aḥádíth*) compiled by the Shí'ih scholar Allámah Muḥammad Báqir al-Majlisi, in the section on *Kitabul Ghaibah* (Book of Occultation).[650]

The Qur'án (25:25, Rodwell) also predicts that 'On that day shall the heaven with its clouds be cleft, and the angels shall be sent down, descending.' In other words, the Sun of the Revelation associated with the Godhead will break through the dark clouds of superstition, tradition and misunderstanding and illumine humanity with new understandings. This event will be accompanied by a myriad of angelic hosts – a reference to individuals who are transformed through the creative power of the Divine Word.

See also Annotations 113, 279, 499 and 609.

499. p. 112 ¶ 167. What can such expect but that God should come down to them overshadowed with clouds?

This is from Qur'án 2:210 (Rodwell): 'What can such expect but that God should come down to them overshadowed with clouds, and the angels also, and their doom be sealed? And to God shall all things return.' The 'such' refers to those people who wait for God to reveal Himself to them in canopies of clouds but fail to recognize the signs when it happens. Thus, they rely on their own limited understanding rather than listening to the Voice of God.

See also Annotations 113, 279, 498 and 609.

500. p. 112 ¶ 167. Mufaḍḍal

Mufaddal bin 'Umar al-Ju'fi al-Kufi, one of the prominent and great companions of Imám Ja'far-i-Ṣádiq. He authored the book *Tawḥíd al-Mufaḍḍal* which consists of a long hadith narrated to him by the Imám. Al-Majlisi (see Annotation 498) quotes this hadith:

> Imám Ja'far Sadiq (a.s.) said: O Mufaddal every allegiance taken

> before the reappearance of the Qá'im is heresy, hypocrisy and a deception. And curse of God be on one who takes allegiance on his behalf or one who demands allegiance from him.
>
> O Mufaddal, the Qá'im will lean on the Kaaba and stretch his hand. An effulgence will emit from his palm. And he will say: this is the hand of God, and God commands you to pledge allegiance. Then he will recite the following verse [Qur'án 48:10]: 'Surely those who swear allegiance to you do but swear allegiance to God; the hand of God is above their hands. Therefore, whoever breaks (his faith), he breaks it only to the injury of his soul . . .[651]

The Báb undertook a pilgrimage to Mecca and Medina in 1260 AH. In Mecca He addressed an epistle to the Sherif of Mecca 'wherein He set forth, in clear and unmistakable terms, the distinguishing features of His mission, and called upon him to arise and embrace His Cause.[652] He also met Mírzá Muḥiṭ-i-Kirmání, the self-appointed successor of Siyyid Káẓim-i-Ras͟htí, in the vicinity of the Black Stone of Kaaba. He addressed him in these words:

> You regard yourself as one of the most outstanding figures of the S͟hayk͟hi community and a distinguished exponent of its teachings. In your heart you even claim to be one of the direct successors and rightful inheritors of those twin great Lights, those Stars that have heralded the morn of Divine guidance. Behold, we are both now standing within this most sacred shrine. Within its hallowed precincts, He whose Spirit dwells in this place can cause Truth immediately to be known and distinguished from falsehood, and righteousness from error. Verily I declare, none besides Me in this day, whether in the East or in the West, can claim to be the Gate that leads men to the knowledge of God. My proof is none other than that proof whereby the truth of the Prophet Muḥammad was established.[653]

501. p. 112 ¶ 167. The Commander of the Faithful

The Commander of the Faithful (Amir al Mu'minin) is a title of 'Alí ibn Abi Ṭálib, the first Imám of S͟hí'ih Islam.

See also ¶ 32 and ¶ 166.

502. p. 112 ¶ 167. I am He Who can neither be named, nor described . . . Outwardly I am an Imám; inwardly I am the Unseen, the Unknowable

These statements attributed to Imám 'Ali are recorded in *Mashdáriq Anwar al-Yaqín fi Asrár Amir Mu'minín* by Hafiz Rajab al-Bursi.[654] They allude to the inner and outer reality of those who are inspired by the Divinity. The inner reality is the unknowable Essence and the outer reality is what humanity sees and understands. Thus the inner reality may be disguised by a new outer form, but nevertheless it is the same reality that spoke in earlier times.

503. p. 112 ¶ 167. Abú-Ja'far-i-Ṭúsí

Also known as Abu Jafar Muḥammad Ibn Ḥassan Tusi (995–1067 CE), he was born in Tus in Khurasan, Iran and studied in Baghdad. He established the Hawza 'Ilmiyya (a seminary for the training of Shí'ih clergymen) in Najaf, Iraq, and was a compiler of hadith handed down from the sixth Imám, Imám Ja'far-i-Ṣádiq. He emigrated to Najaf due to an upheaval in Baghdad during which they burned his many books as well as the chair in which he sat and spoke to people.

504. p. 113 ¶ 167. You are the Way mentioned in the Book of God

This statement attributed to Imám Ja'far-i-Ṣádiq and narrated by Abú-Ja'far-i-Ṭúsí is recorded in volume 7 of *Bihár al-Anwár* by Allámah Muḥammad Báqir al-Majlisi.

In every Dispensation God's intermediary is 'the Way'. For 1,500 years God through the Dispensation of Moses showed the 'Way' to the Children of Israel (Is. 48:17): 'thus saith the Lord, thy Redeemer, the Holy One of Israel; I am the Lord thy God which teacheth thee to profit, which leadeth thee by the way that thou shouldest go.'

Notably, John the Baptist came to prepare and to 'straighten the way' for the Messiah (John 1:23): 'He said, I am the voice of one crying in the wilderness, Make straight the way of the Lord, as said the prophet Esaias (Isaiah).' Jesus also represented 'the way, the truth and the life . . .' (John 14:6). Again, for 1,400 years Muslims have been praying to be guided to the 'Right Way' or the Straight Path. Bahá'u'lláh is the Right Way for this day and age (see Annotation 302).

505. p. 113 ¶ 167. the Impost

In other words, you embody all the essentials of faith. The phrase in Arabic is 'you are the *Zakát*': that is, one of the five pillars of Islam. *Zakát* is a religious obligation for Muslims who meet the necessary criteria of wealth. It is akin to tax, or obligatory alms, given annually and used for charitable and religious purposes.

The Impost is the block which supports an arch of a building – in other words, you are a pillar that maintains the structure of God's Faith in place.

506. p. 113 ¶ 167. the Pilgrimage

In Shí'ih Islam the focus of pilgrimage was Imám 'Alí, as the Shrines of the Báb and Bahá'u'lláh are the focus of pilgrimage today.

507. p. 113 ¶ 167. We are the Sacred Month

The Muslim calendar consists of twelve lunar months: four of these are regarded as sacred, and three of the sacred months occur in succession. Prior to Islam, many of the Arabs regarded these months as holy, and this tradition continued in Islam. According to the commentary of Ibn Kathir, the main purpose of the sacred months was to allow the Hajj and 'Umrah pilgrimage to be performed in safety and with ease:

> Dhul-Qa'dah, the month before the Hajj month, was made sacred because they refrained from fighting during that month. Dhul-Hijjah, the next month, was made sacred because it is the month of Hajj, during which they performed Hajj rituals. Muharram, which comes next, was made sacred so that they are able to go back to their areas in safety after performing Hajj. Rajab, in the middle of the lunar year, was made sacred so that those coming from the farthest areas of Arabia are able to perform 'Umrah and visit the House and then go back to their areas safely.[655]

As Bahá'u'lláh is today the 'Sacred Month', the new Hajj, the Bahá'í calendar celebrates the events associated with God's twin Manifestations.

508. p. 113 ¶ 167. We are the Sacred City

The sacred city in Islam is Mecca, the site of the Great Mosque of Mecca (*al-Masjid al-Ḥarám*, literally 'The Sacred Mosque') which surrounds the Kaaba, Islam's holiest place and the cynosure or Qiblih for Muslims. The Grand Mosque includes other important significant sites to Muslims, including the Black Stone, the Well of Zamzam, the Station of Abraham, and Safá and Marwá.

Before appointing Mecca as the Qiblih for Muslims, Muhammad, together with Jews and Christians and His followers, prayed facing Jerusalem. Thus, the Qiblih is dictated by God. Bahá'u'lláh alerts the Muslim world that today He is the Sacred City, and the cynosure of all Dispensations and all mankind.

509. p. 113 ¶ 167. We are the Kaaba of God, and We are the Qiblih of God

The Qiblih is the Point of Adoration in a religion – the place that the faithful turn to in prayer. For Jews it is the Temple in Jerusalem and for Christians it is the Church of the Holy Sepulchre in Jerusalem. For Muslims the Qiblih changed whilst Muhammad was in Medina. During the middle of prayers, Muhammad turned 180 degrees so that instead of facing Jerusalem he faced the Kaaba and Mecca as the new Qiblih of Islam. Many left Him that day, occasioning the revelation of the following verse (2:177):

> It is not righteousness that ye turn your faces towards East or West;
> But it is righteousness – to believe in God and the Last Day . . . and the Book, and the Messengers . . .

In other words, it is more important for Jews, Christians and Muslims to recognize the Manifestation of God, the true cynosure, and the Day of Resurrection (the Advent of Bahá'u'lláh). The Qiblih in this Dispensation is the Shrine of Bahá'u'lláh at Bahjí known as 'the Heart and Qiblih of the Bahá'í world'.[656]

510. p. 113 ¶ 167. We are the Face of God

The Báb, writing to Sulaymán, a Muslim clergyman in Masqat, capital of Oman, who had failed to respond to His Cause, states:

> Hadst thou observed the contents of the Epistle We sent unto thee, it would have been far more profitable to thee than worshipping thy Lord from the beginning that hath no beginning until this day, and indeed more meritorious than proving thyself wholly devoted in thine acts of worship. And hadst thou attained the presence of thy Lord in this land, and been of them that truly believe that the Face of God is beheld in the person of the Primal Point, it would have been far more advantageous than prostrating thyself in adoration from the beginning that hath no beginning until the present time . . .[657]

Referring to Bahá'u'lláh, the Báb wrote:

> If, on the day of His Revelation, all that are on earth bear Him allegiance, Mine inmost being will rejoice, inasmuch as all will have attained the summit of their existence, and will have been brought face to face with their Beloved, and will have recognized, to the fullest extent attainable in the world of being, the splendour of Him Who is the Desire of their hearts. If not, My soul will indeed be saddened. I truly have nurtured all things for this purpose. How, then, can anyone be veiled from Him?[658]

To the 'leaders of religion', Bahá'u'lláh announced: 'this is the Face of your Lord' (see ¶ 188 quoting the *Kitáb-i-Aqdas*). And in the Súriy-i-Haykal He thus admonished the Czar of Russia (see ¶ 95):

> Incline thine ear unto the voice of God, the King, the Holy, and turn thou unto Paradise, the Spot wherein abideth He Who, among the Concourse on high, beareth the most excellent titles, and Who, in the kingdom of creation, is called by the name of God, the Effulgent, the All-Glorious. Beware lest thy desire deter thee from turning towards the face of thy Lord.

See also Annotation 569.

511. p. 113 ¶ 167. Jábír

Jábír bin Yazíd bin al-Ḥárith al-Ju'fí (died 128 AH) was a 'Tabi'un', one of a select group of Muslims who had met the companions of Muhammad. He was an early Shí'ih jurist of the Qur'án and a companion of both Imám al-Báqir and Imám Ja'far al-Ṣádiq (the fifth and sixth Imáms respectively). Several Sunni scholars such as at-Tirmidhi and al-Razi considered him reliable, although modern Sunni scholars have denounced him. Al-Majlisi recounts a number of traditions from Jábir in *Bihár al-Anwár*, vol. 11.

512. p. 113 ¶ 167. 'Abú-Ja'far

'Abú-Ja'far refers to Muḥammad bin 'Ali bin al-Ḥusayn bin Ali bin Abi Tálib, who was also known simply as al-Báqir (677–733 CE). He was related to Imám 'Alí through both his father and mother. He was the fifth Imám, whose leadership lasted nineteen years after the death of his father, the fourth Imám. He died at the age of 57 years, poisoned by the order of Ibráhim bin Walid bin Yazid.

513. p. 113 ¶ 167. O Jábír! Give heed unto the Bayán (Exposition) and the Má'ání (Significances)

This statement attributed to Imám Báqir is recorded in Háfiz Rajab al-Bursi's *Mashári̇q Anwar al-Yaqín fi Asrár Amir Mu'minín*:[659]

> And the Imám said O Jábir it is your lot to appreciate the Bayán and the Ma'ání. . . by Bayán is meant that thou should realize that God is without equal or comparison, and hath no partners. And by Ma'ání is meant us, we are with God and are His Hand and Tongue – we are the Decree and Command of God, and His Word, and His Knowledge and Truth. Our wish is His Wish, Our Desire is His Desire. We are the masání (Súrih Fátihah, or the seven oft repeated verses of the Qur'án), we are the countenance of God that walk amongst you. Anyone who recognizes us has recognized the Leader and Exponent of Truth and Certitude, and anyone who rejects us is a follower of the devil and an inhabitant of hell. If it is our wish we cleave the earth (of human understanding) and we ascend to the

heavens. The resurrection and the reckoning of these people is by our direction and the fate of all matters is in our hands.

514. p. 113 ¶ 167. How can I worship a Lord Whom I have not seen?

This statement of Imám 'Alí is recorded in al-Majlisi, *Bihár al-Anwár*, vol. 2, ch. 29, and vol. 14, ch. 12. In other words, the invisible and unknowable God is represented by One Who is tangible and Who manifests the divine attributes and personifies the divine Will.

515. p. 114 ¶ 168. that thou mayest hear what no ear hath ever heard, and gaze on that which no eye hath ever seen

In other words, perchance you will not fall into the category of individuals described in the Qur'án (2:7): 'God hath set a seal on their hearts and on their hearing, and on their eyes is a veil; great is the penalty they (incur).' This was indeed the sorry condition of the people at the time of Christ (Mark 8:18): 'Having eyes, see ye not? and having ears, hear ye not? and do ye not remember?' Hopefully, he would instead be amongst those characterized by the Prophet Isaiah (52:15): 'that which had not been told them shall they see; and that which they had not heard shall they consider.'

516. p. 115 ¶ 170. Ponder a while upon the verses concerning the Divine Presence

Bahá'u'lláh draws the attention of the Shaykh to the fact that there are many verses in the Qur'án (more than fifty) which speak of the coming of the Lord, seeing God and attaining His Presence. He challenges the Shaykh to meditate on the collective meaning of these verses.

Clearly, they cannot apply to the invisible and unknowable Essence of essences. A reasonable conclusion and one advanced in the *Kitáb-i-Íqán* is that 'Divine Presence' is a reference to the Manifestation of God. Muhammad, the Apostle of God, had 'sealed' an era of prophecy and prophethood and had warned of the advent of the Divine Manifestation and God's Vicegerent, the Dawning Place of His Revelation – 'The day when mankind shall stand before the Lord of the worlds'

(¶ 168). Knowledge of Him will be the extent to which mankind can know God, and obedience to Him is tantamount to obedience to God.

Hence, the consummation of the Dispensation of Muhammad would be the spiritual resurrection that will occur when some of His followers attain the Presence of the 'Lord of the worlds' (Qur'án 83:4–6, 10). In this Epistle (see Annotations 510, 516, and 525) and in the *Kitáb-i-Íqán*[660] Bahá'u'lláh refers to several of the verses of the Qur'án about the Divine Presence. He explains that 'Attainment unto the Divine Presence can be realized solely by attaining His presence'.[661]

517. p. 115 ¶ 170. It is God Who hath reared the heavens without pillars thou canst behold . . .

Bahá'u'lláh quotes Qur'án 13:2 in its entirety. This verse explains that the heaven of God's Revelation will be independent of any props, that is, it will not need existing civil or ecclesiastical systems to sustain it. The Qur'án asserts that humanity has a tendency to choose 'for intercessors others besides God' (39:43), but in the Promised Day God will be enthroned and will subject the sun and the moon (spiritual and social laws) to His Law (39:44).

518. p. 116 ¶ 170. To him who hopeth to attain the Presence of God, the set time of God will surely come

This is a quotation from Qur'án 29:4 (Rodwell) which associates the individual's meeting with God with a fixed term or time-span (*ajal*) appointed by God for the end of the previous Dispensation and the beginning of a new era. The promise of attaining the Presence of God, that is, the advent of Bahá'u'lláh, is thus linked with the concept of a predestined end (*ajal*) of every *Ummah* including the Dispensation of Islam (7:34–35).

The Bible states that 'God dwells in unapproachable light, whom no man has seen or can see . . .' (I Tim. 6:16) – His Manifestation, Christ, is described as the 'image of the invisible God' (Col. 1:15), and 'the brightness of his glory, and the express image of his person' (Heb. 1:3). Hence, to see God is equivalent to recognizing His Manifestation (John 14:8–9).

See Annotation 529 for 'set time'.

519. p. 116 ¶ 170 As for those who believe not in the signs of God, or that they shall ever attain His Presence

This understanding is implicit in Qur'án 10:7–8 and 29:23.

520. p. 116 ¶ 170. And they say, What! when we shall have lain hidden in the earth, shall we become a new creation? Yea, they deny that they shall attain the Presence of their Lord

This is a quotation from Qur'án 32:9–10 (Rodwell). Bahá'u'lláh uses the term 'new creation' (*khalq-i-jadid*) to describe a spiritually transformed community of faith.

According to the Qur'án (2:28), the people of Arabia were 'dead' prior to Islam but then were endowed with spiritual life. However, God decreed that they would undergo a second (spiritual) death and would have to be again revived by God (through the Revelations of the Báb and Bahá'u'lláh). In the passage quoted by Bahá'u'lláh, the unbelievers, interpreting the second part of 2:28 literally, doubt that God would physically resuscitate them (to become a new creation) after they had been dead and 'lain in the ground' – in this way, they are in fact denying that they will at a future time 'attain the Presence of their Lord' and recognize God's Manifestation and Faith.

Notably, this 'new creation' also occurred when Christ appeared (II Cor. 5:17) and there is an anticipation of a further spiritual rebirth and times of refreshing and restitution/restoration of all things at the Second Coming (Acts 3:21–22).

521. p. 116 ¶ 170. They truly doubt the Presence of their Lord. He, verily, overshadoweth all things

This is a quotation from Qur'án 41:50, 54 (Abdel Haleem):

> he [disbeliever] is sure to say, '. . . I do not think the Hour will ever come, but even if I were to be taken back to my Lord, the best reward would await me with Him . . .'
>
> Truly, they doubt that they will meet their Lord; truly He encompasses everything.

In other words, in spite of the fact that in every Dispensation man has attained to the Presence of God, the people doubt that they will, in turn, witness God's Revelation and attain His Presence in the promised 'Day of God', and the spiritual resurrection of mankind.

522. p. 116 ¶ 170. Verily, they who hope not to attain Our Presence, and find their satisfaction in this world's life, and rest on it, and who of Our signs are heedless – these! their abode the fire

This is from Qur'án 10:9–11 (Rodwell) which also states:

> But they who believe and do the things that are right, shall their Lord direct aright because of their faith. Rivers shall flow at their feet in gardens of delight:
>
> Their cry therein, 'Glory be to thee, O God!' and their salutation therein, 'Peace!'
>
> And the close of their cry, 'Praise be to God, the Lord of the worlds!'
>
> . . . So leave we those who hope not to meet Us, bewildered in their error.

523. p. 116 ¶ 170. But when Our clear signs are recited to them, they who look not forward to attain Our Presence, say, 'Bring a different Qur'án from this, or make some change in it'

This is a quotation from Qur'án 10:16 (Rodwell). Those who objected to what was being revealed in the Qur'án and selfishly wanted it changed to suit their own ideas and fancies, are categorized as not wishing to attain the Presence of God and Muhammad, His Manifestation. The same is true today, for there are many who do not wish to follow what has been written in the Scripture, and would rather follow the dictates of their own desires. The Manifestation of God reveals only what God discloses to Him, whether or not it displeases those who hear it.

524. p. 117 ¶ 170. Then gave We the Book to Moses – complete for Him who should do right, and a decision for all matters, and a

guidance, and a mercy, that they might believe in the Presence of their Lord

The above verse quoted by Bahá'u'lláh is from Qur'án (6:155, Rodwell). It confirms that Moses was provided with a complete Revelation that explained all things. Indeed, every Dispensation represents a complete divine Revelation for its prescribed period of time. It is inconceivable that God will send a Messenger to humanity but leave His intention and purpose incomplete. In spite of persecutions, 'God will complete the revelation of His Light . . .' (Qur'án 61:8). Thus, Islam also represented complete faith, guidance and mercy (Qur'án 5:3). The Dispensation of Moses testified that the Jews will meet with their Lord at the end of time (Amos 4:12): 'Prepare to meet thy God, O Israel.'

525. p. 117 ¶ 170. They are those who believe not in the signs of the Lord, or that they shall ever attain His Presence

This is from Qur'án 18:104 (Rodwell) which states that those that deny God's Revelations and disbelieve in the imperative to attain His Presence are the greatest losers because all their efforts and achievements in this world are in vain. Such people may delude themselves that they are righteous, but their deeds will come to nothing because of their unbelief, and deeds without faith will not be counted.

526. p. 117 ¶ 170. no weight will We allow them on the Day of Resurrection.

The Báb provides the following lucid explanation of 'resurrection':

> what is meant by the Day of Resurrection is this, that from the time of the appearance of Him Who is the Tree of divine Reality, at whatever period and under whatever name, until the moment of His disappearance, is the Day of Resurrection.[662]

The Báb then explains the resurrections of the Dispensations of Moses, Christ and Muhammad. Notably, Muslims are to pray that they will not bring shame on themselves by not recognizing the Promise of all Dispensations:

> Our Lord! Grant us what Thou didst promise unto us through Thy messengers, and save us from shame on the Day of Judgment: For Thou never breakest Thy promise. (Qur'án 3:194)

See also Annotations 591 and 592.

527. p. 117 ¶ 170. Hath the history of Moses reached thee? . . . Verily, I am Thy Lord

The Bible and the Qur'án describe Moses's encounter with God, Who spoke to Him through the burning bush (Ex. 3:1–17). Bahá'u'lláh here quotes Qur'án 10:9, 11 (Rodwell).

528. p. 117 ¶ 170. pull off Thy shoes, for Thou art in the holy vale of Towa . . . Verily, I am God . . . worship Me

This is from Qur'án 20:12–14 (Rodwell). Towa or Túwá is the name of the Holy Valley below Mount Sinai; it is the sacred spot where Moses became aware of God's Presence and was ordered to take off His sandals.

529. p. 117 ¶ 170. Have they not considered within themselves that God hath not created the heavens and the earth and all that is between them but for a serious end, and for a fixed term?

This is from Qur'án 30:7 (Rodwell). The 'serious end' also refers to Qur'án 54:6–8, which warns that the Divine Summoner or Caller (Bahá'u'lláh) will invite Muslims as well as the rest of humanity to a momentous or serious 'affair' that they will find difficult and severe. This important event will signify attaining 'the Presence of their Lord':

> Therefore, (O Prophet) turn away from them. The day that the Caller will call (them) to a terrible affair [Rodwell: 'stern business'; Pickthall: 'a painful thing']. They will come forth . . . towards the Caller! – 'Hard is this Day!' the unbelievers will say.

The Qur'án (7:34–35) explains that for every people or Dispensation (*Ummah*) there is a preordained end or fixed term (*ajal)*, and that the *ajal* of the Dispensation of Islam will coincide with the appearance of other Messengers from God. The 'fixed term' is a reference to the fact that each Dispensation has a defined beginning and a predicted end.

530. p. 117 ¶ 170. But truly most men believe not that they shall attain the Presence of their Lord

This is from Qur'án 30:7 (Rodwell). Other verses (12:103; 40:59) also warn that if individuals imitate and follow the majority they will likely be led astray at the Promised Day and Hour when men must attain the Presence of God.

See also Annotations 522 and 525.

531. p. 117 ¶ 170. What! Have they no thought that they shall be raised again for the Great Day, the Day when mankind shall stand before the Lord of the worlds?

This is a quotation from Qur'án 83:5–6 (Rodwell). The followers of all Dispensations will be summoned and given life again (raised) at the time of the promised Great Day of the Lord. In other words, all humanity will attain the Presence of God.

The Gospel of Matthew (25:32) states that on the Day of Resurrection: 'before him shall be gathered all nations . . .'

532. p. 118 ¶ 170. We heretofore gave the Book to Moses. Have thou no doubt as to His attaining Our Presence

This is a quotation from Qur'án 32:23 (Rodwell) which states that Moses also received a Revelation from God and that He undoubtedly attained the Presence of God (see also 89:21): 'We heretofore gave the Book of the law to Moses: have thou no doubt as to our meeting with him: and we appointed it for the guidance of the children of Israel.'

533. p. 118 ¶ 170. And He saith: 'Aye! But when the earth shall be crushed . . .

This is a quotation from Qur'án 89:22 (Rodwell); God will destroy the 'earth' of previous human understandings and values. Isaiah predicted (24:1): 'Behold, the Lord maketh the earth empty, and maketh it waste, and turneth it upside down.' Also (24:19): 'The earth is utterly broken down, the earth is clean dissolved (New International Version: 'split asunder'; JPS: 'crumbled in pieces'), the earth is moved exceedingly.'

Bahá'u'lláh declares:

> This is the Day whereon the All-Merciful hath come down in the clouds of knowledge, clothed with manifest sovereignty. He well knoweth the actions of men. He it is Whose glory none can mistake, could ye but comprehend it. The heaven of every religion hath been rent, and the earth of human understanding been cleft asunder . . .[663]

534. p. 118 ¶ 170. and thy Lord shall come and the angels rank on rank

This is a quotation from Qur'án 89:23 (Rodwell) which states that the Lord God will come with the hosts of heaven. Qur'án 78:38 (Rodwell) also predicts: 'On the day whereon the Spirit and the Angels shall be ranged in order, they shall not speak: save he whom the God of Mercy shall permit, and who shall say that which is right.'

The Lord of Hosts or the Lord of Heaven's armies is one of the names of God (Hosea 12:15) and is mentioned about 260 times in the Hebrew Bible. The Torah (Deut. 33:2) promises the advent of the Lord with ten thousand saints (*kodesh*, angelic, holy ones or heavenly beings). The Prophet Jeremiah (46:10) announced: 'For that day belongs to the Lord God of hosts . . .'

535. p. 118 ¶ 170. Fain would they put out the light of God with their mouths! But though the infidels hate it, God will perfect His light

This is a quotation from Qur'án 9:32 (Rodwell) (also 61:9). It is restated by Bahá'u'lláh in ¶ 157 and ¶ 249.

Religious leaders who do not believe in God's latest Revelation feel threatened by it and arise to eliminate the truth. This is what the Shaykh did, and what many of his fellow Shí'ih clerics have done in Persia since the Declaration of the Báb to silence God's Faith, and it was precisely what the Jewish and Christian leaders attempted in Medina at the time of Muhammad: hence the revelation of the above verse in the Qur'án, which is also quoted in the *Kitáb-i-Íqán*. In other words, in every Dispensation, the religious leaders try to extinguish the divine light of guidance by speaking out against it, but the divine light is irresistible; it cannot be extinguished by their opposition.

The Qur'án (64:8) further admonishes: 'Believe, therefore, in God and His Messenger, and in the Light which we have sent down. And God is well acquainted with all that ye do.'

536. p. 118 ¶ 171. In all the Divine Books the promise of the Divine Presence hath been explicitly recorded

The following examples are briefly presented here:

Hinduism – Bhagavad Gita:

> My true form is unborn and changeless, I am the Lord who dwells in every creature. Through the power of my own *maya* (spiritual power), I manifest myself in a finite form. Whenever dharma (righteousness) declines and the purpose of life is forgotten, I manifest myself on earth. I am born in every age to protect the good, to destroy evil, and to reestablish dharma.[664]

Judaism – The Hebrew Bible (Ps. 24:7–10):

> Lift up your heads, O ye gates; and be ye lift up, ye everlasting doors; and the King of glory shall come in.
>
> Who is this King of glory? The Lord strong and mighty, the Lord mighty in battle.
>
> Lift up your heads, O ye gates; even lift them up, ye everlasting doors; and the King of glory shall come in.
>
> Who is this King of glory? The Lord of hosts; He is the King of glory.

And Is. 9:6:

> . . . his name shall be called Wonderful, Counseller, the mighty God, the everlasting Father, the Prince of Peace.

A Christian evangelist has explained:

> The Hebrew word for visitation [Divine Presence, *paqad*] indicates a time when the Eternal God breaks into human history in order to bless or to punish individuals or nations. This visitation always changes the destiny of the person or nation, whether they are ready for it or not. In fact, very few people are ready for a visitation from God.[665]

Christianity – The Lord's Prayer:

> Our Father which art in heaven, Hallowed be thy name.
> Thy kingdom come. Thy will be done on earth, as it is in heaven . . . (Matt. 6:9–10)

And:

> And I heard a great voice out of heaven saying, Behold, the tabernacle of God is with men, and he will dwell with them, and they shall be his people, and God himself shall be with them, and be their God. (Rev. 21:3)

Islam – The Qur'án (6:31):

> Lost indeed are they who treat it as a falsehood that they must meet God, until on a sudden the hour is on them, and they say: 'Ah! woe unto us that we took no thought of it . . .'

Also, 10:15, 45; 25:21 and 29:23.

537. p. 119 ¶ 171. there hath been revealed in the Kitáb-i-Íqán (Book of Certitude) concerning the Presence and Revelation of God

The *Kitab-i-Íqán* explains 'Presence of God' (paras. 148–151, pp. 138–43) and the 'Revelation of God' (para. 118, p. 112).

538. p. 119 ¶ 172. Repudiation hath not veiled it, and ten thousand hosts arrayed against it were powerless to withhold it

from shining. Thou canst excuse thyself no longer. Either thou must recognize it, or – God forbid – arise and deny all the Prophets!

All Revelations have been rejected. Bahá'u'lláh states that the fierce opposition has not obscured the light of His Faith. The Shaykh has therefore a clear choice: either to accept God's Faith and stop persecuting it, or to deny Bahá'u'lláh. The latter course of action would necessarily mean that he has also denied Muhammad and all the earlier Messengers.

'Ten thousand hosts' is likely a reference to the number of people gathered to witness the martyrdom of the Báb in Tabriz.[666]

On one occasion Christ accused the Jewish leaders of not loving God and not believing in Moses, for had they been in tune with the reality of Moses and the Scriptures, they would have recognized Him also, instead of laying traps for Him and being primarily concerned with their titles and rank (John 5:42–47).

Similarly, the Qur'án (17:72) states that those who are spiritually blind in the Dispensation of Muhammad will remain blind in the future Dispensation and will be led even further astray: 'And he who has been blind here, shall be blind hereafter, and wander yet more from the way.'

Bahá'u'lláh issues the following challenge:

> O people, if ye deny these verses, by what proof have ye believed in God? Produce it, O assemblage of false ones. Nay, by the One in Whose hand is my soul, they are not, and never shall be able to do this, even should they combine to assist one another.[667]

Notably, Ḥájí Mírzá Siyyid 'Alí, the maternal uncle of the Báb who had raised Him from childhood, made the following response when pressured to either deny his faith or face martyrdom:

> My repudiation of the truths enshrined in this Revelation would be tantamount to a rejection of all the Revelations that have preceded it. To refuse to acknowledge the Mission of the Siyyid-i-Báb would be to apostatise from the Faith of my forefathers and to deny the Divine character of the Message which Muḥammad, Jesus, Moses, and all the Prophets of the past have revealed. God knows that whatever I have heard and read concerning the sayings and doings of those Messengers, I have been privileged to witness the

same from this Youth, this beloved Kinsman of mine, from His earliest boyhood to this, the thirtieth year of His life. Everything in Him reminds me of His illustrious Ancestor and of the imáms of His Faith whose lives our recorded traditions have portrayed. I only request of you that you allow me to be the first to lay down my life in the path of my beloved Kinsman.[668]

539. p. 119 ¶ 173. Shí'ih sect

Almost immediately after the death of Muhammad, there was a fundamental difference of opinion as to who should be His successor, and Islam split into two sects: Shí'ih and Sunni. The word 'Shí'ih' in Arabic means 'follower', or belonging to a particular sect or group. It refers to the followers of 'Alí and his descendants, the Imáms. The Shí'ihs reject the first three Caliphs of the Sunnis, and believe that by divine right the successorship in Islam belonged rightfully to 'Alí (the first Imám and fourth Caliph) and to his descendants, the 'Vicars of the Prophet'.

Despite admonishments in the Qur'án (49:10) for Muslims to remain united, sadly almost every one of the world's more than one billion Muslims is part of a sect of Islam. Shí'ihs even derive their name from the very word used in the Qur'an (6:159 and 30:32) for sect – *shiyaAAan*.

540. p. 119 ¶ 173. How many the edifices which they reared with the hands of idle fancies and vain imaginings, and how numerous the cities which they built!

Rather than actual buildings, this refers metaphorically to the elaborate traditions and constructs of Shí 'ih Islam concerning the advent of their Promised Qá'im. As part of a vast collection of hadith and 'idle fancies and vain imaginings', they believe that the Twelfth Imám, Imám Ḥasan Askari, disappeared at the age of five years and currently lives in the mythical cities of Jabilqá and Jabilsá with his wife and children. He is expected to return as the Qá'im on the Day of Resurrection.

541. p. 119 ¶ 173. At length those vain imaginings were converted into bullets and aimed at Him

This refers to the Báb, Who represented the Promised One (Qá'im) of the Shí'ih sect. For more than a thousand years the Shí'ihs had prayed for His advent, but when the Báb appeared they suspended Him in the barrack square of Tabriz and fired 750 muskets at Him. They failed to recognize the Báb as their Qá'im because of the misrepresentations of the scriptures by the religious scholars and their misdirection of their followers. Thus their vain imaginings became deadly weapons that were directed at Him.

A hadith warns against religious scholars who will stray from God's Path:

> Abu Dharr said, 'I was with the Prophet one day and I heard him saying: "There is something I fear for my Ummah more than the Dajjal." It was then that I became afraid, so I said: "Oh Messenger of God which thing is that?" He said; "Misguided and astray scholars."'[669]

Again:

> It was narrated from 'Umar bin al Khattab that the Messenger of Allah said: 'The thing that I fear most for my *ummah* is every hypocrite who speaks with knowledge.'[670]

542. p. 120 ¶ 173. the Prince of the world

Sayyid Álam (the Prince of the world) refers in this context to the Báb. Elsewhere, it also refers to His twin Manifestation, Bahá'u'lláh.[671]

The word 'prince' translates as 'ruler' – someone endowed with authority (as in I Kings 20:14; Dan. 6:1, 3, 4, 6; Hos. 3:4). The term is used in the Bible for two distinct and different rulers, namely, Satan and profane and wicked rulers of the forces of evil, as in Ezek. 21:25; John 12:31; and, ruler(s) of heavenly forces and those who enact the divine Will on earth.

In the context of the latter, an accepted interpretation of Dan. 8:11 is that it is God Who is described as the 'prince of the host' in that He is the ruler of the host of heaven and the ruler of the holy army below – God as the One with authority over the temporal and spiritual affairs of humanity.[672] Christ is also referred to as the 'Prince of Life' (Acts 3:15), and because of His spiritual dominion is described as the 'Prince of the kings of the earth' (Rev. 1:5). Acts 5:31 refers to Him as 'Prince and Saviour'.

The Bible also refers to the one expected by the Jews and Christians as the 'Prince'. For example, The Messiah is also referred to as the 'Prince of Peace' expected to come in the latter days (Is. 9:6–7) and as 'the Prince' (Dan. 9:25). Daniel (12:1) predicts the arrival of the Archangel Michael, 'the great prince'. Ezekiel (34:23–24) refers to the advent of King David as follows:

> And I will set up one shepherd over them, and he shall feed them, even my servant David; he shall feed them, and he shall be their shepherd.
>
> And I the Lord will be their God, and my servant David a prince among them; I the Lord have spoken it.

Notably, the expectation in the Lord's Prayer is that God will exert His dominion on earth: 'Thy Kingdom come. Thy will be done on earth, as it is in heaven.' It is therefore consistent with this hope that the divine Manifestation who is expected to reveal God's will for mankind in the Day of the Father should be also referred to as the Prince of this world.

543.   p. 120 ¶ 174.   The followers of <u>Sh</u>ay<u>kh</u>-i-Aḥsá'í (<u>Sh</u>ay<u>kh</u> Aḥmad)

<u>Sh</u>ay<u>kh</u> Aḥmad-i-Aḥsá'í and his successor Siyyid Káẓim-i-Ra<u>sh</u>tí are the 'twin resplendent lights' who heralded the Báb and Bahá'u'lláh. Born in 1753, <u>Sh</u>ay<u>kh</u> Aḥmad-i-Aḥsá'í died near Medina in 1826.[673] His followers are known as <u>Sh</u>ay<u>kh</u>is. Remnants of this sect, now fragmented, continue to exist in Iran.

544. pp. 120–21 ¶ 175. this Wronged One requesteth thee and the other divines . . . to appoint some person . . . and despatch him to these regions

Bahá'u'lláh states that the clergy that have opposed Him and spoken against Him have never met Him. He encourages them to visit Him in prison and ascertain the truth directly, and also to visit Mírzá Yaḥyá in Cyprus. There is no record that they complied with this reasonable request and challenge.

545. p. 121 ¶ 175. the island of Cyprus

'The fateful decision was eventually arrived at to banish Bahá'u'lláh to the penal colony of 'Akká, and Mírzá Yaḥyá to Famagusta in Cyprus. This decision was embodied in a strongly worded Farmán, issued by Sulṭán 'Abdu'l-'Azíz.'[674]

546. p. 121 ¶ 176. Wert thou now to exert thyself, the truth of this Cause would be made apparent unto mankind, and the people would be delivered from this grievous and oppressive darkness

Bahá'u'lláh states that the deliverance of His followers from their grievous plight and oppressive darkness is only possible if the ruling clergy arise to investigate fairly the new Revelation rather than make hasty erroneous assumptions and adopt dogmatic positions.

547. 121 ¶ 177. Rawḍih-khání

This refers to the traditional ceremonies that mark the tragedy of Karbila and the martyrdom of Imám Ḥusayn, especially during the month of Muharram. The anniversary is variously commemorated by pilgrimage to the shrine of Imám Ḥusayn, re-enacting in passion plays the Battle of Karbila (*taziyeh*), and organizing or participating in a ritual when a specially trained orator, the *Rawḍih-khán*, recites aloud the book *Rawzat al-shuhadá* with a great deal of improvisation.

> The objective of the oration is to move the audience to tears through recitation of the tragedy of the Battle of Karbala. This type of

> mourning ritual is viewed by Shiite Muslims as a means of achieving salvation by developing empathy and sympathy for the martyrs. This belief is illustrated by the oft-repeated quotation, 'Anyone who cries for Husayn shall go directly to paradise.'[675]

To His followers from a Shí'ih background, Bahá'u'lláh represents the return of Imám Ḥusayn. The Bábís believed that the Imáms had been resurrected and there was therefore no point in holding *Rawḍih-khání.* Those who regularly held the ceremony in their houses, such as Mírzá Hádí Dawlat-Ábádi, the self-appointed successor of Mírzá Yaḥyá, did so in an attempt to dissimulate their faith. In contrast, as a sign of the preeminence of the new Revelation, Ṭáhirih refused to wear the traditional mourning clothes at the remembrance day of the martyrdom of Imám Ḥusayn.

548. p. 122 ¶ 178. Our loved ones have been arrested in the land of Ṭá

A reference to the arrest in 1891 of three eminent Bahá'ís – Ibn-i-Abhar, Mullá 'Alí-Akbar and Ḥájí Amín – by Kámrán Mírzá, the Náyibu's-Salṭanih (Governor of Tehran). He imprisoned a group of political agitators and, despite all the evidence, was under the misapprehension that Bahá'ís also participated in partisan politics. Mullá 'Alí-Akbar and Ḥájí Amín were put in chains, and then taken to the prison of Qazvin, where they remained for eighteen months.[676] Afterwards, they were transferred to the prison of Tehran. Mullá 'Alí-Akbar was released after six months, while Ḥájí Amín's imprisonment was prolonged further; he was released after the Ascension of Bahá'u'lláh. The Lawḥ-i-Dunyá refers to their imprisonment:

> Praise and thanksgiving beseem the Lord of manifest dominion Who hath adorned the mighty prison with the presence of their honours 'Alí Akbar and Amín, and hath illumined it with the light of certitude, constancy and assurance. The glory of God and the glory of all that are in the heavens and on the earth be upon them.[677]

549. 123: ¶ 180. The officials of the Persian Embassy in the Great City (Constantinople).

See ¶ 162 and Taherzadeh, *The Revelation of Bahá'u'lláh*, vol. 4, pp. 393–402.

550. p. 123 ¶ 180. Flingest thou thy calumnies unto the face of Them Whom the one true God hath made the Trustees of the treasures of His seventh sphere?

This is from the *Mathnaví* of Jalálu'ddín Rúmí, the celebrated Persian Sufi poet. It is also quoted in the *Kitáb-i-Íqán*. It is an implicit warning to the Shaykh and his fellow clerics to restrain their attacks against the One whose station was exalted beyond their comprehension.

Bahá'u'lláh warns Muslims that it is unreasonable and reckless to treat His mighty Revelation frivolously and reject it out of hand.

> Could such a thing be made manifest except through the power of a divine Revelation, and the potency of God's invincible Will? By the righteousness of God! Were any one to entertain so great a Revelation in his heart, the thought of such a declaration would alone confound him! Were the hearts of all men to be crowded into his heart, he would still hesitate to venture upon so awful an enterprise. He could achieve it only by the permission of God, only if the channel of his heart were to be linked with the Source of divine grace, and his soul be assured of the unfailing sustenance of the Almighty. To what, We wonder, do they ascribe so great a daring? Do they accuse Him of folly as they accused the Prophets of old? Or do they maintain that His motive was none other than leadership and the acquisition of earthly riches?[678]

551. 124 ¶ 180. Mu'ínu'l-Mulk, Mírzá Muḥsin Khán

Shaykh Muḥsin Khán (c. 1819–1899) was initially employed in the Persian Foreign Service in the capital of Russia, St Petersburg, as well as in France, Britain and Germany. He became the Persian Ambassador to Istanbul in 1872, a position which he held for about nine years. He was dismissed from this post by Náṣiri'd-Dín Sháh for reasons that are uncertain.

552. p. 124 ¶ 181. These, verily, are men who if they come to cities of pure gold will consider them not; and if they meet the fairest and most comely of women will turn aside

Compare:

> Say: He is not to be numbered with the people of Bahá who followeth his mundane desires, or fixeth his heart on things of the earth. He is My true follower who, if he come to a valley of pure gold, will pass straight through it aloof as a cloud, and will neither turn back, nor pause. Such a man is, assuredly, of Me. From his garment the Concourse on high can inhale the fragrance of sanctity . . . And if he met the fairest and most comely of women, he would not feel his heart seduced by the least shadow of desire for her beauty. Such an one, indeed, is the creation of spotless chastity. Thus instructeth you the Pen of the Ancient of Days, as bidden by your Lord, the Almighty, the All-Bountiful.[679]

Paraphrasing the Epistle to Diogenitus which defends the unconventional character of early Christians, and is believed to have been written in the second Christian century, Shoghi Effendi thus describes the true followers of Bahá'u'lláh:

> Of such men and women it may be truly said that to them 'every foreign land is a fatherland, and every fatherland a foreign land.' For their citizenship, it must be remembered, is in the Kingdom of Bahá'u'lláh. Though willing to share to the utmost the temporal benefits and the fleeting joys which this earthly life can confer, though eager to participate in whatever activity that conduces to the richness, the happiness and peace of that life, they can, at no time, forget that it constitutes no more than a transient, a very brief stage of their existence, that they who live it are but pilgrims and wayfarers whose goal is the Celestial City, and whose home the Country of never-failing joy and brightness.[680]

553. p. 124 ¶ 181. the Emperor of Paris

See ¶ 76.

554. p. 124 ¶ 181. Rejoicest thou in that thou rulest a span of earth . . .?

See ¶ 92.

555. p. 125 ¶ 182. Every day bringeth a fresh report of stories

See ¶ 59 and ¶ 160.

556. p. 125 ¶ 182. In the newspapers

See ¶ 59 and ¶ 160.

557. p. 125 ¶ 182. Touching the fraudulent dealings of some of the exiles of 'Akká

See Taherzadeh, *The Revelation of Bahá'u'lláh*, vol. 4, pp. 393–402.

558. p. 125 ¶ 182. the intention of the writer is evident

A reference to Mírzá Áqá Khán, the Grand Vizir of the Shah.

559. p. 125 ¶ 182. Glory to Thee, O my God! But for the tribulations which are sustained in Thy path, how could Thy true lovers be recognized . . .

See ¶ 149 and Bahá'u'lláh, *Prayers and Meditations*, CXII, p. 155.

560. p. 126 ¶ 184. the Shi'ih sect, which regarded itself as the most learned, the most righteous, and the most pious of all the peoples of the world

The Shí'ih sect of Islam believes that, based on certain verses of the Qur'án, their version of Islam is the exclusive and complete Faith of God, and that they are following the right religion – it considers any religion other than their own to be false, abrogated or defunct:

> The true religion before God Is Islam . . .

> As for those who are infidels, and die infidels . . . These! A grievous punishment awaited them; and they shall have none to help them. (3:19, 85, Rodwell)

> This day have I perfected your religion for you, and have filled up the measure of my favours upon you: and it is my pleasure that Islam be your religion . . . (5:5, Rodwell)

The Shí'ih hadith confirms the superiority of Islam:

> The Messenger of Allah has said, 'People of the Holy Qur'án are of the highest degree among men, except the prophets and the messengers of Allah, thus you should not consider them weak in the matter of their rights with Allah . . . they have a special status.'[681]

Shí'ih belief presumes that it is superior to other religious denominations, including the majority Sunni sect. Also, referencing contested hadith, Shí'ihs maintain that they are the ones truly guided who will go to heaven, as they follow Imám 'Alí and the Family of Muhammad (*Ahlul Bayt*):

> The Messenger of Alláh stood up among us and said: 'Those who came before you of the People of the Book split into seventy-two sects, and this Ummah will split into seventy-three sects, seventy-two of which will be in the fire [hell], and one in Paradise.'[682]

Towards the end of His life, Muhammad is reported by the Shí'ihs to have declared to His followers at *Ghadir Khumm* oasis:

> The time approaches when I shall be called away by God and I shall answer that call. I am leaving you with two precious things and if you adhere to both of them, you will never go astray. They are the Qur'án, the Book of God, and my family, the People of the House, *Ahl al Bayt*. The two shall never separate from each other until they come to me by the pool of paradise.[683]

The Qur'án states that God is with the righteous:

> . . . be not grieved about the infidels, and be not troubled at their devices; for God is with those who fear him and do good deeds. (16:128, Rodwell)

Therefore, as Muslims in the righteous camp, the Shí'ihs believe that they must be 'the best of creation' (*khayru albariyyati*):

> But the unbelievers among the people of the Book [Jews and Christians], and among the Polytheists, shall go into the fire of Gehenna [hell] to abide therein aye. Of all creatures are they the worst!
>
> But they who believe and do the things that are right – these of all creatures are the best! (98:5–6, Rodwell)

The pretensions and nefarious actions of the Shaykh, his father the 'Wolf', the 'She-Serpent' Imám-Jum'ih, and many of their celebrated fellow Shí'ih clergymen, which stood in contrast to the purity of the King of Martyrs and the Beloved of Martyrs, fulfilled the prediction of Imám 'Ali, perhaps the most prominent member of the *Ahlalbayt* (family of Muhammad):

> *Amir al-mu'minin*, peace be upon him said: A time will come when nothing will remain of the Qur'án except its writing, and nothing of Islam except its name. The mosques in those days will be busy with regards to construction but desolate with regard to guidance. Those staying in them and those visiting them will be the worst of all on earth. From them mischief will spring up and towards them all wrong will turn. If anyone isolates himself from it (mischief) they will fling him back to it. And if any one steps back from it they will push him towards it.[684]

The Báb states in the *Bayán* that the acceptance of Muslims is contingent on their response to His Revelation:

> O people of the Qur'án! Ye are as nothing unless ye submit unto the Remembrance of God and unto this Book. If ye follow the Cause of God, We will forgive you your sins, and if ye turn aside from Our command, We will, in truth, condemn your souls in Our Book, unto the Most Great Fire . . .[685]

561. pp. 127/128 ¶ 187. O concourse of rulers and divines! Incline your ears unto the Voice calling from the horizon of 'Akká

This statement of Bahá'u'lláh is quite similar to several other summons He issued from 'Akká:

> O kings of the earth! He who is the sovereign lord of all is come. The Kingdom is God's . . .[686]

> Say: O King of Berlin! Give ear unto the Voice calling from this manifest Temple: 'Verily, there is none other God but Me, the Everlasting, the Peerless, the Ancient of Days.'[687]

> O kings of the earth! give ear unto the voice of God, calling from this sublime, this fruit-laden tree . . .[688]

562. p. 128 ¶ 187. O people of <u>Sh</u>ín!

A reference to Shiraz, the dawning place of the Revelation of the Báb.

563. p. 128 ¶ 187. God Who layeth low the necks of men

To 'lay low the necks' means to humble the proud and arrogant. The Qur'án states that those who invent a lie against God (accuse His Revelation falsely) will face shame and disgrace (6:93). It warns that if it is God's will, He will through a Revelation cause humanity to bow themselves in servitude (Yusuf Ali: bend their necks in humility) (26:4).

The Prophet Isaiah (13:11) teaches that God will humble the proud: 'I will cause the arrogancy of the proud to cease, and will lay low the haughtiness of the terrible.' Again (24:21): 'And it shall come to pass in that day, that the Lord shall punish the host of the high ones that are on high, and the kings of the earth upon the earth.' And (26:4–5): 'Trust in the Lord forever . . . For he bringeth down them that dwell on high . . .'

That Day has dawned:

> 'From two ranks amongst men,' is His [Bahá'u'lláh's] terse and prophetic utterance, 'power hath been seized: kings and ecclesiastics.'

> 'If ye pay no heed,' He thus warned the kings of the earth, 'unto the counsels which . . . We have revealed in this Tablet, Divine chastisement will assail you from every direction . . . On that day ye shall . . . recognize your own impotence.' And again: 'Though aware of most of Our afflictions, ye, nevertheless, have failed to stay the hand of the aggressor.' And, furthermore, this arraignment: '. . . We . . . will be patient, as We have been patient in that which hath befallen Us at your hands, O concourse of kings!'[689]

564. p. 128 ¶ 188. Kitáb-i-Aqdas

The 'Most Holy Book' of Bahá'u'lláh, revealed in 'Akká circa 1873 and described by Shoghi Effendi as

> the Charter of His World Order, the chief repository of His laws, the Harbinger of His Covenant, the Pivotal Work containing some of His noblest exhortations, weightiest pronouncements, and portentous prophecies, and revealed during the full tide of His tribulations, at a time when the rulers of the earth had definitely forsaken Him . . .[690]

> the principal repository of that Law which the Prophet Isaiah had anticipated . . . whose provision must remain inviolate for no less than a thousand years, and whose system will embrace the entire planet, may well be regarded as the brightest emanation of the mind of Bahá'u'lláh, as the Mother Book of His Dispensation, and the Charter of His New World Order.[691]

565. p. 128 ¶ 188. the Book itself is the unerring Balance established amongst men. In this most perfect Balance whatsoever the peoples and kindreds possess must be weighed

Bahá'u'lláh here quotes verses 99–105 of the *Kitáb-i-Aqdas*.

In every Dispensation, God provides the standard of what is right and what is wrong, and differentiates between justice and injustice, between moderation and extremism or fanaticism. The Book (Bahá'u'lláh's Revelation) is referred to here as the 'Balance' by which previously understood moral and ethical principles are redefined according the needs of a new age, and by which all human conduct is ultimately judged.

It was with this balance that the Prophet Daniel found King Belshazzar to be spiritually deficient (5:27): 'Thou art weighed in the balances, and art found wanting.' And in the Gospels (John 8:32), it is according to the balance: 'you shall know the truth, and the truth shall make you free [from error and sin]' that Christians will be judged. Revelation (6:5) predicts the coming of a balance at the Second Coming.

The Qur'án (57:25) explains that this balance was set up by all of the Divine Messengers: 'We sent aforetime Our apostles with clear signs and sent down with them the Book and the Balance (of right and wrong), that men may stand forth in justice . . .'; his 'Balance' was also revealed in the Qur'án in the Dispensation of Muhammad (42:17): 'It is God Who has sent down the Book in truth, and the Balance . . .'

Bahá'u'lláh has once again brought the balance, as he repeats later in the *Kitáb-i-Aqdas*:

> Say: This is the infallible Balance which the Hand of God is holding, in which all who are in the heavens and all who are on the earth are weighed, and their fate determined, if ye be of them that believe and recognize this truth.[692]

Addressing Sulṭán 'Abdu'l-'Azíz in the Súriy-i-Mulúk, Bahá'u'lláh admonishes: 'Set before thine eyes God's unerring Balance and, as one standing in His Presence, weigh in that balance thine actions every day, every moment of thy life. Bring thyself to account ere thou art summoned to a reckoning . . .'[693]

See also Annotation 597.

566. pp. 128/129 ¶ 188. Advance, O people, with snow-white faces

Bahá'u'lláh summons mankind to recognize Him as God's latest Manifestation, and to partake of the light of His Revelation. 'Snow-white faces' is used figuratively to mean purity. The phrase in the Scriptures (white as snow) denotes purity of faith and is considered a sign of divinity. For example, the Psalmist prays, '. . . wash me, and I shall be whiter than snow' (Ps. 51:7). Again, God promises through sincere reasoning: '. . . though your sins be as scarlet, they shall be as white as snow' (Is. 1:18). Daniel describes 'the Ancient of days' (a title of Bahá'u'lláh) as having a garment as 'white as snow' (Dan. 7:9).

There are several passages where Bahá'u'lláh makes this reference:

> The Pen of Holiness, I solemnly affirm before God, hath writ upon My snow-white brow and in characters of effulgent glory these glowing, these musk-scented and holy words: 'Behold ye that dwell on earth, and ye denizens of heaven, bear witness, He in truth is your Well-Beloved. He it is Whose like the world of creation hath not seen . . .'[694]

> The Celestial Youth hath, in this Day, raised above the heads of men the glorious Chalice of Immortality, and is standing expectant upon His seat, wondering what eye will recognize His glory, and what arm will, unhesitatingly, be stretched forth to seize the Cup from His snow-white Hand and drain it.[695]

> Erelong shall the snow-white hand of God rend an opening through the darkness of this night and unlock a mighty portal unto His City.[696]

> Grieve not if none be found to accept the crimson wine proffered by Thy snow-white hand and to seize it in the name of Thy Lord, the Most Exalted, the Most High . . .[697]

567. p. 129 ¶ 188. the blest and crimson Spot, wherein the Tree beyond which there is no passing is calling

The 'crimson Spot' is a reference to 'Akká. *Buq'atu'l-Hamrá* (Crimson Spot) was also the name of a hill called *Samaríyyih*, which overlooks Bahjí and where red flowers grew in abundance. Balyuzi writes: 'In the springtime . . . Bahá'u'lláh would have pitched His tent there.'[698]

The 'Tree beyond which there is no passing' refers to Bahá'u'lláh as the Manifestation of God. See Annotations 191 and 333 for the symbolic meaning of the Divine Lote-Tree in previous Scriptures. See also Notes 127 and 128 in Bahá'u'lláh, *The Kitáb-i-Aqdas*, p. 220. For other uses of 'crimson' see Annotations 222, 420, 578 and 618.

568. p. 129 ¶ 188. O ye leaders of religion in Persia!

This is addressed specifically to the Shí'ih clergy of Iran. Bahá'u'lláh admonishes them that their fallible human learning is not a valid criterion for assessing a divine Revelation.

569. p. 129 ¶ 188. this is the face of your Lord

The Qur'án (55:26–27) warns: 'All that is on earth will perish, But [what] will abide (forever) [is] the Face of thy Lord, – full of Majesty, Bounty and Honour.' It reiterates (28:88):

> And call not, besides God, on another god. There is no god but He. Everything (that exists) will perish except His own Face; to Him belongs the Command (*Amr*), and to Him will ye (all) be brought back.

The Bible states that the prayer of those who humbly seek the face of God will be heard and their sins will be forgiven (II Chron. 7:14). Isaiah (59:2) warns: 'your iniquities have separated between you and your God, and your sins have hid his face from you . . .' The Book of Revelation (22:4) promises: 'they shall see His [God's] face'.

Clearly, God does not have a physical face and, as stated in the Qur'án (6:103):

> No vision can grasp Him, but His grasp is over all vision: He is above all comprehension, yet is acquainted with all things.

By the Face of God is meant His Manifestation and the Author of His Revelation. It is in this context that Jesus stated (John 14:9): 'he that hath seen me hath seen the Father . . .'

As attested by Himself, Bahá'u'lláh has today revealed the Face of God.

570. p. 129 ¶ 188. behold how ye have allowed your learning to shut you out, as by a veil, from Him Who is the Dayspring of this Light

Religious learning often becomes a severe test and an impediment to recognizing a fresh Revelation when earlier concepts and scholarship are considered to be at variance with the new divine teachings. This in part explains why the ecclesiastical authorities in every age oppose God's latest Faith. They often fail to appreciate that human learning and Revelation (God's wisdom) can differ, as they do not emanate from the same source.

The Hebrew Bible teaches that 'the Lord gives wisdom; from his mouth come knowledge and understanding' (Prov 2:6). The Apostle Paul wrote that what man regarded as foolish God had made the wisdom of this world (I Cor. 1:20). And again (I Cor. 2:13–14):

> Which things also we speak, not in the words which man's wisdom teacheth, but which the Holy Ghost teacheth; comparing spiritual things with spiritual.
>
> But the natural man receiveth not the things of the Spirit of God: for they are foolishness unto him: neither can he know them, because they are spiritually discerned.

The Qur'án states (2:13) that the unbelievers say: '"Shall we believe as the fools believe?" Nay, of a surety they are the fools, but they do not know.'

571. p. 129 ¶ 188. Mother Book

See Note 128 in Bahá'u'lláh, *The Kitáb-i-Aqdas*, pp. 220–21; see also Annotation 197 above.

572. p. 129 ¶ 188. Who hath caused the Rock to shout

To 'shout' means to express strong emotions. The implication is that the Revelation of the Father has made Christ's primary Apostle, Peter, to cry out for joy.

See Annotation 418.

573. p. 129 ¶ 188. the Mount rising above the Holy Land

A reference to Mount Sinai. See Annotation 66.

574. 129 ¶ 188. We have not entered any school, nor read any of your dissertations

See Annotation 87.

575. p. 129 ¶ 188. Incline your ears to the words of this unlettered One, wherewith He summoneth you unto God, the Ever-Abiding

See Annotation 87.

576. p. 130 ¶ 188. Lucid Book

Arabic: *Kitábun mubínun*, which refers to a Book or Revelation that is 'clear' 'luminous', 'illuminating', and 'evident' in the various translations of the Qur'án. Lucid is also a translation of mubin (as in ¶ 153 and ¶ 198). The word 'lucid' is also a translation of the Arabic word *vázeh*, as in ¶ 230. It implies that what is being described is rational, reasonable, cogent, intelligible, understandable, clear and comprehensive, that is, perspicuous.

The Qur'án describes God's Revelation as follows (5:15): 'There hath come to you from God a (new) light and a perspicuous Book.' The same Arabic word *mubín* is used, but is translated here as 'perspicuous'. 'Perspicuous' as in 'perspicuous verses' (3:5: Rodwell) is also a translation of another Arabic word *muḥkamát* (see ¶ 192).

577. p. 130 ¶ 189. The heedless ones have hamstrung Thy white She-Camel

An allusion to attempts to paralyse the Cause of God, and the suffering inflicted in the process.

See Annotations 421, 472.

578. p. 130 ¶ 189. Thy Crimson Ark

Crimson is associated with love, royalty, nobility and spiritual power. It is also associated with sacrifice, crimson being the colour of fresh blood. The Crimson Ark (*Safina Al-Hamrá*) is a symbol of salvation.

In His commentary on the Súrih of Joseph, the Qayyúmu'l-Asmá', and the Qur'án (12:56), the Báb refers to the 'people of Bahá' as the only 'companions of the Crimson-Coloured Ark':

> Indeed God hath created everywhere around this Gate oceans of divine elixir, tinged crimson with the essence of existence and vitalized through the animating power of the desired fruit; and for them God hath provided Arks of ruby, tender, crimson-coloured, wherein none shall sail but the people of Bahá . . .[699]

Shoghi Effendi has written that 'the companions of the Crimson Colored Ark, lauded in glowing terms in the Qayyúmu'l-Asmá'' refers to 'the community of the Most Great Name'.[700] Bahá'u'lláh writes:

> Blessed is he who preferreth his brother before himself. Verily, such a man is reckoned, by virtue of the Will of God, the All-Knowing, the All-Wise, with the people of Bahá who dwell in the Crimson Ark (*ahl al-Bahá fí al-safínat al-hamrá*).[701]

> How great the blessedness that awaiteth the king who will arise to aid My Cause in My Kingdom, who will detach himself from all else but Me! Such a king is numbered with the companions of the Crimson Ark – the Ark which God hath prepared for the people of Bahá.[702]

Notably, the Book of Revelation (11:19) refers to the 'the ark of His (God's) Testament' which Shoghi Effendi interprets[703] as referring to the Covenant of Bahá'u'lláh:

> And the temple of God was opened in heaven, and there was seen in his temple the ark of his [God's] testament: and there were lightnings, and voices, and thunderings, and an earthquake . . .

The story of Noah's Ark, related in the Hebrew Bible, may be understood to also refer symbolically to God's Ark of deliverance and salvation during an earlier Dispensation.

See also Annotations 420, 567 and 618.

579. p. 130 ¶ 189. and wished to put out Thy Light, and to veil the face of Thy Cause

The Qur'án forbids religious leaders to conceal (veil) the truth (2:42): 'And cover not Truth with falsehood, nor conceal the Truth when ye know (what it is).'

580. p. 130 ¶ 189. The true Faith hath laid fast hold, in this day, on the hem of Our bounty, and circleth about Our Person

In other words, the one, pure, eternal and primordial faith of God is represented today by Bahá'u'lláh. All must turn to Him to appreciate the Truth in this Day.

See also Annotations 208 and 236.

581. p. 131 ¶ 190. Wings that are besmirched with mire can never soar

The mire is 'self' and 'desire' that prevent spiritual development:

> Wert thou to attain to but a dewdrop of the crystal waters of divine knowledge, thou wouldst readily realize that true life is not the life of the flesh but the life of the spirit.[704]

> Ye are even as the bird which soareth, with the full force of its mighty wings and with complete and joyous confidence, through the immensity of the heavens, until, impelled to satisfy its hunger, it turneth longingly to the water and clay of the earth below it, and, having been entrapped in the mesh of its desire, findeth itself impotent to resume its flight to the realms whence it came. Powerless to shake off the burden weighing on its sullied wings, that bird, hitherto an inmate of the heavens, is now forced to seek a dwelling-place upon the dust. Wherefore, O My servants, defile not your wings

> with the clay of waywardness and vain desires, and suffer them not to be stained with the dust of envy and hate, that ye may not be hindered from soaring in the heavens of My divine knowledge.[705]

In another sense the phrase refers to the literal interpretation of the scriptures and expectation of the physical fulfilment of prophecies – 'vain imaginings' of religious leaders that prevent the soul of man from ascending to the heaven of divine Will through recognition of the fulfilment of God's promise. A distinct form of vain imaginings is literal translation of prophecies. In this connection, Christ stated that at both the First and Second Coming truth would have to be appreciated spiritually (John 4:23–24):

> But the hour cometh, and now is, when the true worshippers shall worship the Father in spirit and in truth: for the Father seeketh such to worship him.
>
> God is a Spirit: and they that worship him must worship him in spirit and in truth.

582. p. 131 ¶ 192. these perspicuous verses have, in answer to certain individuals, been sent down

Annotations 582 to 614 on ¶ 192 illustrate the realized eschatology of the Qur'án. The 'perspicuous verses' were initially revealed by Bahá'u'lláh for unknown persons. They were revealed again for Jalíl-i-Khu'i, a coppersmith and a well-known believer from Azerbaijan, in the Tablet of Splendours (Ishráqát).[706] They are re-revealed here in Epistle ¶ 192 and enumerate the events expected in the Qur'án that will attend the Day of Resurrection.

583. p. 131 ¶ 192. Have the verses been sent down?

This is a reference to the expectation of a new divine Revelation. The Qur'án predicts:

> Soon will We show them Our Signs (verses) in the (furthest) regions (of the earth), And in their own souls, until it becomes manifest to them that this is the Truth . . . (41:53)

The Qur'án also states:

> None of Our revelations do We abrogate or cause to be forgotten, but We substitute something better or similar: knowest thou not that God hath power over all things? (2:106)

This implies that some previous verses will be abrogated.

According to Shí'ih traditions, the Qá'im (He Who shall Arise) will usher in a new Dispensation:

> Imám Mahdi (the Guided One) will bring new Sharia (divine law) and commandments.[707]

> *Al-Qá'im* will bring a new teaching, a new book and a new law.[708]

584. p. 131 ¶ 192. Hath the Hour come?

The Day when 'the Hour' will come, 'the Final (last) Hour', 'the Hour of Judgement', and the terrible Hour of 'Convulsions' and of the 'Resurrection' is referred to in the Qur'án and the Bible. The Qur'án states that it is a certain event (15:85; 18:21; 34:3); it is close at hand and will be a terrible experience (42:17–18; 20:15; 22:1; 22:55; 30:12, 14; 54:46); the knowledge thereof is with God (7:187; 43:85; 45:27); and those who deny or dispute about the Hour are misled (25:11). The knowledge as to when it will occur is with God (41:47).

The Gospel of John (5:25) also speaks of the coming of the apocalyptic 'hour': 'Verily, verily, I say unto you, The hour is coming, and now is, when the dead shall hear the voice of the Son of God: and they that hear shall live.' And again (4:23): 'But the hour cometh, and now is, when the true worshippers shall worship the Father in spirit . . .'

585. p. 132 ¶ 192. by Him Who is the Revealer of clear tokens!

'Clear tokens' refers to the divine Revelation which establishes clearly God's Purpose for mankind.

586. p. 132 ¶ 192. the Inevitable is come

This is a quotation from Súrih 69 of the Qur'án which alludes to the advent of the *Ḥáqqa*, 'the Sure Reality' or 'the Inevitable' – a great calamity that humanity will experience. A new Revelation is always a catastrophic day for the followers and institutions of earlier Dispensations.

587. p. 132 ¶ 192. The Plain is disclosed

This is from Qur'án 18:45 (Rodwell):

> And call to mind the day . . . thou shalt see the earth a levelled plain [*al-arda bárizatan*], and we will gather mankind together, and not leave of them any one.

The Qur'án (79:14) also states that humanity in the Day of Resurrection will suddenly find itself awakened to life on the Plain (of supreme gathering), a land that God will create for the Day of Resurrection traditionally known as *al-Sáhira*. The accepted traditional meaning of *al-Sáhira* is clean, white, untrodden land[709] – the place from which Christ ascended to heaven.[710] In his *Safarnáma* (Book of Travels), Násir-i-Khusraw (1004–1088 CE) writes that near Jerusalem:

> there lies before you a great level plain, called the *Sáhirah* which, it is said, will be the place of the Resurrection, where all mankind shall be gathered together. For this reason men from all parts of the world come hither to make their sojourn in the Holy City till death overtakes them, in order that when the day fixed by God – be He praised and exalted! – shall arrive, they may thus be ready and present at the appointed place.[711]

However, it is generally believed that the location of the Plain will be disclosed on the Day of Judgement. The Báb prophesies:

> they shall, upon the Plain of Resurrection, behold how the Lord of Mercy and His Remembrance were near. Thereupon they shall exclaim: 'Would that we had followed the path of the Báb! Would that we had sought refuge only with Him, and not with men of

perversity and error! For verily the Remembrance of God appeared before us [see Qur'án 7:63, 69], behind us, and on all sides, yet we were, in very truth, shut out as by a veil from Him.'[712]

Thus, according to Bahá'í understanding, the Plain refers to the advent of spiritual resurrection associated with the Faith of Bahá'u'lláh – an event destined to assemble the diverse sections of humanity together, when nothing hidden will remain undisclosed or concealed.

588. p. 132 ¶ 192. mankind is sore vexed and fearful

The Qur'án (14: 42) warns that the new divine Day and new Revelation will cause a great deal of consternation: 'Think not that God doth not heed the deeds of those who do wrong. He but giveth them respite against a Day when the eyes will fixedly stare in horror.' Again (19:39): 'warn them of the Day of Distress, when the matter will be determined: for (behold) they are negligent and they do not believe!' And it will be a stern, fateful, or wrathful Day; a Day of commotions; a spiritually distressing Day; a Day of regret and remorse; a Grievous Day; a Painful Day; a Woeful Day; and a Momentous Day (*yawmin-aleem*) (11:26; also, 54:46; 74:9; 76:10; 79:6–9).

589. p. 132 ¶ 192. Earthquakes have broken loose, and the tribes have lamented

'Earthquakes' refers to the tectonic shifts affecting societies caused by the new Revelation. The advances in the physical and spiritual realms are destructive of old understandings and moral and ethical values.

The Qur'án (39:67) predicts that on the Day of Judgement the 'whole earth shall be but his handful, and in his right hand shall the Heavens be folded together'. There will be violent commotions and the 'earth' will be subject to 'earthquakes' (*al-zilzál*):

> O mankind! Fear your Lord! For the convulsion of the Hour (of Judgement) will be a thing terrible! (22:1)

And:

> When the earth with her quaking shall quake.
> And the earth shall cast forth her burdens,
> And man shall say, What aileth her?
> On that day shall she tell out her tidings,
> Because thy Lord shall have inspired her. (99:1–5)

Earthquakes are also expected in the Bible (Is. 29:6): 'Thou shalt be visited of the Lord of hosts with thunder, and with earthquake, and great noise . . .' And in the Gospel of Matthew (24:7): 'For nation shall rise against nation, and kingdom against kingdom: and there shall be famines, and pestilences, and earthquakes, in divers places.'

In one sense this refers to the advent of the Báb and Bahá'u'lláh and the profound changes that have occurred in every sphere of human learning:

> by the term 'earth' is meant the earth of understanding and knowledge, and by 'heavens the heavens of divine Revelation. Reflect . . . how, in one hand, He hath, by His mighty grasp, turned the earth of knowledge and understanding, previously unfolded, into a mere handful, and, on the other, spread out a new and highly exalted earth in the hearts of men . . .[713]

Bahá'u'lláh remarks on the impact of His Revelation on faulty human understanding and religious beliefs, as well as on false objects of religious adoration:

> This is the Cause that hath caused all your superstitions and idols to tremble.[714]

590. p. 132 ¶ 192. The stunning trumpet blast hath been loudly raised

Divine Revelation is described as a trumpet blast indicating the spiritual resuscitation of humankind through the operation of the Holy Spirit (in Hebrew, *rûach*, and in Greek, *pneumatos* and *pneuma*, meaning breath of life – hence the 'trumpet blast' is a sudden blowing of the breath of God). The Prophet Joel (2:1) declares:

> Blow ye the horn in Zion . . . For the day of the Lord cometh, for it is nigh at hand.

The New Testament (I Cor. 15:52) speaks of the Day when humanity will be resurrected by the sound of the trumpet:

> In a moment, in the twinkling of an eye, at the last trump: for the trumpet shall sound, and the dead shall be raised incorruptible, and we shall be changed.

The Qur'án also anticipates a divine blast of the Trumpet that shall reanimate mankind:

> The trumpet shall be sounded, when behold! From the sepulchres (men) will rush forth to their Lord! (36:51)
>
> And the Trumpet shall be blown: that will be the Day whereof warning (had been given). (50:20)
>
> The Day that the Trumpet shall be sounded, and ye shall come forth in crowds. (78:1)
>
> And the Day that the Trumpet will be sounded – then will be smitten with terror those who are in the heavens, and those who are on earth, except such as God will please (to exempt): and all shall come to His (Presence) as beings conscious of their lowliness. (27:87)

The 'stunning trumpet blast' (*alsákhatu* in Arabic, also translated as the 'Deafening Noise' or 'Piercing Cry') is also described in Qur'án 80:33–36 (Rodwell):

> But when the stunning trumpet-blast shall arrive.
> On that day shall a man fly from his brother,
> And his mother and his father,
> And his wife and his children . . .

This will be truly an 'overwhelming event' (88:1). The trumpet blast refers to the Revelation of Bahá'u'lláh:

> Verily We have sounded the Trumpet which is none other than My Pen of Glory . . .[715]

And,

> We have chosen thee to be our most mighty Trumpet, whose blast is to signalize the resurrection of all mankind.[716]

See also Annotations 601 and 681.

591. 132 ¶ 192. Hath the Catastrophe come to pass?

This is a direct reference to Qur'án 79:34: 'Therefore, when there comes the great, overwhelming (Event) . . .' The Arabic phrase used in the Epistle and the Qur'án is *alttammatu alkubrá* – translated also as 'the great disaster', and 'the Great Catastrophe'. It refers to the momentous changes associated with the Day of the Supreme Manifestation of God, Bahá'u'lláh. Shoghi Effendi quotes the following hadith:

> In the latter days a grievous calamity shall befall My people at the hands of their ruler, a calamity such as no man ever heard to surpass it.[717]

He writes further:

> The violent derangement of the world's equilibrium; the trembling that will seize the limbs of mankind; the radical transformation of human society; the rolling up of the present-day Order; the fundamental changes affecting the structure of government; the weakening of the pillars of religion; the rise of dictatorships; the spread of tyranny; the fall of monarchies; the decline of ecclesiastical institutions; the increase of anarchy and chaos; the extension and consolidation of the Movement of the Left; the fanning into flame of the smouldering fire of racial strife; the development of infernal engines of war; the burning of cities; the contamination of the atmosphere of the earth – these stand out as the signs and portents that must either herald or accompany the retributive calamity which, as decreed by Him Who is the Judge and Redeemer

> of mankind, must, sooner or later, afflict a society which, for the most part, and for over a century, has turned a deaf ear to the Voice of God's Messenger in this day –a calamity which must purge the human race of the dross of its age-long corruptions, and weld its component parts into a firmly-knit world-embracing Fellowship.[718]

> The whole of mankind is groaning, is dying to be led to unity, and to terminate its age-long martyrdom. And yet it stubbornly refuses to embrace the light and acknowledge the sovereign authority of the one Power that can extricate it from its entanglements, and avert the woeful calamity that threatens to engulf it.[719]

On another note, Ṭáhirih was described thus by 'Abdu'l-Bahá:

> In eloquence she was the calamity of the age [that is. considered a great threat by the old order], and in ratiocination the trouble of the world.[720]

592. p. 132 ¶ 192. Is the Resurrection come?

There are numerous references in the Qur'án to the Day of Resurrection (*Yawm al-Qiyámah*). The title of Súrih 75 is called *Qiyámat* or the Resurrection.

In both Shí'ih and Sunni eschatology, the *al-Mahdi* (the 'Guided One') will come before the Day of Judgement and, alongside Jesus, will rid the world of wrongdoing, injustice and tyranny, and reform Islam. In Shí'ih Islam, the belief in the Qá'im ('He Who Arises' or 'the One Who will resurrect') is closely related to the appearance or return of the Twelfth Imám, *Muhammad al-Mahdi*.

By 'Resurrection' is meant the spiritual resuscitation associated with the appearance of the divine Manifestation of God. Man is either in heaven or hell, depending on whether or not he accepts Him. Bahá'u'lláh continues by stating that the Resurrection has taken place.

593. p. 132 ¶ 192. Seest thou men laid low?

As a warning to Muslims, the Qur'án relates that the people of 'Ád, who were an unjust people spoilt by their prosperity and did not listen to their Messenger, Húd, were as a consequence destroyed (69:6–7): 'the people laid low, as though they had been the trunks of hollow palms'.

Christ taught that 'whosoever shall exalt himself shall be abased [humbled]; and he that shall humble himself shall be exalted' (Matt. 23:12). The Apostle Peter (I Peter 5:6) admonished: 'Humble yourselves, therefore, under God's mighty hand, so that in due time He may exalt you.'

See also Annotation 563.

594. p. 132 ¶ 192. Have the tree-stumps been uprooted?

Proverbs predicts (2:22): 'the wicked will be cut off from the earth, and the transgressors shall be rooted out of it.' Christ warned (Matt. 15:13): 'Every plant, which my heavenly Father hath not planted, shall be rooted up.'

The Qur'án (14:26–27) compares evil teachings to a tree that has no permanence and which will be uprooted:

> And the parable of an evil Word is as an evil tree: it is torn up by the root from the surface of the earth: it has no stability.
>
> God will establish in strength those who believe, with the Word that stands firm, in this world and in the hereafter; but God will leave, to stray, those who do wrong: God doeth what He willeth.

Furthermore, the Qur'án states that insincere individuals 'are like timber propped up' (63:4). In this connection, the men of 'Ád who rejected the divine warnings are described as having been plucked out 'as if they were roots of palm-trees torn up (from the ground)' (54:20).

595. p. 132 ¶ 192. the mountains have been scattered in dust

The destruction of mountains is predicted in several verses of the Qur'án, where it is described in diverse ways, perhaps indicative of a common spiritual explanation for seemingly disparate events. For example:

> And the Day We will cause (to) move the mountains and you will see the earth (as) a leveled plain and We will gather them and not We will leave behind from them anyone. (18:47)

> They ask thee concerning the mountains: say 'My Lord will uproot them and scatter them as dust; He will leave them as plains smooth and level; Nothing crooked or curved wilt thou see in their place. (20:105–107)

> And you will see the mountains and think them solid, but they shall pass away as the passing away of the clouds. (27:88; quoted by Shoghi Effendi as describing the Day of Bahá'u'lláh in *God Passes By*, p. 98)

> And the mountains shall be made to crumble with an awful crumbling. So that they shall be scattered as dust. (56:5–6)

> . . . the earth and the mountains are borne and crushed . . . (69:14)

> On the day when the earth and the mountains shall quake and the mountains shall become heaps of sand let loose. (73:14)

> When the mountains are scattered (to the winds) as dust. (77:9–10)

> . . . the mountains shall be moved . . . (78:20)

> And when the mountains are moved away . . . (81:3)

> . . . the mountains shall be like flocks of carded wool. (101:5) [stated as having been fulfilled: *Proclamation of Bahá'u'lláh*, p. 98]

The Bible also speaks of the demise of the mountains (Micah 1:4): 'And the mountains shall be molten under him . . .' The prophet Isaiah (40:4–5) predicts that mountains will be reduced but simultaneously the valleys (lowly people who are untrained in theology) will be filled and the crooked paths (clerical misinterpretations) will be corrected:

> . . . every mountain and hill shall be made low: and the crooked shall be made straight, and the rough places plain. And the glory of the Lord [in Arabic, Bahá'u'lláh] shall be revealed, and all flesh shall see it together; for the mouth of the Lord hath spoken it.

'Mountain(s)' is often used in the Writings of the Báb and Bahá'u'lláh figuratively. For example:

> God had, in truth, proposed Our Mission unto the heavens and the earth and the mountains, but they refused to bear it and were afraid thereof . . .[721]

> As it hath been revealed: 'Almost might the heavens be rent and the earth be cleft asunder and the mountains fall down in fragments' [Qur'án 19:92]. And yet how much harder than these mountains their hearts must be to have remained unmoved![722]

> Be ye as firmly settled as the immovable mountain in the Cause of your Lord, the Mighty, the Loving.[723]

> He shall so persevere in the Cause of God, and evince such firmness in the path of His might, that even if all the powers of earth and heaven were to deny Him, He would not waver in the proclamation of His Cause, nor flee from His command in the promulgation of His Laws. Nay rather, He will stand as firm as the highest mountains and the loftiest peaks. He will remain immovable in His obedience to God and steadfast in revealing His Cause and proclaiming His Word.[724]

'Abdu'l-Bahá is reported to have said that in one sense:

> The mountains are men of high renown, whose famous names sink into insignificance, when the dawn of the Manifestation fills the world with light. The pomp of Annas and Caiaphas is outshone by the simple glory of the Christ. The earthquake is the wave of spiritual life that moves through all things and makes creation quiver.[725]

Mountains could also refer to seemingly unassailable clerical authorities and precepts that occupy exalted (lofty) and unassailable positions in the eyes and minds of the people of earlier Dispensations, such as the sacrosanct provisions of the Talmud, Church dogma and rituals, and the voluminous and often spurious traditions and commentaries in Islam. These were shattered by the Dispensations of the Báb and Bahá'u'lláh.

596. p. 132 ¶ 192. Where is Paradise, and where is Hell?

The Qur'án (50:31) states that in the Day of Resurrection, paradise will be made accessible to the righteous: 'And Paradise shall be brought near to the pious, – not far off.' It adds that hell has been prepared for those who deny the Resurrection (25:11): 'Nay, they deny the Hour but We have prepared a Blazing Fire for such as deny the Hour.' Also:

> And Hell-Fire shall be placed in full view for (all) to see . . . (79:36)

> And paradise shall be brought near to the pious; and hell shall lay open for those who go astray. (26:90–91, Rodwell)

> It shall be said to them (unbelievers), 'Enter ye the gates of Hell, therein to dwell for ever;' and wretched the abode of the arrogant!
>
> But those who feared their Lord shall be driven on by troops to Paradise, until when they reach it, its gates shall be opened, and its keepers shall say to them, 'All hail! virtuous have ye been: enter then in, to abide herein for ever.' (39:72–73, Rodwell)

Notably, a well-known Shí'ih hadith equates paradise with attaining the presence of the Promised One:

> The Messenger of Allah (peace be upon him and his family) has said: '. . . Paradise is for that person who meets him (al-Mahdi), and paradise is for that person who loves him, and paradise is for that person who has belief in him.'[726]

It is also clear from the New Testament that heaven and paradise are not physical places but conditions of the soul and spirit. Whilst on earth Christ stated that He was in heaven, inferring that it was His Word that came from heaven:

> And no man hath ascended up to heaven, but he that came down from heaven, even the Son of man which is in heaven. (John 3:13)

Bahá'u'lláh states that He represents paradise today:

> O Czar of Russia! Incline thine ear unto the voice of God, the King, the Holy, and turn thou unto Paradise, the Spot wherein abideth He Who, among the Concourse on high, beareth the most excellent titles, and Who, in the kingdom of creation, is called by the name of God, the Effulgent, the All-Glorious.[727]

597. p. 132 ¶ 192. We see not the Balance

According to the Qur'án every Dispensation has brought the balance of what is right and wrong (57:5, Rodwell): 'We have sent our apostles with the clear tokens, and we caused the Book and the balance to descend with them that men might observe fairness.' The balance is also expected to appear in the Day of Resurrection in which according to tradition, the sins of every individual will be weighed. It refers to the teachings of a new Dispensation which will determine between right and wrong. The Qur'án promises:

> The balance that Day will be true: those whose scale (of good) will be heavy, will prosper.
>
> Those whose scale will be light, will find their souls in perdition, for that they wrongfully treated Our Signs [Revelations]. (7:8–9)

Again:

> Just balances will be set up for the day of resurrection, neither shall any soul be wronged in aught . . . (21:47, Rodwell)

Unequivocally, Bahá'u'lláh declares that His Revelation, and that of the Báb, represent the fulfilment of that expectation:

> Verily this is that Most Great Beauty, foretold in the Books of the Messengers, through Whom truth shall be distinguished from error and the wisdom of every command shall be tested.[728]

And, as He has just stated in ¶ 188, quoting verse 99 of the *Kitáb-i-Aqdas*:

> O leaders of religion! Weigh not the Book of God with such standards and sciences as are current amongst you, for the Book itself is

> the unerring Balance established amongst men. In this most perfect Balance whatsoever the peoples and kindreds of the earth possess must be weighed, while the measure of its weight should be tested according to its own standard, did ye but know it.

See also Annotation 565.

598. p. 132 ¶ 192. Have the stars fallen?

In the Qur'án 'stars' are equated with guidance and protection from evil (the function of religious leaders).

> And it is He who hath ordained the stars for you that ye may be guided thereby in the darknesses of the land and of the sea! Clear have we made our signs to men of knowledge. (6:97)

> We have adorned the lower heaven with the adornment of the stars [likely holy or angelic individuals]. They serve also as a guard against every rebellious Satan. (37:6–7, Rodwell)

The passage is a reference to the following verses of the Qur'an:

> And when the stars are scattered [dispersed; fall]. (81:2; 82:2)

The Bible equates 'stars' with those whose function is to guide others to a virtuous life:

> And they that be wise shall shine as the brightness of the firmament; and they that guide many to righteousness as the stars for ever and ever. (Dan. 12:3)

It also predicts the fall of the stars:

> Immediately after the tribulation of those days shall the sun be darkened, and the moon shall not give her light, and the stars shall fall from heaven, and the powers of heaven shall be shaken. (Matt. 24:29)

Bahá'u'lláh explains that by the falling of stars is meant the fall of religious leaders who, because they denied the Revelation of Bahá'u'lláh, are losing their influence over mankind:

> O concourse of bishops! Ye are the stars of the heaven of My knowledge. My mercy desireth not that ye should fall upon the earth. My justice, however, declareth: 'This is that which the Son hath decreed.'[729]

'Stars' also refer to the laws of a Revelation, as in the case of the *Kitáb-i-Aqdas*, the Most Holy Book of the Revelation of Bahá'u'lláh.

> 'This Book', He [Bahá'u'lláh] Himself testifies, 'is a heaven which We have adorned with the stars of Our commandments and prohibitions.' 'Blessed the man,' He, moreover, has stated, 'who will read it, and ponder the verses sent down in it by God, the Lord of Power, the Almighty.'[730]

599. p. 132 ¶ 192. Yea, when He Who is the Self-Subsisting dwelt in the Land of Mystery

The 'Land of Mystery' refers to Edirne (Adrianople). The *abjad* numerical value[731] of 'Adirnih' and '*sirr*' (Mystery) is the same: 260 (referring to 1260 AH, which is 1844 CE). The spectacular meteoric display while Bahá'u'lláh was in Adrianople may be considered a literal fulfilment of the prophecies:

> In November 1866 when Bahá'u'lláh was residing in the house of Riḍá Big, a spectacular meteoric shower took place. Thousands of shooting-stars lit up the sky as they blazed their way through the atmosphere. This event, which has been called the 'star-fall' of 1866, was watched by millions in the East and West and for many the experience was terrifying.[732]

600. p. 132 ¶ 192. Verily, the Crier hath cried out, when the promised time came

The Qur'án (7:44) refers to the Promised One as 'the Summoner' or 'the Caller' and 'The Crier' (a person who makes announcements in a public forum, in Arabic *mu-a<u>th</u><u>th</u>in*):

> The companions of the Garden [Rodwell: 'inmates of paradise'] will call out to the companions of the Fire: 'We have indeed found the promises of our Lord to us true: have you also found your Lord's promises true?' They shall say 'yes'; but a Crier shall proclaim between them: 'the curse of God is on the wrong-doers;
>
> 'Those who would hinder (men) from the path of God and would seek in it something crooked: they were those who denied the Hereafter.' (7:44–45)

The word 'summons' (*nedá*) as in the Summons of the Lord of Hosts (*Nedá Rabbu'l-Junud*) and the Call of the Kingdom (*Nedá Malakút*) is related to the words *Munádi* and *alddaAAi* (the Caller).

The Qur'án (54:6–8) admonishes that the Summoner will invite humanity to an affair that the unbeliever will find difficult or terrible. And, in 20:108–112 (Rodwell): 'No deception or crookedness will be acceptable, and all faces will be humbled and all voices will be hushed before Him.'

Furthermore, the Qur'án states that in that Day the Crier or *Munádi* will proclaim His Mission from a near place (50:41). On His journey to Mecca, the Báb's announcement at the Kaaba occurred in the City where Muhammad had declared His Faith – hence the statement of Bahá'u'lláh about His forerunner: 'The Herald hath cried out, and the Summoner raised His voice saying: "The Kingdom is God's, the Most Powerful, the Help in Peril, the Self-Subsisting."'[733]

Bahá'u'lláh's own Declaration occurred in the Garden of Riḍván in Baghdad on 21 April 1863, also in close proximity to where Muhammad had revealed the verse of the Qur'án in Medina, Arabia. Referring to the fulfilment of this prophecy, and then to Qur'án 89:23, Bahá'u'lláh writes:

> The Crier hath cried out . . . The earth [of human understanding; human affairs] hath been shaken, and the mountains have passed away, and the angels have appeared, rank on rank, before Us.[734]

Again, the Qur'án promises (21:103):

> The Great Terror will bring them no grief: but the angels will meet them (with mutual greetings): 'This is your Day (the Day) that ye were promised.'

Malachi alerted the Jews to expect their Prophet Elijah, who had risen to heaven in a fiery chariot, to return before 'the great and terrible Day of the Lord' (Mal. 4:5). Christ stated (Luke 1:17) that John the Baptist represented the return of the 'power and spirit' of Elijah, who would return in the future (Luke 1:17). The Gospel of John (1:23) refers to John the Baptist as a Crier in the desert. The Báb, representing the second coming of Elijah, is the Crier Who announced the coming of Bahá'u'lláh.

See also Bahá'u'lláh, *Gems of Divine Mysteries*, para. 75.

601. p. 133 ¶ 192. The trumpet asketh: 'Hath the Bugle been sounded?'

In Judaism trumpets were mainly used for convening the people. The Psalms declare that 'with trumpets and the blast of the ram's horn' (Ps. 98:6) the Jews should joyfully announce the coming of the Lord, the King. It is in this sense that Christ in the Gospel of Matthew (24:31) states that at the Second Coming, 'he shall send his angels with a great sound of a trumpet, and they shall gather together his elect from the four winds, from one end of heaven to the other'. The New Testament also mentions that 'the last Trumpet will sound, and the dead will be raised', and the living will be transformed (I Cor. 15:52).

The Qur'án (39:68) anticipates two trumpet blasts: that is, two Revelations in rapid succession:

> And the trumpet shall be blown, so all those that are in the heavens and all those that are in the earth shall swoon, except such as God please; then it shall be blown a second time, then lo! They shall stand up awaiting.

The Dispensation of the Báb, which had its own independent scripture and laws, preceded the Revelation of Bahá'u'lláh by only 19 years. Therefore, in a sense 'the trumpet asketh' may be taken to refer to the expectation of earlier Dispensations as to the proclamation of the Promised One (namely the second event, 'the Bugle'). In this connection, Bahá'u'lláh declares:

> Once more hath the eternal Spirit breathed into the mystic trumpet, and caused the dead to speed out of their sepulchres of heedlessness

> and error unto the realm of guidance and grace. And yet, that expectant community still crieth out: When shall these things be? When shall the promised One, the object of our expectation, be made manifest . . .?[735]

See also Annotations 590 and 681.

602. p. 133 ¶ 192. Darkness hath been chased away by the dawning-light of the mercy of thy Lord, the Source of all light

God, the Source of the spiritual light in all Dispensations, a light that illuminates the spiritual and social teachings of faith, causes the darkness of spiritual ignorance to recede through the revelation of His new Dispensation. The Qur'án states:

> And say: 'Truth has (now) arrived, and Falsehood perished: for Falsehood is (by its nature) bound to perish.' (17:81)

> God is the Light of the heavens and the earth . . . (24:35)

> for any to whom God giveth not light, there is no light! (24:40)

> It is God Who alternates the Night and the Day . . . (24:44)

603. p. 133 ¶ 192. the souls have been quickened in the tombs of their bodies

'Tombs' here refers to spiritual death. Christ described the scribes and Pharisees as 'whited sepulchres, which indeed appear beautiful outward, but are within full of dead men's bones, and of all uncleanness' (Matt. 23:27). It is the expectation of the Bible and the Qur'án that mankind will be quickened. For example, Qur'án 22:7:

> And verily the Hour will come: there can be no doubt about it, or about (the fact) that God will raise up all who are in the graves.

This quickening is also a promise of the Gospel of John (5:25, 28):

> Verily, verily, I say unto you, The hour is coming, and now is, when the dead shall hear the voice of the Son of God: and they that hear shall live . . .
>
> . . . for the hour is coming, in the which all that are in the graves shall hear his voice.

See also Annotation 82.

604. p. 133 ¶ 192. When were the heavens cleft asunder?

This refers to Qur'án 77:9: 'when the heaven shall cleft asunder' (see also 55:37; 73:18; 82:1 and 84:1).

Mark 1:10 describes that as Christ came out of the water following His baptism He saw the heavens opened (NIV: 'being torn open'; Berean Study Bible: 'breaking open'; International Standard Version: 'split open'; English Revised Version: 'rent asunder').

The prophet Isaiah prays for God to rend the heavens so that Messiah may come down (Is. 64:1). The prophet Joel (2:10) predicted: 'the heavens shall tremble', and the Gospels anticipate (Matt. 24:29 and Mark 13:25) that 'the powers of the heavens shall be shaken'.

Bahá'u'lláh provides the following explanation of the cleaving of the heaven in this connection:

> By 'heaven' is meant the heaven of divine Revelation, which is elevated with every Manifestation, and rent asunder with every subsequent one. By 'cloven asunder is meant that the former Dispensation is superseded and annulled. I swear by God! That this heaven being cloven asunder is, to the discerning, an act mightier than the leaving of the skies! Ponder a while. That a divine Revelation which for years hath been securely established; beneath whose shadow all who have embraced it have been reared and nurtured; by the light of whose law generations of men have been disciplined; the excellency of whose word men have heard recounted by their fathers; in such wise that human eye hath beheld naught but the pervading influence of its grace, and mortal eye hath heard naught but the resounding majesty of its command – what act is mightier than that such a Revelation should, by the power of God, be 'cloven asunder' and be abolished at the appearance of one soul?[736]

605. 133 ¶ 192. Among the heedless is he who rubbeth his eyes . . . Blinded art thou. No refuge hast thou to flee to

This passage depicts the heedless as waking from a deep slumber and being ill-prepared spiritually when resurrection takes place. The Bible warns about spiritual somnolence:

> So wake up! Rub the sleep from your eyes! (Is. 51:17)

> But ye, brethren, are not in darkness, that that day should overtake you as a thief.
>
> Ye are all the children of light, and the children of the day: we are not of the night, nor of darkness.
>
> Therefore let us not sleep, as do others; but let us watch and be sober. For they that sleep sleep in the night; and they that be drunken are drunken in the night.
>
> But let us, who are of the day, be sober . . . (I Thess. 5:4–8)

Bahá'u'lláh writes:

> The peoples of the world are fast asleep. Were they to wake from their slumber, they would hasten with eagerness unto God, the All-Knowing, the All-Wise. They would cast away everything they possess, be it all the treasures of the earth, that their Lord may remember them to the extent of addressing to them but one word.[737]

Notably, Shoghi Effendi referred to the Universal House of Justice as the 'the last refuge of a tottering civilization'.[738]

See also Annotation 174.

606. 133 ¶ 192. Have men been gathered together?

The Day of Resurrection is also referred to in the Qur'án (64:9) as the Day of Assembly – *yawmi-aljam:*

> The Day that He assembles you (all) for a Day of Assembly, – that will be a day of mutual loss and gain (among you). And those who believe in God and work righteousness, – He will remove from them

their ills, and He will admit them to gardens beneath which rivers flow, to dwell therein for ever: that will be the supreme achievement.

Again:

> And warn (them) of the Day of Assembly, of which there is no doubt. (42:7)

And:

> In that is a Sign for those who fear the Penalty of the Hereafter: that is a Day for which mankind will be gathered together: that will be a Day of Testimony.
>
> Nor shall We delay it but for a term appointed.
>
> The day it arrives no soul shall speak except by His leave: of those (gathered) some will be wretched and some will be blessed. (11:103–105)

607. 133 ¶ 192. Hath the Book been sent down through the power of the true Faith?

Divine teachings and scripture are referred to as 'the Book'. A new Revelation is anticipated in the Qur'án:

> That is the Book [*thálika alkitábu*, or future scripture – often mistranslated as 'this Book'], wherein is no doubt, a guidance to the God-fearing . . . (2:2)

> On the Day of Judgment We shall bring out for him a scroll [Arabic *kitában* or Book], which he will see spread open. (17:13)

> For each period [age or *ajal*] is a Book (revealed). (13:38)

> One day we will summon all men with their leaders: they whose book shall be given into their right hand, shall read their book, and not be wronged a thread. (17:73: Rodwell)

A hadith attributed to Imám 'Abú-Ja'far (fifth Imám of the Shí'ihs) states:

> By God, as if I see him (Imam Mahdi) between Rukn and Maqám (of Kaaba, Mecca), people are declaring allegiance (to the Mahdi) based on a new, powerful matter, a new Book (scripture), and a new authority from Heaven.[739]

The New Testament also expects a Day when followers of all Dispensations, high and low, will be judged by their own scriptures, a Day when God will bring a new Book or Revelation that will be the cause of life for the spiritually dead:

> And I saw the dead, small and great [that is, all classes], stand before God; and the books were opened: and another book was opened, which is the book of life: and the dead were judged out of those things which were written in the books, according to their works. (Rev. 20:12)

See also Annotation 583.

608. p. 133 ¶ 192. Have I been assembled with others, blind?

This is a reference to the following verses of the Qur'án:

> the Day the trumpet shall be blown, and We shall gather the guilty on that Day, blind (20:102, *The Study Qur'án*)

> It is he whom God guides, that is on true Guidance; but he whom He leaves astray – for such wilt thou find no protector besides Him. On the Day of Judgment We shall gather, them together, prone on their faces, blind, dumb, and deaf: their abode will be Hell . . . (17:97)

The Qur'án also promises a Day when humanity will be assembled:

> God! . . . of a surety He will gather you together against the Day of Judgment, about which there is no doubt. And whose word can be truer than God's? (4:87; also 11:103; 19:95; 56:49–50)

At the time of resurrection (Qur'án 39:69) the Prophets will also be brought up; that is, their Revelations will be renewed and their followers will be united in one common Faith. The Qur'án also states that animals (spiritually-untrained sections of humanity) will also be assembled (41:19), but warns elsewhere that 'the worst of beasts in the sight of God' are those who do not believe (8:55). It further states that the enemies of God will be gathered in Hell (41:19).

God promises in the Book of Isaiah (42:16): 'And I will bring the blind by a way that they knew not; I will lead them in paths that they have not known: I will make darkness light before them, and crooked things straight . . .'

Christ similarly stated (John 9:39): 'I am come into this world, that they which see not might see; and that they which see might be made blind.'

There are four types of gathering or ingathering mentioned in the Bible:

1. A reference to Christ as the Sower (Matt. 13:3–8) and the ingathering of the harvest by the Lord of harvest (Matt. 9:36–38).
2. The ingathering of Jewish exiles from amongst nations (Is. 56:8; Jer. 29:14; Ezek. 11:17).
3. The gathering and unification of the sheep of many flocks into one flock and under one shepherd (Zech. 2:11; John 10:16).
4. The gathering of wild animals (antagonistic sections of humanity) who will live in harmony (Is. 11:6).

609. p. 133 ¶ 192. Him that rideth upon the clouds

The Torah speaks of God arising and riding on His chariots of salvation on the clouds or heavens at the head of His hosts:

> There is no one like the God of Jeshurun [the Upright One], who rides across the heavens to help you and on the clouds in his majesty. (Deut. 33:26, New International Version)

> Sing to God, sing in praise of his name, extol him who rides on the clouds [KJV: him that rideth upon the heavens] by his name; rejoice before him – his name is the Lord. (Ps. 68:4, New International Version)

> He maketh the clouds His chariot; who walketh upon the wings of the wind . . . (Ps. 104:3)

Christ (Matt. 24:30) prophesied that the Son of Man shall come on the clouds of heaven, and the Book of Revelation (1:7) confirms this event.

See also Annotations 113, 279, 498 and 499.

610. p. 133 ¶ 192. Paradise is decked with mystic roses, and hell hath been made to blaze

That is, the Heaven of Revelation is decorated with wonderful meanings, concepts, or illuminations, and simultaneously, there is a conflagration of hellish impiety.

611. p. 134 ¶ 192. the whole earth hath been illumined at the coming of Him Who is the Lord of the Day of the Covenant

A hadith states that the whole earth was created pure and as a place of worship.[740] Bahá'u'lláh has come to restore that purity, to enlighten the earth of human understanding, and to establish the worship of God throughout the world. The appearance of a promised Dispensation is the Day when God renews His Covenant with mankind.

See also Annotations 47, 432, 564 and 736.

612. p. 134 ¶ 192. The doubters have perished

The book that Bahá'u'lláh wrote before His formal declaration in Baghdad in answer to questions posed by an uncle of the Báb was entitled the *Kitáb-i-Íqán* or the Book of Certitude. By the incontrovertible evidences of His Revelation, Bahá'u'lláh has eliminated any doubts about the validity of His Mission. He reveals in the Tablet of Aḥmad:

> And be thou so steadfast in My love that thy heart shall not waver . . . and be not of those who doubt . . .Be thou assured in thyself that verily, he who turns away from this Beauty hath also turned away from the Messengers of the past and showeth pride towards God from all eternity to all eternity.[741]

The Apostle Paul states that God will do something that they will scoff at and not believe. This will lead to the demise of the doubters (Acts 13:41; see also Hab. 1:5). On one occasion Christ (Matt. 21:19–20) cursed a fruitless fig tree, which quickly withered and died. He then reassured His disciples of what they could achieve if they possessed assured faith (21:21):

> Verily I say unto you, If ye have faith, and doubt not, ye shall not only do this which is done to the fig tree, but also if ye shall say unto this mountain, Be thou removed, and be thou cast into the sea; it shall be done.

The Qur'án also admonishes against having reservations, and emphasizes the importance of certitude (10:94, Rodwell): 'Now hath the Truth come to thee from thy Lord: be not therefore of those who doubt.'

613. p. 134 ¶ 192. the mountain of knowledge was crushed, and men's feet have slipped

The Qur'án states that at the time of the anticipated 'Inevitable Event' the mountains will be crushed and reduced to dust (56:5). One reading of this is that the vast accumulations of man-made religious knowledge will be invalidated and crumble away.

'Slipping of feet' refers to spiritual back-sliding, and to stumbling at the last hurdle. It is an allusion to humanity's tendency not to do what is right. Thus, the Hebrew Bible praises God 'Which holdeth our soul in life, and suffereth not our feet to be moved' (Ps. 66:9). He must have certitude that God will assist him:

> Hold up my goings in thy paths, that my footsteps slip not. (Ps. 17:5)

> When I said, My foot slippeth; thy mercy, O Lord, held me up. (Ps. 94:18)

> My help cometh from the Lord, Who made heaven and earth. He will not suffer thy foot to be moved . . . (Ps. 121:2–3)

The term 'slipping of feet' is also in the Qur'án to describe falling from grace. For example, the fall of Adam and Eve is described as 'slipping' from heaven and a deflection from the right path (2:34, Rodwell).

614. 134 ¶ 192. Be patient, for thy Lord is patient

The Qur'án teaches that God loves patience. His Prophets had persevered in the face of adversity and the believers should also be patient:

> O ye who believe! Seek help with patient perseverance and prayer; for God is with those who patiently persevere. (2:153)

> Rejected were the Messengers before thee: with patience and constancy they bore their rejection and their wrongs, until Our aid did reach them . . . (6:34)

> Our Lord! Pour out on us patience and constancy . . . (7:126)

> For thy Lord's (Cause) be patient and constant! (74:7)

Patience is also one of the virtues in the Bible; Christians are taught to await Christ patiently (II Thess. 3:5): 'And the Lord direct your hearts into the love of God, and into the patient waiting for Christ.'

615. p. 134 ¶ 193. These are verses We sent down previously

The passage in Ishráqát[742] is similar to the Epistle and includes the phrase 'previously', indicating the existence of an even earlier source. A Tablet revealed by Bahá'u'lláh early after His incarceration in 'Akká, part of a compilation called Kitáb-i-Mubín,[743] includes the segment in ¶ 192 but does not contain the phrase 'These are verses We sent down previously'. It is therefore likely that this is the original source.

616. p. 134 ¶ 193. Our Arrival in the prison-city of 'Akká

This occurred during the 'afternoon of the 12th of Jamádíyu'l-Avval 1285, AH (August 31, 1868)'.[744]

617. 135 ¶ 194. to fear God, a fear which is the fountain-head of all goodly deeds and virtues

This paragraph is quoted from Bahá'u'lláh, Ishráqát (Splendours), in *Tablets of Bahá'u'lláh Revealed After the Kitáb-i-Aqdas*, p. 120.

See also Annotations 33, 198, 200 and 673 on the fear of God.

618. p. 135 ¶ 194. the Companions of the Crimson Ark . . . mentioned in the Qayyúm-i-Asmá

The Qayyúmu'l-Asmá, literally, 'Self-Subsisting of the Names (of God)', also named *Tafsír Súrat Yúsuf*, and *Ahsanil-Qisas* (the Best of Stories), is the Báb's Commentary on the Súrih of Joseph (the twelfth chapter of the Qur'án). The number of the Súrihs of the Qayyúmu'l-Asmá is exactly the same as the number of verses in Súrih of Joseph, that is, 111 verses, not counting '*Bismi Alláhi al-raḥmáni al-raḥím* – 'In the name of God, the Most Gracious, the Most Merciful' (see Rodwell's translation of the Qur'án). The Qayyúmu'l-Asmá is the Báb's principal scriptural Writing and is revealed entirely in Arabic. Bahá'u'lláh has characterized it as 'the first, the greatest, and mightiest of all books'[745] in the Bábí Dispensation, as described by Shoghi Effendi:

> It was this Book which the Bábís universally regarded, during almost the entire ministry of the Báb, as the Qur'án of the people of the Bayán; whose first and most challenging chapter was revealed in the presence of Mullá Ḥusayn, on the night of its Author's Declaration; some of whose pages were borne, by that same disciple, to Bahá'u'lláh, as the first fruits of a Revelation which instantly won His enthusiastic allegiance; whose entire text was translated into Persian by the brilliant and gifted Ṭáhirih . . . a single page of which had captured the imagination and entranced the soul of Ḥujjat; and whose contents had set afire the intrepid defenders of the Fort of Shaykh Ṭabarsí and the heroes of Nayríz and Zanján.[746]

> [Its] fundamental purpose was to forecast what the true Joseph (Bahá'u'lláh) would, in a succeeding Dispensation, endure at the hands of one who was at once His arch-enemy and blood brother [Mírzá Yaḥyá]. This work, comprising above nine thousand three

> hundred verses, and divided into one hundred and eleven chapters, each chapter a commentary on one verse of the above-mentioned súrih, opens with the Báb's clarion-call and dire warnings addressed to the 'concourse of kings and of the sons of kings'; forecasts the doom of Muḥammad Sháh; commands his Grand Vizir, Ḥájí Mírzá Aqásí, to abdicate his authority; admonishes the entire Muslim ecclesiastical order; cautions more specifically the members of the Shí'ah community; extols the virtues, and anticipates the coming, of Bahá'u'lláh, the 'Remnant of God', the 'Most Great Master'; and proclaims, in unequivocal language, the independence and universality of the Bábí Revelation, unveils its import, and affirms the inevitable triumph of its Author. It, moreover, directs the 'people of the West' to 'issue forth from your cities and aid the Cause of God'; warns the peoples of the earth of the 'terrible, the most grievous vengeance of God'; threatens the whole Islamic world with 'the Most Great Fire' were they to turn aside from the newly-revealed Law; foreshadows the Author's martyrdom; eulogizes the high station ordained for the people of Bahá, the 'Companions of the crimson-colored ruby Ark'; prophesies the fading out and utter obliteration of some of the greatest luminaries in the firmament of the Bábí Dispensation; and even predicts 'afflictive torment', in both the 'Day of Our Return' and in 'the world which is to come', for the usurpers of the Imamate, who 'waged war against Ḥusayn (Imám Ḥusayn) in the Land of the Euphrates'.[747]

See also Annotations 420 and 578.

619. p. 135 ¶ 196. O thou who hast fixed thy gaze upon My countenance!

The prophet Isaiah states that humanity did not receive God's mercies because of any divine limitations, but because transgressions had concealed the face of God from individuals. After overcoming his shortcomings, the true believer or seeker should steadfastly fix his gaze on the Source of all blessings:

> Behold, the Lord's hand is not shortened, that it cannot save, or his ear dull, that it cannot hear; but your iniquities have made a

> separation between you and your God, and your sins have hidden his face from you. (Is. 59:1–2)

Compare Bahá'u'lláh, Ishráqát (Splendours), in *Tablets of Bahá'u'lláh Revealed After the Kitáb-i-Aqdas*, p. 120.

620. p. 136 ¶ 197. We will now mention unto thee Trustworthiness

Compare Bahá'u'lláh, Ishráqát (Splendours), in *Tablets of Bahá'u'lláh Revealed After the Kitáb-i-Aqdas*, p. 120–21, and Tarázát (Ornaments), ibid. pp. 37–8. Also revealed in a Tablet in honour of Ḥájí Mírzá Buzurg-i-Afnán, a custodian of the House of the Báb in Shiraz.

621. p. 136 ¶ 197. Our Green Island

A reference to the Garden of Riḍván near 'Akká (see Taherzadeh, *The Revelation of Bahá'u'lláh*, vol. 4, p. 16.)

622. p. 137 ¶ 200. Kamál Páshá

Kamál Páshá was a former Ṣadr-i-A'ẓam (Grand Vizier, Prime Minister) of the Sultan of the Ottoman Empire. He visited Bahá'u'lláh in Istanbul, the traditional seat of both the Sultanate and the Caliphate, but Bahá'u'lláh maintained dignified aloofness, and did not, as was the custom, return his visit or the visits of other high-ranking officials. Kamál Pashá and these others reminded him of this custom. Bahá'u'lláh exhorted them to accept the divine commandments and to abandon their effete traditions:

> Call Thou to remembrance Thine arrival in the City, how the Ministers of the Sulṭán thought Thee to be unacquainted with their laws and regulations, and believed Thee to be one of the ignorant. Say: Yea, by My Lord! I am ignorant of all things except what God hath, through His bountiful favour, been pleased to teach Me. To this We assuredly testify, and unhesitatingly confess it.
>
> Say: If the laws and regulations to which ye cleave be of your own making, We will, in no wise, follow them. Thus have I been

instructed by Him Who is the All-Wise, the All-Informed. Such hath been My way in the past, and such will it remain in the future, through the power of God and His might. This, indeed, is the true and right way. . .

Say: It behoveth you, O Ministers of State, to keep the precepts of God, and to forsake your own laws and regulations, and to be of them who are guided aright. Better is this for you than all ye possess, did ye but know it.[748]

623. p. 138 ¶ 200. choose one of the divers languages . . . or . . . create a new language and a new script

Compare:

The sixth Ishráq is union and concord amongst the children of men. From the beginning of time the light of unity hath shed its divine radiance upon the world, and the greatest means for the promotion of that unity is for the peoples of the world to understand one another's writing and speech. . . We have enjoined upon the Trustees of the House of Justice either to choose one language from among those now existing or to adopt a new one, and in like manner to select a common script, both of which should be taught in all the schools of the world. Thus will the earth be regarded as one country and one home. The most glorious fruit of the tree of knowledge is this exalted word: Of one tree are all ye the fruit, and of one bough the leaves. Let not man glory in this that he loveth his country, let him rather glory in this that he loveth his kind.[749]

624. p. 138 ¶ 201. At present, a new language and a new script have been devised

Realizing that linguistic differences were a barrier to communication and unity, Dr Ludwik Lejzer Zamenhof (1859–1917), a Polish physician, constructed the Esperanto language. (His daughter, Lidia, impressed also with the other Bahá'í principles, accepted the Faith around 1925. She died in a Nazi concentration camp in 1942.)

At an Esperanto banquet given in Paris in February 1913, 'Abdu'l-Bahá is reported to have said:

> Today one of the chief causes of the differences in Europe is the diversity of languages. We say this man is a German, the other is an Italian, then we meet an Englishman and then again a Frenchman. Although they belong to the same race, yet language is the greatest barrier between them. Were a universal auxiliary language in operation they would all be considered as one.
>
> His Holiness Bahá'u'lláh wrote about this international language more than forty years ago. He says that as long as an international language is not adopted, complete union between the various sections of the world will be unrealized, for we observe that misunderstandings keep people from mutual association, and these misunderstandings will not be dispelled except through an international auxiliary language . . .[750]

While there are several allusions to Esperanto that are specific and encouraging, it remains true that until the Universal House of Justice has acted on the matter in accordance with Bahá'u'lláh's instruction (see Annotation 623) the Bahá'í Faith is committed neither to Esperanto nor to any other living or artificial language. 'Abdu'l-Bahá Himself is reported to have said: 'The love and effort put into Esperanto will not be lost, but no one person can construct a Universal Language.'[751]

625. p. 140 ¶ 203. I beseech Thee by Thy most glorious light

The name Bahá and its derivatives are mentioned five times in the *Du'a al-Sahar*, also known as the *Du'a al-Bahá*, attributed to Muḥammad al-Báqir, the fifth Imám, and transmitted by Imám Ja'far al-Ṣádiq (the sixth Imám), and Imám 'Alí ibn Músá, Imám Riḍá (the eighth Imám). Traditions associated with Imám Ja'far al-Ṣádiq and Imám Ridá indicate that the prayer contains 'the Greatest Name' (*al-Ismi al-A'zam*) of God.[752] The prayer mentions nineteen attributes which are the source of the names of the months of the Badí' Calendar. It is read by Muslims before dawn during the fasting month of Ramadan, and begins as follows:

> O my God! I beseech Thee by Thy Glory [or Splendour: *bahá*] at its most Glorious [or Splendid: *abhá*] for all Thy Glory [or Splendour: *bahá*] is truly Glorious: [or Resplendent: *bahiyy*]. I, verily, O my God! beseech Thee by all Thy Glories [or Splendours: *bahá*].[753]

626. p. 141 ¶ 204. My Forerunner, Who laid down His life for this Great Announcement, this Straight Path

A reference to the Báb.[754] Compare ¶ 230: 'John [the Baptist], son of Zacharias, said what My Forerunner hath said.'

627. p. 141 ¶ 204. I have written down in My mention of Him

See Shoghi Effendi, *God Passes By*, p. 30.

628. p. 141 ¶ 204. Exalted and glorified is He

See Shoghi Effendi, *God Passes By*, p. 30.

629. p. 141 ¶ 204. In the year nine ye will attain unto the Presence of God

The year nine is a reference to 1269 AH marking the termination of the Bábí Dispensation, nine years after the declaration of the Báb in 1260 AH (1844 CE). In the Síyáh-Chál (1852) Bahá'u'lláh had a vision of a Maiden from God and was made aware of His future mission. Shoghi Effendi describes these statements by the Báb:

> 'In the year nine', He, referring to the date of the advent of the promised Revelation, has explicitly written, 'ye shall attain unto all good'. 'In the year nine, ye will attain unto the presence of God.' And again: 'After Ḥín (68) a Cause shall be given unto you which ye shall come to know.' 'Ere nine will have elapsed from the inception of this Cause', He more particularly has stated, 'the realities of the created things will not be made manifest. All that thou hast as yet seen is but the stage from the moist germ until We clothed it with flesh. Be patient, until thou beholdest a new creation. Say: "Blessed, therefore, be God, the most excellent of Makers!"' 'Wait thou', is His statement to 'Azím, 'until nine will have elapsed from the time of the Bayán. Then exclaim: "Blessed, therefore, be God, the most excellent of Makers!"' 'Be attentive', He, referring in a remarkable passage to the year nineteen, has admonished, 'from the inception of the Revelation till the number of Vaḥíd (19).' 'The Lord of the

Day of Reckoning', He, even more explicitly, has stated, 'will be manifested at the end of Vaḥíd (19) and the beginning of eighty (1280 AH).'⁷⁵⁵

Shoghi Effendi describes the 'Year Nine' as coinciding with the Revelation descending upon Bahá'u'lláh in the Síyáh-<u>Ch</u>ál:

the 'Year Nine', anticipated 2,000 years ago as the 'third woe' by St. John the Divine, alluded to by both <u>Sh</u>ay<u>kh</u> Aḥmad and Siyyid Káẓim – the twin luminaries that heralded the advent of the Faith of the Báb – specifically mentioned and extolled by the Herald of the Bahá'í Dispensation in His Writings, and eulogized by both the Founder of our Faith and the Center of His Covenant. In that year, the year 'after Ḥín', mentioned by <u>Sh</u>ay<u>kh</u> Aḥmad, the year that witnessed the birth of the Mission of the promised 'Qayyúm', specifically referred to by Siyyid Káẓim, the 'requisite number' in the words of Bahá'u'lláh 'of pure, of wholly consecrated and sanctified souls' had been 'most secretly consummated'. In that year, as testified by the pen of the Báb, the 'realities of the created things' were 'made manifest', 'a new creation was born' and the seed of His Faith revealed its 'ultimate perfection'. In that year, as borne witness by 'Abdu'l-Bahá, a hitherto 'embryonic Faith' was born. In that year, while the Blessed Beauty lay in chains and fetters, in that dark and pestilential pit, 'the breezes of the All-Glorious', as He Himself described it, 'were wafted' over Him. There, whilst His neck was weighted down by the Qará-Guhar, His feet in stocks, breathing the fetid air of the Síyáh-<u>Ch</u>ál, He dreamed His dream and heard, 'on every side', 'exalted words', and His 'tongue recited' words that 'no man could bear to hear'.⁷⁵⁶

See also Annotations 634, 702 and 704; 'God, the most excellent of Makers'. The phrase is also related to the following verse of the Qur'án:

He is God, the Producer [Creator], the Maker, the Fashioner [Originator of all Dispensations]; to Him are ascribed excellent titles [belongs the Most Beautiful Names]. Whatever is in the heavens and earth praiseth [glorifies] Him. He is the Almighty, the Wise! (59:24, Rodwell)

630. pp. 141–2 ¶ 204. These melodies, uttered by the Birds of the cities of Knowledge, conform with that which hath been sent down by the All-Merciful in the Qur'án

There are many verses in the Qur'án about the awe-inspiring Day of Resurrection, verses that urge piety and receptivity, and for humanity to act in a manner that would befit attaining the presence of God (Bahá'u'lláh's Revelation), and thereby attain unto all good.

631. p. 142 ¶ 205. The River of Mercy floweth, and the Ocean of Utterance surgeth, and the Sun of Revelation shineth forth resplendent

This is a reference to the divine outpourings of the Revelations of the Báb and Bahá'u'lláh. In scripture, water, river and sun are often used as metaphors for revelation:

> There is a river [divine grace and mercy], the streams whereof shall make glad the city of God, the holy place of the tabernacles of the most High.
>
> God is in the midst of her; she shall not be moved: God shall help her . . . (Ps. 46:4–5)

> For the Lord God is a sun and shield: the Lord will give grace and glory: no good thing will he withhold from them that walk uprightly. (Ps. 84:11)

> When the poor and needy seek water, and there is none, and their tongue faileth for thirst, I the Lord will hear them, I . . . will not forsake them.
>
> I will open rivers in high places, and fountains in the midst of the valleys: I will make the wilderness a pool of water, and the dry land springs of water. (Is. 41:17–18)

> And he shewed me a pure river of water of life, clear as crystal, proceeding out of the throne of God . . . (Rev. 22:1)

God in the Qur'án (5:12) states: 'Verily I will wipe out from you your evils, and admit you to gardens with rivers flowing beneath.'

632. p. 142 ¶ 205. 'Aẓím

Mullá 'Alí ('Alí Mírzá Mullá Shaykh, a nephew of the Imám-Jum'ih of the Masjid-i-Vakíl), and a well-known disciple of the Báb.

> Some of His disciples the Báb assiduously prepared to expect the imminent Revelation. Others He orally assured would live to see its day. To Mullá Báqir, one of the Letters of the Living, He actually prophesied, in a Tablet addressed to him, that he would meet the Promised One face to face. To Sayyáh, another disciple, He gave verbally a similar assurance. Mullá Ḥusayn He directed to Ṭihrán, assuring him that in that city was enshrined a Mystery Whose light neither Ḥijáz nor Shíráz could rival. Quddús, on the eve of his final separation from Him, was promised that he would attain the presence of the One Who was the sole Object of their adoration and love. To Shaykh Ḥasan-i-Zunúzí He declared while in Máh-Kú that he would behold in Karbilá the countenance of the promised Ḥusayn. On Dayyán He conferred the title of 'the third Letter to believe in Him Whom God shall make manifest', while to 'Azím He divulged, in the Kitáb-i-Panj-Sha'n, the name, and announced the approaching advent, of Him Who was to consummate His own Revelation.[757]

633. p. 142 ¶ 205. This, verily, is the thing We promised thee

The Báb revealed Bahá'u'lláh's name and His approaching advent to 'Azím in the Kitáb-i-Panj-Sha'n.

634. p. 142 ¶ 205. In the year nine this Most Great Revelation arose

> His imprisonment [in the Síyáh-Chál] lasted for a period of no less than four months, in the middle of which the 'year nine' (1269), anticipated in such glowing terms by the Báb, and alluded to as the year 'after Ḥín'. . . was ushered in, endowing with undreamt-of

> potentialities the whole world. Two months after that year was born, Bahá'u'lláh, the purpose of His imprisonment now accomplished, was released from His confinement, and set out, a month later, for Baghdád, on the first stage of a memorable and life-long exile which was to carry Him, in the course of years, as far as Adrianople in European Turkey, and which was to end with His twenty-four years' incarceration in 'Akká.[758]

> 'Behold', Bahá'u'lláh Himself, years later, testified, in refutation of the claims of those who had rejected the validity of His mission following so closely upon that of the Báb, 'how immediately upon the completion of the ninth year of this wondrous, this most holy and merciful Dispensation, the requisite number of pure, of wholly consecrated and sanctified souls has been most secretly consummated.' 'That so brief an interval', He, moreover has asserted, 'should have separated this most mighty and wondrous Revelation from Mine own previous Manifestation is a secret that no man can unravel, and a mystery such as no mind can fathom. Its duration had been foreordained.'[759]

See also Annotation 629.

635. p. 142 ¶ 205. I am the first servant to believe in Him

This is one of the many acknowledgements of the Báb of Bahá'u'lláh's Dispensation:

> 'I have written down in My mention of Him', He thus extols the Author of the anticipated Revelation, 'these gem-like words: "No allusion of Mine can allude unto Him, neither anything mentioned in the Bayán."' 'I, Myself, am but the first servant to believe in Him and in His signs . . .'[760]

Compare ¶ 230:

> Wherefore, hath My Forerunner, as a sign of submissiveness and humility, said: 'The whole of the Bayán is only a leaf amongst the leaves of His Paradise.' And likewise, He saith: 'I am the first to adore Him, and pride Myself on My kinship with Him.'

It is noteworthy that in an earlier time the sixth Imám is reported to have made a similar statement about the Qá'im (the Báb):

> Imám Ja'far ibn Muḥammad as-Sádiq (peace be upon both of them) said: 'Indeed if I were to live to see him (*al-Mahdí*) then I would have been his servant for the duration of my life.[761]

The statement in ¶ 205 is in keeping with the understanding that the first to believe in the voice of God is the Manifestation of God, and the first to believe in the Manifestation of God is the prior Manifestation. According to the Qur'án, when Moses heard the Voice of God from the Burning Bush He said, 'To Thee I turn in repentance, and I am the first to believe' (7:143). Similarly, Muhammad stated (6:14): 'I am commanded to be the first of those who bow to God [submit to His Will] . . .'

See also Annotation 727.

636. p. 142–3 ¶ 205. He, verily, is the One Who, under all conditions, proclaimeth: 'I, in very truth, am God!'

This is a quotation from the Báb, *Persian Bayán*, Váḥid I, Chapter 1.

637. p. 143 ¶ 205. That which is meant by Divinity and Godhead hath previously been stated

See ¶ 67 to ¶ 75.

638. p. 143 ¶ 206. O <u>Sh</u>ay<u>kh</u>! Hearken unto the melodies of the Gospel

The <u>Sh</u>ay<u>kh</u> is admonished to study the Gospels, a Scripture that the Qur'án confirms (3:84). He would then learn from the statement of Christ that the exact knowledge of the circumstances when the Father would come, an event that was the main theme of the Gospels, was not available to His followers. Therefore, he too should be humble in assessing His prophecies.

'Abdu'l-Bahá inscribed in the old Bible of the City Temple Church in London: 'This book is the Holy Book of God, of celestial Inspiration.

It is the Bible of Salvation, the Noble Gospel. It is the mystery of the Kingdom and its light. It is the Divine Bounty, the sign of the guidance of God.'[762] Bahá'ís consider the Bible and the Qur'án to be part of their Holy Scriptures:

> Verily, the people are veiled from comprehending the meanings of the Gospel, the Bible and the Koran and know not the interpretation of the scriptures of God, except those whose eyes are opened by the outpouring of the Spirit of God. Thou shalt behold men-servants and maid-servants of Baha' [sic] in those far-distant lands and wide countries, speaking the secrets of the Gospel and the mysteries of the Bible and the allusions of the Koran and the explanation of the Words of the Merciful One. Those are the servants to whomsoever God hath assigned His mercy which overfloweth the existence.[763]

> Thou hast written that thou lovest the Bible. Undoubtedly, the friends and the maid-servants of the Merciful should know the value of the Bible, for they are the ones who have discovered its real significances and have become cognizant of the hidden mystery of the Holy Book.[764]

> Fifty years ago no one would touch the Christian Bible in Persia. Bahá'u'lláh came and asked, 'Why?' They said, 'It is not the Word of God.' He said, 'You must read it with understanding of its meanings, not as those who merely recite its words.' Now Bahá'ís all over the East read the Bible and understand its spiritual teaching. Bahá'u'lláh spread the Cause of Christ and opened the book of the Christians and Jews. He removed the barriers of names. He proved that all the divine Prophets taught the same reality and that to deny One is to deny the Others, for all are in perfect oneness with God.[765]

> Consider attentively and with assiduity in the New Testament, as well as the Bible, and thou shalt find new significances, very clear of this great Manifestation.[766]

> Thank God, for He hath uncovered the veil from before thine eye, and that thou hast witnessed the great signs of the greatest

> glad-tidings which have been revealed in the Gospel, Bible and the Psalms; and wert confirmed that verily those glad-tidings have been allusions to the appearance of the Kingdom of God during this time.[767]

> The Heavenly Books, the Bible, the Qur'án, and the other Holy Writings have been given by God as guides into the paths of Divine virtue, love, justice and peace.[768]

In *Tablets of the Divine Plan* 'Abdu'l-Bahá links the creation of unity and religious harmony with elucidation of the mysteries of the Bible and the Qur'án:

> Although in most of the states and cities of the United States, praise be to God, His fragrances are diffused, and souls unnumbered are turning their faces and advancing toward the Kingdom of God, yet in some of the states the Standard of Unity is not yet upraised as it should be, nor are the mysteries of the Holy Books, such as the Bible, the Gospel, and the Qur'án, unraveled. Through the concerted efforts of all the friends the Standard of Unity must needs be unfurled in those states, and the Divine teachings promoted, so that these states may also receive their portion of the heavenly bestowals and a share of the Most Great Guidance.[769]

639. p. 143 ¶ 206. But of that Day and Hour knoweth no man

The need for spiritual receptivity is highlighted by the fact that Jesus gave the good news of the Second Coming and alluded to events that would signal its advent. Notably, in the Gospel of Mark (13:32–33; 35–37) Christ indicates that His Revelation did not contain the precise knowledge of the manner in which it would unfold. This passage quoted by Bahá'u'lláh also appears in the Gospel of Matthew (24:36). Of the 28 most commonly used Bible translations in English,[770] seventeen, including the New International version working directly from the original Greek, include the phrase 'nor the Son'.[771] Eleven, including the King James version, relying on certain Greek translations, omit 'neither the Son', because of difficulty reconciling this with the conviction of an omniscient Christ.

Elsewhere, the New Testament similarly states: 'And He (Jesus) said unto them, "It is not for you to know times or the seasons which the Father hath put in his own power"' (Acts 1:7).

The Qur'án also states:

> They ask thee about the (final) Hour – when will be its appointed time? Say: 'The knowledge thereof is with my Lord (alone): None but He can reveal as to when it will occur . . .' (7:187)
>
> To Him (God) is referred The Knowledge of the Hour . . . (41:47)

640. p. 143 ¶ 206. By Father in this connection is meant God – exalted be His glory

'Father' is one of the many names of God in the Bible. It often refers to the divine Revelation at the end of times or the Second Coming, as in Is. 9:6: 'his name shall be called Wonderful, Counseller, The mighty God, The everlasting Father, The Prince of Peace'. Again, (Matt. 6:9–10): 'Our Father which art in heaven . . . Thy kingdom come.' And the Apostle Paul wrote (I Cor. 8:6): 'But to us there is one God, the Father, of whom are all things . . .'

641. p. 143 ¶ 206. He, verily, is the True Educator, and the Spiritual Teacher

'The Lord' is frequently used in the Bible and the Qur'án to refer to God. The Arabic word for 'Lord' is *ar-Rabb*. This is related to the word *murabbi* which means educator and teacher.

642. p. 143 ¶ 207. For the Day of the Lord is great

The great 'Day of the Lord' is anticipated in the Hebrew Bible:

> . . . for the day of the Lord is great and very terrible; and who can abide it? (Joel 2:11)
>
> The sun shall be turned into darkness, and the moon into blood, before the great and the terrible day of the Lord come. (Joel 2:31)

> The great day of the Lord is near, it is near, and hasteth greatly . . . (Zeph. 1:14)

> Behold, I will send you Elijah the prophet [John the Baptist at the First Coming; the Báb at the Second Coming] before the coming of the great and dreadful day of the Lord . . . (Mal. 4:5)

The New Testament reiterates:

> The sun shall be turned into darkness, and the moon into blood, before that great and notable day of the Lord come. (Acts 2:20)

The Qur'án similarly states that there is no refuge for humanity other than God's Revelation in the Day of Resurrection (75:6, 10).

643. p. 143 ¶ 207. Of what ask they of one another? Of the Great Announcement

A major theme of the Qur'án concerns a future spiritual experience and commotion – a momentous and truly awesome and dreadful occurrence, the like of which has not been witnessed by humanity. Its very anticipation must regulate the conduct of all Muslims.

The quotation in ¶ 207 is from Qur'án 78:1–2, the chapter of the Qur'án entitled *al-Naba* or 'the Announcement'. The Súrih speaks of the 'Great Announcement or *naba-e Azim* (also translated as the 'Great News', 'Great Tiding' or 'Great Event'). Other Súrihs also refer to this event: 'When the Event Inevitable cometh to pass, Then will no (soul) entertain falsehood concerning its coming.' (56:1–2); and 'that Day shall the (Great) Event [also translated as 'the Inevitable Event'] come to pass' (69:15).

Bahá'u'lláh unambiguously declares that His Revelation is the *naba-e Azim* (the Great Announcement) that humanity and all religions, and particularly Islam, must heed:

> Say: I am come to you, O people, from the Throne of glory, and bear you an announcement from God, the Most Powerful, the Most Exalted, the Most Great.[772]

> By Him Who is the Great Announcement! The All-Merciful is come invested with undoubted sovereignty.[773]

Notably, the Qur'án alludes to two closely related Revelations (78:4–5). It states: 'Verily, they [humanity] shall soon come to know!' (about the Great Announcement, that is, the Báb); and then repeats: 'Verily, verily [*thumma* which means thereafter] they shall soon come to know!' (that is, Bahá'u'lláh).

644. p. 144 ¶ 208. Oh, for great is that Day

Compare Jer. 30:7: 'Alas! for that day is great, so that none is like it,' and Rev. 6:17: 'For the great day of his wrath is come; and who shall be able to stand?'

The Qur'án also describes the Promised 'Day of God' (45:14) as 'a Great Day' (*Yawmin A<u>th</u>ím*) (7:59).

See also Annotation 642.

645. p. 144 ¶ 208. greatness of the Day

Bahá'u'lláh, concerning the greatness of this Day, further states:

> Great indeed is this Day! The allusions made to it in all the sacred Scriptures as the Day of God attest its greatness. The soul of every Prophet of God, of every Divine Messenger, hath thirsted for this wondrous Day. All the divers kindreds of the earth have, likewise, yearned to attain it.[774]

And:

> Should the greatness of this Day be revealed in its fullness, every man would forsake a myriad lives in his longing to partake, though it be for one moment, of its great glory – how much more this world and its corruptible treasures![775]

Shoghi Effendi gives further quotations:

'None among the Manifestations of old, except to a prescribed degree, hath ever completely apprehended the nature of this Revelation.' 'I testify before God to the greatness, the inconceivable greatness of this Revelation. Again and again have We, in most of Our Tablets, borne witness to this truth, that mankind may be roused from its heedlessness.' 'How great is the Cause, how staggering the weight of its Message!' 'In this most mighty Revelation all the Dispensations of the past have attained their highest, their final consummation.'[776]

646. p. 144 ¶ 208. song of David

A reference to the Book of Psalms (also known as the Psalter) consisting of an anthology of 150 sacred odes and poems of hope, praise, thanksgiving, anguish and despair, composed between c. 1407–586 BCE). A number of authors are mentioned in the titles, including Moses, David and Solomon. The Psalms are part of the *Ketuvim* (Writings) of the Hebrew Bible and are meant to be sung (from Greek *psalmos*, a sacred ode sung accompanied by a plucked musical instrument such as a harp). Bahá'u'lláh refers to the Psalms as *Naghmeh* or Melody of David (plural, *Naghamát*, as in *naghamáté Injil*, 'the melodies of the Gospel', see ¶ 206).

The Qur'án refers to the Psalms three times as *Zabúr*. The scripture gives equal prominence to the Twarat (Torah), the Injil (Gospels), and the Qur'án: 'We did bestow on some prophets more (and other) gifts than on others: and We gave to David (the gift of) the Psalms' (17:55).

Az-Zubúr is the plural of *Zabúr* and refers to earlier scriptures (26:196).

647. p. 144 ¶ 208. Who will bring me into the Strong City?

This is a reference in the Psalms (108:10) to 'Akká. Bahá'u'lláh was forcefully banished to Zion as a prisoner of the Ottoman Empire. The Prophet Micah (7:7, 9, 12) traces the journeys and multiple banishments of Bahá'u'lláh from Persia to the Holy Land:

> In that day also he shall come even to thee from Assyria [Persia], and from the fortified cities [in several translations such as English Revised Version: 'cities of Egypt'; Bahá'u'lláh landed in Alexandria

> and Port Said], and from the fortress [other translations: 'from Egypt'] even to the river [the Riḍván Garden is a small island situated in the middle of Na'mayn river or Nahr Na'mein near 'Akká in north-western Israel], and from sea to sea [the Black Sea to the Mediterranean Sea], and from mountain to mountain [Sar-Galú mountain in Kurdistan to Mount Carmel in Israel].

The final place of banishment of Bahá'u'lláh was 'Akká, a penal colony of the Ottoman Empire. Because of its foul weather and dire conditions at that time, He was sent there to die, away from any prestigious centres where He could exert His influence. Notably, the Prophet Hosea (2:15) promised that Achor (lit. trouble) or 'Akká, a fortified city with a violent history, would become a gateway of optimism and aspiration:

> And I will give her her vineyards from thence, And the valley of Achor for a door of hope; And she shall respond there, as in the days of her youth, And as in the day when she came up out of the land of Egypt.

648. p. 144 ¶ 208. 'Akká

The following description of 'Akká is provided by Shoghi Effendi:

> 'Akká, itself, flanked by the 'glory of Lebanon', and lying in full view of the 'splendor of Carmel', at the foot of the hills which enclose the home of Jesus Christ Himself, had been described by David as 'the Strong City', designated by Hosea as 'a door of hope', and alluded to by Ezekiel as 'the gate that looketh towards the East', whereunto 'the glory of the God of Israel came from the way of the East', His voice 'like a noise of many waters'. To it the Arabian Prophet had referred as 'a city in Syria to which God hath shown His special mercy', situated 'betwixt two mountains . . . in the middle of a meadow', 'by the shore of the sea . . . suspended beneath the Throne', 'white, whose whiteness is pleasing unto God'. 'Blessed the man', He, moreover, as confirmed by Bahá'u'lláh, had declared, 'that hath visited 'Akká, and blessed he that hath visited the visitor of 'Akká'. Furthermore, 'He that raiseth therein the call to prayer, his voice will be lifted up unto Paradise'. And again: 'The poor of 'Akká are the kings of Paradise

and the princes thereof. A month in 'Akká is better than a thousand years elsewhere.' Moreover, in a remarkable tradition, which is contained in Shaykh Ibnu'l-'Arabí's work [1165–1240 CE], entitled 'Futúḥát-i-Makkíyyih', and which is recognized as an authentic utterance of Muḥammad, and is quoted by Mírzá Abu'l-Faḍl in his 'Fará'íd', this significant prediction has been made: 'All of them (the companions of the Qá'im) shall be slain except One Who shall reach the plain of 'Akká, the Banquet-Hall of God.'[777]

The arrival of Bahá'u'lláh in 'Akká marks the opening of the last phase of His forty-year long ministry, the final stage, and indeed the climax, of the banishment in which the whole of that ministry was spent. A banishment that had, at first, brought Him to the immediate vicinity of the strongholds of Shí'ah orthodoxy and into contact with its outstanding exponents, and which, at a later period, had carried Him to the capital of the Ottoman empire, and led Him to address His epoch-making pronouncements to the Sulṭán, to his ministers and to the ecclesiastical leaders of Sunní Islám, had now been instrumental in landing Him upon the shores of the Holy Land – the Land promised by God to Abraham, sanctified by the Revelation of Moses, honored by the lives and labors of the Hebrew patriarchs, judges, kings and prophets, revered as the cradle of Christianity, and as the place where Zoroaster, according to 'Abdu'l-Bahá's testimony, had 'held converse with some of the Prophets of Israel', and associated by Islám with the Apostle's night-journey, through the seven heavens, to the throne of the Almighty. Within the confines of this holy and enviable country, 'the nest of all the Prophets of God', 'the Vale of God's unsearchable Decree, the snow-white Spot, the Land of unfading splendor' was the Exile of Baghdád, of Constantinople and Adrianople condemned to spend no less than a third of the allotted span of His life, and over half of the total period of His Mission. 'It is difficult', declares 'Abdu'l-Bahá, 'to understand how Bahá'u'lláh could have been obliged to leave Persia, and to pitch His tent in this Holy Land, but for the persecution of His enemies, His banishment and exile.'[778]

649. p. 144 ¶ 208. the Most Great Prison

Shoghi Effendi wrote:

> His arrival at the penal colony of 'Akká, far from proving the end of His afflictions, was but the beginning of a major crisis, characterized by bitter suffering, severe restrictions, and intense turmoil, which, in its gravity, surpassed even the agonies of the Siyáh-Chál of Ṭihrán, and to which no other event, in the history of the entire century can compare, except the internal convulsion that rocked the Faith in Adrianople. 'Know thou', Bahá'u'lláh, wishing to emphasize the criticalness of the first nine years of His banishment to that prison-city, has written, 'that upon Our arrival at this Spot, We chose to designate it as the "Most Great Prison." Though previously subjected in another land (Ṭihrán) to chains and fetters, We yet refused to call it by that name. Say: Ponder thereon, O ye endued with understanding!'[779]

See also Annotations 227, 648 and 814.

650. p. 144 ¶ 209. Get thee up into the high mountain

This is a quotation from the Book of Isaiah (40:9):

> O Zion, that bringest good tidings, get thee up into the high mountain . . .

Isaiah reiterates:

> And it shall come to pass in the last days, that the mountain of the Lord's house shall be established in the top of the mountains, and shall be exalted above the hills; and all nations shall flow unto it.
>
> And many people [or 'many nations', that is other than Jews: Gentiles or *Goyim rabbim]* shall go and say, Come ye, and let us go up to the mountain of the Lord, to the house of the God of Jacob; and he will teach us of his ways, and we will walk in his paths: for out of Zion shall go forth the law, and the word of the Lord from Jerusalem. (2:2–3; see also Micah 4:1–3)

Again:

> How beautiful upon the mountains are the feet of him that bringeth good tidings, that publisheth peace; that bringeth good tidings of good, that publisheth salvation; that saith unto Zion, Thy God reigneth! (Is. 52:7)

651. p. 145 ¶ 209. Behold your God! Behold the Lord God will come with strong hand, and His arm shall rule for Him

This is the continuation of the above quotation from the Book of Isaiah (40:9–11) explaining that God, faithful to His promises, will bring the good tidings of His return to Zion. The proclamation that their God is come is to be announced from a mountain so that the joyful news can be heard by the inhabitants of the city or the land:

> Go on up to a high mountain, O Zion, herald of good news; lift up your voice with strength, O Jerusalem, herald of good news; lift it up, fear not; say to the cities of Judah, 'Behold your God!'
>
> Behold, the Lord God comes with might [King James Version: 'Behold, the Lord God will come with strong hand'], and his arm rules for him; behold, his reward is with him, and his recompense before him.
>
> He will tend his flock like a shepherd . . .
>
> All the nations are as nothing before him, they are accounted by him as less than nothing and emptiness. (Is. 40:9–11, 17)

652. p. 145 ¶ 209. This Day all the signs have appeared

This is a declaration of realized Christian eschatology. Amongst the prominent fulfilled prophecies of the Hebrew Bible and the New Testament is the date 1260 (AH) coinciding with 1844 (CE), and the return of the Jews to their homeland at the Second Coming following their dramatic dispersion at the First Coming of the Messiah (Christ) – this would occur after the Gospel had been preached to all nations, the darkening of the sun and the moon and the falling of the stars.[780]

653. p. 145 ¶ 209. A Great City hath descended from heaven

Bahá'u'lláh explains that the Holy City refers to God's Revelation:

> When the channel of the human soul is cleansed of all worldly and impeding attachments, it will . . . attain and enter the City of Certitude . . . How unspeakably glorious are the signs, the tokens, the revelations, and splendors which He, Who is the King of Names and Attributes, hath destined for that City! The attainment of this City quencheth thirst without water, and kindleth the love of God without fire . . . It bestoweth wealth without gold, and conferreth immortality without death . . .
>
> . . . Once in about a thousand years shall this City be renewed and re-adorned.
>
> . . . That City is none other than the Word of God revealed in every age and dispensation. In the days of Moses it was the Pentateuch; in the days of Jesus, the Gospel; in the days of Muḥammad, the Messenger of God, the Qur'án; in this day, the Bayán; and in the Dispensation of Him Whom God will make manifest, His own Book – the Book unto which all the Books of former Dispensations must needs be referred, the Book that standeth amongst them all transcendent and supreme.[781]

'Abdu'l-Bahá provides the following explanation of the verses:

> Verily, verily the new heaven and the new earth are come. The holy City, new Jerusalem, hath come down from on high in the form of a maid of heaven, veiled, beauteous, and unique, and prepared for reunion with her lovers on earth. The angelic company of the celestial Concourse have joined in a call that hath rung throughout the universe, all loudly and mightily acclaiming: 'Hail, O City of God! Abide Thou, and make Thy habitation with the pure, virtuous and holy servants of Thine; for they are Thy people, and Thou art their Lord.'
>
> He hath wiped away their tears, kindled their light, rejoiced their hearts and enraptured their souls. Death shall no more overtake them, neither shall sorrow, crying and tribulation afflict them. The

> Lord God Omnipotent hath been enthroned in His Kingdom and hath made all things new. This is the truth, and what truth greater than the Revelation of St. John the divine? He is the Alpha and Omega. He is the One that will give unto him that is athirst of the fountain of the water of life, and bestow upon the sick the remedy of true salvation. He whom such grace aideth is verily he that receiveth the most glorious heritage from the prophets of God and His holy ones. The Lord will be his God, and he His dearly-beloved son.[782]

> By 'that great city, the holy Jerusalem, descending out of heaven from God' is meant the holy Law of God, and this is set forth in many Tablets and still to be read in the Scriptures of the Prophets of the past: for instance, that Jerusalem was seen going out into the wilderness.[783]

In a vision of Ezekiel, a new city is built that will symbolize the centre of the Messianic Kingdom: 'and the name of the city from that day shall be, the Lord is there [*YHWH-shamma*]' (Ezek. 48:35). And the Psalms proclaim: 'Glorious things are spoken of thee, O city of God' (Ps. 87:2).

The Book of Revelation, written towards the end of the first Christian century, deals almost exclusively with the subject of the Second Coming. It speaks of the demise of the first heaven and the first earth, and their replacement by a new heaven and a new earth, and a new Jerusalem (21:1–3). God Himself will 'make all things new' (21:5), and will 'give unto him that is athirst to drink of the fountain of the water of life freely' (21:6).

The anticipated Dispensation would be associated with the presence of God's 'tabernacle' amongst men (21:3), and be given 'a new name' written on clean tablet, that is, unsullied by earlier traditional notions of faith. Those that overcome the spiritual difficulties of those days will witness the advent of the City of God, a new Jerusalem:

> I will write upon him the name of my God, and the name of the city of my God, which is new Jerusalem, which cometh down out of heaven from my God: and I will write upon him my new name. (3:12)

And:

> And he carried me away in the spirit to a great and high mountain, and shewed me that great city, the holy Jerusalem, descending out of heaven from God, Having the glory of God: and her light . . . (21:10–11)

Entrance to the City is promised to those who have heeded the divine call:

> Blessed are they that do his commandments, that they may have right to the tree of life, and may enter in through the gates into the city. (22:14–15)

The Book of Revelation also advises that the promised City will not require the light of earlier Dispensations (their spiritual and social principles) for illumination:

> And the city had no need of the sun, neither of the moon, to shine in it: for the glory of God ['Bahá'u'lláh' in Arabic] did lighten it . . .
>
> And the gates of it shall not be shut at all by day: for there shall be no night [no spiritual darkness due to the firmness of the new Covenant] there.
>
> And they shall bring the glory and honour of the nations into it.
>
> And there shall in no wise enter into it any thing that defileth, neither whatsoever worketh abomination, or maketh a lie. (21:23, 25–27)

Further, the followers of all religions, both high and low, will be judged by the content of their own scripture (Rev. 20:12).

The Lawḥ-i-Karmil (Tablet of Carmel) mentions 'the City of God that hath descended from heaven':

> Call out to Zion, O Carmel, and announce the joyful tidings: He that was hidden from mortal eyes is come! His all-conquering sovereignty is manifest; His all-encompassing splendour is revealed. Beware lest thou hesitate or halt. Hasten forth and circumambulate the City of God that hath descended from heaven, the celestial Kaaba round which have circled in adoration the favoured of God, the pure in heart, and the company of the most exalted angels.[784]

654. p. 145 ¶ 209. Zion trembleth

This is reminiscent of Joel 2:1, 10:

> Blow ye the trumpet in Zion, and sound an alarm in my holy mountain: let all the inhabitants of the land tremble: for the day of the Lord cometh, for it is nigh at hand . . . The earth shall quake before them; the heavens shall tremble.

Also, Isaiah 33:14 states that the sinners in Zion will be terrified and trembling will grip the godless. He promised (59:20): 'the Redeemer [God] shall come to Zion . . . ', and (66:2) that God will look to 'him that is poor and of a contrite spirit, and trembleth at my word [that fears me and reveres my commands]'. Isaiah rejoices:

> Then shall the lame man leap as an hart, and the tongue of the dumb sing: for in the wilderness shall waters break out, and streams in the desert.
>
> And the parched ground shall become a pool, and the thirsty land springs of water . . .
>
> And an highway shall be there, and a way, and it shall be called the way of holiness; the unclean shall not pass over it; but it shall be for those: the wayfaring men, though fools, shall not err therein . . .
>
> . . . the redeemed shall walk there:
>
> And the ransomed of the Lord shall return, and come to Zion with songs and everlasting joy upon their heads: they shall obtain joy and gladness, and sorrow and sighing shall flee away. (35:4–10)

Zephaniah gave the glad-tidings:

> Sing aloud, O daughter of Zion; shout, O Israel! Rejoice and exult with all your heart. (3:14)

Also Zechariah:

> Sing and rejoice, O daughter of Zion: for, lo, I come, and I will dwell in the midst of thee, saith the Lord. (2:10)

655. p. 145 ¶ 209 This Day Jerusalem hath attained unto a new Evangel

In the gospels 'Jerusalem' refers to God's Faith and in particular the Dispensation of Moses (Matt. 23:37). Both the Hebrew Bible (Ezek. 48:35) and the New Testament (Rev. 21:2) anticipate the advent of a 'new Jerusalem', also referred to as 'the Holy City'. The Prophet Isaiah announced the glad-tidings, as quoted in ¶ 209.

'Abdu'l-Bahá has written:

> This is a prophetic symbol, meaning the coming again of the Divine Teaching to enlighten the hearts of men . . . now, at last, the Holy City of the New Jerusalem has come again to the world . . .[785]

Again:

> . . . Jerusalem encompasses the reality of the religion of God, which is the Holy of Holies, as well as all the laws, mutual relationships, rites, and material ordinances, which constitute the city. That is why it is called the heavenly Jerusalem.[786]

The 'Evangel' of the First Coming consisted of the 'good news' of the advent of the Kingdom of the Father. The 'new Evangel' is the glad tiding that the Kingdom of God is now being established. Thus, Bahá'u'lláh has announced:

> The Breath hath been wafted, and the Breeze hath blown, and from Zion hath appeared that which was hidden, and from Jerusalem is heard the Voice of God, the One, the Incomparable, the Omniscient.[787]

Again:

> Call out to Zion, O Carmel and announce the joyful tidings: He that was hidden from mortal eyes is come! His all-conquering sovereignty is manifest . . .[788]

Bahá'u'lláh uses the term 'new Evangel' to refer to His evolving World

Order. In contrast, the Catholic Church has recently used a similar expression 'New Evangelization' to refer to a renewed general call to evangelization, to re-energize Christians who have fallen away, and to teach those who do not know Christ or who have always rejected Him.[789]

656. p. 145 ¶ 209. it hath heard the Voice of God on every side

The followers of all Dispensations have been praying for their Promised One, and today Bahá'u'lláh has addressed all humanity. 'Praise be to God', reveals 'Abdu'l-Bahá, 'for kindling the fire of divine love in the Holy Tree on the summit of the loftiest mount: that Tree which is "neither of the East nor of the West" (Qur'án 24:35).'[790]

The whole 'earth will shine with the Glory of her Lord' (Qur'án 39:69).

And the Hebrew Bible resonates with the glad tiding of His Voice. Whatever direction the seeker turns, he will be directed to God:

> Whether you turn to the right or to the left, your ears will hear a voice behind you, saying, 'This is the way; walk in it.' (Is. 30:21)

> Holy, holy, holy, is the Lord of hosts: the whole earth is full of his glory. (Is. 6:3)

> The voice of the Lord is upon the waters [many faiths]; The God of glory thundereth, The Lord is upon many waters. The voice of the Lord is powerful; yea, The voice of the Lord is full of majesty. (Is. 29:3–9)

The joy is evident in the Psalms:

> Make a joyful noise unto God, all ye lands: Sing forth the honour of his name: make his praise glorious . . . All the earth shall worship thee, and shall sing unto thee; they shall sing to thy name. (Ps. 66:1–2, 4)

> All the people praise thee. O let the nations [Jews and Gentiles, hence a reference to the end of times] be glad and sing for joy:

> for thou shalt judge the people righteously, and govern the nations upon earth . . . Let the people praise thee, O God; let all the people praise thee. (Ps. 67:3–5)

The prophet Ezekiel also announced:

> And, behold, the glory of the God of Israel was coming from the way of the east: and His voice was like a noise of many waters; and the earth shined with His glory. (Ezek. 43:2)

657. p. 145 ¶ 209. This Day Jerusalem hath attained unto a new Evangel

'Evangel' or Gospel (*Injil* in Arabic, referring to Christian scriptures in the Qur'án) is a term derived from the Greek *euangelion* which means good news. Christ was the good news of the Hebrew Bible and the fulfilment of the Messianic expectations of the Jews. The Jewish scriptures also gave good news of the coming of a universal Redeemer at the end of time. Christ referred to this good news as the coming of the Day of the Father. God has once again revealed His healing Message to mankind, and laid the foundations of His Kingdom on earth.

See also Annotation 310.

658. p. 145 ¶ 209. in the stead of the sycamore standeth the cedar

The Prophet Isaiah illustrates the concept of progressive revelation figuratively by portraying the divinely ordained social and spiritual evolution as improvements in the building blocks of faith:

> The bricks are fallen, but we will build with hewn stones. (Is. 9:10)

The following explanation is provided by the Bible scholar Albert Barnes:

> Bricks, in oriental countries, were made of clay and straw, and were rarely turned. Hence, exposed to suns and rains, they soon dissolved. Walls and houses constructed of such materials would not be

> very permanent, and to build with them is strongly contrasted with building in a permanent and elegant manner with hewn stone. The meaning is, that their former state was one of less splendor . . .[791]

For double emphasis, Isaiah goes on to state in the same vein:

> The sycamores are cut down, but cedars will we put in their place. (Is. 9:10)

Sycamore trees grew abundantly on the lowlands of Judea, and were very little esteemed (II Chron. 9:27). Cedar was a much more rare and precious wood that was smoother, more beautiful, and long-lasting. Zechariah spoke of the demise of faith, as the falling of the glorious and stately cedars:

> Howl, fir tree; for the cedar is fallen; because the mighty are spoiled: howl, O ye oaks of Bashan; for the forest of the vintage is come down.
>
> There is a voice of the howling of the shepherds; for their glory is spoiled . . . (Zech. 11:2–3)

Christ portrayed progressive revelation as a greater abundance of spiritual life: 'I am come that they might have life, and that they might have it more abundantly' (John 10:10).

I Cor 3:2 provides another figurative illustration of progressive revelation: 'I fed you with milk, not with meat; for ye were not yet able to bear it: nay, not even now are ye able.'

659. p. 145 ¶ 209. Jerusalem is the place of pilgrimage for all the peoples of the world

Jerusalem is a holy City for Jews, Christians and Muslims. It was where Abraham was about to sacrifice his son before being commanded by God not to do so. It was chosen by King David as his capital; his son Solomon built the Temple there. It is the city where Christ preached and was crucified. It is also where Muhammad came during his night journey and had a vision of God. The Al Aqsa Mosque, the third holiest place for Muslims, was built on the site of Solomon's Temple on the Temple Mount.

660. p. 145 ¶ 209. Blessed is the man that hath migrated to 'Akká

A hadith records:

> The Apostle of God – may the blessings of God and His salutations be upon Him – is reported to have said: 'Blessed the man that hath visited Akka, and blessed he that hath visited the visitor of Akka.'[792]

See also ¶ 59 and ¶ 265.

661. p. 145 ¶ 210. Amos

Amos (c. 750 BCE) was a simple and unlearned shepherd before He became a prophet.[793] He lived during a period of political stability and prosperity, accompanied by a collapse of moral standards. The great ideals and commandments of the Torah to help the poor, and to practise justice and loving-kindness, were ignored. The rich oppressed the poor; might was right; it was an age of corruption. The degeneration of the morals of the people and neglect of the divine law led to increased idolatry. People built many altars on mountains to serve the Canaanite gods, Baal and Ashtarte. The Golden Calves were worshipped more than before and the teachings of the Torah and the holy commandments were viewed with contempt. God sent several prophets, including Amos, to admonish the people and to warn them that unless they mended their ways, they and the land would be doomed. Yet the admonitions were, for the most part, unheeded. The people continued to go their own way. Amos is reputed to have been the first prophet to write down the divine messages he received. His major teaching concerned social justice.

662. p. 145 ¶ 210. The Lord will roar from Zion, and utter His Voice from Jerusalem; and the habitations of the shepherds shall mourn, and the top of Carmel shall wither

This statement follows the citation by Bahá'u'lláh of prophecies in the books of Psalms, Isaiah and Amos concerning 'Akká, Jerusalem, Palestine and Zion. It is a verse from Amos (1:2) and alludes to four consecutive Dispensations: Moses (Mount Zion is a hill in Jerusalem: it is a term used in the Hebrew Bible for the City of David); Jesus (uttered His Voice in Jerusalem); Muhammad (habitations of the shepherd: Muhammad was at one time a shepherd and used to meditate in the cave of Hirá on *Jabal an Nour*, the Mountain of Light), and Bahá'u'lláh (Zion is a synonym for Jerusalem as well as the Holy Land as a whole; Bahá'u'lláh designated Mount Carmel the administrative centre of His Cause in the Tablet of Carmel).

The statement is similar to Joel (3:16–17), attesting to the oneness of the mission of the two prophets – to prepare people for the coming judgements of God:

> The Lord also shall roar out of Zion, and utter his voice from Jerusalem; and the heavens and the earth shall shake: but the Lord will be the hope of his people, and the strength of the children of Israel.
> So shall ye know that I am the Lord your God dwelling in Zion, my holy mountain, then shall Jerusalem be holy . . .

663. p. 145 ¶ 210. Carmel, in the Book of God, hath been designated as the Hill of God, and His Vineyard

The word 'Carmel' means 'the vineyard of God'; it is derived from the Hebrew words *kerem*, which means vineyard, and *El*, which means God. A vineyard produces wine, which is a scriptural metaphor for divine Revelation. Both terms, the 'Hill of God' and the 'Mountain of God', have been used for Carmel and Zion by Bible translators. For example, Psalm 99:9 reads: 'Exalt the Lord our God, and worship at his holy hill [The New International Version and the English Standard Version: 'his holy mountain']; for the Lord our God is holy.'

See also Annotations 238 and 676.

664. p. 145 ¶ 210. His Vineyard

In the parable of the wicked tenants (Matt 21:33–46; Luke 20:9–16) God (the householder) has planted a vineyard (His Revelation) and when it is time to pick the fruit, He sends a series of servants (prophets) to the tenants who work in the vineyard. The tenants beat, stone and kill them. He then sends His Son (Jesus) who is also killed by the tenants. Thereafter Jesus explains that the Lord of the Vineyard (a reference to Bahá'u'lláh)[794] will come Himself, take away the vineyard from the tenants, and give it to others who will produce the fruit.

It is important to note that, despite all man's trespasses and evil, the Father does not destroy the earth but arranges for it to realize its full potential. Today Mount Carmel, the Biblical vineyard, is the site of the administrative centre of the Bahá'í Faith.

665. p. 145 ¶ 210. It is here that, by the grace of the Lord of Revelation, the Tabernacle of Glory hath been raised

The Tabernacle of Glory (*Shekinah*) refers to the dwelling or presence of God. God commands in the Torah (Ex. 25:8): 'let them make me a sanctuary; that I may dwell among them'. It also describes when for the first time the Lord came down and filled the tabernacle (Ex. 40:34–35). The Book of Revelation (21:3) promises that God will again dwell with men: 'And I heard a loud voice from the throne saying: "Behold, the dwelling place of God is with man, and He will live with them. They will be His people, and God Himself will be with them as their God."'

Notably, after the Báb's martyrdom in 1850 in Persia, His remains were brought to the Holy Land and have been placed in a shrine on Mount Carmel. Bahá'u'lláh visited Mount Carmel several times while still a prisoner of the Ottoman Empire, and revealed the Lawḥ-i-Karmil.

Simultaneously, a German evangelical Protestant sect, the Templers (no relationship to the Templar Crusaders), a splinter group from the Lutheran Church that was persecuted in its homeland, settled in the Holy Land at the urging of its leaders, Christoff Hoffman and David Hardegg, in anticipation of the Second Coming of Christ. They landed in Haifa in 1868 and built one of their colonies at the foot of Mount Carmel. The front of one of their buildings is engraved with a verse in German from Isaiah 60:1: 'Arise, shine, for thy light is come, and the glory of the Lord is risen upon thee.' Another has an inscription quoting Psalms 87:2: 'The Lord loveth the gates of Zion more than all the dwellings of Jacob.' Yet another inscription on a building dated 1871 reads: '*Der Herr ist nahe*' or 'The Lord is nigh'.

Bahá'u'lláh has announced: 'O thou who art waiting, tarry no longer, for He is come. Behold His Tabernacle and His Glory dwelling therein. It is the Ancient Glory, with a new Manifestation.'[795]

See also Annotations 44 and 63.

666. p. 145 ¶ 210. Our God will come, and He will not be silent

This refers to Psalms 50:2–4:

> Out of Zion, the perfection of beauty, God shines forth.
> Our God comes; he does not keep silence; before him is a devouring fire, around him a mighty tempest.
> He calls to the heavens above and to the earth, that he may judge his people.

The advent of Bahá'u'lláh, the Supreme Manifestation of God, is represented in the Bible not merely as the coming of another prophet but as the advent of God Himself and His Day. In spite of attempts to silence Him, Bahá'u'lláh voiced His summons to the civil and ecclesiastical rulers and to all humanity.

667. p. 145 ¶ 211. words addressed by Him Who is the Desire of the world to Amos

The 'Desire of the world' refers to the Divinity that is worshipped by all humanity. The phrase is similar to 'the Desire of all nations' which appears in the Book of Haggai (Hagg. 2:6–7, 9), and is a title of Bahá'u'lláh in the Bible, for He is the Promise of all Dispensations, and His Revelation addresses the needs of all humanity.

See also Annotations 56 and 480.

668. p. 145 ¶ 211. Prepare to meet thy God, O Israel, for, lo, He that formeth the mountains and createth the wind, and declareth unto man what is his thought

This is quoted directly from the Book of Amos (4:12–13). It is yet another scriptural reference to the coming of God Himself. It warns that humanity must acknowledge the supreme Manifestation of God and receive with all eagerness His advent.

669. p. 146 ¶ 211. the morning darkness

This appears in the continuation of the preceding quotation from Amos 4:13.

In one of His Tablets revealed in 'Akká, Bahá'u'lláh states that this prophecy refers to Him, that it concerns the year 80 (1280 AH, 1863 CE) and that the 'high places of the earth' are Constantinople (Istanbul) and the Holy Land (Mount Carmel).[796]

Isaiah (45:6–7) states:

> I am the Lord, and there is none else, there is no God beside me: I girded thee, though thou hast not known me:
>
> I form the light, and create darkness: I make peace, and create evil: I the Lord do all these things.

God in every Dispensation defines light, peace and salvation and in so doing simultaneously defines, and in a sense creates, darkness and evil. Today is the dawn of a new light, and opposition to it represents darkness. Also, the brilliance of the light today necessarily eclipses the light of earlier Dispensations.

A Bible commentatory provides the same explanation of the phrase 'the morning darkness':

> If the light become darkness, how great that darkness! From the knowledge of man's heart, the prophet goes on to retribution. Morning is the symbol of all which is beautiful, cheering, radiant, joyous to man; darkness effaces all these . . .
>
> Such was He, who made Himself 'their God', The Author of all, the Upholder of all, the Subduer of all which exalted itself, who stood in a special relation to man's thoughts, and who punished. At His command stand all the hosts of heaven. Would they have Him for them, or against them? Would they be at peace with Him, before they met Him, face to face?[797]

There is yet another consideration: 'alluding to Mírzá Yaḥyá's title Ṣubh-i-Azal (Morn of Eternity), [Bahá'u'lláh] asserts that through His power the untrue morn was completely darkened'.[798]

670. p. 146 ¶ 211. the Manifestation of Him Who conversed on Sinai

The Sermon of the Gulf by Imám 'Ali, *Al-Khutbah al-Tutunjiyyah*, states: 'anticipate ye then the Revelation of the Speaker of Mount Sinai. This will appear with manifest signs visible unto all, clearly perspicuous to them.'[799]

The 'Speaker' Who conversed with Moses on Mount Sinai was God. Bahá'u'lláh, Whose advent represents the coming of the Father and the Day of the Lord, is identified with the Supreme Manifestation of God.

See also Annotation 262.

671. p. 146 ¶ 211. woe unto such as follow him without a clear token from God

The Qur'án (17:36) admonishes: 'pursue not that of which thou hast no knowledge' and states (2:99, 6:57, 6:104) that for His part God manifests the truth of His Revelation through *áyát* (revealed verses, clear tokens, manifest signs, proofs, evidences). The *áyát* (verses) of the Qur'an (27:1) are from a book that is *mubeen* (a Revelation that makes it clear). However, the leaders of earlier Dispensations make statements and oppose God's Faith without any direction from God and by concealing the scriptures and passing over many things (Qur'án 5:15). Similarly, the New Testament states that individuals should not follow somebody who has no proof of the validity of what he states: 'Prove all things; hold fast that which is good' (I Thess. 5:21).

672. p. 146 ¶ 212. The Lord alone shalt be exalted in that day

This is a quotation from Isaiah (2:11, 17) which states that no secular or religious leader has the right to gainsay the Inaugurator of the anticipated Lord in His Day:

> The lofty looks of man shall be humbled, and the haughtiness of men shall be bowed down, and the Lord alone shall be exalted in that day.
>
> And the loftiness of man shall be bowed down, and the haughtiness of men shall be made low: and the Lord alone shall be exalted in that day.

673. p. 146 ¶ 212. Enter into the rock

A direct quotation from Isaiah 2:10–12: 'Enter into the rock, and hide thee in the dust, for fear of the Lord, and for the glory of his majesty.' The following explanation is offered by the Bible scholar Albert Barnes:

> *Enter into the rock* – That is, into the 'holes or caverns' in the rocks, as a place of refuge and safety . . . This expression is highly figurative and poetic. The prophet warns them to flee from danger. The sense is, that such were their crimes that they would certainly be punished; and he advises them to flee to a place of safety.
> *And hide thee in the dust* – this is 'caves of the dust'.
> *For fear of the Lord* – 'From the face of the terror of the Lord.' That is, the punishment which God will inflict will sweep over the land, producing fear and terror.
> *And for the glory . . .* – That is, the honor or splendor which will attend him when he comes forth to inflict judgment on the people.[800]

674. p. 146 ¶ 212. The wilderness and the solitary place shall be glad for them

This is a direct quotation from Isaiah 35:1–2:

> The wilderness and the solitary place [New International Version: desert and parched land] shall be glad for them; and the desert [New International Version: wilderness] shall rejoice, and blossom as the rose.
>
> It shall blossom abundantly, and rejoice even with joy and singing . . .

The phrase 'wilderness and the solitary place' is evidently meant figuratively and denotes a dry place, a place without springs and streams of water; as such places produce no verdure, and nothing to sustain life, the word comes to mean a desert. Such expressions are often used in the Scriptures to express dearth of divine teachings, and moral or spiritual desolation. In keeping with this prophecy and figurative interpretation, Isaiah also states:

> the poor and needy seek water, and there is none, and their tongue faileth for thirst, I the Lord will hear them . . . I will open rivers in high places, and fountains in the midst of the valleys: I will make the wilderness a pool of water, and the dry land springs of water. (41:17–18)

675. p. 146 ¶ 212. the glory of Lebanon . . . splendor of Carmel

This is a quotation from Isaiah 35:2:

> the glory of Lebanon shall be given unto it, the excellency of Carmel and Sharon, they shall see the glory of the Lord, and the excellency of our God.

Isaiah 60:13 reiterates:

> The glory of Lebanon shall come to you, the cypress, the plane, and the pine, to beautify the place of my sanctuary, and I will make the place of my feet glorious.

Symbolically, the Prophet sees in the New Jerusalem a revival of the glories of Solomon – the cedars of Lebanon and materials from different nations will adorn God's footstool. 'The place of my feet' refers to God's sanctuary.[801]

See also Annotation 238.

676. p. 146 ¶ 212. Carmel

Mount Carmel is where Elijah confronted and destroyed the 450 priests of Baal, and saved, through the miraculous power of the Lord God, Israel from gross idolatry (I Kings 18:1–40). The Hebrew Bible states that it is also on Mount Carmel that God will again reveal His Purpose, and this time, address all humanity. Shoghi Effendi has provided the following summary:

> Carmel is a mountain in the Holy Land characterized by Bahá'u'lláh as the 'Hill of God and His Vineyard', the home of Elijah, extolled by Isaiah as the 'mountain of the Lord' to which 'all nations shall flow'.[802]

See also Annotations 238 and 663.

677. p. 146 ¶ 212. Sharon

The Plain of Sharon is a roughly triangular region in Israel's Mediterranean coastal plain, stretching from the coast of Mount Carmel south towards Tel Aviv and bounded to the east by the Mount Carmel range and by the hills of Samaria.

678. p. 146 ¶ 212. the glory of the Lord

Hebrew prophecies speak of the advent of the 'Glory of the Lord [God]'. The Torah anticipated a time when 'all the earth shall be filled with the glory of the Lord' (Num. 14:21). In a vision, the Prophet Ezekiel was transported by God to the land of Israel and to a very high mountain. From this vantage point he had visions of the coming of the glory of the God of Israel from the east:

> Afterward he brought me to the gate, even the gate that looketh toward the east [literally, eastward looking gate of the court of priests, 'the Báb' in Arabic]
>
> And, behold, the glory of the God of Israel came from the way of the east; and His voice was like the sound of many waters [multiple Dispensations]; and the earth did shine with His glory.
>
> And the glory of the Lord came into the house by the way of the gate whose prospect is toward the east. (Ezek. 43:1–2, 4)

Isaiah prophesied (40:3–5):

> And the glory of the Lord shall be revealed, And all flesh shall see it together: for the mouth of the Lord hath spoken it. (Is. 40:5)

Predicting the glorious future that awaited Zion, he exhorted:

> Arise, shine; for thy light is come, and the glory of the Lord is risen upon thee.
>
> For, behold, the darkness shall cover the earth, and gross darkness

> the people: but the Lord shall arise upon thee, and his glory shall be seen upon thee. (Is. 60:1–2)

The Book of Habakkuk states:

> For the earth shall be filled with the knowledge of the glory of the Lord, as the waters cover the sea. (Hab. 2:14)

The New Testament also speaks of the Glory of God as being the source of the light of the Holy City[803] (new Dispensation) expected to descend from heaven (Rev. 21:10–11, 23–27).

See also ¶ 213.

679. p. 147 ¶ 213. follow not the doubts of such as shout aloud, who have broken the Covenant of God

Doubts have plagued every Dispensation, particularly the misgivings expressed by those who break God's Covenant. In the Dispensation of Muhammad, the Qur'án states:

> The Truth hath indeed come to thee from thy Lord: so be in no wise of those in doubt. (10:94)

And:

> The parable of those who reject Faith is as if one were to shout Like a goat-herd, to things that listen to nothing but calls and cries: Deaf, dumb, and blind, they are void of wisdom. (2:171)

Further:

> These are they who have bartered Guidance for error: But their traffic is profitless, and they have lost true direction,
>
> Their similitude is that of a man who kindled a fire; when it lighted all around him, God took away their light and left them in utter darkness. So they could not see.
>
> Deaf, dumb, and blind, they will not return (to the path). (2:16–18)

In the New Testament (John 20:24–29) the Apostle Thomas, known as 'doubting Thomas', refused to believe that Christ had appeared to the ten other disciples, until he could see and feel the holes in Christ's hands. The Lord urged him: 'Do not doubt but believe.'

Bahá'u'lláh emphasizes the importance of constancy and certitude of faith in the face of the doubts as to His Dispensation of those who have been untrue to the Covenant that God made with their prophets. The statement applies particularly to the disbelieving clergy and the Bábís who broadcasted their doubts about God's new Revelation from the pulpits. Bahá'u'lláh instructs: 'And be thou so steadfast in My love that thy heart shall not waver, even if the swords of the enemies rain blows upon thee and all the heavens and the earth arise against thee.'[804] He thus describes His true follower:

> He shall so persevere in the Cause of God, and evince such firmness in the path of His might, that even if all the powers of earth and heaven were to deny Him, He would not waver in the proclamation of His Cause, nor flee from His command in the promulgation of His Laws. Nay rather, He will stand as firm as the highest mountains and the loftiest peaks. He will remain immovable in His obedience to God and steadfast in revealing His Cause and proclaiming His Word. No obstacle will hinder Him, nor will the censure of the froward deter Him or the repudiation of the infidels cause Him to waver. All the hatred, the rejection, the iniquity, and the unbelief that He witnesseth serve but to strengthen His love for God, to augment the yearning of His heart, to heighten the exultation of His soul, and to fill His breast with passionate devotion.[805]

At the time of the passing of Bahá'u'lláh, the Centre of the Covenant wrote:

> O ye beloved of the Lord! Beware, beware lest ye hesitate and waver. Let not fear fall upon you, neither be troubled nor dismayed. Take ye good heed lest this calamitous day slacken the flames of your ardour, and quench your tender hopes. Today is the day for steadfastness and constancy. Blessed are they that stand firm and immovable as the rock, and brave the storm and stress of this tempestuous hour. They, verily, shall be the recipients of God's grace; they, verily, shall

> receive His divine assistance, and shall be truly victorious. They shall shine amidst mankind with a radiance which the dwellers of the Pavilion of Glory laud and magnify.[806]

680. p. 147 ¶ 214. Say to them that are of a fearful heart: be strong, fear not, behold your God

This is a quotation from Isaiah – almost the entire Chapter 35 (4–10) is devoted to the advent of the Glory of the Lord which will coincide with the redemption and the return of the dispersed Jews to their homeland.

681. p. 147 ¶ 214. the blast of the trumpet must needs spread confusion

Bahá'u'lláh explains that His Revelation, described in the Bible and the Qur'án as the blast of the trumpet, necessarily results in confusion. Indeed, the advent of every Manifestation of God is associated with disturbance, confusion and division because of the challenge the new Revelation poses to the old order. The upheavals are in part caused by the fact that old concepts are discarded and are replaced by new principles, which in turn results in a separation of communities into those who recognize, and those who oppose and deny the new Faith. The Qur'án describes the event thus:

> On that day there shall be a blast on the trumpet, and all that are in the heavens, and all that the on the earth shall be terror-stricken, save him whom God pleaseth to deliver; and all shall come to him in humble guise. (27:87, Rodwell)

See ¶ 192 and also Annotations 590 and 601.

682. p. 147 ¶ 214. trust and detachment

Led by Bahá'u'lláh, the Bábís imprisoned in the Síyáh-Chál chanted with great fervour:

> God is sufficient unto me; He verily is the All-sufficing! In Him let the trusting trust.[807]

These two qualities, Bahá'u'lláh states in the *Kitáb-i-Íqán*, are prerequisites to the recognition of the Manifestation of God:

> That seeker must at all times put his trust in God, must renounce the peoples of the earth, detach himself from the world of dust, and cleave unto Him Who is the Lord of Lords.[808]

They are necessary for success in service to Bahá'u'lláh:

> It behoveth whosoever willeth to journey for the sake of God, and whose intention is to proclaim His Word and quicken the dead, to bathe himself with the waters of detachment, and to adorn his temple with the ornaments of resignation and submission. Let trust in God be his shield, and reliance on God his provision, and the fear of God his raiment. Let patience be his helper, and praise-worthy conduct his succorer, and goodly deeds his army. Then will the concourse on high sustain him. Then will the denizens of the Kingdom of Names march forth with him, and the banners of Divine guidance and inspiration be unfurled on his right hand and before him.[809]

683. p. 147 ¶ 214. The tribulations of that Day will not hinder or alarm him

Acquisition of the qualities of 'trust and detachment' is essential for one's protection during the tribulations attending the Advent of the Day of God:

> Let the flame of the love of God burn brightly within your radiant hearts. Feed it with the oil of Divine guidance, and protect it within the shelter of your constancy. Guard it within the globe of trust and detachment from all else but God, so that the evil whisperings of the ungodly may not extinguish its light.[810]

684. p. 147 ¶ 214. It is now incumbent upon them who are endowed with a hearing ear and a seeing eye to ponder these

sublime words, in each of which the oceans of inner meaning and explanation are hidden

A hearing ear and a seeing eye are essential if the seeker is to fathom the many mysteries enshrined in the Revelation of Bahá'u'lláh. This in turn is only feasible if one renounces imitation and tradition, and focuses on the spiritual rather than the mundane. Bahá'u'lláh explains in the *Kitáb-i-Íqán*:

> they that thirst for the wine of certitude, must cleanse themselves of all that is earthly – their ears from idle talk, their minds from vain imaginings, their hearts from worldly affections, their eyes from that which perisheth. They should put their trust in God . . . Then will they be made worthy of the effulgent glories of the sun of divine knowledge and understanding . . . inasmuch as man can never hope to attain unto the knowledge of the All-Glorious . . . unless and until he ceases to regard the words and deeds of mortal men as a standard for the true understanding and recognition of God and His Prophets.[811]

'Abdu'l-Bahá taught the importance of raising people's awareness:

> The first remedy is to guide the people, so that they may turn unto God, hearken unto the divine commandments and go forth with a hearing ear and seeing eye . . .[812]

685. p. 148 ¶ 215. in the sayings of Him Who is the Spirit (Jesus) unnumbered significances lie concealed. Unto many things did He refer, but . . . He found none possessed of a hearing ear or a seeing eye

Christ, facing the difficult challenge of speaking to a people that lacked spiritual perception and receptivity, stated (Matt. 13:14–16):

> And in them is fulfilled the prophecy of Esaias, which saith, By hearing ye shall hear, and shall not understand; and seeing ye shall see, and shall not perceive:
>
> For this people's heart is waxed gross, and their ears are dull of

> hearing, and their eyes they have closed; lest at any time they should see with their eyes, and hear with their ears, and should understand with their heart, and should be converted, and I should heal them.
>
> But blessed are your eyes, for they see: and your ears, for they hear.

The Qur'án (2:171) similarly likens inviting the disbelievers to hearken to God's Revelation as the calling of a shepherd to sheep who hear only the sound of his voice and not the meaning of his call.

686. p. 148 ¶ 215. He chose to conceal most of these things

A reference to a statement that Christ made towards the end of His Ministry as recorded in the Gospel of John (see Annotation 687). He indicated that there were many truths that He had to conceal from His disciples because they were not ready for the teachings. These truths would be revealed at the Second Coming. Indeed, the Dispensation of Christ is characterized by the relative lack of specific commandments that must govern society. He had come not to establish the Kingdom of God on earth but to proclaim the good news of its advent. Today, Bahá'u'lláh has brought many of the social laws that Christ did not reveal because His disciples could not bear them two thousand years ago. These include the principle of the oneness of mankind (slavery is condoned in the Bible); the equality of women and men (women are taught to be subservient to men in the New Testament); and the declaration that 'the earth is but one country'[813] (the whole world had not been explored at the time of Christ).

687. p. 148 ¶ 215. But ye cannot bear them now . . . on that Day He Who is the Promised One will reveal the things which are to come . . . the Sublime Pen

These are the words of Christ recorded in the Gospel of John (16:12–13):

> I have yet many things to say unto you, but ye cannot bear them now.
>
> Howbeit when he, the Spirit of truth, is come, he will guide you into all truth . . . and he will shew you things to come.

Here Bahá'u'lláh asserts that He is the Promised One foretold by Christ, and He has revealed 'things to come'. He gives examples of some of His Writings and Tablets in which He accurately foretells future events, such as the fate of some of the world's rulers.

See also Annotation 686.

688. p. 148 ¶ 215. Dawning-Place of Revelation

This is a reference to Jesus as the Bearer of God's Revelation, but the title refers to all the Manifestations of God.

> The Person of the Manifestation hath ever been the representative and mouthpiece of God. He, in truth, is the Day Spring of God's most excellent Titles, and the Dawning-Place of His exalted Attributes.[814]

> Thou art He, O my God, Who hast summoned all men to turn in the direction of Thy mercy, and called them unto the horizon of Thy grace and bounties. None, however, heeded Thy call, except such as have forsaken all things save Thee, and hastened unto the Dayspring of Thy beauty, and the Dawning-Place of Thine inspiration and Thy revelation.[815]

'Abdu'l-Bahá explains:

> The Sun of Reality is one Sun but it has different dawning-places, just as the phenomenal sun is one although it appears at various points of the horizon.[816]

The Bible also states that God is the Source of all light, revelation and guidance (Gen. 1:3; Ps. 32:8; 86:11; 143:10; Heb. 1:1); for example: 'All Scripture is breathed out by God and profitable for teaching, for reproof, for correction, and for training in righteousness' (II Tim. 3:16).

Muhammad in the Qur'án (48:28) also states: 'It is He [God] Who has sent His Apostle with Guidance and the Religion of Truth, to proclaim it over all religion: and enough is God for a Witness.'

689. p. 148 ¶ 215. Lawḥ-i-Ra'ís

The Lawḥ-i-Ra'ís, which . . . contains passages directed to 'Álí Páshá, was revealed shortly after Bahá'u'lláh's incarceration in the citadel of 'Akká and includes a chilling denunciation of the character of the Minister . . . the Lawh-i-Fu'ád, revealed in 1869 shortly after the death of Fu'ád Páshá, the Ottoman Minister to whose machinations it refers, describes the spiritual consequences of the abuse of power, and foretells the imminent downfall of his colleague, 'Álí Páshá, and the overthrow of the Sulṭán himself –prophecies that were widely circulated and whose dramatic fulfilment added greatly to the prestige of their Author.[817]

Soon will He seize you in His wrathful anger, and sedition will be stirred up in your midst, and your dominions will be disrupted. Then will ye bewail and lament, and will find none to help or succour you.[818]

690. p. 148 ¶ 215. Lawḥ-i-Fu'ád

See above, Annotation 689; Bahá'u'lláh, *The Summons of the Lord of Hosts*, pp. 175–81; and Taherzadeh, *The Revelation of Bahá'u'lláh*, vol. 3, pp. 87–107.

691. p. 148 ¶ 216. O Land of Ṭá

Tehran is referred to as the 'the land of Ṭá' nine times in the Epistle. The English alphabet letter 'T' is represented by two letters in Arabic and Persian: Ṭá with an *abjad* numerical value of nine (equalling the numerical value of the word 'Bahá') and Te. Originally, Ṭehran was written with Ṭá but later the name was Persianized by changing the Ṭá to Te.[819]

692. p. 148 ¶ 216. God hath chosen thee to be the source of the joy of all mankind

Addressing the city of Tehran Bahá'u'lláh has written:

O Land of Ṭa! Thou art still, through the grace of God, a centre around which His beloved ones have gathered. Happy are they; happy every refugee that seeketh thy shelter, in his sufferings in the path of God, the Lord of this wondrous Day![820]

As soon as thine eyes behold from afar My native city (Ṭihrán), stand thou and say: I am come to thee out of the Prison, O Land of Ṭá, with tidings from God, the Help in Peril, the Self-Subsisting. I announce unto thee, O mother of the world and fountain of light unto all its peoples, the tender mercies of thy Lord, and greet thee in the name of Him Who is the Eternal Truth, the Knower of things unseen. I testify that within thee He Who is the Hidden Name was revealed, and the Unseen Treasure uncovered. Through thee the secret of all things, be they of the past or of the future, hath been unfolded.

O Land of Ṭá! He Who is the Lord of Names remembereth thee in His glorious station. Thou wert the Dayspring of the Cause of God, the fountain of His Revelation, the manifestation of His Most Great Name – a Name that hath caused the hearts and souls of men to tremble. How vast the number of those men and women, those victims of tyranny, that have, within thy walls, laid down their lives in the path of God, and been buried beneath thy dust with such cruelty as to cause every honoured servant of God to bemoan their plight.[821]

Shoghi Effendi thus describes the city of Tehran:

a city which, by reason of so rare a privilege conferred upon it, had been glorified by the Báb as the 'Holy Land', and surnamed by Bahá'u'lláh 'the Mother of the world', the 'Dayspring of Light', the 'Dawning-Place of the signs of the Lord', the 'Source of the joy of all mankind'.[822]

693. p. 148 ¶ 216. one who will rule with justice

Bahá'u'lláh's prediction about Tehran is recorded in the *Kitáb-i-Aqdas*:

Let nothing grieve thee, O Land of Ṭá, for God hath chosen thee to be the source of the joy of all mankind. He shall, if it be His Will, bless thy throne with one who will rule with justice, who will gather together the flock of God which the wolves have scattered . . .

> Rejoice with great joy, for God hath made thee 'the Dayspring of His light', inasmuch as within thee was born the Manifestation of His Glory.[823]

Notably, Bahá'u'lláh reminds the kings and rulers of the world of their duty: 'God hath committed into your hands the reins of the government of the people, that ye may rule with justice over them, safeguard the rights of the downtrodden, and punish the wrongdoers.'[824]

694. p. 148 ¶ 216. who will gather together the flock of God

The flock of God refers to humanity. Using this analogy, the Shepherd tending and guiding the flock is the Manifestation of God. Bahá'u'lláh states: 'Regard men as a flock of sheep that need a shepherd for their protection.'[825]

Christ saw the people of His time as 'sheep without a shepherd' (Mark 6:34). He also stated that God intends to unify the diverse flocks of mankind:

> And I have other sheep that are not of this fold. I must bring them also, and they will listen to my voice. So there will be one flock, one shepherd. (John 10:16)

The Hebrew Bible speaks of false shepherds who have misled humanity:

> My people have been lost sheep. Their shepherds have led them astray . . . They have forgotten their fold. (Jer. 50:6)

It explains that the Lord God is the true Shepherd:

> Behold, the Lord God will come with strong hand . . . He shall feed his flock like a shepherd . . . (Is. 40:10–11)

King David became a revered ruler and a true 'shepherd' of Israel (II Sam. 5:1–3). The Hebrew Bible anticipates the return of King David and the coming of the (One) Shepherd:

> Therefore will I save my flock, and they shall no more be a prey . . .
> And I will set up one shepherd over them, and he shall feed them, even my servant David; he shall feed them, and he shall be their shepherd.
> And I the Lord will be their God, and my servant David a prince among them . . . (Ezek. 34:22–24)

Notably, the New Testament anticipates the coming of the Chief Shepherd:

> And when the chief Shepherd shall appear, ye shall receive a crown of glory that fadeth not away. (I Peter 5:4)

695. p. 148 ¶ 216. which the wolves have scattered

Individuals who prey on humanity and scatter the flock (Jer. 23:1; John 10:12) are castigated as wolves. They often come in the guise of sheep, pretending to be of the faithful. Bahá'u'lláh addresses these individuals in the *Hidden Words*:

> O ye that are foolish, yet have a name to be wise! Wherefore do ye wear the guise of shepherds, when inwardly ye have become wolves, intent upon My flock? Ye are even as the star, which riseth ere the dawn, and which, though it seem radiant and luminous, leadeth the wayfarers of My city astray into the paths of perdition.[826]

The continued dispersion of the Persian believers to the four corners of the world, accelerated by their persecution by the clergy of the Islamic Republic of Iran, is an illustration of the scattering of the flock of God by wolf-like leaders.

696. p. 148 ¶ 216. These verses were revealed previously

As mentioned at the start of this paragraph, they were revealed in the *Kitáb-i-Aqdas*.

697. p. 149 ¶ 216. Bahá beseecheth Thee and imploreth Thee . . . to aid the Sháh

Bahá'u'lláh promises that the throne of Persia will be occupied by one who will rule with justice. Many of the prominent clergy were involved in undermining the rule of the Shah either directly, or indirectly by not providing him with sound advice. In particular, the Shaykh worked against the interests of king and country, which eventually led to his downfall. In contrast, Bahá'u'lláh prays for the Shah's welfare, and supplicates that God aid the monarch to be 'fair and equitable', perchance the Shah would be the king whose throne is blessed with authority and 'sovereignty'.

In the Kitáb-i-'Ahd Bahá'u'lláh exhorts His followers to pray also for the kings and rulers of the earth:

> O ye the loved ones and the trustees of God! Kings are the manifestations of the power, and the daysprings of the might and riches, of God. Pray ye on their behalf. He hath invested them with the rulership of the earth and hath singled out the hearts of men as His Own domain.[827]

698. p. 149 ¶ 216. Rejoice with great joy, O Land of Ṭá . . . for God hath made thee the dayspring of His light, inasmuch as within thee was born the Manifestation of His glory

Compare ¶ 215: 'O Land of Ṭá (Ṭihrán)! Let nothing grieve thee, for God hath chosen thee to be the source of the joy of all mankind.'

See also Annotations 691 and 692.

699. p. 150 ¶ 217. Neither is there a thing green nor sere, but it is noted in a distinct writing

This is a quotation from the Qur'án concerning the divine attributes 'the All-Knowing' and 'the All-Aware':

> And with Him are the keys of the secret things; none knoweth them but He: He knoweth whatever is on the land and in the sea; and no leaf falleth but He knoweth it; neither is there a grain in the

> darknesses of the earth, nor a thing green or sere [dry, withered], but it is noted in a Book with clear evidence in a distinct writing. (6:59, Rodwell)

Also:

> And the words of thy Lord are perfect in truth and in justice: none can change his words: He is the Hearing, Knowing.
>
> But if thou obey most men in this land, from the path of God will they mislead thee: they follow but a conceit, and they are only liars. (6:115–116, Rodwell)

Bahá'u'lláh's Revelation is from the All-Knowing. He points out here that if the Shaykh would read His Writings with fairness and honesty he would readily agree that they contain prophecies of future events, such as the final outcome of the monarchs who were recipients of His Tablets.

700. p. 150 ¶ 218. He, verily, hath manifested that which was hidden, when He, upon His return, mounted the throne of the Bayán

An allusion to the return of Bahá'u'lláh from Kurdistan to Baghdad (19 March 1856) after an absence of two lunar years, when it became clear that He was the One alluded to in the Báb's Writings. Shoghi Effendi writes of this:

> Now at last, in spite of Bahá'u'lláh's reluctance to unravel the mystery surrounding His own position, the Bábís found themselves able to centre both their hopes and their movements round One Whom they believed (whatever their views as to His station) capable of insuring the stability and integrity of their Faith. The orientation which the Faith had thus acquired and the fixity of the centre towards which it now gravitated continued, in one form or another, to be its outstanding features, of which it was never again to be deprived . . .
>
> The ascendancy achieved by Bahá'u'lláh was nowhere better demonstrated than in His ability to broaden the outlook and transform the character of the community to which He belonged. Though Himself nominally a Bábí, though the provisions of the Bayán were still regarded as binding and inviolable, He was able to inculcate a

standard which, while not incompatible with its tenets, was ethically superior to the loftiest principles which the Bábí Dispensation had established. The salutary and fundamental truths advocated by the Báb, that had either been obscured, neglected or misrepresented, were moreover elucidated by Bahá'u'lláh, reaffirmed and instilled afresh into the corporate life of the community, and into the souls of the individuals who comprised it. The dissociation of the Bábí Faith from every form of political activity and from all secret associations and factions; the emphasis placed on the principle of non-violence; the necessity of strict obedience to established authority; the ban imposed on all forms of sedition, on back-biting, retaliation, and dispute; the stress laid on godliness, kindliness, humility and piety, on honesty and truthfulness, chastity and fidelity, on justice, toleration, sociability, amity and concord, on the acquisition of arts and sciences, on self-sacrifice and detachment, on patience, steadfastness and resignation to the will of God – all these constitute the salient features of a code of ethical conduct to which the books, treatises and epistles, revealed during those years, by the indefatigable pen of Bahá'u'lláh, unmistakably bear witness.[828]

701. p. 151 ¶ 220. Behold ye Him with His own eyes. Were ye to behold Him with the eyes of another, ye would never recognize and know Him

Scholars and religious leaders are apt to evaluate the truth of a new Dispensation by their own limited understanding. Thus the Pharisees objected to the Revelation of Christ although the Prophet Isaiah had warned:

> Remember ye not the former things, neither consider the things of old.
>
> Behold, I will do a new thing; now it shall spring forth; shall ye not know it? I will even make a way in the wilderness, and rivers in the desert. (Is. 43:18–19)

Similarly, the Christians rejected the Revelation of Muhammad by ignoring the declaration of God in the Book of Revelation (21:5) that He shall 'make all things new'.

The Báb stated that 'divine acceptance can in no wise be achieved except through the acceptance of Him Who is the Exponent of His Revelation'.[829] Furthermore, He imposed limits on His own Dispensation:

> the Bayán shall constitute God's unerring balance till the resurrection which is the Day of Him Whom God will make manifest [Bahá'u'lláh].[830]

He warned:

> in the Day of the appearance of Him Whom God shall make manifest a thousand perusals of the Bayán cannot equal the perusal of a single verse to be revealed by Him Whom God shall make manifest.[831]

Bahá'u'lláh, quoting the Báb, admonishes individuals that His Dispensation must also be understood through the perspective of a new Revelation. He elaborates:

> Among them also were those who inquired of the darkness about the light. Say: Open thine eyes, that thou mayest behold the brightness which hath visibly enveloped the earth! This, verily, is a light which hath risen and shone forth above the horizon of the Dayspring of divine knowledge with manifest radiance. Would ye ask the Jews whether Jesus was the True One from God, or the idols if Muhammad was an Apostle of His Lord, or inquire from the people of the Qur'án as to Him Who was the Remembrance of God [the Báb], the Most Exalted, the Most Great?[832]

702. p. 151 ¶ 220. The year-old germ that holdeth within itself the potentialities of the Revelation that is to come is endowed with a potency superior to the combined forces of the whole of the Bayán

In this statement from the Persian *Bayán* (VII:15) the Báb alludes to the as yet unrealized creative power of Bahá'u'lláh's Revelation. He also writes:

> By the righteousness of Him Whose power causeth the seed to germinate and Who breatheth the spirit of life into all things . . .[833]

> Today the Bayán is in the stage of seed; at the beginning of the manifestation of Him Whom God shall make manifest its ultimate perfection will become apparent . . . Ere nine will have elapsed from the inception of this Cause the realities of the created things will not be made manifest. All that thou hast as yet seen is but the stage from the moist-germ until We clothed it with flesh. Be patient until thou beholdest a new creation. Say: Blessed, therefore, be God, the Most Excellent of Makers![834] (See also Annotation 704)

> Well is it with him who fixeth his gaze upon the Order of Bahá'u'lláh, and rendereth thanks unto his Lord. For He will assuredly be made manifest. God hath indeed irrevocably ordained it in the Bayán.[835]

The process of human development from conception is used as a metaphor for the stages of the maturation of humanity in recognizing the new Manifestation. It is a reference to the following verses in the Qur'án:

> Now of fine clay have we created man:
> Then we placed him, a moist germ, in a safe abode;
> Then made we the moist germ a clot of blood [in some translations, 'a clot of clay']: then made the clotted blood into a piece of flesh; then made the piece of flesh into bones: and we clothed the bones with flesh: then brought forth man of yet another make – Blessed therefore be God, the most excellent of Makers. (23:12–14, Rodwell)

703. p. 152 ¶ 221. The whole of the Bayán is only a leaf amongst the leaves of His Paradise

The Báb here alludes to the Revelation of Bahá'u'lláh. Shoghi Effendi in *God Passes By* brings together several statements of the Báb in this vein.[836] Bahá'u'lláh repeats this quotation later in the Epistle (see Annotation 726).

As revealed in the Epistle, this passage is not found in the available published Writings of the Báb. However, as an approximation, the Persian *Bayán* (VIII:15) states that if believers marry, their offspring who recognize Him Whom God shall make manifest will become leaves of paradise, otherwise they may become leaves consigned to the Fire.

Also, the following:

> There is no paradise, in the estimation of the believers in the Divine Unity, more exalted than to obey God's commandments, and there is no fire in the eyes of those who have known God and His signs, fiercer than to transgress His laws and to oppress another soul, even to the extent of a mustard seed. On the Day of Resurrection God will, in truth, judge all men, and we all verily plead for His grace.[837]

704. p. 152 ¶ 222. Ere nine will have elapsed from the inception of this Cause, the realities of the created things will not be made manifest . . . Be patient, until thou beholdest a new creation. Say: 'Blessed, therefore, be God, the most excellent of Makers!'

This is a statement of the Báb that is recorded in a Tablet addressed to Mulla 'Abdu'l-Karím Qazvíní, a secretary of the Báb, also called Mírzá Aḥmad Kátib ('the Scribe') or Mírzá Aḥmad Qazvíní. He and his brother 'Abdu'l-Hamid were imprisoned in the Síyáh-Chál with Bahá'u'lláh and were both martyred by being hacked to pieces with swords by the artillerymen of the royal bodyguard.[838]

The Báb several times mentions the 'year nine' as the date for the coming of 'Him Whom God shall make manifest'. The Báb's Mission began in the year 1260 AH (1844 CE). The 'year nine' was 1269 AH when Bahá'u'lláh was confined for two months in the Síyáh-Chál of Tehran, and received the first intimations of His Divine Mission.

See also Annotations 629, 634 and 702.

705. p. 152 ¶ 222. Lawful is it for Him Whom God will make manifest to reject him who is greatest on earth

This statement of the Báb is also quoted by Bahá'u'lláh in the Kalímát-i-Firdawsíyyih (Words of Paradise):

> Were the Point of the Bayán present in this day and should He, God forbid, hesitate to acknowledge this Cause, then the very blessed words which have streamed forth from the wellspring of His Own Bayán would apply to Him. He saith, and His word is the truth, 'Lawful is it for Him Whom God will make manifest to reject him who is the greatest on earth.' Say, O ye that are bereft of understanding! Today that Most Exalted Being is proclaiming: 'Verily, verily, I

am the first to adore Him.' How shallow is the fund of men's knowledge and how feeble their power of perception. Our Pen of Glory beareth witness to their abject poverty and to the wealth of God, the Lord of all worlds.[839]

706. p. 152 ¶ 222. After Ḥín

The numerical *abjad* of Ḥin is 68, meaning after the year 1268 AH. See Annotations 629 and 634 for explanations provided by Shoghi Effendi, and also Annotation 704.

707. p. 153 ¶ 222. Know thou with absolute certainty . . . that He . . . maketh each thing to be known through its own self; who then can know Him through any one except Himself?

This is from a statement of the Báb[840] to Mullá Báqir Tabrízí, the thirteenth Letter of Living (see Annotations 727 and 797 for further information about him). The *Bayán* states:

> No creature hath ever recognized Him [God] as befitteth His recognition, nor hath any created being ever praised Him as is worthy of His praise. Through Him all things are made known, while too lofty is His reality to be known through anyone but Him.[841]

Bahá'u'lláh, as His Manifestation, will only be known through Himself.

708. 153 ¶ 222. Beware, beware lest, in the days of His revelation, the Váḥid of the Bayán (eighteen Letters of the Living) shut thee not out as by a veil from Him

This is also from a statement of the Báb to Mullá Báqir Tabrízí, the thirteenth Letter of the Living, warning that none of His disciples should become a barrier to recognizing 'He whom God shall make manifest'.

709. p. 153 ¶ 222. the Váḥid of the Bayán

This refers to the Báb and eighteen of His early disciples, whom He named the Letters of the Living (*Ḥurúf-i-Ḥayy*). 'The Living' (*al-Ḥayy*) is one of the names of God (Jer. 10:10; Matt. 16:16; Qur'án 2:255). The numerical value of *Ḥayy* and *Váḥid* is 19. A list of the Letters of the Living is provided by the historian Nabíl.[842]

710. p. 153 ¶ 222. And beware, beware that the words sent down in the Bayán shut thee not out as by a veil from Him

These words of the Báb addressed to Mullá Báqir Tabrízí warn the Bábís that nothing in His Writings should be made the reason for rejecting the Revelation of Bahá'u'lláh. Indeed, the Báb directed His followers to read this particular verse every nineteen days so that when 'He Whom God shall make manifest' appeared, they would not fail to recognize Him (see Annotation 724).

711. p. 153 ¶ 222. Look not upon Him with any eye except His own

This is from a Tablet of the Báb addressed to Mullá Báqir Tabrízí and to Siyyid Yaḥyá Dárábí (surnamed *Vaḥíd Akbar* – the great peerless one – by the Báb).[843]

See also Annotation 701.

712. p. 153 ¶ 222. Better is it for thee to recite but one of the verses of Him Whom God shall make manifest than to set down the whole of the Bayán

This is from the *Bayán* (V:8) eulogizing Bahá'u'lláh's Revelation. Also quoted by Shoghi Effendi.[844]

713. p. 154 ¶ 224. I, verily, am a believer in Him

This is from a letter addressed to Mullá Báqir Tabrízí (see Annotations 707, 708, 710, 711, 727 and 797).

714. p. 154 ¶ 224. O congregation of the Bayán . . . Recognize ye the limits imposed upon you, for such a One as the Point of the Bayán Himself hath believed in Him Whom God shall make manifest, before all things were created

A statement of the Báb to all His followers warning them of the limitations of the Revelation that He had entrusted to them, and that He Himself had been a believer in 'Him Whom God shall make manifest' from the beginning.[845]

715. pp. 154–5 ¶ 225. Suffer not yourselves to be shut out as by a veil from God after He hath revealed Himself. and I Myself am, verily, but a ring upon the hand of Him Whom God shall make manifest . . .

This continues the quotation in ¶ 224.[846] *Kh͟átam* means ring, ornament, or jewel. A different pronunciation, *kh͟átem*, means the 'ender' as in the 'Seal of the Prophets'.

716. p. 155 ¶ 225. Were He to make of every one on earth a Prophet, all would, in very truth, be accounted as Prophets in the sight of God . . . For the will of God can in no wise be revealed except through His will, nor His wish be manifested save through His wish

This is a quotation from the Arabic *Bayán* (VII:5) indicating that in the next Dispensation, God's Will shall be manifested through Bahá'u'lláh. Compare:

> In confirmation of the exalted rank of the true believer, referred to by Bahá'u'lláh, He reveals the following: 'The station which he who hath truly recognized this Revelation will attain is the same as the one ordained for such prophets of the house of Israel as are not regarded as Manifestations 'endowed with constancy.'[847]

717. p. 155 ¶ 225. In the day of the revelation of Him Whom God shall make manifest all that dwell on earth will be equal in His estimation

This is from a letter addressed to Mullá Báqir Tabrízí. It is a declaration that the principle of the oneness of mankind will be a major theme of the Revelation of Bahá'u'lláh.

718. p. 156 ¶ 227. He – glorified be His mention – resembleth the sun. Were unnumbered mirrors to be placed before it, each would, according to its capacity, reflect the splendor of that sun . . .

This passage is quoted by Bahá'u'lláh in the Kitáb-i-Badí'. The Báb warns the mirrors that they must face the Sun of Truth, which will continue to shine even if the mirrors are 'veiled from its light'.[848]

719. p. 156 ¶ 227. mirrors

The Báb had bestowed the title 'Mirror' of His Dispensation upon several of His followers, including Mírzá Yaḥyá. The designation was not supposed to be taken as a badge of honour and authority but as an indication of a duty to arise and mirror the light of the Sun of Bahá'u'lláh's Revelation.

See also Annotations 364, 718, 738, 739, 743 and 783.

720. p. 156 ¶ 228. They will even refuse unto that Tree, which is neither of the East nor of the West, the name believer

Bahá'u'lláh here points out that the enmity of some of the disciples of the Báb towards 'He whom God shall make manifest' was such that they would not even admit that He was a believer. This is reminiscent of the verse of the Qur'án (4:95) forbidding Muslims from condemning others as unbelievers (*takfir*) without proper investigation.

Christ had stated that it is the fruits that define a tree:

> Ye shall know them by their fruits. Do men gather grapes of thorns, or figs of thistles?

> Even so every good tree bringeth forth good fruit; but a corrupt tree bringeth forth evil fruit.
>
> A good tree cannot bring forth evil fruit, neither can a corrupt tree bring forth good fruit.
>
> Every tree that bringeth not forth good fruit is hewn down, and cast into the fire.
>
> Wherefore by their fruits ye shall know them. (Matt. 7:16–20)

He had also stated that the Heavenly Father is merciful to all humanity (Matt. 5:45): 'he maketh his sun to rise on the evil and on the good, and sendeth rain on the just and on the unjust.' The Qur'án states similarly that God's blessed tree has its roots firmly fixed and its branches reach to the sky, and that in every Dispensation it yields its spiritual fruits (14:24) – this divine tree does not favour the East or the West (24:35). Hence, the Bábís were expected to judge the Tree of Bahá'u'lláh's Revelation by its wonderful fruits, by its universality and by its transformative power.

721. p. 157 ¶ 229. For none knoweth the time of the Revelation except God

The Báb referred to 'He whom God shall make manifest', as the *Mustaghá<u>th</u>* ('He Who is invoked') – the inaugurator of the Latter Resurrection, i.e. the Advent of Bahá'u'lláh.[849] Numerically, the letters of *Mustaghá<u>th</u>* add up to 2001 according to the *abjad* reckoning – assumed by some to be the limit of time assigned by the Báb for the advent of the Promised One. With these words of the Báb, Bahá'u'lláh refutes the claims of certain Bábís who claimed that the Promised One would not appear until 2001.

There are many signs and allusions to the timing of the advent of Christ in the Dispensation of Moses but the Jews failed to perceive their true meaning. Similarly, despite many signs describing the Second Coming in the Gospels, including its timing (1260 AH or 1844 CE), most Christians have failed to recognize the Faith of Bahá'u'lláh. In part, this has been because the religious leaders have tried to interpret the prophecies through their limited understanding, despite the clear warnings of the New Testament (Acts 1:7): 'Jesus replied, "It is not for you to know the times or the seasons, which the Father hath put in his own power.' Again (I Thess. 5:2 and II Peter 3:10): 'For yourselves know perfectly that the day of the Lord so cometh as a thief in the night.'

The Qur'án (3:7) also warns that the explanation of the abstruse parts of the Revelation, such as the timing of the Day of Resurrection, belongs to God: 'no one knows its hidden meanings except God . . .' Similarly, in spite of the allusions in the Writings of the Báb to the fact that nine years will separate His Dispensation from that of 'Him Whom God shall make manifest', some of the Bábís, like the followers of John the Baptist, objected to the timing of Bahá'u'lláh's Dispensation. In a Tablet addressed to 'Him Who will be made manifest' the Báb wrote:

> Shouldst Thou dismiss the entire company of the followers of the Bayán in the Day of the Latter Resurrection by a mere sign of Thy finger even while still a suckling babe, Thou wouldst indeed be praised in Thy indication. And though no doubt is there about it, do Thou grant a respite of nineteen years as a token of Thy favour so that those who have embraced this Cause may be graciously rewarded by Thee. Thou art verily the Lord of grace abounding.[850]

The Declaration of Bahá'u'lláh in Baghdad occurred at the end of nineteen lunar years from the time of the Declaration of the Báb.

See also Annotations 629 and 639.

722. p. 157 ¶ 229. the followers of John (the Baptist)

There are striking similarities between the advents of John the Baptist, the Forerunner of Christ, and the Báb, the Forerunner of Bahá'u'lláh.

The last lines and verses of Malachi (4:5–6), the final book of the Tanakh, indicate that the Prophet Elijah will return from heaven 'before the coming of the great and terrible day of the Lord', and restore the broken relationship of the older and newer generations. His followers believed that John the Baptist was the Prophet Elijah who had returned after having been transported to heaven in a fiery chariot several centuries earlier. They had their own teachings and rituals which were different from the disciples of Christ. However, to the dismay of his followers, the earthly life of John the Baptist was brief; he was beheaded by King Herod.

Many Bábís believed that the Dispensation of the Báb, the Promised

Qá'im, would last much longer than it did. They objected to their practices being abrogated so soon after the martyrdom of their leader, similar to the disciples of John (Matt. 9:14): 'Then came to him the disciples of John, saying, Why do we and the Pharisees fast oft, but thy disciples fast not?'

The Bible records that when John the Baptist languished in the prison of Herod, he asked his bewildered disciples to investigate the truth of Christ for themselves (Matt 11:2–3): 'Now when John had heard in the prison the works of Christ, he sent two of his disciples, And said unto him, Art thou he that should come, or do we look for another?' This passage has been interpreted by some Christian scholars as indicating that John the Baptist had last-minute doubts. However, a more likely interpretation is that John the Baptist did not have concerns about his own mission and future, otherwise he would have recanted and not been martyred for his faith. Rather, the indirect dialogue between John and Jesus was intended to allay the fears of his disciples and to convert their doubt into certitude.

The Gospel of Luke (1:41) records that when Elisabeth, John's mother and the cousin of Mary, Jesus's mother, came to visit and 'heard the salutation of Mary, the babe leaped in her womb; and Elisabeth was filled with the Holy Ghost'. John expressed his humility when He baptized Jesus. In turn, Christ (Luke 1:17) acknowledged that John exhibited the spirit and power of the Prophet Elijah, and there had not been anyone as great as his predecessor. Through the teachings of John the Baptist many came to accept Christ:

> And many resorted unto him, and said, John did no miracle: but all things that John spake of this man were true.
>
> And many believed on him there. (John 10:41–42)

However, many of the followers of John the Baptist failed to recognize Jesus as the Messiah. They not only had their differences with the Jews but resented the increasing popularity and influence of Christ:

> Then there arose a question between some of John's disciples and the Jews about purifying.
>
> And they came unto John, and said unto him, Rabbi, he that was with thee beyond Jordan, to whom thou barest witness, behold,

the same baptizeth, and all men come to him.

John answered and said, A man can receive nothing, except it be given him from heaven.

Ye yourselves bear me witness, that I said, I am not the Christ, but that I am sent before him. (John 3:25–28)

There are still a few followers of John the Baptist today in southern Iraq and south-western Iran who practise a Gnostic religion called Sabean-Mandaeism or simply Mandaeism. Their numbers are dwindling because of persecution and the fact that they do not accept converts. Some have emigrated to Jordan, Syria, Australia and the United States. Mandaeism has an extensive scripture and expresses belief in one God and several but not all of the Jewish prophets. Their scripture describes the Prophet Yaḥyá ibn Zakariyya (John the Baptist), known also as Enosh-Uthra, the 'good man', as having come in the days of Pilate, healed the sick, gave sight to the blind, and raised the dead. They continue to practise the ritual of baptism in the Tigris to purify both their body and our soul. Before starting with the ritual in the Tigris, they recite a passage of the *Ginza*, the Mandaeans' sacred book.

723. p. 158 ¶ 229. eighth Chapter of the sixth Váḥid

The Persian *Bayán* or *Bayán-i-Farsí* is the principal work of the Báb which He wrote while imprisoned in Máh-Kú (1847/1848). The Báb also wrote a smaller Arabic *Bayán*. The Persian *Bayán* was originally intended to comprise nineteen sections (*váḥids* or unities: the numerical value of *váḥid* is 19) each consisting of 19 chapters (in Arabic, *báb*). The Báb completed nine and intended that the remaining revelation be completed by 'Him Whom God shall make manifest'. The *Kitáb-i-Íqán* represents that completion.[851]

724. p. 158 ¶ 229. Once every nineteen days this Chapter should be read

The Persian *Bayán* has not been officially translated in its entirety. The translation of Edward G. Browne of the 'eighth báb of the sixth váhid' begins as follows:

He who seeks to bring proofs from other than the book of God and the verses of the Bayán, the like of which none are able to produce, it is no argument from him: and he who recounteth a miracle other than the verses of the Bayan, has no witness for it. But he who assumes to produce (revealed) verses, none should oppose him. You must read this chapter once every 19 days, and ponder on that which has revealed by night and day, that perchance ye may not be veiled from Him whom God shall manifest by states other than the (revealed) verses.

After the cessation of the [Islamic] revelation, till the manifestation of these verses, no one appeared to produce revealed verses. And you have not so much sagacity as to see that none but God can reveal verses. Know therefore that this is the same Primal Reality to whom God revealed verses in the beginning of Islám. If ye had understood the proof of your own religion, you would also have understood this Dispensation. Just as from the time of Muḥammad until now, which is 1270 years, no one has been able to produce verses like it, so after the setting of this sun will it be, till He who God shall manifest shall appear. It is impossible for anyone other than He who God shall manifest can claim to this Matter . . .[852]

725. p. 158 ¶ 230. John, son of Zacharias

This is a reference to John the Baptist who, according to the Bible, was the forerunner of Jesus and expressed his humility towards Christ (Matt. 3:1–3, 11).

726. p. 158 ¶ 230. The whole of the Bayán is only a leaf amongst the leaves of His Paradise

Bahá'u'lláh states here that His Forerunner, the Báb, showed a similar submissiveness and humility towards His Revelation. This quotation from the Báb is referenced by Shoghi Effendi in *God Passes By*, p. 30.

See also Annotation 703.

727. p. 158 ¶ 230. I am the first to adore Him, and pride Myself on My kinship with Him

This passage is from a letter of the Báb addressed to the thirteenth Letter of Living, Mullá Báqir Tabrízí, in reply to his question about 'Him Whom God will make Manifest'. The Tablet begins:

> In the Name of God, the Transcendent, the Most Holy. Praised be to God, no god is there except Him, the Mighty, the Beloved One. The Splendour (*Bahá*) which cometh from God (*al-bahámin*) – exalted be His Remembrance – be upon Him Whom God shall make manifest – exalted be His command – and upon whomsoever is created through His command, for naught can be seen in Him except what God hath caused to be manifested unto Him, through Him, by virtue of His Utterance, 'Verily, no God is there save Him, the Help in Peril, the Self-Subsisting.'[853]

The kinship of the Báb and Bahá'u'lláh is demonstrated by the fact that they are referred to as the 'Twin Manifestations' of God. 'Abdu'l-Bahá explains that 'all [the peoples of the world] are promised two Manifestations, Who will come one following on the other'.[854]

See also Annotations 635, 707–713 and 797.

728. p. 158 ¶ 230. Dhi'l-Jawshan

Shimr bin Dhi'l-Jawshan (*jawshan* means armour – he was the second Arab to wear this) was chief of an Arab tribe and an early believer and member of a select group of Muslims (*Tabi'un*) who had met with one or more of the disciples of Muhammad (the *Sahaba*). He was a respected judge and learned man of Kufah known for his piety, as exemplified by his removing thorns in the desert so that they would not hurt the feet of any Muslim. He was initially one of the companions of Imám 'Alí and participated in the Battle of Siffin between the Imám and Mu'awiya (657 CE). When the forces of Mu'awiya were about to be defeated, they resorted to the ruse of putting copies of the Qur'án on the tips of their spears, and thus discouraged part of Imám 'Alí's army from attacking a side that clearly had the Qur'án and believed in Muhammad's Revelation. He later became an enemy of Imám 'Alí and a fierce opponent of Imám Ḥusayn.

In 680 CE Shimr arrived in Karbila as a commander in the army of Caliph Yazid, the son of Mu'awiya, that fought the vastly outnumbered army of Imám Ḥusayn. His soldiers shot the Imám with several arrows, following which Shimr allegedly decapitated him and rode his horse over the body. Members of the Imám's family, including his six-month-old son, were martyred. The Imám's head and those of seventy-two of his followers were mounted on spears and taken as trophies to Kufah.

729. p. 158 ¶ 230. Ibn-i-Anas

A reference to Sinán bin Anas al-Nakha'í, a resident of Kufah, who participated in the Battle of Karbila. Some sources allege that he was responsible for the murder of Imám Ḥusayn – according to these, when no one dared to kill the surrounded Imám, Sinán bin Anas struck him in the chest with a spear, dismounted his horse and decapitated him.

730. p. 158 ¶ 230. Aṣbahí

A reference to Khawlí bin Yazíd al-Aṣbahí al-Iyádí al-Dárimí. He was part of the army of Yazid at the Battle of Karbila and participated in the martyrdom of Imám Ḥusayn. By the order of 'Umar bin Sa'd he took the head of the Imám to Kufah. But because it was late he took the head to his house first, which caused his wife to seriously admonish him and to detest him thereafter because of his enmity towards the household of the Prophet. He was caught during an uprising that sought justice for the tragedy of Karbila when his wife revealed his hiding-place. He was beheaded and his body was burnt.

731. p. 159 ¶ 231. Recognize Him by His verses

Taherzadeh comments:

> In one of His Writings, the Báb declares that at the time of the coming of 'Him Whom God shall make manifest', all those who dwell in the Sinai of God's Revelation will be found awestruck at His glory. He urges the learned among His followers to withhold their pens from writing epistles and books when 'Him Whom God shall make manifest' has revealed Himself. He further urges His

followers to recognize and acknowledge Bahá'u'lláh with no hesitation or delay and warns them:

> Recognize Him by His verses. The greater your neglect in seeking to know Him, the more grievously will ye be veiled in fire.[855]

See also Annotations 701 and 707.

732. p. 159 ¶ 231. On that Day

The Báb thus refers to the Day of Bahá'u'lláh:

> That Day is indeed an infinitely mighty Day, for in it the Divine Tree proclaimeth from eternity unto eternity, 'Verily, I am God. No God is there but Me.'[856]

The Hebrew Bible frequently alludes to a future Dispensation as 'in that Day' or 'on that Day' (Is. 4:2; 11:10–11; 24:21; 26:1; Ezek. 38:14; Micah 4:6; Zeph. 3:11; Hagg. 2:23; Zech. 9:16; 14:20). Other phrases are also used to refer to the anticipated day: for example, 'that time' (Dan. 12:1); 'latter days' (Micah 4:1); 'end times' (Dan. 12:4); 'the great and awesome day of the Lord comes' (Joel 2:30–31); 'the day cometh (Mal. 4:1); and 'the coming of the great and terrible day of the Lord' (Mal. 4:5).

The New Testament also often mentions 'that Day', 'that Hour', or 'that Time(s)' (Matt. 7:22: Mark 13:32; Acts 3:18; I Thess. 5:4; II Tim. 1:12; 4:8; II Peter 3:10). The Apostle Paul refers to the event simply 'as the day of the Lord' (I Thess. 5:2); the Apostle Peter (II Peter 3:12) as the 'coming of the day of God,' and (Acts 2:20) as 'the great and notable day of the Lord'.

The term 'that Day' or 'that Hour' is used to refer to a future time (the Second Coming, the Day of the Father), in contrast to an Hour that has come (the First Coming; the Day of the Son). For example (John 4:23): 'But the hour cometh, and now is, when the true worshippers shall worship the Father in spirit and in truth: for the Father seeketh such to worship him'; and (John 5:25): 'Truly, truly, I tell you, the hour is coming and has now come when the dead will hear the voice of the Son of God, and those who hear will live.'

The Qur'án similarly alludes to the future Revelation in several ways, including 'that' or 'the' Day (20:105–106; 25:25; 27:87; 50:41; 80:34,38; 83:6, 15).

733. p. 159 ¶ 231. Say: O ye unbelievers! I worship not that which ye worship

This is from a súrih of the Qur'án (109:1–6) entitled 'the Unbelievers' or *al-Káfirún*. It was revealed in Mecca at the time when Muhammad and His followers had suffered severely at the hands of the leaders of Mecca. It was revealed in response to a proposal by them that their deities should be worshipped side by side with God. Muhammad tells them that despite certain superficial relationships between what they believed, and He believed, the two were quite distinct.

As quoted by Bahá'u'lláh in this paragraph, the Báb stated that 'On that Day, the Daystar of Truth [Bahá'u'lláh] will address the people of the Bayán and will recite this Súrih of the Qur'án.' This illustrates the extent to which some of the Bábís had violated the Covenant of the Báb. The Báb considers it inexplicable that some of His followers will reject Bahá'u'lláh but express their allegiance to Him (the Báb):

> From the beginning that hath no beginning all men have bowed in adoration before Him Whom God shall make manifest and will continue to do so until the end that hath no end. How strange then that at the time of His appearance ye should pay homage by day and night unto that which the Point of the Bayán hath enjoined upon you and yet fail to worship Him Whom God shall make manifest.[857]

He also admonishes:

> God hath apprised you in the Bayán that no similarity existeth between the Cause of Him Whom God will make manifest and the cause of others.[858]

The above references take on an added significance when we see how Bahá'u'lláh stigmatizes Mírzá Yaḥyá as an idol of the Bábí community:

> These creatures are the same creatures who for three thousand years have worshipped idols, and bowed down before the Golden Calf. Now, too, they are fit for nothing better. What relation can there be between this people and Him Who is the Countenance of Glory? What ties can bind them to the One Who is the supreme embodiment of all that is lovable?[859]

734. p. 159 ¶ 231. The tree of affirmation, by turning aside from Him, is accounted as the tree of denial, and the tree of denial, by turning towards Him, is accounted as the tree of affirmation

This is a quotation from the Persian *Bayán* (IV:3). The Báb counsels that it is 'He Whom God shall make manifest' Who ultimately decides what is good and what is evil, and what is and what is not acceptable to God. This should have been an adequate warning to His nominee Mírzá Yaḥyá and his followers.

735. pp. 159–60 ¶ 231. Should anyone lay claim unto a Revelation, and fail to produce any proof, do not protest, and sadden Him not

This is a quotation from the Persian *Bayán* (VI:8) which expresses the desire that His followers refrain from opposing anyone who makes a claim that he is the promise of the Bábí Dispensation, in case by doing so they reject 'Him Whom God shall make manifest' and cause Him grief.

Compare:

> Take ye good heed in your night [By 'night' is meant the period between two divine Revelations when the Sun of Truth is not manifest among men] lest ye be a cause of sadness to any soul, whether ye be able to discover proofs in him or not, that haply on the Day of Resurrection ye may not grieve Him within Whose grasp lieth every proof.[860]

736. p. 160 ¶ 232. through this Book, I have covenanted with all created things concerning the Mission of Him Whom Thou shalt make manifest

The Kitáb-i-Badí' revealed by Bahá'u'lláh is a defence of His Faith.[861] It makes it clear that the purpose of the Báb in revealing Himself was none other than to prepare His followers for the coming of Bahá'u'lláh. It contains many passages from the Writings of the Báb in which He makes a firm covenant with His followers concerning 'Him Whom God shall make manifest'.

> The whole of the Bayán is only a leaf amongst the leaves of His Paradise.[862]

Again:

> The Bayán . . . is, from beginning to end, the repository of all His attributes, and the treasury of both His fire and His light.[863]

In other passages He affirms:

> The purpose underlying this Revelation, as well as those that preceded it, has, in like manner, been to announce the advent of the Faith of Him Whom God will make manifest. And this Faith – the Faith of Him Whom God will make manifest – in its turn, together with all the Revelations gone before it, have as their object the Manifestation destined to succeed it.[864]

And:

> Bear Thou witness that, through this Book, I have covenanted with all created things concerning the Mission of Him Whom Thou shalt make manifest, ere the covenant concerning Mine own Mission had been established.[865]

Hence, the Bábís who opposed Bahá'u'lláh broke the Covenant of the Báb.

See ¶ 203, ¶ 224 and ¶ 245.

737. p. 160 ¶ 233. O Sun-like Mirrors!

See Annotations 718, 719, 738, 739, 743 and 783.

738. p. 160 ¶ 233. Look ye upon the Sun of Truth

Mírzá Yaḥyá used to employ the title of 'Mirror' to impress the followers of the Báb. Bahá'u'lláh clarifies the position of the 'Mirrors'. He quotes many statements of the Báb that the Mirrors had no light of their own, that their radiance depended upon their turning to the source of light, 'Him Whom God shall make manifest'. Bahá'u'lláh exhorts the Mirrors of the Dispensation of the Báb to turn to the Sun of His Revelation.

See also Annotations 364, 718, 719, 739, 743 and 783.

739. p. 160 ¶ 233. I complain unto thee, O Mirror of My generosity

The Báb, addressing Ḥájí Siyyid Javád-i-Karbilá'í, complains that the Mirrors (the Báb designated certain leading believers as 'Mirrors', 'Guides' and 'Witnesses'[866]) have not detached themselves from the things of this world and would therefore not be able to teach His Cause effectively. 'Mirror of My generosity' refers to Ḥájí Siyyid Javád-i-Karbilá'í who had met Shaykh Aḥmad Aḥsá'í and had been a capable student of Siyyid Káẓim-i-Rashtí. He became a devoted follower of the Báb and Bahá'u'lláh:

> He had known the Báb from the days of His childhood, years before His Declaration, and was fascinated by the remarkable qualities which were so strikingly apparent in Him . . . He dedicated his life to the service of the Cause in Karbilá. It was in this city in the year 1851 that he met Bahá'u'lláh for the first time, but did not appreciate His glorious station until sometime later. . .
>
> Early in 1852 Bahá'u'lláh returned from Karbilá to His native city and was imprisoned a few months later in the Síyáh-Chál of Ṭihrán. Ḥájí Siyyid Javád was in Karbilá when Bahá'u'lláh was exiled to 'Iráq after His release from that dungeon. During the ten years of Bahá'u'lláh's sojourn in 'Iráq, he was a faithful companion, one who truly recognized the station of Bahá'u'lláh before His Declaration.

When Bahá'u'lláh was exiled to Adrianople, Ḥájí Siyyid Javád travelled to Persia and lived in various parts of the country, serving the Faith with great distinction.[867]

740. p. 161 ¶ 234. this Siyyid stood by this Wronged One

The followers of Mírzá Yaḥyá (Azal) falsely broadcast that Ḥájí Siyyid Javád-i-Karbilá'í was one of his followers. To that end they published his picture amongst that of others under the picture of Mírzá Yaḥyá, whereas in actual fact he remained a loyal and steadfast follower of Bahá'u'lláh to the end of his life. He died in Kirman *circa* 1882 when he was about 100 years of age.

741. p. 161 ¶ 234. Ḥaydar-'Alí

Ḥájí Mírzá Ḥaydar 'Alí Iṣfáhání was a believer in the Báb. He later met Bahá'u'lláh in Adrianople and became one of His ardent followers, an outstanding disciple who endured patiently and with fortitude many calamities, and staunchly defended the Covenant of Bahá'u'lláh. He travelled to Egypt to teach the Faith at the request of Bahá'u'lláh and was imprisoned. After being exiled to Khartoum in Sudan, he spent a further ten years in prison. Following his release he travelled and taught the Faith in several countries, including Iran and Turkey. During the time of 'Abdu'l-Bahá he lived in Haifa and became known as the Angel of Carmel. He is the author of the narrative *Bihjatu'ṣ-Ṣudúr* (The Delight of Hearts) and *Dalá'il al-'Irfán*. He passed away in 1920 CE.[868]

742. p. 161 ¶ 234. They have, on one occasion, secured a picture of this Siyyid and pasted it on a sheet with that of others, surmounted by the portrait of Mírzá Yaḥyá

This refers to an attempt by the plotters against Bahá'u'lláh to convey the false impression that Ḥájí Siyyid Javád-i-Karbilá'í was a follower of Mírzá Yaḥyá (see Annotation 740).

743. p. 162 ¶ 235. the complaint of the Primal Point

This alludes to the fact that the Báb was disappointed by the knowledge that not all the Bábís whom he had designated as 'Mirrors' would lead the people to Bahá'u'lláh (see Annotation 739). However, the Báb did foresee that Ḥájí Siyyid Javád-i-Karbilá'í would be able to do this.

744. p. 162 ¶ 235. Mirrors

See Annotations 718, 738, 739, 743 and 783.

745. p. 162 ¶ 235. Consecrate Thou, O my God, the whole of this Tree unto Him, that from it may be revealed all the fruits created by God . . . I have not wished that this Tree should ever bear any branch, leaf, or fruit that would fail to bow down before Him, on the day of His Revelation, or refuse to laud Thee through Him

A statement by the Báb indicating that all the fruits of His Dispensation have been revealed for the sake of Bahá'u'lláh.[869]

Notably, the Báb referred to Himself as the letter 'Thá' which is the first letter of 'Thamárih' which means 'fruit'. Shoghi Effendi, in his writings, refers to the Báb as the 'Thamárih' (fruit) of the Tree of God's successive Revelations.[870]

746. p. 163 ¶ 237. O Hádí

A reference to Mírzá Hádí Dawlat-Ábádí, a Muslim clergyman in Isfahan who became a follower of Mírzá Yaḥyá Azal (see Annotation 427).

747. p. 163 ¶ 237. in the end all pronounced the sentence of His death, and caused Him to suffer martyrdom

Bahá'u'lláh points out that after supplicating for 1,200 years that the Qá'im hasten His coming, the Shí'ihs were the eventual cause of the martyrdom of the selfsame Qá'im they were expecting (the Báb). Similarly, despite the warnings of the Báb, a number of His followers nevertheless caused Bahá'u'lláh intense suffering.

748. p. 163 ¶ 237. the Seal of the Prophets, and . . . the Chosen Ones

'Seal of the Prophets' refers to the Prophet Muhammad, and 'the Chosen Ones' in this context are the Imáms. The Shí'ihs interpret a verse of the Qur'án (35:32) as referring to the Imáms, whom they believe were chosen by God: 'Moreover, we have made the Book an heritage to those of our servants whom we have chosen . . .'

In other words, for all their professed expressions of belief in God and Muhammad and love for the Imáms, the Shí'ihs still killed their Promised One Who represented the return of their Twelfth Imám.

The Bábís should have learnt from this tragedy of Islam and, in their turn, not persecuted Bahá'u'lláh, who was 'He Whom God will make manifest' anticipated in the Dispensation of the Báb.

749. p. 164 ¶ 239. Every one of this people well knoweth that Siyyid Muḥammad was but one of Our servants

It was prior to the Báb's martyrdom that Siyyid Muḥammad-i-Iṣfáhání became one of his followers in Karbilá.

See also Annotations 752, 765 and 809.

750. p. 164 ¶ 239. as requested by the Imperial Ottoman Government

This refers to the extradition of Bahá'u'lláh from Baghdad to Istanbul by decree of the Ottoman Government: 'on a Wednesday afternoon (April 22, 1863), thirty-one days after Naw-Rúz, on the third of Dhi'l-Qa'dih, 1279 A.H., He set forth on the first stage of His four months' journey to the capital of the Ottoman Empire'.[871]

751. p. 164 ¶ 239. their Capital

Istanbul, also known in the West at that time as Constantinople, was named after Constantine I, the first Roman Emperor to convert to Christianity. Originally the capital city of the Byzantine Empire, it was conquered by the Ottoman Sultan Mehmed II in 1453, and replaced Adrianople as the capital of the Ottoman Empire.

752. p. 164 ¶ 239. he committed that which . . . hath caused the Pen of the Most High to weep and His Tablet to groan

Siyyid Muḥammad-i-Iṣfáhání committed many disreputable acts and was the source of a great deal of mischief when Bahá'u'lláh was living in Baghdad.

> As to Siyyid Muḥammad . . . he had surrounded himself, as Nabíl . . . categorically asserts, with a band of ruffians, whom he allowed, and even encouraged, to snatch at night the turbans from the heads of wealthy pilgrims who had congregated in Karbilá, to steal their shoes, to rob the shrine of the Imám Ḥusayn of its divans and candles, and seize the drinking cups from the public fountains.[872]

(Ishráq-Khávarí recounts in his *Qámús* that Siyyid Muḥammad stole and sold brass cups from various shrines, and lived on the pigeons that flocked there.)

In their efforts to discredit Bahá'u'lláh, the followers of Mírzá Yaḥyá, aided by Siyyid Muḥammad-i-Iṣfáhání, complained to the authorities that they had insufficient means of livelihood, blaming Bahá'u'lláh for depriving them of their share of the allowances made to the family by the government, and that Bahá'u'lláh had made an alliance with Bulgaria with the purpose of conquering Istanbul. The Persian ambassador in that city took advantage of the disturbance in Turkey to inform Persian consuls in Iraq and in Egypt that the Turkish government had withdrawn protection from the 'Bábí sect'.

At his instigation, Mírzá Yaḥyá betrayed the trust of the Báb, claimed to be His successor, and intrigued against Bahá'u'lláh, even attempting to have Him murdered.

> [Siyyid Muḥammad-i-Iṣfáhání] was a man of corrupt character and great personal ambition who induced Mírzá Yaḥyá to oppose Bahá'u'lláh and to claim prophethood for himself. Although he was an adherent of Mírzá Yaḥyá, Siyyid Muḥammad was exiled with Bahá'u'lláh to 'Akká. He continued to agitate and plot against Bahá'u'lláh.[873]

See also Annotations 765 and 809.

753. p. 164 ¶ 239. order of the Mawlavis

The Order of dancing dervishes or Mawlavis, one of several Sufi Orders, was established by Rumi's son, Sulṭán Valad. However, the spiritual founder was Mevlana Celaleddin Rumi, a great mystic Turkish scholar who lived in the 13th century CE in Konya. Their name derives from his title *Mawlá*, meaning Master.

754. p. 164 ¶ 239. until the time when We were summoned to depart

Shoghi Effendi describes this:

> On the twenty-second of the month of Rabí'u'th-Thání 1285 A.H. (August 12, 1868) Bahá'u'lláh and His family, escorted by a Turkish captain, Ḥasan Effendi by name, and other soldiers appointed by the local government, set out on their four-day journey to Gallipoli . . . It was eventually decided that all the exiles, numbering about seventy, should be banished to 'Akká. Instructions were, moreover, issued that a certain number of the adherents of Mírzá Yaḥyá, among whom were Siyyid Muḥammad and Áqá Ján, should accompany these exiles, whilst four of the companions of Bahá'u'lláh were ordered to depart with the Azalís for Cyprus.[874]

755. p. 165 ¶ 240. thou hast striven to lay hands on and destroy every copy of the Bayán

A reference to Mírzá Hádí Dawlat-Ábádí (see Annotation 437) who had at one stage made it his mission to destroy all copies of the Báb's preeminent Writings.

756. p. 165 ¶ 241. Apprehend now the cry of Him Who is the Point as raised by His utterance. He supplicateth God that if there should appear from this Tree – which is His blessed Self – any fruit, or leaf, or branch that would fail to believe in Him, God should cut it off forthwith

The Báb writes:

> And shouldst Thou behold, O my God, any branch, leaf, or fruit upon Me that hath failed to bow down before Him, on the day of His Revelation, cut it off, O My God, from that Tree, for it is not of Me, nor shall it return unto Me.[875]

See also Annotation 745.

757. p. 165 ¶ 241. 'Should any one make a statement, and fail to support it by any proof, reject him not.' And yet, now, though supported by a hundred books, thou hast rejected Him and rejoicest therein!

The claim to be Him Whom God shall make manifest was so daunting that few would consider it. The Báb was anxious that the Bábís not reject Bahá'u'lláh under any circumstances even if He failed to produce any proof that He was the expected Manifestation of God. However, despite His copious writings as a proof of His claim, and the warning that the Báb had given His followers, Bahá'u'lláh states that nevertheless they rejected Him as Him Whom God shall make manifest.

758. p. 166 ¶ 242. two months after Our arrival in 'Iráq

Bahá'u'lláh arrived in Baghdad on the 28th of Jamádíyu'th-Thání 1269 AH (8 April 1853 CE).[876]

759. p. 166 ¶ 242. Mírzá Músá

Shoghi Effendi writes:

> Of the two brothers who accompanied Him on that journey the first was Mírzá Músá, commonly called Áqáy-i-Kalím, His staunch and valued supporter, the ablest and most distinguished among His brothers and sisters, and one of the 'only two persons who', according to Bahá'u'lláh's testimony, 'were adequately informed of the origins' of His Faith.[877]

'Abdu'l-Bahá provides an account of his life in *Memorials of the Faithful.*

760. p. 166 ¶ 242. Subsequently, this Wronged One departed from Baghdád, and for two years withdrew from the world

A reference to Bahá'u'lláh's withdrawal to the inhospitable mountains of Sulaymaniyyih in Kurdistan where He lived alone in the wilderness as a wandering seeker, a dervish, at times in a cave or in a crude rock shelter. Despite the physical deprivation, despite deep grief over the decline of the Bábí community, His soul spent blissful days in communion with God. In that loneliness Bahá'u'lláh's spirit could be filled with the completeness of the love of God:

> Our withdrawal contemplated no return, and Our separation hoped for no reunion. The one object of Our retirement was to avoid becoming a subject of discord among the faithful, a source of disturbance unto Our companions, the means of injury to any soul, or the cause of sorrow to any heart. Beyond these, We cherished no other intention, and apart from them, We had no end in view.[878]

761. p. 167 ¶ 243. We especially appointed certain ones to collect the writings of the Primal Point

It was especially important to have the original Writings of the Báb, since Mírzá Yaḥyá, after his rebellion against Bahá'u'lláh, wrote passages using similar calligraphy to that of the Báb – even corrupting the text of the original Writings in some instances – which contained false statements that were used by him to, for example, back up his claims to be the successor to the Báb. Any authentic copies were made under the direction of Bahá'u'lláh.

762. p. 167 ¶ 243. Mírzá Vahháb-i-Khurásání, known as Mírzá Javád

This early believer went by both names, since *Vahháb* (the Bestower) has the same numerical value (14) as *Javád* (the Generous). During the Báb's incarceration in Máh-Kú Mírzá Javád lived in Tabriz where he met the followers of the Báb and studied His Writings. He is mentioned in the *Dalá'il-i-Sab'ih* (Seven Proofs) which the Báb revealed while incarcerated in Máh-Kú, setting out the truth of His mission.

After the martyrdom of the Báb he accepted Bahá'u'lláh and met Him in Baghdad. On the instructions of Bahá'u'lláh he collaborated with Mírzá Yaḥyá to collate and copy the writings of the Báb.

763. p. 167 ¶ 243. When We arrived in Mossoul, We found that Mírzá Yaḥyá had left before Us for that city, and was awaiting Us there

Mosul is a major city in northern Iraq some 250 miles north of Baghdad and stands on the west bank of the Tigris River. It was the first city where Bahá'u'lláh stopped on His way to Istanbul. Shoghi Effendi describes this incident:

> Mírzá Yaḥyá had, ever since the return of Bahá'u'lláh from Sulaymáníyyih, either chosen to maintain himself in an inglorious seclusion in his own house, or had withdrawn, whenever danger threatened, to such places of safety as Ḥillih and Basra. To the latter town he had fled, disguised as a Ba<u>gh</u>dád Jew, and become a shoe merchant. So great was his terror that he is reported to have said on one occasion: 'Whoever claims to have seen me, or to have heard my voice, I pronounce an infidel.' On being informed of Bahá'u'lláh's impending departure for Constantinople, he at first hid himself in the garden of Huvaydar, in the vicinity of Ba<u>gh</u>dád, meditating meanwhile on the advisability of fleeing either to Abyssinia, India or some other country. Refusing to heed Bahá'u'lláh's advice to proceed to Persia, and there disseminate the writings of the Báb, he sent a certain Ḥájí Muḥammad Káẓim, who resembled him, to the government-house to procure for him a passport in the name of Mírzá 'Alíy-i-Kirmán<u>sh</u>áhí, and left Ba<u>gh</u>dád, abandoning the writings there, and proceeded in disguise, accompanied by an Arab Bábí, named Ẓáhir, to Mosul, where he joined the exiles who were on their way to Constantinople.[879]

764. p. 167 ¶ 243. We despatched the writings unto another place and another country

The precise destination is uncertain but was likely in Persia.

765. p. 168 ¶ 244. The Siyyid of Iṣfáhán, however, surreptitiously duped him

Shoghi Effendi refers to Siyyid Muḥammad-i-Iṣfáhání as the 'Antichrist of the Bahá'í Revelation',[880] and 'the black-hearted scoundrel who befooled and manipulated' Mírzá Yaḥyá 'with consummate skill and unyielding persistence'.[881] Shoghi Effendi adds that he was 'notorious for his inordinate ambition, his blind obstinacy and uncontrollable jealousy' and writes that Bahá'u'lláh later referred to him in the *Kitáb-i-Aqdas* as 'the one who had "led astray" Mírzá Yaḥyá, and stigmatized him, in one of His Tablets, as the "source of envy and the quintessence of mischief"'.[882] Together with Mírzá Yaḥyá he created a great deal of trouble for Bahá'u'lláh and His followers.

> This supreme crisis Bahá'u'lláh Himself designated as the Ayyám-i-Shidád (Days of Stress), during which 'the most grievous veil' was torn asunder, and the 'most great separation' was irrevocably effected. It immensely gratified and emboldened its external enemies, both civil and ecclesiastical, played into their hands, and evoked their unconcealed derision. It perplexed and confused the friends and supporters of Bahá'u'lláh, and seriously damaged the prestige of the Faith in the eyes of its western admirers. It had been brewing ever since the early days of Bahá'u'lláh's sojourn in Baghdád, was temporarily suppressed by the creative forces which, under His as yet unproclaimed leadership, reanimated a disintegrating community, and finally broke out, in all its violence, in the years immediately preceding the proclamation of His Message. It brought incalculable sorrow to Bahá'u'lláh, visibly aged Him, and inflicted, through its repercussions, the heaviest blow ever sustained by Him in His lifetime. It was engineered throughout by the tortuous intrigues and incessant machinations of that same diabolical Siyyid Muḥammad, that vile whisperer who, disregarding Bahá'u'lláh's advice, had insisted on accompanying Him to Constantinople and Adrianople, and was now redoubling his efforts, with unrelaxing vigilance, to bring it to a head.[883]

Notably, the New Testament states (I John 2:18) that many Antichrists had come at the First Coming but the Antichrist will also appear at the last hour (Second Coming).

The expected Antichrist in Islam is called *Dajjal* (the deceiver, liar, and the one who will cause *fitnah* (mischief or sedition). The Arabic root is *dajala*, which means to mix truth with falsehood, that is, to equivocate.

See also Annotations 752 and 809.

766. p. 168 ¶ 244. Would that thou wouldst inquire from the officials of the government concerning the conduct of Mírzá Yaḥyá in that land

The catalogue of shameful actions of Mírzá Yaḥyá in Baghdad was ample evidence that he was not 'Him Whom God shall make manifest' promised by the Báb and frequently referred to in His Book the *Bayán*.[884]

767. p. 168 ¶ 244. communications . . . to the Primal Point

Bahá'u'lláh lovingly protected His younger half-brother, Mírzá Yaḥyá for many years. These were communications that Bahá'u'lláh sent to the Báb on his behalf and possibly in some cases in the name of Mírzá Yaḥyá. The Báb responded by encouraging Mírzá Yaḥyá. No other details are available. However, the letters, undeserved by Mírzá Yaḥyá, would have been clear evidence of Bahá'u'lláh's generosity.

768. pp. 168–9 ¶ 244. thou hadst ascribed the authorship of the Kitáb-i-Íqán and of other Tablets unto others

Bahá'u'lláh wrote the *Kitáb-i-Íqán* in Baghdad in the year preceding His Declaration, in response to questions put to Him by one of the maternal uncles of the Báb. Mírzá Hádí Dawlat-Ábádí shamefully circulated the rumour that Mírzá Yaḥyá was the author of the *Kitáb-i-Íqán*, Lawḥ-i-Ḥikmat (Tablet of Wisdom), the Tablet to Náṣiri'd-Dín Sháh and other Writings of Bahá'u'lláh. However, all his efforts came to nothing. Also, Bahá'u'lláh refers to the fact that, with the help of Siyyid Muḥammad-i-Iṣfáhání, Mírzá Yaḥyá had disseminated some of His Writings among the believers in his own name.

769. p. 169 ¶ 245. Haṣan-i-Mázindaráni

Muḥammad Ḥasan was a believer from Mázindarán, the ancestral province of Bahá'u'lláh. He was a son of Mírzá Zaynu'l-'Ábidín, a paternal uncle of Bahá'u'lláh and much loved by Him and 'Abdu'l-Bahá. He made several trips to 'Akká and each time he carried back many Tablets for the believers living in the northern cities of Persia. He was present when the Purest Branch passed away and assisted Shaykh Maḥmud in washing his body. Bahá'u'lláh revealed the Lawḥ-i-Pisar-'Amm (Tablet to the Cousin) in honour of him. On his arrival in Tehran to transmit the Tablets of Bahá'u'lláh to their recipients he was arrested and imprisoned. Seventy-two Tablets were stolen from him by a woman who later gave them to Bahá'u'lláh's half-sister, Sháh Sulṭán Khánum. No one knows what happened to these Tablets, but it is suspected that she distributed them in her own name and/or in the name of Mírzá Yaḥyá.

770. p. 169 ¶ 245. one of the sisters of this Wronged One

Bahá'u'lláh had six sisters. Two, a full sister, Sárih Khánum and a half-sister, Sakínih Khánum, became His faithful followers. The rest became the followers of Mírzá Yaḥyá Azal.

The reference here is to Sháh Sulṭán Khánum known as Khánum Buzurg, the oldest of five children of Mírzá Buzurg Núrí and Kulthúm Khánum-i-Núrí, and half-sister of Bahá'u'lláh. The followers of Azal refer to her as 'Izziyya Khánum. They attribute to her a book which attacks Bahá'u'lláh, named *Tanbih al-Na'imin* (Punishment of Sleepers), a title very similar to the book written by Mírzá Yaḥyá inciting violence against Dayyán. This is perhaps a fabrication, as she was mostly illiterate and had little education. According to Edward Granville Browne, the author of the book was in fact Shaykh Aḥmad Rúḥí, the son-in-law of Mírzá Yaḥyá.

'Abdu'l-Bahá wrote her a long letter, Lawḥ-i-'Ammih (Tablet to the Aunt), in which He addressed her as 'O my affectionate Aunt'. In this letter He responded to her objections, in an effort to make her see how untenable the position of Mírzá Yaḥyá was. Her supposed answer to 'Abdu'l-Bahá's Tablet, Risáliy-i-'Ammih (The Aunt's Treatise), is an apologia for Mírzá Yaḥyá.[885]

Sháh Sulṭán Khánum never married and died at the age of 95 years.

She never lived with Bahá'u'lláh and never saw Mírzá Yaḥyá. This was the same sister and aunt who prevented the marriage of the daughter of Áqá Mírzá Ḥasan (an older faithful half-brother of Bahá'u'lláh and much esteemed by Him) with 'Abdu'l-Bahá (see Annotation 778).

771. 169 ¶ 245. We, a few days prior to Our departure, visited her and her mother

Bahá'u'lláh briefly met Sháh Sulṭán Khánum and her mother, Kulthúm Khánum-i-Núrí, briefly before His banishment to Baghdad.

772. p. 169 ¶ 245. After We were exiled and had departed from 'Iráq to Constantinople

This took place on 8 April 1863.

773. p. 169 ¶ 245. Mírzá Riḍá-Qulí

The third of the five children of Mírzá Buzurg Núrí and Kulthúm Khánum-i-Núrí (see above, Annotation 770) and a half-brother of Bahá'u'lláh. His title was 'Hakim' as he was a physician. He neither recognized the station of Bahá'u'lláh nor that of the Báb. He kept apart from Bahá'u'lláh and tried to conceal the fact of his relationship to Him. His wife, however, was an ardent follower of Bahá'u'lláh. Mírzá Riḍá-Qulí had no antipathy towards Bahá'u'lláh and it was in his home that Bahá'u'lláh stayed after His release from the Síyáh-Chál, when He was bedridden for one month.

774. p. 170 ¶ 245. Farmán-Farmá

Several individuals in the history of Persia have had the title 'Farmán-Farmá' (Commander-in-Chief), such as Ḥusayn-'Alí Mírzá Farmán-Farmá, the governor of Fárs, referred to here by Bahá'u'lláh. He was a prince and, as the son of Fatḥ-'Alí Sháh, a paternal uncle of Náṣiri'd-Dín Sháh.

Bahá'u'lláh's father, Mírzá 'Abbás-i-Núrí, was a friend of Mírzá Abu'l-Qásim Farahání, Qá'im Maqám, the Prime Minister of Iran (1834–35 CE). The latter was later betrayed and murdered on the orders of

Muḥammad Sháh Qájár in 1835, at the instigation of the perfidious Ḥájí Mírzá Áqásí, who would become Qá'im Maqám's successor. Consequently, when Mírzá Áqásí came to power he harboured enmity to all Qá'ím Maqám's associates. As a result Bahá'u'lláh's father lost his considerable wealth and came to owe a great deal of money to his lenders. He was forced to live in the house of his son, Mírzá Riḍá-Qulí. After the passing of Mírzá 'Abbás-i-Núrí his debtors demanded payment. Bahá'u'lláh paid all His father's debts out of His own resources. To achieve this He had to sell His magnificent house and furnishings for a paltry sum to Farmán-Farmá and Ḥisámu's-Salṭanih. Mírzá Áqá Khán Núrí (1807–65 CE) who later became Prime Minister under Náṣiri'd-Dín Sháh Qájár (1851–58 CE) forcefully and deceitfully took possession of the lands belonging to Bahá'u'lláh and in the end paid not a cent for them. Thus, by the time Bahá'u'lláh left for Baghdad He had lost almost all His wealth.

775. p. 170 ¶ 245. Ḥisámu's-Salṭanih

Title of Sulṭán Murád Mírzá (1818–83 CE). He too was a prince and a paternal uncle of Náṣiri'd-Dín Sháh, and governor-general of Khurasan.

776. p. 170 ¶ 245. Masjid-i-Sháh

Masjid-i-Sháh or the Shah Mosque, also known as the Royal Mosque (Masjid-i-Sulṭání) was renamed the Imam Mosque after the 1979 Islamic Revolution. It is situated in the northern section of the Grand Bazaar in Tehran.

777. p. 170 ¶ 245. Gate of Shimírán

One of the twelve gates of the old city of Tehran. Shimírán was an area with several villages to the north of the city.

778. p. 170 ¶ 245. Mírzá Muḥammad-Ḥasan's daughter

Taherzadeh recounts this incident:

> When 'Abdu'l-Bahá was a child in Ṭihrán, they chose for Him Shahrbánú, a cousin, and betrothed her to Him . . . When Bahá'u'lláh and

His family were exiled to 'Iráq, Shahr-bánú remained in the district of Núr in Mázindarán, until in 1285 A.H. (1868). Bahá'u'lláh instructed His uncle Mullá Zaynu'l-'Ábidín to conduct Shahr-bánú to Ṭihrán and from there arrange her journey to Adrianople.

No sooner had this news reached Sháh Sulṭán Khánum . . . than she arose in enmity to prevent the marriage from taking place. She took Shahr-bánú to her home in Ṭihrán and practically forced her to marry instead Mírzá 'Alí-Khán-i-Núrí the son of the Prime Minister.[886]

779. p. 171 ¶ 246. Were He to appear this very moment

Bahá'u'lláh here makes reference to the Báb, Who revealed that He would be the first to worship 'Him Whom God shall make manifest'. Compare also the Báb's words:

> Glorified is He before Whom all the dwellers of earth and heaven bow down in adoration and unto Whom all men turn in supplication.[887]

780. p. 171 ¶ 246. The purpose of the Most Exalted One (the Báb) was to insure that the proximity of the Revelation should not withhold men from the Divine and everlasting Law

Many of the statements of the Báb were intended to allay concerns about the appearance of Bahá'u'lláh as 'Him Whom God shall make Manifest' so soon after the inception of the Báb's own Dispensation. Bahá'u'lláh wrote the following in this regard:

> Shake off, O heedless ones, the slumber of negligence, that ye may behold the radiance which His glory hath spread through the world. How foolish are those who murmur against the premature birth of His light. O ye who are inly [inwardly] blind! Whether too soon or too late, the evidences of His effulgent glory are now actually manifest. It behooveth you to ascertain whether or not such a light hath appeared. It is neither within your power nor mine to set the time at which it should be made manifest. God's inscrutable Wisdom hath fixed its hour beforehand.[888]

781. p. 171 ¶ 246. even as the companions of John (the Baptist) were prevented from acknowledging Him Who is the Spirit (Jesus)

The disciples of John the Baptist also objected to Jesus declaring to be the Messiah so soon after the inception of the ministry of their leader.

See also Annotations 722 and 725.

782. p. 171 ¶ 246. Suffer not the Bayán . . . to withhold you from the Essence of Being

The Báb had repeatedly emphasized that His Revelation (the *Bayán*) should not prevent the Bábís from recognizing the Promised One (Bahá'u'lláh).

783. p. 172 ¶ 247. Let not names shut you out as by a veil from Him

In the *Kitáb-i-Aqdas* (verse 167), Bahá'u'lláh cautions, 'Take heed lest the word "Prophet" withhold you from this Most Great Announcement'. A note on this passage reads:

> Bahá'u'lláh cautions people 'of insight' not to allow their interpretations of the Holy Scriptures to prevent them from recognizing the Manifestation of God. Followers of each religion have tended to allow their devotion to its Founder to cause them to perceive His Revelation as the final Word of God and to deny the possibility of the appearance of any subsequent Prophet. This has been the case of Judaism, Christianity and Islám. Bahá'u'lláh denies the validity of this concept of finality both in regard to past Dispensations and to His own. With regard to Muslims, He wrote in the *Kitáb-i-Íqán* that the 'people of the Qur'án . . . have allowed the words "Seal of the Prophets" to veil their eyes', 'to obscure their understanding, and deprive them of the grace of all His manifold bounties'. He affirms that 'this theme hath . . . been a sore test unto all mankind', and laments the fate of 'those who, clinging unto these words, have disbelieved in Him Who is their true Revealer'. The Báb refers to this same theme when He warns: 'Let not names shut you out as by a veil from Him Who is their Lord, even the name Prophet, for such a name is but a creation of His utterance.'[889]

Thus the Bábís were warned not to allow nominal titles such as 'Mirrors', and the titles of Mírzá Yaḥyá – *Mir'átu'lláh* (Mirror of God), *Mir'átu'l-Azalíyyih* (Everlasting Mirror), *Ismu'l-Azal* (Name of Eternity), *Thamara-i-Azalíyyih* (the Eternal Fruit) and *Ṣubḥ-i-Azal* (Morn of Eternity) – to prevent them from recognizing 'Him Whom God shall make manifest' and acknowledging Bahá'u'lláh.

Compare the following declaration in the Long Obligatory Prayer: 'I testify that Thou hast been sanctified above all attributes and holy above all names.'[890] Also:

> Magnified art Thou, O Lord my God! I ask Thee by Thy Name which Thou hast set up above all other names . . .[891]

784. p. 172 ¶ 247. O people of the Bayán! Act not as the people of the Qur'án have acted, for if ye do so, the fruits of your night will come to naught

This admonition occurs in the Persian *Bayán* (II:7). 'The fruits of your night' refers to all the achievements of Islam from the appearance of Muḥammad until the advent of the Báb. Compare:

> Those who have deprived themselves [Muslims] of this Resurrection by reason of their mutual hatreds or by regarding themselves to be in the right and others in the wrong, were chastised on the Day of Resurrection [Dispensation of the Báb] by reason of such hatreds evinced during their night. Thus they deprived themselves of beholding the countenance of God, and this for no other reason than mutual denunciations.
>
> O ye that are invested with the Bayán! Ye should perform such deeds as would please God, your Lord, earning thereby the good-pleasure of Him Whom God shall make manifest . . .
>
> Be ye sincere in your allegiance to Him Whom God shall make manifest, for the sake of God, your Lord, that perchance ye may, through devotion to His Faith, be redeemed on the Day of Resurrection. Beware lest ye suffer one another to be wrapt in veils by reason of the disputes which may, during your night . . .[892]

A note to this quotation reads: 'By 'night' is meant the period between two divine Revelations when the Sun of Truth is not manifest among men.'[893]

785. p. 172 ¶ 247. If thou attainest unto His Revelation, and obeyest Him, thou wilt have revealed the fruit of the Bayán

This statement of the Báb is quoted by Shoghi Effendi in *God Passes By*, p. 29. In other words, if the *Bayán* causes you to acknowledge His Revelation then it would have accomplished its purpose. The following appears in the Persian *Bayán*:

> For today the Bayán is in the stage of seed; at the beginning of the manifestation of Him Whom God shall make manifest its ultimate perfection will become apparent. He is made manifest in order to gather the fruits of the trees He hath planted; even as the Revelation of the Qá'im [He Who ariseth], a descendant of Muḥammad - may the blessings of God rest upon Him – is exactly like unto the Revelation of the Apostle of God Himself [Muḥammad]. He appeareth not, save for the purpose of gathering the fruits of Islám from the Qur'ánic verses which He [Muḥammad] hath sown in the hearts of men. The fruits of Islám cannot be gathered except through allegiance unto Him [the Qá'im] and by believing in Him.[894]

786. p. 172 ¶ 247. If not . . . If though aidest not Him

If in spite of the admonitions in the *Bayán* you refuse to recognize Bahá'u'lláh, then you are not worthy of mention – if you are not going to assist Him, at least endeavour not to be the cause of His sorrow.

787. p. 172 ¶ 248. to blot out the Bayán

This is a reference to Mírzá Hádí Dawlat-Ábádí's determination to destroy all copies of the *Bayán* (see ¶ 139 and ¶ 240; Annotations 437 and 755.)

788. p. 172 ¶ 248. the pillars of the Bayán

Shoghi Effendi describes the Báb's prominent early disciples and the Letters of Living as the pillars of His infant Faith.[895]

789. p. 172 ¶ 248. Chihríq

The fortress to which the Báb was transferred from Máh-Kú (10 April 1848) and where He was incarcerated for a total of 27 months. He wrote: 'Now, in My thirtieth year, Thou beholdest Me, O My God, in this Grievous Mountain (*Jabal-i-Shadíd*) where I have dwelt for one whole year.'[896]

790. p. 172 ¶ 248. Mákú

Máh-Kú literally means 'where is the moon?' – the cave-like fortress in the side of a mountain prevented a clear view of the sky. It was where the Báb was imprisoned for seven or nine months, and is located near the border of Persia and Russia. Referred to by Him as *Jabal-i-Básiṭ* (The Open Mountain). The numerical value of *Básiṭ* (meaning 'open') is 72 which is equal to the numerical value of Máh-Kú.

791. p. 173 ¶ 248. Siyyid Ḥusayn

The eighth Letter of the Living and a native of Yazd, who was a companion of the Báb in Máh-Kú and Chihríq. His later life is described by Shoghi Effendi:

> The fierce gale of persecution that had swept Bahá'u'lláh into a subterranean dungeon and snuffed out the light of Ṭáhirih also sealed the fate of the Báb's distinguished amanuensis, Siyyid Ḥusayn-i-Yazdí, surnamed 'Azíz, who had shared His confinement in both Máh-Kú and Chihríq. A man of rich experience and high merit, deeply versed in the teachings of his Master, and enjoying His unqualified confidence, he, refusing every offer of deliverance from the leading officials of Ṭihrán, yearned unceasingly for the martyrdom which had been denied him on the day the Báb had laid down His life in the barrack-square of Tabríz. A fellow-prisoner of Bahá'u'lláh in the Síyáh-Chál of Ṭihrán, from Whom he derived inspiration and solace as he recalled those precious days spent in the company of his Master in Ádhirbayján, he was finally struck down, in circumstances of shameful cruelty, by that same 'Azíz Khán-i-Sardár who had dealt the fatal blow to Ṭáhirih.[897]

792. p. 173 ¶ 248. Mírzá Aḥmad

A reference to Mullá 'Abdu'l Karím-i-Qazvíní. 'Abdu'l-Bahá is reported to have said:

> The first person who recognized the sublimity and holiness of Bahá'u'lláh and became certain that He would manifest a momentous Cause was Mullá 'Abdu'l-Karím-i-Qazvíní, whom the Báb had named Mírzá Aḥmad. He was the intermediary between the Báb and Bahá'u'lláh and was aware of the truth of the matter.[898]

And Shoghi Effendi writes:

> He Himself had already foreshadowed His own approaching death. In the Kitáb-i-Panj-Sha'n, one of His last works, He had alluded to the fact that the sixth Naw-Rúz after the declaration of His mission would be the last He was destined to celebrate on earth. In His interpretation of the letter Há, He had voiced His craving for martyrdom, while in the Qayyúmu'l-Asmá' He had actually prophesied the inevitability of such a consummation of His glorious career. Forty days before His final departure from Chihríq He had even collected all the documents in His possession, and placed them, together with His pen-case, His seals and His rings, in the hands of Mullá Báqir, a Letter of the Living, whom He instructed to entrust them to Mullá 'Abdu'l-Karím-i-Qazvíní, surnamed Mírzá Aḥmad, who was to deliver them to Bahá'u'lláh in Ṭihrán.[899]

Mírzá Aḥmad was martyred in Tehran in 1852 during the great massacre of the Bábís following the attempt on the life of Náṣiri'd-Din Sháh.[900]

793. p. 173 ¶ 249. continually surrounded by five of the handmaidens of God

This is an allusion to Mírzá Yaḥyá, who was always accompanied by at least five of his wives. His own son Riḍván-'Ali reports him to have had 11 or 12 wives[901] while another source mentions 14 wives.[902] In his 84 years of life he fathered nine sons and five daughters; the names of fourteen of his wives are detailed by Ishráq-Khávarí in his *Qámús* of the *Epistle to the Son of the Wolf*.

794. p. 173 ¶ 250. How many the fires which God converteth into light through Him Whom God shall make manifest; and how numerous the lights which are turned into fire through Him!

Compare the following supplication of the Báb:

> I beseech Thee, O my Lord, by Thy most effulgent splendour . . . before whose radiance fire is turned into light, the dead are brought to life and every difficulty is changed into ease. I entreat Thee . . . [to] enable us to become fountains of Thy light.[903]

And:

> Verily God transmuteth fire into light as He willeth, and indeed potent is He over all things.[904]

'Fire' and its derivative, 'light', are frequently mentioned in several contexts in the Writings of Bahá'u'lláh. A dominant context is briefly mentioned here – the eternal fire of the love of God and the light of unity. In one sense therefore, through the Revelation of 'Him Whom God shall make manifest' (Bahá'u'lláh) the divine fire of the love of God has been reborn. This fire has caused the light of unity to shine – the realization of the oneness of God, oneness of Faith and oneness of mankind. The light of oneness and amity has in turn created the love of God to burn in the hearts of humanity.

Bahá'u'lláh underlines the central role of God's manifestations:

> . . . through the rise of these Luminaries of God the world is made new, the waters of everlasting life stream forth, the billows of loving-kindness surge . . . It is the warmth that these Luminaries of God generate, and the undying fires they kindle, which cause the light of the love of God to burn fiercely in the heart of humanity.[905]

This fire or flame of the love of God, which Moses experienced on Mount Sinai, has been re-ignited, illuminating the light of guidance:

> O my Lord! O my Lord! This is a lamp lighted by the fire of Thy love and ablaze with the flame which is ignited in the tree of Thy mercy. O my Lord! Increase his enkindlement, heat and flame, with the fire which is kindled in the Sinai of Thy Manifestation.[906]

> I know not, O my God, what the Fire is which Thou didst kindle in Thy land. Earth can never cloud its splendour, nor water quench its flame.[907]

Bahá'u'lláh exhorts His followers that a soul 'called forth by the Word of God' must 'be kindled with the fire of the love of its Lord'.[908] Without this fire there is no illumination: 'It is clear and evident that until a fire is kindled the lamp will never be ignited'.[909] Again:

> Be as brilliant as the light and as splendid as the fire that blazed in the Burning Bush. The brightness of the fire of your love will no doubt fuse and unify the contending peoples and kindreds of the earth, whilst the fierceness of the flame of enmity and hatred cannot but result in strife and ruin.[910]

> Burn thou brightly with the flame of this undying Fire which the All-Merciful hath ignited in the midmost heart of creation, that through thee the heat of His love may be kindled within the hearts of His favoured ones.[911]

> Be most loving one to another. Burn away, wholly for the sake of the Well-Beloved, the veil of self with the flame of the undying Fire, and with faces joyous and beaming with light, associate with your neighbour.[912]

> Be thou as a flame of fire to My enemies and a river of life eternal to My loved ones, and be not of those who doubt.[913]

795. p. 174 ¶ 250. far astray

Remote from divine mercies and God's Truth.

796. p. 174 ¶ 251. The Bayán is from beginning to end the repository of all of His attributes, and the treasury of both His fire and His light

The Báb links fire and light in a different but related context from the one discussed in Annotation 794. He explains that an individual's exposure to Revelation can result in either the destructive 'fire' of unbelief or the divine 'light' of illumination. The *Bayán* is hence not only the light of the Báb's Revelation but also its fire:

> These verses, clear and conclusive, are a token of the mercy of thy Lord and a source of guidance for all mankind. They are a light unto those who believe in them and a fire of afflictive torment for those who turn away and reject them.[914]

And 'Abdu'l-Bahá explains:

> Every man trained through the teachings of God and illumined by the light of His guidance, who becomes a believer in God and His signs and is enkindled with the fire of the love of God, sacrifices the imperfections of nature for the sake of divine perfections . . . May the divine light become manifest upon your faces . . .[915]

Writing to the Sherif of Mecca (steward of the holy cities of Mecca and Medina) who failed to respond to His Cause, the Báb stated:

> Shouldst thou return unto Us while revelation still continueth through Us, We shall transform thy fire into light. Truly We are powerful over all things. But if thou failest in this task, thou shalt find no way open to thee other than to embrace the Cause of God and to implore that the matter of thine allegiance be brought to the attention of Him Whom God shall make manifest, that He may graciously enable thee to prosper and cause thy fire to be transformed into light.[916]

In the Qur'án 'fire' is associated with hell and 'light' with Revelation. A similar understanding of fire as spiritual error and disbelief is implied in the following passages by Bahá'u'lláh:

> They hasten forward to Hell Fire, and mistake it for light . . .[917]

> I entreat Thee, O my Lord, by Thy Most Great Name whereby Thou didst separate light from fire, and truth from denial, to send down upon me and upon such of my loved ones as are in my company the good of this world and of the next.[918]

797. p. 174 ¶ 251. Mullá Báqir

Mullá Báqir Tabrízí was a learned individual who originally was a follower of the Shaykhi school (the followers of Shaykh Aḥmad-i-Aḥsá'í and Siyyid Káẓim-i-Rashtí. He embraced the Cause of Bahá'u'lláh and remained loyal and devoted to Him all his life.

> Some of His disciples the Báb assiduously prepared to expect the imminent Revelation. Others He orally assured would live to see its day. To Mullá Báqir, one of the Letters of the Living, He actually prophesied, in a Tablet addressed to him, that he would meet the Promised One face to face.[919]

> He accompanied Bahá'u'lláh to the Fort of Shaykh Ṭabarsí and was also present at the Conference of Badasht . . . Soon after Bahá'u'lláh's release from the Síyáh-Chál of Ṭihrán, Mullá Báqir attained the presence of Bahá'u'lláh in Baghdád and, remembering the promise of the Báb, recognized His station and became filled with the glory of His Revelation. He was an outstanding believer and teacher of the Cause. It was to him that the Báb, shortly before His martyrdom, entrusted a coffer containing all His important documents and Tablets, seals and agate rings, which was to be handed to Mullá 'Abdu'l-Karím-i-Qazvíní, surnamed Mírzá Aḥmad, who was instructed to deliver it to Bahá'u'lláh.
>
> Soon after the declaration of the Message of Bahá'u'lláh, Mullá Báqir arose to teach His Cause with great determination and devotion among his fellow countrymen in the province of Ádhirbáyján. He wrote an epistle in which he refuted the claims and rejected the writings of Mírzá Yaḥyá. Longing to attain the presence of His Lord, he travelled twice to 'Akká, and on his last visit he obtained

permission from Bahá'u'lláh to reside in Constantinople where he died around the year 1881.[920]

He had received a letter from the Báb saying he would attain 'Him whom God shall make manifest' in the year 'eight' (1268 AH). He outlived the other Letters and died in Istanbul around 1881.

See also Annotations 707–13, and 727.

798. p. 174 ¶ 252. Thou, however, art still alive

Most of the true followers of the Báb who were active supporters of His Faith suffered martyrdom. Bahá'u'lláh asks how it was that Ḥájí Mírzá Hádí Dawlat-Ábádí, who professed to be an ardent follower of the Báb, had been spared death – clearly, despite his pretences, he was not active in teaching the Faith of the Báb and had been insincere, practising *taqíyyah* (dissimulation).

See also Annotation 427.

799. p. 174 ¶ 253. Dayyán

Mírzá Asadu'lláh of Khuy, surnamed Dayyán by the Báb – the numerical (*abjad*) value of Dayyán (65) is equal to that of 'Asad' or lion (Asadu'lláh means 'the lion of God'). Shoghi Effendi describes him as 'the zealous, the famous Mírzá Asadu'lláh, surnamed Dayyán, a prominent official of high literary repute, who was endowed by the Báb with the "hidden and preserved knowledge" and extolled as the "repository of the trust of the one true God"' [921]

See also Annotations 364, 632, 800–804 and 806.

800. p. 175 ¶ 253. O thou who art the third Letter to believe in Him Who God shall make manifest

A reference to Dayyán (see Annotation 799.) The Báb had promised that he would be the third person to believe in 'Him Whom God shall make manifest'. Dayyán understood the significance of the Báb's prediction when he met Bahá'u'lláh and recognized Him as the One promised in the Bayán.

801. p. 175 ¶ 253. Should God, however, be willing, He will make thee known through the words of Him Whom God shall make manifest.

This is a reference to the promise of the Báb to Dayyán, who realized the falsity of Mírzá Yaḥyá by reading the latter's answers to his questions, but recognized the station of Bahá'u'lláh during a meeting with Him. The Báb had stated:

> God desireth that all men should be guided aright through the potency of the Words of Him Whom God shall make manifest. However, such as are conceited will not suffer themselves to be guided. They will be debarred from the Truth, some by reason of their learning, others on account of their glory and power, and still others due to reasons of their own, none of which shall be of any avail at the hour of death.[922]

802. p. 175 ¶ 253. so cruel a martyrdom

A reference to the brutal death of Dayyán. Mírzá Yaḥyá in his book *Mustayqiz* had instructed the Bábís to kill Dayyán, who had written an epistle refuting his claims to be the successor of the Báb, and whom he regarded as a potential adversary. He sent his servant Mírzá Muḥammad-i-Mázindarání to Azerbaijan 'with explicit orders to kill Dayyán',[923] but by the time he arrived, Dayyán was already on his way to Baghdad to attain the presence of Bahá'u'lláh, Who Himself was returning to Baghdad from Sulaymaniyyih in Kurdistan. Dayyán met Bahá'u'lláh and recognized Him as the One foretold by the Báb. Within a few days, Mírzá Muḥammad did find Dayyán and, while journeying with him from Kazimayn to Baghdad, killed him.[924]

See also ¶ 252 and Annotation 804.

803. p. 175 ¶ 253. He it is whom He (the Báb) had taught the hidden and preserved knowledge

The Báb revealed a Tablet in honour of Dayyán during His incarceration in Chihríq for the two remaining years of His life. 'The hidden and preserved knowledge' refers to the mysteries concealed in this abstruse and difficult Writing called the Tablet of the Letters (Lawḥ-i-Ḥuru'fát), or the Tablet of Nineteen Temples (Lawḥ-i-Ḥayákil-i-Váḥid). There are nineteen Temples each with eleven parts and each section is devoted to a Name of God. The primary purpose of this Tablet, believed to have been written calligraphically in the form of a pentacle, was to indicate the nineteen years between the beginning of the Dispensation of the Báb and the declaration of Bahá'u'lláh (1844–1863).

> . . . the Lawḥ-i-Ḥuru'fat (Tablet of the Letters) . . . however misconstrued at first as an exposition of the science of divination, was later recognized to have unravelled, on the one hand, the mystery of the Mustaghá<u>th</u>, and to have abstrusely alluded, on the other, to the nineteen years which must needs elapse between the Declaration of the Báb and that of Bahá'u'lláh.[925]

> . . . the last temple ends with *Huva'l-Mustaghíth* [He is the One Who is invoked] – the name of Him Whom God shall make manifest . . . the Báb is alluding to the fact that in nineteen years, corresponding to the Primal Unity of His Dispensation, the year of Mustagháth will be realized and He Whom God shall make manifest will reveal Himself. The fact that this tablet was revealed for Dayyán, who was to become the third believer in Him Whom God shall make manifest, makes the meaning of the Tablet even more evident. The Báb's identification of the year of Mustagháth . . . and the name of the Promised One, *Huva'l-Mustaghíth*, with the nineteenth temple clearly shows that the Bábí cycle will be completed in nineteen years, corresponding to the nineteen temples.[926]

804. p. 176 ¶ 253. Mírzá 'Alí-Akbar

A paternal cousin of the Báb and an intimate friend of Dayyán who also accepted Bahá'u'lláh:

> He [Mírzá Yaḥyá] even, as a further evidence of the enormity of his crimes, ordered that the cousin of the Báb, Mírzá 'Alí-Akbar, a fervent admirer of Dayyán, be secretly put to death – a command which was carried out in all its iniquity.[927]

The *fatwá* was carried out by Mírzá Muḥammad-i-Mázindarání, the same servant of Mírzá Yaḥyá who had murdered Dayyán.

805. p. 176 ¶ 253. Abu'l-Qásim-i-Ká<u>sh</u>í

A disciple of the Báb who had attained His presence in Kashan. He suffered extensively and became bedridden as a result of the beatings he received on account of his new faith. Following the martyrdom of the Báb he went to Baghdad where he recognized the station of Bahá'u'lláh and became an ardent lover of the Blessed Beauty. Consequently, 'Abu'l-Qásim-i-Ká<u>sh</u>í and several others suffered martyrdom through the decree pronounced by Mírzá Yaḥyá.[928]

806. p. 176 ¶ 254. Mustayqiz

Mustayqiz (Sleeper awakened) is one of the writings of Mírzá Yaḥyá (c. 1854/1855) intended to prove his claims and to refute the objections of several prominent followers of the Báb including Dayyán and Nabíl-i-Zarandí. The brunt of his attack was on Dayyán, who had written a treatise proving that Mírzá Yaḥyá could not be and was not the successor of the Báb.[929] Mírzá Yaḥyá was infuriated by this exposure and he reprimanded Dayyán, calling him the 'Father of Calamities'. He also denounced Siyyid Ibráhím-i-<u>Kh</u>alíl, another prominent Bábí who had turned away from him, as the 'Father of Iniquities' (*Abu'<u>sh</u>-<u>Sh</u>urúr*). He urged the Bábís to arise and take their lives. The orientalist Edward Granville Browne wrote:

> Ṣubḥ-i-Azal [Mírzá Yaḥyá] . . . not only reviles him in the coarsest language, but expresses surprise that his adherents 'sit silent in their places and do not transfix him with their spears,' or rend his bowels with their hand ['to cut the tongues of his bowels'].[930]

Bahá'u'lláh encourages Ḥájí Mírzá Hádí Dawlat-Ábádí, who supported Mírzá Yaḥyá Azal, to study *Mustayqiz*, as this may help him reconsider his views concerning the pretensions of Azal.

807. p. 176 ¶ 255. Siyyid Ibráhím

He was a native of Tabriz, a learned divine of the Shaykhí sect, and a disciple of Siyyid Káẓim-i-Rashtí. He became a disciple of the Báb and attained His presence in Azerbaijan. He was the recipient of several Tablets and also received the title *Khalíl* (Friend) from Him. The Báb transmitted to his care some of His Writings revealed in Máh-Kú:

> During His incarceration in Máh-Kú, nine commentaries on the whole of the Qur'án had been revealed by Him [the Báb]. The texts of these commentaries were entrusted, in Tabríz, to the keeping of a certain Siyyid Ibráhím-i-Khalíl, who was instructed to conceal them until the time for their publication might arrive. Their fate is unknown until now.[931]

> I (Shaykh Ḥasan-i-Zunúzí, a Bábí convert from the Shaykhi school) was instructed by Him (the Báb) to collect all the available Tablets that He had revealed during His incarceration in the castles of Máh-Kú and Chihríq, and to deliver them into the hands of Siyyid Ibráhím-i-Khalíl, who was then living in Tabríz, and urge him to conceal and preserve them with the utmost care.[932]

He attained the presence of Bahá'u'lláh in Baghdad and was protected by him so that Mírzá Yahyá's attempt to have him killed came to nothing (see Annotation 806).

808. p. 176 ¶ 255. O thou who art mentioned as My friend in My scriptures

Address of the Báb to Siyyid Ibráhím (The title of Ibráhím or Abraham is *Khalil-u-lláh* or 'the Friend of God' or 'the Intimate of God'). This title appears in the scriptures of three earlier Abrahamic Dispensations, namely, in the Hebrew Bible (II Chron. 20:7); the New Testament (James 2:23); and the Qur'án (4:125).

809. p. 176 ¶ 256. Reflect a while upon the dishonor inflicted upon the Primal Point

The Qur'án calls the wives of Muhammad *Ummahat al-Mumineen*, or the Mothers of the believers (33:6). It forbids Muslims to marry them after His passing:

> And you must not trouble the Apostle of God, nor marry his wives, after him, for ever. This would be a grave offence with God. (33:53, Rodwell)

The Báb gave a similar injunction concerning His spouses. In nineteenth-century Persia social and religious circumstances almost required a man (especially if he were an eminent person) to take more than one wife. The Báb's first wife was Khadíjih Bagum, the first to accept Him. During His six-months' travel to Isfahan, and after much insistence by Manúchihr Khán, the Governor of Isfahan, the Báb took a second wife, Fáṭimih, who was a sister of Mullá Rajab 'Alíy-i-Qahír, a Bábí from Isfahan. The brothers of Fáṭimih came under the influence of Mírzá Yaḥyá. In violation of the Báb's wishes, after His passing Mírzá Yaḥyá married Fáṭimih. One month later he followed this shameful act by giving her in marriage to Siyyid Muḥammad-i-Iṣfáhání, the arch-enemy of the Faith, who in turn threw her out of his house. Fáṭimih went on a journey to Adrianople with her brother, became blind in her later years and died in Tehran.

This episode, which occurred in Baghdad, was a source of great pain to Bahá'u'lláh and delayed, but did not prevent, the acceptance of the Faith by the Báb's mother, Fáṭimih Bagum.

> His shamelessness and effrontery had waxed so great as to lead him to perpetrate himself, and permit Siyyid Muḥammad to repeat after him, an act so odious that Bahá'u'lláh characterized it as 'a most grievous betrayal', inflicting dishonor upon the Báb, and which 'overwhelmed all lands with sorrow'.[933]

810. p. 176 ¶ 256. after a retirement of two years

Unwilling to speak out against His half-brother, Bahá'u'lláh decided to remove Himself from the situation:

> Attired in the garb of a traveller, coarsely clad, taking with Him nothing but his kashkúl (alms-bowl) and a change of clothes, and assuming the name of Darvísh Muḥammad, Bahá'u'lláh retired to the wilderness, and lived for a time on a mountain named Sar-Galú, so far removed from human habitation that only twice a year, at seed sowing and harvest time, it was visited by the peasants of that region . . . 'From My eyes', He, referring in the Kitáb-i-Íqán to those days, testifies, 'there rained tears of anguish, and in My bleeding heart surged an ocean of agonizing pain. Many a night I had no food for sustenance, and many a day My body found no rest . . . Alone I communed with My spirit, oblivious of the world and all that is therein.'[934]

Amongst the people that Bahá'u'lláh interacted with during the days of His retirement to the mountains of Kurdistan was a group of Sufis in Sulaymaniyyih. In response to their request He revealed the Qasídiy-i-Varqá'iyyih (Ode of the Dove), in praise of the Maiden personifying the Spirit of God that had recently descended upon Him. Shoghi Effendi describes this:

> Amazed by the profundity of His insight and the compass of His understanding, [the Sufis] were impelled to seek from Him what they considered to be a conclusive and final evidence of the unique power and knowledge which He now appeared in their eyes to possess. 'No one among the mystics, the wise, and the learned', they claimed, while requesting this further favour from Him, 'has hitherto proved himself capable of writing a poem in a rhyme and meter identical with that of the longer of the two odes, entitled Qaṣídiy-i-Ta'iyyih composed by Ibn-i-Fárid. We beg you to write for us a poem in that same meter and rhyme.' This request was complied with, and no less than two thousand verses, in exactly the manner they had specified, were dictated by Him, out of which He selected one hundred and twenty-seven, which He permitted them to keep,

deeming the subject matter of the rest premature and unsuitable to the needs of the times.[935]

811. p. 176 ¶ 256. as a result of the intervention of a few

Shoghi Effendi recounts:

> Bahá'u'lláh was still pursuing His solitary existence on that mountain when a certain Shaykh, a resident of Sulaymáníyyih, who owned a property in that neighborhood, sought Him out, as directed in a dream he had of the Prophet Muḥammad. Shortly after this contact was established, Shaykh Ismá'íl, the leader of the Khálidíyyih Order, who lived in Sulaymáníyyih, visited Him, and succeeded, after repeated requests, in obtaining His consent to transfer His residence to that town. Meantime His friends in Baghdád had discovered His whereabouts, and had dispatched Shaykh Sulṭán, the father-in-law of Áqáy-i-Kalím, to beg Him to return; and it was now while He was living in Sulaymáníyyih, in a room belonging to the Takyiy-i-Mawláná Khálid (theological seminary) that their messenger arrived. 'I found', this same Shaykh Sulṭán, recounting his experiences to Nabíl, has stated, 'all those who lived with Him in that place, from their Master down to the humblest neophyte, so enamoured of, and carried away by their love for Bahá'u'lláh, and so unprepared to contemplate the possibility of His departure that I felt certain that were I to inform them of the purpose of my visit, they would not have hesitated to put an end to my life.'[936]

And in the words of Bahá'u'lláh Himself:

> Upon Our arrival in 'Iráq We found the Cause of God sunk in deep apathy and the breeze of divine revelation stilled. Most of the believers were faint and dispirited, nay utterly lost and dead.[937]

Bahá'u'lláh said to Shaykh Sulṭán:

> But for My recognition of the fact that the blessed Cause of the Primal Point was on the verge of being completely obliterated, and all the sacred blood poured out in the path of God would have

been shed in vain, I would in no wise have consented to return to the people of the Bayán, and would have abandoned them to the worship of the idols their imaginations had fashioned.[938]

812. p. 177 ¶ 256. Mírzá Muḥammad-'Alí of Rasht came to see Him, and related, before a large gathering of people, that which had been done, affecting the honor of the Báb

This individual portrayed himself as a seeker and associated with the Bahá'ís in Baghdad, but was apt to find excuses for not accepting the Faith. He put several questions to Bahá'u'lláh after His return from Kurdistan. One of the issues was that if the Báb was a Manifestation of God, then His widow should also have been regarded as the Mother of the believers and not have remarried. The Báb had also stated clearly in the *Tafsir Súrat Yúsuf*, also known as the *Qayyúm al-asmá* and *Ahsan al-qasas*, that the same restriction applied to His widows. Why did then Mírzá Yaḥyá, who considered himself successor to the Báb, inflict this dishonour on the Báb? As a result of his questioning, this issue became widely known.

813. p. 177 ¶ 257. He that was hidden in the Treasury of Knowledge, and inscribed by the Pen of the Most High in His Books, and His Scriptures, and His Scrolls, and His Tablets, is come!

This refers to Bahá'u'lláh, Whose reality was alluded to but in part concealed in the Holy Scriptures. He had become manifest.

The Epistle ends with a number of references that eulogize 'Akká where Bahá'u'lláh was incarcerated in 1863 and lived until His passing in 1892. These represent realized eschatology of Muslim traditions.

814. p. 177 ¶ 258. traditions . . . recorded regarding the blessed and honored city of 'Akká

Shoghi Effendi gives the following description of 'Akká at the time of the arrival of Bahá'u'lláh to that city:

'Akká, the ancient Ptolemais, the St. Jean d'Acre of the Crusaders,

> that had successfully defied the siege of Napoleon, had sunk, under the Turks, to the level of a penal colony to which murderers, highway robbers and political agitators were consigned from all parts of the Turkish empire. It was girt about by a double system of ramparts; was inhabited by a people whom Bahá'u'lláh stigmatized as 'the generation of vipers'; was devoid of any source of water within its gates; was flea-infested, damp and honey-combed with gloomy, filthy and tortuous lanes. 'According to what they say', the Supreme Pen has recorded in the Lawḥ-i-Sulṭán, 'it is the most desolate of the cities of the world, the most unsightly of them in appearance, the most detestable in climate, and the foulest in water. It is as though it were the metropolis of the owl.' So putrid was its air that, according to a proverb, a bird when flying over it would drop dead.[939]

For other descriptions of 'Akká by Shoghi Effendi, see *God Passes By*, pp. 183–5, quoted in Annotations 227, 648 and 649.

Despite the above, a number of Sunni and Shí'ih traditions quoting the Prophet Muhammad extol the sanctity of 'Akká, Ashkelon and other neighbouring regions of the Holy Land, indicating that its importance lay in the fact that Bahá'u'lláh graced it with His Presence. Some of these are recorded in the following sources: *Majma'-ul-Bahrain* (The Mingling of the Two Oceans), by Prince Muḥammad Dara Shikuh (1615–1659 CE); *Kitáb Muhit Al-Muhit*, by Burus Ibn Blus Bustn (1818; published in 1867, Beirut); *Fada'il 'Akká wa 'Asqalan* (Merits of 'Akká and Ashkelon), a compilation of hadith by Bahá ad-Din Abu Muḥammad al-Qasim ibn Abu'l-Qasim 'Ali ibn al-Hasan ibn Hibatullah ibn 'Abdullah ash-Shafi'i. Amongst these is the work of Abu'l-Hasan 'Ali ibn Muḥammad ar-Ruba'i al-Maliki (d. 1052 CE), entitled *Faḍá'al Shám wa Dimashq* (The Merits of Shám and Dimashq); Shám refers to the lands of present-day Syria, Palestine, Lebanon and Jordan, and Dimashq to Damascus). This manuscript, which begins with the refrain 'In the name of God, the Compassionate, the Merciful' describes a number of the hadith recounted by Bahá'u'lláh here.

815. p. 178 ¶ 260. Aynu'l-Baqar

Aynu'l-Baqar (The Spring of the Cow) is the name of an ancient spring in 'Akká. There are a number of statements attributed to Muhammad concerning the beneficial effects of the water drunk from this spring because of its location. Bahá'u'lláh quotes one of statements about it later in the Epistle (¶ 262): 'Whoso drinketh a draught therefrom, God will fill his heart with light, and will protect him from the most great terror on the Day of Resurrection.'

816. p. 178 ¶ 261. 'Abdu'l-'Azíz

Son of 'Abdu'-Ṣalám.[940]

817. p. 178 ¶ 261. 'Abdu'-Ṣalám

A famous Muslim ecclesiastic of the Sunni sect.

818. p. 178 ¶ 262. Ibn-i-Mas'úd

'Abd Allah ibn Maṣúd, also known as Kunya and Abú Abdu'l-Raḥmán (594–c. 653 CE) was a shepherd in his youth and met Muhammad when the latter was fleeing with Abú Bakr from the Quraysh. He was an early Companion of Muhammad (a *sahabah*) and the nineteenth individual to believe in Him. As a foreigner coming from a lower Arab social class and being without any influential supporter he was vulnerable to attacks by the Quraysh aristocracy. He is known for reciting the Qur'án in clear tones to the Quraysh and suffering a beating for his efforts. He migrated (one of the *muhájirún*) with the rest of the Muslims to Medina. He took care of the Prophet, and participated in all the battles defending the new religion. He was said to be the 'keeper of secrets'. He was a contemporary of another Companion of Muhammad, Abú Dhar (see Annotation 142).

819. p. 178 ¶ 262. Askelon

Askelon (Ashkelon) is a coastal Mediterranean town about 30 miles south of Tel Aviv, and about eight miles north of Gaza. Initially a Palestinian city, it was conquered by the tribe of Judah after the death of Joshua. It is mentioned several times in the Hebrew Bible: Judges 14:19; Jer. 25:20, 47:5, 47:7; Amos 1:8; Zeph. 2:7; Zech. 9:5. The Arab village of al-Majdal or al-Majdal Asqalan was established a few kilometres inland from the ancient site by the late 15th century, under Ottoman rule. It was conquered by Israeli forces in 1948.

820. p. 178 ¶ 262. two mountains

'Akká is in a valley between Mount Hermon, *Jabal el-Shaykh* (Mountain of the Shaykh) which borders the Golan Heights, and Mount Carmel, which would have been part of ancient Syria.

821. p. 178 ¶ 263. Anas, son of Málik

Anas ibn Málik ibn Nadar (c. 612–712 CE) was from the Bani Khazraj tribe of Ansárs – the inhabitants of Medina who welcomed and helped Muhammad and His followers who migrated to their city. He became one of the Companions of Muhammad. After the passing of Muhammad he went to Damascus and died in Basra. He is one of the major narrators of hadith, and as a *sahaba* his traditions are considered trustworthy.

822. p. 179 ¶ 264. And He . . . hath said

The verses that follow are from the Prophet Muhammad.

823. p. 179 ¶ 264. I announce unto you a city, on the shores of the sea, white, whose whiteness is pleasing unto God

A description of the Mediterranean Sea is 'the white sea' (Turkish: *Akdeniz*) and 'the middle white sea' (Arabic: *Al Bahr Al-Abyad Al-Muttawasit*), because the shores of the sea are made of chalk and limestone, and when looked at from a far distance the rocks on the shore look white; the city of 'Akká, which is located on the shore, therefore looks white.

824. p. 179 ¶ 264. Khiḍr

Khiḍr is mentioned amongst the traditions relating to 'Akká in the commentaries on the Qur'án (*tafsir*). Although not mentioned by name, the Qur'án describes him as the 'servant' (18:65) who accompanied Moses during His sojourn through the desert to the Holy Land. He is portrayed as a prophet who possessed divine knowledge and who mentored

Moses (18:66–83). The Qur'án mentions many stories about him – the wondrous works ascribed to him only make sense once their hidden purpose is explained. The lesson is that one must be patient in the face of God's inscrutable decrees and await the unfoldment of His will.

Although the accounts of Khiḍr, like the 'Companions of the Cave', may represent legends there is some validity in mentioning them:

> The fact that Bahá'u'lláh makes such statements for the sake of illustrating the spiritual principles that He wishes to convey, does not necessarily mean that He is endorsing their historical accuracy.[941]

> For certain matters are in reality just stories, but the Divine Manifestations bring them out as though it were truth and discourse upon them. For if they were to deny well-known and established matters, others would consider this evidence of their ignorance. Therefore, they bring them out as though they were truth.[942]

825. p. 180 ¶ 265. the black-eyed damsels quaff the camphor in Paradise

The black-eyed damsels is a translation of the Arabic phrase *al-húr'al-Ain*. These heavenly maidens or *húrís* are mentioned several times in the Qur'án (44:54; 52:20; 55:56; 71–72; 78:33) – as virgins, or companions with 'large dark eyes' (52:20, Rodwell) and 'damsels with retiring glances' (55:56, Rodwell) destined to serve the righteous believers in Paradise (of God's future Revelation).

Qur'án 76:5 describes that the righteous are also destined to drink from a cup containing camphor. This is akin to Qur'án 83:22–26 which state that the pious will quaff the choice sealed wine, whose seal is musk, that is, partake of the previously hidden divine truths.

In the Writings of Bahá'u'lláh, the *húrís* are symbolically the countless inner meanings of Revelation that are hidden and remain untouched by the human mind (that is, are in a virginal state):

> By God! however great Our desire to be brief, yet We feel We cannot restrain Our pen. Notwithstanding all that We have mentioned, how innumerable are the pearls which have remained unpierced in the shell of Our heart! How many the húrís of inner meaning that

> are as yet concealed within the chambers of divine wisdom! None hath yet approached them; – húrís, 'whom no man nor spirit hath touched before'.[943]

Though in the Writings of Bahá'u'lláh there are isolated references to the 'maids of heaven' serving the believers in the next life, they are symbols of the inaccessible holiness of God:

> Say: Step out of Thy holy chamber, O Maid of Heaven, inmate of the Exalted Paradise! Drape thyself in whatever manner pleaseth Thee in the silken Vesture of Immortality, and put on, in the name of the All-Glorious, the broidered Robe of Light. Hear, then, the sweet, the wondrous accent of the Voice that cometh from the Throne of Thy Lord, the Inaccessible, the Most High. Unveil Thy face, and manifest the beauty of the black-eyed Damsel, and suffer not the servants of God to be deprived of the light of Thy shining countenance.[944]

826. p. 180 ¶ 265. Spring of Salván (Siloam)

The Pool of Salván (or Siloam in Hebrew) was a pool cut from a rock on the southern slope of the City of David, the original site of Jerusalem, located outside the walls of the Old City to the south-east. The pool was originally fed by the waters of the Gihon Spring via an aqueduct, but this was replaced by the underground Siloam tunnel. It was built during the reign of Hezekiah (715–687/6 BCE) to provide it with a water supply inside the city to protect it from a siege, and is mentioned several times in the Hebrew Bible.

827. p. 180 ¶ 265. Well of Zamzam

Zamzam is a sacred well in the Masjid al-Haram mosque of Mecca in close proximity to the Kaaba. It is identified in Islamic tradition with the spring from which Hagar and Ishmael drank (Gen. 16:14.). *Zam* means 'fill' and it has been suggested that the duplication of '*zam*' (or 'fill, fill') was because Hagar commanded Ishmael to fill the jar as soon as she saw the water. Visiting the well and drinking its water is part of the Hajj pilgrimage:

The spring is naturally regarded as miraculous, and the water, which is held in high esteem, is used for drinking and ablutions. It is exported to distant countries, and religious Moslems break their fasts with it; it is also applied to the eyes to brighten the sight, thus presenting a close analogy to the beverage of the Habdalah cup, with which many Jews moisten their eyes on the night of the Sabbath.[945]

828. p. 181 ¶ 268. the Rukn

Al-Rukn al-Aimani is the right-hand side corner of the Kaaba opposite the Black Stone (*Hajar al-Aswad*). In Islamic tradition it is a revered place.

829. p. 181 ¶ 268. the Maqám

The *Maqám-e-Ibráhím*, also known as the Station of Abraham, is a large stone that is located in an ornate structure near the Kaaba. According to Islamic tradition Abraham stood on the stone while he was rebuilding the Kaaba. It is said to bear an imprint of Abraham's feet. The *Maqám-e-Ibráhím* is referenced in the Qur'án (2:125), and is distinct from the sacred Black Stone that is in the Kaaba. It is a Muslim belief that both the Maqám-e-Ibráhím and the Black Stone were sent from heaven.

830. p. 181 ¶ 269. Verily, the Apostle of God – may the blessings of God, exalted be He, and His salutations be upon Him – hath spoken the truth

That is, the truth of the Prophet Muhammad's statements about 'Akká have now become evident.

BIBLIOGRAPHY

'Abdu'l-Bahá. *'Abdu'l-Bahá in London* (1912). London: Bahá'í Publishing Trust, 1982.

— *Memorials of the Faithful.* Trans. Marzieh Gail. Wilmette, IL: Bahá'í Publishing Trust, 1971.

— *Min Makátíb 'Abdu'l-Bahá.* Vol 1. Rio de Janeiro: Editora Bahá'í Brasil, 1982.

— *Makátib-i Ḥaḍrat 'Abdu'l-Bahá.* Talks of 'Abdu'l-Bahá in Europe and America. Vol. 1. Cairo: Faraju'llah Zaki al-Kurdi, 1921.

— *Muntakhabátí az Makátib-i-Ḥaḍrat-i-'Abdu'l-Bahá* (Selections from the Tablets of 'Abdu'l-Bahá). Langenhain, Germany: Bahá'í Publication Committee in Persian and Arabic, 2000.

— *Paris Talks: Addresses given by 'Abdu'l-Bahá in 1911* (1912). London: Bahá'í Publishing Trust, 12th ed. 1995.

— *The Promulgation of Universal Peace: Talks Delivered by 'Abdu'l-Bahá During His Visit to the United States and Canada in 1912* (1922, 1925). Comp. H. MacNutt. Wilmette, IL: Bahá'í Publishing Trust, 2nd ed. 1982.

— *The Secret of Divine Civilization.* Trans. Marzieh Gail. Wilmette, IL: Bahá'í Publishing Trust, 1957.

— *Selections from the Writings of 'Abdu'l-Bahá.* Comp. Research Department of the Universal House of Justice. Haifa: Bahá'í World Centre, 1978.

— *Some Answered Questions* (1908). Comp. and trans. Laura Clifford Barney. Haifa: Bahá'í World Centre, rev. ed. 2014.

— *Tablets of 'Abdu'l-Bahá* (etext in the Ocean search engine; originally published as *Tablets of Abdul-Baha Abbas.* 3 vols. Chicago: Bahá'í Publishing Society, 1909–1916). Wilmette, IL: National Spiritual Assembly of the Bahá'ís of the United States, 1980.

— *Tablets of the Divine Plan.* Wilmette, IL: Bahá'í Publishing Trust, rev. ed. 1977.

— *A Traveler's Narrative Written to Illustrate the Episode of the Báb* (1891). Trans. E. G. Browne. Wilmette, IL: Bahá'í Publishing Trust, rev. ed. 1980.

— 'Twelve Table Talks Given by 'Abdu'l-Bahá in 'Akká between 1904 and 1906'.

Available online in *Writings and Talks of 'Abdu'l-Bahá*, https://www.bahai.org/library/authoritative-texts/abdul-baha/.

— *Will and Testament of 'Abdu'l-Bahá.* Wilmette, IL: National Spiritual Assembly of the Bahá'ís of the United States, 1944.

Abrahamian, Ervand. *Tortured Confessions: Prisons and Public Recantations in Modern Iran.* Oakland: University of California Press, 1999.

Afnán, Muhammad; Hatcher, William S. 'Western Islámic scholarship and Bahá'í origins', in *Religion*, vol. 15. London: Academic Press, 1985.

Ahmad Bin Hanbal. *Musnad.* Cairo: Dar el-Hadith, 1995. Available at: https://books-library.online/d-22-download; see also: https://www.ummah.com/.../466881-misguided-and-astray-scholars.

— *Musnad.* Trans. Nasiruddin Al-Khattab. Riyadh, Houston, New York: Maktaba Darussalam, 2012.

'Alawí, Núrúralláh Dáneshvar. *Táríkh-e enqeláb-e mashrúṭíyat-e Írān o jonbesh-e waṭanparastán-e Eṣfahén o Baktiárí*, Tehran, 1956.

'Alí ibn Abí Tálib. *Nahjul Balaghah* (Sermons, Letters and Sayings). Qum, Islamic Republic of Iran: Ansariyan Publications, 1971.

— 'The Sermon of *Ma'rifat bin-Nuráníyyat* (Recognition with Luminousness) of 'Alí ibn 'Abú Tálib, the First Imám'. Trans. and explanatory note by Khazeh Fananapazir, 2001. Available at: https://bahai-library.com/imam-ali_marifat_nuraniyyat.

Ameer Ali, Syed. *The Spirit of Islam: A History of the Evolution and Ideals of Islam, with a Life of the Prophet.* University of California Libraries, 1922.

al-Amili, Shaykh al-Hurr (comp.). *Wasa'il ash-Shi'a.* 10 vols. Manshurat Dhawi'l-Qurba, 2008.

Áyatí, 'Abdu'l-Ḥusayn (Avarih). *Al-Kawákibud-Durríyah fí ta'rikh ẓuhúr al-Bábíyah wa-al-Bahá'íyah*, vol. 1. Cairo: Matba'ah sa'aadah, 1923.

The Báb. *Selections from the Writings of the Báb.* Comp. Research Department of the Universal House of Justice. Haifa: Bahá'í World Centre, 1976.

— 'Twenty-two letters from the Bāb addressed to different individuals by Bāb, 'Alī Muḥammad Shīrāzī, 1819–1850', E. G. Browne Collection, F. 21, Cambridge University Library.

Bahá'í Prayers: A Selection of Prayers Revealed by Bahá'u'lláh, The Báb, and 'Abdu'l-Bahá. Wilmette, IL: Bahá'í Publishing Trust, rev. ed. 2002.

Bahá'í Reference Library. Authoritative online source of Bahá'í writings. Available at: https://www.bahai.org/library/.

The Bahá'í World: An International Record. Vol. XVIII (1979–1983). Haifa: Bahá'í World Centre, 1986.

Bahá'í World Faith: Selected Writings of Bahá'u'lláh and 'Abdu'l-Bahá. Wilmette, IL: Bahá'í Publishing Trust, rev. ed. 1956.

Bahá'u'lláh. *Á<u>th</u>ár-i-Qalam-i-A'lá* (Traces of the Supreme Pen). Hamilton, Ont.: Muassasih Maarif Bahá'í, Association for Bahá'í Studies in Persian, 2002.

— *The Call of the Divine Beloved: Selected Mystical Works of Bahá'u'lláh.* Haifa, Bahá'í World Centre, 2018.

— *Epistle to the Son of the Wolf.* Trans. Shoghi Effendi. Wilmette, IL: Bahá'í Publishing Trust, rev. ed. 1976.

— *Gems of Divine Mysteries: Javáhiru'l-Asrár.* Haifa: Bahá'í World Centre, 2002.

— *Gleanings from the Writings of Bahá'u'lláh.* Trans. Shoghi Effendi. Wilmette, IL: Bahá'í Publishing Trust, 2nd ed. 1976.

— *The Hidden Words of Bahá'u'lláh.* Trans. Shoghi Effendi. Wilmette, IL: Bahá'í Publishing Trust, 1970; New Delhi: Bahá'í Publishing Trust, 1987.

— Iran National Bahá'í Archives (INBA), series of Writings of Bahá'u'lláh.

— *I<u>sh</u>ráqát va Chand Lawḥ-i-Digar.* Bombay: Dutt Prashad Press, circa 1892. Available at: https://www.h-net.org/~bahai/areprint/baha/G-L/I/ishraqat/ishraqat.htm.

— *The Kitáb-i-Aqdas: The Most Holy Book.* Haifa: Bahá'í World Centre, 1992.

— *Kitáb-i-Íqán: The Book of Certitude.* Trans. Shoghi Effendi. Wilmette, IL: Bahá'í Publishing Trust, 2nd ed. 1950, 1981.

— *La'Aaliyul Hikmat Jild Awwal.* Vol. 1. Rio de Janeiro: Editora Bahá'í Brasil, 1986.

— *Prayers and Meditations by Bahá'u'lláh.* Trans. Shoghi Effendi. Wilmette, IL: Bahá'í Publishing Trust, 1938, 1987.

— *The Proclamation of Bahá'u'lláh to the Kings and Leaders of the World.* Haifa: Bahá'í World Centre, 1967.

— *The Summons of the Lord of Hosts: Tablets of Bahá'u'lláh.* Haifa: Bahá'í World Centre, 2002.

— *The Tabernacle of Unity.* Haifa: Bahá'í World Centre, 2006.

— *Tablets of Bahá'u'lláh Revealed After the Kitáb-i-Aqdas.* Comp. Research Department of the Universal House of Justice. Haifa: Bahá'í World Centre, 1978.

Bahíyyih <u>Kh</u>ánum, the Greatest Holy Leaf: A Compilation from Bahá'í Sacred Texts and Writings of the Guardian of the Faith and Bahíyyih <u>Kh</u>ánum's Own Letters. Haifa: Bahá'í World Centre, 1982.

al-Bahraani, Sayyid Hashim. *The Qa'em in the Qur'an.* Trans. Sayyid Mohsen al-Husaini al-Milani, 2006. Available at: www.shiabooks.ca.

Bakhtiari, Ali Mortezá Samsam. *The Last of the Khâns: The Life of Morteza Quli Khân Samsam Bakhtiari.* New York: Universe, 2006.

Balyuzi, H. M. *'Abdu'l-Bahá.* Oxford: George Ronald, 1971.

— *Bahá'u'lláh, The King of Glory.* Oxford: George Ronald, 1980.

— *Edward Granville Browne and the Bahá'í Faith.* Oxford: George Ronald, 1975.

— *Eminent Bahá'ís in the Time of Bahá'u'lláh.* Oxford: George Ronald, 1985.

Barnes, Rev. Albert. *Notes, Critical, Explanatory, and Practical, of the Book of the Prophet Isaiah with a New Translation.* Glasgow: Bell and Bain, 1845.

— *Notes on the Bible* (1834). Available at: sacred-texts.com; see also https://biblehub.com/commentaries/daniel/8-11.htm.

Benson, Joseph. *The Holy Bible: Containing the Old and New Testament (according to the Present Authorized Version) with Critical, Explanatory, and Practical Notes.* G. Lane & C. B. Tippett, for the Methodist Episcopal Church, 1846.

Bible. *Holy Bible.* King James version. London: Eyre and Spottiswoode, various dates. Unless otherwise stated this translation is used.

— *Holy Bible.* English Standard Version (ESV). London: Collins, various dates.

— New American Standard Bible (NAS). Trans. Lockman Foundation. New York: Broadman and Holman, 1986. Available at: https://www.biblestudytools.com/nas/.

— New English Translation (NET). See https://www.biblegateway.com/versions/New-English-Translation-NET-Bible/; and netbible.com.

— New International Version (NIV). Trans. Biblica. Available at: https://www.biblestudytools.com/niv/.

Blomfield, Lady. *The Chosen Highway.* London: Bahá'í Publishing Trust, 1940. RP Oxford: George Ronald, 2007.

Browne, E.G. *Materials for the Study of the Bábí Religion.* Cambridge: Cambridge University Press, 1918.

— 'Personal Reminiscences of the Bábí Insurrection at Zanjan in 1850, written by Aqa 'Abdu'l-Ahad-i-Zanjani', in *Journal of the Royal Asiatic Society* (1897), pp. 761–827.

al-Bursi, Hafiz Rajab. *Mashâriq Anwar al-Yaqín fi Asrár Amir Mu'minín.* Beirut: Dar al-Andalus, 1978. Sections translated by Dr Khazeh Fananapazir, available at: bahai-library.com/fananapazir_khutbih_tutunjiyyih.

A Compilation on Women. Research Department of the Universal House of Justice. Haifa: Bahá'í World Centre, 1986.

Cornell, Vincent J. *Voices of Islam: The Passion of 'Ashura in Shiite Islam.* Westport, Conn.: Praeger, 2007.

Curzon, George N. *Persia and the Persian Question* (1892). 2 vols. Facsimile reprint. London: Frank Cass,1966.

The Dawn-Breakers: Nabíl's Narrative of the Early Days of the Bahá'í Revelation. Trans. Shoghi Effendi. Wilmette, IL: Bahá'í Publishing Trust, 1932, 1999.

De Wette, W. M. L. *A Critical and Historical Introduction to the Canonical Scriptures of the Old Testament.* Vol. II. New York: D. Appleton and Company, 4th ed. 1864.

Elad, Amikam. *Medieval Jerusalem and Islamic Worship: Holy Places, Ceremonies, Pilgrimage.* Leiden and New York: Brill Academic Publishers, 1994.

Ellicott, Charles John (ed). *An Old Testament Commentary for English Readers.* London, Paris and New York: Cassell, 1884.

Encyclopaedia Iranica. Available at: www.iranicaonline.org.

Esslemont, J. E. *Bahá'u'lláh and the New Era* (1923). Wilmette IL: Bahá'í Publishing Trust, 1980.

Fáḍil-i-Mázindarání. *Amr Va Khalq* (Revelation and Creation). Tehran: Bahá'í Publishing Trust, 1971 (128 BE).

Fananapazir, Lameh. *Islam at the Crossroads.* Oxford: George Ronald, 2015.

Fire and Light. Trans. Habib Taherzadeh et al. Hofheim-Langenhain: Bahá'í Verlag, 1982. Originally published in *The Bahá'í World*, vol. 18 (1979–1983), pp. 9–38.

Firestone, Reuven. 'Muslim-Jewish Relations', in *Oxford Research Encyclopedia: Religion.* New York and London: Oxford University Press, 2016.

Foran, John. *A Century of Revolution: Social Movements in Iran.* University of Minnesota Press, 1994.

Gail, Marzieh. *Bahá'í Glossary: A Glossary of Persian and Arabic Words Appearing in the Bahá'í Writings.* Wilmette, IL: Bahá'í Publishing Trust, 1955.

Gibson, Dave. *Expect God's Visitation: Preaching Today.* Available online at: www.preachingtoday.com/Sermons.

Ḥaydar-'Ali, Ḥájí Mírzá. *Stories from The Delight of Hearts: The Memoirs of Ḥájí Mírzá Ḥaydar-'Ali.* Trans. and abridged A.-Q. Faizi. Los Angeles, Kalimát Press, 1980.

Hazelton, Lesley. *After the Prophet: The Epic Story of the Shia–Sunni Split in Islam.* New York: Anchor Books, 2009.

Ibn al-'Arabí, *The Bezels of Wisdom* (Fuṣúṣ al-Ḥikam). The Classics of Western Spirituality Series. Trans. R. W. J. Austin. New York and Ramsey: Paulist Press, 1980.

Ibn-Babwayh (Shaykh Ṣaduq). *I'tiqadat fi Deen Al-Imamiyyah.* Beirut: Dar Al-Mufid Wa An Nashr, 1993 (1414 AH).

Iran National Bahá'í Archives (INBA). https://www.h-net.org/~bahai/diglib/INBA/INBA018.pdf.

al-Irbili, Ali b. Isa. *Kashf al-ghumma fi ma'rifat al-a'imma* (Lifting the Hardship in Knowing the Imams). In Arabic. Beirut, Dar al-Adwa', 1403/1983.

Ishráq-Khávarí, 'Abdu'l-Ḥamid (comp.). *Má'idiy-i-Ásamání*, A compilation of Bahá'í Writings. Tehran: Bahá'í Publishing Trust, 1972.

— *Qámús Lawḥ Shaykh Najafí.* A commentary on the Tablet of Shaykh Najafi, the Son of the Wolf. Tehran: Mu' assasih Matbu'at Amri, 1972. Republished by Asre Jadid in Germany, 2001 (158 BE).

Jámi 'At-Tirmidhi. Trans. Abu Khalyl. Riyadh, Jeddah, London, Houston, New York: Maktaba Darussalam. 2007.

Keddie, Nikki R. *Religion and Rebellion in Iran: The Tobacco Protest of 1891–1892.* New York: Humanities Press, 1967.

al-Kulayni, Abu Ja'far Muhammad ibn Ya'qub (Thigatu Al-Islam) (comp.). *Al-Kafi* (a collection of Shí'ih traditions). Trans. Muhammad Sarwar. 8 vols. Vol. 1: *The Meanings of the Names of Allah and Their Derivatives*; vol. 2: *The Book of Belief and Disbelief.* New York: The Islamic Seminary, 2015.

Lambden, Stephen. 'Tablet to Mullá Muhammad Báqir-i Tabrízí', provisional translation posted by Jonah Winters in Bahá'í Library Online, 1 January 2013. Available at: bahai-library.com/bab_lawh_muhammad_baqir-tabrizi.

— 'The Word *Bahá*: Quintessence of the Greatest Name', in *Bahá'í Studies Review*, vol. 3 (1993), no. 1.

Lewis, Frank. 'Overview of the Abjad numerological system', in Bahá'í Library Online, 1999-04.

Lights of Guidance: A Bahá'í Reference File. Comp. H. Hornby. New Delhi: Bahá'í Publishing Trust, 5th ed. 1997.

Lings, Martin. *Muḥammad: His Life Based on the Earliest Sources.* London: Allen and Unwin, 1983; Rochester, VT: Inner Traditions, 2006.

al-Majlisi, Allamah Muhammad Baqir. *Bihár al-Anwár*, Vols. 51-52-53 (new ed.). *Kitabul Ghaibah* (Book of Occulation), Part II: 'The Promised Mihdi. Trans. Sayyid Athar Husain S.H. Rizvi. Mumbai: Ja'fari Propagation Centre. Also: vol. 22 (originally vol. 6). Beirut: Mu'assasat–al-Wafá,. 1983.

Malik-Khusravi, Muḥammad 'Alí. *'Iqlim-i-Nur.* Tehran: Mu'assisih Matbu'at Amri, 1958 (115 BE).

Manuchehri, Sepehr. 'The practice of taqiyyih (dissimulation) in the Bábí and Bahá'í religions', in *Australian Bahá'í Studies*, vol. 2 (2000), pp. 219–251. Available at: manuchehri_taqiyyih_babi_bahai.pdf.

Momen, Moojan. 'The 'Akká traditions in the Epistle to the Son of the Wolf: A research note', in *Lights of 'Irfán,* Papers Presented at the 'Irfán Colloquia and Seminars, vol. 4, pp. 167–178. Evanston, IL: Bahá'í National Center, 2003.

Available at: http://irfancolloquia.org/pdf/lights4_momen.pdf; and at: https://bahai-library.com/momen_hadith_esw.

— (ed). *Selections from the Writings of E. G. Browne on the Bábí and Bahá'í Religions.* Oxford: George Ronald, 1987.

Násir-i-Khsrau. *Diary of a Journey Through Syria and Palestine by Násir-i-Khsrau in 1047 A.D.* Trans. Guy Le Strange, The Library of the Palestine Pilgrims Text Society. London: Committee of the Palestine Exploration Fund, 1896.

Nasr, Seyyed Hossein. *The Study Qur'án.* New York: Harper Collins, 2015.

al-Numani, Sheikh Muhammad bin Ibraheem bin Jafar. *Kitab al-Ghayba: The Book of Occultation.* Qum, Islamic Republic of Iran: Ansariyan Publications, n.d.

Osborn, Eric. *Irenaeus of Lyons.* Cambridge: Cambridge University Press, 2001.

— *Tertullian: First Theologian of the West.* Cambridge: Cambridge University Press, 1997, 2003.

Purcell, Rev. Edward. (ed.). 'Bells', in *The Catholic Telegraph*, 19 January 1850. Catholic Research Resources Alliance, The Catholic News Archive.

Pusey, Rev. E. B. *The Minor Prophets with a Commentary Explanatory and Practical, and Introductions to the Several Books.* New York: Funk and Wagnalls, 1885.

al-Qummi, Shaykh Abbas. *Mafátih al-Jinan* (A Treasury of Islamic Piety). Trans. Ali Quli Qarai. CreateSpace Independent Publishing Platform, 2018.

Qur'an. *The Holy Qur'an.* Trans. Abdullah Yusuf Ali. Lahore: Sh. Muhammad Ashraf, 1934. Rev. ed. 2009/10 available at sacred-texts.com. Unless otherwise stated this translation is used.

— *The Koran.* Trans. J. M. Rodwell. New York: Dutton, 1971.

— *The Meaning of the Glorious Koran.* Trans. Marmaduke Pickthall, 1930. Many editions.

al-Sadiq, Imam Ja'far. *Misbah al-Shariah.* Beirut: Mu'assasah A'lami, 2nd ed. 1983. English translation: *Lantern of the Path: Misbah Al-Shariah*, Trans. Shaykh Haeri. CreateSpace Independent Publishing Platform, 2017.

Sahih Muslim (compendium of traditions). 7 vols. Book 31, ch. 4: 'The Merits of 'Ali B. Abi Talib'. Trans. Nasiruddun al-Khattab. Available at: HadithCollection.com; Book 45: 'The Book of Virtue, Enjoining Good Manners, and Joining of the Ties of Friendship'. Available at: https://sunnah.com/muslim.

Sahih al-Bukhari (compendium of Sunni traditions). Trans. Muhammad Muhsin Khan. Riyadh: Darussalam, 1997. See also: https://muflihun.com/bukhari/56/662.

Saiedi, Náder. *Gate of the Heart: Understanding the Writings of the Báb.* Waterloo, Ont.: Wilfred Laurier, 2008.

Salmání, Ustád Muḥammad-ʿAlí. *My Memories of Bahá'u'lláh*. Trans. Marzieh Gail. Los Angeles: Kalimát Press, 1982.

Schaff, Philip; Wace, Henry. *A Select Library of Nicene and Post-Nicene Fathers of the Christian Church.* Second Series, Translated into English with Prolegmena and Explanatory Notes. New York: The Christian Literature Company. 1898.

Shoghi Effendi. *The Advent of Divine Justice* (1939). Wilmette, IL: Bahá'í Publishing Trust, 1984, 1990.

— *Citadel of Faith: Messages to America, 1947–1957.* Wilmette, IL: Bahá'í Publishing Trust, 1965, 1980.

— *Directives from the Guardian.* Comp. Gertrude Garrida. New Delhi: Bahá'í Publishing Trust, 1973.

— *God Passes By* (1944). Wilmette, IL: Bahá'í Publishing Trust, rev. ed. 1974.

— *Messages to America 1932–1946.* Wilmette, IL: Bahá'i Publishing Trust, 1947. Published online by the Project Gutenberg and by Bahá'í Publishing Trust, Wilmette as *This Decisive Hour* (see below).

— *Messages to the Bahá'í World 1950–1957.* Wilmette, IL: Bahá'í Publishing Trust, 2nd ed. 1971.

— *The Promised Day Is Come* (1941). Wilmette, IL: Bahá'í Publishing Trust, rev. ed. 1980.

— *This Decisive Hour: Messages from Shoghi Effendi to the North American Bahá'ís 1932–1946.* Wilmette, IL: Bahá'í Publishing Trust, 1992.

— *Unfolding Destiny: The Messages from the Guardian of the Bahá'í Faith to the Bahá'í Community of the British Isles.* London: Bahá'í Publishing Trust, 1981.

— *The World Order of Bahá'u'lláh: Selected Letters by Shoghi Effendi* (1938). Wilmette, IL: Bahá'í Publishing Trust, 2nd rev. ed. 1974.

Singer, Isidore; Seligsohn, M. 'Zamzam', in *The Jewish Encyclopedia.* 12 vols. 1901-1906. Available at: JewishEncyclopedia.com.

Smith, Rev. George Adam. *The Expositor's Bible.* Vol. 1. London: Hodder and Stoughton, 1907.

Smith, Peter. *A Concise Encyclopedia of the Bahá'í Faith.* Oxford: Oneworld, 2000.

Star of the West: The Bahai Magazine. Periodical, 25 vols. 1910–1935. Vols. 1–14 RP Oxford: George Ronald, 1978. Complete CD-ROM version: Talisman Educational Software/Special Ideas, 2001.

Sunan Abu Dawud. Comp. Imám Háfiz Abu Dawud Sulaiman bin Ashʿath. Trans. Nasiruddin al-Khattab. Riyadh, Houston, New York: Darrussalam, 2008.

Suyuti, Jalal-ud Din. *Al-Jami'u Sagheer Fi Ahadeeth Al-Basshee An-Nadheer.* Beirut: Dar Al Kutub Al-Ilmiyyah DKI, 2016.

Taherzadeh, Adib, *The Revelation of Bahá'u'lláh*. 4 vols. Oxford: George Ronald, 1974–1987.

Universal House of Justice, The. *The Constitution of the Universal House of Justice.* Haifa: Bahá'í World Centre, 1972. Available at: https://www.bahai.org/documents/the-universal-house-of-justice/constitution-universal-house-justice.

— 'Diacritics; meaning of "Self-subsisting"', letter on behalf of the Universal House of Justice to an individual, 21 January 1993. Available at: https://bahai-library.com/uhj_translation_subsisting.

— Memorandum on Socrates, 22 October 1995. Available at: http://bahai-library.com/compilation_socrates_bwc#15.

— *A Synopsis and Codification of the Kitáb-i-Aqdas*. Haifa: Bahá'í World Centre, 1973.

— *A Wider Horizon: Selected Messages of the Universal House of Justice*. Riviera Beach, FL: Palabra Publications, 1992.

Van Voorst, Robert E. *Anthology of World Scriptures.* Belmont, CA: Wadsworth, 2nd ed. 2016.

Walbridge, John. 'Some Bábi Martyrs' in Walbridge, *Essays and Notes on Bábi and Bahá'í History*, in *Occasional Papers in Shaykhi, Babi and Bahá'í Studies*, vol. 6, no. 1. East Lansing, MI: H-Bahai Digital Library, 2002–03. Available at: https://bahai-library.com/walbridge_babi_martyrs.

Walcher, Heidi A. *In the Shadow of the King: Zill Al-Sultán and Isfahan under the Qájars*. London: Tauris, 2008.

Zarzecny, Matthew. *Religion in Napoleonic France, Part II: Napoleon III and Religion; Part III: Religious Goals of The Two Emperors.* The Napoleon Series, 2003. Available at: https://www.napoleon-series.org/research/napoleon/c_religion2.html.

Zürcher, Erik-Jan. 'The Ottoman conscription system in theory and practice, 1844–1918', in *International Review of Social History*, vol. 43 (1998), no. 3, pp. 437–449.

REFERENCES

Foreword

1. Shoghi Effendi, *This Decisive Hour*, no. 78. The first part of the translation was received on 7 May 1940. The Guardian sent the remaining part on 26 November 1940.
2. Shoghi Effendi, *God Passes By*, pp. 219–20.

Introduction

1. The Epistle mentions the arrest of three eminent Bahá'ís by the governor of Tehran, Kámrán Mírzá, which occurred in 1891, and Bahá'u'lláh passed away on 29 May 1892.
2. The Lord's Prayer, Matt. 6:9–11.
3. Súrih 78 of the Qur'án, *an Naba'*: the Announcement or the Tidings.
4. Qur'án 1:4.
5. Qur'án 1:6.
6. Qur'án 14:5; 30:43; and 45:14.
7. Qur'án 3:194.
8. Qur'án 39:69.
9. The Books of Daniel and Revelation.
10. Qá'im-i-Al-i-Muḥammad, literally, 'He Who shall arise from the family of Muhammad' expected by Shí'ihs. See for example al-Irbili, *Kashf al-ghumma*, vol. 3. p. 255: Imám Jafar Sádiq said, 'when the Qá'im shall arise, he will rule with justice, the tyrants of his time shall fear him, the righteous will be safe, the earth shall reveal its treasures, all the truth-seekers will seek his company . . .'
11. Shoghi Effendi, *God Passes By*, p. 94.
12. Shoghi Effendi, *The Advent of Divine Justice*, para. 29, p. 17.
13. ibid. para. 31, p. 18.
14. *The Dawn-Breakers*, p. 200.
15. The cleric or Imam who leads the Muslims in prayer on Fridays.
16. Armenian–Jewish quarter in Isfahan.
17. Marzieh Gail, Introduction to 1953 edition of *Epistle to the Son of Wolf*, pp. x–xi.
18. Doctor of Islamic jurisprudence.
19. The castigation 'wolf' perhaps refers to the animal's alleged tendency to destroy more prey, particularly when excited by the carnage, than it can immediately eat.
20. A son of the king, Násiri'd-Dín Sháh, and the ruler of the town and province of Isfahan.
21. Taherzadeh, *The Revelation of Bahá'u'lláh*, vol. 4, ch. 5, p. 76.
22. Bahá'u'lláh, Lawḥ-i-Burhán (Tablet of the Proof), in *Tablets of Bahá'u'lláh Revealed After the Kitáb-i-Aqdas*, p. 216.
23. ibid. pp. 214–15.
24. Shoghi Effendi, *God Passes By*, pp. 233.
25. ibid. p. 232.

26. Taherzadeh, *The Revelation of Bahá'u'lláh*, vol. 4, ch. 6, pp. 100–101, quoting Shoghi Effendi (see above, notes 23 and 24).
27. *Encyclopaedia Iranica*: 'term used to designate the processes of exposition, analysis, and argument which constitute human effort to express God's law (*shari'ah*)'. Available at: www.iranicaonline.org.
28. Walcher, *In the Shadow of the King*, p. 49.
29. *Encyclopaedia Iranica*: Áqá Najafí Eṣfahání.
30. ibid.
31. Bahá'u'lláh, *Epistle to the Son of the Wolf*, p. 18.
32. *The Dawn-Breakers*, p. 90.
33. Walcher, *In the Shadow of the King*, p. 49.
34. ibid. p. 51.
35. *Encyclopaedia Iranica*: Áqá Najafí Eṣfahání.
36. Walcher, *In the Shadow of the King*, p. 10.
37. Also, on his orders, three Bahá'ís were arrested in Nayriz (province of Fars) in 1897; see Momen, 'A Chronology of some of the persecutions of the Bábís and Bahá'ís in Írán, 1844–1978, in *The Bahá'í World*, vol. XVIII, pp. 383–4.
38. Walcher, *In the Shadow of the King*, pp. 112–13.
39. ibid. p. 115.
40. ibid. p. 112.
41. ibid. p. 113.
42. ibid. p. 51.
43. Bahá'u'lláh, *Kitáb-i-Íqán*, para. 162, pp. 153–4.
44. Shoghi Effendi, *The Promised Day Is Come*, p. 107.
45. Bahá'u'lláh, *Gleanings from the Writings of Bahá'u'lláh*, CXXXII, pp. 287–8.
46. 'Abdu'l-Bahá, *Paris Talks*, no. 18, p. 57.
47. Quoted in Balyuzi, *'Abdu'l-Bahá*, p. 145.
48. 'Abdu'l-Bahá, *Tablets of the Divine Plan*, no. 5: Tablet to the Bahá'is of Canada and Greenland, p. 27.
49. Bahá'u'lláh, *Epistle to the Son of the Wolf*, p. 143.
50. ibid. p. 28.
51. Bahá'u'lláh, *Gleanings from the Writings of Bahá'u'lláh*, CXXXII, p. 288.

Annotations

1. See https://www.bahai.org/documents/the-universal-house-of-justice/constitution-universal-house-justice.
2. Bahá'u'lláh, *The Kitáb-i-Aqdas*, para. 1, p. 19.
3. 'Abdu'l-Bahá, Tafsír-i-Bismilláh, in *Min Makátíb 'Abdu'l-Bahá*, vol. 1, pp. 32–48.
4. al-Kulayni (comp.), Al-Kafi, vol. 1, The Meanings of the Names of Allah and Their Derivatives, H 305, ch. 16, h 1, p. 98.
5. See for example Bahá'u'lláh, *Prayers and Meditations*, LXXIII, p. 121.
6. Bahá'u'lláh, *Gems of Divine Mysteries* (Javáhiru'l-Asrár), p. 34.
7. Bahá'u'lláh, *Gleanings from the Writings of Bahá'u'lláh*, CXXI, p. 258.
8. Bahá'u'lláh, in *Bahá'í Prayers*, p. 220.
9. 'Diacritics; meaning of "Self-subsisting"', letter on behalf of the Universal House of Justice to an individual, 21 January 1993.
10. 'Abdu'l-Bahá, *Will and Testament*, p. 9.

11. 'Abdu'l-Bahá, *Tablets of Abdul-Baha Abbas*, p. 393.
12. Bahá'u'lláh, *Tablets of Bahá'u'lláh Revealed After the Kitáb-i-Aqdas*, p. 231.
13. Bahá'u'lláh, Lawḥ-i-Karmil (Tablet of Carmel), in *Tablets of Bahá'u'lláh Revealed After the Kitáb-i-Aqdas*, p. 4.
14. Bahá'u'lláh, quoted in Shoghi Effendi, *The Advent of Divine Justice*, pp. 82–3.
15. Bahá'u'lláh, *Tablets of Bahá'u'lláh Revealed After the Kitáb-i-Aqdas*, p. 231.
16. Bahá'u'lláh, *Prayers and Meditations*, LXIX, p. 113.
17. 'Abdu'l-Bahá, *Some Answered Questions*, pp. 118–121.
18. 'Abdu'l-Bahá, in *Bahá'í World Faith*, p. 405; see also Shoghi Effendi, *Unfolding Destiny*, p. 5.
19. The Báb, *Selections from the Writings of the Báb*, p. 52.
20. Bahá'u'lláh, *Prayers and Meditations*, XXIV, pp. 27–8.
21. Bahá'u'lláh, *Kitáb-i-Íqán*, para. 281, p. 252.
22. Bahá'u'lláh, Lawḥ-i-Dunyá (Tablet of the World), in *Tablets of Bahá'u'lláh Revealed After the Kitáb-i-Aqdas*, p. 89.
23. Bahá'u'lláh, *Gleanings from the Writings of Bahá'u'lláh*, XLIII, p. 97.
24. ibid. XCII, p. 183.
25. ibid. XIV, p. 29.
26. Bahá'u'lláh, quoted in Shoghi Effendi, *The Advent of Divine Justice*, pp. 82–3.
27. Bahá'u'lláh, *Prayers and Meditations*, XCVII, p. 162.
28. Bahá'u'lláh, *Kitáb-i-Íqán*, para. 148, p. 136.
29. ibid. para. 182, p. 171.
30. Bahá'u'lláh, *The Kitáb-i-Aqdas*, para. 7, pp. 21–22.
31. 'Abdu'l-Bahá, *Some Answered Questions*, p. 173.
32. 'Ali ibn Abi Tálib, *Nahjul Balaghah*, vol. 2, p. 736, Sermon 369.
33. Sahih al-Bukhari, Darussalam reference, hadith 3456; USC-MSA web (English) reference, vol. 4, Book 56, hadith 662. Available at: https://muflihun.com/bukhari/56/662.
34. Bahá'u'lláh, Súriy-i-Haykal, in *The Summons of the Lord of Hosts*, p. 28.
35. Bahá'u'lláh, Tablet of Aḥmad, in *Bahá'í Prayers*, pp. 210–11.
36. Osborn, *Irenaeus of Lyons*, pp. 104–6.
37. Osborn, *Tertullian: First Theologian of the West*, pp. 44–5.
38. Ibn al-'Arabí, *The Bezels of Wisdom* (Fuṣúṣ al-Ḥikam), ch. I, pp. 51–5; and ch.. XXVII, p. 272.
39. 'Abdu'l-Bahá, *Some Answered Questions*, pp. 196, 222.
40. 'Abdu'l-Bahá, *Paris Talks*, p. 51.
41. Bahá'u'lláh, quoted in Shoghi Effendi, *God Passes By*, pp. 82–3.
42. 'Abdu'l-Bahá, *Tablets of the Divine Plan*, no. 9: Tablet to the Bahá'ís of the North-eastern States, p. 62.
43. Bahá'u'lláh, I<u>sh</u>ráqát (Splendours), in *Tablets of Bahá'u'lláh Revealed After the Kitáb-i-Aqdas*, p. 119.
44. Bahá'u'lláh, *Gleanings from the Writings of Bahá'u'lláh*, XXXVIII, pp. 87–8.
45. Bahá'u'lláh, quoted in Shoghi Effendi, *The World Order of Bahá'u'lláh*, p. 167.
46. Shoghi Effendi, *God Passes By*, p. 94.
47. Bahá'u'lláh, *The Summons of the Lord of Hosts*, para. 197, p. 101.
48. Bahá'u'lláh, *Prayers and Meditations*, CLXXXIII, p. 320.
49. 'Abdu'l-Bahá, *The Promulgation of Universal Peace*, p. 156.

50. Shoghi Effendi, *The Promised Day Is Come*, pp. v–vi.
51. 'Abdu'l-Bahá, *The Promulgation of Universal Peace*, p. 151.
52. Bahá'u'lláh, *Gleanings from the Writings of Bahá'u'lláh*, LXX, p. 136.
53. Shoghi Effendi, *The World Order of Bahá'u'lláh*, p. 42.
54. ibid. p. 203.
55. Shoghi Effendi, *God Passes By*, p. 94.
56. Bahá'u'lláh, Súriy-i-Haykal, in Bahá'u'lláh, *The Summons of the Lord of Hosts*, para. 21, p. 12.
57. Medium Obligatory Prayer revealed by Bahá'u'lláh, in *Bahá'í Prayers*, p. 5.
58. Shoghi Effendi, *The Promised Day Is Come*, pp. 13–20, and *God Passes By*, pp. 104–26, 163–91.
59. Bahá'u'lláh, Tablet of Visitation, in *Bahá'í Prayers*, p. 232.
60. Bahá'u'lláh, quoted in Shoghi Effendi, *The World Order of Bahá'u'lláh*, pp. 118–19.
61. Fananapazir, *Islam at the Crossroads*, chs. 13-16.
62. Bahá'u'lláh, *Tablets of Bahá'u'lláh Revealed After the Kitáb-i-Aqdas*, pp. 258–9.
63. Shoghi Effendi, *God Passes By*, pp. 94–100.
64. Bahá'u'lláh, *Prayers and Meditations*, CLV, p. 248.
65. Bahá'u'lláh, *Hidden Words*, Arabic no. 1, p. 3.
66. 'Abdu'l-Bahá, *Paris Talks*, ch. 16, p. 49.
67. Bahá'u'lláh, *Gleanings from the Writings of Bahá'u'lláh*, CXXIX, pp. 279–80.
68. Bahá'u'lláh, Súriy-i-Vafá (Tablet to Vafá), in *Tablets of Bahá'u'lláh Revealed After the Kitáb-i-Aqdas*, pp. 189–90.
69. The Báb, *Selections from the Writings of the Báb*, p. 62.
70. Bahá'u'lláh, *Kitáb-i-Íqán*, para. 251, p. 224.
71. 'Abdu'l-Bahá, *Will and Testament*, pp. 10–11.
72. Shoghi Effendi, *The Advent of Divine Justice*, p. 7.
73. Bahá'u'lláh, *Tablets of Bahá'u'lláh Revealed After the Kitáb-i-Aqdas*, p. 155.
74. Bahá'u'lláh, *Kitáb-i-Íqán*, para. 76, p. 69.
75. Bahá'u'lláh, *Gleanings from the Writings of Bahá'u'lláh*, CXXI, p. 256.
76. Bahá'u'lláh, *Tablets of Bahá'u'lláh Revealed After the Kitáb-i-Aqdas*, p. 63.
77. Bahá'u'lláh, Ishráqat (Splendours), ibid. p. 120.
78. Shoghi Effendi, *The World Order of Bahá'u'lláh*, pp. 186–7.
79. Letter on behalf of Shoghi Effendi to an individual believer, 26 July 1946, in *Lights of Guidance*, p. 185.
80. Bahá'u'lláh, *Gleanings from the Writings of Bahá'u'lláh,* CXXXIV, p. 290.
81. Bahá'u'lláh, *Hidden Words*, Persian no. 20.
82. Shoghi Effendi, *God Passes By*, p. 129.
83. ibid. p. 360.
84. ibid. pp. 356–60.
85. ibid. pp. 176–7.
86. *Sahih Muslim*, Book 31, ch. 4: The Merits of 'Ali B. Abi Talib, hadith 5923.
87. Bahá'u'lláh, quoted in Shoghi Effendi, *The Advent of Divine Justice*, p. 31.
88. Bahá'u'lláh, *Gleanings from the Writings of Bahá'u'lláh*, XCIV, p. 192.
89. ibid. LXXVIII, p. 151.
90. Bahá'u'lláh, *Prayers and Meditations*, CLXXXIII, p. 320.
91. ibid. LVIII, p. 88.

92. ibid. CLXXXIII, pp. 319–20.
93. ibid. X, p. 13.
94. ibid. XXXVIII, p. 51.
95. ibid. LXXIX, p. 31.
96. ibid. LXXIX, p. 131.
97. ibid. XLIX, p. 72.
98. ibid. XXXVIII, pp. 51–2.
99. *Bahá'í Prayers*, p. 242.
100. Bahá'u'lláh, quoted in Shoghi Effendi, *The Promised Day Is Come*, p. 82.
101. Bahá'u'lláh, 'The Seven Valleys', in *The Call of the Divine Beloved*, p. 17.
102. Bahá'u'lláh, *Prayers and Meditations* by Bahá'u'lláh, CLXXVI, p. 268.
103. ibid. CL, p. 240.
104. ibid. LXXIX, p. 131.
105. *Bahá'í Prayers*, p. 150.
106. The Báb, *Selections from the Writings of the Báb*, p. 208.
107. ibid. p. 199.
108. Bahá'u'lláh, Lawḥ-i-Ḥikmat (Tablet of Wisdom), in *Tablets of Bahá'u'lláh Revealed After the Kitáb-i-Aqdas*, p. 145.
109. Bahá'u'lláh, *Prayers and Meditations*, CLXXXIV, p. 329.
110. Bahá'u'lláh, *Gleanings from the Writings of Bahá'u'lláh*, V, p. 7.
111. Bahá'u'lláh, *Gems of Divine Mysteries* (Javáhiru'l-Asrár), p. 7.
112. Bahá'u'lláh, *The Kitáb-i-Aqdas*, para. 106, p. 139.
113. Bahá'u'lláh, Súriy-i-Haykal, in *The Summons of the Lord of Hosts*, para. 218, p. 112.
114. Bahá'u'lláh, *Prayers and Meditations*, CVI, p. 178.
115. ibid. CXLIX, p. 239.
116. ibid. CL, p. 240.
117. Bahá'u'lláh, *Kitáb-i-Íqán*, para. 128, p. 120.
118. Bahá'u'lláh, Lawḥ-i-Manikchí-Ṣáḥib, para. 1, in Bahá'u'lláh, *The Tabernacle of Unity*, p. 1.
119. Bahá'u'lláh, *Kitáb-i-Íqán*, para. 1, p. 3.
120. Bahá'u'lláh, Súriy-i-Haykal, in *The Summons of the Lord of Hosts*, para. 128, p. 66.
121. Bahá'u'lláh, *Prayers and Meditations*, CLXXXI, p. 314.
122. 'Abdu'l-Bahá, quoted in *The Bahá'í World*, vol. 18, p. 21; also in *Fire and Light*, p. 21.
123. *Tablets of 'Abdu'l-Bahá*, p. 543.
124. 'Abdu'l-Bahá, *Some Answered Questions*, no. 29, p. 132.
125. See Bahá'u'lláh, *The Kitáb-i-Aqdas*, note 168, p. 237.
126. Bahá'u'lláh, Súriy-i-Haykal, in *The Summons of the Lord of Hosts*, para. 23, pp. 13–14.
127. Bahá'u'lláh, *Gleanings from the Writings of Bahá'u'lláh*, XCV, p. 195.
128. Bahá'u'lláh, *Kitáb-i-Íqán*, para. 22, pp. 22–3.
129. Bahá'u'lláh, Lawḥ-i-Aqdas, in *Tablets of Bahá'u'lláh Revealed After the Kitáb-i-Aqdas*, p. 16.
130. Bahá'u'lláh, *Prayers and Meditations*, VII, p. 9.
131. See explanation in *Star of the West*, vol. III, no. 14 (23 Nov. 1912), p. 11.

132. Bahá'u'lláh, Lawḥ-i-Aqdas, in *Tablets of Bahá'u'lláh Revealed After the Kitáb-i-Aqdas*, pp. 12–13.
133. Bahá'u'lláh, *Prayers and Meditations*, CLXXIX, p. 306.
134. ibid. CXIX, p. 202.
135. Bahá'uláh, *Gleanings from the Writings of Bahá'u'lláh*, XLIX, p. 103.
136. Bahá'u'lláh, Aṣl-i-Kullu'l-Khayr (Words of Wisdom), in *Tablets of Bahá'u'lláh Revealed After the Kitáb-i-Aqdas*, p. 155.
137. Bahá'u'lláh, *Kitáb-i-Íqán*, para. 2, p. 1.
138. The Báb, *Selections from the Writings of the Báb*, p. 68.
139. ibid. p. 215.
140. Bahá'u'lláh, Kalímát-i-Firdawsíyyih (Words of Paradise), in *Tablets of Bahá'u'lláh Revealed After the Kitáb-i-Aqdas*, p. 75.
141. Bahá'u'lláh, Súriy-i-Haykal, in *The Summons of the Lord of Hosts*, para. 194, p. 99.
142. Bahá'u'lláh, *Prayers and Meditations*, CXXV, p. 212.
143. ibid. p. 211.
144. Bahá'u'lláh, *Gleanings from the Writings of Bahá'u'lláh*, CXLIII, p. 313.
145. ibid. LXIX, p. 135.
146. 'Abdu'l-Bahá, *The Secret of Divine Civilization*, p. 44.
147. 'Abdu'l-Bahá, *Tablets of 'Abdul-Bahá*, p. 192.
148. 'Abdu'l-Bahá, *Memorials of the Faithful*, p. 12.
149. *The Dawn-Breakers: Nabíl's Narrative of the Early Days of the Bahá'í Revelation*, p. 295.
150. Arabic text in *Makátib-i Ḥaḍrat 'Abdu'l-Bahá*, vol. 1, pp. 102–8.
151. Bahá'u'lláh, Bishárát (Glad Tidings), in *Tablets of Bahá'u'lláh Revealed After the Kitáb-i-Aqdas*, p. 25.
152. Bahá'u'lláh, Ishráqát (Splendours), ibid. p. 118.
153. Bahá'u'lláh, *The Kitáb-i-Aqdas*, para. 2, p. 20.
154. Bahá'u'lláh, quoted in Shoghi Effendi, *The Promised Day Is Come*, p. 107.
155. Bahá'u'lláh, *Gleanings from the Writings of Bahá'u'lláh*, CXLIII, pp. 312–13.
156. Bahá'u'lláh, Lawḥ-i-Burhán, in *Tablets of Bahá'u'lláh Revealed After the Kitáb-i-Aqdas*, pp. 210, 214–15.
157. Bahá'u'lláh, *Kitáb-i-Íqán*, para. 169, p. 158
158. Bahá'u'lláh, Lawḥ-i-Dunyá (Tablet of the World), in *Tablets of Bahá'u'lláh Revealed After the Kitáb-i-Aqdas*, pp. 86–7.
159. Bahá'u'lláh, *Prayers and Meditations*, CXXXVII, p. 225.
160. 'Abdu'l-Bahá, *Some Answered Questions*, no. 36, p. 163.
161. 'Abdu'l-Bahá, *Tablets of the Divine Plan*, no. 1: Tablet to the Bahá'ís of Canada and Greenland, p. 96.
162. Bahá'u'lláh, Tablet to Mánikchí Ṣáḥib, in *The Tabernacle of Unity*, p. 6.
163. 'Abdu'l-Bahá, *Tablets of Abdul-Baha Abbas*, pp. 596–7.
164. Bahá'u'lláh, *Kitáb-i-Íqán*, para. 98, p. 89.
165. ibid.
166. ibid. para. 144, p. 132.
167. *The Dawn-Breakers*, p. 379.
168. 'Abdu'l-Bahá, *Tablets of the Divine Plan*, no. 14, p. 106.
169. Bahá'u'lláh, *Hidden Words*, Persian no. 24.

170. ibid. Persian no. 2.
171. Bahá'u'lláh, Tablet to Mánikchí Ṣáḥib, in *The Tabernacle of Unity*, p. 9; see also Lawḥ-i-Maqṣúd, in *Tablets of Bahá'u'lláh Revealed After the Kitáb-i-Aqdas*, p. 169.
172. Bahá'u'lláh, Tablet to Mánikchí Ṣáḥib, in *The Tabernacle of Unity*, p. 8.
173. See Fananapazir, *Islam at the Crossroads.*
174. Bahá'u'lláh, *The Kitáb-i-Aqdas*, para. 104, p. 57.
175. Balyuzi, *Bahá'u'lláh, The King of Glory*, p. 20.
176. Taherzadeh, *The Revelation of Bahá'u'lláh*, vol. 1, p. 22.
177. Balyuzi, *Bahá'u'lláh, The King of Glory*, pp. 20–21.
178. ibid. p. 39.
179. Bahá'u'lláh, Lawḥ-i-Ḥikmat, in *Tablets of Bahá'u'lláh Revealed After the Kitáb-i-Aqdas*, p. 149.
180. Bahá'u'lláh, Súriy-i-Haykal, paras. 186–276, in Bahá'u'lláh, *The Summons of the Lord of Hosts*, pp. 96–137; see also Shoghi Effendi, *God Passes By*, p. 173.
181. Shoghi Effendi, *The Promised Day Is Come*, pp. 20 and 67.
182. Shoghi Effendi, *God Passes By*, p. 197.
183. ibid. p. 225.
184. Bahá'u'lláh, *Prayers and Meditations*, XVIII, pp. 20–21.
185. ibid. CLXXIX, p. 306.
186. 'Abdu'l-Bahá. *Some Answered Questions,* no. 16, pp. 95–6.
187. Shoghi Effendi, *Messages to America*, p. 99.
188. Bahá'u'lláh, quoted in Shoghi Effendi, *God Passes By*, p. 102.
189. Shoghi Effendi, *God Passes By*, p. 94.
190. Bahá'u'lláh, Kitáb-i-'Ahd, in *Tablets of Bahá'u'lláh Revealed After the Kitáb-i-Aqdas*, p. 219.
191. 'Abdu'l-Bahá, *The Promulgation of Universal Peace*, pp. 5–6.
192. Bahá'u'lláh, *Hidden Words*, Arabic no. 2.
193. Bahá'u'lláh, *Gleanings from the Writings of Bahá'u'lláh*, CXXXI, p. 286.
194. *The Dawn-Breakers*, pp. 188–9.
195. Bahá'u'lláh, *Prayers and Meditations*, CLXXXI, p. 240.
196. Bahá'u'lláh, *Hidden Words,* Arabic no. 69.
197. Bahá'u'lláh, *Prayers and Meditations*, LVIII, p. 92.
198. Bahá'u'lláh, *Kitáb-i-Íqán*, para. 103, p. 97.
199. 'Abdu'l-Bahá, in *Bahá'í Prayers*, p. 102.
200. Bahá'u'lláh, *Gleanings from the Writings of Bahá'u'lláh*, CXXXII, p. 287.
201. Bahá'u'lláh, Lawḥ-i-Maqṣúd (Tablet of Maqṣúd), in *Tablets of Bahá'u'lláh Revealed After the Kitáb-i-Aqdas*, p. 162.
202. The Báb, *Selections from the Writings of the Báb*, p. 203.
203. Bahá'u'lláh, *Kitáb-i-Íqán*, para. 104, p. 98.
204. 'Abdu'l-Bahá, *Paris Talks*, no. 44, p. 146.
205. Bahá'u'lláh, *Ishráqát va Chand Lawḥ-i-Digar*, p. 134, line 7.
206. For more information see the article 'Russo-Turkish War 1876–1878', available at: https://www.onwar.com/aced/chrono/c1800s/yr70/frussoturk1876.htm:

> The last Russo-Turkish War (1877–78) was also the most important one. In 1877 Russia and its ally Serbia came to the aid of Bosnia and Herzegovina and Bulgaria in their rebellions against Turkish rule. The Russians attacked through Bulgaria, and after successfully concluding

the Siege of Pleven they advanced into Thrace, taking Adrianople (now Edirne, Turkey) in January 1878. In March of that year Russia concluded the Treaty of San Stefano with Turkey. This treaty freed Romania, Serbia, and Montenegro from Turkish rule, gave autonomy to Bosnia and Herzegovina, and created a huge autonomous Bulgaria under Russian protection. Britain and Austria-Hungary, alarmed by the Russian gains contained in the treaty, compelled Russia to accept the Treaty of Berlin (July 1878), whereby Russia's military-political gains from the war were severely restricted.

207. Shoghi Effendi, *Directives from the Guardian*, p. 61.
208. Shoghi Effendi, *The World Order of Bahá'u'lláh*, p. 42.
209. Bahá'u'lláh, Ishráqát, in *Tablets of Bahá'u'lláh Revealed After the Kitáb-i-Aqdas*, pp. 127–8.
210. Shoghi Effendi, *The World Order of Bahá'u'lláh*, pp. 42–3.
211. ibid.
212. Bahá'u'lláh, *Kitáb-i-Íqán*, paras. 79–80, pp. 71–2.
213. Bahá'u'lláh, *Gleanings from the Writings of Bahá'u'lláh*, XIII, p. 26.
214. Bahá'u'lláh, *Kitáb-i-Íqán*, paras. 28 and 29. pp. 29–31.
215. Bahá'u'lláh, *Gleanings from the Writings of Bahá'u'lláh*, LXXX, p. 155.
216. Bahá'u'lláh, Súriy-i-Haykal, in Bahá'u'lláh, *The Summons of the Lord of Hosts*, p. 54.
217. Bahá'u'lláh, *The Kitáb-i-Aqdas*, para. 165, p. 79.
218. Shoghi Effendi, *God Passes By*, p. 220.
219. Bahá'u'lláh, Ṭarázát (Ornaments), in *Tablets of Bahá'u'lláh Revealed After the Kitáb-i-Aqdas*, pp. 35–6.
220. Bahá'u'lláh, *The Kitáb-i-Aqdas*, para. 144, p. 72.
221. 'Abdu'l-Bahá, *Will and Testament* of 'Abdu'l-Bahá, p. 14.
222. 'Abdu'l-Bahá, *The Promulgation of Universal Peace*, p. 454.
223. Shoghi Effendi, *The Advent of Divine Justice*, p. 65.
224. Bahá'u'lláh, Ishráqát, in *Tablets of Bahá'u'lláh Revealed After the Kitáb-i-Aqdas*, p. 129.
225. Shoghi Effendi, *The World Order of Bahá'u'lláh*, pp. 57–8.
226. Bahá'u'lláh, *Gleanings from the Writings of Bahá'u'lláh*, CXXVIII, p. 279.
227. Shoghi Effendi, *God Passes By*, pp. 139–40.
228. ibid. p. 140.
229. ibid. p. 347.
230. *Jámi 'At-Tirmidhi*, vol. 4, ch. 59, hadith 2404.
231. Bahá'u'lláh, *Kitáb-i-Íqán*, para. 28, p. 29.
232. Hadith attributed to Imám Ja'far al-Ṣadiq, *Misbah al-Shariah* (Lantern of the Path), ch. 2, p. 8.
233. Shoghi Effendi, *The Promised Day Is Come*, para. 271, pp. 110–11.
234. Qaṣídiy-i-Tá'íyyih: the shorter ode consists of 45 verses and the longer ode consists of 600–750 verses.
235. Shoghi Effendi, *God Passes By*, p. 123.
236. Bahá'u'lláh, *Prayers and Meditations*, VIII, p. 7.
237. 'Abdu'l-Bahá, Tablet to the Bahá'ís in Iran, quoted in *Fire and Light*, no. X, p. 24.
238. Bahá'u'lláh, Kalímát-i-Firdawsíyyih (Words of Paradise), in *Tablets of Bahá'u'lláh Revealed After the Kitáb-i-Aqdas*, pp. 72–3.

239. *Bahíyyih Khánum, the Greatest Holy Leaf*, no. 72, p. 195.
240. Shoghi Effendi, *God Passes By*, p. 221.
241. Bahá'u'lláh, Súriy-i-Ra'ís, in *The Summons of the Lord of Hosts*, para. 14, p. 147.
242. Bahá'u'lláh, *The Kitáb-i-Aqdas*, para. 5, p. 21.
243. ibid. note 2, p. 166.
244. Shoghi Effendi, *The Promised Day Is Come*, p. 31.
245. Bahá'u'lláh, Lawḥ-i-Síyyid-i-Mihdíy-i-Dahájí (Tablet to Siyyid Mihdíy-i-Dahájí), in *Tablets of Bahá'u'lláh Revealed After the Kitáb-i-Aqdas*, p. 195.
246. Bahá'u'lláh, *Prayers and Meditations*, CIX, p. 183.
247. Bahá'u'lláh, *Tablets of Bahá'u'lláh Revealed After the Kitáb-i-Aqdas*, p. 248.
248. Shoghi Effendi, *God Passes By*, p. 139.
249. 'Diacritics; meaning of "Self-subsisting"', letter on behalf of the Universal House of Justice to an individual, 21 January 1993.
250. Bahá'u'lláh, Fire Tablet, in *Bahá'í Prayers*, p. 218.
251. Bahá'u'lláh, *Hidden Words*, Persian no. 69.
252. ibid. Persian no. 2.
253. Bahá'u'lláh, *Gleanings from the Writings of Bahá'u'lláh*, CLI, p. 319.
254. 'Abdu'l-Bahá, *The Promulgation of Universal Peace*, p. 244.
255. 'Abdu'l-Bahá, *Tablets of the Divine Plan*, no. 8, p. 53.
256. Bahá'u'lláh, *Kitáb-i-Íqán*, para. 204, p. 187; and para. 213, p. 192.
257. Bahá'u'lláh, *Hidden Words*, Arabic no. 68.
258. Bahá'u'lláh, *Kitáb-i-Íqán*, para. 272, pp. 240–41.
259. Bahá'u'lláh, quoted in Shoghi Effendi, *The Advent of Divine Justice*, pp. 82–3.
260. Bahá'u'lláh, *Gleanings from the Writings of Bahá'u'lláh*, LXXIV, p. 141.
261. Shoghi Effendi, *The Advent of Divine Justice*, p. 68; see also Matt. 16:13–19.
262. Shoghi Effendi, *The Promised Day Is Come*, p. 109.
263. Lings, *Muhammad, His Life . . .*, p. 56.
264. The Sermon of *Ma'rifat bin-Nuráníyyat* (Recognition with Luminousness) of 'Alí ibn 'Abú Tálib, the First Imám, translation and explanatory note by Khazeh Fananapazir, 2001.
265. *The Dawn-Breakers*, p. 99.
266. Shoghi Effendi, *God Passes By*, p. 10; *The Dawn-Breakers*, p. 90–91.
267. Bahá'u'lláh, *The Kitáb-i-Aqdas*, para. 166, pp. 79–80.
268. Letter from Shoghi Effendi to an individual, 15 February 1947, in Shoghi Effendi, *Unfolding Destiny*, p. 445.
269. 'Abdu'l-Bahá, *A Travelers Narrative*, pp. 31–2.
270. *The Dawn-Breakers*, pp. 586-7, 593-4.
271. Shoghi Effendi, *God Passes By*, p. 71; see also *The Dawn-Breakers*, p. 599.
272. *The Dawn-Breakers*, pp. 559–60.
273. Shoghi Effendi, *God Passes By*, p. 63.
274. ibid. p. 71.
275. ibid. p. 101.
276. Blomfield, *The Chosen Highway*, pp. 41-2.
277. Shoghi Effendi, *God Passes By*, p. 102.
278. *Sahih Muslim*, Book 45: The Book of Virtue, Enjoining Good Manners, and Joining of the Ties of Friendship, ch. 15, hadith 2577.
279. Esslemont, *Bahá'u'lláh and the New Era*, p. 39.
280. Account by Bahíyyih Khánum in Blomfield, *The Chosen Highway*, pp. 40–41.

281. Abrahamian, *Tortured Confessions: Prisons and Public Recantations in Modern Iran*, p. 19.
282. ibid. p. 17.
283. ibid. p. 21.
284. Shoghi Effendi, *God Passes By*, pp. 132–3.
285. Bahá'u'lláh, Súriy-i-Haykal, paras. 6–7, in Bahá'u'lláh, *The Summons of the Lord of Hosts*, pp. 5–6.
286. Shoghi Effendi, *God Passes By*, p. 101.
287. The Báb, quoted in *The Dawn-Breakers*, p. 317.
288. 'Abdu'l-Bahá, *Selections from the Writings of 'Abdu'l-Bahá*, no. 203, p. 250.
289. Bahá'u'lláh, Súriy-i-Haykal, para. 8, in Bahá'u'lláh, *The Summons of the Lord of Hosts*, p. 6.
290. Shoghi Effendi, *God Passes By*, pp. 105–6.
291. ibid. p. 106.
292. ibid. pp. 137–8.
293. ibid. p. 72.
294. ibid. p. 101.
295. Bahá'u'lláh, *La'Aaliyul Hikmat Jild Awwal*, vol. 1, p. 136.
296. *A Compilation on Women*, no. 95, from a Tablet translated from the Persian and Arabic.
297. Bahá'u'lláh, Lawḥ-i-Ra'ís, para. 19, in Bahá'u'lláh, *The Summons of the Lord of Hosts*, p. 168.
298. Bahá'u'lláh, Súriy-i-Mulúk, para. 5, ibid. p. 187.
299. ibid. para. 93, pp. 223–4.
300. Bahá'u'lláh, Lawḥ-i-Aqdas, in *Tablets of Bahá'u'lláh Revealed After the Kitáb-i-Aqdas*, pp. 16–17.
301. Esslemont, *Bahá'u'lláh and the New Era*, p. 256.
302. *A Compilation on Women*, no. 53, from a Tablet translated from the Persian and Arabic.
303. Shoghi Effendi, *God Passes By*, p. 94.
304. Bahá'u'lláh, Kalímát-i-Firdawsíyyih, in *Tablets of Bahá'u'lláh Revealed After the Kitáb-i-Aqdas*, pp. 70–71.
305. Bahá'u'lláh, *Hidden Words*, Persian no. 43.
306. Bahá'u'lláh, *The Kitáb-i-Aqdas*, para. 145, p. 72.
307. Bahá'u'lláh, Lawḥ-i-Siyyid-i-Mihdíy-i-Dahají, in *Tablets of Bahá'u'lláh Revealed After the Kitáb-i-Aqdas*, pp. 198–9.
308. Bahá'u'lláh, Ṭarazát, in *Tablets of Bahá'u'lláh Revealed After the Kitáb-i-Aqdas*, p. 36.
309. Letter from Shoghi Effendi to the American Bahá'I Community, 23 November 1951, in Shoghi Effendi, *Citadel of Faith*, p. 105.
310. Bahá'u'lláh, *Áthár-i-Qalam-i-A'lá*, vol. 2, p. 34.
311. Shoghi Effendi, *God Passes By*, pp. 216–17.
312. 'Abdu'l-Bahá, *The Promulgation of Universal Peace*, p. 5.
313. ibid.
314. Bahá'u'lláh, *The Kitáb-i-Aqdas*, para. 148, p. 72.
315. ibid. para. 64, p. 42.
316. Shoghi Effendi, *God Passes By*, p. 94.

317. Bahá'u'lláh, *Prayers and Meditations,* LXXXVII, p. 148.
318. Bahá'u'lláh, *Á<u>th</u>ár-i-Qalam-i-A'lá*, vol. 2, p. 34.
319. Bahá'u'lláh, Bi<u>sh</u>árát (Glad-Tidings), in *Tablets of Bahá'u'lláh Revealed After the Kitáb-i-Aqdas*, p. 21.
320. Bahá'u'lláh, *Gleanings from the Writings of Bahá'u'lláh,* CXXXVI, p. 296.
321. Bahá'u'lláh, *The Kitáb-i-Aqdas*, para. 165, p. 79.
322. Bahá'u'lláh, *Kitáb-i-Íqán*, para. 162, pp. 153–4.
323. Shoghi Effendi, *The World Order of Bahá'u'lláh*, p. 58.
324. Bahá'u'lláh, Súriy-i-Haykal, para. 63, in Bahá'u'lláh, *The Summons of the Lord of Hosts,* pp. 33–4.
325. Bahá'u'lláh, *Gleanings from the Writings of Bahá'u'lláh,* XCVI, pp. 195-6.
326. 'Abdu'l-Bahá, *Selections from the Writings of 'Abdu'l-Bahá*, no. 29, p. 60.
327. Bahá'u'lláh, I<u>sh</u>ráqát (Splendours), in *Tablets of Bahá'u'lláh Revealed After the Kitáb-i-Aqdas,* p. 126.
328. Bahá'u'lláh, Tajallíyát (Effulgences), ibid. pp. 51–2.
329. Bahá'u'lláh, *The Kitáb-i-Aqdas*, para. 103 and note 129, pp. 220–21.
330. The Báb, Qayyúmu'l-Asmá', ch. XIX, in *Selections from the Writings of the Báb*, p. 70.
331. Bahá'u'lláh, Tablet of Aḥmad, in *Bahá'í Prayers*, p. 209.
332. Bahá'u'lláh, Kalímát-i-Firdawsíyyih (Words of Paradise), in *Tablets of Bahá'u'lláh Revealed After the Kitáb-i-Aqdas*, p. 75.
333. Bahá'u'lláh, I<u>sh</u>ráqát (Splendours), in *Tablets of Bahá'u'lláh Revealed After the Kitáb-i-Aqdas*, p. 125.
334. Bahá'u'lláh, *Gleanings from the Writings of Bahá'u'lláh*, XXXIV, p. 81.
335. Shoghi Effendi, *The World Order of Bahá'u'lláh*, p. 187.
336. Bahá'u'lláh, Kalímát-i-Firdawsíyyih (Words of Paradise), in *Tablets of Bahá'u'lláh Revealed After the Kitáb-i-Aqdas*, pp. 66–7.
337. Shoghi Effendi, *God Passes By,* p. 218.
338. Shoghi Effendi, *The Promised Day Is Come*, pp. 7–8.
339. Bahá'u'lláh, Tablet of Aḥmad, in *Bahá'í Prayers*, p. 210.
340. Afnán and Hatcher, 'Western Islámic scholarship and Bahá'í origins', pp. 38-9.
341. Iran National Bahá'í Archives (INBA) no. 18, p. 125.
342. Letter from Shoghi Effendi to the Bahá'ís in Great Britain, 24 September 1924, in Shoghi Effendi, *Unfolding Destiny*, p. 28.
343. Bahá'u'lláh, *Gleanings from the Writings of Bahá'u'lláh,* CIX, p. 215.
344. Shoghi Effendi, *The World Order of Bahá'u'lláh*, p. 114.
345. *Sahih al-Bukhari*, vol. 2, Book 23: 'Funerals' (Al-Janá'iz), hadith 1358, p. 253, and hadith 1385, p. 267.
346. Shoghi Effendi, quoting Bahá'u'lláh, *Kitáb-i-Íqán*, in *The World Order of Bahá'u'lláh*, p. 58.
347. Based on Shoghi Effendi's explanation of a quotation from the *Kitáb-i-Íqán*, ibid. p. 59.
348. Bahá'u'lláh, Kalimát-i-Firdawsíyyih, in *Tablets of Bahá'u'lláh Revealed After the Kitáb-i-Aqdas,* p. 64.
349. Shoghi Effendi, *The Advent of Divine Justice*, pp. 77–8.
350. al-Majlisi, *Bihár al-Anwár*, vols. 51-52-53 (New Edition), Kitabul Ghaibah (Book of Occultation), Part II, The Promised Mihdi, sections 208–209.

351. Bahá'u'lláh, Kalimát-i-Firdawsíyyih, in *Tablets of Bahá'u'lláh Revealed After the Kitáb-i-Aqdas*, p. 64. The Tablet revealed in Persian is included in Bahá'u'lláh, *Má'idiy-i-Ásamání*, vol. 8.
352. Bahá'u'lláh, *Tablets of Bahá'u'lláh Revealed After the Kitáb-i-Aqdas*, pp. 240–41.
353. Shoghi Effendi, *God Passes By*, p. 206.
354. Bahá'u'lláh, *Gleanings from the Writings of Bahá'u'lláh*, CXIX, p. 254.
355. Bahá'u'lláh, Bi<u>sh</u>árát, in *Tablets of Bahá'u'lláh Revealed After the Kitáb-i-Aqdas*, p. 23.
356. Bahá'u'lláh, Lawḥ-i-Dunya, ibid. p. 89.
357. Bahá'u'lláh, Lawḥ-i-Maqsúd, ibid. p. 165.
358. Letter from the Universal House of Justice to an individual, 19 April 2001, regarding the unity of nations and the establishment of the Lesser Peace. Available at: https://www.bahai.org/library/authoritative-texts/the-universal-house-of-justice.
359. Shoghi Effendi, *God Passes By*, p. 218.
360. Zürcher, 'The Ottoman conscription system in theory and practice, 1844–1918'.
361. Bahá'u'lláh, Lawḥ-i-Maqsúd, in *Tablets of Bahá'u'lláh Revealed After the Kitáb-i-Aqdas*, p. 164.
362. Shoghi Effendi, *Directives from the Guardian*, no. 33, p. 17.
363. Bahá'u'lláh, Kitáb-i-'Ahd, in *Tablets of Bahá'u'lláh Revealed After the Kitáb-i-Aqdas*, p. 221.
364. ibid. p. 220.
365. Bahá'u'lláh, Aṣl-i-Kullu'l-<u>Kh</u>ayr (Words of Wisdom), ibid. p. 156.
366. 'Abdu'l-Bahá, *Selections from the Writings of 'Abdu'l-Bahá*, no. 183, pp. 208–9.
367. Shoghi Effendi, *God Passes By*, p. 238.
368. Bahá'u'lláh, *Hidden Words*, Persian no. 27.
369. Bahá'u'lláh, quoted in Shoghi Effendi, *The Promised Day Is Come*, p. 80.
370. Bahá'u'lláh, Súriy-i-Haykal, para. 30, in Bahá'u'lláh, *The Summons of the Lord of Hosts*, pp. 17–18.
371. Shoghi Effendi, *God Passes By*, pp. 143–4.
372. Benson, *The Holy Bible*, vol. 1, ch. VII, p. 81.
373. Bahá'u'lláh, *Gleanings From the Writings of Bahá'u'lláh*, CLXIII, p. 341.
374. I<u>sh</u>ráq-<u>Kh</u>ávarí, *Qámús Lawḥ <u>Sh</u>ay<u>kh</u> Najafí.*
375. Bahá'u'lláh, *Prayers and Meditations*, LXV, p. 105.
376. Shoghi Effendi, *The Promised Day Is Come*, p. 77.
377. Bahá'u'lláh, *The Kitáb-i-Aqdas*, para. 63, p. 196.
378. Bahá'u'lláh, *Prayers and Meditations*, XCI, p. 153.
379. Shoghi Effendi, *God Passes By*, p. 185.
380. ibid. p. 205.
381. Shoghi Effendi, *The Promised Day Is Come*, p. 77
382. 'Abdu'l-Bahá, *Tablets of Abdul-Baha*, p. 359.
383. ibid. p. 198.
384. ibid. p. 114.
385. ibid. p. 25.
386. Shoghi Effendi, *Unfolding Destiny*, p. 67.
387. Shoghi Effendi, *Citadel of Faith*, p. 96.
388. *Bahíyyih <u>Kh</u>ánum, the Greatest Holy Leaf*, no. 30. p. 61.
389. Shoghi Effendi, *God Passes By*, pp. 185–6.

390. 'Abdu'l-Bahá, *Memorials of the Faithful*, pp. 26–7.
391. ibid. pp. 29–32.
392. Bahá'u'lláh, Lawḥ-i-Siyyid-i-Mihdíy-i-Dahají, in *Tablets of Bahá'u'lláh Revealed After the Kitáb-i-Aqdas*, p. 196.
393. Bahá'u'lláh, quoted in Shoghi Effendi, *The Advent of Divine Justice*, p. 83.
394. Letter from Shoghi Effendi to the British Bahá'í Community, 24 September 1924, in Shoghi Effendi, *Unfolding Destiny*, p. 28.
395. Schaff and Wace, *A Select Library of Nicene and Post-Nicene Fathers of the Christian Church*, vol. 13, part 2, p. 167.
396. Bahá'u'lláh, Súriy-i-Mulúk, in Bahá'u'lláh, *The Summons of the Lord of Hosts*, para. 38, p. 201.
397. Bahá'u'lláh, *The Kitáb-i-Aqdas*, para. 38. pp. 32–3.
398. Bahá'u'lláh, in *Tablets of Bahá'u'lláh Revealed After the Kitáb-i-Aqdas*, p. 264.
399. E. G. Browne, quoted in *The Proclamation of Bahá'u'lláh*, p. ix.
400. Bahá'u'lláh, Kitáb-i-'Áhd (Book of the Covenant), in *Tablets of Bahá'u'lláh Revealed After the Kitáb-i-Aqdas*, p. 223.
401. Bahá'u'lláh, *Gleanings from the Writings of Bahá'u'lláh*, C, p. 203.
402. Tribute by the Universal House of Justice to Bahá'u'lláh on the Centenary of His Passing – first read at the Shrine of Bahá'u'lláh in May 1992. In The Universal House of Justice, *A Wider Horizon*, pp. 239–40.
403. The Báb, Qayyúmu'l-Asmá', LIII, in *Selections from the Writings of the Báb*, p. 72.
404. *Star of the West*, vol. 19, no. 3, p. 69.
405. 'Abdu'l-Bahá, from the frontispiece to Ali-Kuli Khan's translation of the *Kitáb-i-Íqan.*
406. Bahá'u'lláh, *Gleanings from the Writings of Bahá'u'lláh*, CXXXIV, p. 290.
407. Bahá'u'lláh, quoted in *The Dawn-Breakers*, p. 583.
408. Ibn-Babwayh (Shaykh Ṣaduq), *I'tiqadat fi Deen Al-Imamiyyah*, p. 107. *Al-Kafi*, a compilation of Shí'ih traditions by al-Kulayni, also quotes the following concerning taqíyyah: 'Protect your religion and veil it with al-Taqiyyah (protective measures); one who does not observe al-Taqiyyah has no belief' (vol. 2, hadith 2234, p. 196).
409. *The Dawn-Breakers*, pp. 315–16.
410. Manuchehri, 'The practice of taqiyyih (dissimulation) in the Bábí and Bahá'í religions'.
411. See Bahá'u'lláh, *The Summons of the Lord of Hosts*, p. 96, where it appears as part of the Súriy-i-Haykal.
412. The Báb, *Selections from the Writings of the Báb*, p. 27.
413. ibid. p. 12.
414. Bahá'u'lláh, *The Summons of the Lord of Hosts*, p. 99.
415. Bahá'u'lláh, *Gleanings from the Writings of Bahá'u'lláh*, CXXXII, p. 288.
416. Bahá'u'lláh, *Kitáb-i-Íqán*, para. 170, p. 160.
417. Bahá'u'lláh, *Tablets of Bahá'u'lláh Revealed After the Kitáb-i-Aqdas*, p. 257.
418. Bahá'u'lláh, Ishráqát (Splendours), ibid. p. 107.
419. Ḥaydar-'Alí, *Stories from The Delight of Hearts*, p. 104.
420. Ishráq-Khávarí, *Qámús Lawḥ Shaykh Najafí*, p. 257.
421. Bahá'u'lláh, *Gleanings from the Writings of Bahá'u'lláh*, XCIV, pp. 192–3.
422. ibid. p. 193.

423. Shoghi Effendi, *The World Order of Bahá'u'lláh*, p. 112.
424. Bahá'u'lláh, *Gleanings from the Writings of Bahá'u'lláh*, LXXXIV, p. 167.
425. ibid. XX, p. 49.
426. Note 160 in Bahá'u'lláh, *The Kitab-i-Aqdas*, p. 234.
427. Bahá'u'lláh, *Kitáb-i-Íqán*, para. 196, pp. 178–9.
428. ibid. para. 57, p. 53.
429. Bahá'u'lláh, Lawḥ-i-Burhan, in *Tablets of Bahá'u'lláh Revealed After the Kitáb-i-Aqdas*, p. 210.
430. Bahá'u'lláh, *Kitáb-i-Íqán*, para. 172, p. 162, and para. 178, p. 166.
431. Bahá'u'lláh, *Prayers and Meditations*, XXV, p. 29.
432. al-Qummi, *Mafatih al-Jinan*, vol. 2: The Book of Ziyárah, p. 141.
433. *Sahih al-Bukhari*, Book 6: 'The Book of Commentary', hadith 4851.
434. ibid.
435. Bahá'u'lláh, *Kitáb-i-Íqán*, para. 3. p. 4.
436. Bahá'u'lláh, quoted in Shoghi Effendi, *The Advent of Divine Justice*, pp. 77–8.
437. Ameer Ali, *The Spirit of Islam: A History of the Evolution and Ideals of Islam*, p. 254; see also Gail, *Bahá'í Glossary*, p. 7.
438. The Sermon of the Gulf, trans. Khazeh Fananapazir, from al-Bursi, *Masháriq Anwar al-Yaqín fi Asrár Amir Mu'minín*, pp. 160–70, originally written as *Khutbih-i-Tutunjiyyih* in Arabic.
439. Iran National Bahá'í Archives (INBA) series of Bahá'u'lláh's Writings, vol. 35.
440. Bahá'u'lláh, *Kitáb-i-Íqán,* para. 135, p. 126.
441. See Shoghi Effendi, *God Passes By*, p. 94.
442. Bahá'u'lláh, *Gleanings from the Writings of Bahá'u'lláh*, IX, p. 12.
443. Saiedi, *Gate of the Heart: Understanding the Writings of the Báb*, p. 352.
444. Shoghi Effendi, *God Passes By*, p. 94.
445. Bahá'u'lláh, *Prayers and Meditations*, CLXXXII, pp. 316; see also Ishráqát (Splendours), in *Tablets of Bahá'u'lláh Revealed After the Kitáb-i-Aqdas*, p. 111.
446. Bahá'u'lláh, Ishráqát (Splendours), *Tablets of Bahá'u'lláh Revealed After the Kitáb-i-Aqdas*, p. 107.
447. Bahá'u'lláh, quoted in Shoghi Effendi, *The Promised Day Is Come*, p. 86.
448. Shoghi Effendi, *God Passes By*, p. 173.
449. Shoghi Effendi, *The Promised Day Is Come*, pp. 51–2.
450. ibid. p. 51.
451. Partially quoted ibid.
452. A note in the French edition of the Epistle (*Épître au fils du Loup*) refers to him as 'César Ketfagou, fils d'un consul de France en Syrie.'
453. The Universal House of Justice, 'Introduction', in Bahá'u'lláh, *The Summons of the Lord of Hosts*, pp. i–ii.
454. Purcell, 'Bells'.
455. Zarzecny, *Religion in Napoleonic France, Part II: Napoleon III and Religion.*
456. ibid.
457. ibid.
458. Rev. George Adam Smith, 'The Book of Isaiah', in *The Expositor's Bible*, vol. 1, p. 254.
459. al-Bahraani, *The Qa'em in the Qur'an*, p. 267.
460. Bahá'u'lláh, *Gleanings from the Writings of Bahá'u'lláh,* XCIX, p. 200.

461. 'Abdu'l-Bahá, *The Promulgation of Universal Peace*, p. 161.
462. Shoghi Effendi, *The World Order of Bahá'u'lláh*, pp. 180–81
463. Bahá'u'lláh, *Kitáb-i-Íqán*, para. 3, p. 4.
464. Shoghi Effendi, *The Promised Day Is Come*, p. 112.
465. Bahá'u'lláh, *Gleanings from the Writings of Bahá'u'lláh,* CLXIII, p. 343.
466. Bahá'u'lláh, *Hidden Words*, Persian no. 71.
467. Bahá'u'lláh, *Kitáb-i-Íqán*, para. 10, p. 9–10.
468. ibid. para. 219, pp. 199–200.
469. Bahá'u'lláh, *Gems of Divine Mysteries, Javáhiru'l-Aṣrár*, para. 107, pp. 72–3.
470. Bahá'u'lláh, Lawḥ-i-Aqdas (The Most Holy Tablet), in *Tablets of Bahá'u'lláh Revealed After the Kitáb-i-Aqdas*, p. 13.
471. 'Abdu'l-Bahá, *The Promulgation of Universal Peace*, pp. 384–5.
472. 'Abdu'l-Bahá, *Paris Talks*, no. 27, p. 80.
473. Bahá'u'lláh, Lawḥ-i-Dunyá (Tablet of the World), in *Tablets of Bahá'u'lláh Revealed After the Kitáb-i-Aqdas*, pp. 96–7.
474. Bahá'u'lláh, Lawḥ-i-Aqdas (The Most Holy Tablet), ibid. p. 14.
475. Bahá'u'lláh, *Kitáb-i-Íqán*, para. 34, p. 36.
476. Bahá'u'lláh, *Gleanings from the Writings of Bahá'u'lláh*, XCVI, pp. 195–6..
477. Bahá'u'lláh, *The Kitáb-i-Aqdas*, para. 173, p. 82.
478. Bahá'u'lláh, Súriy-i-Haykal, para. 127, in *The Summons of the Lord of Hosts*, pp. 65–6.
479. Bahá'u'lláh, Kalimát-i-Firdawsíyyih, in *Tablets of Bahá'u'lláh Revealed After the Kitáb-i-Aqdas*, p. 71.
480. Bahá'u'lláh, Lawḥ-i-Aqdas, (The Most Holy Tablet), ibid. pp. 9–10.
481. Bahá'u'lláh, Súriy-i-Haykal, para. 154, in *The Summons of the Lord of Hosts*, pp. 80–81.
482. Bahá'u'lláh, Lawḥ-i-Aqdas, (The Most Holy Tablet), in *Tablets of Bahá'u'lláh Revealed After the Kitáb-i-Aqdas*, p. 14.
483. Taherzadeh, *The Revelation of Bahá'u'lláh*, vol. 3, ch. 6, p. 110.
484. Bahá'u'lláh, Ishráqát (Splendours), in *Tablets of Bahá'u'lláh Revealed After the Kitáb-i-Aqdas*, p. 101.
485. Bahá'u'lláh, *Tablets of Bahá'u'lláh Revealed After the Kitáb-i-Aqdas*, p. 248.
486. ibid. p. 251.
487. ibid. p. 254.
488. The Báb, Qayyúmu'l-Asmá', in *Selections from the Writings of the Báb*, p. 45.
489. ibid. p. 63.
490. Bahá'u'lláh, Ishráqát (Splendours), in *Tablets of Bahá'u'lláh Revealed After the Kitáb-i-Aqdas*, p. 101.
491. Bahá'u'lláh, Lawḥ-i-Maqṣúd, ibid. p. 169.
492. Bahá'u'lláh, *The Kitáb-i-Aqdas*, para. 186, p. 87.
493. Bahá'u'lláh, *Prayers and Meditations*, CLXXVI, p. 275.
494. Bahá'u'lláh, *The Kitáb-i-Aqdas*, para. 14, p. 24.
495. Bahá'ú'lláh, Lawḥ-i-Burhán (Tablet of the Proof), in *Tablets of Bahá'u'lláh Revealed After the Kitáb-i-Aqdas*, p. 205.
496. Bahá'u'lláh, *Gleanings from the Writings of Bahá'u'lláh*, LXXXI, p. 156.
497. Shoghi Effendi, *God Passes By*, pp. 147–8.
498. ibid. p. 225.

499. ibid. p. 182.
500. ibid. p. 185.
501. Bahá'u'lláh, Tablet to Napoleon III, Súriy-i-Haykal, para. 148, in *The Summons of the Lord of Hosts*, p. 78.
502. Bahá'u'lláh, *Gleanings from the Writings of Bahá'u'lláh*, CIII, p. 209.
503. Taherzadeh, *The Revelation of Bahá'u'lláh*, vol. 3, p. 114.
504. ibid. pp. 121-2.
505. ibid. pp. 122-3.
506. Shoghi Effendi, *God Passes By*, p. 106.
507. ibid. p. 104.
508. Bahá'u'lláh, Is͟hráqát, in *Tablets of Bahá'u'lláh Revealed After the Kitáb-i-Aqdas*, p. 122.
509. Bahá'u'lláh, *Gleanings from the Writings of Bahá'u'lláh,* XLVI, p. 99.
510. 'Abdu'l-Bahá, *The Promulgation of Universal Peace*, p. 282.
511. Curzon, *Persia and the Persian Question*; quoted in *The Dawn-Breakers*, p. xlvi.
512. Bahá'u'lláh, *Gems of Divine Mysteries, Javáhiru'l-Aṣrár*, para. 8, p. 8.
513. Bahá'u'lláh, *Tablets of Bahá'u'lláh Revealed After the Kitáb-i-Aqdas*, p. 247.
514. Max Fisher, in *The Washington Post*, 17 October 2014.
515. Bahá'u'lláh, quoted in Shoghi Effendi, *The World Order of Bahá'u'lláh*, p. 203.
516. Bahá'u'lláh, *Kitáb-i-Íqán*, para. 162, pp. 153–4.
517. Shoghi Effendi, *The World Order of Bahá'u'lláh*, pp. 57–8.
518. 'Abdu'l-Bahá, *The Promulgation of Universal Peace*, pp. 408–409.
519. Bahá'u'lláh, *The Kitáb-i-Íqán*, para. 118, pp. 112–113.
520. Bahá'u'lláh, Lawḥ-i-Ra'ís, in *The Summons of the Lord of Hosts*, pp. 161-2.
521. al-Majlisi, *Bihár al-Anwár*, vol. 22 (originally vol. 6), p. 453.
522. Taherzadeh, *The Revelation of Bahá'u'lláh*, vol. 4, p. 394.
523. 'Abdu'l-Bahá, *Memorials of the Faithful*, p. 7; see also Taherzadeh, *The Revelation of Bahá'u'lláh*, vol. 4, pp. 402–5.
524. Shoghi Effendi, *God Passes By*, pp. 146, 159.
525. Taherzadeh, *The Revelation of Bahá'u'lláh*, vol. 2, pp. 399–401.
526. Encyclopaedia Britannica: Sublime Porte, Ottoman Empire. Available at: https://www.britannica.com/topic/Sublime-Porte.
527. Bahá'u'lláh, Súriy-i-Mulúk, para. 24, in *The Summons of the Lord of Hosts*, p. 195; see also *Gleanings from the Writings of Bahá'u'lláh,* LXV, pp. 122–3.
528. Taherzadeh, *The Revelation of Bahá'u'lláh*, vol. 2, p. 4.
529. 'Abdu'l-Bahá, *A Traveler's Narrative*, p. 92, quoted in Taherzadeh, *The Revelation of Bahá'u'lláh*, p. 5.
530. Is͟hráq-K͟hávarí (comp.), *Má'idiy-i-Ásamání*, vol. IV, p. 369, quoted in Taherzadeh, *The Revelation of Bahá'u'lláh*, p. 5.
531. Bahá'u'lláh, Súriy-i-Mulúk, para. 39, in *The Summons of the Lord of Hosts*, pp. 201–2.
532. Bahá'u'lláh, Tablet of Visitation, in *Bahá'í Prayers*, pp. 232–3.
533. Shoghi Effendi, *God Passes By*, pp. 158–9.
534. ibid. p. 165.
535. Balyuzi, *Bahá'u'lláh, The King of Glory,* p. 248.
536. Shoghi Effendi, *God Passes By*, pp. 112–13.
537. Taherzadeh, *The Covenant of Bahá'u'lláh,* p. 65.

538. Shoghi Effendi, *God Passes By*, pp. 164–5.
539. ibid. pp. 165–6.
540. Bahá'u'lláh, *Kitáb-i-Íqán*, para. 175, p. 164, referring to Qur'án 2:19.
541. Bahá'u'lláh, Lawḥ-i-Burhán, in *Tablets of Bahá'u'lláh Revealed After the Kitáb-i-Aqdas*, p. 216.
542. Bahá'u'lláh, Ishráqát, in *Tablets of Bahá'u'lláh Revealed After the Kitáb-i-Aqdas*, p. 108.
543. Shoghi Effendi, *God Passes By*, p. 78.
544. *Encyclopaedia Iranica*: Kámrán Mírzá Náyeb-al-Salṭana.
545. Taherzadeh, *The Revelation of Bahá'u'lláh*, vol. 4, p. 383; vol. 2, pp. 245–9; Balyuzi, *Eminent Bahá'ís*, pp. 63–4, 70, 201, 204–5.
546. Balyuzi, *Eminent Bahá'ís*, pp. 33–51, 231–2, 261.
547. Taherzadeh, *The Revelation of Bahá'u'lláh*, vol. 4, pp. 384–5.
548. Paraphrased in English from Áyatí (Avarih), *Al-Kawákibud-Durríyah fí ta'ríkh ẓuhúr al-Bábíyah wa-al-Bahá'íyah*, vol. 1, pp. 420. Avarih wrote this book before he was declared a Covenant-breaker. It was praised by Shoghi Effendi: 'His forthcoming book . . . which has been partly revised by the Pen of our Beloved Master is beyond any doubt the most graphic, the most reliable and comprehensive of its kind in all Bahá'í literature' (Shoghi Effendi, *Unfolding Destiny*, p. 11).
549. ibid. p. 421.
550. Shoghi Effendi, *God Passes By*, p. 201.
551. *The Dawn-Breakers*, pp. 625–6.
552. 'Abdu'l-Bahá, *Memorials of the Faithful*, pp. 148–50.
553. ibid.
554. Shoghi Effendi, *God Passes By*, p. 199. See also: Balyuzi, *Bahá'u'lláh, The King of Glory*, pp. 293–310; Salmání, *My Memories of Bahá'u'lláh*, pp. 89, 137; Balyuzi, *Eminent Bahá'ís*, pp. 179, 261–2; Taherzadeh, *The Revelation of Bahá'u'lláh*, vol. 3, ch. 9.
555. Taherzadeh, *The Revelation of Bahá'u'lláh*, vol. 2. p. 222.
556. Shoghi Effendi, *God Passes By*, p. 178. See also: Taherzadeh, *The Revelation of Bahá'u'lláh*, vol. 2, pp. 222–3; Ḥaydar-'Alí, *Stories from The Delight of Hearts*, p. 15; Salmání, *My Memories of Bahá'u'lláh*, pp. 18, 25, 142; Balyuzi, *Bahá'u'lláh, The King of Glory*, p. 144.
557. Shoghi Effendi, *God Passes By*, p. 201. See also: Ḥaydar-'Alí, *Stories from The Delight of Hearts*, pp. 101–3; Taherzadeh, *The Revelation of Bahá'u'lláh*, vol. 4, p. 387.
558. Salmání, *My Memories of Bahá'u'lláh*, pp. 71, 135. See also: Shoghi Effendi, *God Passes By*, p. 199; Taherzadeh, *The Revelation of Bahá'u'lláh*, vol. 2, pp. 226–7.
559. Shoghi Effendi, *God Passes By*, pp. 199–200. See also: Bahá'u'lláh, *Gleanings from the Writings of Bahá'u'lláh*, p. 135; Taherzadeh, *The Revelation of Bahá'u'lláh*, vol. 2, pp. 223–30; Balyuzi, *Bahá'u'lláh, The King of Glory*, p. 470; Salmání, *My Memories of Bahá'u'lláh*, pp. 71, 143.
560. *The Dawn-Breakers*, pp. 562–3.
561. Bahá'u'lláh, Súriy-i-Haykal, in *The Summons of the Lord of Hosts*, para. 211, p. 109.
562. Bahá'u'lláh, *The Kitáb-i-Aqdas*, p. 95.
563. Taherzadeh, *The Revelation of Bahá'u'lláh*, vol. 2, pp. 39–40.

564. Shoghi Effendi, *God Passes By*, p. 200.
565. ibid. p. 136. See also: *The Dawn-Breakers*, pp. 170, 387; Taherzadeh, *The Revelation of Bahá'u'lláh*, vol. 1, pp. 101–3.
566. Shoghi Effendi, *God Passes By*, pp. 68, 293; see also *The Dawn-Breakers*, pp. 368–78.
567. Shoghi Effendi, *God Passes By*, pp. 117–18.
568. Browne (trans.) *New History of the Báb*, p. 132, quoted in Esslemont, *Bahá'u'lláh and the New Era*, p. 17.
569. Shoghi Effendi, *God Passes By*, pp. 202–3. See also: Taherzadeh, *The Revelation of Bahá'u'lláh*, vol. 4, p. 342.
570. Peter Smith, 'Síyah-Chál', in *A Concise Encyclopedia of the Bahá'í Faith*, pp. 323–67.
571. Bahá'u'lláh, *Tablets of Bahá'u'lláh Revealed After the Kitáb-i-Aqdas*, pp. 205–16.
572. Shoghi Effendi, *God Passes By*, p. 219.
573. *Yasna*, ix. 18–21.
574. See www.defenders.org/gray-wolf/fact-vs-fiction.
575. See www.dictionary.com/browse/serpent.
576. 'Abdu'l-Bahá, *Some Answered Questions*, no. 13, p. 79.
577. *Sahih al-Bukhari*, Book 24, hadith 486.
578. Bahá'u'lláh, Lawḥ-i-Burhán, in *Tablets of Bahá'u'lláh Revealed After the Kitáb-i-Aqdas*, pp. 207–8.
579. al-Amili, (comp.), *Wasa'il ash-Shi'a*, vol. 7, p. 26, hadith 10.
580. Bahá'u'lláh, *Prayers and Meditations*, XLIV, p. 63.
581. al-Majlisi, *Bihár al-Anwár*, vol. 52, p. 373, Tafsir Furat ibn Ibrahim.
582. Firestone, 'Muslim-Jewish Relations', p. 7.
583. Bahá'u'lláh, *Kitáb-i-Íqán*, para. 15, p. 15.
584. ibid. paras. 3–4, pp. 4–5.
585. Shoghi Effendi, *God Passes By*, pp. 185, 196, 224.
586. ibid. pp. 93, 101; and Bahá'u'lláh, *Kitab-i-Íqán*, pp. 50, 89, 117, 164–5.
587. Bahá'u'lláh, Tablet of Aḥmad, in *Bahá'í Prayers*, p. 210.
588. *The Dawn-Breakers*, pp. 106–7.
589. Bahá'u'lláh, *Tablets of Bahá'u'lláh Revealed After the Kitáb-i-Aqdas*, p. 254.
590. Bahá'u'lláh, *The Kitáb-i-Aqdas*, para. 103, p. 57. Bahá'u'lláh quotes this passage in the Epistle, para. 188, p. 129.
591. Bahá'u'lláh, Tablet to Pope Pius IX, Súriy-i-Haykal, para. 113, in *The Summons of the Lord of Hosts*, p. 59.
592. 'Abdu'l-Bahá, *Tablets of 'Abdul-Bahá*, p. 364.
593. Shoghi Effendi, *The Promised Day Is Come*, p. 52.
594. Note 115 in Bahá'u'lláh, *The Kitáb-i-Aqdas*, p. 216.
595. Shoghi Effendi, *God Passes By*, pp. 17, 25, 28.
596. Bahá'u'lláh, Ṭarazát (Ornaments), in *Tablets of Bahá'u'lláh Revealed After the Kitáb-i-Aqdas*, p. 42.
597. Shoghi Effendi, *God Passes By*, p. 233.
598. Shoghi Effendi, *The World Order of Bahá'u'lláh*, p. 126.
599. Shoghi Effendi, *God Passes By*, pp. 57–8.
600. ibid. p. 57.
601. ibid. pp. 44–6 and *The Dawn-Breakers*, ch. XXIV.

602. ibid. pp. 42–4 and *The Dawn-Breakers*, ch. XXII.
603. ibid. pp. 41–2 and *The Dawn-Breakers*, ch. XIX and XX.
604. ibid. p. 62.
605. See www.iranicaonline.org/articles/aqa-najafi-esfahani.
606. ibid.
607. ibid; see also Keddie, *Religion and Rebellion in Iran*, p. 94; Foran, *A Century of Revolution*, pp. 13–16.
608. Bakhtiari, *The Last of the Khāns*, pp. 108–23.
609. Suyuti, *Al-Jami'u Sagheer Fi Ahadeeth Al-Basshee An-Nadheer*, vol. 2, p. 127.
610. Bahá'u'lláh, *Kitáb-i-Íqán*, para. 267, p. 238.
611. ibid.
612. ibid. paras. 13–14, pp. 12–14.
613. Bahá'u'lláh, Tablet to Náṣiri-Dín Sháh, Súriy-i-Haykal, in *The Summons of the Lord of Hosts*, pp. 101–2.
614. Bahá'u'lláh, *Áthár-i-Qalam-i-A'lá*, vol. 2, p. 15.
615. Shoghi Effendi, *God Passes By*, p. 319.
616. See Fananapazir, *Islam at the Crossroads*, ch. 16.
617. Bahá'u'lláh, *Prayers and Meditations*, CII.
618. Bahá'u'lláh, Tablet to Náṣiri'd-Dín Sháh, Súriy-i-Haykal, in *The Summons of the Lord of Hosts*, p. 136.
619. Bahá'u'lláh, Súriy-i-Mulúk, para. 109, in *The Summons of the Lord of Hosts*, p. 232; also quoted in Shoghi Effendi, *The Promised Day Is Come*, p. 89.
620. Bahá'u'lláh, Súriy-i-Haykal, in *The Summons of the Lord of Hosts*, p. 8.
621. Bahá'u'lláh, *Tablets of Bahá'u'lláh Revealed After the Kitáb-i-Aqdas*, p. 246.
622. *Bahíyyih Khánum, the Greatest Holy Leaf*, no. 15, p. 61.
623. ibid. no. 30, p. 110.
624. Bahá'u'lláh, Tablet of Aḥmad, in *Bahá'í Prayers*, p. 210.
625. Shoghi Effendi, *God Passes By*, pp. 138–9.
626. Walcher, *In the Shadow of the King*, p. 51.
627. Nasr, *The Study Qur'án*, p. 96 (Qur'án 2:20); p. 428 (Qur'án 7:56); and p. 1108 (Qur'án 38:28).
628. Shoghi Effendi, *God Passes By*, p. 232.
629. *The Dawn-Breakers*, p. 418.
630. Shoghi Effendi, *God Passes By*, p. 14.
631. The cleric or Imám who leads the Muslims in prayer on Fridays.
632. 'Núrayn-i-Nayyirayn', in Wikipedia.
633. Shoghi Effendi, *God Passes By*, pp. 200–01.
634. ibid. pp. 232–3.
635. Encyclopaedia Iranica: Áqá Najafí Eṣfahání, at www.iranicaonline.org/articles/aqa-najafi-esfahani.
636. Shoghi Effendi, *The World Order of Bahá'u'lláh*, p. 59.
637. Bahá'u'lláh, Súriy-i-Vafá, in *Tablets of Bahá'u'lláh Revealed After the Kitáb-i-Aqdas*, p. 188.
638. Bahá'u'lláh, Ishráqát, ibid. p. 120.
639. Bahá'u'lláh, Tablet of Aḥmad, in *Bahá'í Prayers*, p. 211.
640. Bahá'u'lláh, Tablet to Náṣiri'd-Dín Sháh, Súriy-i-Haykal, in *The Summons of the Lord of Hosts*, p. 97.

641. Bahá'u'lláh, 'The Seven Valleys' in *The Call of the Divine Beloved.*
642. Bahá'u'lláh, *Hidden Words*, Persian no. 67.
643. Balyuzi, *Edward Granville Browne and the Bahá'í Faith*, p. 23.
644. Shoghi Effendi, *The Advent of Divine Justice*, p. 16.
645. ibid. pp. 17–18.
646. Shoghi Effendi, *The World Order of Bahá'u'lláh*, p. 155.
647. 'Abdu'l-Bahá, First Tablet to the Hague, 17 December 1919, in 'Abdu'l-Bahá, *Selections from the Writings of 'Abdu'l-Bahá* (1982 edition), no. 1.
648. al-Sadiq, *Misbah al-Shariah*, ch. 2.
649. al-Majlisi, *Kitabul Ghaibah* (Book of Occultation) in *Bihár al-Anwár*, vol. 13 (old edition), vols. 51/52/53 (new edition), section 77.
650. ibid. p. 330.
651. ibid. section 298.
652. *The Dawn-Breakers*, p. 138.
653. ibid. p. 134.
654. Beirut: Dar al-Andalus, 1978.
655. 'The Four Sacred Months – Tafseer Ibn Kathir'. Available at: https://abdurrahman.org/2016/10/02/the-four-sacred-months-tafseer-ibn-kathir/.
656. Shoghi Effendi, *God Passes By*, pp. 110, 277.
657. The Báb, *Selections from the Writings of the Báb*, p. 36.
658. ibid. p. 156.
659. See Ishráq-Khávarí, *Qámús Lawḥ Shaykh Najafí*, p. 244.
660. See Bahá'u'lláh, *Kitáb-i-Íqán*, paras. 149–51, 189; pp. 139–42, 169.
661. Bahá'u'lláh, Tajallíyát (Effulgences), in *Tablets of Bahá'u'lláh Revealed After the Kitáb-i-Aqdas*, p. 50.
662. The Báb, Persian Bayán, II:7, in *Selections from the Writings of the Báb*, pp. 106–8.
663. Bahá'u'lláh, *Gleanings from the Writings of Bahá'u'lláh*, XVIII, p. 45.
664. Van Voorst, 'Selections from the Bhagavad Gita', in Van Voorst, *Anthology of World Scriptures*, p. 59.
665. Gibson, *Expect God's Visitation*, *Preaching Today.*
666. Shoghi Effendi, *God Passes By*, pp. 52–3.
667. Bahá'u'lláh, Tablet of Aḥmad, in *Bahá'í Prayers*, p. 211.
668. *The Dawn-Breakers*, pp. 447–8.
669. Ahmad Bin Hanbal, *Musnad* (Cairo, 1995), hadith 21193.
670. Ahmad Bin Hanbal, *Musnad* (trans. Nasiruddin al-Khattab), hadith 143.
671. Shoghi Effendi, *God Passes By*, p. 95.
672. See Barnes, *Notes on the Bible.*
673. Shoghi Effendi, *God Passes By*, p. 92; see also *The Dawn-Breakers*, p. 42.
674. ibid. p. 179.
675. Cornell, *Voices of Islam*, p. 119.
676. See illustration in Taherzadeh, *The Revelation of Bahá'u'lláh*, vol. 3, facing p. 61.
677. Bahá'u'lláh, Lawḥ-i-Dunyá, in *Tablets of Bahá'u'lláh Revealed After the Kitáb-i-Aqdas*, p. 83.
678. Bahá'u'lláh, *Kitáb-i-Íqán*, para. 257, pp. 230–31.
679. Bahá'u'lláh, *Gleanings from the Writings of Bahá'u'lláh*, LX, p. 118.
680. Shoghi Effendi, *The World Order of Bahá'u'lláh*, p. 198.
681. al-Kulayni (comp.), *Al-Kafi*, vol. 2, hadith 3469, ch. 2, h1, p. 496.

682. *Sunan Abu Dawud*, vol. 5, hadith 4597.
683. Hazelton, *After the Prophet: The Epic Story of the Shia–Sunni Split in Islam*, p. 51.
684. 'Ali ibn Abi Tálib, *Nahjul Balaghah*, Saying 369, vol. 2, p. 736.
685. The Báb, Qayyúmu'l-Asmá, ch. LXII, in *Selections from the Writings of the Báb*, p. 61.
686. Bahá'u'lláh, *The Kitáb-i-Aqdas*, para. 78, p. 48.
687. ibid. para. 86, p. 51.
688. Bahá'u'lláh, Súriy-i-Mulúk, para. 2, in *The Summons of the Lord of Hosts*, p. 185.
689. Shoghi Effendi, *God Passes By*, pp. 230–31.
690. Shoghi Effendi, *The Promised Day Is Come*, p. 24.
691. Shoghi Effendi, *God Passes By*, p. 213.
692. Bahá'u'lláh, *The Kitáb-i-Aqdas*, para. 183, p. 86.
693. Bahá'u'lláh, Súriy-i-Mulúk, para. 69, in *The Summons of the Lord of Hosts*, p. 213.
694. Bahá'u'lláh, quoted in Shoghi Effendi, *The World Order of Bahá'u'lláh*, p. 104.
695. Bahá'u'lláh, *Gleanings from the Writings of Bahá'u'lláh*, LIII, p. 107.
696. Bahá'u'lláh, Súriy-i-Haykal, in *The Summons of the Lord of Hosts*, p. 135.
697. ibid. p. 13.
698. Balyuzi, *Bahá'u'lláh, The King of Glory*, p. 364.
699. The Báb, Qayyúmu'l-Asmá', ch. LXVII, in *Selections from the Writings of the Báb*, p. 57.
700. Shoghi Effendi, *God Passes By*, p. 151.
701. Bahá'u'lláh, Kalímát-i-Firdawsíyyih, in *Tablets of Bahá'u'lláh Revealed After the Kitáb-i-Aqdas*, p. 71.
702. Bahá'u'lláh, *The Kitáb-i-Aqdas*, para. 84, p. 50.
703. Shoghi Effendi, *God Passes By*, p. 239.
704. Bahá'u'lláh, *Kitáb-i-Íqán*, para. 128, p. 120.
705. Bahá'u'lláh, *Gleanings from the Writings of Bahá'u'lláh*, CLIII, p. 327.
706. Bahá'u'lláh, Ishráqát, in *Tablets of Bahá'u'lláh Revealed After the Kitáb-i-Aqdas*, pp. 117–121.
707. al-Majlisi, *Bihár al-Anwár*, vol. 10, p. 597.
708. ibid. vol. 52, p. 354.
709. Elad, *Medieval Jerusalem and Islamic Worship*, pp. 141–4.
710. ibid. p. 144.
711. Násir-i-Khsrau, *Diary of a Journey Through Syria and Palestine*, vol 4, P. 24.
712. The Báb, Qayyúm'l-Asmá', ch. VII, in *Selections from the Writings of the Báb*, p. 47.
713. Bahá'u'lláh, *Kitáb-i-Íqán*, para. 51, p. 48.
714. Bahá'u'lláh, *The Kitáb-i-Aqdas*, para. 167, p. 80.
715. Bahá'u'lláh, Kalimát-i-Firdawsíyyih, in *Tablets of Bahá'u'lláh Revealed After the Kitáb-i-Aqdas*, p. 61.
716. Bahá'u'lláh, *Gleanings from the Writings of Bahá'u'lláh*, XIV, p. 31.
717. Shoghi Effendi, *The World Order of Bahá'u'lláh*, p. 179.
718. Message from Shoghi Effendi to the Bahá'is of the World, April 1957, in Shoghi Effendi, *Messages to the Bahá'í World 1950–1957*, p. 103.
719. Shoghi Effendi, *The World Order of Bahá'u'lláh*, p. 201.
720. 'Abdu'l-Bahá, quoted in Shoghi Effendi, *God Passes By*, p. 75.
721. The Báb, Qayyúmu'l-Asmá', ch. XII, in *Selections from the Writings of the Báb*, p. 70.

722. The Báb, Persian Bayán, II:6, ibid. p. 103.
723. Bahá'u'lláh, *Gleanings from the Writings of Bahá'u'lláh*, LXX, p. 137.
724. Bahá'u'lláh, *Gems of Divine Mysteries*, p. 55.
725. 'Abdu'l-Bahá, quoted in Balyuzi, *'Abdu'l-Bahá*, p. 499.
726. al-Amili, *Wasa'il ash-Shi'a*, vol. 7, p. 327, hadith 1.
727. Bahá'u'lláh, Súriy-i-Haykal, in *The Summons of the Lord of Hosts*, p. 83.
728. Bahá'u'lláh, Tablet of Aḥmad, in *Bahá'í Prayers*, p. 210.
729. Bahá'u'lláh, Lawḥ-i-Aqdas, in *Tablets of Bahá'u'lláh Revealed After the Kitáb-i-Aqdas*, p. 14.
730. Shoghi Effendi, *God Passes By*, p. 216.
731. The *abjad* is a decimal numerical system in which the 28 letters of the Arabic alphabet are assigned numerical values. See Lewis, 'Overview of the Abjad numerological system'.
732. Taherzadeh, *The Revelation of Bahá'u'lláh*, vol. 2, p. 270.
733. Bahá'u'lláh, *Gleanings from the Writings of Bahá'u'lláh*, XVIII, pp. 43–44.
734. ibid. XVII, p. 40.
735. Bahá'u'lláh, *Kitáb-i-Íqán*, para. 25, pp. 26–7.
736. ibid. para. 46, pp. 44–45.
737. Bahá'u'lláh, *The Kitáb-i-Aqdas*, para. 39, p. 33.
738. Shoghi Effendi, *The World Order of Bahá'u'lláh*, p. 89.
739. al-Numani, *Kitab al-Ghayba: The Book of Occultation*, p. 107.
740. *Sahih al-Bukhari*, hadith 335.
741. Bahá'u'lláh, Tablet of Aḥmad, in *Bahá'í Prayers*, pp. 210–12.
742. Bahá'u'lláh, Ishráqát (Splendours), in *Tablets of Bahá'u'lláh Revealed After the Kitáb-i-Aqdas*, pp. 119–120.
743. Kitáb-i-Mubín, in Bahá'u'lláh, *Athár-i-Qalam-i-A'lá*, no. 40, pp. 228–9.
744. Shoghi Effendi, *God Passes By*, p. 182.
745. Bahá'u'lláh, *Kitáb-i-Íqán*, p. 231, para. 260.
746. Shoghi Effendi, *God Passes By*, pp. 23–4.
747. ibid. p. 23.
748. Bahá'u'lláh, Súriy-i-Mulúk, in *The Summons of the Lord of Hosts*, p. 195, para. 24–26.
749. Bahá'u'lláh, Ishráqát (Splendours), in *Tablets of Bahá'u'lláh Revealed After the Kitáb-i-Aqdas*, pp. 127–8: compare ibid. pp. 68, 89, 127 and 165; *Gleanings from the Writings of Bahá'u'lláh*, pp. 87 and 117; Shoghi Effendi, *The Promised Day Is Come*, p. 121; and *The World Order of Bahá'u'lláh*, p. 39.
750. Quoted in Esslemont, *Bahá'u'lláh and the New Era*, pp. 164–5.
751. 'Abdu'l-Bahá, *'Abdu'l-Bahá in London*, p. 94.
752. According to the scholar Abdu'l-Hamíd Ishráq-Khávarí, Bahá' al-Dín ibn Husayn al Ámilí, also known as Shaykh-i Bahá'í, was a Muslim scholar (1532–1621 CE) who adopted the pen name 'Bahá' after being inspired by words of Imám Báqir and Imám Jafar al-Ṣádiq who had stated that the Greatest Name of God was included in the Du'a al-Sahar.
753. This prayer is recorded as 'Du'a al-Sahar' in al-Qummi, *Mafátih al-Jinan*, vol. 1, pp. 474–7.
754. Shoghi Effendi, *God Passes By*, p. xvi.
755. ibid. p. 29.

756. Letter from Shoghi Effendi to the Bahá'is of the United States, 23 November 1951, in Shoghi Effendi, *Citadel of Faith*, p. 101.
757. Shoghi Effendi, *God Passes By*, p. 28; see also *The Dawn-Breakers*, pp. 87, 109, 123, 222, 227–8, 370, 481, 440, 466, 473 and 467.
758. Shoghi Effendi, *God Passes By*, p. 104.
759. ibid. p. 92.
760. The Báb, quoted ibid. p. 30.
761. al-Majlisi, *Bihár al-Anwár*, vol. 51, p. 148; see also al-Numani, *Kitab al-Ghayba: The Book of Occultation.*
762. 'Abdu'l-Bahá, *'Abdu'l-Bahá in London*, p. 18.
763. 'Abdu'l-Bahá, *Tablets of Abdul-Baha*, p. 685.
764. ibid. p. 218.
765. 'Abdu'l-Bahá, *The Promulgation of Universal Peace*, p. 212.
766. 'Abdu'l-Bahá, *Tablets of Abdul-Baha*, pp. 477–8.
767. ibid. p. 475.
768. 'Abdu'l-Bahá, *Paris Talks*, no. 18, p. 57.
769. 'Abdu'l-Bahá, *Tablets of the Divine Plan*, p. 27, quoted in Shoghi Effendi, *The Advent of Divine Justice*, pp. 57–8.
770. See http://biblehub.com/matthew/24-36.htm.
771. The Zondervan Parallel New Testament in Greek and English.
772. Bahá'u'lláh, *Gleanings from the Writings of Bahá'u'lláh*, CXXIX, p. 281.
773. ibid. XVII, p. 40.
774. ibid. VII, p. 11.
775. ibid. XCVI, p. 197.
776. Bahá'u'lláh, quoted by Shoghi Effendi in *The Advent of Divine Justice*, p. 77.
777. Shoghi Effendi, *God Passes By*, p. 184.
778. ibid. p. 183.
779. ibid. p. 185.
780. See Fananapazir, *Islam at the Crossroads*, chs. 15 and 16.
781. Bahá'u'lláh, *Kitáb-i-Íqán*, paras. 217–19, pp. 197–200.
782. *Bahá'í World Faith*, pp. 350–51.
783. 'Abdu'l-Bahá, *Selections from the Writings of 'Abdu'l-Bahá*, no. 142, p. 165.
784. Bahá'u'lláh, Lawḥ-i-Karmil (Tablet of Carmel), in *Tablets of Bahá'u'lláh Revealed After the Kitáb-i-Aqdas*, pp. 3–5.
785. 'Abdu'l-Bahá, *Paris Talks*, no. 28, p. 82.
786. 'Abdu'l-Bahá, *Some Answered Questions*, no. 11, pp. 68–9.
787. Bahá'u'lláh, quoted in Shoghi Effendi, *The Promised Day Is Come*, p. 79.
788. Bahá'u'lláh, Lawḥ-i-Karmil (Tablet of Carmel), in *Tablets of Bahá'u'lláh Revealed After the Kitáb-i-Aqdas*, p. 4.
789. United States Conference of Catholic Bishops, 'New Evangelization'. Available at: Usccb.org. See also https://www.uscatholic.org/articles/what-new-evangelization-26744.
790. 'Abdu'l-Bahá, in *Bahá'í Prayers*, pp. 200-01.
791. See Barnes, *Notes on the Bible* (1834), at sacred-texts.com.
792. See Momen, 'The Akká traditions in the Epistle to the Son of the Wolf: A research note':

    The Akka Traditions quoted by Bahá'u'lláh in the *Epistle to the Son of the*

Wolf probably came from a work named Fadáil 'Akká wa 'Asqalán: This work was compiled in the late sixth century C.E. based on Traditions transmitted by Bahá ad-Dín Abú Muhammad al-Qasim, the son of the famous historian Ibn 'Asákir, in lectures that he gave in Damascus in 581 and 585 C.E. The compiler was one of the students of Bahá ad-Dín al-Qasim.

793. De Wette, *A Critical and Historical Introduction to the Canonical Scriptures of the Old Testament*, vol. II, p. 445.
794. Shoghi Effendi, *God Passes By*, p. 194.
795. Quoted in Esslemont, *Bahá'u'lláh and the New Era*, p. 23.
796. Bahá'u'lláh, in Ishráq-Khávarí (comp.), *Má'idiy-i-Ásamání*, vol. 7, p. 192; see also Taherzadeh, *The Revelation of Bahá'u'lláh*, vol. 2, p. 2.
797. Pusey, *The Minor Prophets*, p. 288.
798. Taherzadeh, *The Revelation of Bahá'u'lláh*, vol. 2, p. 2.
799. Sermon of the Gulf (al-Khutbah al-Tutunjiyyah) of Imám 'Ali, as printed in Hafiz Rajab al-Bursi's *Masháriq Anwar al-Yaqín fi Asrár Amir Mu'minín*, pp. 160–170; translated by Dr Khazeh Fananapazir, bahai-library.com/fananapazir_khutbih_tutunjiyyih.
800. Barnes, *Notes, Critical, Explanatory, and Practical, of the Book of the Prophet Isaiah*, p. 69.
801. Adapted from commentaries by Ellicott, *An Old Testament Commentary for English Readers*, vol. IV. p. 563; and Benson, *The Holy Bible . . .*, vol. III, p. 287.
802. Shoghi Effendi, *God Passes By*, p. 194.
803. See 'Abdu'l-Bahá, *Some Answered Questions*, p. 48.
804. Bahá'u'lláh, Tablet of Aḥmad, in *Bahá'í Prayers*, p. 210.
805. Bahá'u'lláh, *Gems of Divine Mysteries, Javáhiru'l-Aṣrár*, p. 55.
806. 'Abdu'l-Bahá, *Selections from the Writings of 'Abdu'l-Bahá*, no. 5, pp. 17–18.
807. *The Dawn-Breakers*, pp. 631–2.
808. Bahá'u'lláh, *Kitáb-i-Íqán*, para, 213, p. 193; also in *Gleanings from the Writings of Bahá'u'lláh*, CXXV, p. 264.
809. Bahá'u'lláh, quoted in a letter from Shoghi Effendi to the North American Bahá'ís, 4 July 1939, in *Messages to America*, pp. 25–6 (republished as *This Decisive Hour*, no. 57).
810. Bahá'u'lláh, *Gleanings from the Writings of Bahá'u'lláh*, CLIII, pp. 325–6.
811. Bahá'u'lláh, *Kitáb-i-Íqán*, para. 2, p. 3–4.
812. 'Abdu'l-Bahá, *Tablets of 'Abdul-Bahá*, p. 36.
813. Bahá'u'lláh, Lawḥ-i-Maqṣúd (Tablet of Maqṣúd), in *Tablets of Bahá'u'lláh Revealed After the Kitáb-i-Aqdas*, p. 167.
814. Bahá'u'lláh, *Gleanings from the Writings of Bahá'u'lláh*, XXVIII, p. 70.
815. Bahá'u'lláh, *Prayers and Meditations*, CXII, p. 189.
816. 'Abdu'l-Bahá, *The Promulgation of Universal Peace*, p. 94.
817. The Universal House of Justice, Introduction to Bahá'u'lláh, *The Summons of the Lord of Hosts*, p. vi.
818. Bahá'u'lláh, Lawḥ-i-Ra'ís, para. 7, ibid. p. 164.
819. *Encyclopædia Iranica:* 'Tehran'.
820. Bahá'u'lláh, *Gleanings from the Writings of Bahá'u'lláh,* LV, pp. 109–10.
821. ibid. LXIII, pp. 120–21.

822. Shoghi Effendi, *God Passes By*, p. 102.
823. Bahá'u'lláh, *The Kitáb-i-Aqdas*, para. 91–92, pp. 53–4.
824. Bahá'u'lláh, Súriy-i-Mulúk (Súrih to the Kings), para. 21, in *The Summons of the Lord of Hosts*, p. 194.
825. Bahá'u'lláh, *The Kitáb-i-Aqdas*, para. 124, p. 63.
826. Bahá'u'lláh, *Hidden Words*, Persian no. 24.
827. Bahá'u'lláh, *Tablets of Bahá'u'lláh Revealed After the Kitáb-i-Aqdas*, pp. 220–21.
828. Shoghi Effendi, *God Passes By*, pp. 127–8, 132–3.
829. The Báb, Persian Bayán, VIII:19, in *Selections from the Writings of the Báb*, p. 81.
830. ibid. II:6, p. 102.
831. ibid. V:8, p. 104.
832. Bahá'ú'lláh, Súriy-i-Haykal, para. 79, in *The Summons of the Lord of Hosts*, p. 42.
833. The Báb, quoted in Shoghi Effendi, *The World Order of Bahá'u'lláh*, p. 101.
834. The Báb, quoted in Shoghi Effendi, *God Passes* By, p. 98.
835. Note 189 in Bahá'u'lláh, *The Kitáb-i-Aqdas*, p. 247.
836. The Báb, quoted in Shoghi Effendi, *God Passes By*, p. 30.
837. The Báb, Persian Bayán, V:19, in *Selections from the Writings of the Báb*, p. 79.
838. Walbridge, 'Some Bábi Martyrs'.
839. Bahá'u'lláh, *Tablets of Bahá'u'lláh Revealed After the Kitáb-i-Aqdas*, p. 75.
840. 'Twenty-two letters from the Bāb addressed to different individuals . . .'. E. G. Browne Collection, F. 21, No. 32 Twaqi (Scripts or Writings) of Hazrat Alá.
841. The Báb, *Selections from the Writings of the Báb*, p. 125.
842. *The Dawn-Breakers*, pp. 80–81.
843. See *The Dawn-Breakers*, chs. IX and XX.
844. Shoghi Effendi, *God Passes By*, p. 30.
845. The Báb, *Selections from the Writings of the Báb*, p. 168.
846. ibid.
847. Shoghi Effendi, *The World Order of Bahá'u'lláh*, p. 111.
848. See The Báb, *Selections from the Writings of the Báb*, p. 156; and the description of the Kitáb-i-Badí' in Taherzadeh, *The Revelation of Bahá'u'lláh*, vol. 2, ch. 17.
849. See Bahá'u'lláh, *Kitáb-i-Íqán*, para. 256, p. 229; para. 276, p. 248.
850. The Báb, *Selections from the Writings of the Báb*, p. 7.
851. Peter Smith, 'Bayán', in *A Concise Encyclopedia of the Bahá'í Faith*, p. 91.
852. See 'A Summary of the Persian Bayán' in Momen (ed.), *Selections from the Writings of E. G. Browne on the Bábí and Bahá'í Religions.*
853. Provisional translation by Stephen Lambden.
854. 'Abdu'l-Bahá, quoted in Shoghi Effendi, *God Passes By*, p. 92.
855. Taherzadeh, *The Revelation of Bahá'u'lláh*, vol. 2, pp. 380–81.
856. The Báb, Persian Bayán, VIII:9, in *Selections from the Writings of the Báb*, p. 78.
857. The Báb, *Selections from the Writings of the Báb*, p. 155.
858. The Báb, Kitáb-i-Asmá', ibid. p. 134.
859. Bahá'u'lláh, quoted in Shoghi Effendi, *God Passes By*, p. 119.
860. The Báb, Kitáb-i-Asmá', in *Selections from the Writings of the Báb*, pp. 134–5.
861. See Taherzadeh, *The Revelation of Bahá'u'lláh*, vol. 2, ch. 17.
862. Bahá'u'lláh, quoted by Shoghi Effendi, *God Passes By*, p. 30.
863. ibid. p. 29.
864. The Báb, Persian Bayán, IV:12, in *Selections from the Writings of the Báb*, p. 106.

865. The Báb, quoted by Bahá'u'lláh in the Kitáb-i-Badí'; also quoted in Shoghi Effendi, *God Passes By*, p. 30.
866. Shoghi Effendi, *God Passes By*, p. 114.
867. Taherzadeh, *The Revelation of Bahá'u'lláh*, vol. 1, pp. 221–4; see also vol. 2, pp. 376–7; vol. 3 pp. 279–80; and Shoghi Effendi, *God Passes By*, p. 130.
868. Balyuzi, *Eminent Bahá'ís*, pp. 236–50 and *Bahá'u'lláh, The King of Glory*, pp. 236, 248–50; Taherzadeh, *The Revelation of Bahá'u'lláh*, vol. 1, pp. 28–9; vol. 2, pp. 68–73, 194–202; Shoghi Effendi, *God Passes By*, p. 178.
869. The Báb, *Selections from the Writings of the Báb*, p. 155.
870. Letter from Shoghi Effendi to the Bahá'ís of the East, dated Naw-Rúz 110, p. 5. See also The Báb, *Selections from the Writings of the Báb*, a Tablet addressed to 'Him Who Will be made Manifest', note on p. 3.
871. Shoghi Effendi, *God Passes By*, p. 148.
872. ibid. p. 125.
873. Note 192 in Bahá'u'lláh, *The Kitáb-i-Aqdas*, p. 249. See also ibid. Note 190.
874. Shoghi Effendi, *God Passes By*, pp. 180–81.
875. The Báb, *Selections from the Writings of the Báb*, pp. 155-6.
876. Shoghi Effendi, *God Passes By*, p. 109.
877. ibid. p. 108.
878. Bahá'u'lláh, *Kitáb-i-Íqán*, para. 278, p. 251.
879. Shoghi Effendi, *God Passes By*, p. 164.
880. ibid. pp. 164, 112.
881. ibid. p. 112.
882. ibid.
883. ibid. pp. 163–4.
884. ibid. pp. 163–8.
885. Balyuzi, *Edward Granville Browne and the Bahá'í Faith*, p. 44.
886. Taherzadeh, *The Revelation of Bahá'u'lláh*, vol. 2, pp. 205–6.
887. The Báb, Tablet Addressed to Him Who Will be Manifest, in *Selections from the Writings of the Báb*, p. 3.
888. Bahá'u'lláh, *Gleanings from the Writings of Bahá'u'lláh*, L, p. 103.
889. Note 180 in Bahá'u'lláh, *The Kitáb-i-Aqdas*, pp. 243-4.
890. Bahá'u'lláh, *The Kitáb-i-Aqdas*, p. 95.
891. Bahá'u'lláh, *Prayers and Meditations by Bahá'u'lláh*, LXXXIV, p. 142.
892. The Báb, Kitáb-i-Asmá' (The Book of Names), in *Selections from the Writings of the Báb*, pp. 129–30.
893. ibid. p. 129.
894. The Báb, Persian Bayán, II:7, in *Selections from the Writings of the Báb*, p. 108.
895. Shoghi Effendi, *God Passes By*, p. 49.
896. The Báb, *Selections from the Writings of the Báb*, p. 181.
897. Shoghi Effendi, *God Passes By*, p. 77.
898. 'Abdu'l-Bahá, 'Twelve Table Talks . . ., no. 11, para. 6.
899. Shoghi Effendi, *God Passes By*, pp. 50-51.
900. Taherzadeh, *The Revelation of Bahá'u'lláh*, vol. 3, p. 425.
901. Browne, 'Personal Reminiscences of the Bábí Insurrection at Zanjan in 1850, written by Aqa 'Abdu'l-Ahad-i-Zanjani', in *Journal of the Royal Asiatic Society* (1897) p. 767.

902. Malik-Khusravi, *'Iqlim-i-Nur*, pp. 202–5.
903. The Báb, *Selections from the Writings of the Báb*, p. 180.
904. The Báb, Kitáb-i-Asmá', XVII, 4, ibid. p. 142.
905. Bahá'u'lláh, *Kitáb-i-Íqán*, para. 31, p. 34.
906. 'Abdu'l-Bahá, in *Bahá'í Prayers*, p. 153.
907. Bahá'u'lláh, *Prayers and Meditations*, LIII, p. 76.
908. Bahá'u'lláh, Súriy-i-Ra'ís, para. 32, in *The Summons of the Lord of Hosts*, p. 153.
909. Bahá'u'lláh, *Gleanings from the Writings of Bahá'u'lláh*, XXVII, p. 66.
910. Bahá'u'lláh, Lawḥ-i-Dunyá (Tablet of the World), in *Tablets of Bahá'u'lláh Revealed After the Kitáb-i-Aqdas*, p. 88.
911. Bahá'u'lláh, Súriy-i-Haykal (Napoleon III), para. 145, in *The Summons of the Lord of Hosts*, p. 76.
912. Bahá'u'lláh, *Gleanings from the Writings of Bahá'u'lláh*, CXLVII, p. 316.
913. Bahá'u'lláh, Tablet of Aḥmad, in *Bahá'í Prayers*, p. 211.
914. The Báb, *Selections from the Writings of the Báb*, p. 163.
915. 'Abdu'l-Bahá, *The Promulgation of Universal Peace*, p. 452.
916. The Báb, *Selections from the Writings of the Báb*, p. 30.
917. Bahá'u'lláh, *Gleanings from the Writings of Bahá'u'lláh*, XVII, p. 42.
918. Bahá'u'lláh, in *Bahá'í Prayers*, p. 125.
919. Shoghi Effendi, *God Passes By*, p. 28.
920. Taherzadeh, *The Revelation of Bahá'u' lláh*, vol. 2, pp. 146–7.
921. Shoghi Effendi, *God Passes By*, p. 20; see also Balyuzi, *The Báb*, p. 136 and note 2 on p. 237.
922. The Báb, *Selections from the Writings of the Báb*, p. 96.
923. Taherzadeh, *The Revelation of Bahá'u'lláh*, vol. 1, p. 250.
924. Balyuzi, *Bahá'u'lláh: The King of Glory*, pp. 123–4.
925. Shoghi Effendi, *God Passes By*, p. 27.
926. Saiedi, *Gate of the Heart: Understanding the Writings of the Báb*, p. 357.
927. Shoghi Effendi, *God Passes By*, p. 125.
928. Taherzadeh, *The Revelation of Bahá'u'lláh*, vol. 4, Appendix III, Notes for the Study of *Epistle to the Son of the Wolf*, pp. 339–440.
929. See Balyuzi, *Bahá'u'lláh, The King of Glory*, pp. 123–4; Taherzadeh, *The Revelation of Bahá'u'lláh*, vol. 1, pp. 249–52.
930. Browne, *Materials for the Study of the Bábí Religion*, p. 218. quoted in Balyuzi, *Edward Granville Browne and the Bahá'í Faith*, p. 43.
931. *The Dawn-Breakers*, p. 31.
932. ibid. p. 307.
933. Shoghi Effendi, *God Passes By*, p. 125.
934. ibid. p. 120.
935. ibid. p. 123.
936. ibid. pp. 121–2.
937. Bahá'u'lláh, Ishráqát (Splendours), in *Tablets of Bahá'u'lláh Revealed After the Kitáb-i-Aqdas*, p. 131.
938. Shoghi Effendi, *God Passes By*, p. 126.
939. ibid. pp. 185–6.
940. See Momen, 'The 'Akká traditions in the Epistle to the Son of the Wolf: A Research Note'.

941. The Universal House of Justice, Memorandum on Socrates, 22 October 1995. Available at: http://bahai-library.com/compilation_socrates_bwc#15.
942. Fáḍil-i-Mázindarání, quoting 'Abdu'l-Bahá in *Amr va Khalq*, vol. 2, p. 211.
943. Bahá'u'lláh, *Kitáb-i-Íqán*, para. 78, pp. 70–71.
944. Bahá'u'lláh, *Gleanings from the Writings of Bahá'u'lláh*, CXXIX, pp. 282–3.
945. See Singer and Seligsohn, 'Zamzam', at *JewishEncyclopedia.com*.

ABOUT THE AUTHOR

Lameh Fananapazir was born in Iran and spent his youth in Africa. He is a graduate of Edinburgh Medical School, where he trained in Cardiovascular Diseases and was elected as a Fellow of the Royal College of Physicians of Edinburgh. He further specialized in Electrophysiology at Duke Medical Center, following which he was recruited to study causes of sudden death in athletes and patients with familial cardiac diseases at the National Institutes of Health where he became the chief of the Section of Inherited Heart Diseases. He has written and presented several hundred articles. He spent two and half years in Haifa, Israel where he was the director of the Health Services at the Bahá'í World Centre and Visiting Professor of Molecular Genetics at Technion, Israel Institute of Technology. Dr Fananapazir recently retired from his private practice in Cumberland, Maryland. Post 9/11 he wrote *Islam at the Crossroads* which examines the issues that Islam increasingly faces and their potential solutions.

CPSIA information can be obtained
at www.ICGtesting.com
Printed in the USA
BVHW031645131120
593063BV00007B/494

9 780853 986317